# Understanding Global Poverty

*Understanding Global Poverty* introduces students to the study and analysis of poverty, helping them to understand why it is pervasive across human societies, and how it can be reduced through proven policy solutions.

The book uses the capabilities and human development approach to foreground the human aspects of poverty, keeping the voices, experiences, and needs of the world's poor central to the analysis. Starting with definitions and measurement, the book goes on to explore the causes of poverty and how poverty reduction programs and policy have responded in practice. The book also reflects on the ethics of why we should work to reduce poverty and what actions readers themselves can take. This new edition has been revised and updated throughout, featuring:

- a new chapter on migration and refugees
- additional international examples, including material on Mexico, Covid-19 in global perspective, and South–South development initiatives
- information on careers in international development
- insights into how various forms of social difference, including race, ethnicity, social class, gender, and sexuality relate to poverty

Fully interdisciplinary in approach, the book is also supplemented with case studies, discussion questions, and further reading suggestions in order to support learning. Perfect as an introductory textbook for students across sociology, global development, political science, anthropology, public health, and economics, *Understanding Global Poverty* will also be a valuable resource to policy makers and development practitioners.

**Serena Cosgrove** is an Associate Professor in International Studies at Seattle University, USA.

**Benjamin Curtis** is a Director and Principal Consultant at Development Insights Partners, Czech Republic.

"This exceptional cross-disciplinary and cross-cultural work on one of the most pressing issues of humanity must be read not only by scholars and university students but also by policy makers. The authors show vividly and compassionately how poverty is a human problem and how it is related to capabilities. This book hands a mirror to its readers."

**Gül İnanç**, *Co-Director, Centre for Asia Pacific Refugee Studies, University of Auckland*

"*Understanding Global Poverty* is an excellent resource that lives up to its name in offering readers a rich understanding of poverty as more than low income. The authors use clear language and compelling case studies as they untangle complex issues of global poverty in a manner that is sure to engage students."

**Lori Keleher**, *PhD, Professor of Philosophy, New Mexico State University; President of the International Development Ethics Association*

"This smartly revised second edition of *Understanding Global Poverty* is an exemplary go-to resource. Each chapter's clearly articulated learning goals and discussion questions are ideal for the student-centered classroom. While unapologetically grounded in ethical approaches to development, the authors nevertheless consider both the strengths and weaknesses of each using empirical evidence and vignettes to illustrate core concepts and debates. Its multi-disciplinarity will attract a wide variety of students eager to understand the challenges of global poverty and engage in solutions to meet them."

**Daniel J. Whelan,** *Bill and Connie Bowen Odyssey Professor of Politics, Hendrix College, USA*

# Understanding Global Poverty

Causes, Solutions, and Capabilities

Second Edition

**Serena Cosgrove and Benjamin Curtis**

Routledge
Taylor & Francis Group

LONDON AND NEW YORK

Second edition published 2022
by Routledge
2 Park Square, Milton Park, Abingdon, Oxon OX14 4RN

and by Routledge
605 Third Avenue, New York, NY 10158

*Routledge is an imprint of the Taylor & Francis Group, an informa business*

First edition published by Routledge 2018

*British Library Cataloguing-in-Publication Data*
A catalogue record for this book is available from the British Library

*Library of Congress Cataloging-in-Publication Data*
A catalog record has been requested for this book

ISBN: 978-0-367-48985-4 (hbk)
ISBN: 978-0-367-48983-0 (pbk)
ISBN: 978-1-003-04382-9 (ebk)

Typeset in Bembo
by Newgen Publishing UK

# Contents

# Figures

# Contributors

**Paula E. Brentlinger**, MD, MPH, Clinical Assistant Professor, Department of Global Health, University of Washington

**Serena Cosgrove**, PhD, Associate Professor in International Studies, Seattle University

**Benjamin Curtis**, PhD, Director and Principal Consultant, Development Insights Partners

**Audrey Hudgins**, EdD, Associate Clinical Professor, Seattle University

# Preface

*Serena Cosgrove and Benjamin Curtis*

This book has three main objectives. First, it presents an interdisciplinary perspective on the problem of global poverty. Despite common rhetoric about the benefits of interdisciplinary approaches, research and teaching often remain firmly siloed within individual disciplines. The authors of this book are an anthropologist/sociologist and a political scientist, with one chapter written by a medical doctor who is a public health specialist, and another written by an academic researcher/practitioner who works at the intersection of human and national security. Some vignettes or text boxes were prepared by former students of ours whose majors were interdisciplinary as well: Humanities and International Studies. The primary authors have decades of experience in global health, international humanitarian assistance, sustainable development, and public policy. The endeavor to harmonize disciplinary perspectives within this book has not been easy, but we believe it was both necessary and rewarding. It was necessary because poverty's multi-dimensional nature requires an interdisciplinary approach; no single academic discipline can provide an adequate understanding of such a complex phenomenon. It was rewarding because it forced us to think outside our own narrow academic specializations, which should help readers think outside narrow bounds too. The book thereby presents a more holistic and insightful understanding of poverty than if it were written from the perspective of a single academic discipline.

The chapters that follow draw on academic literature from philosophy; economics; anthropology; sociology; women, gender, and sexuality studies; political science; and public health. We also draw on research written by international and national practitioners about what does and does not work for poverty reduction programs. And we draw on our own fieldwork. For this book, we have carried out research in Latin America (Mexico, Chile, Argentina, Guatemala, El Salvador, Panama, Nicaragua, Costa Rica, and Brazil), Asia (Malaysia, Indonesia, India, and Kyrgyzstan), Africa (Zambia, Ghana, Rwanda, and the Democratic Republic of the Congo) and several post-socialist countries in Europe (Bosnia-Herzegovina, Croatia, Hungary, and Slovakia).

The second main objective of the book is to introduce undergraduate and graduate students to the capabilities approach: what capabilities/opportunities do people need to lead a life that they value? Though there is a considerable literature on this approach to poverty and development, there are few introductory survey texts. Those that do exist we have found too specialized, or more philosophical than empirical, or otherwise not written in an accessible way to students new to the topic. We aimed to write a book that would present readers with some of the key concepts of the capabilities approach, then apply those concepts to a number of causes of and solutions to poverty. Because this book is a survey, we emphasize breadth rather than depth in our coverage; there are certainly subtleties and specificities that we neglect. We do not pretend to be exhaustive, but do suggest additional readings at the end of each chapter for those who want to deepen their knowledge about a particular theme or topic. That same caveat applies to our coverage of the causes and solutions. We do not pretend to be comprehensive. We chose to cover causes and solutions where we had expertise, and which we thought would be interesting to analyze through the lens of capabilities.

The third main objective is pedagogical in nature. We wanted the book to be *teachable*, much more so than most of what academics write, including other textbooks. This book emerged from a course on global poverty that we developed to complement an existing course at our academic institution called Poverty in America. Given all the research and teaching that had been synthesized for the Poverty in America course, we decided it was important to examine many of the same questions from a global perspective, preferencing voices from the global south but also recognizing that some of the same causes contribute to poverty in the global north. We believe – given that we live in an interconnected, globalized world where economic, political, cultural, and environmental issues affect us all – it is just as important to understand poverty and inequality at home as well as abroad. And though the primary focus of this book is poverty in low- and middle-income countries (where most of the world's poor live), the reader should understand that poverty and inequality pervade many societies. Inequality in high-income countries can mean that certain groups have levels of deprivation in life expectancy, hunger, or illiteracy comparable to low-income countries.

In contrast to many textbooks, this one has (unapologetically) an ethical perspective. In Chapter 1 we state our fundamental ethical assumptions for studying poverty, which depend above all on conceiving poverty as a human problem. This means that for all the diverse definitions and methods we utilize, the focus must always be on how poverty affects human beings as individuals and not just on abstract, aggregate statistics. For this reason, the book includes vignettes about real individuals affected by the topics we discuss. Ethnographic description helps us visualize and understand how it might feel to be that particular person. Compassion is an essential quality when considering the causes of and solutions to poverty because it helps us appreciate the urgency of the topic. Focusing on poverty as a human problem, too, connects to our collective responsibility to achieve the book's goals of understanding what causes poverty and how it can be reduced.

Just as the book does not aim to be exhaustive and comprehensive, nor does it aim to be definitive. We try to avoid authoritatively pronouncing on what students and readers should conclude. Instead, we encourage debate and discussion. On one issue we do presume a bedrock definitiveness, namely on the need to address the injustice of poverty. Besides our own ethics and beliefs on what constitutes good pedagogy, in this aspect of the book's approach we rely on some influential inspiration. This inspiration comes from Amartya Sen – the founder of the capabilities approach – who wrote that "the greatest relevance of ideas of justice lies in the identification of patent injustice, on which reasoned agreement is possible" (Sen 1999: 287). We hope this book promotes both reasoning and agreement on at least this bedrock issue. Beyond that, the book is very much aligned with Paulo Freire's pedagogy that those who have been invisibilized and marginalized by poverty and exclusion can be the authors of the solutions to the challenges they confront. In this, our book's objectives, approach, and inspiration are wonderfully summed up by Melanie Walker: "The key question is: what do I as a human being become as a consequence of what I experience in learning about human development?" For us as teachers of human development, "the essential question is therefore: what kinds of human beings do I hope my students might one day become?" (Walker 2009: 335). We hope that this book provides some useful answers to both of these questions.

When Routledge approached us to do this second edition, it seemed a confirmation that the book had been successful in many of its goals. Besides being used at many different universities around the world, the first edition was also translated into Spanish. The first edition also served as part of the inspiration for the documentary *Hunger and Hope: Lessons from Ethiopia and Guatemala* (available for viewing at www.ricksteves.com/watch-read-listen/video/tv-show/hunger-and-hope). For this second edition, all of the chapters have received a thorough revision, which included updating with the latest statistics and most recent scholarship. Some chapters were significantly restructured, such as Chapter 3 ("Multidimensional measurements of poverty and wellbeing") and Chapter 6 (formerly focused on gender, now titled "Race, class, gender, and poverty"). Our colleague Audrey Hudgins also contributed an all-new chapter on migration and poverty (Chapter 9) to provide a much-needed analysis of one of the highest profile and most controversial phenomena in global development in recent years. Finally, it bears mentioning that this second edition was prepared primarily during the pandemic year of 2020. While the chapter on health and poverty (Chapter 4) was updated with an addendum on the pandemic, at the time of writing, the impacts of the SARS-CoV-2 virus on a range of development outcomes remain to be seen. The coming years will reveal just how much this massive global challenge will require a new analysis of relationships between poverty, capabilities, and human wellbeing.

## Works cited

Sen, Amartya. 1999. *Development as Freedom*. New York: Knopf.

Walker, Melanie. 2009. "Teaching the Human Development and Capability Approach: Some Pedagogical Implications", in Séverine Deneulin and Lila Shahani, eds. *An Introduction to the Human Development and Capability Approach*. London: Earthscan:.

# Acknowledgments

Over a decade of researching and writing this book, in both its first and second editions, we have been fortunate to work with, learn from, and be assisted by many inspirational people on five continents. Our list of gratitude is long and deep, and an acknowledgement here is a frustratingly incomplete attempt to repay our debts, not least because the list is actually so much longer than what we can mention below. Thank you to all who helped us along the way, and if we have not mentioned you by name, accept our apologies for the oversight. And, of course, the standard disclaimer applies: any errors in this text are our own.

Thanks to the staff at Seattle University's Lemieux Library who tracked down research materials from far and wide. Thanks to current and former colleagues at Seattle University, particularly in the Matteo Ricci Institute and the International Studies Department in the College of Arts and Sciences, for providing a worthy intellectual home. Jodi O'Brien and Tanya Hayes provided useful feedback on chapters 6 and 10 respectively. This book would not have been possible without support from the Seattle University Endowed Mission Fund and SU's Global Engagement Grants program. Ben also thanks his former colleagues in the United Kingdom at the Behavioural Insights Team and the National Foundation for Educational Research for the opportunity to work on impactful development projects.

Thanks to all the many people at development organizations we have met over the course of our fieldwork. Particular thanks to: Arturo Aguilar, Jennifer Anderson, Robin Bush, Kizzy Gandy, Merit Hietanen, David Holiday, Jessica Olney, Ciaran O'Toole, and Andrew Russell for participating in the international development careers interviews; Thomas Awiapo and CRS staff, and Cole Hoover and Lumana staff in Ghana; Sabina Čehajić-Clancy, Amir Telibečirović, Sanel Marić, and Kurt Bassuener in Bosnia; Rafael and Shirley Luna and Moisés Leon in Costa Rica; Peter Henriot, SJ, Leonard Chiti, SJ, and the staff of the Jesuit Centre for Theological Reflection in Zambia; Modestine Etoy and the amazing young women she works with in Goma, Democratic Republic of the Congo; the faculty, staff, and students at the Gashora Girls Academy in Gashora, Rwanda; the faculty and students at Universitas Sanata Dharma in Indonesia; in India, staff from the Ernakulam, Trivandrum, and Kochi Social Service Societies, from Caritas and the Karunya Trust, and from Pratham Mumbai; Danessa Luna and her staff at the Guatemalan women's organization, Asociación Generando, in Chimaltenango, Guatemala as well as their friends and contacts around the country; Gül Inançand the other team members at Opening Universities for Refugees; and, last but not least, José (Chepe) Idiáquez, SJ, the rector of the Universidad Centroamericana (UCA) in Managua, Nicaragua, and students and colleagues at the UCA.

Thanks to Helena Hurd, Matthew Shobbrook, and Kelly Watkins at Routledge for shepherding this project to publication. Helena saw the relevance of an interdisciplinary textbook from her first read of the manuscript, and we are very grateful for her keen eye and support. An enormous debt of gratitude to Audrey Hudgins for many reasons, one in particular that she will understand. A huge thanks to Paula Brentlinger, not only for contributing an excellent chapter on health and poverty, but also for being a brilliant mind and dear friend over many years. Emily Lieb, a colleague at Seattle University and US historian, made valuable suggestions for including historical perspective when applicable. Serena also thanks her writing companions, Shady Cosgrove and Irina Carlota Silber; her children, Meme García, Alexandra Bosworth, and Raquel Idiáquez; and her partner, Marty Bosworth. Ben also thanks Rick Steves, for using his bully pulpit to help raise awareness of global poverty; Gretchen Hund and Ted Andrews, for all their support and encouragement over the years; and Eric and Lisa Sieberson, for being family despite sharing no DNA.

Finally, and perhaps most importantly, thanks to our students. It has been a great joy to teach many remarkable young people over the years. They helped us create a wonderful learning community, both in the classroom in Seattle and in the field in a number of countries. We cannot mention all their names, but several shouldered extra duty. Janie Bube, Morgan Marler, Feeza Mohammad, Mark Olmstead, Helen Packer, Kelsea Shannon, Mara Silvers, and Callie Woody accompanied us on a research trip to Bosnia in 2014. Kelly Armijo, Meme García, Andrew Gorvetzian, Lauren Kastanas, Michael Keenen, Lindsay Mannion, Jacqueline Shrader, and Caitlin Terashima accompanied a research trip to Guatemala in 2013. Erika Bailey, Phillip Bruan, Emily Chambers, Raine Donohue, Laura Gomez, Melissa Howlett, Sophia Sanders, Caitlin Terashima, and Kimberly Whalen assisted us on a trip to Ghana in 2012. A special thanks to former student Anna Pickett for recommended readings about disability rights in global perspective as well as former students who worked as our research assistants and/or contributed vignettes: Sy Bean, Mason Bryan, Sophia Dex, Jill Douglas, Julian Fellerman, Meme García, Andrew Gorvetzian, Michael Kaemingk, Alex Ozkan, Sophia Sanders, and KJ Zunigha.

*In gratitude,*

*Serena Cosgrove and Benjamin Curtis*

# 1 Building a framework for understanding poverty

*Benjamin Curtis and Serena Cosgrove*

## Learning objectives

- Explain how poverty is multidimensional and depends on deprivation and thresholds.
- Describe income and monetary definitions of poverty, and analyze their strengths and weaknesses.
- Describe the capabilities definition of poverty, and analyze its strengths and weaknesses.
- Understand the distinction between capabilities and functionings, and how entitlements can be enshrined in laws but not actualized in reality.
- Summarize how human rights, structural violence, wellbeing, absolute and relative poverty relate to capabilities.
- Explain what it means to conceive of poverty as a human problem.

## Introduction

It may have been the most troubling place we have ever visited. It was an informal settlement (often called a "slum") in a major city in the developing world; for the moment, it does not matter exactly where. An estimated one million people were living in an area of about 500 acres, creating one of the highest population densities in the world. Sometimes families of eight people would be living in houses of maybe 100 square feet, roughly the same size as a bedroom in an average home in a high-income country. If they were fortunate, people would have running water in their house for about three hours a day. Otherwise, they had to get water from a communal spigot. In either case, the water was not safe to drink. Very few people in this community had bathrooms in their homes. Instead, they had to use the public toilets. Because of the scarcity of services and the very high population density, one public toilet would serve around 1500 people. The stench was horrifying. There were few paved streets in this settlement. Rather, it was mostly pathways through dilapidated structures, and many of those pathways had open sewage running along them. There was garbage everywhere. One children's playground was on top of a giant mound of trash.

Though people might own the precarious structure where they lived, very few owned the land beneath it, which means that their housing options remain insecure. If people did earn an income, they might be lucky to make the equivalent of USD 2 a day. Oftentimes, the working conditions were appalling. Some people worked in a small plastics recycling industry. All day long they would sort by hand through giant piles of plastic – including things like discarded syringes – then melt the plastic down into other things. They had little to no protection from the melting plastic's hazardous fumes, and yet this is what they did every day just to earn two dollars. There was actually a whole range of jobs in this community. Some people made pottery, some made food, some made clothing. As hard as life here may sound, many people came because they could make more money than trying to farm land in the rural areas. Why, then, was this place so troubling? It was not just the sewage, the cramped living conditions, the fumes, or the paltry wages. It was that human beings should not have to live with their opportunities so drastically restricted. And yet for most people in the community, they had no better option. They were poor.

Poverty can be found virtually everywhere. It is a universal human problem. However, poverty may not be the same everywhere. The very definition of "poor" can change from place to place – and yet it can also remain the same. There are some traps that will make you poor no matter where you are. This chapter is concerned with definitions because a study of global poverty must start with trying to understand what "poverty" means. We will first consider how poverty is multidimensional and predicated on deprivation. We will then review several ways of defining poverty, though we will ultimately suggest that a lack of opportunities is a basic, underlying definition. We examine monetary/income understandings of poverty before turning to the theory of capabilities and functionings. We will also discuss the idea of wellbeing, and a basic set of rights to which all humans are entitled. This is a necessary foundation for understanding what poverty is, what causes it, how it affects people, and how it can be reduced. Subsequent chapters will build on this foundation to expand upon the chapter's themes. One idea will remain consistent, however: poverty is a human problem, so just as with the example of the informal settlement above, we must never lose sight of the experiences, hopes, aspirations, and opportunities human beings have to live a life that they value.

## What is poverty?

How can we define poverty? This is one of those words that people use conversationally, with a meaning they think they understand, but often without thinking deeply about possible definitions. Stop right now and take a minute to think about how you would define poverty. What does it mean to be poor?

On the one hand, the definition could seem simple – but it is not nearly as simple as it initially seems. The most common way of defining poverty is "not having enough money." But why use money (or the lack thereof) to define poverty? What is money good for? The idea is that money (or income more broadly) is really a proxy to indicate a person's or family's ability to acquire goods necessary to survive. Money can be used to buy food, for example. Therefore, another potential definition of poverty is "not having enough food." If a person is starving not by his own choice, then he is almost certainly poor; he is lacking the means necessary to survive. This food definition of poverty is most applicable in low income countries, since in high income countries it is very rare that people do not get enough calories (though the calories they get may not be optimally nutritious). When we add the idea of food poverty to monetary poverty, the definition of poverty becomes more complex, since we recognize that poverty is a *multidimensional* phenomenon. There is more than one way that a person can be poor, and thus there is more than one way of defining poverty.

As this chapter progresses, we will be exploring how poverty is multidimensional. There is nonetheless a core idea to all definitions of poverty, namely a shortfall or deprivation of something, whether something tangible such as money or food, or intangible such as rights or respect. The specific meaning of *deprivation* is key here: it assumes that a person is deprived of something to which he or she is entitled. Does this presume that every person is somehow entitled to a certain amount of money? Not necessarily. What it does presume is that every person is entitled to a basic material standard of living (such as having enough food) that a certain amount of money can buy. Therefore, a shortfall of money below the threshold necessary to acquire the basic necessities (such as food) deprives a person of a minimally adequate standard of living. In addition to deprivation, then, also essential to the idea of poverty is some conception of a *threshold*: above this threshold, whether it relates to money, food, rights, respect, etc., a person is not poor, but below it, he or she is. The question of what constitutes the threshold for an adequate minimum in the areas of income, food, rights, and respect is a debatable one that we will return to repeatedly.

## Income definitions of poverty

Combining the ideas of deprivation and a threshold, we need to examine the definition of income poverty in greater detail. Income is certainly a vital component of meeting one's needs. At the individual level, one's income is the sum of all income-generating activities. Those activities can be in formal sector jobs, that is, those jobs that are regulated and taxed by the government, and/or in the informal sector, which is commonly thought of as "under the table" work that is not reported to the government. Informal sector jobs can include domestic service work, construction, farm work, food preparation, sales in the marketplace, etc., and they are very common in lower income countries. At the national level, the gross domestic product (GDP) – or the total market value of all goods and services produced in the country – is a way of measuring a country's economic prosperity. When this figure is divided by the number of people in a country, you have the GDP per capita, often used as an indicator of a country's standard of living. According to International Monetary Fund data from 2020, GDP per capita in the United States was USD 67,426, compared to USD 873 in the Democratic Republic of the Congo (DRC). While much more will be said in Chapter 3 about such measurements, a quick glance at these figures suggests that there is much more poverty in the DRC than in the United States.

Since the end of the Second World War, lack of income has been the principal definition economists have used to describe poverty. However, given what we have already said about multidimensionality, do income/monetary definitions of poverty tell the whole story? In this book, we argue that monetary or income definitions of poverty are useful, but do not include many critical dimensions of what it means to be poor. Income has an instrumental value, which means it can be used for certain other ends, such as acquiring things that enable a person to live a life that she values. The instrumental value of income is a prime reason why economists use it as a proxy for wellbeing or poverty. Having enough money alone, however, does not guarantee that a person will be able to live a life that she values. For example, those who are rich but sick will probably not rate themselves high on wellbeing, even if money may help them get treatment. Similarly, it is conceivable that someone who is rich but still subject to legal or cultural discrimination of various kinds, or denied basic civil rights, cannot be said to have escaped forms of poverty.

Part of the problem is that income (or other resources, including money) are not always easily converted into things a person values. Personal, environmental, and institutional factors can all limit the instrumental or proxy value of income. This is an example of how institutional factors can complicate using income as a proxy: imagine two sets of parents, each with the same income, but they live in two different countries. In country A, there is a good public education system, but in country B the public system is shoddy, so parents who want a good education for their children will pay for private schools (Sen 1999: 70). Who is better off, the parents in country A or country B? They have the same level of income, but in this example the parents in country A are better off because they are not spending additional money to send their children to school. The point of this example is that income cannot fully capture wellbeing. As another example, imagine a family whose income is somewhat above the poverty line, but where the parents squander the money on alcohol, presents for themselves, or unwise investments rather than spending the money to ensure that their children are adequately fed, educated, and otherwise cared for. In this example, because the family's income is above the poverty line, it may seem that they have a basically adequate standard of living. However, the way that income is distributed within the family disadvantages the children. Such unequal distribution of income is all too common in many societies, with women and children most often getting less than a fair share.

It is also important to remember that income is not the same as employment. In the case of someone who has lost their job, income may be state welfare disbursements, but their self-esteem may be affected by not generating their own income. In this case again, income cannot equate to wellbeing. The problems with using income as the sole indicator of poverty magnify at the aggregate level. Imagine a country, such as the United States, with a high GDP per capita but also substantial levels of income inequality. In such a case where income is so unevenly distributed, there will be a small group of people with high incomes while the majority of the people have lower incomes. However, because of the way the numbers have been averaged, it appears that people are richer than they actually are: the few rich people have skewed the average. Poverty may be much more widespread, and much more severe, than the numbers indicate. Furthermore, economic growth – particularly in countries with high income inequality – is not the same as increased income for everyone. Because of income inequality and other structures of discrimination and marginalization, the theory that economic growth automatically benefits the poor – that is, that "a rising tide lifts all boats" – is not necessarily correct. When a country's economy is growing, many people might not get to share in the wealth.

Few theorists argue against the utility of income at the individual or aggregate level as one potential indicator of poverty, but it is important to recognize that income as an indicator has its limitations. The simplest definition of poverty as "not having enough money" is therefore inadequate. To reiterate, poverty is multidimensional: it cannot be truly understood via a single perspective, whether money, food, or some other dimension. We should also return to the idea of deprivation. What does it really mean? Deprivation of what? Deprivation can take many forms, not just of the income needed to sustain oneself. In fact, a lack of money does not serve as an adequate proxy for lack of political rights, lack of safety or control over one's body, or a lack of adequate health and education. If deprivations of income and economic growth are insufficient for understanding poverty, then what other deprivations should we consider?

### The capabilities approach

The capabilities approach calls attention to deprivation of opportunities, choices, and freedoms. This is a powerful, provocative, and multidimensional way of understanding what constitutes a good human life. It is most associated with the Nobel Prize-winning economist and philosopher Amartya Sen, but its ideas have been elaborated by a number of others as well, including the philosophers Martha Nussbaum and Ingrid Robeyns, and the development ethicist David Crocker, to name but a few. Sen developed this approach in part from a series of lectures at the World Bank in which he encouraged the Bank to expand its thinking about what poverty is. He agreed that income is an important asset in helping people get out of poverty, but he argued for a more comprehensive approach in which the goal of public policy should be securing the basic abilities necessary for a human to lead a fulfilled life. The capabilities approach thus provides a means of evaluating minimum requirements for quality of life, which then constitute demands of social justice for government policy to guarantee those minimum requirements.

Rather than focusing on a country's economy, the capabilities approach focuses on individual humans. It prioritizes "the actual freedom of choice a person has over alternative lives that he or she can live" (Sen 1990: 114). The words "freedom" and "choice" are key: this approach emphasizes that every human being must have the opportunity to choose aspects of a life that he or she will value. As Nussbaum has written, the capabilities approach holds "that the crucial good societies should be promoting for their people is a set of opportunities, or substantial freedoms, which people then may or may not exercise in action: the choice is theirs" (Nussbaum 2011: 18). People may value different things, both because of their individual desires and how those desires are (at least partially) socially constructed. What matters is that people have the freedom to choose what they want their lives to be.

What are capabilities? Capabilities are the processes that allow freedom of action and decisions. They are best thought of as opportunities for life choices. Can you choose your profession? Can you participate in your society? Can you choose where to live? Can you live to a ripe old age? Essentially, capabilities are the freedom to do things that are important to you. A capability is not the choice or the opportunity itself; rather, it is the *potential* to choose, the freedom to choose. Writers in this tradition describe capabilities as the answer to the question, "What is this person able to do and to be?" (Nussbaum 2011: 20), and as the freedom to enjoy functionings (Comim 2008: 4). The term "functionings" is another fundamental concept in this approach. Think of it as the other side of the coin to "capabilities." It is not enough to be able to do something, to have the capability. Do you actually do it? If capabilities are what you can possibly do, then functionings are what you *actually* do, the outcomes or realizations of your choices. Functionings are people putting their capabilities into action (Sen 1999: 17). A functioning, Sen explains, "is an achievement of a person, what she or he manages to do or be" (Sen 1985: 10).

The distinction between capabilities and functionings is not merely philosophical quibbling – it is a very important consideration in evaluating wellbeing. For example, a woman may have the education and vocational skill to carry out a particular job, but she is unable to use those skills in the marketplace because women are not allowed to work outside the home in her society. In this case, she is denied the capability to hold a job: she does not have the freedom to choose to work outside the home. Nussbaum gives an example of how an important capability is often not actualized as a functioning: "Many societies educate people so that they are capable of free speech on political matters – internally – but then deny them free expression in practice through repression of speech" (2011: 21). You could have the capability to engage in political participation, but you might not choose to do so. In such a case, you have chosen not to actualize your capability as a functioning, which is justifiable because it is your own personal choice. But it is also possible that the actualization of your capability is thwarted not through your own volition, as for example, when a government prevents your political participation, or you are unable to achieve the functioning of reading because you have been denied an adequate education.

A common example that may help clarify these concepts is the bicycle. The bicycle is a resource that allows its rider to convert a capability into a functioning. The capability is the opportunity to move around faster than walking, something a person might choose because she values it. A person could have this capability – for example, if she knows how to ride, owns a bike, and social norms permit women to ride – but she may choose not to convert it to a functioning for whatever reason. The functioning itself is mobility: it is the realization of the capability to move around faster than walking. When a person is able to convert her capability to a functioning – actualizing her opportunity to move around by becoming mobile on the bike – then she derives (hopefully) some utility, some satisfaction, from doing so (Alkire and Deneulin 2009: 42). This example helps demonstrate why the twinned concepts of capabilities and functionings are important. A person could have many capabilities but might not realize any of them. This means that a person could have a great deal of freedom in theory – she could have the freedom to choose a variety of things that she could value – but that freedom may be insufficient if her choices cannot be converted to actions. Both capabilities (freedoms, opportunities) and functionings (actualizations, realizations) matter for a person's life.

*Defining the central capabilities*

We have already given some examples of capabilities, such as political participation or mobility. An important (but contentious) topic within the capabilities approach concerns the central capabilities, that is, the basic capabilities to which every human being is entitled. There is considerable room for disagreement in identifying the basic capabilities, in that the capabilities approach recognizes that different societies will value different things, and hence there will be some acceptable difference among cultures and individuals as to what constitutes a valuable human life. The imperative nonetheless is that communities decide democratically on the central capabilities for their society. The hope is that through a participatory, deliberative process, a society can arrive at some prioritization of what every person should be free to be and to do. However, such a process must be truly democratic, inclusive of all voices in a society, so that people or groups in power are not able to dominate and impose their values.

Where the discussion truly gets contentious, however, is with identifying what the basic, *universal* capabilities should be, those that have a value regardless of cultural or societal specificities. Interestingly, Sen, the father of the capabilities approach, has refused to specify a list of basic, central capabilities, insisting on the need for the democratic process mentioned above to determine them in culturally specific contexts. Other writers, though, have proposed such a list, chief among them Nussbaum (see also Gough 2003, Qizilbash 2002). Nussbaum claims that it is possible to identify a consensus about what constitutes a valuable human life – what basic capabilities every human is entitled to – that transcends cultures. Part of her rationale is to establish a kind of moral authority with such a list, so that students, researchers, policy makers and indeed anyone can identify when a person falls below the minimum thresholds of capabilities and is thereby deprived of some basic rights. The list of all potential human capabilities could be very long, but the objective of a list of "basic" capabilities is to set out the aspects of a life essential to wellbeing.

What are the basic capabilities? Despite the disputes, there is some consensus, in that most writers on the subject do find areas of common ground. Many writers mention having adequate health, enough food and nutrition, and at least enough education to ensure basic knowledge and the capability of independent thought and expression (see Saith 2001, Desai 1995). Sen himself, despite his avoidance of an explicit list, tends to mention these same features, and adds the ideas of political participation and freedom from discrimination on the basis of race, religion, and gender. These common areas have not been arrived at purely theoretically; empirical research has made some similar findings as to what people consistently value. From their massive ethnographic research project, *Voices of the Poor*, Narayan and Petesch point to these as basic capabilities that people value: bodily health; bodily integrity; respect and dignity; social belonging; cultural identity; imagination, information, and education; organizational capacity; and political representation (Narayan and Petesch 2002). In David Clark's research in South Africa, people mentioned jobs, housing, education, income, family and friends, religion, health, food, good clothes, recreation and relaxation, and safety and economic security as the major aspects of a valuable life (Clark 2005a). While the specific meanings people may assign to each of those (admittedly somewhat vague) labels may vary, it is nonetheless apparent that some consonance holds for the fundamental *categories*, such as with health, education/information, sociability, and safety.

Nussbaum's own list embraces many of these same categories and adds a few idiosyncratic particulars. Box 1.1 enumerates and briefly explains Nussbaum's list. Her list is by no means canonical or exhaustive; it has definitely sparked debate, and we include it here not as a complete endorsement on her view of the central capabilities but rather because it is one of the most influential lists and, as such, a useful springboard for discussions of what the central human capabilities are or should be. Note how the list is phrased: "being able" expresses the idea that these are capabilities that people must be free to choose to realize if they want to, but they do not have to choose to realize them. That is why this is a list of basic capabilities and not basic functionings.

---

**Box 1.1 Martha Nussbaum's list of the central capabilities**

1  **Life**. "Being able to live to the end of a human life of normal length, not dying prematurely, or before one's life is so reduced as to be not worth living." The principle here relates to life expectancy, asserting that no one should have to accept a life of seriously foreshortened mortality.

2  **Bodily health**. "Being able to have good health, including reproductive health; to be adequately nourished; to have adequate shelter." These capabilities relate to food security and shelter security, but also to the fact that no one should have to accept a life with especially high morbidity (i.e. susceptibility to disease).

3  **Bodily integrity**. This capability is about an individual's right to have control over and security for his or her own body. It includes freedom from violence of all kinds, including sexual assault, as well as mobility, and choice over one's sex life and reproduction.

4  **Senses, imagination, and thought**. This range of capabilities upholds the principles of freedom of expression, freedom of conscience, and the right to education; it is about being able to use one's mind freely and imaginatively.

The idea is that everyone should be able to think creatively and individually. Education up to minimum standards of literacy, mathematics, and science is necessary to support that ability, but also to support the capability for practical reason, listed below.

5   **Emotions**. "Being able to have attachments to things and people outside ourselves," to those who love us, to feel longing, gratitude, anger, and the full complement of emotions. This item connects to the freedom that everyone must have to form intimate relationships, but it is also part of freedom of association.

6   **Practical reason**. This is intellectual freedom broadly construed, including freedom of religion. It stipulates that every human should be able to think for him or herself, and to make reasoned choices about the life one leads.

7   **Affiliation**. This refers to a bundle of ideas on being able to live beneficially in society. It again relates to freedom of association, but it is conceived not just in political terms as the freedom to form or join political parties or other societal organizations. It is also about sociability, the capability to have a variety of social relations, and to do so without being discriminated against because of one's race, gender, sexual orientation, ethnicity, caste, religion or any other ascriptive category.

8   **Other species**. "Being able to live with concern for and in relation to animals, plants, and the world of nature."

9   **Play**. "Being able to laugh, to play, to enjoy recreational activities."

10  **Control over one's environment**. This is another bundle of political and civil rights that relate to being able to shape the conditions in which a person lives. This includes political participation and freedom of speech, freedom from unreasonable search and seizure, and the equal right to hold property. It also relates to work, including freedom from employment discrimination and other unfair working conditions.

Source: adapted from Nussbaum (2011).

There is a degree of overlap or repetition in Nussbaum's list, such as with the multiple mentions of freedom of association and expression. Part of the reason for the overlap is Nussbaum's insistence that affiliation and practical reason play an "architectonic role" for the other capabilities (Nussbaum 2011: 39). This means that affiliation and reason are essential to a person's deciding what sort of life she values. They are also essential, in Nussbaum's view, to human dignity. She envisions a situation whereby someone might be well nourished and well educated, enjoying many of the basic capabilities, and yet without the freedom to express herself politically because of government restrictions. In such a case, that person is denied her dignity, since she is being treated like an infant. She is not truly free to make choices for herself, nor is she free to participate adequately in the life of her community, which must necessarily include helping make decisions about how her community is governed. Nussbaum's list also leaves some room for societally contextualized variation. While the list attempts to establish levels below which no one should fall, different societies may establish minimum thresholds above the levels that Nussbaum suggests. In other words, there is the potential that different societies could adapt Nussbaum's central capabilities to their own cultural context, as long as they do not violate the minimum guarantees.

Because these are basic capabilities, considerations of equality and equity are important. While everyone is equally entitled to these capabilities, sometimes equality is not a sufficient standard. Nussbaum alludes to the possibility that women could have an "equal" right to vote as men, but that their votes would only be counted as one-quarter of a man's. Similarly, everyone might have an equal right to the minimum threshold of a primary education, but that threshold is almost meaningless unless one also considers the *quality* of the primary education. Some schools may be well equipped and provide an excellent education, while others may lack resources and teach children relatively little (Nussbaum 2011: 41). Thus, though Nussbaum regards these capabilities as the "bare minimum" that any government must secure for its people at a minimum threshold level, sometimes getting everyone to that threshold is not enough to satisfy justice concerns. The reason is that the threshold level may be inequitable, disproportionately disadvantaging some people.

Imagine for instance that everyone gets one anti-malaria pill. For people who live in high or dry areas, where malaria is not endemic, one pill may be adequate. But for people who live in malaria endemic areas, the equal standard of one pill will not do enough to help them. They may need more than one pill – an unequal distribution if the people in the high, dry areas get only one – in order to enjoy the same health as the people who do not live in malaria endemic areas. In this case, because systemic or other contextual factors create disproportionate disadvantage, an equitable (rather than equal) distribution of resources is required. Equity means ensuring that people who are disadvantaged receive proportionately more resources based on what they need to overcome the disadvantage.

The idea of basic entitlements that all people must be guaranteed should bring to mind the Universal Declaration of Human Rights (see Box 1.2), and indeed there are many affinities between human rights and the capabilities approach (see i.a. Vizard *et al.* 2011, Sen 2005 and 2004, Nussbaum 1997). Both paradigms insist that human beings be treated as ends and not as means, which implies protections for certain fundamental things such as freedom of conscience, political participation, and personal security. Both depend upon principles of universality, equality, and interdependence necessary to safeguard our own specific rights plus each other's rights (Deneulin 2009: 60). There are, however, meaningful differences between human rights and capabilities, such that these two approaches are not identical. For instance, human rights primarily depend upon state and legal institutions, while the fulfilment of capabilities depends upon a more diverse network of formal and informal institutions, including government, cultural norms, civil society organizations, and businesses. The capabilities approach also adds the idea of functionings, paying more attention to the dynamics of the *realization* of fundamental guarantees than does the human rights approach.

---

**Box 1.2 Selected rights from the Universal Declaration of Human Rights**

**Article 3:**

Everyone has the right to life, liberty, and security of person.

**Article 7:**

All are equal before the law and are entitled without any discrimination to equal protection of the law. All are entitled to equal protection against any discrimination in violation of this Declaration and against any incitement to such discrimination.

**Article 13:**

1   Everyone has the right to freedom of movement and residence within the borders of each state.
2   Everyone has the right to leave any country, including his own, and to return to his country.

**Article 18:**

Everyone has the right to freedom of thought, conscience, and religion; this right includes freedom to change his religion or belief, and freedom, either alone or in community with others and in public or private, to manifest his religion or belief in teaching, practice, worship, and observance.

**Article 19:**

Everyone has the right to freedom of opinion and expression; this right includes freedom to hold opinions without interference and to seek, receive, and impart information and ideas through any media and regardless of frontiers.

**Article 20:**

1   Everyone has the right to freedom of peaceful assembly and association.
2   No one may be compelled to belong to an association.

**Article 21:**

1   Everyone has the right to take part in the government of his country, directly or through freely chosen representatives.
2   Everyone has the right of equal access to public service in his country.
3   The will of the people shall be the basis of the authority of government; this will shall be expressed in periodic and genuine elections which shall be by universal and equal suffrage and shall be held by secret vote or by equivalent free voting procedures.

**Article 23:**

1   Everyone has the right to work, to free choice of employment, to just and favourable conditions of work and to protection against unemployment.
2   Everyone, without any discrimination, has the right to equal pay for equal work.
3   Everyone who works has the right to just and favourable remuneration ensuring for himself and his family an existence worthy of human dignity, and supplemented, if necessary, by other means of social protection.
4   Everyone has the right to form and to join trade unions for the protection of his interests.

**Article 25:**

1   Everyone has the right to a standard of living adequate for the health and well-being of himself and of his family, including food, clothing, housing and medical care and necessary social services, and the right to security in the event of unemployment, sickness, disability, widowhood, old age, or other lack of livelihood in circumstances beyond his control.

2   Motherhood and childhood are entitled to special care and assistance. All children, whether born in or out of wedlock, shall enjoy the same social protection.

**Article 26:**

1   Everyone has the right to education. Education shall be free, at least in the elementary and fundamental stages. Elementary education shall be compulsory. Technical and professional education shall be made generally available and higher education shall be equally accessible to all on the basis of merit.

2   Education shall be directed to the full development of the human personality and to the strengthening of respect for human rights and fundamental freedoms. It shall promote understanding, tolerance, and friendship among all nations, racial or religious groups, and shall further the activities of the United Nations for the maintenance of peace.

3   Parents have a prior right to choose the kind of education that shall be given to their children.

Source: www.un.org/en/universal-declaration-human-rights/.

Ultimately, though, these two approaches complement each other. The capabilities approach benefits from the moral legitimacy that human rights grant to the fundamental guarantees, and the accountability of institutions for respecting them. As the 2000 United Nations Human Development Report declared:

> Human rights express the bold idea that all people have claims to social arrangements that protect them from the worst abuses and deprivations – and that secure the freedom for a life of dignity. Human development, in turn, is a process of enhancing human capabilities – to expand choices and opportunities so that each person can lead a life of respect and value. When human development and human rights advance together, they reinforce one another – expanding people's capabilities and protecting their rights and fundamental freedoms.
>
> (UNDP 2000: 2)

Much more could be said about the relationship between rights and capabilities, and in subsequent chapters this theme will return. Throughout the book we will sometimes speak of "rights to capabilities," since that is an area where these two approaches intersect: as human beings, we all have inalienable rights to certain opportunities that are encapsulated by the notion of capabilities. For example, we all have the right to realize our capability of political participation. Thus, legal rights can be a way of guaranteeing capabilities. Box 1.2 gives a partial list of some rights from the Universal Declaration of Human Rights that could be considered congruent with basic capabilities; we encourage readers to read the Declaration's complete list for themselves.

*Other important concepts in the capabilities approach*

The capabilities approach moves quickly from asking whether or not someone can do something (has the capability) to whether or not they are actually doing it (realizing the capability, i.e. the functioning). The reason is that there is so much variability and heterogeneity of people's choices and differences of distribution of opportunities, not to mention the unreliability of preferences (Nussbaum 2011: 59). For this reason, in using the capabilities approach to understand poverty, we have to be careful with what "choice" really means. Take for example the problem of "adaptive preference," which means that our preferences (and hence our choices) adapt to our circumstances. "When society has put some things out of reach for some people," Nussbaum writes, "they typically learn not to want those things" (2011: 54). If a person has no conception that she could potentially choose *not* to get married at age 14 and become a mother by 15, then she has no knowledge of how her choices are unfairly limited. Her preferences have adapted to her circumstances. One of the normative assumptions of the capabilities approach, though, is that people deserve to be aware of a full range of life choices – they must have the freedom to choose from that range.

The freedom–limiting dynamic of adaptive preference may be especially severe for oppressed groups, in which members adjust their expectations to the restrictions (social, cultural, political, economic) in which they are embedded. This is why the capabilities approach also stresses the idea of *agency*; it is defined as "one's freedom to bring about achievements one values and which one attempts to produce" (Sen 1992: 57). In other words, it is the ability to actualize functionings, but most generally to pursue one's own goals, to effect change in one's life. A person's agency is important to consider because it is a way of thinking about the control that person exerts over his or her own destiny. We have to keep our attention on what people actually do because capabilities are only half of the story. As an example, a woman raised in a society that discourages her from working outside of the home may, because of adaptive preference, never seek a profession. Or she might have the capability of getting a job, but if her functioning is limited by discrimination, she is not free to choose. In this latter case, her agency is constricted.

Freedom to choose which capabilities to actualize into functionings is also a fundamental normative assumption for the capabilities approach. The choices a person makes here are rarely simple, however, nor is the principle of freedom of choice. Sen insists that evaluating a person's freedom to choose must incorporate some perspective on the quality, quantity, and diversity of available opportunities (Sen 1985, 1983). If a person is forced to choose between two evils – such as whether to stay in the village that the government has burned down, or flee to a refugee camp – then is it really accurate to say that he has adequate freedom of choice? And sometimes capabilities do not involve a meaningful choice. Does a person choose to live long, or choose whether or not to have good health? People typically have no choice about contracting such things as malaria and cholera, for example (Clark 2005a). The point of these questions about choice is this: while freedom to choose is a principle worth adhering to, in practice it is often easier to evaluate achieved functionings rather than possible choices when trying to determine a person's quality of life or poverty status. How to evaluate achieved functionings – in other words, to use the capabilities approach to measure human wellbeing and poverty – is a topic we will return to in Chapter 3.

Choice and agency can work differently for different people when it comes to achieving a life that one values. Many factors will impact the choices a person makes, including her evaluation of the possibility of attaining the functioning she desires. Another essential consideration are *conversion factors*, which are the factors that influence whether a person is able to convert a capability into a functioning. Sen cites three broad categories of conversion factors (Sen 2005: 153; see also Robeyns 2005):

1   Physical or mental heterogeneities among persons (including such things as disability, metabolism, sex, intelligence, and being prone to illness)
2   Variations in non-personal resources (including such social factors as norms, gender roles, societal hierarchies, societal cohesion, and public policies, such as on public health care or anti-discrimination laws and their enforcement)
3   Environmental diversities (such as climatic conditions, infrastructure such as roads, buildings, and bridges, geographical factors such as isolation, or varying threats from diseases or local crime).

Returning to the bicycle example, this is a resource that enables a person to convert a capability to a functioning, but several factors can limit the conversion possibilities. If someone has a physical disability, she might not be able to ride the bike. Or, as Robeyns explains, "if there are no paved roads or if a government or the dominant societal culture imposes a social or legal norm that women are not allowed to cycle without being accompanied by a male family member, then it becomes much more difficult or even impossible to use the good [i.e. the bicycle] to enable the functioning" (Robeyns 2005: 99). This example reminds us of two important things. First, that it is not just the goods, services, and resources a person has access to that will influence how she is able to convert capabilities to functionings. Various social institutions such as cultural norms are also influential, and for this reason it is necessary to study the situation and circumstances of people's actual lives in order to evaluate what they can choose and achieve.

Second, the example reinforces the earlier point about equity because some people may require more resources to convert the same capabilities to functionings (Walker 2004, 2003). A blind person may have the capability for mobility but will need different resources compared to the sighted person. In Walker's example, girls in South African schools may have difficulty converting the same capabilities as boys (they are equally able to read, do math etc.) to the same functionings because of certain factors such as cultural devaluing of girls' education, or threats of sexual harassment or violence, or sexist employment practices after completing an education. Thus, one must be very careful in assumptions about equality of opportunity, since even if such initial equality truly exists, it still does not mean that there is an equal chance to achieve the life choices that a person values. Initial opportunities are at best half of the story; achieved functionings are again essential for evaluating wellbeing. And in order to assist deprived or disadvantaged people to achieve those functionings, they may need disproportionate attention or resources compared to those who are not deprived or disadvantaged.

It should be clear that an idea of freedom is absolutely central to the capabilities approach. However, this is not the shallow understanding of freedom that one might assume. Freedom is not only what are known as positive liberties, that is, the freedom to do certain things, such as criticize the government, practice your own religion, live where you want, or marry whom you want. The idea of freedom does include positive liberties, but it also includes negative liberties, that is, freedom *from* hunger, fear, and shame. The capabilities approach embraces both notions of freedom. It does so by emphasizing the imperative of a person's freedom to choose to live a life that he values. That is a positive liberty, but it can include the freedom to avoid other things, that is, the negative liberty to be free from things the person does not value, such as hunger or discrimination or ignorance. Why freedom is so central to the capabilities approach is because often people who are poor simply are not free to escape their destitution. They lack alternatives; they lack agency and choice. Hence, they are condemned to the unfreedom of poverty, where they do not have adequate power to change their lives.

Another way that the capability approach's emphasis on freedom avoids simplistic, jejune understandings is by recognizing that freedom is not purely individualistic. Someone who crassly insists that freedom amounts to his positive liberty to do whatever he wants fails to realize how any individual's freedom depends upon the broader society. As noted above, many social factors can impinge upon the choices we make, whether norms about gender behavior, public policies connected to education or health care, or economic arrangements, including the distribution of wealth and power. How other people exercise their freedoms impacts how you or I exercise our freedoms. The choices we can make depend upon broader social circumstances, and we must be attentive to those circumstances when making our choices. Sometimes certain people (because of their relative status in society) will have more choices – and hence more freedoms – than other people. Sometimes, too, the actual attainment of a person's choice is not so important. Imagine a girl in the global south who decides to pursue a PhD: what matters is that she has the reasonable freedom to make that choice and is not unfairly constrained in the actual achievement of the goal. For the purposes of the capabilities theory, though, not everyone who wants to do a PhD must complete it in order for that person to be "free." As Sen explains, "the freedom to have any particular thing can be substantially distinguished from actually having that thing" (Sen 2005: 155).

---

### Box 1.3 Freedom and human wellbeing

On the roads around Lusaka, the capital city of Zambia, men and women sit by piles of stones. They sit right next to the asphalt, cars and trucks whizzing past them. They sit there all day long, in the intense heat or in the torrential downpours. All day long, day in and day out, they sit there with a hammer, breaking large stones into smaller stones. They breathe in the pollution from the vehicles and the dust from smashing rocks. They endure injuries to their hands and muscles from the grueling work. Every so often they will sell a pile of stones to someone who needs it for a construction project. They will earn the equivalent of a few dollars for a week's worth of work. Who would choose this work, if they had a choice? The stone breakers are often the poorest of the poor, lacking education, skills, or assets such as tools besides a hammer that might help them earn a less brutal living. What freedom do people in this situation have to choose a different life for themselves?

On an island in the southern Indian state of Kerala there is a village of Dalit people. The Dalit are the lowest in India's caste system, formerly known as "untouchables," victims of systemic cultural discrimination. The island where they live often floods during the monsoon season, which means their dwellings are insecure. Most of the men from the village work as day laborers, which is also insecure: some days you get work and money, and others you do not. The women make money by harvesting coconuts. They earn three cents for every coconut they sell. When a girl gets married, according to custom her family has to pay a dowry. Dowries can cost up to USD 1600, plus gold. How can you amass that kind of money if you earn three cents per coconut? Families often have to take on massive debt to be able to afford a dowry. Fortunately, Kerala has a decent system of public education, so many of the villagers go to school up to the tenth grade. Beyond that, however, tuition is no longer free, so they cannot continue. Why not leave the island and go live somewhere less flood-prone? Why not find some other means of generating an income besides harvesting coconuts? Why not refuse to pay the dowry if it is such a financial burden? These choices are not open to the villagers – they are not free to choose. In many ways, they live in unfreedom, and that is what it means to be poor.

## Poverty and capabilities

This book, in accordance with the capabilities approach, defines poverty as unfreedom, the deprivation of freedoms necessary to lead a fulfilled life. A person is poor when she lacks the capabilities to live the life she has reasonably chosen. Sen describes a number of unfreedoms that a person would surely not choose if she were free to choose something else: famine, malnutrition, excessive morbidity, lack of access to adequate health care and clean water, violations of political and civil rights (Sen 1999). These deprivations of inherent dignity, of basic capabilities – these unfreedoms to choose something better for oneself – qualify a person as poor. In this book we do presume that there are basic or central capabilities. Our bedrock definition of poverty is being deprived of the basic capabilities to which every human is entitled. Such deprivation places a person below the minimum threshold necessary for an adequate, dignified human life. Everyone by virtue of being human has dignity, but sometimes people live in situations where their dignity is compromised or unrealized. When such situations – whether social, political, familial, or economic – deny a person her dignity, then that person is deprived (Nussbaum 2011: 30). Such deprivation denies a person the freedom to choose a life that she has reason to value.

This conception of poverty links to two other important analytical perspectives. The first is again human rights: poverty is the denial of basic rights, which can be understood as rights to the basic capabilities (see Osmani 2005). People who are poor routinely suffer human rights violations because they are not able to access their basic capabilities. Hence for people to escape poverty, their human rights must be secure. The second analytical perspective – structural violence – expands on this link between rights and poverty. Structural violence is defined as "the avoidable disparity between the potential ability to fulfil basic needs and their actual fulfilment" (Ho 2007: 1). "Basic needs" refers to human rights and basic capabilities. "Structural" here relates to the unequal distribution of power in societies and around the globe. Such structures create inequalities of race, class, and gender which shape interactions in political and economic systems and via global institutions such as the United Nations and the World Trade Organization. These systemic inequalities mean that people with power get much more than their fair share of resources, while those who have little or no power are exploited – they have much reduced chances to meet their basic needs.

"Violence" in this case is both direct (e.g. physical brutality) but also indirect such as human rights violations. It is indirect because it is built into the unequal power structures. The idea of "avoidable disparity" entails that all people should be free to realize their capabilities and functionings, but some are not because structures disproportionately disadvantage them, creating fundamentally unequal life chances. So, the concept of structural violence holds that people are poor in part because they are systematically exploited, and one of the reasons they are systematically exploited is because they are poor. As Paul Farmer has written, "the poor are not only more likely to suffer; they are also more likely to have their suffering silenced" (Farmer 2009: 25). The poor not only disproportionately suffer human rights violations but find it harder to change their situation because of existing power structures. To use a term that we introduced earlier, we can say that such social structures unjustly limit some individuals' opportunity to exercise their agency. In subsequent chapters we will examine specific domains that contribute to poverty (health, geography, conflict, etc.); what the idea of structural violence adds to such focused empirical analysis is an underlying conceptual frame for how systemic power imbalances contribute to poverty.

A few other initial observations will help in applying the capabilities definition of poverty. First, one has to consider the extent of deprivation. A person might be denied a number of capabilities, but is it conceivable that he still might not be poor? Imagine, for example, that someone is denied (for whatever reason) the capability of enjoying nature, such as by taking a walk in the mountains. Number 8 on Nussbaum's list involves being able to live in relation to nature. Is that person who is denied his hike "poor"? Probably not, though the reasons for the deprivation may help determine the answer. More powerfully, though, most people would presumably not regard taking a hike in the mountains as a basic capability to which everyone is inherently entitled, the deprivation of which would fundamentally harm his dignity or the life that he values. Again, there is a permissible vagueness or uncertainty here; the individual himself has to determine what sort of life he values. Nonetheless, a principle that Clark and Qizilbash (2005) have proposed is that poverty is best defined as a shortfall in any core or basic dimension. So if a person experienced deprivation of one single core capability – such as being able to get an education – he would be considered poor, even if he had ample freedom in non-core capabilities such as taking a hike. From Clark and Qizilbash's research, the people who were "core poor" because of deprivations in the basic capabilities were the homeless, those with no access to water at all, those with no education, and the unemployed (2005: 21).

Also, be attentive to the difference between absolute and relative poverty. The idea of absolute poverty holds that there are some standards by which anyone is poor. Someone who is starving not by his own volition, someone who cannot read, someone who is so sick that he cannot work or lead the life that he wants – all of these people experience poverty according to an absolute standard. The list of basic capabilities sets out such an absolute standard for determining poverty: if someone falls below the minimum threshold of the basic capabilities then, by definition, he is poor. Absolute definitions of poverty have a binary aspect, that is, you either are or are not poor. A relative definition of poverty, in contrast, is contingent upon a particular society or culture. A famous example from Adam Smith illustrates this point. In Smith's example, a person who could not afford a linen shirt and leather shoes would feel shame in public. A linen shirt and leather shoes were a standard relative to eighteenth-century Britain, and if you did not have them then you were poor. Shame, however, is an absolute standard. No one should be forced to feel shame because he lacks some basic material good, or has a disability, or is a member of a minority ethnic group, or has made a life choice that contravenes an oppressive social norm. Shame is a deprivation of dignity, another absolute standard to which we are all entitled (see Sen 1983).

In any practical application, both absolute and relative standards have to be applied to define poverty. Why this matters is that occasionally some uninformed people will claim something to the effect of "poor people in the United States don't know how good they have it – they have cars, public schools, health care at the emergency room, plenty to eat, not like *real* poor people" in some developing country. The misguided assumption is that poor people in rich societies such as the United States are not really poor in comparison to poor people in lower income societies such as Haiti or Malawi. While there could seem to be a grain of truth in this thinking, it fails to recognize that the United States will have its own relative poverty thresholds that are completely irrelevant to Malawi. Every society will rightly require poverty measures specific and contextual to that society, while other aspects of poverty corresponding to the basic capabilities will be absolute and apply everywhere.

### Wellbeing and happiness

Though poverty conceived as capability deprivation is this book's main focus, it is also worth considering what is perhaps the opposite of poverty, namely wellbeing. Within the capability approach, different writers take slightly divergent perspectives on what wellbeing means, but most agree that it depends on wellbeing freedom and wellbeing achievement (see i.a. Dalziel *et al.* 2018, Robeyns 2017, Clark 2005b). Wellbeing freedom refers to the choices a person can make, the potential "doings" and "beings" she might choose. It is not the choices themselves that necessarily grant wellbeing, but rather the freedom to make them. Sen (1999) insists that not just any capabilities are fundamental for wellbeing, rather, only the choices we make that are informed by reasoned judgements about the kind of life we value. This is why wellbeing is partially relative and predicated on an individual's particular values. What matters is that we each have the freedom to select from a range of options that matter to us. Wellbeing achievement relates to functionings, that is, the realization of our choices for a valued life and whether we achieve them. Wellbeing would be only partial if we had the freedom to make valuable choices but were unable to convert those choices into achieved functionings.

To put this in the perspective of poverty, freedom is again key. A person who is poor is denied wellbeing freedom and wellbeing achievement. Poverty equates to *ill*being when people are not free to make choices about a life they have reason to value, or are systematically prevented from converting those choices into functionings. The basic capabilities establish a minimum, absolute threshold: without them, a person is in illbeing. However, the basic capabilities amount to only a partial definition of wellbeing. Just because a person's basic capabilities are secure, that does not mean she has achieved wellbeing. She may have reason to value certain possibilities that are not captured by the list of basic capabilities. These choices will be contextual to the individual and/or the society, but ultimately we must all determine what wellbeing means for ourselves. Helping people to escape poverty and achieve wellbeing means helping them to secure their capability freedoms, in other words to expand their opportunities (Smith and Reid 2018).

Though the choices that constitute wellbeing can be subjective to a person's own values, in most cases the achieved functionings can be measured objectively. For example, assume that a person would choose good health, career advancement, and societal engagement as key to her wellbeing. These achievements can all be measured through externally observable indicators for health, salary, or social capital. There are other measures of wellbeing that are more subjective, such as happiness. In some ways, happiness as an aspect of wellbeing would seem obvious. Ask someone about their overall life satisfaction, and/or their satisfaction in certain areas such as income, work, relationships, etc., and you can get a picture of what they want out of life and whether they feel they are achieving it. Mental states do matter for wellbeing, and Sen (2008) regards happiness as one relevant indicator, since the capability to be happy is an important freedom that most people will value.

However, from a capabilities perspective, subjective measures such as happiness have only a partial and problematic relationship to wellbeing. There are several reasons. The first relates back to adaptive preference: people whose freedoms are limited may not know they are limited, and so could report themselves "happy" even if their agency is seriously compromised. Imagine someone who is starving and bedridden but considers himself happy; is he truly in a state of wellbeing? Additionally, some achievements that are fundamental to a capabilities conception of wellbeing have a weak empirical relationship to happiness. Education, for example, does not consistently improve subjective reported wellbeing. Empirical evidence also shows that reported life satisfaction differs systematically between groups, with men consistently rating themselves less satisfied than women (Robeyns and van der Veen 2007). Furthermore, many of the factors that have been shown to affect happiness – such as genetics, age, or religion – are not realistic targets for development policy (Stewart 2014). Though religious people may report higher wellbeing, making people religious is not a reasonable development project. These and other problems mean that happiness is insufficient as an indicator of wellbeing and as a focus of programs to improve people's lives. Nonetheless, happiness can be included as part of a "dashboard" of wellbeing measures, a topic we will discuss in Chapter 3.

*Critiques of the capabilities approach*

Inevitably, the capabilities approach has attracted criticism from some scholars of development and poverty, who raise several objections. One objection is that the capabilities approach is too individualistic, since its emphasis is on the freedoms enjoyed by individuals and not groups. However, the approach's proponents, such as Sen, have always emphasized that an analysis of capabilities is not incompatible with application to groups or social structures. In fact, the approach explicitly acknowledges that social and group factors can impinge upon the conversion of capabilities to functionings, for instance through norms or formal state institutions. It is certainly possible to consider the freedoms and rights of groups, or the possibilities of collective action, via the capabilities approach; Chapter 5 on geography and spatial poverty, and Chapter 11 on the environment both do so.

Nonetheless, Sen has given powerful reasons for why individuals need to be the primary focus for capabilities. The individual, in his account, is the main unit of moral concern. What we have to care about with social justice is individuals, because individuals are what constitute groups, whether the family, the ethnicity or whatever other collectivity. Also, prioritizing an analysis of the group or its rights can overlook deprivations or inequalities within the group. The classic example is with women or children, who may be disadvantaged with resource allocation within the family (Alkire and Deneulin 2009).

Two other objections are worth mentioning for their relevance to this book's application of the capabilities approach. The difficulty of agreeing upon a set of basic capabilities has attracted much attention because, critics allege, it makes the approach very difficult to operationalize, that is, to use, to apply, to measure in the real world. We will turn to some of the issues with measuring capabilities in Chapter 3. But one of the alleged problems with operationalizing the approach is that consensus on the basic capabilities is unattainable, certainly at the global level, and perhaps even within countries. Even if Sen's ideal of a democratic, deliberative approach to arrive at societally contextualized basic capabilities were tried, so the complaint goes, it will be distorted by power imbalances within the society. Critics claim that disputes about what counts as "basic" will be politically impossible to overcome. For the time being, we will leave the validity of this objection open for debate and return to the question in the book's conclusion.

Lastly, it has been alleged that the capabilities approach (particularly Nussbaum's list of the central capabilities) is a product of imperialistic, western thinking. The claim is that Nussbaum's philosophy, heavily inspired by Aristotle, ignores or excludes potential non-western views of "the good life" and valuable freedoms. In its extreme form, this argument accuses the capabilities approach of justifying further imposition of western values on non-western societies. Nussbaum not surprisingly rejects such accusations, pointing out that many of the capabilities approach's main theorists are from non-western societies (Nussbaum 2011: 104). She also says that the only imposition the approach justifies is to protect the weak from the strong. While Nussbaum mounts a cogent defense of the approach from this accusation, we will again leave this debate open for discussion as the book proceeds.

## This book's method

These open questions point to the book's method of studying poverty, which incorporates these three features: (1) a multidisciplinary approach, (2) a consistent emphasis on poverty as a *human* problem, and (3) debates and deliberation. First, our multidisciplinary approach grows out of the multidimensional nature of poverty. Poverty is not just a topic for economics and economists. It relates to health, education, civil rights, international politics, gender, cultural norms, and environmental concerns, among other things. Anthropology, psychology, political science, law, philosophy, history, cultural studies, biology, chemistry, and theology can add a great deal to the study of poverty. While a scholarly inquiry cannot fuse all of these different disciplines, we have tried to blend insights from a number of them into the chapters that follow.

Second, studying poverty from multiple disciplines has a deep connection to studying poverty as a human problem. The ultimate object of improving wellbeing is not states, economies, businesses, or cultures but human beings. Theory and analysis should not lose sight of the people who are suffering but could be thriving. This is why the book will continually emphasize the faces and voices of people in poverty: because they are a constant reminder of why, as fellow human beings, we should care about this problem, and why we should work to remedy it. Faces and voices give an immediacy that provides a more compelling entry point into studying poverty than some distant, high-altitude, purely analytical approach. Moreover, reading individual stories as they relate to poverty should help stimulate empathy by appealing to our common humanity. Emphasizing the human aspects of poverty also makes a direct connection to the ethical demands of poverty, namely what we (whether professors, students, those who have much, or those who have little) owe those who are suffering.

The method we use in this book is well attuned to the overall ethos of the capabilities approach. The capabilities approach avowedly puts human beings at the heart of its concerns. Remember that its fundamental question is: what are people able to be and to do? As Drèze and Sen have written, this "is essentially a 'people-centered' approach, which puts human agency (rather than organizations such as markets or governments) at the center of the stage. The crucial role of social opportunities is to expand the realm of human agency and freedom, both as an end in itself and as a means of further expansion of freedom" (Drèze and Sen 2002: 6). The idea is again that the individual human is the fundamental unit of analysis, and the point of the analysis is to determine the opportunities (and the constraints on those opportunities) that a person has to live a life that she values. Nussbaum's emphasis on dignity also connects here. When people are unjustly denied the development of their capabilities, the inherent dignity to which they are entitled is violated.

Third, this book will consistently include debates and encourage deliberation. The reasons are several. Intense debates rage around certain topics in development, and many of the book's chapters consider these debates in some detail. Occasionally we will offer what we judge to be the most justifiable answers to a controversial question, but we generally avoid definitive pronouncements, as definitiveness is hard to attain in development. Rather, in our view the best approach is more provisional, and embraces competing perspectives. This approach is also partly motivated by capabilities theory. Sen says in *The Idea of Justice*, "When we try to determine how justice can be advanced, there is a basic need for public reasoning, involving arguments coming from different quarters and divergent perspectives" (2009: 92). This book therefore aims to inculcate and support the general belief (espoused by other writers in the capabilities tradition such as Crocker 2008) in deliberation. By presuming debate and competing viewpoints on many topics, rather than a single definitive answer, we want to encourage careful, open-minded, analytical reasoning about those viewpoints. Our hope is that the chapters stimulate readers to debate divergent analyzes and perspectives for themselves.

## Conclusion

The multidimensional perspective, the human focus, and the emphasis on debate and deliberation are all essential for answering questions on what poverty is, what causes it, and how it can be reduced. They all aid in understanding the possibilities for human wellbeing. They are pedagogical strategies to shed some light on this book's ultimate question: what does it mean to be a human living in poverty? This is an enormous question, with many different potential answers, and we do not intend to answer it at the outset. Instead, we hope that readers return to the question again and again, seeking new answers in every chapter. For now, and to launch this book into its subsequent chapters, we will return to the community we mentioned at the beginning of the chapter to pose a series of questions that all stem from the objective of treating poverty as a human problem.

The community itself was Dharavi, a neighborhood in Mumbai, India, known as one of the largest slums in the world. This is a place where, with its deprivations, so many people are struggling and sometimes succeeding to build a flourishing life. From the description we have given, how might poverty be multidimensional in Dharavi? What might it mean to be a human living in absolute poverty versus relative poverty in this community? What could be the basic entitlements, the central capabilities to which all people in Dharavi should have a right? How does lacking those basic entitlements affect the human being? How might living in Dharavi affect one's physical health and learning? How might it affect one's psychological health? How would you imagine that living in poverty might affect one's sense of self-worth? How, in sum, might living in poverty affect one's ability "to do and to be" in the capabilities sense?

This book is not an ethics manual, though ethical concerns will pervade its inquiry. Focusing on poverty as a human problem connects to our collective responsibility as human beings to achieve the goals of understanding what causes poverty and how suffering can be alleviated. Studying poverty is fundamentally about our *own* humanity. This is because we humanize ourselves by considering the basic rights and capabilities to which we are all entitled (Walker 2009). We humanize ourselves, and hopefully our societies and the world, when we take on the challenges of understanding the minimum requirements of human dignity, how people are unjustly deprived of their dignity, and how we can justly help them to recover it. In the final chapter of the book, we examine ethical questions in more detail, but throughout all the chapters that follow, we urge readers to think consistently and profoundly about their own ethical engagement with poverty, what it means to study it, and what you owe those who are living in unfreedom.

## Discussion questions

1   What does freedom have to do with poverty?
2   What are the problems with examining global poverty only in terms of the global south and not the global north?
3   What do you see as the relative advantages and disadvantages of the income and capabilities approaches? Is the capabilities approach relevant only for "developing countries," or could it work for any country around the world?
4   What does it mean to treat human beings as ends and not as means?
5   What capabilities do you think are essential for a dignified life? Do you think the list should be left open like Sen advocates or do you think the global community needs to agree on a list like Nussbaum's? What would you add to or subtract from Nussbaum's list?
6   What would the deliberative process look like for a society to decide on its list of central capabilities?
    • Attempt to construct such a process in your class and conduct a debate to identify agreed-upon central capabilities.
    • Do you think it is possible to come to a truly democratic agreement on basic capabilities, whether globally, within countries, or even within your classroom?
7   What do you think of the critiques that the capabilities approach is guilty of imposing western values on the rest of the world?

## Online resources

• This interview with Amartya Sen from 1999 covers a number of ideas in the capabilities approach: www.youtube.com/watch?v=-6A7k6peWRM
• The short documentary *Dharavi Diary* is available at https://vimeo.com/40813441

## Further reading

Clark, David A. 2006. "The Capability Approach," in David A. Clark, ed. *The Elgar Companion to Development Studies*. Cheltenham, UK: Edward Elgar.
Comim, Flavio, Mozaffar Qizilbash and Sabina Alkire, eds. 2008. *The Capability Approach: Concepts, Measures and Applications*. Cambridge, UK: Cambridge University Press.

Deneulin, Séverine and Lila Shahani, eds. 2009. *An Introduction to the Human Development and Capability Approach*. London: Earthscan.

Nussbaum, Martha. 2006. "Poverty and Human Functioning: Capabilities as Fundamental Entitlements," in David B. Grusky and Ravi Kanbur, eds. *Poverty and Inequality*. Stanford, CA: Stanford University Press.

Pogge, Thomas, ed. 2007. *Freedom from Poverty as a Human Right*. Oxford: Oxford University Press.

Sen, Amartya. 1999. *Development as Freedom*. New York, NY: Anchor Press.

Sen, Amartya. 2003. "Capability and Well-Being," in Martha Nussbaum and Amartya Sen, eds. *The Quality of Life*. Oxford: Oxford University Press.

Universal Declaration of Human Rights: www.un.org/en/documents/udhr/

## Works cited

Alkire, Sabina and Séverine Deneulin. 2009. "The Human Development and Capability Approach," in Séverine Deneulin and Lila Shahani, eds. *An Introduction to the Human Development and Capability Approach*. London: Earthscan.

Clark, David A. 2005a. "The Capability Approach: Its Development, Critiques and Recent Advances," Global Poverty Research Group paper, GPRG-WPS-032.

Clark, David A. 2005b. "Sen's capability approach and the many spaces of human well-being." *The Journal of Development Studies* 41.8: 1339–1368.

Clark, David A. and Mozaffar Qizilbash. 2005. "Core Poverty, Basic Capabilities and Vagueness: An Application to the South African Context," Global Poverty Research Group paper GRPG-WPS-026, July.

Comim, Flavio. 2008. "Measuring Capabilities," in Flavio Comim, Mozaffar Qizilbash and Sabina Alkire, eds. *The Capability Approach: Concepts, Measures and Applications*. Cambridge, UK: Cambridge University Press.

Crocker, David A. 2008. *Ethics of Global Development: Agency, Capability, and Deliberative Democracy*. Cambridge, UK: Cambridge University Press.

Dalziel, Paul; Saunders, Caroline; Saunders, Joe. 2018. *Wellbeing Economics: The Capabilities Approach to Prosperity*. London: Palgrave Macmillan.

Deneulin, Séverine. 2009. "Ideas Related to Human Development," in Séverine Deneulin and Lila Shahani, eds. *An Introduction to the Human Development and Capability Approach*. London: Earthscan.

Desai, Meghnad. 1995. "Poverty and Capability: Towards an Empirically Implementable Measure," in *Poverty, Famine and Economic Development: The Selected Essays of Meghnad Desai, Volume II*. Aldershot, UK: Edward Elgar.

Drèze, Jean and Amartya Sen. 2002. *India: Development and Participation*. Oxford: Oxford University Press.

Farmer, Paul. 2009. "On suffering and structural violence: A view from below." *Race/Ethnicity: Multidisciplinary Global Contexts* 3.1: 11–28.

Gough, Ian. 2003. "*Lists and Thresholds: Comparing Our Theory of Human Need with Nussbaum's Capabilities Approach,*" WeD Working Paper 01, The Wellbeing in Developing Countries Research Group, University of Bath.

Ho, Kathleen. 2007. "Structural violence as a human rights violation." *Essex Human Rights Review* 4.2: 1–17. September.

Narayan, Deepa and Patti Petesch. 2002. *Voices of the Poor from Many Lands*. Washington, DC: The World Bank.

Nussbaum, Martha. 1997. "Capabilities and human rights." *Fordham Law Review* 66: 273–300.

Nussbaum, Martha. 2011. *Creating Capabilities: The Human Development Approach*. Boston, MA: Harvard University Press.

Osmani, Siddique Rahman. 2005. "Poverty and human rights: building on the capability approach." *Journal of Human Development* 6.2: 205–219.

Qizilbash, Mozaffar. 2002. "Development, common foes and shared values." *Review of Political Economy* 14.4: 463–480.

Robeyns, Ingrid. 2005. "The capability approach: a theoretical survey." *Journal of Human Development* 6.1: 93–114.

Robeyns, Ingrid. 2017. *Wellbeing, Freedom and Social Justice: The Capability Approach Re-examined.* Online: Open Book Publishers.

Robeyns, Ingrid and Robert-Jan Van der Veen. 2007. *Sustainable Quality of Life. Conceptual Analysis for a Policy-Relevant Empirical Specification.* Bilthoven: Netherlands Environmental Assessment Agency.

Saith, Ruhi. 2001. "Capabilities: The Concept and its Operationalisation," Queen Elizabeth House Working Paper 66, February.

Sen, Amartya. 1983. "Poor, relatively speaking." *Oxford Economic Papers*, New Series, 35.2: 153–169.

Sen, Amartya. 1985. "A sociological approach to the measurement of poverty: a reply to Professor Peter Townsend." *Oxford Economic Papers*, New Series, 37.4: 669–676.

Sen, Amartya. 1990. "Justice: means versus freedoms." *Philosophy and Public Affairs* 19 : 111–121.

Sen, Amartya. 1992. *Inequality Re-examined.* Oxford: Oxford University Press.

Sen, Amartya. 1999. *Development as Freedom.* New York: Knopf.

Sen, Amartya. 2004. "Elements of a theory of human rights." *Philosophy & Public Affairs* 32.4: 315–356.

Sen, Amartya. 2005. "Human rights and capabilities." *Journal of Human Development* 6.2: 151–166.

Sen, Amartya. 2008. "The Economics of Happiness and Capability," in Luigino Bruni, Flavio Comim and Maurizio Pugno, eds. *Capabilities and Happiness*, 16–27. Oxford: Oxford University Press.

Sen, Amartya. 2009. *The Idea of Justice.* London: Allen Lane.

Smith, Tom and Reid, Louise. 2018. "Which 'being' in wellbeing? Ontology, wellness and the geographies of happiness." *Progress in Human Geography* 42.6: 807–829.

Stewart, Frances. 2014. "Against happiness: a critical appraisal of the use of measures of happiness for evaluating progress in development." *Journal of Human Development and Capabilities* 15.4: 293–307.

United Nations Development Programme. 2000. *Human Development Report: Human Rights and Human Development.* Oxford: Oxford University Press.

Vizard, Polly, Sakiko Fukuda-Parr and Diane Elson. 2011. "Introduction: the capability approach and human rights." *Journal of Human Development and Capabilities* 12.1: 1–22.

Walker, Melanie. 2003. "Framing social justice in education: what does the 'capabilities' approach offer?" *British Journal of Educational Studies* 51.2: 168–187.

Walker, Melanie. 2004. "Human Capabilities, Education and 'Doing the Public Good': Towards a Capability-Based Theory of Social Justice in Education", paper presented at the Australian Association for Research in Education, November—December.

Walker, Melanie. 2009. "Teaching the Human Development and Capability Approach: Some Pedagogical Implications", in Séverine Deneulin and Lila Shahani, eds. *An Introduction to the Human Development and Capability Approach.* London: Earthscan.

# 2 Development and its debates

*Benjamin Curtis and Serena Cosgrove*

## Learning objectives

- Explain what is meant by "development," including the history of this concept.
- Analyze how human development and capabilities are relevant to poverty reduction.
- Summarize who does development, distinguishing between the major actors at the national and international levels.
- Discuss how the meaning and practice of development are contested, characterizing some of the major controversies in this field.

## Introduction

Busia, in western Kenya, has long been one of the poorest parts of the country. According to one estimate, 60 percent of the population live below the poverty line (Gugerty and Kremer 2008). Most people get by as subsistence farmers, earning a little bit of money selling crops such as cotton or sugarcane. Very few farmers are able to irrigate their land, and few possess livestock such as cattle. In this situation of chronic deprivation, a well-regarded Dutch non-governmental organization (NGO) came up with a plan to help. This NGO had previously worked in Busia, and concluded that a program to boost agricultural productivity, incomes, and nutrition could lift people out of poverty. The program the NGO implemented focused on the most disadvantaged groups, aiming to help them with the fields that they collectively farmed. Specifically, the program provided women's community organizations with managerial training (such as leadership skills, book-keeping, and administrative techniques) and agricultural training and resources (such as seeds, fertilizer, pesticides, and tools, as well as classes on farming and animal husbandry).

Both the intentions and the expertise behind this program were admirable. Its results, however, proved disappointing. According to a rigorous evaluation, most of the program's benefits accrued to the more *advantaged* members of the community (Gugerty and Kremer 2008). For example, significant numbers of new people joined the community organizations once the NGO money started flowing. That might seem beneficial, except that these new members were already better off than the members of longer standing: they were more likely to come from outside the village, and to have higher levels of education and formal jobs (rather than just depending on farming income). The leadership composition of the organizations also changed, with men increasingly assuming positions of authority. In fact, many of the older women members left, often because of conflicts sparked by the new resources.

Even the resources and trainings did not produce benefits. The groups' assets in terms of livestock, cash, and other capital did not meaningfully increase. Most groups distributed the resources such as tools so that individuals could use them on their own private properties rather than on the communal land. The trainings were usually not full, and were disproportionately attended by men. One reason might be that the older women lacked either the literacy level and/or the freedom to take time away from childcare that the trainings necessitated. Agricultural productivity also grew only slightly, on average only by about 28 USD although each group received about 700 USD in resources. So it was a very poor return on investment for the money the NGO put into the program. In one positive sign, group members who were surveyed said the program was useful. Nonetheless, the evaluation found that the program inputs failed to strengthen the organizations. For instance, group members did not assist each other more, did not meet more frequently, and did not invest more in the community resources. It seems that when program participants gave positive reviews, they were just telling the NGO what they thought it wanted to hear.

What can we learn from this project about helping people escape poverty? What are the complexities, both practical and conceptual, of doing development? This chapter explores these questions and, in particular, some of the controversies in the development field. As with the program in Busia, development efforts can be informed by good intentions, relevant expertise, and yet still become deeply problematic. Most chapters in this book will provide an analysis of anti-poverty programs, including in health, education, and financial services. But before diving into those details, it is necessary to think in broader terms about how the global community can promote prosperity and wellbeing. A range of philosophies, practices, and actors are working to accomplish those goals, and some are even opposed to each other, or mutually contradictory. This chapter lays out several competing philosophies, explains the major actors who work in the development sector, and discusses some of the most salient critiques and debates. In some cases, there is no "right answer" to these debates – but we will show that there are nonetheless principles for doing development that are most strongly justified, and most recommendable for reducing poverty and improving people's lives.

## What is development?

Most scholars agree that the idea of "international development" begins shortly after the Second World War. In its broadest form, this idea holds that via the application of certain policies, the parts of the world that are "underdeveloped" can be brought up to the levels of prosperity and wellbeing of the rich western countries. Since the 1940s, the theory and practice of development have transitioned through multiple paradigms, some of which actively disagree with each other. The importance of these development paradigms is that they all, in one way or another, espouse a particular vision of what poverty is and how it can be reduced. There are many different periodizations of these paradigms, but a few of the major categories include:

1   **Modernization theory** predominated in the 1950s and the 1960s as the wave of decolonization created many new, "developing" countries. According to modernization theory, a society's path to prosperity involves overcoming backward traditions to acquire the social and economic characteristics of the high-income western countries. Scholars such as Walt Rostow (1960) argued that societies progress along a series of stages from an agricultural economy with more rigid social structures towards a

"modern," industrialized, consumer society. The focus of much development policy in these decades was to identify the strategies that would help countries transition to an industrial economy.

2   **Dependency theory** inverts the modernization perspective to examine economic development from the perspective of the "periphery," that is, the non-industrialized countries. Influential in the 1960s and 1970s, dependency theory argued that the economic development of the West retarded the development of the rest by exploiting the latter's resources, making them dependent on the high-income industrialized countries. Further, according to this perspective, globally unequal development actually serves the interests of elites in western countries, who benefit by keeping the periphery poor. Representative writers include Raúl Prebitsch, Paul Baran, André Gunder Frank, and Immanuel Wallerstein.

3   **Neo-liberalism** was dominant in the 1980s and 1990s, though its ideas remain influential today. This approach generally stresses free market economics as the optimal route to development, including liberalizing trade policies and privatizing state-run enterprises to spur more rapid economic growth. It is famously associated with the so-called "Washington consensus," a prescriptive set of policies promoted by Washington, DC-based institutions including the World Bank and the International Monetary Fund. As conditions for loans to developing countries, these institutions often insisted on "structural adjustment," which required developing countries to adopt measures including tax reform, deregulation, strict budget discipline, and policies to encourage foreign direct investment. Writers commonly associated with neo-liberalism are Friedrich Hayek and Milton Friedman.

4   **Human development** is in some ways a reaction against the economic focus of modernization theory and particularly neo-liberalism. It emerged in the later 1970s and gained momentum in the 1990s. Because it is this book's guiding approach to poverty, human development is discussed in more detail below.

5   **Sustainable development** is a broad collection of ideas questioning the costs to the environment of existing models of economic growth. Attention to these issues has grown since 1987 when the Brundtland Commission called for "development that meets the needs of the present without compromising the ability of future generations to meet their own needs" (Brundtland 1987). The sustainable development ethos focuses on how to encourage conservation and more sustainable management of natural resources. Though sustainability is usually conceived in environmental terms, it can have additional dimensions such as social sustainability, which emphasizes that economic growth must be more equitably shared at national and global levels. The sustainability ethos can be compatible with other paradigms including human development. (See i.a. Elliott 2012, Redclift 2005, and this book's Chapter 11 on the environment and poverty reduction.)

This is by no means a complete listing of development theories, and even when theories (such as modernization) become passé or discredited, some of their ideas often form part of the intellectual heritage of subsequent paradigms, so there is not a strict sequence in development theories either. Similarly, none of these paradigms is without its critics, and most of the theories do offer some insights. Depending on one's viewpoint, the entire idea of development itself is riddled with flaws and problems, as we discuss in a subsequent section. In fact, there is now a field of "post-development" studies (see e.g. Sidaway 2007, Rapley 2004, Rahnema and Bawtree 1997). While we will use the language of development, our strong preference is to emphasize human development, and in particular poverty reduction.

## Human development: strengthening capabilities

Human development is often identified with the capabilities approach, though they are not identical (see e.g. Nussbaum 2011, Deneulin and Shahani 2009). The capabilities approach is fundamentally a theory for evaluating what should count as wellbeing and illbeing. Human development is inspired by capabilities theory, but seeks to operationalize it for practical implementation. For example, human development builds on the capabilities approach by insisting that the purpose of development is not merely to improve individuals' economic conditions, but rather to "enlarge people's choices" (Alkire and Deneulin 2009: 26), to expand "the opportunities open to each person" (Nussbaum 2011: 14), in short to promote freedom. It aims to implement these goals in specific areas, whether politics, economics, social opportunities, or basic security. Mahbub ul Haq, one of the principal theorists of human development, proclaimed that it should be operationalized in "all aspects of development – whether economic growth or international trade; budget deficits or fiscal policy; savings, investment or technology, basic social services or safety nets for the poor" (ul Haq 2004: 17).

How can human development encompass such diverse areas? The answer is the guiding goal of "creating an enabling environment for people to enjoy long, healthy, creative lives," in short to widen people's choices and enrich the lives they lead (ul Haq 2004: 17). Ul Haq points to these five key principles of human development:

1  Development must put people at the center of its concerns.
2  The purpose of development is to enlarge all human choices and not just income.
3  The human development paradigm is concerned both with building human capabilities (through investment in people) and with using those human capabilities more fully (through an enabling framework for growth and employment).
4  Human development has four essential pillars: equality, sustainability, productivity, and empowerment. It regards economic growth as essential, but emphasizes the need to pay attention to its quality and distribution, analyzes at length its link with human lives, and questions its long-term sustainability.
5  The human development paradigm defines the ends of development and analyzes sensible options for achieving them (ul Haq 2004: 19).

These principles need to be examined in some detail. The first principle means that the fundamental locus of concern is human beings and human lives – not economic systems, governments, or industrial policies. This principle accords with one of the guiding ideas of this book, which is that poverty is a human problem, and problems of poverty and development must never lose sight of the individuals who are both suffering and potentially flourishing. The second principle connects directly to the perspective of capabilities. People must be free to make choices – they must have the capability to choose, and to actualize their capabilities as functionings. The third principle states that development must secure people's basic capabilities, and that doing so requires society-wide programs to create an "enabling framework" that can help people convert capabilities to functionings.

The fourth principle is a bundle of concepts which Sabina Alkire and Séverine Deneulin (2009) have elucidated. The pillar of equality (more appropriately stated in this case as "equity") recognizes that some people, such as those who are poor, women, or from minority groups, may be chronically and systematically disadvantaged in terms of their opportunities in life. They therefore may need additional resources to guarantee their basic capabilities. Sustainability, they explain, refers to achieving positive results that will endure over time. Besides the need to protect environmental resources for future generations, there are also financial and social dimensions of sustainability. The former refers to the need to finance development so that future generations are not harmed through countries falling into debt traps. The latter refers to involving communities in development projects to ensure that those projects have lasting positive effects. The pillar of productivity relates to the idea that everyone is entitled to an economic livelihood and that economic growth can enlarge people's choices. The final pillar, empowerment, relates again to community involvement. It stresses the need for people to have agency in political processes that affect them, so that they can ensure that development projects do truly benefit them, and so they can hold politicians and development professionals accountable.

As the fifth principle indicates, the conception of development's purpose is different between the economic and human development paradigms. Classically, in the economic development paradigm the purpose of development is to increase people's incomes. The rationale again is that higher incomes will translate to higher wellbeing. Sen reminds us, however, that the objective of building a manufacturing economy is ultimately not to expand a country's exports and raise the value of the goods it produces. Economic growth and higher incomes should be conceived above all as means of expanding human freedoms, not as ends in themselves. One reason why is that economic development does not always lead to poverty reduction. If only a small slice of the population accrues the benefits of economic growth while vast numbers remain hungry, sick, illiterate, or disempowered, then clearly economic growth is not a sufficient solution. Furthermore, some scholars have claimed that economic growth is unsustainable without a focus on the key aspects of human development such as education and health (Ranis *et al.* 2000).

The human development perspective holds that people must be free to decide what sort of life they want to live. Yet like the other development paradigms, it is still prescriptive, since it emphasizes human freedom as the central moral good. Remember that poverty (as explained in Chapter 1) can be defined as unfreedom. "Development," Sen has written, "requires the removal of major sources of unfreedom: poverty as well as tyranny, poor economic opportunities as well as systematic social deprivation, neglect of public facilities as well as intolerance or overactivity of repressive states" (Sen 1999: 3). Thus, Sen defines things such as education and health not as "outcomes" of development, but as "constituent components" of development. They can contribute to economic growth, but that is not the only rationale to pursue improvements in education and health. The additional and more powerful rationale is that improving individuals' education and health should strengthen their freedoms and rights, and doing so is the definition of development. The idea of "development as freedom" directs attention to the ends of development, its ultimate goals, rather than stopping at its means, namely increasing incomes. Again, this is not to deny the utility of studying economic development – it is just to emphasize that though economic development has dominated research and policy, it is a decidedly incomplete way of understanding poverty.

It should be clear by now that the capabilities approach's conceptual lens for defining poverty and wellbeing presumes a normative view on what development should be. "The purpose of global development," according to Nussbaum, "is to enable people to live full and creative lives, developing their potential and fashioning a meaningful existence commensurate with their equal dignity" (2011: 185). The perspective of the capabilities approach on development is convincingly summarized by Ingrid Robeyns:

> [The capabilities approach] asks whether people are being healthy, and whether the means or resources necessary for this capability are present, such as clean water, access to doctors, protection from infections and diseases, and basic knowledge on health issues. It asks whether people are well-nourished, and whether the conditions for this capability, such as having sufficient food supplies and food entitlements, are being met. It asks whether people have access to a high-quality educational system, to real political participation, to community activities that support them to cope with struggles in daily life and that foster real friendships. For some of these capabilities, the main input will be financial resources and economic production, but for others it can also be political practices and institutions, such as the effective guaranteeing and protection of freedom of thought, political participation, social or cultural practices, social structures, social institutions, public goods, social norms, traditions and habits.
>
> (Robeyns 2005: 95)

In other words, the policies, programs, institutions, and structures must be in place to guarantee people their basic capabilities. Designing development programs with the objective of guaranteeing those capabilities should be the overarching goal of development. In the chapters that follow, we will be examining a number of prominent causes of poverty, and studying in particular how these causes deprive people of basic capabilities. Our study of programs to reduce poverty will focus on how basic capabilities can be supported along the lines Robeyns sketches above.

## Development or poverty reduction or poverty eradication?

Is there a difference between development and "poverty reduction"? What should the global community be aiming for – poverty eradication? Though there is some overlap between these terms, they are not synonymous, and their differences in meaning are (not surprisingly) contentious. In fact, just as there are different paradigms of development, different actors can have different definitions of poverty reduction. For instance, the United Nations Development Program has said that reducing poverty involves "public policy interventions that help to modify the social, cultural, and economic conditions that created poverty in the first place" (UNDP 2013). Those interventions can target a number of areas, such as gender equality and women's empowerment, democratic governance, adaptation to climate change and the elimination of stigma with HIV/AIDS. As another example, the Asian Development Bank has characterized poverty reduction as depending upon pro-poor, sustainable economic growth, and sound macroeconomic management with good governance. It also involves strengthening human capital, social capital, the status of women, and social safety net protections for people who suffer from disabilities, natural disasters, or conflict. Lastly, according to the Asian Development Bank, poverty reduction necessitates attention to environmental issues including air and water pollution and degradation of natural resources, such as deforestation, which disproportionately affect the poor (Deolalikar *et al.* 2002).

The World Bank has emphasized that poverty reduction must involve empowerment, security, and opportunity for poor people. Empowerment is defined as making state institutions more responsive and accountable to poor people. It can be achieved by strengthening poor people's participation in political processes and local decision making, and removing discriminatory barriers to participation whether because of gender, ethnicity, race, religion etc. Security refers to protecting the poor from adverse shocks such as ill health, crop failure, natural disasters, and violence. It can be achieved by better management of the economy and through a more robust social safety net. Opportunity means increasing poor people's access to assets such as land and education, and increasing the rates of return to these assets (World Bank 2000). Clearly, poverty reduction can mean many different things. But note some consistencies here. First, the idea of poverty reduction depends upon a multidimensional understanding of poverty: poverty is more than one thing, and people can suffer from it in a variety of ways. Second, definitions of poverty reduction do tend to emphasize economic growth with equity, good governance, certain aspects of human development such as health and education, and social protection policies specifically designed to benefit the poor.

However, the broad scope of poverty reduction also raises some difficult questions. Owen Barder points to several problematic trade-offs with both the idea and practice of poverty reduction. One is the "broad versus deep" trade-off: should poverty reduction aim to help as many people as possible, or focus on a smaller number of people in more severe, chronic poverty? The "today versus tomorrow" trade-off asks whether poverty reduction should focus resources on helping people in poverty today, or on reducing the conditions that may make people poor in the future? Similarly, there is a trade-off between poverty reduction programs with a more temporary focus – to help people in the short term – versus programs that aim for a long-term, sustainable impact (Barder 2009). Further complicating the picture is that many of the criticisms of development (see the section below) can also be levelled at poverty reduction. It is accused of still following a neo-liberal model of development, letting large donors set priorities and thereby preserving the clout of the big international development agencies (Hydén n.d.).

Given these difficulties, should one focus on "poverty alleviation" or "poverty relief" or "poverty eradication"? These terms appear in the study and practice of global development (and occasionally in this book), though they, too, are not without their complications. Poverty alleviation is akin to the idea of poverty reduction, in that it presumes an amelioration of the suffering and/or deprivation associated with poverty. However, some critics claim that the "alleviation" term connotes not a real elimination of the factors causing poverty, but just their temporary lessening – a Band-Aid, perhaps, but not a cure. Poverty relief, likewise, can connote a short-term focus, merely relieving the suffering of poverty at the immediate time. Such a focus is necessary sometimes, as in situations of famine, natural disaster, or insecurity provoked by armed conflict. But "relief" as a term does not embrace the idea of systemic change to prevent poverty in the future. So why not use the term "poverty eradication"? Ultimately, the goal should be that no human suffers from poverty. But is that a realistic goal? On the one hand, the push to eliminate extreme poverty – the deprivations of basic entitlements of food, health, rights, or central capabilities – is a moral imperative for which the global community should strive. On the other hand, poverty may never be fully eradicated because even if absolute poverty came to an end, there would still be relative poverty.

Keeping all these definitional complications in mind, this book favors the terminology of poverty reduction. One reason is that this is a book primarily about *poverty* rather than development. Additionally, the idea of poverty reduction is more closely attuned to the multidimensional and multidisciplinary approach to poverty the book espouses, in a way that economic development is not. Remember that the ultimate end of poverty reduction and development broadly conceived is improvements in human wellbeing, not just increases in income. Poverty reduction through a focus on development of basic human capabilities can thus avoid some of the problematic assumptions inherent in prioritizing economic growth. In their most simplistic form, those assumptions can treat capitalism as an unquestioned good. The perspective of "poverty reduction" can help to avoid the strain of neo-liberal ideology that holds a doctrinaire view of US-style capitalism as the highest, or only valid, model of economic organization.

Additionally, by emphasizing poverty reduction and human development, we hope to avoid the sometimes implicit, sometimes explicit attitude in development discourse and practice that the rich world can "save" the poor. Such paternalistic attitudes fail to respect people's own agency, and can fall prey to even more offensive stereotypes about people in lower-income countries. It is not the job of the richest countries to "save" the poor. Rather, what this book will explore is what ethical global citizens owe people whose basic capabilities are threatened. While we will offer several answers that we think are well reasoned, this should be a debate, albeit one conducted without unexamined paternalistic attitudes.

## Who does development?

There are many different actors in the development landscape, and many different forms of poverty reduction programs. For instance, there are multi-year programs targeting multiple countries supported by international agencies; projects by national governments; projects implemented by international non-governmental organizations (INGOs) or local non-governmental organizations; and other types besides. This section surveys both the broad categories of such programs as well as who implements them. In general, most development initiatives fall under three broad categories:

1 Official development assistance (ODA), which typically involves financial transfers (grants or low-interest loans) from a donor government. When the donor government gives to another government, it is bilateral aid. Multilateral aid is given by a government to an international organization such as the United Nations. By total dollar amounts, most aid is ODA. Because these investments can be quite large, they have the potential to be big projects tackling big problems. However, this kind of aid is also the most criticized, as we discuss in a subsequent section.

2 Humanitarian aid provided in cases of natural disasters, widespread famine or drought, and human disasters such as armed conflict. Funds for humanitarian aid can come from governments, individuals, foundations, or businesses. Whereas ODA is generally intended for long-term ends, humanitarian aid aims to reduce suffering in the short term. Examples of this kind of aid can be supplying food or water, providing medical care or shelter, or protecting civilians in conflict situations. Even fierce critics of ODA often agree that humanitarian assistance is necessary to help local populations cope with unexpected shocks. However, there is an emerging body of research that points to how this type of aid, too, can get misused if it falls into the greedy hands of rebel groups or corrupt officials.

3 Development assistance provided by INGOs and national and local NGOs. As with humanitarian aid, funds for development projects run by any kind of NGO can come from governments, individuals, foundations, or businesses. Many international development researchers and practitioners agree that strengthening civil society

organizations such as NGOs is beneficial on two levels. First, it can channel aid dollars to a local organization capable of implementing the project, and, second, it can strengthen civil society, which helps people hold local governments accountable. Nonetheless, critics have claimed that INGOs sometimes play such a prominent role in development projects that a country's government becomes less accountable as citizens look more to INGOs, such as Save the Children and World Vision, to help them meet their needs (see Esquith 2013, Moratti and Sabric-El-Rayess 2009).

The different actors involved in international development can be broken down into the following categories. These actors can be involved in all three kinds of development programs listed above.

1   **Multilateral and supranational institutions**. This category refers to when countries work together (multilateralism) to create governance that operates above national governments. Examples of institutions in this category include the International Monetary Fund, the World Bank, the World Trade Organization, and the United Nations and its many agencies (such as the United Nations Children's Fund, UNICEF; the United Nations High Commissioner for Refugees, UNHCR; the United Nations Development Program, UNDP; and United Nations Entity for Gender Equality and the Empowerment of Women, UN Women). The Organization for Economic Cooperation and Development (OECD, a club of high- and middle-income countries), the African Union, and the Asian Development Bank also fit in here.

2   **Development agencies associated with national governments**. The agencies of high-income countries are major players around the world, such as the United States Agency for International Development (USAID), the German Agency for Technical Cooperation (GTZ), the British Department for International Development (DFID), or the Canadian International Development Agency (CIDA), to name but a few. The Development Assistance Committee (DAC) is a grouping of the world's largest donor agencies; its membership is almost exclusively made up of the richest countries. These agencies give ODA and often work with the development agency, or ministries of agriculture, economics, or health of the recipient government to implement projects. Development agencies from non-DAC countries in the global south are also becoming more important as donors. The Brazilian Cooperation Agency (ABC) is involved in multiple projects in the Portuguese-speaking parts of Africa, for example, and China's International Development Cooperation Agency (CIDCA) has projects worldwide.

3   **Non-governmental organizations**. As mentioned above, there is an extensive network of NGOs and INGOs working to address poverty, and they operate both in individual and multiple countries. Some of the best-known NGOs include BRAC (Building Resources Across Communities, which started in Bangladesh but now works many places), CARE, Save the Children, Médecins Sans Frontières, the International Red Cross, and Mercy Corps. Sometimes these organizations, such as World Vision, have a religious affiliation; other development NGOs with a faith connection include Caritas and Catholic Relief Services, Muslim Aid, and World Jewish Relief.

4   **Foundations**. Often supporting INGOs, these foundations also work with local NGOs to fund development projects. The most famous example is the Gates

Foundation, but there are many others, such as the Ford Foundation and the Open Society Foundation. Besides funding NGOs, such foundations can work together with multilateral institutions and governments. These collaborations have formed prominent partnerships such as the Global Alliance for Vaccination and Immunization (GAVI) and the Global Agriculture and Food Security Program (GAFSP).

5  **Businesses**. The activities of for-profit enterprises sometimes contribute to poverty reduction and development. The range of relevant businesses is very wide, including small, local social enterprises (which are organizations that apply commercial strategies to achieve positive social impact), on up to huge multinational corporations that bring jobs to an area (e.g. Nestlé has worked with farmers in some lower-income countries to source ingredients for its products). Foreign direct investment (FDI) can bring both capital and know-how that improves productivity in firms, as for example via investments in Latin America in manufacturing, mining, or infrastructure. Public–private partnerships (PPPs) typically involve governments contracting a private enterprise to provide social services. As one example, governments in Sub-Saharan Africa have contracted with private firms to build and run schools. Of course, multinational corporations' activities can be hugely controversial, but it is important to recognize that they are sometimes important players in development.

6  **Universities and think tanks**. In both the global north and the global south, universities play a role in development through research and sometimes project implementation. Examples include major public health research centers at the University of Washington or Johns Hopkins University, the Abdul Latif Jameel Poverty Action Lab (J-PAL, affiliated with the Massachusetts Institute of Technology) which has specialized in impact evaluations, and the London International Development Research Centre, founded by a consortium of higher education institutions in the United Kingdom. Prominent development think tanks include the Center for Global Development headquartered in Washington, DC, the International Development Research Centre in Ottawa, the Indira Gandhi Institute of Development Research in Mumbai, and the African Population and Health Research Center in Nairobi. Universities and think tanks partner with governments, multilateral institutions, or civil society organizations to improve development policy or focus on a particular problem such as malaria, HIV/AIDS, tuberculosis, or gender inequality.

The project in Busia, Kenya with which the chapter opened can serve as an example of how these different actors work together. The Dutch INGO International Child Support planned and carried out the project in consultation with the Kenyan Ministry of Agriculture and local women's civil society groups. The funding came from several different sources, including institutional donors such as the World Bank and individual donations to the Dutch organization. Researchers from Harvard University conducted the outcomes evaluation for the project. Not all development projects work this way, but many do involve partnerships with multiple actors at the international and national levels.

From the perspective of the capabilities approach, we would affirm that governments have a particular duty when it comes to development. As Nussbaum states, "the job of government is understood to be that of raising all citizens above the threshold on all ten [central] capabilities" (2011: 109). Concerted public action in the form of government policy is one of the most effective ways of mobilizing resources to make people's capabilities more secure.[1] Poor people often lack security, whether of food, income, or bodily integrity. So, for example, a policy to guarantee women access to reproductive control or other services for bodily health would be a way of securing their capabilities to make choices about their sexual and reproductive lives. Women would not have to choose to avail themselves of these services. What matters is that they have opportunity freedom (so that the services exist, they are available to be chosen) as well as process freedom (so that women could make the choice for themselves, they are not constrained or prevented from choosing what they want).

The reason basic capabilities are so important as objects of government policy is, first, because they are the fundamental rights to which all human beings are entitled. Second, these capabilities are foundational to many others. Without bodily health one will simply not have the opportunity to choose many other aspects of a life that one might value. Therefore, basic capabilities are a sensible focus for development projects. Programs to guarantee people access to these opportunities – such as reproductive health, or schooling – are a way of ensuring that people have the freedom they should have. Government's role is vital because escaping poverty does not depend solely on individual effort; it requires concerted, societal effort. It is unreasonable to assume that poor people can simply "lift themselves up by their own bootstraps" to get out of poverty. If an adolescent child must work as a trash picker on an urban dump site so that his family has enough to eat, and he is therefore suffering from poverty by having his health harmed by terrible working conditions and being denied an opportunity to get an education, it is senseless to urge that child to "pull himself up by his own bootstraps." While all development actors should support pro-poor policies to expand people's opportunities, governments have a special obligation to assure basic capabilities, especially for the most vulnerable people such as the child in this example.

## The "rise of the south," and insiders vs. outsiders

One important change since roughly 2000 is the so-called "rise of the south," which has affected who does development and how development is done (see Mawdsley 2012, 2017). This is a multifaceted phenomenon. Rapid economic growth in some countries has lifted many millions out of poverty; improved living standards in China and India account for most of this trend, though others such as Brazil and Indonesia have also seen significant periods of growth. While growth has typically increased inequality, and significant populations within these countries remain deprived, the greater prosperity has nonetheless brought an expanded presence on the global stage. These governments now have more resources to deal with their own societal problems, so they depend less on outside aid, and are becoming influential aid donors themselves. The highest-profile grouping of these "emerging countries" is known as the BRICS (Brazil, Russia, India, China, and South Africa). Other countries such as Mexico, Indonesia, Nigeria, Saudi Arabia, and Turkey are likewise helping to reshape the nature and governance of development assistance.

Emerging countries are contributing an increasing share of global aid totals, and in some cases, the kind of aid they give is different. Funds from the high-income DAC group still account for around 75 percent of total aid dollars, but China draws a lot of attention as the biggest "southern" player (Mawdsley 2017). China does not transparently report expenditures that can count as ODA, though analysis suggests that it still gives far less than countries such as the United States or the United Kingdom, and to different kinds of development projects (Bräutigam 2011). For instance, Chinese projects more commonly take the form of loans to recipient governments, pursuit of commercial/trade ties, and investment in infrastructure. Almost anyone who has travelled around Sub-Saharan Africa in recent years can tell stories of new roads, railways, dams, or power plants built with Chinese involvement. In contrast, DAC countries are somewhat more likely to give grants, and invest in social programs such as education. Another frequent contrast in the nature of development projects is that emerging countries are less likely to attach conditions such as democratic politics as a requirement for receiving aid. Where the DAC countries typically regard such conditions as important for fostering the rule of law and human rights, recipient countries may be glad to receive China's assistance without perceived meddling in their domestic affairs. Note that this is a complex picture, since some BRICS countries, such as Brazil and South Africa, have highlighted democracy as important to their own development policies, and some DAC countries, such as the United States, have often supported dictatorships.

The example of democratic conditionality shows how south–south cooperation is providing alternatives to the traditional development models. South–south cooperation may appeal to some aid recipients as a counter to a perceived neo-colonial dependence on rich "northern" countries. Assistance from the BRICS is still deeply shaped by geo-strategic concerns, however. China's development policy can be just as self-interested as that of northern governments; the goal of seeking raw materials in Africa to fuel Chinese industries is one obvious example (Breslin 2013). Another alternative to older models is "triangular" or "trilateral" cooperation, which involves donor countries from both the DAC and the south working with a recipient (or "partner") country also in the south (McEwan and Mawdsley 2012). For instance, Germany has been collaborating with Brazil in several Latin American and African countries on AIDS treatment programs. In addition to these specific projects, southern actors are fundamentally transforming the basic structures of development governance. In perhaps the clearest example, China has led the creation of the Asian Infrastructure Investment Bank (AIIB) to finance development projects throughout Asia. Though a number of northern countries have now joined this endeavor, the United States has refused, evidently regarding the AIIB as a competitor to the DAC-dominated World Bank.

It remains to be seen whether development will look significantly different in coming years thanks to the "rise of the south," or how much older institutions and patterns will persist. Regardless of whether a development project is led by a "northern" or "southern" actor, it is important to interrogate the relationship between who actually implements the project and who benefits from it. Scholars in development ethics such as David Crocker (1991) call for a critical reflection on the balance between "insiders" and "outsiders" in planning, carrying out, and evaluating projects. Insiders in this case are the local people who have an intimate understanding of their situation and its cultural contexts; outsiders are the foreigners who may have a thematic or issue-specific knowledge necessary to implement a project. In Crocker's view, the ideal is for insiders and outsiders to reach a shared vision and plan for what is to be achieved. Crocker aligns more with a "universalist" camp, who argue that the most effective development will be a result of finding common ground and getting locals and foreigners to work together. A more "particularist" perspective is that only members of a group should assess a group's needs and propose projects. The divide here is not merely philosophical. It applies on a daily basis in development work, since outsiders seeking to make change routinely come into communities about which they may know little.

The most sensible perspective is to recognize that there are liabilities and merits to being either an insider or an outsider. We are all cultural insiders and outsiders in different contexts, places, and times. Sometimes insiders need to carry out development, and sometimes an outsider view is useful to see something taken for granted. The key challenge for insiders is not to overlook contributing factors to poverty or suffering because they see it as "natural or acceptable." The challenge for outsiders is to avoid ethnocentric responses to local situations and acknowledge the limits of their contextual knowledge. Ultimately, a crucial principle we emphasize throughout this book is local buy-in and participation: without it, there is little chance that projects will be sustainable. If local populations, including project beneficiaries, are not included in the design, implementation, or evaluation of development projects, those projects may fail. They may not be financially sustainable, since without the participation of local populations the project's benefits might end when funding ends. They may also not be socially sustainable, since without the participation of local populations the project might not benefit those populations. Thus, an answer for who does development, and how to make development sustainable, requires the inclusion of local people and institutions in planning and implementation.

---

### Box 2.1 Deprivation and dignity in a rich city, by Mason Bryan

Jeffrey shuffled into the coffee shop wearing a black trench coat over a black dress, with black leather loafers on his feet. Five lighters – blue, red, green, yellow, purple – dangled from the coat buttons. Behind him he lugged a rickety rolling suitcase. He approached the counter, a flustered and irritated look on his face, and ordered a hot chocolate and oatmeal. He paid with a crumpled up ten dollar bill, then planted himself at a table near a plug, where he set up his laptop, situated his suitcase neatly beside him, and began charging his phone. He stood up to use the bathroom or to go smoke a cigarette. Sometimes he would tell me – his barista – a joke.

This was the pattern Jeffrey followed for months: After a couple of hours panhandling in the morning, he ambled into the cafe, spent time writing, watching videos, and surfing the internet, then ambled out just as the barista locked the door, his life's possessions in tow. At that point he'd head back to the streets for another round of panhandling before finally retiring to a quiet space in a park, under a bridge, or in the doorway of a small business. If he had cardboard, he laid it down. Then he'd unroll his sleeping bag and settle in for some YouTube or metal music on his phone. With luck, he'd doze off. With a little extra, he'd wake up spared by the rain.

Over the years I've known him, Jeffrey has shared bits about his life – both traumas from the past and aspirations for the future. He has said he resigned himself to homelessness some years after his mother died and he lost his young children to Child Protective Services (this, following a complicated situation with the mother of his children).

He learned how to survive on the streets, but not without sacrifice. At various times, bad actors have accosted him and stole his belongings; police officers have arrested him for sleeping in a park or in a parking garage; and he has endured a whole host of illnesses and injuries while exposed to harsh weather. No matter how bad his circumstance, he has refused traditional shelters – too many bad experiences with lice and hostile men.

Through it all, Jeffrey has held on to hopes for a better life. He longs to play music in a band, tell jokes in front of a crowd, start a podcast, write a book. Thoughts of achieving his goals sustain him when times are hard.

Jeffrey suffers from complex post-traumatic stress disorder, a condition that makes it challenging to complete basic tasks. It leaves him depressed, irritable, and deeply distrustful of others. The cumulative effects of his condition prevent him from working, and, because of this, he qualifies for supplemental security income. The monthly payment of just over USD 700 is enough for food, clothing, his phone bill, acid reflux medicine, cigarettes, a bus pass, cat food and litter, and subscriptions to Netflix and ad-free YouTube, among other minor incidentals which help preserve his sanity. It's barely enough to survive on, let alone to live a life with some material comforts. During a month when he's hit with unexpected expenses, he is forced to make impossible choices.

For Jeffrey, being poor is expensive.

He's not alone. Jeffrey is one of roughly 11,200 people living in shelters and outdoors in the biggest county in Washington state. Seattle is the county seat. A booming west coast tech hub in the wealthiest country in the world, the city's average household income is over USD 100,000; the median value of a single family home is around USD 800,000, which makes Seattle one of the most expensive housing markets in the nation. The region is also home to two of the world's richest men, Amazon CEO Jeff Bezos and Microsoft co-founder Bill Gates.

The spoils of this chart-topping wealth do not reach all residents. On the edges of freeways, under bridges, and in both sanctioned and unsanctioned encampments throughout the city, visible signs of homelessness abound. According to one count, Seattle has the third largest homeless population in the country, after New York City and Los Angeles.[2] Soaring rental costs, a tattered safety net, insufficient access to mental health treatment, and an opioid and amphetamine crisis are all factors that fuel what the city has for years called "a state of emergency."[3]

On more than one occasion Jeffrey has attempted to abandon homelessness and find a better place to live. But affordable housing is scarce and the channels for finding it prohibitively complex. Tens of thousands of people are in need of housing vouchers, yet only a couple thousand are available in any given year. The bureaucratic landscape of social services – a constellation of public, private, and nonprofit agencies and organizations – is opaque and confusing.

A couple years ago, Jeffrey had a stroke of luck while panhandling. He'd encountered one of the city's wealthy tech workers, who offered to buy him a used van. At USD 2500, it was a luxury Jeffrey could scarcely imagine affording. The van ran precariously, but reliably, for a few months, strengthening his sense of safety and affording him freedom he'd long been without.

The 25-foot van is defunct now and parked illegally in the city's industrial district, a popular area for people living in RVs. The engine is shot, the tires are flat. The doors won't lock from the outside. But it remains Jeffrey's primary form of shelter, what he calls his "home on wheels." Inside, with his cat Rebel, he feels more secure than he did in storefronts or under bridges. He has no bathroom, electricity, or stove to cook on, but he has a bed and he has a roof. Jeffrey says the van is the most important thing he's ever owned.

In the last year, police have ticketed him over a half dozen times for illegal parking. The pink slip slapped on his window explains that if the vehicle isn't moved within

72 hours, it'll be impounded. His only option is to enlist people to push the van a few blocks away, or to have it towed. Both options buy time. The former is unreliable. The latter costs USD 180, an unexpected expense Jeffrey can't afford.

And yet, if he can, he pays it – and suffers the consequences, even when this means going without food for a few days or longer. In his eyes, he has no other choice. To lose the van would be to lose a fragile but profound sense of safety and dignity.

## Problematizing development

Jeffrey's case (Box 2.1) poses a critical question: if he and many others live in chronic deprivation in one of the richest cities in the world, then could the United States be considered a "developing" country? This is just one of the many questions, terminological and otherwise, that problematize both the concept and practice of development. To begin with the terminological issues, the postwar conception of development has generally hinged on a binary: countries are either "developed" or "developing."[4] Yet as Jeffrey's story reminds us, poverty and basic capability deprivations exist in the richest countries too. This is why the term "developing countries" itself can be problematic – all countries are actually developing in the sense of trying to improve human wellbeing. For this reason, the Sustainable Development Goals were conceived to apply not just to lower-income countries, but to all countries. In this book we focus on societies where the incidence and severity of poverty is greatest, which tends to be countries in the global south. However, nearly all of the analytical concepts and tools we present can and should be applied to the global north as well.

These categories – "north," "south," "western" – present another terminological issue. They can be a useful shorthand, but it is worth considering how accurate or oversimplified they may be. For instance, though the label "global south" is typically used to refer to countries that have not dominated global economics and politics, this is by no means a homogeneous lot. Is it really meaningful to lump such different countries as China and Mali into the same "southern" category? The terms "rich country" and "poor country" are also rather crude since poverty exists in both. Instead, it is more accurate to follow the terminology of "low income," "middle income," and "high income" countries. In this book we do occasionally still use the problematic categories because they appear widely in development practice and scholarship. One term it is best to avoid is "Third World," an outdated reference to the least-developed countries.

We must also dig deeper than terminology to consider some of the critiques of development from scholars in post-development studies (see i.a. Escobar 2011, Sachs 2009, Rist 2002). Ideas of what development entails have changed over the decades and will doubtless continue to change in the future. Yet to one extent or another, most development paradigms have presumed that the end goal of becoming "developed" involves adopting the social-political model of the rich western countries. An operating assumption has been that industrialization, international trade, impersonal bureaucratic management, and more or less free markets have brought enormous wealth to western societies, and later, non-western industrializers such as Japan, South Korea, or Singapore have all become rich following the same basic model. Implicit in this assumption is that achieving progress – whether defined as income growth or improvement in human development – depends upon accepting the western conception of what "progress" looks like. Often that western conception has envisioned progress as a linear, deterministic, one-size-fits-all path from "undeveloped" to "developed."

Besides pointing out how this entire notion of development is derived from western models; post-development scholars have also raised the question of whether such models are applicable around the world. Can development policies truly transform a traditional tribal pastoralist society into a high-wage, export-oriented, industrial democracy such as Germany? The assumption behind many development efforts is that they can. Indeed, the assumption is that the right policies can help less-developed countries speed up their development, achieving in a matter of decades what many western countries took centuries to accomplish. Hence the conception and practice of development has been extremely policy prescriptive. It has assumed that the key to success in the development endeavor is to get policies right. In other words, if Peru would only adopt the same policies as Canada, then Peru could attain Canadian-style levels of prosperity. But according to development critics, this assumption is problematic because the policies simply may not work in a different societal context.

Policies typically depend on plans, which means that development is based on another assumption: that planning leads to results. Plans are typically devised by technical experts. However, development critics also raise the point of "insiders" versus "outsiders" by asking who those experts are and what they know about local conditions. For example, how responsive are plans to the needs and desires of the individuals/communities who are their objects or beneficiaries? It is undeniable that development has been guided by a belief in the power of technocratic management – that smart people, accurately identifying the key problems and solutions, can prescribe the steps necessary for progress. Critics are not alleging that all planning is futile, or that western policy blueprints are inevitably faulty. Some planning is necessary to make almost any endeavor successful. The criticism is rather that too strong a faith in planning can lead to inflexibility and a homogenizing mindset that insufficiently respects diverse contexts. Critics question at what point planning becomes excessively top-down and unaccountable, failing to incorporate the voices of the people being affected by the planning.

Combining the previous critiques of development leads to another, and very important, question: Is development just a new form of paternalistic western politics, colonialism in another guise? In previous centuries, western imperialism was motivated by ideas of the "civilizing mission" and the "white man's burden." This overtly racist ideology asserted that western countries had the power and the duty to lift up benighted peoples in other parts of the world, to make them more modern for their own good. Some development critics claim that the belief in the civilizing mission did not die with colonialism, that it still informs many western attitudes about non-western countries, even if unconsciously.

This critique targets not only western countries' governments but also the major institutions of global development such as the International Monetary Fund (IMF) and the World Bank. Critics claim that many of these institutions are products of western dominance. It is difficult to deny that the IMF and the World Bank in particular have been "heavily influenced by the material and intellectual power of the United States, OECD countries, corporate capitalism and neo-classical economics in US universities" (Hulme 2010: 51). Historically, the head of the IMF has always been from Europe, and the head of the World Bank from the United States. These two institutions in particular are often attacked for being excessively top-down and technocratic, lacking in accountability to those whom their policies affect. Critics charge that the IMF and the World Bank, as major promoters of neo-liberalism, have often harmed developing countries with their policies (see i.a. Babb 2005, Gore 2000, Sheppard and Leitner 2010, Wade 2002 ). The structural adjustment program is especially criticized for increasing poverty by forcing countries that receive loans to slash spending on social services.

According to some critics, the western model of development has essentially tried to remake the world along the lines of the consumer societies of Europe and North America. At worst, development could be an imposition of a model unsustainable on a planetary scale: if a billion Chinese want to consume like Americans, then the Earth will be despoiled in no time at all. But how can people in western countries tell people in China *not* to aspire to western levels of comfort and consumption? At best, even if not an imposition, development might just be empty posturing on the part of western governments. In another line of the critique, attaining North American or European levels was never realistic for the vast proportion of the world's population, so development was a false promise that the west never intended to keep. Indeed, by holding out a development model based on western ideas and experience, countries across the globe were being asked to buy into a system that was not only unsustainable, but predicated on inequalities (Sachs 2000). Critics claim that capitalism and global governance as they have been instituted since the 1940s so consistently benefit western countries that "development" never really envisioned an equal share of prosperity and resources for all the "developing" countries.

Finally, problematizing development involves questioning whether people from non-western, or traditional, or rural cultures really aspire to "development" as it has typically been conceived. It is possible that by encouraging societies around the world to follow the development model, much has been lost in traditional cultures. Unquestionably those cultures have been disrupted by urbanization, industrialization, and globalization. Ancient ways of life practiced by peoples in Africa, Asia, Latin America and elsewhere have been irrevocably altered by economic and social changes. A post-development perspective asks whether those peoples had any choice in the matter; are they really any better off if they become "developed"? This question, and the others above, are ripe for debate, and are only a small sample of the critiques problematizing development. Here we will offer no conclusive answers. Instead, we encourage readers to think hard for themselves about which perspectives are most justified.

## The aid debate

Whereas most of the preceding critiques are perhaps more conceptual in nature, another of the perennial debates about development is more policy focused, namely whether "foreign aid" is beneficial or harmful. Periodically producing a flurry of books and articles, the fundamental dispute is whether ODA is effective – and some critics doubt that ODA should be given at all (see Engel 2014 for a survey). Because this debate about aid continually percolates in the development industry, and connects to many of the critical questions about development raised above, it is worth rehearsing in some detail. First, we will survey the usual arguments against development assistance, then the arguments for, and finally suggest a synthesis between the opposing sides. The goal is to explore this debate but simultaneously transcend it. By examining the opposing arguments, ultimately we will suggest not only which of them are most convincing, but more importantly, what the future of development assistance could be to promote poverty reduction.

The argument against aid incorporates many of the previous criticisms of development as a whole. The most prominent critics include William Easterly (2006, 2014) and

Dambisa Moyo (2009). Among the many varying critiques, it is commonly claimed that since the development age began in the late 1940s, aid has generally failed for four interlocking reasons. First, the foundational premise for aid to developing countries is based on a false analogy. The Marshall Plan, implemented between 1948 and 1952 to rebuild the economy in several western European countries, was largely successful. But it is not a reasonable point of comparison for development assistance to countries in the global south. The Marshall Plan was aid for reconstruction: there was a foundation upon which to rebuild much of war-ravaged Europe, since the countries that received Marshall Plan aid had been industrialized before the war. This is different from development's typical task of bringing industrialization and democratic political systems to countries with limited or no experience of such things. Moreover, the Marshall Plan worked because the aid flows never represented significant portions of national income. Dambisa Moyo claims, "At their peak, aid flows were only 2.5 per cent of GDP of the larger recipients like France and Germany, while never amounting to more than 3 per cent of GDP for any country for the five-year life of the program" (Moyo 2009: 36). In contrast, ODA often amounts to a much larger percentage of GDP (around 30 percent for the least developed countries in the last decade), so it is very different in kind and amount from the assistance given to Europe after the Second World War (Action Aid 2011).

This leads to the second claim why aid fails: aid dollars can actually harm economic development. When aid flows comprise over 60 percent of a government's budget, the influx of dollars creates an effect eerily similar to diamonds, gold, or oil. Aid dollars begin to resemble the rents received from natural resources under a phenomenon called "Dutch disease." These dollar flows can raise prices and choke off economic growth in areas such as manufacturing or agriculture (Rajan and Subramanian 2011). Aid can also promote corruption. Like the rents from commodities such as diamonds and oil, aid comes into a government's coffers – whether as a loan or a grant – and officials are tempted to misuse the money, even putting it into their own pockets. The extent to which this routinely happens is disputed, but there is some empirical support. As one example, in Chad only 1 percent of the money intended for rural health clinics reached them (Collier 2007). Increased levels of corruption harm economic development partly because companies are less likely to invest in an environment where bribes and under-the-table negotiations drive up the cost of doing business.

Third, aid can harm political development. Corruption in the political system is only one aspect. There is also empirical support for the idea that aid promotes autocracy. Rents from commodities such as oil and diamonds often result in authoritarian political systems – and aid can act in a similar way to these rents (Bueno de Mesquita and Smith 2009, Collier 2007). One way that aid can foment repressive government is through the need to protect the corruption cycle. In corrupt systems, government officials want to keep their bribes coming. They therefore have an incentive to undermine or suppress the NGOs acting as watchdogs. Autocrats and corrupt officials do not want citizens requesting budget transparency (Kono and Montinola 2009). In short, aid dollars can act in a way similar to the "resource curse," in which too great a reliance on inflows of aid or an export such as oil can retard development and poverty reduction. (For more on corruption and the resource curse, see Chapter 7 on state institutions and governance.)

Fourth, and finally, despite these well-known problems, aid keeps flowing. According to this argument, despite a lot of rhetoric about the importance of meeting anti-corruption milestones, seldom is anyone held accountable. Organizations such as the IMF and the World Bank are sufficiently satisfied with the status quo that they do not radically re-evaluate the impact of their development assistance. Project evaluation can be so short term that there is no long-term evidence to sustain the policies in place, and hence no incentive to examine the contradictions caused by aid. It is not in the interests of the stakeholders (whether international institutions or national governments) to change the rules of the game. At the bottom of it all, critics allege, aid is not about helping countries emerge from aid. Aid is about furthering a neo-colonial model of resource extraction and profit, as well as assuring a world view that represents the political commitments and economic interests of northern countries. Aid flows to Iraq, the Congo, Sierra Leone, El Salvador, Colombia, and Mexico are not about supporting locally-led development and increased self-determination. The United States and other countries from the global north are not interested in facilitating deep democracy and local economic development. Rather, they are interested in preserving the currently unequal distribution of global power and wealth.

From the opposite camp, arguments *for* development assistance are led by people such as Jeffrey Sachs (2005) and Peter Singer (2009). Singer, in particular, emphasizes the essential facts on the distribution of world wealth. Roughly three-quarters of a billion people live below the poverty line of USD 1.90 a day. There is no denying the extent of poverty on the planet – there are many, many people who need help. On the flip side, countries just in North America and Europe, whose population accounts for about 15 percent of the world total, control some 50 percent of the world's net worth. Thus, there is also no denying that some countries have vastly more resources than others. By any reasonable calculation, these rich countries (and people in those countries) can afford to devote more of their budgets to aiding poorer people around the world – the most common target is 0.7 percent of GDP. Aid proponents say that this is not too much to ask.

The case for foreign aid rests on the powerful ethical claim that because the rich world *can* help, it *should* help. The vast resources that high-income countries possess can alleviate suffering and catalyze improvement in economies and lives throughout the world. Development aid, in its various forms, has the power to combat diseases like malaria, HIV/AIDS, and even less headline-grabbing afflictions such as river blindness or schistosomiasis. It also has the power to build roads, ports, electricity grids, dams, sewage systems, and communications networks. Aid can help transfer technologies such as medicines or pest-resistant crops, it can provide on-the-ground technical assistance, and of course it can build schools and hospitals. In the direst circumstances, aid can supply food, shelter, and medicine for victims of disasters, whether natural or human-caused.

It is indisputable that aid can work – and it does work. In addition to the ethical argument, an empirical argument supports the case for aid. A tremendous amount of evidence demonstrates the benefits of development assistance. For instance, the World Health Organization helped push for the distribution of around 300 million bed nets between 2008 and 2010, and malaria deaths for children in Sub-Saharan Africa dropped by 51 percent in roughly a decade. Thanks in part to support from the US President's Emergency Plan for AIDS Relief (PEPFAR), some ten million people infected with HIV received anti-retroviral medications. Money from the Global Fund to Fight AIDS, Tuberculosis and Malaria has led to the global mortality rate from tuberculosis dropping by 45 percent since 1990. The GAVI Alliance (founded and funded in part by the World Bank) has helped immunize more than 500 million children. Aid helped spread the Green Revolution, bringing vastly increased agricultural productivity – and with it, food security – to communities around the globe. In education, aid has massively expanded children's access to schools; as but one example, the German government spent millions of euros to help

Ghana eliminate school fees. Subsequent chapters in this book will contain many more stories of development programs that work to reduce poverty. Many of these programs have received ODA from governments in the DAC group. These are aid dollars that have obvious, measurable benefits.

The case for aid does not assume that development projects are flawless or always beneficial. One can still argue for aid while acknowledging the critics' valid points. It is true that aid has sometimes imposed a neo-colonial model on southern countries. It is also true that some aid has been wasted by corrupt regimes. And historically aid has sometimes been hamstrung by narrow political and economic interests in the donor country. Likewise, more aid dollars do not necessarily mean more improvement, and aid can contribute to Dutch disease. Too often there has indeed been a lack of accountability for donor organizations and too little consultation with the people who are supposed to benefit from poverty reduction programs. However, it is empirically false to claim that all of these problems are omnipresent or unavoidable. For example, the assertion that aid *causes* corruption, repression, and civil society breakdown is problematic because often aid has gone to states that *already* had problems with corruption, repression, and weak civil society, such as Iraq, Sierra Leone, and El Salvador. Counter-examples are abundant: Botswana, Namibia, South Korea, and Malaysia are just a few places where aid has clearly helped economic and human development.

Beyond those four cases, there is strong empirical evidence for aid's benefits. A number of studies suggest that overall aid does have a positive economic effect, even if it may be modest. As Paul Collier (2007) concluded from his survey of the literature, over three decades aid added probably one percent to the economic growth of the poorest countries, which though not huge is important because otherwise they might not have grown at all. Similarly, a review of influential studies concluded that on the whole, increases in aid are associated with increases in economic growth and investment (Clemens *et al.* 2012). As Collier states, even a modest contribution to growth means that aid "has made the difference between stagnation and severe cumulative decline. Without aid, cumulatively the countries of the bottom billion would have become much poorer than they are today" (Collier 2007: 100). Even if some scholars will contest that particular finding, it is easy to see aid's positive effects aside from economic growth. Aid has made great contributions to human development, for example, by nearly wiping out polio, and helping over two billion people gain access to safe drinking water in the past 20 years. Thus, even if aid were somehow conclusively shown not to foster positive economic growth, the evidence base for how aid has expanded capabilities for poor people throughout the world is consistent, generalizable, and readily apparent.

In the end, the question of whether aid is "good" or "bad" is so overbroad that the debate becomes simplistic. Instead, the more productive question is to ask, "how can aid work *better*?" (See i.a. Birdsall *et al.* 2005, Cohen and Easterly 2009, Ramalingam 2013, Riddell 2007). As a set of guiding principles for all development assistance, doing "better" involves asking questions such as these:

- Does the development project respond to local needs? In other words, does the project include an assessment of on-the-ground conditions rather than having been devised in far-away Geneva, London, or Washington, DC? Aid projects should be designed taking account of what local people want, not so much what donors think they need or want to give them. In general, the more that people affected by development are consulted, the better.

- How are local/national actors and institutions involved? Most of the time, the closer development is planned to where it will be carried out the better. Doing so will help the project respond to local needs, as above. Additionally, employing local experts and partners (rather than relying exclusively on international experts) supports capacity building. Capacity building strengthens project sustainability so that local actors and institutions can conceive, implement, and carry development initiatives forward. Also, procuring supplies, labor, and expertise at a local level can help the community economically.
- Does the project empower local groups, including civil society? This goes beyond mere consultation: development projects *must* include participation and buy-in, not just from local authorities, but also from the people whom the project is intending to help. The more that local people participate, the more they can strengthen their agency, and demand accountability and responsiveness from local, national, and international institutions. This is capacity building of a different kind, namely to secure democratic practices, which is constituent of human development and the capabilities approach.
- Is development inclusive and equitable? Sometimes elites at local, national, and international levels perpetuate discriminatory practices. These discriminatory practices lead to or reinforce the exclusion of individuals and communities from certain rights, resources, and capabilities. Inclusive development projects take account of the disadvantaged positions of women and marginalized groups, for example. They ensure that the people who most need help receive it.
- How has the recipient country committed to the rule of law and human rights? Because development projects usually involve governments in the recipient country, and because bad governance is consistently associated with poverty, development assistance should be given preferably only when the recipient country has already demonstrated commitment to improving its institutions such as its civil service and legal system. This is another aspect of supporting democratic practices.
- How are donor agencies coordinating and evaluating their projects? This is necessary, first, so that development projects avoid needless replication. For instance, having both Swedish and Turkish agencies funding similar projects in the same locality may well be wasteful. Second, all development projects should pursue rigorous, independent evaluation of project outcomes to make sure that aid dollars are well spent, and that local communities are really benefiting.

Much of the aid debate has centered on the role of ODA, overlooking the development assistance provided by other actors such as NGOs and foundations. That is to an extent understandable, since ODA has accounted for much larger sums of development dollars. But another way of transcending the aid debate is to examine the effective work done by these other actors. Their programs may be smaller, sometimes pilot projects with a limited impact. Yet there are consistent efforts to take such projects to scale. For example, the Gates Foundation has partnered with the INGO PATH to scale up research and programs for getting vaccines to wider populations. The International Fund for Agricultural Development has for a number of years pushed to scale up its rural development programs in countries including Albania, Ethiopia, and Peru, in areas such as market access, village-level investment planning, and small-scale irrigation. There are many other similar, innovative projects that have not cost millions of dollars to be successful, things such as training for small entrepreneurs, education to improve health and hygiene practices, programs to empower women and girls, low-technology water delivery systems, or community forest management programs. These projects may rely more on bottom–up approaches that do not require large influxes of money but instead leverage local economies, ownership, and knowledge.

Doing development better can also involve focusing on areas where aid has most often had positive effects and should therefore receive a preponderance of resources in the future. Health programs are critical here, and continued support for reducing the disease burden in poor communities is a tangible area where rich countries can help ameliorate the conditions that lead to poverty. A chief strategy, and one of the most recommendable based on its past success, is technology transfer. For instance, transferring technologies in the health field, such as licenses for pharmaceuticals, or technical materials and equipment, has had many benefits. Creating partnerships to transfer technologies for renewable energy is another promising and necessary field as both developed and developing countries confront the challenges of climate change. Likewise, technical assistance – partnerships for capacity building in various fields – can be beneficial when done right. Examples of technical assistance include expert advising on climate adaptation strategies, programs for urban water supplies, reform of the judicial system, or efforts to improve agricultural productivity. There will also always remain a role for humanitarian assistance. No one deserves to be left on their own when they are desperate after a disaster.

And despite the many criticisms, there will always remain a role for ODA. Systemic aid, bilateral flows from government to government, or large projects financed through the IMF and World Bank, will not cease. Nor should they. A purely bottom–up approach relying on entrepreneurship or individuals' economic incentives is not going to counter the big, structural causes of poverty such as disadvantageous geography, armed conflict, the disease burden, or bad institutions. Microfinance alone is not going to solve Somalia's problems. Moreover, individuals working individually are rarely going to provide public goods. As noted previously, there is a reason government exists: neither individuals, entrepreneurs in lower-income countries, or foreign direct investment is reliably going to undertake large-scale health or education interventions, or build roads, railways, sanitation, electricity and communication grids, or other infrastructure that can demonstrably improve not only poor people's lives, but poorer countries' economies. Whatever ODA's problems, such projects typically rely on governments to make a wider impact, so a critical role for development assistance will continue to be supporting these public goods when no one else will.

What one always has to remember in debates about development is that people's lives are at stake. The question, again, should not be whether aid is good or bad, but rather how aid can prevent human beings from dying prematurely, how it can help people live lives that they value. Though controversies about how to achieve those goals will continue, the objective should be that all forms of development assistance reach the people who most need it, and embolden citizens to know where aid dollars are going and how they can help steer development in their own societies.

## Conclusion

The recommendations we have just given are in some ways facile. Broad principles such as technical assistance, capacity building, and local buy-in are useful as guidelines, but they admittedly fall short in their detailed, practical application. For instance, in a new maternal health program in a remote village in South Asia, how *specifically* can one build capacity and generate local buy-in? A major difficulty is that once beyond broad principles, the precise answers on how best to carry out anti-poverty programs can vary considerably based on the local context. The good news is that today in the development field there is more awareness of the need to pursue policies based on a society's historical, social, and political context. Moreover, there is acknowledgement from development professionals that the entire idea of "development" needs to be reconsidered to some extent. A country's level of development should be evaluated based not on how well it approximates to, say, Canada, but rather in relation to the progress it has made compared to where it started.

One of the key things to remember is that doing development is *hard*. As in the example of the program in Kenya with which this chapter opened, the best of intentions and careful planning can still sometimes go awry. Any development project – and "development" as a whole – can have many different, sometimes contradictory components. For a perspective on those different components, consider the Center for Global Development's Commitment to Development Index. This measure ranks high-income countries on how much they do to help the poor around the world. The analysis relies on seven different dimensions of development: development finance, investment, migration, trade, environment, security, and technology. Some countries, such as Luxembourg, top the chart for development finance, but score much less well on their contributions to security. Overall, Sweden, France, Norway, and the United Kingdom are ranked highest for their overall commitment to development, and the United States in 2020 ranked 18th out of 40 countries – ahead of some other wealthy countries such as Japan and South Korea, but well behind countries with much smaller economies, such as Portugal or New Zealand. According to this index, the United States could be doing much more to promote development around the world.

But what should it be doing? That question returns to the dilemmas and controversies of this field. Ultimately, in a book analyzing causes of and solutions to poverty, it is nearly impossible to avoid some of the problematic assumptions of development and poverty reduction. The important thing is to acknowledge those problems, and throughout the rest of the book as well as in one's individual engagement with the world, continue to interrogate the flaws in our knowledge of how to promote human flourishing.

## Discussion questions

1   Why is it so hard to do development well?
2   What do you see as the distinctions between the terms "development," "poverty reduction," "poverty alleviation," and "poverty eradication"? Which terms or goals are preferable, and why?
3   Think about the project in Busia, Kenya. What might have been the reasons the project was not successful? Based on the principles outlined in this chapter, what could the NGO possibly have done better to plan and implement the project?
4   In what ways is Jeffrey from the vignette in Box 2.1 poor? Based on the principles laid out in this chapter, what might a development program look like to help homeless people in high-income countries?
5   Does one side of the aid debate seem more convincing? Why? What key conclusions should we take from this debate?

6   Examine the Commitment to Development Index at www.cgdev.org/initiative/
    commitment-development-index/index. What do you see as the benefits and flaws
    of this index?

- What do the seven different dimensions of development consist of? In your view,
  which seem the most important for poverty reduction?
- Explore how the different countries rate on this index. Compare several different
  countries in their respective strengths and weaknesses.

## Online resources

- This short video provides a concise explanation of Mahbub ul Haq's ideas on human
  development: https://www.youtube.com/watch?v=IDPmmYDY7Z0
- The Human Development Reports produced annually by UNDP are an excellent
  source of information: www.report.hdr.undp.org/
- The Gates Foundation's "Goalkeepers" report provides a summary of progress toward
  the Sustainable Development Goals: https://www.gatesfoundation.org/goalkeepers/
- The Council on Foreign Relations offers concise backgrounders on a range of issues
  related to development: https://world101.cfr.org/
- The Brookings Institution's "Future Development" blog has articles on many different
  issues relevant to development: www.brookings.edu/blog/future-development/

## Notes

1  The basic capabilities do not necessarily need to be those from Nussbaum's list. Though we
   agree with her general perspective that there are some fundamental, universal entitlements, what
   counts as "basic" in any given society could be partially context specific.
2  Kate Walters, "Seattle homeless population is third largest in US, after LA and NYC," Kuow.org,
   18 December 2018, www.kuow.org/stories/here-s-how-seattle-and-washington-compare-to-
   national-homeless-trends, accessed December 2020.
3  Jake Goldstein-Street, "Seattle's oldest emergency," Capitol Hill Seattle Blog, 22 July 2020, www.
   capitolhillseattle.com/2020/07/seattles-oldest-emergency/, accessed December 2020.
4  Note, too, that the usual assumption is about countries rather than societies or peoples. The
   western model of the nation-state dominates the international order, and so also structures
   thinking and practice about how development must take place.

## Further reading

Gates Foundation. 2014. Annual Letter, "Three Myths that Block Progress for the Poor."
    www.gatesfoundation.org/Who-We-Are/Resources-and-Media/Annual-Letters-List/
    Annual-Letter-2014.
Moyo, Dambisa. 2009. *Dead Aid: Why Aid Is Not Working and How There Is a Better Way for Africa.*
    New York, NY: Farrar, Straus and Giroux.
Payne, Anthony and Nicola Phillips. 2010. *Development.* Cambridge: Polity Press.
Sachs, Wolfgang. 2000. "Development: The Rise and Decline of an Ideal," Wuppertal Institut für
    Klima, Umwelt, und Energie, Paper no. 108, August.
Stewart, Frances, Gustav Ranis, and Emma Samman. 2018. *Advancing Human Development: Theory
    and Practice.* Oxford: Oxford University Press.
Ziai, Aram. 2017. "Post-development 25 years after *The Development Dictionary.*" *Third World
    Quarterly* 38.12: 2547–2558.

## Works cited

Action Aid. 2011. *Real Aid: Ending Aid Dependency*. London: Action Aid. www.actionaid.org.uk/sites/default/files/doc_lib/real_aid_3.pdf. Accessed September 2020.

Alkire, Sabina, and Séverine Deneulin. 2009. "The Human Development and Capability Approach," in Séverine Deneulin and Lila Shahani, eds. *An Introduction to the Human Development and Capability Approach*. London: Earthscan.

Babb, Sarah. 2005. "The social consequences of structural adjustment: recent evidence and current debates." *Annual Review of Sociology* 31.1: 199–222.

Barder, Owen. 2009. "What is Poverty Reduction?" Center for Global Development, Working Paper 170, April.

Birdsall, Nancy, Dani Rodrik and Arvind Subramanian. 2005. "How to help poor countries." *Foreign Affairs* 84.4: 136–152.

Bräutigam, Deborah. 2011. *The Dragon's Gift: The Real Story of China in Africa*. Oxford: Oxford University Press.

Breslin, Shaun. 2013. "China and the South: Objectives, actors and interactions." *Development and Change* 44.6: 1273–1294.

Brundtland Commission on Environment and Development. 1987. *Our Common Future*. Vol. 383. Oxford: Oxford University Press.

Bueno de Mesquita, Bruce, and Alastair Smith. 2009. "Political survival and endogenous institutional change." *Comparative Political Studies* 42.2: 167–197.

Clemens, Michael A., Steven Radelet, Rikhil R. Bhavnani and Samuel Bazzi. 2012. "Counting chickens when they hatch: timing and the effects of aid on growth." *The Economic Journal* 122: 590–617.

Cohen, Jessica, and William Easterly, eds. 2009. *What Works in Development? Thinking Big and Thinking Small*. Washington, DC: Brookings Institution Press.

Collier, Paul. 2007. *The Bottom Billion: Why the Poorest Countries Are Failing and What Can Be Done About It*. New York, NY: Oxford University Press.

Crocker, David A. 1991. "Insiders and outsiders in international development." *Ethics & International Affairs* 5.2: 149–173.

Deneulin, Séverine, and Lila Shahani, eds. 2009. *An Introduction to the Human Development and Capability Approach*. London: Earthscan.

Deolalikar, Anil B., Alex B. Brillantes Jr., Raghav Gaiha, Ernesto M. Pernia and Mary Racelis. 2002. "Poverty Reduction and the Role of Institutions in Developing Asia," ERD Working Paper No. 10, Asian Development Bank, May.

Easterly, William. 2014. *The Tyranny of Experts: Economists, Dictators, and the Forgotten Rights of the Poor*. New York: Basic Books.

Easterly, William. 2006. *The White Man's Burden: Why the West's Efforts to Aid the Rest Have Done So Much Ill and So Little Good*. New York: Penguin.

Elliott, Jennifer. 2012. *An Introduction to Sustainable Development*. New York: Routledge.

Engel, Susan. 2014. "The not-so-great aid debate." *Third World Quarterly* 35.8: 1374–1389.

Escobar, Arturo. 2011. *Encountering Development: The Making and Unmaking of the Third World*. Princeton, NJ: Princeton University Press.

Esquith, Stephen L. 2013. "The political responsibility of bystanders: the case of Mali." *Journal of Global Ethics* 9.3: 377–387.

Gore, Charles. 2000. "The rise and fall of the Washington Consensus as a paradigm for developing countries." *World Development* 28.5: 789–804.

Gugerty, Mary Kay and Kremer, Michael 2008. "Outside funding and the dynamics of participation in community associations." *American Journal of Political Science* 52.3: 585–602.

Hulme, David. 2010. *Global Poverty: How Global Governance Is Failing the Poor*. London: Routledge.

Hydén, Göran. n.d. "Governance, Development and Poverty Eradication," mimeo.

Kono, Daniel Yuichi and Gabriella R. Montinola. 2009. "Does foreign aid support autocrats, democrats, or both?" *The Journal of Politics* 71: 704–718.

Mawdsley, Emma. 2017. "Development geography 1: Cooperation, competition and convergence between 'North' and 'South'." *Progress in Human Geography* 41.1: 108–117.

Mawdsley, Emma. 2012. *From Recipients to Donors: The Emerging Powers and the Changing Development Landscape*. London: Zed Books.

McEwan, Cheryl and Emma Mawdsley. 2012. "Trilateral development cooperation: Power and politics in emerging aid relationships." *Development and Change* 43.6: 1185–1209.

Moratti, Massimo and Amra Sabic-El-Rayess. 2009. "Transitional Justice and DDR: The Case of Bosnia and Herzegovina," International Center for Transitional Justice Research Unit, June.

Moyo, Dambisa. 2009. *Dead Aid: Why Aid Is Not Working and How There Is a Better Way for Africa*. New York: Farrar, Straus and Giroux.

Nussbaum, Martha. 2011. *Creating Capabilities: The Human Development Approach*. Boston, MA: Harvard University Press.

Rahnema, Majid, and Victoria Bawtree, eds. 1997. *The Post-Development Reader*. London: Zed Books.

Rajan, Raghuram G., and Arvind Subramanian. 2011. "Aid, Dutch disease, and manufacturing growth." *Journal of Development Economics* 94.1: 106–118.

Ramalingam, Ben. 2013. *Aid on the Edge of Chaos: Rethinking International Cooperation in a Complex World*. Oxford: Oxford University Press.

Ranis, Gustav, Frances Stewart and Alejandro Ramirez. 2000. "Economic growth and human development." *World Development* 28.2: 197–219.

Rapley, John. 2004. "Development studies and the post–development critique." *Progress in Development Studies* 4.4: 350–354.

Redclift, Michael. 2005. "Sustainable development (1987–2005): an oxymoron comes of age." *Sustainable Development* 13.4: 212–227.

Riddell, Roger. 2007. *Does Foreign Aid Really Work?* Oxford: Oxford University Press.

Rist, Gilbert. 2002. *The History of Development: From Western Origins to Global Faith*. London: Zed Books.

Robeyns, Ingrid. 2005. "The capability approach: a theoretical survey." *Journal of Human Development* 6.1: 93–114.

Rostow, Walt. 1960. *The Stages of Economic Growth: A Non-Communist Manifesto*. Cambridge, UK: Cambridge University Press.

Sachs, Jeffrey. 2005. *The End of Poverty*. New York: Penguin.

Sachs, Wolfgang. 2000. "Development: The Rise and Decline of an Ideal," Wuppertal Institut für Klima, Umwelt, und Energie, Paper no. 108, August.

Sachs, Wolfgang, ed. 2009. *The Development Dictionary*. London: Zed Books.

Sen, Amartya. 1999. *Development as Freedom*. New York: Knopf.

Sheppard, Eric, and Helga Leitner. 2010. "Quo vadis neoliberalism? The remaking of global capitalist governance after the Washington Consensus." *Geoforum*, 41.2: 185–194.

Sidaway, James D. 2007. "Spaces of postdevelopment." *Progress in Human Geography* 31.3: 345–361.

Singer, Peter. 2009. *The Life You Can Save*. New York: Random House.

ul Haq, Mahbub. 2004. "The Human Development Paradigm," in Sakiko Fukuda-Parr and AK Shiva Kumar, eds. *Readings in Human Development: Concepts, Measures and Policies for a Development Paradigm*. New York: Oxford University Press.

United Nations Development Program. 2013. *Fast Facts: Poverty Reduction and UNDP*. New York: UNDP.

Wade, Robert Hunter. 2002. "US hegemony and the World Bank: the fight over people and ideas." *Review of International Political Economy* 9.2: 215–243.

World Bank. 2000. *World Development Report 2000: Attacking Poverty*. New York: Oxford University Press.

# 3 Multidimensional measurements of poverty and wellbeing

*Benjamin Curtis*

## Learning objectives

- Describe how poverty lines are constructed, and where relevant data come from.
- Interpret major monetary measures of poverty and inequality.
- Interpret multidimensional measures of poverty and wellbeing.
- Understand qualitative measures such as participatory poverty assessments.
- Explain strengths and weaknesses of the various measures.

## Vignette 3.1

*Aneni is a 28-year-old woman who lives in a little town outside of Masvingo, Zimbabwe. She works as a small trader in the market, selling fruit, vegetables, and some basic products such as soap and soft drinks. Aneni is smart and hard working, and she has successfully built her business up from scratch. In a good month, she may earn the equivalent of as much as USD 400, which is impressive since the average income in Zimbabwe is closer to USD 200 a month. Aneni even earns enough to be able to afford to send her two older children to school, which is important to her since she herself completed only the first grade. On the other hand, though Aneni is the main breadwinner for her family, partly because of cultural norms she has to give much of what she earns to her husband, Chindori. He has had very little paid work in months, and too often spends some of the family's money on alcohol. Sometimes there is not enough money for when a family member falls sick, as happened to Aneni last year when she was incapacitated for a week with a bout of malaria. The line between good and ill health can be precarious for Aneni and her family. One of her children died when he was only three months old, and Aneni worries about having to endure another childbirth as complicated as her last one. Fortunately, she has been able to convince her husband to use a condom. When you ask her about her life, Aneni says that overall she is mostly satisfied and happy.*

## Introduction

Given Aneni's situation – by no means an unusual one for a woman in the developing world – should she be considered poor? In terms of her income, she is fairly well off when compared to many Zimbabweans. But does a lack of control over one's own earnings constitute a kind of poverty? And what about the fact that Aneni has had so little formal education? Likewise, do her health problems allow us to classify her as poor in some ways? The often complex task of identifying and measuring poverty is the focus of this chapter. This task – and the question of whether Aneni is poor – is obviously important, since identifying who is poor can determine who needs help, and what kind of help they need. Good measures of the breadth and depth of poverty are necessary because without them, how can we know if we are making progress in the fight against the various dimensions and causes of poverty, helping people to live lives that they value?

Deriving accurate measures to understand "who is poor" is not simple. There are many different statistics to consider, most of which come with methodological disagreements and conceptual challenges. As an initial example of such complications, estimations for the percentage of people who were poor in 17 Latin American countries ranged from 13 to 66 percent, depending on which definition and measurements for poverty were used (Szekely *et al.* 2000). This chapter primarily takes a practical and empirical approach, presenting a variety of ways to measure both poverty and wellbeing, and how they are applied around the world. We begin with some conceptual issues before examining specific monetary and multidimensional measures, including those inspired by the capabilities approach. We will also consider a methodology called participatory poverty assessments, as well as subjective measures of wellbeing. The level of analysis is mostly global: though individual countries do develop their own specific measures of poverty, our focus is on indicators that are comparable across countries. At the end of the chapter we will discuss some methodological difficulties behind the statistics presented.

### Establishing a poverty line

As we discussed in Chapter 1, poverty is often conceived of as deprivation. Measuring deprivation in areas such as monetary income, food, health, education and/or rights presumes first establishing a threshold above which a person is not deprived, and below which she is. This threshold is referred to as a *poverty line*. Constructing a poverty line involves identifying elementary, minimum requirements for the different potential dimensions of poverty such as income or nutrition. Different dimensions can have different poverty lines, and poverty lines can apply differently for different groups of people. For instance, a food poverty line that is often used is 2100 calories a day: a person whose consumption of food falls below that limit is considered to be deprived, or food poor. But the 2100 number is for an "average person" – a small child will need less, or someone doing hard physical labor in extreme conditions could well need more. Constructing a poverty line is essential as part of the process to establish a target of basic requirements to which every human is entitled. Poverty lines are also useful because they establish a measure – whether of income, caloric intake, minimum years of schooling, etc. – that enables comparisons between different years, locations, and people.

Poverty lines, like poverty itself, can be absolute (i.e. a common threshold across all humanity) or relative (a threshold contextualized to certain societies or groups of people). Absolute poverty lines are useful for cross-country comparison. But poverty lines are also often constructed to be relative; a minimum of monetary income or years of schooling will be different in Denmark than in Sudan. The comparison between Denmark and Sudan illustrates a common principle: in low and middle income countries, deprivation in "absolute consumption" tends to define poverty. This means the absolute minimum that people need to live. In higher income countries, the minimum is drawn not according to what is needed merely to survive, but rather according to what is needed to live a life which is considered acceptable in that country. The most prominent measure of global absolute poverty is the percentage of population living on USD 1.90 or less a day (see Figure 3.1). The precise numbers have changed over the years (the threshold has risen

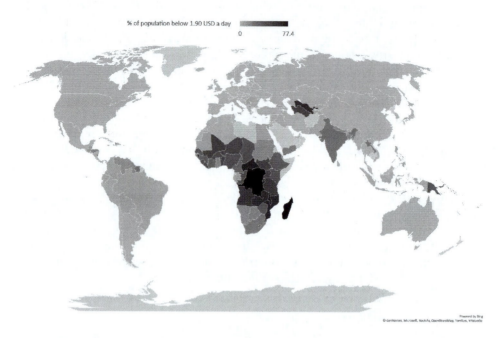

% of population below 1.90 USD a day

0                    77.4

*Figure 3.1* Population in extreme poverty, percentage of country's population living below 1.90
USD a day

Source: World Bank data, most recent year. Created by the author. Powered by Bing. © GeoNames,
Microsoft, Navinfo, OpenStreeMap, TomTom, Wikipedia.

from USD 1.08 to 1.25 to 1.90), but this measure is important because it enables a cross-
country comparison on where the poorest people are. As an easily comprehensible, stark
indicator of deprivation, the measure helps generate awareness and concern, and focuses
policymakers' attention on the neediest.

Measuring income is one way to determine which households or individuals fall
below the poverty line, but measuring consumption is more likely to produce an
accurate picture of deprivation. Consumption refers to the usage of a variety of goods
and services, everything from food to transportation. It is typically measured through
household surveys, which can provide a finer-grained picture of a family's standard of
living than their incomes, which really serve to enable that consumption. Income may
be difficult to calculate, especially in the poorest countries. Time can be a critical consideration in identifying poverty: a person's income can fluctuate radically according
to the season (e.g. if it is harvest season) or across years (years of drought will harm
harvests and hence depress incomes). Similarly, valuing the income from agriculture,
particularly subsistence agriculture (when the family's production does not enter the
market) can be difficult. Households may also be reluctant to report accurately on
income rather than consumption because they are seeking to avoid taxation on that
income (Sahn and Younger 2010). For all these reasons, most governments throughout
low and middle income countries conduct household surveys of consumption, sending
workers around cities, towns, and villages to interview families on their consumption
levels. Those reported levels then help the government establish a poverty line and
who falls below it.

---

**Box 3.1 Example of questions from a household survey**

- What is the main source of drinking water for members of your household (e.g. piped water, dug well, water from spring, rainwater, surface water, bottled water)?
- How long does it take to go to your water source and come back? Who usually goes to collect the water?
- In the last month, has there been any time when your household did not have sufficient quantities of drinking water when needed?
- What kind of toilet facility do members of your household usually use (e.g. flush or pour flush toilet, pit latrine, composting toilet, bucket toilet, no facility/bush/field)?
- Do you share this toilet facility with other households? Including your household, how many other households use the facility?
- In your household, what type of cookstove is mainly used for cooking (e.g. electric stove, solar cooker, biogas stove, open fire)?
- Does the stove have a chimney? Is cooking usually done in the house, in a separate building, or outdoors?
- What type of fuel or energy source is used in this cookstove (e.g. gasoline, kerosene, charcoal, wood, straw/grass, dung, garbage)?
- Does the household own any livestock, herds, other farm animals, or poultry?
- Does your household have: electricity, a radio, a tv, a non-mobile telephone, a computer, a refrigerator?
- Does any member of this household have an account in a bank or other financial institution?
- Does the household have any mosquito nets?

Source: adapted from DHS (2019).

---

## Monetary measures of poverty

Poverty lines and consumption play into both monetary and multidimensional approaches to measuring poverty and wellbeing. Monetary measures are the most widely used, in part because data are relatively available and sometimes simpler to interpret. Multidimensional approaches to measure capability poverty can be more complicated, but efforts have been made in recent decades to devise better ways of calculating capability deprivation. We will consider in turn the concepts behind both approaches' measurements, as well as the measurements themselves.

Monetary poverty measurements involve calculating a person's income, consumption, and production at market prices, and calculating whether these three things add up to meet the minimum needs set by the poverty line. There are several key assumptions behind the monetary approach to measuring poverty. First is the claim that measurements such as a person's annual income are the best, easiest proxy for measuring all sorts of other deprivations that are often more difficult to capture. For example, if a person's income is below 50 percent of the society's poverty line, then he seriously lacks what has been established as the minimum income necessary for basic wellbeing, and he might be deeply deprived in a variety of ways. Therefore, though other measures such as health and education are also appropriate, a lack of income is held to represent fundamental deficiencies.

*Table 3.1* List of countries by GDP (PPP) per capita

| World rank | Country | PPP $ |
|---|---|---|
| 1 | Qatar | 132,886 |
| 2 | Luxembourg | 108,951 |
| 3 | Singapore | 103,181 |
| 4 | Ireland | 83,399 |
| 5 | Brunei | 80,384 |
| 6 | Norway | 76,684 |
| 7 | United Arab Emirates | 69,435 |
| 8 | Kuwait | 66,387 |
| 9 | Switzerland | 66,197 |
| 10 | United States | 65,112 |
| 176 | Sierra Leone | 1,690 |
| 177 | South Sudan | 1,602 |
| 178 | Liberia | 1,414 |
| 179 | Mozambique | 1,303 |
| 180 | Malawi | 1,240 |
| 181 | Niger | 1,106 |
| 182 | Eritrea | 1,060 |
| 183 | Democratic Republic of Congo | 849 |
| 184 | Central African Republic | 822 |
| 185 | Burundi | 727 |

Source: International Monetary Fund data (2020).

Two other assumptions behind monetary measures are objectivity and externality. These assume that poverty can be objectively measured by an external observer such as a researcher or government worker. These ideas are valid, but they contrast with the view that poverty is best measured subjectively by those who experience it. Finally, monetary measures also depend upon an individualistic approach that presumes that poverty should be defined with reference to individuals rather than to groups (Stewart *et al.* 2007).

Income levels as measured by gross domestic product (GDP) per capita present a picture of overall monetary assets for a country's population. Using these numbers, countries are often classified into low income, low–middle, high–middle and high income categories (see Table 3.1's list of highest and lowest income countries). Comparisons of income across countries have to be converted using a standard metric so that income in India is measured with the same yardstick as income in Paraguay. The most common metric is purchasing power parity (PPP), which is a way of comparing prices and incomes across countries with different currencies; a PPP dollar is a standardized, universally comparable unit of currency to allow for monetary comparisons.

Income data also factor into measurements of inequality. Wealth or income inequality is an indicator of relative deprivation. Measuring income inequality can therefore provide a valuable perspective on poverty in a country. Amartya Sen (2006) notes that the absolute deprivation of capabilities typically depends on relative deprivation of incomes, and Andy Sumner (2012) reminds us that to understand poverty we must ask the question "Who gets what?" The most used measurement of income inequality, known as the Gini coefficient (or index), helps answer that question. This measure computes the statistical distribution of wealth in a country. It ranges theoretically from 0 (where all income would be completely equally distributed) to 100 (where a single person would control all

*Table 3.2* List of highest and lowest countries by Gini coefficient

| Country | Gini (%) |
| --- | --- |
| Ukraine | 25 |
| Belarus | 25.4 |
| Slovenia | 25.4 |
| Moldova | 25.9 |
| Czech Republic | 25.9 |
| Slovakia | 26.5 |
| Azerbaijan | 26.6 |
| Finland | 27.1 |
| Kyrgyz Republic | 27.3 |
| Norway | 27.5 |
| Belize | 53.3 |
| Brazil | 53.3 |
| Botswana | 53.3 |
| Mozambique | 54 |
| Lesotho | 54.2 |
| Central African Republic | 56.2 |
| Zambia | 57.1 |
| Suriname | 57.6 |
| Namibia | 59.1 |
| South Africa | 63 |

Source: World Bank data.

income). In practice, values typically range from around 25 to around 63 (see Table 3.2). The United States has a Gini score of 41.5 (which is high for the advanced industrial democracies); Canada's is 34 (roughly average for similar countries); and Mexico's is 48.3 (high in global terms but not unusual for Latin America). There are a number of variations to the Gini coefficient – such as whether it is calculated from before-tax or after-tax numbers – as well as alternative inequality measures, such as the Palma ratio or the Theil index. The Gini index remains the most common *monetary* measure of inequality, though disparities in multidimensional measures are another way of analyzing inequalities.

---

**Box 3.2 How many extremely poor people are there, and where are they?**

According to monetary measures, around the world in 2020 there were about 600 million extremely poor people living below the USD 1.90 poverty line. This is an appalling number – yet it represents amazing progress. In 1990, roughly 1.9 billion people lived in extreme poverty. In the last several decades, monetary poverty rates have fallen sharply in a number of countries, including Ethiopia, Indonesia, Ghana, and above all India and China, which have experienced blazing economic growth that has lifted hundreds of millions of people into the middle class. Recent data suggest that less than 10 percent of the world's population lives in extreme poverty, with another approximately 15 percent living below the USD 3.20 line for poverty in lower-middle income countries. Estimates are that about 380 million of the extreme poor live in Africa, 320 million in Asia, 19 million in South America, and 13 million in North America. The countries with the most extremely poor people are Nigeria (95.9 million people, which is 47 percent of Nigeria's population, and represents 16 percent of the total number of extreme poor in the world) and the Democratic Republic of Congo (63.6 million, 74 percent of the country's population, and 10.7 percent of the world total). India, which for many years had high shares of extreme poverty, now accounts for only 5 percent of the world total; less than 3 percent of the country's population lived in extreme poverty in 2020.

This distribution of global poverty has also changed significantly in recent years. By total numbers, most of the world's poor people now live in middle income countries, not low income countries. This is because of the aforementioned swift economic growth that has improved average incomes, though it has not benefited these countries' populations equally. Thus absolute poverty tends to be concentrated in communities that suffer from geographic/spatial disadvantages (see Chapter 5 of this book), and/or who are marginalized or disempowered in broader social structures (see Chapter 6), and/or who are discriminated against or underrepresented in institutions and governance (see Chapter 7). People who are in chronic poverty (i.e. for years at a time) make up a large proportion of the extremely poor, and unfortunately, chronic poverty is often passed on from generation to generation. Even people who escape absolute poverty may end up in an insecure group known as the "precariat" because they are at higher risk of falling back into poverty due to shocks such as in income or health. The Covid-19 pandemic is one such shock that at the time of writing is predicted to throw tens of millions of people back into poverty, and end the world's recent streak of declining poverty numbers.

Note that all these numbers are estimates, and such estimates are often contested on methodological and ideological grounds. Different calculation formulae will give different pictures of the number of people in poverty. For example, when in 2008 the World Bank revised its poverty line from USD 1.08 to USD 1.25, some 1.4 billion people were counted as extremely poor – 300 million more than according to the Bank's 2005 estimate. This kind of recalculation has led to some critics accusing the World Bank of "shifting the goalposts" on poverty reduction. As one example, Robert Wade argues that because of a litany of problems such as unreliability of data sources and changes in calculation methods that make the data from different years non-comparable, the World Bank actually *under*estimates the number of people in poverty. On the other end of the spectrum, critics such as Surjit Bhalla have claimed that in the household survey data underlying many World Bank statistics, poor people consistently understate their income or consumption, which means that the Bank drastically *over*estimates poverty rates. Another critic, Philip Alston, claims that the USD 1.90 poverty line does not adequately cover the cost of food and housing, and obscures poverty among women and neglected groups such as migrants. Though there will always be disagreements and data problems, in general the World Bank's statistics set the standard and are considered "official," and we rely on them throughout this book.

Sources: World Data Lab, Alston 2020, Bhalla 2009, Roser and Ortiz-Espina 2020, Sumner 2016, Wade 2004.

## Multidimensional measures

Though monetary measurements may be somewhat simplistic, they have an obvious advantage in that they are relatively easy to calculate and understand. They provide one useful lens for measuring poverty. Multidimensional measurements offer a more nuanced picture of poverty and wellbeing, but are typically more complex. They are more nuanced because they seek to gauge factors that support capabilities, capturing more aspects of quality of life than income alone. As an example, women educated through a literacy program in Pakistan might not see a boost in incomes, but they may report a major boost in feelings of self-esteem, empowerment, and autonomy (Alkire 2002). The complexity comes in how to quantify such positive outcomes – which is nonetheless a vital task for conceptualizing what development means and how poverty reduction can be achieved.

Various indicators provide information on capability deprivation and quality of life for people around the world. Health measures are some of the most fundamental: studies have shown that they are not highly correlated with incomes, which means that they capture aspects of wellbeing that monetary measures miss (Sahn and Younger 2010). The information that goes into the health measures is often more reliable than that derived from consumption surveys, since health measures are typically done at the individual level, and they use nearly universal units such as kilograms. Thus, measuring a child's weight and height relative to others her age provides a fairly uncomplicated insight into that child's healthy physical development. Educational attainment is another oft-used indicator of functionings. The idea is that schooling empowers people through knowledge applicable to the kind of life they want to live, and that the capability to get educated can be measured through functioning outcomes such as literacy rates. (See Table 3.3 for examples of human development indicators in health and education.)

The Sustainable Development Goals (SDGs) for 2030 are built upon a multidimensional conception of deprivation and wellbeing. The SDGs bundle together 17 goals, 169 targets and 300 or so indicators – see the list of goals below. The SDGs were designed in part to respond to some of the criticisms of the Millennium Development Goals (MDGs),

*Table 3.3* Examples of human development indicators

| Some key health indicators | Some key education indicators |
| --- | --- |
| Rates of child malnutrition | Net enrolment in primary education and secondary education |
| Infant mortality rate; under age 5 mortality rate | Proportion of pupils in grade 1 who reach grade 5 |
| Adult mortality rate | Adult literacy rate |
| Maternal mortality rate | Learning outcomes measurements such as passing rates on standardized tests |
| HIV/AIDS prevalence | Mean years of schooling (adults) |
| Proportion of population at risk of malaria; death rates associated with malaria | Expected years of schooling (children) |
| Prevalence of tuberculosis; death rates associated with tuberculosis | Ratio of girls to boys in primary, secondary, and tertiary education |
| Percentage of population without access to an improved water source | Government expenditure on education as a percentage of GDP |
| Percentage of population without access to improved sanitation facilities | |

which covered the period 2000 to 2015. For example, the MDGs did not specifically mention human rights, and in practice they were goals only for developing countries, not for high-income countries. The SDGs are also more attentive to inequality than the MDGs were. There are naturally some criticisms of the SDG agenda: the number of indicators can seem like a laundry list; some of the data required may be difficult to come by, especially in the poorest countries; and it is debatable how many of the SDGs can realistically be achieved. Though accountability for achieving the targets may be lacking, the SDGs do represent a relatively coherent, internationally valorized, and highly visible attempt to agree upon development definitions, objectives, and measurements for the coming years.

---

**Box 3.3 The sustainable development goals**

Goal 1: End poverty in all its forms everywhere

Goal 2: End hunger, achieve food security and improved nutrition and promote sustainable agriculture

Goal 3: Ensure healthy lives and promote wellbeing for all at all ages

Goal 4: Ensure inclusive and quality education for all and promote lifelong learning

Goal 5: Achieve gender equality and empower all women and girls

Goal 6: Ensure access to water and sanitation for all

Goal 7: Ensure access to affordable, reliable, sustainable and modern energy for all

Goal 8: Promote inclusive and sustainable economic growth, employment and decent work for all

Goal 9: Build resilient infrastructure, promote sustainable industrialization and foster innovation

Goal 10: Reduce inequality within and among countries

Goal 11: Make cities inclusive, safe, resilient and sustainable

Goal 12: Ensure sustainable production and consumption patterns

Goal 13: Take urgent action to combat climate change and its impacts

Goal 14: Conserve and sustainably use the world's oceans, seas, and marine resources

Goal 15: Sustainably manage forests, combat desertification, halt and reverse land degradation, halt biodiversity loss

Goal 16: Promote just, peaceful, and inclusive societies

Goal 17: Revitalize the global partnership for sustainable development

Explore the Sustainable Development Goals and their indicators at the UN's dedicated website: www.un.org/sustainabledevelopment/sustainable-development-goals/

---

A capability understanding of poverty has also inspired several measures that combine multiple indicators into a broader composite or "index" measure. These composite measures include the Human Development Index (HDI), several gender-related index measures, and the Multidimensional Poverty Index. Researchers at the United Nations Development Program devised the HDI to combine both economic and social indicators relevant to "the enlargement of people's choices," and to enable cross-country comparisons (UNDP 2007) (see Table 3.4). The HDI is not focused on deprivation; rather, it seeks to

*Table 3.4* List of countries by Human Development Index score

| Overall HDI rank | Country | HDI score |
|---|---|---|
| 1 | Norway | .954 |
| 2 | Switzerland | .946 |
| 3 | Ireland | .942 |
| 4 | Germany | .939 |
| 4 (tie) | Hong Kong | .939 |
| 6 | Australia | .938 |
| 6 (tie) | Iceland | .938 |
| 8 | Sweden | .937 |
| 9 | Singapore | .935 |
| 10 | Netherlands | .933 |
| 180 | Mozambique | .446 |
| 181 | Sierra Leone | .438 |
| 182 | Eritrea | .434 |
| 182 (tie) | Burkina Faso | .434 |
| 184 | Mali | .427 |
| 185 | Burundi | .423 |
| 186 | South Sudan | .413 |
| 187 | Chad | .401 |
| 188 | Central African Republic | .381 |
| 189 | Niger | .377 |

Source: United Nations Development Program data (2019).

measure a society's overall attainment of wellbeing. It is composed of a "health indicator" (life expectancy at birth), two "knowledge" indicators (mean years of schooling and expected years of schooling), and a "material wellbeing" indicator (gross national income per capita in USD PPP). There is also an inequality-adjusted HDI which reranks countries taking into account the amount of inequality in the society. Some countries that score very high on the HDI – such as the United States, Spain, and South Korea – fall significantly when inequality is factored in.

The Gender Development Index (GDI), the Gender Inequality Index (GII), and the Global Gender Gap Index (GGGI) have been designed to capture important aspects left out of the HDI. The GDI is composed of indicators comparing men and women in terms of life expectancy, education, and earned income. The GII measures the loss of achievement due to gender inequality in the dimensions of health, empowerment, and labor market participation. The GGGI measures gender-based disparities in access to resources and opportunities. It incorporates indicators for women's health and survival, plus others such as the ratio of female participation in the labor force and the ratio of women with seats in parliament. Figure 3.2 shows countries' GII scores. Part of the appeal of these index measures is that by combining a number of indicators, they provide a more cohesive picture of human development that can be easily understood by policymakers and the public.

In response to some of the difficulties with measuring capability poverty, and the limitations of other index measures, the Multidimensional Poverty Index (MPI) has been developed, principally by the scholars Sabina Alkire and James Foster. This measure is focused intentionally on poverty – not development or empowerment or income – and it includes indicators to gauge multiple, simultaneous deprivations. As Alkire and

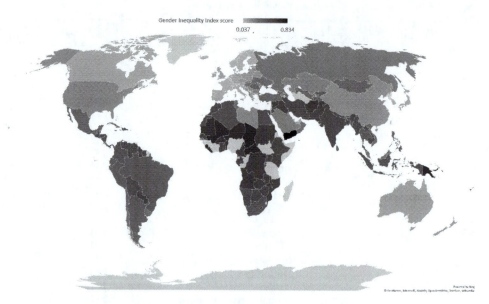

*Figure 3.2* Countries by Gender Inequality Index score
Source: UNDP data, 2018. Created by the author. Powered by Bing. © GeoNames, Microsoft, Navinfo, OpenStreeMap, TomTom, Wikipedia.

Foster have written, "When poor people describe their situation […], part of their description often narrates the multiplicity of disadvantages that batter their lives at once. Malnutrition is coupled with a lack of work, water has to be fetched from an area with regular violence, or there are poor services and low incomes" (Alkire and Foster 2011: 13). The MPI also draws explicitly on the capabilities approach: indicators reflect functionings, and so low scores on the indicators are analogous to states of "unfreedom" (Alkire and Santos 2013). Another advantage of the MPI is that it allows much finer-grained analysis than the HDI or the Human Poverty Index (which was used before the MPI). For instance, the data computed into the MPI make it possible to identify *who* is poor by individuals or groups, *where* poor people are by region or locality, *how* they are poor by which deprivations they suffer from, and *how intense* their poverty is by the number of deprivations.

The MPI's indicators allow for cross-country comparison as well as country-specific modifications. The breakdown of poverty dimensions, indicators, and their weights in computing the MPI is shown in Figure 3.3. A person is defined as multidimensionally poor if he or she is deprived in one-third of these indicators (Alkire and Sumner 2013). A list of countries with the severest multidimensional poverty is presented in Table 3.5. The report on the 2019 MPI revealed a much more detailed picture of global poverty than most of the other measures we have considered. According to this analysis, 23.1 percent of people in countries covered by the MPI count as multidimensionally poor, and two-thirds of them live in middle-income countries. Half of the multidimensionally poor people in the world are children, and 85 percent of them live in South Asia and Sub-Saharan Africa. In several countries – Burkina Faso, Chad, Ethiopia, Niger, and

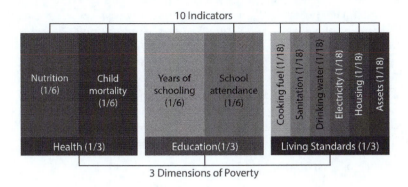

*Figure 3.3* Components of the Multidimensional Poverty Index
Source: © Oxford Poverty and Human Development Initiative (OPHI).

*Table 3.5* Top ten countries by highest Multidimensional Poverty Index score

| Country | MPI score | % Population in severe multidimensional poverty | Intensity of deprivation (average % of weighted deprivations) |
| --- | --- | --- | --- |
| Niger | .59 | 74.8 | 65.2 |
| South Sudan | .58 | 74.3 | 63.2 |
| Chad | .53 | 66.1 | 62.3 |
| Burkina Faso | .52 | 64.8 | 61.9 |
| Ethiopia | .49 | 61.5 | 58.5 |
| Central African Republic | .46 | 54.7 | 58.6 |
| Mali | .46 | 56.6 | 58.5 |
| Madagascar | .45 | 57.1 | 58.2 |
| Mozambique | .41 | 49.1 | 56.7 |
| Burundi | .40 | 45.3 | 54.3 |

Source: Oxford Poverty and Human Development Initiative (2019), www.ophi.org.uk/multidimensional-poverty-index/.

South Sudan – 90 percent or more of children under the age of ten are multidimensionally poor. But there are also major disparities within countries. In some regions in Uganda, for instance, only 6 percent of people are multidimensionally poor, while in others, 96 percent are. A piece of good news is that a few countries, namely India and Cambodia, are reducing their MPI values quite fast, and not leaving the poorest people behind as they do so (OPHI 2019).

One advantage of the MPI is that its weighted dimensions and poverty thresholds can be adjusted for applications to specific countries. For instance, Mexico has adapted the MPI to identify and measure poverty for its own national policies. In Mexico's application, deprivations in one of several indicators help define a person as multidimensionally poor, including access to health care, access to social security, basic services in homes, and housing quality. For access to social security, a person falls below the poverty threshold if she does not receive medical services through a public, voluntary, or family network. For basic services, the poverty threshold is lacking access to piped or fresh water, public drainage services, or public electricity. An analysis of 2010 data concluded that 46.2 percent of Mexico's population (in other words, 52 million people out of a total population of about 112 million) were multidimensionally poor, and on average these 52 million people suffered from deprivations in 2.5 of the indicators (OPHI 2013). Like previous measures we have studied, the MPI is not sufficient in itself. Because its usage is still expanding, and still working out methodological issues of calculation and data collection, the MPI is best used as a complement to income and other measures.

## Participatory poverty assessments

Another approach to measuring poverty differs significantly from the preceding ones in that it does not rely primarily on statistics for cross-national comparisons. Also important is that this approach is not predicated on external observers' ostensibly objective measurements, but depends instead on groups of (usually poor) people defining poverty within the context of their own community. The goal is to understand how poor people themselves would subjectively measure poverty. Known as participatory poverty assessments (PPAs; or sometimes participatory rural appraisals), the participatory aspect is that a group of people gather together to talk about definitions of poverty, how to identify need, and who is deprived in what ways. PPAs can play a vital role in the capabilities approach by providing information about the capabilities or freedoms that individuals deem "fundamental," and what their minimum thresholds would be for an adequate life. Besides giving outsiders an insight into the community's definitions of poverty, these participatory assessments often fulfil other functions, such as promoting self-determination, empowerment, and group cooperation (Laderchi 2001). By helping to highlight the specific concerns or priorities of poor people, PPAs can serve as an important policy tool for governmental or NGO programs. Evidence also suggests that PPAs often do not identify the same people as poor as do monetary measures.

Of course, like any other way of measuring poverty, PPAs have certain limitations. Because they are qualitative research, the results of PPAs can be difficult to use in comparisons from one society to another, or to quantify for econometric analyses. Also, researchers have found that sometimes such participatory assessments can be skewed when the participants think they are more likely to receive some commodity (whether food, health care, or something else) as a result. For instance, it can happen that more people claim they are poor in the hopes of getting help. People are essentially always biased in regard to their own situation. Though subjective reports are part of the rationale of PPAs, they nearly always involve some post-hoc evaluation or synthesis by an external researcher. The external researchers' work must be designed very carefully to avoid methodological problems in the data gathering, and ethical pitfalls in the relationship with the community. There is no guarantee, either, that the actual participants in these assessments are the most representative of poverty in the community; it is certainly possible that the most marginalized people are excluded (Norton *et al.* 2001).

Regardless, PPAs are valuable for providing a "grassroots" picture of poverty that can be different from that provided by the other measures. For instance, results from various PPAs have revealed that income is often not people's primary concern but other considerations such as security and self-respect are. People value a wide variety of things that are probably impossible to capture via monetary measures. These things include freedom to choose jobs and livelihoods; freedom from persecution, humiliation, violence, and exploitation; the ability to participate in decision making; and preservation of and ability to participate in traditional cultural values (Streeten 1998). In Clark and Qizilbash's research in South Africa, people in poor communities identified these ten "essentials of life," in rank order of importance: housing/shelter, food, clean water, work/jobs, money/income, clothes, education/schools, health and health care, electricity/energy, and safety/security (Clark and Qizilbash 2005). A PPA in Laos documented villagers' tribulations with crises such as crop losses from bad weather, pests, or land degradation. Those crises tended to cause food shortages, and human crises such as illness, alcoholism, or death, which led to labor shortages and reduced income. The PPA also identified political/legal problems leading to the unsustainable exploitation of environmental resources, which in turn harmed people's security in other ways (Action Aid 2006). The World Bank's *Consultations with the Poor* series was a monumental project of PPAs interviewing 20,000 people in 200 communities in 23 countries. A very small selection of findings from the project is presented in the box below.

---

### Box 3.4 Findings from the World Bank's *Consultations with the Poor* PPAs

From their roughly 20,000 interviews, the World Bank team synthesized five interconnected dimensions of wellbeing that poor people identified.

- *Material wellbeing.* Defined by a person in Ecuador as "A livelihood that will let you live."
- *Physical wellbeing.* An older man in Egypt described deprivation in this area: "My children were hungry and I told them the rice is cooking, until they fell asleep from hunger."
- *Freedom of action and choice.* A poor woman in Brazil defined freedom in this way: "The rich [person] is the one who says: 'I am going to do it' and does it. The poor, in contrast, do not fulfil their wishes or develop their capacities."
- *Security.* For a person in Russia, security meant "the absence of constant fear."
- *Social wellbeing.* "It is neither leprosy nor poverty which kills the leper, but loneliness," said a person in Ghana.

The World Bank team also identified five consistent, cross-cutting problems that trapped people in poverty: corruption, violence, powerlessness, weakness, and bare subsistence. A person in Bulgaria claimed that "corruption is virtually everywhere," and another in Uzbekistan complained that "the police have become the rich people's stick used against common people." People decried violence in society and in the household: "Women are beaten at the house for any reason that may include failure to prepare lunch or dinner for the husband," said a respondent in Ethiopia. The lack of security also applied to basic living conditions. A woman in Brazil lamented that "the sewage runs in your front door, and when it rains, the water floods into the house and […] the waste brings some bugs, here we have rats, cockroaches, spiders, and even snakes and scorpions." The PPAs showed that poor people around the world routinely felt themselves ignored by both government and NGOs. This powerlessness defined poverty for an old man in Nigeria: "If you want to do something and have no power to do it, it is poverty."

Source: Narayan *et al.* (1999).

## How much overlap is there between these measures?

Having surveyed a range of different measurements, a natural question would be to ask how the measurements relate to each other. Specifically, do they identify the same people as poor? It would be nice, for the sake of simplicity, if the answer were "yes," but in fact the picture is mixed, and ultimately there are many ways that the different measures fail to overlap. Several studies have concluded that monetary and human development measures sometimes overlap, but often do not (see Bourguignon *et al.* 2008, Stewart *et al.* 2007). At the national level, for example, a country might make major strides in eliminating health-related aspects of poverty such as malaria prevalence, yet have no income growth, and hence still be counted as poor according to monetary measures. At the individual level, consider again the example that opened this chapter: Aneni in Zimbabwe would not be considered income poor, but she does suffer from serious deprivations in health and education, and she lacks some fundamental rights of autonomy in her own household. So is she truly poor? One approach, known as the "union" approach, would say that if she has deprivations in *any* dimension – either income, or health, or education, or rights, for instance – then yes, she is poor. But another approach, the intersection approach, would say that she is poor if she has deprivations in *all* dimensions, so income *and* health, and education, and rights (Atkinson 2003). The problem is that these two approaches may not identify the same people as poor. As one example, a study found that 97 percent of India's population was poor according to the union approach, but according to the intersection approach, only 0.1 percent of the population was poor (Alkire and Seth 2009).

This is not to say there is never overlap between measures; sometimes there is, but it can be weak. The weak overlap leads to surprising cases such as that of Nicaragua, which achieved a relatively favorable score of 18 on the Human Poverty Index (HPI), but where 80 percent of the population was living below the old USD 2 a day line. South Africa had the opposite problem, with a relatively high HPI of 31.7 but with only 23.8 percent of the population living on less than USD 2 a day. Further demonstrating how different data sources can complicate analysis, one study found that 12 percent of the population of Bhutan in 2012 was income poor, and 12.6 percent were poor according to the MPI – but only 3.2 percent of the population was poor by both measures (Alkire 2018). Clearly, there are mismatches between these data and indicators. Comparing countries such as Saudi Arabia and Uruguay also complicates definitions of wellbeing: Saudi Arabia has a higher GDP per capita than Uruguay, but Uruguay scores much higher on human development indicators such as adult literacy, life expectancy, child mortality, and political rights (Alkire and Deneulin 2009).

## Wellbeing measures

The flip side to measuring deprivation and poverty is measuring when people are doing well, when they are satisfied with their lives and happy. Think of this as a way of assessing the true goals of human development, and the fulfilment of capabilities and functionings (Gough and McGregor 2007). The idea of measuring wellbeing depends on a number of assumptions already familiar from our discussion thus far. For example, wellbeing is multidimensional. It might depend on aspects of income, health, education, safety, community ties, even work–life balance. But clearly wellbeing goes beyond mere income or economic sufficiency; indeed, sometimes economic growth can lead to people saying they are *less* happy (Lora and Chaparro 2008). Hence measures of wellbeing should focus on the lived experience of human beings, rather than on GDP or economies or countries as a whole (Boarini *et al.* 2014). Measuring wellbeing can involve objective, external indicators such as some of the human development indicators mentioned above. The idea is that low malaria death rates or illiteracy rates are reasonable proxies for a satisfactory life. Additionally, measuring wellbeing has a subjective element; as with PPAs, it should involve asking people about their own quality of life.

Of the various wellbeing measures widely used in the world, among the highest profile is the World Happiness Report (WHR). A country's happiness ranking is derived from data from a worldwide poll asking people to rate their life satisfaction according to a "Cantril Ladder." This "ladder" starts at zero, which would be the worst possible life, and goes up to ten, which would be the best possible life (see Helliwell *et al.* 2019). The WHR's analysis also takes into account additional data from another poll, the World Values Survey. Figure 3.4 shows a map of countries by their happiness score in 2020. Worldwide trends are fairly stable: Nordic countries tend to rank as the happiest (Finland topped the world with a score of 7.81), while very poor and/or conflict-torn countries are the least happy (Afghanistan was bottom of the table at 2.57). This is not surprising, given that over time the WHR has found several variables that tend to be most influential in explaining people's evaluations of their own happiness: healthy life expectancy, social support, freedom, trust, generosity, and yes, income (Helliwell *et al.* 2019). The Better Life Index is another measure which includes several variables similar to these. At present, this index is calculated mostly for high income countries, but a few middle income countries (such as South Africa, Mexico, and Turkey) are included, and that pool could be widened as data become available (Boarini *et al.* 2014). Once

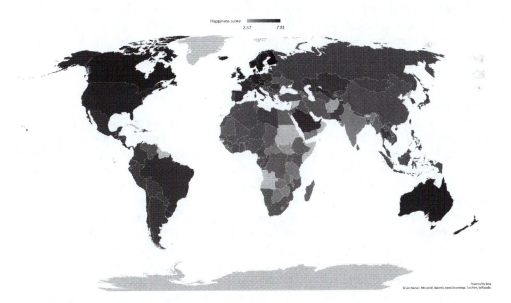

*Figure 3.4* Happiness score by country

Source: World Happiness Report data, 2019. Created by the author. Powered by Bing. © GeoNames, Microsoft, Navinfo, OpenStreeMap, TomTom, Wikipedia.

again, northern European countries (plus Canada and Australia) score the highest on this measure.

The WHR and the Better Life Index incorporate both subjective and objective measures, but it is worth reviewing some of the criticisms of subjective measures that we noted in Chapter 1. Adaptive preference poses a serious problem for gauging a person's happiness because someone used to a deprived life might rate their wellbeing as relatively good if they have never experienced anything better. Alternatively, someone who is well-off might rate his own life relatively poorly because he has no perspective on what genuine suffering looks like (see i.a. Pogge and Wisor 2016, Stewart 2014). Another critique is that understandings of "happiness" may vary so much across time and cultures that people would conceive of "wellbeing" differently. However, there is some evidence that subjective wellbeing measures are at least partially valid across cultures and countries. As we have seen even from the participatory poverty assessments, certain aspects of what makes a "good life" (such as shelter, food, income, health, and education) might be called universal (see i.a. Exton *et al.* 2015). Critics of the subjective wellbeing approach also question how much confidence we can have in the accuracy and honesty of individuals' answers to life satisfaction survey questions. People may forget bad things that have happened to them, for instance, or exaggerate how good they feel. Proponents argue that these problems do not completely compromise the measure (Barrington-Leigh and Escande 2018). Ultimately, though people's self-evaluated quality of life is important, it is problematic enough that "happiness" alone should not be taken as an indicator of wellbeing.

## Measurement difficulties

The critiques of subjective wellbeing measures allude to a broader point: as the World Bank itself has admitted, statistics on global poverty have "considerable uncertainty," and are "flawed but not useless" (World Bank 2017: xvi). Rather than assuming that all the measures we have presented in this chapter are completely accurate, it is wise to treat them with a certain amount of caution. They are the best the development community has available, but nearly all measures have their flaws. In this section we will briefly survey some of the measurement difficulties that motivate a cautious approach to statistics around global poverty.

To begin with, the very idea of poverty lines has to be approached with care (see Ravallion 2019). A "bright line" as a poverty threshold can be somewhat crude. Take, for example, an income poverty line of USD 1000 a year. How much difference is there, really, between a person who makes USD 1050 a year (and is therefore above the poverty line, and not considered poor) and a person who makes USD 950 a year (and is therefore considered poor)? The simplest calculation of poor people using a poverty line – what is known as the "headcount method" – only tallies the number of people below the line. It does not take into account *how far* people fall below the poverty line. There is a method known as the "poverty gap" to calculate how far people fall below the line, but it is relatively seldom used (Deaton 2004). Poverty lines can also be fudged in a variety of ways to achieve political ends. For instance, if a government wants to claim its policies have significantly reduced poverty, it can target those policies at people just below the poverty line, helping them move above the threshold. In so doing, the government has "reduced poverty" according to the headcount numbers, but it has done little for the very poor. In extreme cases, a poverty line can even be recalculated to redraw it downwards, which results in a reduction of the numbers of poor people purely through math and not through improving their lives.

The data that go into constructing poverty lines – and that inform many poverty-related statistics – can also be problematic (see i.a. Deaton 2016). Household surveys often provide the data from the local level. However, different countries use different methods for household surveys, and sometimes even within countries the survey methods may change from year to year. Household data might also neglect specific individual-level deprivations such as inequitable distribution of resources within the family (Ravallion 2010). Because they are self-reports of consumption, household surveys are often at best approximations. For instance, surveys sometimes have trouble accounting for consumption related to public goods such as health care or schools. Certain groups of people may also be over-counted or under-counted. Evidence suggests that richer people are less likely to respond to such surveys and/or they will under-report their consumption or incomes. It can also be hard to reach the poorest of the poor, refugees, people in conflict zones, and the homeless, since they may not have fixed addresses or may avoid contact with government workers for their own reasons (World Bank 2017).

The outcome of these under- or over-counts is that researchers arrive at an inaccurate picture of income or consumption levels in a country or region, which can then lead to incorrect conclusions about the extent and depth of poverty there. As a concrete example, it has been estimated that household surveys reached only 71 percent of the population for Sub-Saharan Africa in the years around 2005; if almost 30 percent of the population remained uncounted, then income and consumption data may very well be unrepresentative (Anand *et al.* 2010).

Where household surveys gather data at the local level, national accounts measures operate at the country level, including macroeconomic statistics such as production outputs of goods and services, wages and salaries, redistribution of income through government taxes, and how income is spent or saved. National accounts statistics thus purport to measure consumption, but they have been found to understate consumption in very poor countries and to overstate rates of growth of average consumption (Deaton 2010). Moreover, economists have observed a growing disparity between poverty counts arrived at via the household survey and national accounts methods. In India, for example, these two measures in 1950 produced poverty count estimates that were roughly "at parity," but more recently the survey data produced poverty counts half those produced by the national accounts data (Deaton 2001). This suggests that the two methods are actually counting different things, and thereby providing highly divergent answers as to who is poor.

Similar caveats should be kept in mind when considering any income measure of poverty. Such measures say almost nothing about how income gets used, for example. Do people spend their income on things that actually improve their wellbeing? Or does the money get spent on drugs/alcohol, frivolous items, or other things not necessary for survival? At the household level, is the income spent to benefit family members fairly, or do women, the elderly, the young, or the sick get short shrift (Alkire and Santos 2009)? PPP measures also have weaknesses. Not all governments gather the relevant data using the same methodology, nor do some governments regularly update those data. The basic formulas by which global PPP comparisons are calculated have also been changed several times, which means that PPP statistics from 1995 may not be strictly comparable with the numbers from 2015. The outcome of this range of methodological controversies is that estimates of the number of people in poverty can swing wildly. For instance, when calculation methods were changed, estimates for the percentage of the population below the poverty line in Sub-Saharan Africa in 1993 jumped from 39 to 49 percent. For Latin America, it declined from 23.5 to 15 percent (Deaton 2001).

Multidimensional composite measures also have certain drawbacks. The very idea of combining indicators in an index such as the HDI can be contentious (Seth and Villar 2017). One reason is that composite indices typically miss out on simultaneous deprivations, which can lead to estimation errors on the number of poor people and how poor they (Alkire *et al.* 2015). The respective weights of the indicators (i.e. their importance in the overall index calculation) have also been called arbitrary, and it has been charged that too many other indicators of human development are left out. The HDI does not address areas potentially relevant to basic capabilities such as political freedoms, justice and equity, personal security, ecology and sustainability, or other fundamental human rights (Streeten 1998). There may be some danger, too, that by enshrining health and education indicators in these indexes, health and education improperly come to define human development to the exclusion of other dimensions. So once again these index measures should only be taken as approximations: they provide a compelling but partial view on poverty and human development at the national – but not the individual – level.

Measuring capabilities – as the MPI aims to do – entails difficulties both conceptual and methodological. One such difficulty is how to define metrics for capabilities: after all, how can one measure "freedoms," or the "freedom to choose" that the capabilities approach holds as the standard for an acceptable life? Moreover, how can you measure achieved capabilities, that is, functionings? There is also the difficulty that different people will require different inputs (such as resources or commodities) to achieve the same level of functionings. Age, health status, characteristics of the physical environment, cultural norms, and societal features such as hierarchies and political arrangements can all impact an individual's ability to convert opportunities to functionings. In practice, MPI data come from the household level, thus obscuring individual-level deprivations, despite the fact that individuals' capabilities are the primary concern in terms of promoting development. Finally, the MPI has been lacking a measure of the depth of deprivation, that is, how far a household falls below the poverty threshold in any given dimension. This blunts its precision as a tool for measuring the severity of poverty (Pogge and Wisor 2016).

---

### Box 3.5  Measuring outcomes with randomized controlled trials

In this chapter we primarily discuss descriptive statistics derived from various measures of poverty. Another type of statistical analysis plays into measuring *outcomes* of poverty reduction programs via randomized controlled trials (RCTs). RCTs are often touted as the "gold standard" of program evaluation because of their ability to isolate causal impacts. The randomization methodology reveals those causal impacts by differentially allocating "treatment" (i.e. participation in the program) to different groups. In an ideal case, the way it works is this: a population is selected for analysis, then randomly divided into "treatment arms," one of which is the "control," meaning it does not actually receive the treatment. Randomly dividing the groups is supposed to eliminate the problem of selection bias, by which too many people sharing some similar characteristics might all get the treatment, which in turn would skew the analysis of the treatment's effects.

A study of a program to help people living in extreme poverty can provide a concrete example of the method. Researchers worked with the NGO BRAC on a program that operated in various countries including Bangladesh, Ethiopia, Honduras, India, and Peru, among others. The program's components included: giving people an asset such as livestock or goods to start a store; training on how to manage the asset; coaching visits to help participants handle challenges; health education and access to health care; basic food or cash support; and a savings account. Randomization took place at the household level in a few countries (which means that some households in a village received the program support, and some did not) and at the village level in other countries (so some villages got the support). This methodology allowed the researchers to control as much as possible for other factors that could influence observed outcomes for the program participants. And the outcomes were impressive: people who received the treatment had more assets and savings, better health, and were hungry less and worked more. In Bangladesh, for instance, poor women increased their earnings by an average 38 percent. The analysis also showed that the program was highly cost effective. In India, for every 1 USD spent on the program, households in extreme poverty saw USD 4.33 in long-term benefits (Banerjee *et al.* 2015).

The ability to pinpoint results like these is one reason that RCTs have grown enormously in international development research and practice in the last 20 years. J-PAL, one of the main research organizations behind RCTs, has estimated that it has conducted 700 projects to date, with around 200 million people reached by programs it has evaluated. Some of the leading lights behind J-PAL – the economists Abhijit Banerjee, Esther Duflo, and Michael Kremer – were awarded a Nobel Prize in 2019 for their work expanding both the methods and evidence base of development research. Of course, like anything else in development, RCTs are not without their controversies (see i.a. Banerjee *et al.* 2020, Deaton and Cartwright 2018). They can be very complex and laborious to implement. Participants and program partners must adhere strictly to the implementation protocols, otherwise the causal analysis can be weakened. Results from an RCT might not be easily scalable, since a program implemented by an NGO with the help of expert researchers might not be as effective when run by a government for a much larger population. Similarly, causal inferences from the statistical analysis of RCT results might not be valid when a similar program is applied in a different context or country. Critics of RCTs also raise ethical questions about denying treatment and/or performing these kinds of social experiments on vulnerable people. Contrary to what "randomistas" (as the most hard-core proponents of RCTs are known) may claim, there are other valuable forms of program evaluation, some of which capture data that RCTs cannot. Hence the most sensible way forward for outcomes measurement is a "mixed methods" toolkit that includes meticulous quantitative analysis like RCTs as well as qualitative research with communities and individuals participating in the program.

## Conclusion

What lesson should you take from measurement difficulties and controversies? The answer is that it is essential to understand where poverty-related data are coming from, how those data were derived, and the relative strengths (and weaknesses) of competing measures. Poverty lines, household surveys, monetary measures, composite indices, and subjective wellbeing reports all have their utility. Because measures of poverty and wellbeing do have limitations, there is no sole optimal measure. No single global poverty line is going to give a reliable picture of poverty around the world. The circumstances of poverty are ultimately too country- and society-specific to allow for single measures in which we can have much confidence. Similarly, an index of a variety of poverty measures will not provide a complete picture. Not all deprivations are relevant in all situations.

Therefore, it is smartest to consult a number of different measures of poverty, with reference to specific societies, to examine deprivation using several indicators. This is akin to what is known in the field as a "dashboard approach." The measures should embrace multiple dimensions, whether income, health, education, empowerment, employment status, housing quality, personal safety, and/or subjective measures of wellbeing. The measures should include both quantitative and qualitative data – statistics, but ideally also interviews, participatory analyses, and ethnographies. A more comprehensive analysis will not be restricted to poverty, but will also examine indicators for inequality (such as the Gini index and the Gender Inequality Index) and quality of life (such as the Human Development Index and World Happiness Report). You cannot expect that different measures will produce one cohesive answer. The dashboard approach typically fails to capture overlapping deprivations that can affect individuals and families. But together, the various measures can identify the people who need help, and point to the dimensions in which concerted action may alleviate their suffering.

Combining measures in this way also lets us see where progress has been made in the last several decades. The Millennium Development Goals for 2015 fell short of many of their targets, but still showed progress according to a variety of indicators. For instance, the proportion of undernourished people worldwide fell between 1990 and 2015 from 23.3 to 12.9 percent. Major gains were made in education – the net enrolment rate in primary education rose from 83 percent in 2000 to 91 percent in 2015. Child and maternal mortality both fell by half, and in gender empowerment, the proportion of women in parliament almost doubled. The incidence and mortality from malaria and the proportion of people without access to safe drinking water were also halved (United Nations 2015). Most of these positive trends have continued into the 2020s. However, the data also show how much work is left to be done. Despite major drops in the total numbers of people in extreme poverty, analysis suggests that the very poorest people are often not benefiting (Ravallion 2016). Those being left behind are increasingly concentrated in Sub-Saharan Africa, which may be home to 90 percent of the world's poorest by 2030. Addressing their multiple deprivations will be a challenge both for measurement and poverty reduction strategies.

## Discussion questions

1  Are there basic capabilities essential to a definition of poverty that have been left out of this discussion? If so, what are they? How should they be measured?
2  Use the internet to explore indicators of poverty, inequality, and wellbeing. What can you learn about individual countries, trends among countries, trends over time, and relationships between different indicators?
   a)  UNDP's data explorer is an excellent source for a variety of measures: www.hdr. undp.org/en/data

b)   Gapminder.org may seem complicated at first, but you can investigate a wide variety of discrete indicators and the relationships between them, as well as statistical trends and videos.

c)   The World Inequality Database (www.wid.world) has a wealth of data at both the global and country levels.

d)   Explore the Social Progress Index (www.socialprogress.org). How is "social progress" defined? What is the range of indicators? Examine how several individual countries perform according to this measurement. How does the Index as a whole relate to the capabilities approach?

3   Envision a participatory poverty assessment for your society. How would you define what constitutes "poverty"? How would you identify who is poor and not poor? What is "deprivation" in your society, and how can you measure it?

4   Examine the full list of Sustainable Development Goals and their indicators online. Is there anything missing from the SDGs, in your view? What do you think are the most important of the 17 goals?

5   If measures such as the SDGs and the HDI have major flaws, then what is the point of using them? What do you see as the advantages and disadvantages of such measures?

## Online resources

- Our World in Data, with many different articles and data visualizations on topics related to poverty and development: www.ourworldindata.org/
- The SDG Tracker, measuring progress on all 17 of the Sustainable Development Goals: www.sdg-tracker.org/
- Global Data Lab, with subnational human development data, useful for zooming in beyond national-level statistics: www.globaldatalab.org/

## Further reading

Edin, Kathryn J. and H. Luke Shaefer. 2015. *$2.00 a Day: Living on Almost Nothing in America*. New York: Mariner Books.

Oxford Poverty and Human Development Initiative. 2015. "Measuring multidimensional poverty: insights from around the world," OPHI Briefing No. 30, May.

Saith, Ruhi. 2001. "*Capabilities: the concept and its operationalisation*," Queen Elizabeth House Working Paper 66, February.

World Happiness Report: www.worldhappiness.report/

## Works cited

Action Aid. 2006. Participatory Poverty Assessment, Attapeu Province, Lao PDR. Mekong Wetlands Project.

Alkire, Sabina. 2002. *Valuing Freedoms: Sen's Capabilities Approach and Poverty Reduction*. Oxford: Oxford University Press.

Alkire, Sabina. 2018. "The research agenda on multidimensional poverty measurement: important and as-yet unanswered questions." Oxford Poverty and Human Development Initiative Working Paper 119, June.

Alkire, Sabina and Andy Sumner. 2013. "Multidimensional poverty and the post-2015 MDGs," Oxford Poverty & Human Development Initiative brief, February.

Alkire, Sabina and James Foster. 2011. "Understandings and misunderstandings of multidimensional poverty measurement." *Journal of Economic Inequality* 9: 289–314.

Alkire, Sabina and Maria Emma Santos. 2009. "Poverty and Inequality Measurement," in Séverine Deneulin and Lila Shahani, eds. *An Introduction to the Human Development and Capability Approach*. London: Earthscan.

Alkire, Sabina and Maria Emma Santos. 2013. "A multidimensional approach: poverty measurement & beyond." *Social Indicators Research* 112: 239–257.

Alkire, Sabina and Séverine Deneulin. 2009. "A Normative Framework for Development," in Séverine Deneulin and Lila Shahani, eds. *An Introduction to the Human Development and Capability Approach*. London: Earthscan.

Alkire, Sabina and Suman Seth. 2009. "Determining BPL status: some methodological improvements." *Indian Journal of Human Development* 2.2: 407–424.

Alkire, Sabina, James Foster, Suman Seth, Maria Emma Santos, Jose M. Roche, and Paola Ballon. 2015. *Multidimensional Poverty Measurement and Analysis*. Oxford: Oxford University Press.

Alston, Philip. 2020. "The parlous state of poverty eradication." Report of the Special Rapporteur on extreme poverty and human rights. United Nations Human Rights Council, July.

Anand, Sudhir, Paul Segal and Joseph Stiglitz. 2010. "Introduction," in Sudhir Anand, Paul Segal and Joseph Stiglitz, eds. *Debates on the Measurement of Global Poverty*. Oxford: Oxford University Press.

Atkinson, A. B. 2003. "Multidimensional deprivation: contrasting social welfare and counting approaches." *Journal of Economic Inequality* 1: 51–65.

Banerjee, Abhijit, Esther Duflo and Michael Kremer. 2020. "The Influence of Randomized Controlled Trials on Development Economics Research and on Development Policy," in Kaushik Basu, David Rosenblatt and Claudia Paz Sepulveda, eds. *The State of Economics, the State of the World*. Cambridge, MA: MIT Press.

Banerjee, Abhijit, *et al.* 2015. "A multifaceted program causes lasting progress for the very poor: Evidence from six countries." *Science* 348.6236: 1260799.

Barrington-Leigh, Christopher, and Alice Escande. 2018. "Measuring progress and well-being: A comparative review of indicators." *Social Indicators Research* 135.3: 893–925.

Bhalla, Surjit S. 2009. "Raising the standard: the war on global poverty," unpublished working paper, March.

Boarini, Romina, Alexandre Kolev, and Allister McGregor. 2014. "Measuring well-being and progress in countries at different stages of development." OECD Development Center Working Paper 325, November.

Bourguignon, François *et al.* 2008. "Millennium Development Goals at midpoint: where do we stand, and where do we need to go?" European Report on Development, September.

Clark, David A. and Mozaffar Qizilbash. 2005. "Core poverty, basic capabilities and vagueness: an application to the South African context," Global Poverty Research Group paper GRPG-WPS-026, July.

Deaton, Angus. 2001. "Counting the world's poor: problems and possible solutions." *The World Bank Research Observer* 16.2: 125–147.

Deaton, Angus. 2004. "Measuring poverty." Paper for the Research Program in Development Studies, Princeton University

Deaton, Angus. 2010. "Measuring Poverty in a Growing World (or Measuring Growth in a Poor World)," in Sudhir Anand, Paul Segal and Joseph Stiglitz, eds. *Debates on the Measurement of Global Poverty*. Oxford: Oxford University Press.

Deaton, Angus. 2016. "Measuring and understanding behavior, welfare, and poverty." *American Economic Review* 106.6: 1221–1243.

Deaton, Angus, and Nancy Cartwright. 2018. "Understanding and Misunderstanding Randomized Controlled Trials." *Social Science and Medicine* 210: 2–21.

DHS Program Demographic and Health Surveys. 2019. Household Questionnaire. www.dhsprogram.com/publications/publication-DHSQ8-DHSDHSQ8--Questionnaires-and-Manuals.cfm. Accessed March 2020.

Exton, Carrie, Smith, Conal and Vandendriessche, Claire. 2015. "Comparing Happiness across the World." OECD Statistics Directorate Working Paper 62.

Gough, Ian, and J. Allister McGregor, eds. 2007. *Wellbeing in Developing Countries: From Theory to Research*. Cambridge: Cambridge University Press.

Helliwell, John, Layard, Richard, & Sachs, Jeffrey. 2019. *World Happiness Report 2019*, New York: Sustainable Development Solutions Network.

International Monetary Fund data. 2020. www.imf.org/en/Data. Accessed March 2020.

Laderchi, Caterina. 2001. "Participatory methods in the analysis of poverty: a critical review," QEH Working Paper QEHWPS62, January.

Lora, Eduardo and Chaparro, Juan Camilo 2008. 'The Conflictive Relationship between Satisfaction and Income.' Inter-American Development Bank, Working Paper 642.

Narayan, Deepa, Robert Chambers, Meera Shah and Patti Petesch. 1999. *Global synthesis: Consultations with the poor*. Washington, DC: World Bank Poverty Group.

Norton, Andy, Bella Bird, Karen Crock, Margaret Kakande and Carrie Turk. 2001. *Participatory Poverty Assessment: An Introduction to Theory and Practice*. London: Overseas Development Institute.

Oxford Poverty and Human Development Initiative. 2013. 'Measuring multidimensional poverty: insights from around the world,' briefing paper, June.

Oxford Poverty and Human Development Initiative (OPHI). 2019. *Global Multidimensional Poverty Index 2019*. www.hdr.undp.org/sites/default/files/mpi_2019_publication.pdf. Accessed March 2020.

Pogge, Thomas and Wisor, Scott. 2016. "Measuring Poverty: A Proposal," in Matthew Adler and Marc Fleurbaey, eds. *Oxford Handbook of Well-Being and Public Policy*: 645–676. Oxford: Oxford University Press.

Ravallion, Martin. 2010. "The Debate on Globalization, Poverty, and Inequality: Why Measurement Matters," in Sudhir Anand, Paul Segal and Joseph Stiglitz, eds. *Debates on the Measurement of Global Poverty*. Oxford: Oxford University Press.

Ravallion, Martin. 2016. "Are the world's poorest being left behind?" *Journal of Economic Growth* 21.2: 139–164.

Ravallion, Martin. 2019. "On measuring global poverty." NBER Working Paper w26211. National Bureau of Economic Research, August.

Roser, Max and Esteban Ortiz-Ospina. 2020. "Global Extreme Poverty." Published online at OurWorldInData.org. www.ourworldindata.org/extreme-poverty. Accessed March 2020.

Sahn, David E. and Stephen D. Younger. 2010. "Living Standards in Africa," in Sudhir Anand, Paul Segal and Joseph Stiglitz, eds. *Debates on the Measurement of Global Poverty*. Oxford: Oxford University Press.

Sen, Amartya. 2006. "Conceptualizing and Measuring Poverty," in David B. Grusky and Ravi Kanbur, eds. *Poverty and Inequality*. Stanford, CA: Stanford University Press.

Seth, Suman, and Antonio Villar. 2017. "Measuring human development and human deprivations." *OPHI Working Papers* 110.

Stewart, Frances. 2014. "Against happiness: A critical appraisal of the use of measures of happiness for evaluating progress in development." *Journal of Human Development and Capabilities* 15.4: 293–307.

Stewart, Frances, Ruhi Saith and Barbara Harriss-White, eds. 2007. *Defining Poverty in the Developing World*. New York, NY: Palgrave Macmillan.

Streeten, Paul. 1998. "Beyond the six veils: conceptualizing and measuring poverty." *Journal of International Affairs* 52.1: 1–31.

Sumner, Andy. 2012. "Where do the world's poor live? A new update," Institute for Development Studies Working Paper 393, June.

Sumner, Andy. 2016. *Global Poverty: Deprivation, Distribution, and Development Since the Cold War*. Oxford: Oxford University Press.

Szekely, Miguel, Nora Lustig, José Antonio Mejía and Martin Cumpa. 2000. "Do we know how much poverty there is?" Inter-American Development Bank Research Working Paper 437, December.

United Nations. 2015. *The Millennium Development Goals Report 2015*. New York: United Nations.

United Nations Development Programme. 2007. *Measuring Human Development: A primer*. New York: United Nations.

United Nations Development Programme data. www.hdr.undp.org/en/data. Accessed March 2020.

Wade, Robert H. 2004. "Is globalization reducing poverty and inequality?" *World Development* 32.4: 567–589.

World Bank. 2017. *Monitoring Global Poverty: Report of the Commission on Global Poverty*. Washington, DC: World Bank. doi: 10.1596/978-1-4648-0961-3.

World Bank data. www.data.worldbank.org/. Accessed March 2020.

World Data Lab. www.worldpoverty.io/. Accessed March 2020.

World Happiness Report data. www.worldhappiness.report/ed/2019/. Accessed March 2020.

# 4 Health and poverty

*Paula E. Brentlinger*

## Learning objectives

- Considering "health" as a central capability, articulate or describe some important links between poverty, ill health, and capabilities.
- Explain how poverty may affect the prevention, diagnosis, and treatment of disease. Describe differences in the ways in which poverty affects different diseases.
- Compare the similarities and differences in the ways in which poorer vs. wealthier populations approach the prevention and treatment of illness.
- Describe how the capabilities approach is reflected in national and international health policies and in international law.
- Analyze linkages between health, poverty, and capabilities in your own community (positively or negatively)?
- Summarize the extent to which individuals can secure their health-related capabilities by themselves, and which health-related capabilities require contributions from the community or government.

## Introduction

Just as there are many definitions of "poverty," there are many definitions of "health."

The Preamble to the Constitution of the World Health Organization (WHO) defines health as "a state of complete physical, mental and social well-being and not merely the absence of disease or infirmity." Though some have criticized WHO for leaning too far towards a utilitarian definition of health, by seeming to conflate health with happiness (Saracci 1997), and others have observed that interpretation of "well-being" will vary markedly across cultures and social classes (Susser 1974), WHO's is now a standard definition. It does not include the term "capabilities," but its conceptual overlap with capabilities theory is substantial. For example, Martha Nussbaum's list of ten central capabilities includes "Bodily Health," and her description of bodily health focuses on "good health" and explicitly addresses the importance of nutrition, housing and reproductive health, not just "the absence of disease" (Nussbaum 2003).

Relationships that involve health, poverty, capabilities, opportunities, human rights and freedoms are complex. Briefly, if we conceptualize capabilities as the freedom and opportunity for a person "to be and to do" what is of value to that person, it is not hard to imagine that physical and/or mental suffering and dysfunction might constrict a person's freedoms and opportunities, and that deficits of freedoms or opportunities might impede a person's ability to prevent or obtain treatment for specific diseases.

In this chapter, we will explore aspects of three diseases or medical conditions (maternal mortality, Hepatitis C, and malaria) to illustrate important principles, and to illuminate similarities and differences between the capabilities approach and other methods of analyzing and addressing health problems. The first discussion, on maternal mortality, will be the longest, and will serve as our introduction to most of the concepts that will also appear in later discussions. The three health problems that will be addressed have been chosen because they illustrate different concepts and challenges, and different ways in which health may influence human capabilities and human capabilities may also influence bodily health.

## Maternal mortality

### Vignette 4.1 Maternal mortality (eclampsia)

*In the late twentieth century, there were armed conflicts in nearly every country in the Central American isthmus, from Panama to southern Mexico. In the particular village where a pregnant woman named Rosa Maria lived, a low-level conflict had gone on for years. (Note that Rosa Maria is not her real name; the details of all of the vignettes in this chapter have been altered to protect personal privacy.) Rosa Maria and her family lived in a mountainous rural area where they grew corn, beans, and a few vegetables, and raised chickens and pigs. They bartered for most of their needs and lived almost entirely outside the cash economy. They spoke an indigenous language with no written form. They had no electricity, telephone, or piped water; their water was drawn from the river.*

*This was not the family's home village – the fighting had driven them from their original village. The conflict had polarized the region. Nearly every village was aligned with one of the two warring factions; the dominant faction drove the minority members out. A few villages were almost physically split, with supporters of the different factions living on opposite sides of a street or other dividing line.*

*Rosa Maria and her family were aligned with one faction, but the other faction controlled most of the local hospitals. Rosa Maria planned to deliver her baby at home with the village midwife, because it would be less expensive than going to the single hospital that she trusted, and also because if her labor was rapid, or if it started at night (when it was dangerous to travel) she did not think that she would be able to get to the hospital. Also, Rosa Maria and the local midwife spoke the same indigenous language, which almost no one spoke at the hospital. The midwife had never been formally trained in pregnancy and delivery care, and there was no clinic, hospital, or higher-level health worker in the village.*

*In the pregnancy's seventh month, Rosa Maria noticed that her ankles were swelling, but neither she nor the midwife worried about this until the swelling worsened. It extended halfway to her knees, and she developed headaches. She did not have a fever, but she took some malaria tablets that her husband bought from a neighbor. The headaches got worse. Then, during the worst headache she had ever had, she fell unconscious to the dirt floor of her house. Her family found her there, convulsing. The midwife did not know what to do. Rosa Maria's husband rounded up some relatives and neighbors, and they put Rosa Maria into a rope hammock and started walking to the hospital they trusted.*

*Eight hours later, they arrived. Rosa Maria was still unconscious and still having seizures. The doctor on duty quickly found that Rosa Maria's face, hands and legs were very swollen, and her blood pressure was dangerously high. Rosa Maria almost certainly had a condition called eclampsia, which occurs only in pregnancy and threatens the life of both mother and baby. At that point, though, the fetal heartbeat could still be heard and seemed normal. Rosa Maria's convulsions were quickly stopped with medications, and an intravenous line was placed to provide a steady drip of medication to prevent further attacks. The blood pressure was soon controlled, but Rosa Maria did not wake up. Immediate delivery of the baby would have been best for both Rosa Maria and the baby, because delivery stops the disease process in the mother. But Rosa Maria was not yet in labor, and the small rural hospital had no surgeon to perform a caesarean section, and no specialists in the care of premature newborns. The nearest hospital with a surgeon and a higher-level nursery was about two hours away, down a road that was closed by the fighting.*

*After long conversations, the family and the hospital opted to try to get Rosa Maria through the military roadblocks by ambulance. There was no telephone link between the two hospitals, and the decision to transport was made based on desperation and faith. And the plan worked, in so far as Rosa Maria and her unborn baby were still alive on arrival to the referral hospital, and the driver made it back safely. Because of the communications difficulties in this conflict zone, the health workers who arranged for Rosa Maria's transfer to the referral hospital were never able to find out whether the higher-level hospital had been able to perform a caesarean section, but they eventually learned that neither mother nor infant had survived.*

This story, with a few variations, could have come from any of many war zones in the region. Rosa Maria's story ended in what is called "maternal mortality." The definition of maternal mortality (per the International Statistical Classification of Diseases, 10th revision [ICD-10]) is: "The death of a woman while pregnant or within 42 days of termination of pregnancy, irrespective of the duration and site of the pregnancy, from any cause related to or aggravated by the pregnancy or its management but not from accidental or incidental causes" (World Health Organization 2014b). If a woman dies during pregnancy or childbirth, it is sometimes, but not always, possible to save her infant. The story of Rosa Maria's death ended with the loss of the infant (fetal or neonatal mortality) as well. How might we analyze this story of poverty and ill health?

### Analysis of disease (eclampsia) and its treatment in one patient

We will start with a disease-focused medical review, focusing on the diagnosis and treatment of the patient and her specific illness(es). Rosa Maria clearly did not enjoy "the absence of disease," and her primary medical problem was almost certainly eclampsia, as noted above. Although eclampsia is one of the most dangerous complications of pregnancy, recognition and treatment in an earlier stage (pre-eclampsia) offers an opportunity to control the mother's high blood pressure and prevent seizures, and early delivery of the baby, if necessary, can occur in a planned way, with attention to the safety of both mother and infant. In the vignette above, the untrained midwife did not recognize the signs or symptoms of pre-eclampsia and did not even know how to measure Rosa Maria's blood pressure. Thus, Rosa Maria did not receive proper medical attention until her condition had become life-threatening, with loss of consciousness and convulsions. The definitive treatment of eclampsia – early delivery of the baby – was not available at the hospital she chose, and it is unclear whether it was ever achieved. A physician (medical doctor) reviewing this case would conclude that it was a case of treatable maternal morbidity (sickness), culminating in avoidable direct maternal and fetal or neonatal mortality (death) because of failure to identify and treat a life-threatening condition before severe complications developed. A conscientious physician would also have concluded that it was a terrible tragedy, and that something should be done about it.

---

**Box 4.1  Disease-focused analysis: Rosa Maria and eclampsia**

•   *What was the most probable medical diagnosis?* Pre-eclampsia with evolution to eclampsia and both maternal and fetal (or neonatal) death.

•   *What medical errors led to adverse outcomes?* Failure to identify signs and symptoms of pre-eclampsia (midwife), late initiation of treatment for pre-eclampsia and eclampsia (midwife and hospital[s]).

---

*A public health analysis of eclampsia*

A disease-focused analysis does not reflect the complexity of this story. A public health analysis would go further. One definition of public health, from the CDC Foundation, is "Public Health is the science of protecting and improving the health of families and communities through promotion of healthy lifestyles, research for disease and injury prevention, and detection and control of infectious disease. Overall, public health is concerned with protecting the health of entire populations" (CDC Foundation 2016). Public health analyses commonly begin with an estimate of the size of a problem – in this case, eclampsia – for the entire population of pregnant women in the country (or state, region, province or planet).

WHO has estimated the burden of maternal mortality on the global level (World Health Organization 2014b and 2019a). Per WHO's calculations, there were approximately 295,000 maternal deaths worldwide in the year 2017 alone. WHO's 2019 report did not calculate the relative burdens of different common causes of maternal mortality (aside from HIV), but WHO's earlier report (World Health Organization 2014b) stated that 343,000 deaths (14.0 percent of global total during the 2003–2009 interval) were caused by "hypertensive disorders," a category that includes eclampsia and other conditions causing very high blood pressure in the mother. During the same period, hypertensive disorders caused approximately 22.1 percent of maternal deaths in Latin America and the Caribbean (the region in which Rosa Maria lived). In both its 2014 and 2019 reports, WHO concluded that the overwhelming proportion of maternal deaths worldwide occur in resource-constrained countries. For example, maternal mortality in the least developed countries is estimated to be 40 times more common than in Europe and almost 60 times more common than in Australia and New Zealand (World Health Organization 2019a). In the worst-affected region, sub-Saharan Africa, one of every 37 women is likely to die of pregnancy-related causes (World Health Organization 2019a). Examining these metrics, it is hard to deny that maternal mortality caused by eclampsia and/or other conditions is a significant problem in the world, especially when we recall that the death of a pregnant or post-partum woman often implies death for the fetus or newborn as well, and orphanhood for older siblings.

Having identified an important problem at the level of the population (global or smaller units), a public health analysis would go on to identify gaps in capacity for prevention, recognition, and treatment of eclampsia at different levels of the population and the health system. With pre-eclampsia and eclampsia, the focus is on identifying women with early signs and symptoms, and then providing treatment to slow progression of pre-eclampsia to eclampsia, with early delivery if required. Because pre-eclampsia can progress quickly, rapid diagnosis and rapid initiation of effective treatment are the highest priorities. For this reason, one commonly used scheme for analysis of factors contributing to maternal mortality focuses on "three delays": delay in recognizing and seeking care for a pregnancy complication, delay in arrival at a health-care facility, and delay in receiving appropriate treatment after arrival at the appropriate health facility (Thaddeus and Maine 1994). The delays are identified based on a review of cases of maternal mortality. Analysing Rosa Maria's case using the "three delays" approach, we can easily see that all three delays occurred.

---

**Box 4.2 Public health analysis step 1: How big is the problem of eclampsia-related mortality, and where is it concentrated?**

- *How many women die of eclampsia or pre-eclampsia?* Tens of thousands per year.
- *Where are they?* Everywhere, but primarily in the poorer countries and in Latin America.

---

A full regional maternal mortality review would be far more complex than what is described above (Averting Maternal Death and Disability Program 2010). For example, a thorough analysis would look beyond the specific situation of just one patient and would address broader questions, such as: How many health workers in the region were trained to identify pre-eclampsia and eclampsia? Where were they located relative to populations of women of child-bearing age? Which health facilities could lower blood pressure, stop convulsions, perform a caesarean section, and care for a premature infant? Were affordable ambulance services available?

---

**Box 4.3 Public health analysis step 2: Review of an eclampsia-related maternal mortality case (identifying the three delays)**

Based on Rosa Maria's story:

- *Delay 1: Recognition of the problem.* No one was trained or able to recognize the signs and symptoms of pre-eclampsia in Rosa Maria's village.
- *Delay 2: Transport.* Rosa Maria and her family were hesitant to use the nearest hospital because of cultural and political barriers. Also, they lacked passable roads, telecommunications, and vehicles. Travel was risky because of the armed conflict.
- *Delay 3: Treatment.* Initial transport did not get Rosa Maria to a hospital that was able to provide adequate emergency obstetrical care. Although Rosa Maria's first-choice hospital was able to control her seizures and reduce her high blood pressure, it had no surgeon (to perform a caesarean section) or premature-infant care, and she had to be transferred elsewhere (a second transport delay).

---

### A capabilities analysis: eclampsia

Now, let us analyse Rosa Maria's case from the perspective of capabilities. Was her illness caused by a deprivation of capabilities or freedoms? Did her illness deprive her of any capabilities or freedoms?

Before and during her illness, Rosa Maria suffered a deprivation of multiple capabilities within Nussbaum's list of the "central capabilities." (See Chapter 1 for complete definitions of central capabilities.) Some of these deprivations are listed below, but the reader may be able to identify others.

1   Bodily health: Because of her pre-eclampsia and eclampsia, Rosa Maria was not able to enjoy good reproductive or other health.
2   Bodily integrity: Because of the armed conflict, Rosa Maria was not able to move from place to place freely and without fear.
3   Senses, imagination, and thought: Rosa Maria was not able to read and had never had the opportunity to attend school.
4   Affiliation: Because Rosa Maria belonged to a particular minority ethnic group, she worried that she would not be treated with dignity at the hospital.
5   Control over one's environment: Rosa Maria's family had been forced out of their original village by the armed conflict.

Rosa Maria's illness also deprived her of the most central of the capabilities – "life."

An alternative summary would be that Rosa Maria's life circumstances deprived her of the freedom and opportunities necessary to obtain timely, life-saving medical treatment for her pre-eclampsia and eclampsia, and the consequences of her eclampsia then deprived her of all other freedoms and opportunities. We will return to the role of capabilities later in this discussion.

### The role of poverty

Let us look briefly at Rosa Maria's story and its association with core definitions of poverty (described in earlier chapters of this book). Pre-eclampsia and eclampsia may occur in pregnant women in any country or economic circumstance. But the availability of diagnosis and treatment is not so evenly distributed.

*Poverty of money*: The family had almost no cash with which to purchase a vehicle, pay for fuel and maintenance, or hire a driver to take Rosa Maria to her preferred hospital. Her preferred hospital did not have enough money to pay for round-the-clock emergency surgery coverage or the construction of an intensive care nursery for sick or very premature babies. The family almost certainly became even poorer because of Rosa Maria's illness, because of the time they spent away from their fields and what they must have paid to get home from the second hospital.

*Poverty of income at the village level*: In Rosa Maria's village of displaced indigenous persons, no one was wealthy enough to own a car or truck, and so no neighbor could have done her the favor of driving her to the hospital.

In so far as the loss (or deprivation) of capabilities can be regarded as a poverty of freedoms, Rosa Maria and her family were impoverished in both capabilities and freedoms.

## Yet another layer of discussion

From the perspectives of medicine, public health, and capabilities, we can affirm that many things went wrong in Rosa Maria's life, and in the course of her pregnancy and her medical care, and that several kinds of poverty and deprivation were implicated. But our analyses are not over until we address an even more complex question: What is to be done to prevent future tragedies of this kind, and how are we to decide where to start? Who had the obligation (or duty) to treat Rosa Maria's pregnancy complications and prevent her death, or to protect other pregnant women in the future? These may be regarded as human rights questions, not just medical ones, and both international law and health activism have created important standards and precedents for problem-solving in the setting of health-related capabilities deprivation.

Martha Nussbaum has emphasized that the relationship between human rights and the central capabilities is very close (Nussbaum 2011). She holds that human rights exist whether or not they are codified in constitutions or legal codes, and that human rights discussions touch on "an especially urgent set of functions" (Nussbaum 2000).

Our discussion of relevant human rights will begin by invoking international humanitarian law, which (among other aims) seeks to protect civilians from the consequences of armed conflict. Legal language referring specifically to the protection of civilians was developed in the aftermath of the Second World War and the conflict in Vietnam. For example, the 1977 "Protocols additional to the Geneva Conventions of 12 August 1949" states, in its "basic rule and field of application" section (Part IV, Section 1, Chapter 1, Article 48), that "the Parties to the conflict shall at all times distinguish between the civilian population and combatants and between civilian objects and military objectives and accordingly shall direct their operations only against military objectives" (Diplomatic Conference on the Reaffirmation and Development of International Humanitarian Law Applicable in Armed Conflicts 1977). The concept of "medical neutrality" has been developed to define and promote the health rights of those affected by war. Physicians for Human Rights, for example, has defined medical neutrality as "the principle of non-interference with medical services in times of armed conflict" (Averting Maternal Death and Disability Program 2010, Geiger and Cook-Deegan 1993, Physicians for Human Rights n.d.).

In Rosa Maria's story, though, the conflict-related aspects are intertwined with other factors that affected her country and village more generally, even before the fighting began. So, in addition to the Geneva Conventions, we will look closely at the International Covenant on Social, Economic, and Cultural Rights (ICESCR) (United Nations 1966).

ICESCR's Article 12 recognized "the right of everyone to the enjoyment of the highest attainable standard of physical and mental health." The United Nations Committee on Economic, Social, and Cultural Rights' General Comment 14 provided practical definitions of the components of the human right to health (as defined by ICESCR), defined governmental duties and obligations in regard to the right to health, and defined mechanisms for securing health rights. It also acknowledged the close links between poverty and health (Committee on Economic Social and Cultural Rights 2000). The resulting definitions of the core components of the right to health (abbreviated for our purposes) are:

1   Availability. Functioning public health and health-care facilities, goods and services, as well as programs, have to be available in sufficient quantity within the State party. ...

They will include … the underlying determinants of health, such as safe and potable drinking water …

2   Accessibility. Health facilities, goods and services have to be accessible to everyone without discrimination, within the jurisdiction of the State party. Accessibility has … overlapping dimensions:

   a.   Non–discrimination: health facilities, goods and services must be accessible to all, especially the most vulnerable or marginalized sections of the population, in law and in fact, without discrimination on any of the prohibited grounds.

   b.   Physical accessibility: health facilities, goods and services must be within safe physical reach for all sections of the population, especially vulnerable or marginalized groups, such as ethnic minorities and indigenous populations, women …

   c.   Economic accessibility (affordability): health facilities, goods and services must be affordable for all, including socially disadvantaged groups. Equity demands that poorer households should not be disproportionately burdened with health expenses as compared to richer households …

3   Acceptability. All health facilities, goods and services must be respectful of medical ethics and culturally appropriate, i.e. respectful of the culture of individuals, minorities, peoples and communities …

4   Quality. As well as being culturally acceptable, health facilities, goods and services must also be scientifically and medically appropriate and of good quality …

There is much more to ICESCR and General Comment 14, but let us stop to compare Rosa Maria's situation to that of the healthy person and functioning health services envisioned above.

Functioning health–care facilities were not available "in sufficient quantity" where Rosa Maria lived, nor were they "accessible to everyone without discrimination." The local hospitals (with one exception) also failed the "acceptability" test, because they did not provide culturally appropriate services for members of her ethnic group. Both the midwife and the first hospital failed the "quality" test – the midwife because she did not know how to recognize or treat danger signs in pregnancy, and the hospital because it did not have adequate capacity for treatment of obstetrical emergencies. Thus, ICESCR and General Comment 14 provide us with the terms we need to describe the principles that were violated in Rosa Maria's case.

Later sections of General Comment 14 defined the core obligations of states parties (countries that have adopted the ICESCR) with regard to health services. Although many of the core obligations are relevant to Rosa Maria's situation, we will only give key excerpts below:

14   The provision for the reduction of the stillbirth rate and of infant mortality and for the healthy development of the child (art. 12.2 (a)) … may be understood as requiring measures to improve child and maternal health … including emergency obstetric services and access to information, as well as to resources necessary to act on that information.

18   By virtue of article 2.2 and article 3, the Covenant proscribes any discrimination in access to health care and underlying determinants of health, as well as to means and entitlements for their procurement, on the grounds of race, color, sex, language, religion, political or other opinion, national or social origin … even in times of severe resource constraints, the vulnerable members of society must be protected by the adoption of relatively low–cost targeted programs.

19  With respect to the right to health, equality of access to health care and health services has to be emphasized. States have a special obligation to provide those who do not have sufficient means with the necessary health insurance and health-care facilities, and to prevent any discrimination …

Upon reading the excerpts above, it becomes clear that the state party (the national government of the country where Rosa Maria lived) had the duty, under the Covenant (which it had endorsed), to see that she had access to emergency obstetrical care (EmOC) as well as access to the information she needed in order to make use of EmOC.

Per General Comment 14, states parties that have not yet fully realized the right to health for their citizens are obliged to make specific plans for the "progressive realization" of those rights, and the plans must have measurable benchmarks. The core obligations of states parties include:

(f) To adopt and implement a national public health strategy and plan of action, on the basis of epidemiological evidence, addressing the health concerns of the whole population; the strategy and plan of action shall be devised, and periodically reviewed, on the basis of a participatory and transparent process; they shall include methods, such as right to health indicators and benchmarks, by which progress can be closely monitored; the process by which the strategy and plan of action are devised, as well as their content, shall give particular attention to all vulnerable or marginalized groups.

After ICESCR, ongoing advocacy for maternal mortality reduction resulted in even more specific definitions of related duties and rights. The United Nations High Commissioner for Human Rights' "Technical guidance on the application of a human-rights based approach to the implementation of policies and programs to reduce preventable maternal mortality and morbidity" (United Nations General Assembly. Human Rights Council 2012) gave detailed guidance on planning, budgeting, implementation, monitoring, review, oversight, and on the use of a "human rights approach" to analyze maternal mortality:

Example of identified problem: women arriving late or failing to seek emergency obstetric care

56  The first step is to analyze the cause of delays and failure to seek care. A human rights-based approach places responsibility on the State for ensuring available, accessible, acceptable and quality facilities, goods and services to address life-threatening delays. Delays in the decision to seek care or opting out of the health system entirely are treated not as idiosyncratic, personal choices or immutable cultural preferences but as human rights failures. …

57  The second step is to identify responsibility for each specific factor leading to delays or failure to seek care …

58  The third step is to suggest and prioritize actions by different duty-bearers required for each factor causing the problem …

The High Commissioner's technical guidance also inserts another remarkable element in the approach to problem-solving – the active participation of civil society in overseeing each country's efforts to reduce maternal mortality: "Social accountability calls for civil society and public participation at all levels of decision-making regarding sexual and reproductive health, and throughout the project cycle." This human–rights–based approach has also been described and amplified by Yamin, Fukuda- Parr, and Freedman, among others (Yamin 2013, Fukuda-Parr 2009, Freedman 2001).

Within the context of maternal mortality reduction, the creation of legal definitions of the right to health (in both wartime and peacetime) has led in turn to creation of standards by which governmental efforts to secure health rights might be developed and evaluated. Real-life examples of health-rights approaches to maternal mortality reduction have begun to appear. In Mexico, for example, national efforts to reduce maternal mortality as part of Mexico's effort to achieve the Millennium Development Goals (MDGs) have been monitored and evaluated over time by the Observatory of Maternal Mortality in Mexico (Observatorio de Mortalidad Materna en México n.d.).

Elsewhere in Latin America and other regions, less formally organized groups of citizens have developed their own approaches to prevention and management of pregnancy-related health problems (Smith *et al.* 2015). In its chapter "Community solutions to make birth safer," the book *Health Actions for Women* describes community-level actions such as forming an emergency health committee, organizing emergency transportation, creating an emergency loan fund, establishing safe motherhood houses, ensuring the safety of blood donation, and creating community medicine kits (Smith *et al.* 2015). Imagine how Rosa Maria's story might have ended if her community had established an emergency health committee and an emergency transportation plan!

At this point the reader may wonder whether we have strayed too far from the capabilities approach. Amartya Sen himself maintained that, while the capabilities approach was not designed specifically for policy making, the capabilities approach could be instrumental in the analyses that support policy decisions (Sen 2009).

## Summary

So, let us now revisit the problem of maternal mortality in light of the preceding comments, emphasizing the complementary contributions of medicine, public health, human rights, and capabilities. The science of medicine has identified risk factors, signs, symptoms, and means of treatment of pre-eclampsia and eclampsia (in the context of EmOC); with this knowledge, we can declare that Rosa Maria's death was almost certainly preventable. The science of public health enables us to know how the problem of eclampsia is distributed within and among populations, and what might be done to identify and treat it in groups of pregnant women, not just in individuals. The capabilities approach shows us that deprivation of Rosa Maria's capabilities contributed to her death, and had repercussions for the capabilities of her family.

A human rights analysis based on the laws of war reveals the contributory role of armed conflict in Rosa Maria's suffering, and a human rights analysis based on ICESCR not only permits us to describe the health system and societal characteristics that would best support diagnosis and treatment of her obstetrical emergency, it identifies the individuals and entities assigned the duty or obligation of preventing maternal mortality, and offers guidance for national or sub-national groups of citizens who wish to define a pathway towards attainment of the relevant human capabilities. Efforts to monitor and reduce maternal mortality in Latin America and elsewhere are illustrative of a pathway – a form of "public discussion," as Amartya Sen might have put it – by which citizens might collectively identify what they value (with respect to "being and doing"), and define the steps they wish to take to secure the associated rights and capabilities for themselves and their neighbors.

All of these approaches have their own implications for poverty, whether defined as material resources or freedoms: the various poverties affecting both Rosa Maria and the local health system rendered medical error and the terrible outcome of maternal mortality more likely. Medical, public health, human rights, and capabilities approaches can be used together to clarify difficult health questions and their interconnectedness with different kinds of poverty, and are now being employed globally. For example, the 2019 WHO Strategic Framework for Ending Preventable Maternal Mortality (EPMM) emphasizes the importance of empowering women, applying a human rights framework, and addressing inequities, among other key recommendations (World Health Organization 2019a).

Below, we will address two other health conditions – Hepatitis C and malaria – that illustrate other aspects of the complementarity of these approaches.

## Hepatitis C

### *Vignette 4.2 Hepatitis C*

*George (again, details of the case of this real person have been changed) was born in the 1960s, in a developed country. In his teens, he injected drugs, including heroin, with friends. They often shared needles, because clean needles were scarce and expensive. This practice did not seem unsafe to them at the time. Eventually, George developed a bloodstream infection caused by bacteria, almost certainly caused by using a contaminated needle, and he had to be hospitalized. He was so sick that he had to stay in the intensive care unit; his blood count dropped so much that he required multiple blood transfusions. He recovered, but his nearly fatal illness scared him so much that he stopped using drugs. He graduated from high school, went on to college and became a social worker. He did his best to live a healthy life and felt fine.*

*Then, in his 40s, George felt unusually tired, and went for a medical check-up. His doctor told him that his liver function was not normal. Because George's earlier transfusions had been given before there was any known way to test blood for chronic viral infections, the doctor tested for three important viruses. George's HIV and Hepatitis B tests were negative (normal), but he tested positive for Hepatitis C antibodies (showing that he had been exposed to Hepatitis C at some point), and follow-up tests confirmed that his Hepatitis C infection was still active and had caused significant scarring in his liver. Although George felt fine aside from the fatigue, his doctor recommended Hepatitis C treatment, because of the liver scarring and the high level of virus detected. The treatment involved multiple medications that had to be taken for six months. On this treatment George felt exhausted, his blood count dropped so much that he required more transfusions, and he became so depressed that he could barely go to work. He dropped out of treatment before finishing, and soon lost his job and his health insurance. Once off the medications his blood count normalized and his depression resolved, and he felt reasonably good aside from fatigue. But the fatigue was better than it had been, because he had taken his doctor's advice and started to avoid alcohol (to prevent further damage to his liver) and to exercise more.*

*George found a new job, with new health insurance. He did not want to think about the Hepatitis C ever again but his wife kept urging him to get checked. He went to a liver specialist. The specialist informed George that his liver function tests and liver scarring both looked worse than before. But there was also good news – new drugs were available for Hepatitis C treatment, and they were much better than the old ones. They had very few side effects, no injections were required, treatment could be completed in 12 weeks rather than six months, and there was a greater than 95 percent chance of eliminating the virus permanently. If the virus was eliminated, George's liver would probably recover, and he would be much less likely to develop liver failure or liver cancer in the future. There was only one problem: George's insurance would not cover the USD 85,000 cost of treatment. George and his family did not have that kind of money.*

*Then, the liver specialist's clinic received enough donated medications (from a drug company) to provide immediate hepatitis treatment for 15 patients. They hoped to have even more donated medication in the future, but for now they could only select 15 of their sickest patients for free treatment. Would George like to have his name entered in a lottery for free Hepatitis C treatment? George thought that this was a really strange way to make treatment decisions, but his doctor explained that a group of the sickest Hepatitis C patients in her clinic had decided that a lottery would be the fairest way of deciding who would be treated first. George's family convinced him to participate because his children were young, and the specialist had told him that he was very close to liver failure. George was one of the lottery winners. By this stage in his life he had avoided drugs and alcohol for years and had a lot of support from family and friends; he never missed a dose of his Hepatitis C medications and finished his treatment with no important side effects. Ultimately, he was declared to have been cured.*

*George and his family felt very lucky. Then, when George found out that one of his old high-school friends also had Hepatitis C complicated by liver cancer, he felt terrible because his friend had not had the same chance at treatment. George is now volunteering with a non-profit organization that is trying to make Hepatitis C drugs more available to those who need them, and he has a big poster with Hepatitis C information hanging in his social work office.*

The illness often called "Hepatitis C" (or "Hep C") is caused by the Hepatitis C virus, which was not identified until the late 1980s (Webster *et al.* 2015). The Hepatitis C virus infects and inflames the human liver and may cause death from its various complications (liver failure, liver cancer, bleeding from the intestinal tract etc.), which usually do not occur until years or even decades after the initial infection. Hepatitis C is usually passed from person to person through contact with contaminated blood – dirty needles used in health-care facilities or for illegal drug use, unscreened blood transfusions, and (much less commonly) sexual activity or the birth of an infant to an infected mother. At the time of infection, there are often no symptoms, and so diagnosis is usually delayed. Although some people's immune systems resolve the infection without any treatment, most of those infected are infected for life. The earliest treatments for Hepatitis C caused many side effects and failed to cure many patients (Webster *et al.* 2015). In the present century, treatments involving combinations of several medications finally succeeded in curing more than half of patients, and cure rates of over 95 percent have now been achieved with combinations of well-tolerated medications that must be taken every day for at least eight weeks (see e.g. Zeuzem *et al.* 2018 and Feld *et al.* 2015).

As above, we will look at George's case from several complementary perspectives, but we will try not to repeat what has already been said about Rosa Maria's illness.

### Analysis of disease (Hepatitis C) and its treatment in one patient

George's case was different from Rosa Maria's. When he first became infected with Hepatitis C, there was no way to diagnose or treat the disease. For many years he had no symptoms. When he finally developed fatigue and sought medical care, his Hepatitis C was diagnosed promptly and treatment was begun – but he could not tolerate the side effects. He was retreated with much better medications shortly after those medications became available, and he was cured.

In George's case, medical errors did not really contribute to his problem. We cannot even argue that there was a failure to screen his early blood transfusions for Hepatitis C, because no test for the virus existed at the time. Here, we need a different perspective on George's illness.

### Public health analysis

Is George's case isolated, or are there others who share or shared his diagnosis and his difficulty in accessing treatment? According to WHO, in 2015 around 70 million people were living with chronic Hepatitis C infection, and about 400,000 people died annually of complications of this disease (World Health Organization 2020b, 2015). The infection is present in all regions of the world. The proportion of persons infected is highest in the Eastern Mediterranean and European regions, but the number of infected persons is almost equally high in the Western Pacific and African regions.

---

**Box 4.4 Disease-focused analysis: George and Hepatitis C**

- *What was the medical diagnosis?* Chronic Hepatitis C infection, with evolution to liver damage and impending liver failure.
- *What medical errors led to adverse outcomes?* In this case, the final outcome was good and there were no significant medical errors. Diagnosis and initial treatment were delayed by the absence of reliable lab tests and safe/effective medications. His first treatment failed because of uncontrollable side effects, and because it was not very effective, not because of medical error. George had his second round of treatment just as the first really effective, well-tolerated treatments for Hepatitis C became available, and his treatment was successful. His doctors acted as quickly and correctly as the available science (which was still evolving) and the fortuitous medication donation permitted.

---

**Box 4.5 Public health analysis step 1: How big is the problem of Hepatitis C, and where is it concentrated?**

- *How many individuals are living with Hepatitis C?* Around 70 million (globally). About 400,000 die each year.
- *Where are they?* On every continent. (Highest-prevalence regions: Eastern Mediterranean, Europe, Western Pacific, and Africa.)

---

The second step in our public health analysis is to identify gaps in prevention, diagnosis, and treatment of Hepatitis C. WHO, the Centers for Disease Control and Prevention (CDC) in the United States, and other agencies have considered these problems in detail within the past decade. WHO's recommendations for prevention have included providing clean injection supplies to those who inject drugs and testing of the blood supply for hepatitis. The American Association for the Study of Liver Disease (AASLD) now recommends that all adults be tested at least once for Hepatitis C (regardless of risk factors or symptoms), and that patients with chronic Hepatitis C be offered effective treatment as soon as they are diagnosed (www.aasld.org).

In George's case, the most likely source of his infection was through injection of heroin, but he could also have been infected by contaminated needles or transfusions during his hospitalization. Because the hospitalization was caused by complications of heroin use, the best prevention for George's infection would have been avoidance of heroin injection in either scenario. However, had he had regular access to clean needles, his heroin addiction would have been less dangerous to his health.

---

**Box 4.6 Public health analysis step 2: Gaps and delays in prevention and in George's care**

- *Prevention*: If there were existing drug-abuse prevention programs when George was an adolescent, they failed to prevent his heroin use or to educate him about blood-borne infections. When he had his original blood transfusions, no test was yet available to screen the transfused blood for Hepatitis C.
- *Diagnosis*: The delay in George's diagnosis was caused by the absence of a blood test and by the absence of symptoms during the earlier years of his chronic infection. Indeed, the Hepatitis C virus had not yet been discovered when he was young.
- *Treatment*: When George was initially infected, there was no good treatment for Hepatitis C. His first attempt to be treated failed, because the available drugs caused intolerable side effects. Fortunately, he returned to medical care just as safe, effective drugs became available, and he was able to access the extremely expensive regimen because of the unusual circumstance of the lottery.

---

This is a different analysis from that of Rosa Maria's case. In the case of eclampsia, the best means of diagnosis and treatment were defined decades ago, although there have been refinements over time. Adequate treatment was theoretically available near Rosa Maria's village, but it was not available to her for reasons related to her poverty, her ethnicity and her status as an internally displaced person. In George's case, Hepatitis C had not even been discovered when he became infected, and good methods for diagnosis and treatment of his illness were not discovered until he had been infected for years.

### Capabilities analysis

What is there to be said about George's Hepatitis C and capabilities that has not already been said earlier, in the discussion of eclampsia? George was fortunate in that his illness was cured before it caused death or disability, and after his cure he was in a good position "to be and to do" what he valued. But there are two other aspects of the capabilities approach that bear exploring here: "agency" and "entitlements."

Amartya Sen has written extensively about agency and capabilities. He has noted that a person's "agency freedom" may support a person's efforts to help others, not just serve more individual desires (Sen 2009). In Rosa Maria's story the utter deprivation of her capabilities also deprived her of agency (although her neighbors and family used their own agency to try to save her). But George's story is different. His goals and values went beyond mere short-term happiness or wellbeing. He gave up both heroin and alcohol (both of which he had originally used because of the feeling of happiness that they initially provided) to pursue other goals that he valued more: to feel healthy, to finish his education and to care for his family. He sought treatment for Hepatitis C a second time, in spite of his fears of medication toxicities, for similar reasons. His fellow Hepatitis C patients used their agency freedom to support what they deemed "fair" distribution of expensive drugs, not just to fight for their own individual advantages. Finally, George became an activist for increased access to Hepatitis C treatment for others, such as his school friend.

George's later role as an activist is also relevant to the issue of entitlements. Martha Nussbaum has stated clearly that her list of central capabilities can also be viewed as a list of freedoms to which human beings are entitled by virtue of being human. "Entitlement" in this descriptive sense does not mean entitlement to money or objects or other tangible things, often referred to as the "normative" meaning of entitlement. Rather, Nussbaum states that the "central capabilities are fundamental entitlements inherent in the very idea of minimum social justice, or a life worthy of human dignity" (Nussbaum 2011). These entitlements, though fundamental in theory, must be "secured" in order to be usable in practice. In the case of George's Hepatitis C, had he not had access to high-quality treatment, he would have progressively lost a multitude of central capabilities as his disease advanced to liver failure and/or liver cancer and death. But he was spared these bad outcomes because he was fortunate enough to win a lottery – not because society had made any arrangements to secure the entitlement of "bodily health" from risks conferred by Hepatitis C. The other 70 million Hepatitis C infected citizens of Earth will not, for the most part, enjoy such lucky circumstances. George became an activist to secure the relevant entitlements for others.

### The role of poverty

As in the case of eclampsia, Hepatitis C has multiple associations with different kinds of poverty. Hepatitis C causes monetary and income poverty and poverty of capabilities in those who are too ill to work. Lack of money or income or freedoms or opportunities at the individual or health-systems level may increase the likelihood of Hepatitis C infection (through unsafe injection and transfusion practices, for example) and decrease the likelihood of early diagnosis and effective treatment.

### Human rights analysis (Hepatitis C)

We will now revisit the question of effective Hepatitis C treatment in terms of General Comment 14's requirements for availability, accessibility, acceptability and quality. For our purposes, effective treatment is defined as treatment with an established, well-studied combination of direct-acting antiviral drugs known to result in high likelihood of disappearance of the Hepatitis C virus from the blood and liver, provided for a period of time that is known to be long enough to yield high cure rates, and administered in a setting that permits proper support for patients and monitoring of response to treatment.

Because the best medications were so expensive, George's chance of receiving adequate treatment for his Hepatitis C did not originally seem much greater than it might have been had he been a resident of a much poorer country. What are the duties and obligations of the countries in which Hepatitis C is present? Is there a process parallel to that defined for maternal mortality reduction? Hepatitis C is not mentioned directly in ICESCR or General Comment 14, but there is a clear intent to support control of important infectious diseases, such as AIDS and malaria. Discussions of inequity in access to Hepatitis C treatment were not as heated when treatments were very toxic and cure rates were low. With the recent development and approval of treatments that are more effective and much less toxic, but very expensive (more than USD 1000 per tablet at times), the debate has become much more active, and links between Hepatitis C treatment access and human rights concerns have become more explicit.

---

**Box 4.7 Effective Hepatitis C treatment and ICESCR**

- *Availability*: Not really available outside the research setting until about 2014, because the most effective drugs had not yet been developed or adequately tested.
- *Accessibility* (1): Non-discrimination. George did not encounter discrimination, except any inherent discrimination described below under "economic accessibility."
- *Accessibility* (2): Physical accessibility. George had physical access to a health facility with a liver specialist, laboratory, and pharmacy capacity.
- *Accessibility* (3): Economic accessibility. Between his first and second rounds of Hepatitis C treatment, George had no health insurance, and could not have afforded to see a specialist or pay for Hepatitis C treatment. When he obtained his new health insurance, he was able to see a specialist without economic hardship but his insurance would not pay for the medications, and he could not afford to pay this price out of his own pocket. The very unusual lottery saved him from the severe accessibility constraints that affect many (if not most) Hepatitis C patients. (Note: since George was treated, access to Hepatitis C drugs has improved in certain settings, because of manufacturers' assistance programs, liberalized insurer policies and price negotiations.)
- *Quality*: The quality of treatment initially available to George was poor. When he was retreated, the treatment was of high quality because new medication regimens had been developed.

---

In mid-2015, WHO added five of the newest, most effective Hepatitis C medications to its Model List of Essential Medicines (World Health Organization 2015). Cheaper, generic versions of the newer standard regimens are now expected to become available in poorer countries. A greater than 90 percent reduction in Hepatitis C drug prices has been negotiated to support treatment in Egypt, where large numbers of persons were infected with contaminated medical syringes (World Health Organization 2014a). Humanitarian organizations such as Médecins sans Frontières (MSF) have engaged in advocacy for increased availability of effective Hepatitis C treatment (Médecins Sans Frontières n.d.).

This is an interesting variant on the concept of "progressive realization of the right to health" as described in General Comment 14. Originally, "progressive realization" was described primarily as a catch-up process for countries that were very resource-constrained and were unable to adopt existing, effective health measures overnight. Rapid advances in the science of Hepatitis C diagnosis and treatment have forced another kind of progressive realization, driven by the imperative to keep up with development of new diagnostics and new medications, rather than by the catch-up model.

## Summary

In contrast to Rosa Maria's story, George's story had a happy ending. The different outcomes were driven by different forces. Before her illness, Rosa Maria did not enjoy the same opportunities or freedoms that George did, because of the armed conflict, her ethnicity, and the extreme poverty of her family, her community, and the local health system. Her illness started abruptly, and she needed to obtain effective treatment within hours or days in order to survive, so there was little time for her health strategy to evolve. She was so ill that she really could not exercise agency. Sometime after her death, human rights law and policy with regard to maternal mortality were expanded, and civil society (in some countries) took on this cause in a way that might have saved Rosa Maria's life had it occurred earlier. Indeed, in the country where Rosa Maria died, free ambulance transport and free treatment for obstetrical emergencies are now guaranteed by law.

In contrast, George lived in a wealthier society, and it took decades for his Hepatitis C to progress to near-failure of his liver. During that period, medical science made immense progress – the Hepatitis C virus was identified, laboratory tests were developed, and newly discovered treatment regimens had few side effects and usually resulted in a cure. George had a college education and health insurance and access to a liver specialist. He had the remarkably good fortune to win a treatment lottery. Because of his successful treatment, he preserved important freedoms and opportunities, and exercised his agency not just to preserve his own health but to advocate for the health of others. His post-treatment advocacy approach was influenced by previous health rights endeavors in support of maternal mortality reduction and HIV/AIDS treatment expansion (Ford *et al.* 2012), among other causes, and may, in the future, help create the normative entitlement of "effective Hepatitis C treatment" to support others' descriptive entitlements to "bodily health." Thus, the concepts of medicine, public health, capabilities, and human rights are relevant to both cases, but in different ways.

## Malaria

### Vignette 4.3 Malaria

*Luz's mother lived near a broad African river that flooded over and over; the floodwaters were paradise for mosquitoes. When the waters were high, local residents traveled to health centers by canoe (they paddled right down the middle of flooded streets), but Ministry of Health vehicles could not transit the roads, so medications and other supplies were not restocked, ambulances were unavailable and the centers lacked staff. Insecticide-treated bednets (ITNs, designed to repel and kill the mosquitoes that bit at night) could be bought in some of the local shops, but Luz's mother could not afford to buy one. Some ITNs were given away for free in the health centers, but only to pregnant women who were infected with HIV. Luz's mother became pregnant during the rainy season, and had malaria twice before Luz was born. In both instances, a Ministry of Health-trained community health worker based in her village diagnosed the malaria with a finger-prick test, and then dispensed malaria tablets. The tablets were provided free by the Ministry of Health, and seemed to work both times. The community health worker did not provide prenatal care, though, and Luz's mother was unable to get to the district health center for even a single prenatal visit. Luz was eventually born at home. She was a month early and was tiny, just over four pounds, but she survived.*

*At first, Luz was usually swaddled in clothes or rags and the mosquitoes could not reach her. When she grew bigger, her older sister took her outside to play. Luz was bitten by mosquitoes many times. Eventually, she developed a fever and became listless; she would not look at her mother, she would not eat or breast-feed; she seemed pale. The community health worker diagnosed malaria. Luz was too sick to swallow malaria tablets, and the community health worker did not have any other way to administer the needed medication. So, Luz's father pedaled his ancient bicycle to the health center; her mother rode behind, holding Luz. The health center nurse pricked Luz's finger again, and informed Luz's parents that she had a dangerously low blood count in addition to malaria. The nurse gave Luz an injection of an antimalarial drug and called the doctor to admit Luz to the small hospital ward for further treatment. Luz, somewhat amazingly, survived and went back home.*

*At about that time, a non-profit aid agency started a program to improve child development in the district. They came to the family house and evaluated Luz. Luz had not learned to roll over or crawl or walk at the usual times for her age group, and she had only learned about half the expected number of words. Her height and weight were also much too low for her age (now 17 months). The project provided Luz and her family with ITNs, iron and vitamin supplements, and a high-energy nut-based food supplement. A volunteer came to visit once a week and showed Luz's parents and older sister how to make homemade toys and play educational games with Luz. Bit by bit, Luz started to grow more quickly; she became physically stronger and more active, and she started to learn new words at a much faster pace.*

Malaria is not just one disease, nor does it have just a single cause or consequence, and we will not be able to describe malaria in all of the detail it deserves (for those who are interested in learning more we would recommend starting with the most recent edition of WHO's annual World Malaria Report: WHO Global Malaria Program). But we will describe some of basic facts here.

Four protozoans of the *Plasmodium* family (*P. falciparum, P. vivax, P. malariae* and *P. ovale*) cause nearly all malaria disease in humans; the most lethal of the four is *P. falciparum*. Malaria is almost exclusively transmitted to humans through the bites of infected mosquitoes. Malaria infection can evolve in several different ways: (1) uncomplicated malaria (primarily featuring fevers, chills, and aching); (2) severe malaria (with seizures, coma, profound anemia, and/or other possibly fatal complications); (3) chronic "asymptomatic" malaria (malaria parasites live in the bloodstream but the human host does not feel ill); (4) relapsing malaria (like acute malaria, except that after the first episode, some malaria parasites remain in the host's liver, where they cause no symptoms until, at an unpredictable later date, they re-emerge and fever and other symptoms recur); and (5) placental malaria (the malaria parasite sequesters in the pregnant woman's placenta, where it may impair fetal growth and/or cause premature labor or pregnancy loss).

With prompt diagnosis and effective treatment, most adults and children recover fully from malaria episodes. But when malaria is severe, consequences may include death or permanent disability. "Asymptomatic" (without symptoms) and recurrent malaria may cause chronic anemia, undernutrition and (for children) delays in both cognitive and motor development. Malaria in pregnancy may cause pregnancy loss (miscarriage), premature birth, and/or low birth weight.

### Analysis of disease and treatment in one patient: malaria

As before, we will start by looking only at issues of medical diagnosis and treatment. But this analysis will be a bit different from the medical analyses of the two previous vignettes, because we have to consider episodes of malaria both in Luz's mother and in Luz.

Our narrow analysis of diagnosis and treatment of acute symptomatic malaria (in Luz and in her mother) is not able to tell us whether Luz's problems were really avoidable or not. As before, we will go on to a more public health-focused analysis.

### Public health analysis

In 2019, WHO estimated that there were 229 million cases of malaria worldwide, resulting in 409,000 deaths. According to the World Malaria Report (World Health Organization 2020a), the burden of malaria disease is largely determined by geography and age: in 2019, approximately 93 percent of malaria deaths occurred in Africa, and 67 percent of all malaria deaths occurred in children under five years of age. Other factors that increase risk of malaria include pregnancy (before the initiation of effective preventive measures, about one in four pregnant women in Sub-Saharan Africa tested positive for the presence of malaria parasites in her blood at the time of delivery: Desai *et al.* 2007) and HIV infection (persons with advanced HIV infection are about 2.5 times more likely to have malaria-related fever than HIV-infected persons with intact immune systems: French *et al.* 2001). Estimates of the number of children who survive but suffer from the consequences of malaria-related low birth weight and neurodevelopmental delay are less precise.

---

**Box 4.8 Disease-focused analysis: Luz and malaria**

- *What was the medical diagnosis?* (A) In Luz's mother, two episodes of acute malaria with symptoms, probably associated with placental malaria. (B) In Luz herself, one episode of acute malaria, with symptoms.
- *What medical errors led to adverse outcomes?* In this two-person case, there were no significant medical errors related to diagnosis or treatment of symptomatic malaria. Both Luz and her mother recovered physically from their episodes of acute symptomatic malaria.

---

Once again, we are examining a problem that takes hundreds of thousands of lives every year, though this particular problem has many known solutions, some of them known for over a century. Malaria was a major health problem in Europe and the United States as recently as the early twentieth century. One economist estimated that the infant death rate from malaria in the United States in 1850 was not significantly different from the infant death rate from malaria in the ten most malaria-affected African countries in 2008: 93 deaths of infants under one year of age per 1000 live births in the United

States, vs. 99 in the ten African countries (Hong 2011). Wealthier countries – such as the United States and Italy – defeated their malaria epidemics decades ago, through reduction of human contact with mosquitoes and through population-wide distribution of antimalarial tablets.

---

**Box 4.9  Public health analysis step 1: How big is the problem and where is it concentrated?**

- *How many people fall ill with malaria?* Over 200 million per year, with over 400,000 deaths.
- *Where are they?* Primarily in Sub-Saharan Africa. (Young children, pregnant women, and persons living with HIV infection are at higher risk.)

---

Current options for malaria prevention include use of larvicides or insecticides to kill mosquitoes, use of long-lasting ITNs to prevent mosquito bites at night, and (for special populations, such as pregnant women and travelers) periodic use of malaria medications to prevent malaria infection and/or to treat malaria infection that has not become symptomatic (World Health Organization 2020a, 2019b, Desai *et al.* 2007). HIV-infected persons can prevent malaria by taking daily doses of co-trimoxazole, a common antibiotic that also helps prevent certain other AIDS-related infections (Church *et al.* 2015, French *et al.* 2001). Vaccines against malaria have been developed, but as of this writing no existing malaria vaccine has been shown to be effective enough to justify population-level rollout (Duffy and Gorres 2020, WHO 2020a). Vaccine research is ongoing, however.

Malaria is not only preventable; it is treatable if effective medications are given promptly. In contrast to the high cost of treating Hepatitis C (as of this writing), malaria can be treated much more cheaply. Non-profit groups such as the Medicines for Malaria Venture (MMV) and the Drugs for Neglected Diseases initiative (DNDi) have contributed to the discovery, development, and/or delivery of effective, affordable antimalarial drugs (Drugs for Neglected Diseases Initiative 2015, Medicines for Malaria Venture 2015). The national malaria control programs of many countries now guarantee free malaria treatment for their citizens. However, where national health systems are weak, the sick may have to buy antimalarial drugs over the counter. Antimalarial medication may still be unaffordable to the most vulnerable families. For example, in one region of Ethiopia, the private sector price for a three-day course of malaria treatment was reported to be equivalent to or higher than "about a week's wages" (SIAPS – Ethiopia PMI/AMDM Program 2014).

Large international initiatives (e.g. the Roll Back Malaria Partnership and the President's Malaria Initiative, among others) have systematically helped malaria-affected countries to implement the most effective measures for mass malaria control. WHO estimated that between 2000 and 2019 the incidence rate of malaria dropped worldwide from 80 to 57 cases per 1000 population at risk, and that malaria deaths declined from 736,000 in 2000 to 409,000 in 2019. During the same time period, reduction in malaria deaths varied widely by region. For example, malaria deaths dropped by 74 percent in the WHO South-East Asia Region, vs. 16 percent in the WHO Eastern Mediterranean Region. (World Health Organization 2020a).

So, let us look at Luz's situation again (see Box 4.10).

---

**Box 4.10 Public health analysis step 2: Gaps and delays in prevention and in Luz's care**

- *Prevention*: During pregnancy, Luz's mother should have been given antimalarial medication to prevent malaria (intermittent preventive treatment of malaria in pregnancy, or IPTp), but she had no prenatal care. Luz's premature birth and low birthweight were probably caused by her mother's malaria. The household should have used ITNs, but they were not available or affordable. The family's house was apparently never sprayed against mosquitoes.
- *Diagnosis*: When Luz and her mother felt sick, they were promptly checked for malaria, using modern rapid tests. But Luz's mother also probably had malaria without symptoms during her pregnancy, and it was not diagnosed or treated. Earlier diagnosis and/or IPTp might have prevented Luz's premature birth and low birth weight. Luz's anemia was diagnosed during her malaria hospitalization, but was not followed up afterward. Her developmental delay (very likely associated with long-standing anemia) was not diagnosed until an aid agency started a program in her district.
- *Treatment*: Once Luz's mother was diagnosed with malaria, she was treated with a medication that appeared to work promptly. But there was a delay in providing effective medications for Luz herself, because the village health worker did not have medications that would work for a child too sick to swallow. Luz's anemia treatment was probably delayed (she may have been born with anemia because of her mother's malaria infection), as was the therapy for her developmental delay.

---

It is clear that the local malaria control program was not able to protect Luz or her mother from this illness. Although both survived their episodes of malaria, the consequences for Luz were alarming.

## Capabilities

What is the association between malaria and Luz's capabilities? Here, we will focus on the special way that the capabilities approach regards children. Martha Nussbaum, in particular, has written about this issue extensively. She (with Rosalind Dixon and others) has emphasized two aspects of capabilities that are different for children: their "special vulnerability" and "the special cost-effectiveness of protecting children's rights" (Nussbaum and Dixon 2012). Briefly, and perhaps too simplistically, the special vulnerability of children is a result of the long period of dependency (more than a decade) that characterizes human development. The special cost-effectiveness principle arises from the fact that if a child is deprived of the opportunity of fully developing the central capabilities that must underpin his or her ability to be, to do, and to live the adult life that he or she values, this period of dependency is prolonged and the cost (to the family and the society) of providing needed services is therefore increased. Nussbaum and Dixon mention, for example, that if inexpensive antiretroviral medications are given to an HIV-infected woman during pregnancy and labor and the post-partum period, the resulting avoidance of HIV infection in the exposed baby may "prevent a spiraling need for state intervention to protect more and more capabilities" (Nussbaum and Dixon 2012).

Although other factors, such as malnutrition or anemia in her mother, may have contributed to Luz's premature delivery and underweight, malaria was certainly a major contributor to this problem. Prematurity and low birth weight are important causes of capability deprivation in children. In 2010, for example, approximately 15 million babies were born at least three weeks early, only 13 million survived, and about 900,000 babies were thought to have some degree of neurodevelopmental impairment (Blencowe *et al.* 2013), and also had elevated risks of infections and heart or lung diseases.

In addition to premature birth and low birth weight, Luz suffered from symptomatic malaria at a very young age. Both symptomatic and asymptomatic malaria have been shown to affect child development. In one study in Zanzibar, children who had had more episodes of malaria were slower to start walking, slower to develop language, and were fussier and less active than children who had no or fewer episodes of malaria (Olney *et al.* 2013). In Sri Lanka, the mean mathematics test score for a child who had not had malaria might be 69.4 percent, vs. 37.6 percent for a child who had had at least six episodes (Fernando *et al.* 2003).

Is Luz doomed to a lifetime of dependency and capabilities deprivation? We do not know yet. As the vignette ends, she is 17 months old. To be effective, interventions to address developmental delay should usually start during the first two or three years of life, to take advantage of a period of active brain development (Doyle *et al.* 2009, Engle *et al.* 2007). The most effective programs combine multiple interventions – for example, nutritional supplementation, prevention of infections (such as malaria and diarrhea), and psychosocial stimulation. The aid agency that has just come to Luz's district appears to understand these principles and it is possible that, with their help, Luz will continue to catch up.

### The role of poverty

As in the preceding vignettes, the role of poverty is pervasive here. Monetary poverty affected both Luz's family and the local health system, as reflected in the family's difficulty in procuring ITNs, prenatal care, IPTp, and treatment for Luz. Income poverty affected the family and the whole region, because the combination of frequent flooding and constant exposure to malaria greatly reduced the productivity of individuals (such as Luz's father) and the society as a whole. Malaney *et al.* (2004) have observed that malaria is a cause of income poverty. One may infer that effective malaria control measures may therefore relieve poverty, and this has been demonstrated. Famously, two decades of intensive malaria control programs in Zambia (then known as Northern Rhodesia) are thought to have prevented approximately 14,000 deaths and nearly a million work-shift losses, and increased national copper-mining revenue (Utzinger *et al.* 2002).

### Human rights

Luz's family had difficulty preventing and treating malaria because of problems with availability, accessibility, and other core elements of the right to health as defined in ICESCR and related documents (discussed in previous vignettes). As in the case of the capabilities approach, human rights law also recognizes that children require special protections. The Convention on the Rights of the Child affirms, in Article 24, that children also have the right "to the enjoyment of the highest attainable standard of health"; Article 27 recognizes children's right "to a standard of living adequate for the child's physical, mental, spiritual, moral and social development," and both articles describe the states parties' obligation to assist families in the securing of these rights (United Nations 1990). In their paper on children and capabilities, Nussbaum and Dixon outline the congruences between the Convention on the Rights of the Child and the capabilities approach.

## Summary

How can we merge the perspectives of medicine, public health, capabilities, and human rights to understand this vignette about malaria and poverty, and to compare its implications to those of the two preceding vignettes? To start with the disease perspective, malaria has been recognized for centuries. The first effective treatment (quinine) has been known for over 400 years, though the causative parasites were not identified until the late nineteenth century. Malaria has caused widespread disease and disability almost worldwide, including in the United States and Europe. Public health approaches to malaria control have existed for over 100 years, but have recently become much more effective and systematized, and malaria–control initiatives are now customized to respond to differences in malaria burden across regions and sites.

Where malaria is still widespread, it poses a significant threat to human capabilities. Because pregnant women and children are particularly vulnerable to malaria, because malaria in a pregnant woman may affect infant health, and because malaria may result in slowing of neurocognitive development in early life, the capabilities of children are more severely affected by malaria. Malaria's adverse effect on the capabilities of children is most likely to occur when children are still unable to live independently, and before they can develop effective agency. Both the capabilities approach and human rights law have recognized that the great dependence and vulnerability of children, and the dire consequences of interruption of normal child development, impose greater duties on families and on society. Thus, malaria may cause the greatest poverty of freedoms and opportunities in its youngest victims; and poverty of freedoms and opportunities may also impede effective prevention and treatment of malaria. With regard to other kinds of poverty: malaria is most rampant in poorer communities, and rampant malaria exacerbates income and monetary poverty. For all of these reasons, intensified efforts to control malaria worldwide may help decrease global poverty, by all of its definitions.

## Poverty reduction and health: some major debates

Within the past few decades, global policies on maternal mortality, Hepatitis C, and malaria have all changed in response to new scientific discoveries and to activism. The relevant scientific discoveries have included identification of new diseases (Hepatitis C), development of newer and better medications (Hepatitis C and malaria), development of better preventive interventions (malaria) and improved descriptions of the actual burden of suffering and of the potential impact of combinations of preventive and curative interventions on that burden of suffering (all three conditions). Many relevant recent and active debates revolve around issues of equity, fairness, rights, and responsibilities. The implications for human capabilities are seldom articulated but may seem obvious to those of you who have read this far. Ongoing debates and open questions that are relevant to these concerns include the following.

*Malaria*: The burden of malaria is greatest in countries with fewer resources. Multiple interventions are now available for the effective prevention and treatment of malaria, but countries with the highest malaria burdens cannot afford to pay for them without external assistance. If combined intelligently and applied across all malarial regions, currently available interventions might even result in the elimination of malaria worldwide (Newby *et al.* 2016). How might the countries, regions and sub-populations of the world organize themselves to achieve malaria elimination?

*Maternal mortality*: In the vignette above, we described a case of avoidable maternal (and fetal or neonatal) mortality that occurred in a poor country. But maternal mortality is not confined to poor countries. In the United States, not only does maternal mortality still occur, the rates are steadily rising (Centers for Disease Control and Prevention 2016). Why might maternal mortality rates increase where resources are thought to be abundant?

*Hepatitis C*: In addition to debates over drug prices and availability (described above), other debates revolve around safe injection practices for heroin and other drug users. In the United States, a recent outbreak driven by needle-sharing among drug users resulted in a cluster of over 150 new cases of HIV infection in a single county in southern Indiana; over 80 percent of the HIV-infected were also infected with Hepatitis C. Needle-exchange programs were illegal in Indiana when this occurred. Public health experts have called for legalization and improvement of needle-exchange programs in order to stop the spread of both HIV and Hepatitis C; but this issue has not yet been settled as of this writing, even though unsafe injections have been linked to a near-explosion in Hepatitis C cases in the region in recent years (Strathdee and Beyrer 2015). What is your opinion?

## Conclusion

This chapter has not addressed all of the most important issues related to health and poverty. For example, we have not directly analyzed problems related to mental health, climate change, racism, or income inequality. But close examination of maternal mortality, Hepatitis C, and malaria should provide an opportunity to understand the multiplicity of pathways that connect health and poverty and capabilities and rights, both for individual human beings and across populations. Many of these pathways are bidirectional; poverty is a threat to good health, and ill health contributes to poverty. But, when sound science and the right-to-health framework are combined, effective medical and public health measures can preserve or increase human capabilities, and alleviate many kinds of poverty.

## Health, capabilities, and the Covid-19 pandemic: an update to this chapter

We imagine that many or most readers of this book have been affected directly or indirectly by the Covid-19 pandemic, and are familiar with this virus and the illness it causes. For those who have not had experience with Covid-19, we will start by describing it briefly.

### *The disease*

In Wuhan, China, in December 2019, dozens of adults suddenly required hospitalization after falling ill with a previously unknown type of pneumonia (lung infection) (Huang *et al.* 2020). Within weeks, scientists identified the cause: a new virus from the corona-virus family. This virus was given the name 2019-nCoVs (later changed to SARS-CoV-2) (Tan *et al.* 2020). The disease it causes became known as Covid-19. Within China, Covid-19 "spread from a single city to the entire country" within a month, and by early February 2020, China had identified more than 70,000 persons sickened by it (Wu and McGoogan 2020). Although the majority of cases were mild, nearly one in five were severe or critical, and about half of the sickest patients died (Wu and McGoogan 2020).

Global spread of Covid-19 began concurrently with or shortly after the first Chinese cases. WHO has now tallied over 93 million confirmed cases of Covid-19, including more than two million deaths, affecting all continents except Antarctica (World Health Organization n.d.). As of today (18 January 2021), Covid-19 caseloads are still increasing rapidly. WHO received reports of 11,136 new deaths and 588,325 cases within the past 24 hours (World Health Organization n.d.) . True case numbers are almost certainly higher, because capacity to test for the presence of the virus is still not adequate, especially in resource-constrained regions (Ondoa *et al.* 2020).

Although medical care for gravely ill Covid-19 patients has improved since the earliest waves of the outbreak, there is as yet no cure, and vaccine rollout is just beginning. This disease has also left many survivors with varying types of long-term disability, some of it quite serious and lasting for months.

Control of Covid-19 has been difficult; it spreads quickly and easily, largely via infected droplets that pass from person to person through coughing, sneezing, singing, breathing hard, or physical contact (Centers for Disease Control 2019). Although most Covid-infected people have symptoms at some time, the disease is most infectious just before symptoms develop, and nearly half of infected people have no symptoms at all. A recent study estimated that 59 percent of new Covid-19 infections are transmitted by infected persons who do not yet have, and may never develop, Covid-19 symptoms ("asymptom-atic" but infected persons) (Johansson *et al.* 2021).

Prevention of transmission is, in theory, simple: where Covid-19 is active, everyone should wear face masks, wash hands frequently, and/or stay at least six feet away from others in order to avoid contact with the virus (the six-foot rule may be expanded to include avoidance of mass gatherings and closure of sites where people congregate, including schools and workplaces). These interventions work. For example, New Zealand actually achieved elimination of Covid-19 in only 103 days, through implementation of strict quarantines, restriction of gatherings, stay-at-home orders, contact tracing, and other public health strategies (Baker *et al.* 2020). However, in other countries, individual, group, and/or societal resistance to these public health measures has been common and sometimes even violent.

## Impact of Covid-19 on capabilities

Certain direct effects of Covid-19 infection on capabilities can be described with con-ventional measures of mortality and morbidity. For example, among nearly 6000 per-sons hospitalized with Covid-19 in New York City at the beginning of the pandemic, 21 percent died, 22 percent suffered kidney damage, and 6 percent were still too ill to return home at the time of hospital discharge (Richardson *et al.* 2020). Among over 500 persons hospitalized with Covid-19 in Chicago, Illinois, approximately one-third developed encephalopathy (an inflammation of the brain), and about one-third of those with encephalopathy were unable to walk or tend to their self-care at the time of hospital discharge (Liotta *et al.* 2020). A study from China reported that more than half of patients who survived a Covid-19 hospital stay still had active health problems six months after onset of illness; these problems included fatigue, weakness, reduced exercise capacity, and breathing or other lung abnormalities (Huang *et al.* 2021). Direct medical complications of Covid-19 clearly impede patients' capacity "to do and become things of value," and often confer disease-related loss of previously acquired capabilities.

Less direct effects of the pandemic have included grief (in the setting of bereavement), social isolation with loss of opportunities for engaging in common pursuits (associated with quarantine or social distancing), loss of income and essential goods (associated with illness, the deaths of breadwinners, and/or loss of employment), and fear or anxiety (which may be provoked or exacerbated by misinformation, refusal to believe that Covid-19 exists, and/or social strife (Seytre 2020). Thus, for example, a child who is never infected personally with Covid-19 may have diminished opportunities to attain desirable capabilities because of orphanhood, social isolation, and/or other pandemic-associated social and economic constraints.

Complex analyses may be required to sort out intertwining associations between capabilities and the direct or indirect effects of Covid-19. For example, López Barreda *et al.* (2019) note that successful completion of a bicycle ride to a health facility may require availability of a bicycle, physical ability to pedal the bike, social acceptability of bicycling, and the presence of navigable local roads, thus demonstrating the importance of resources and conversion factors in the progression from capabilities to functionings; they also comment that "individuals may differ in their ability to transform resources into actual well-being" (López Barreda *et al.* 2019).

The process of developing functionings may be iterative and even bidirectional. For example, the above-imagined bicyclist may have gone to the health center to obtain asthma medications, and, once having received the necessary inhalers, may then be able to breathe more easily and pedal further and faster – higher levels of previous functioning, thanks to the contribution of new resources to support the previous capability.

But if a staff member or fellow patient at the health center is sick with Covid-19, the cyclist may acquire Covid-19 infection at the time of the health center visit, and may develop difficulty breathing that impairs any activity (even walking), and thus lose capabilities and functionings because the disease serves as a negative conversion factor. Worse still, the ailing cyclist may subsequently be turned away from the local hospital because all of the hospital beds are full and the facility is overwhelmed, or because all of the medical staff have resigned or been injured after threats or violence enacted by Covid disbelievers, as has happened in many countries (Devi 2020, Taylor 2020). As Martha Nussbaum (2005) has noted "violence, and its ongoing threat, interferes with every major capability…"

The imagined anecdote above focuses on the evolution of one individual's capabilities. But, because successive waves of Covid-19 infection affect whole communities and nations, not just individuals, we must also think about societal-level, or group-level, capabilities and functionings. For example, when schools and/or medical services are closed for long periods (now over a year in some sites), all children in a community may be deprived of opportunities for learning and socializing and sports, and this deprivation may have long-term impact. When sickness and death affect farmers, widespread food shortages may develop (Adhikari *et al.* 2021). Should coverage of standard maternal and child health programs be reduced significantly, the number of deaths caused by starvation and/or pregnancy complications could rise by nearly half, and would be "devastating" at the community or societal level (Robertson *et al.* 2020).

That said, it is absolutely crucial to note that human societies can be resilient and creative, in spite of threats posed by mass crises such as the Covid-19 pandemic. Sen observed that valuation of the capabilities of groups, rather than just of individuals, "would tend to be based on the importance that people attach to being able to do certain things in collaboration with others" (Sen 2009: 244–246). We have living examples of such collaboration. In various settings, motivated health workers and civilians, faced with shortages and other dilemmas, have invented and built what they and their communities needed to get through the Covid-19 pandemic. For example, the BBC news (www.bbc.com/news/world-africa-53776027) reported that Senegalese students invented a "Doctor Car" robot to help caregivers tend to quarantined Covid-19 patients. These student inventors' capabilities and functionings were used to support the development (or preservation) of better functionings and capabilities at the societal level. Similarly, coronavirus vaccine development has been undertaken by multiple groups and collaborators, networking internationally; their group-level capabilities, some of which have already shown success, should serve to advance the health capabilities of large societies (www.gavi.org/covax-facility). And in Seattle, Washington, a recent call for volunteer assistance in mass Covid-19 vaccination attracted so many volunteers that over 8000 of them had to be placed on a waiting list, because their willingness to come to their communities' aid exceeded the immediate need (Cornwell 2021).

At present, the story of Covid-19 is still evolving. But we believe that even in complex and dangerous situations such as the Covid-19 pandemic, capabilities and functionings will continue to evolve, and will support both individuals and communities in their quest for good health, in spite of great hardships. We must give the last word to Amartya Sen, a child witness to suffering and violence: "I have seen big problems and then their being solved...I don't see that one has to be hopeless before such hopelessness is due" (Chotiner 2019).

## Discussion questions

1   What role did poverty play in causing the maternal mortality, Hepatitis C, and malaria cases described above? Describe and compare the three cases.
2   Did maternal mortality, Hepatitis C or malaria worsen the poverty of those described in the vignettes? Describe and compare the three cases.
3   If Rosa Maria had lived in George's city, or if George had lived in Luz's village, how might their capabilities have been different both before and after their illnesses?
4   Describe an important health problem in your own community, and its association with poverty (any definition) and capabilities. Alternatively, can you think of a way in which illness or treatment of illness has affected your own capabilities, or those of your friends or family?
5   Identify a health-related law or program that is controversial right now in your community or country. Debate its role in increasing or reducing illness, poverty, and capabilities development.

## Online resources

•   The Malaria Atlas Project has tools such as an interactive map for malaria incidence and data visualizations of global, regional, and national trends: www.malariaatlas.org/

- The World Health Organization's Global Health Observatory has extensive resources including data on a wide range of indicators, a map gallery, and analyses of individual countries: www.who.int/data/gho
- The Institute for Health Metrics and Evaluation has country profiles, infographics, and results from health projects around the world: www.healthdata.org/
- The World Food Program is one of the leading global institutions focusing on nutrition, health, and sustainable development: www.wfp.org/
- Survival: The Story of Global Health is a series of videos that takes a big-picture look at the relationships between health and human societies: www.youtube.com/channel/UCyxRuuY1APjPsJzJc89dKOg/videos

## Further reading

Alkire, S. and L. Chen. 2004. "Global health and moral values." *The Lancet* 364.9439: 1069–1074.
Center for Global Development's "Millions Saved" series of success stories in global health: www.millionssaved.cgdev.org/
Dodd, R. and L. Munck. 2001. *Dying for Change: Poor People's Experience of Health and Ill-Health.* Geneva: World Health Organization.
Fox, A. M. and B. Meier. 2009. "Health as freedom: addressing social determinants of global health inequities through the human right to development." *Bioethics* 23.2: 112–122.
Walraven, G. 2013. *Health and Poverty: Global Health Problems and Solutions.* London: Routledge.

## Works cited

Adhikari, J., Timsina, J., Raj Khadka, S., Ghale, Y. and Ojha, H. 2021. "COVID-19 impacts on agriculture and food systems in Nepal: implications for SDGs." *Agricultural Systems* 186: 102990.
Averting Maternal Death and Disability Program. 2010. Needs Assessments of Emergency Obstetric and Newborn Care. New York: Columbia University.
Baker M. G., Wilson N. and Anglemyer A. 2020. "Successful elimination of Covid-19 transmission in New Zealand." *New England Journal of Medicine* 383.8:e56.
Blencowe, H., Lee, A. C. C., Cousens, S., Bahalim, A., Narwal, R., Zhong, R., Chou, D., Say, L., Modi, N., Katz, J., Vos, T., Marlow, N. and Lawn, J. E. 2013. "Preterm birth-associated neurodevelopmental impairment estimates at regional and global levels for 2010." *Pediatric Research* 74: 17–34.
CDC Foundation. 2016. What is Public Health? www.cdcfoundation.org/what-public-health. Accessed 18 January 2021.
Centers for Disease Control and Prevention. 2016. *Pregnancy Mortality Surveillance System.* www.cdc.gov/reproductivehealth/maternalinfanthealth/pmss.html. Accessed 14 November 2016.
Centers for Disease Control. How COVID-19 Spreads. 2019. www.cdc.gov/coronavirus/2019-ncov/prevent-getting-sick/how-covid-spreads.html. Accessed 23 January 2021.
Chotiner, I. 2019. "Amartya Sen's Hopes and Fears for Indian Democracy." *The New Yorker,* 6 October 2019. www.newyorker.com/news/the-new-yorker-interview/amartya-sens-hopes-and-fears-for-indian-democracy.
Church, J. A., Fitzgerald, F., Walker, A. S., Gibb, D. M. and Prendergast, A. J. 2015. "The expanding role of co-trimoxazole in developing countries." *The Lancet Infectious Diseases* 15: 327–339.
Committee on Economic Social and Cultural Rights. 2000. Substantive issues arising in the implementation of the International Covenant on Economic, Social and Cultural Rights. General Comment No. 14. The right to the highest attainable standard of health (Article 12 of the International Covenant on Economic, Social, and Cultural Rights). In: United Nations (ed.) *E/C.12/2000/4.*

Cornwell, P. 2021. "As Washington state aims to vaccinate millions against COVID-19, thousands sign up to help." *Seattle Times*, 23 January.

Desai, M., Ter Kuile, F. O., Nosten, F., Mcgready, R., Asamoaa, K., Brabin, B. and Newman, R. D. 2007. "Epidemiology and burden of malaria in pregnancy." *The Lancet Infectious Diseases* 7: 93–104.

Devi, S. 2020. "COVID-19 exacerbates violence against health workers." *The Lancet*, 5 September: 658.

Diplomatic Conference on the Reaffirmation and Development of International Humanitarian Law Applicable in Armed Conflicts. 1977. *Protocols additional to the Geneva Conventions of 12 August 1949*. Geneva: International Committee of the Red Cross.

Doyle, O., Harmon, C. P., Heckman, J. J. and Tremblay, R. E. 2009. "Investing in early human development: timing and economic efficiency." *Economics & Human Biology* 7: 1–6.

Drugs for Neglected Diseases Initiative. 2015. *2014 Annual Report. Partnerships to Bridge Innovation and Access*. Geneva: Drugs for Neglected Diseases initiative.

Duffy, P. E. and Gorres J. P. 2020. Malaria vaccines since 2000: progress, priorities, products. *NPJ Vaccines* 5: 48.

Engle, P. L., Black, M. M., Behrman, J. R., Carbral De Mello, M., Gertler, P. J., Kapiriri, L., Martorell, R., Young, M. E. and The International Child Development Steering Group. 2007. "Strategies to avoid the loss of development potential in more than 200 million children in the developing world." *The Lancet* 369: 229–242.

Feld, J. *et al*. 2015. "Sofosbuvir and velpatasvir for HCV genotype 1, 2, 4, 5, and 6 infection." *New England Journal of Medicine* 373: 2599–2607.

Fernando, S., Gunawardena, D., Bandara, M., De Silva, D., Carter, R., Mendis, K. and Wickremasinghe, A. 2003. "The impact of repeated malaria attacks on the school performance of children." *American Journal of Tropical Medicine and Hygiene* 69: 582–588.

Ford, N., Singh, K., Cooke, G. S., Mills, E. J., Von Schoen-Angerer, T., Kamarulzaman, A. and Du Cros, P. 2012. "Expanding access to treatment for hepatitis C in resource-limited settings: lessons from HIV/AIDS." *Clinical Infectious Diseases* 54.10: 1465–1472.

Freedman, L. P. 2001. "Averting maternal death and disability. Using human rights in maternal mortality programs: from analysis to strategy." *International Journal of Gynecology & Obstetrics* 75: 51–60.

French, N., Nakiyingi, J., Lugada, E., Watera, C., Whitworth, J. and Gilks, C. F. 2001. "Increasing rates of malarial fever with deteriorating immune status in HIV-1-infected Ugandan adults." *AIDS* 15: 899–906.

Fukuda-Parr, S. 2009. "Human Rights and Human Development," in K. Basu and R. Kanbur, eds. *Arguments for a Better World. Essays in Honor of Amartya Sen*. Oxford: Oxford University Press.

Geiger, H. and Cook-Deegan, R. 1993. "The role of physicians in conflicts and humanitarian crises. Case studies from the field missions of Physicians for Human Rights." *JAMA* 270: 616–620.

Hong, S. C. 2011. "Malaria and economic productivity: a longitudinal analysis of the American case." *Journal of Economic History* 71: 654–671.

Huang, C. *et al*. 2021. "6-month consequences of COVID-19 in patients discharged from hospital: a cohort study." *The Lancet*, published online January 8, 2021.

Huang, C. *et al*. 2020. "Clinical features of patients infected with 2019 novel coronavirus in Wuhan, China." *The Lancet* 395: 497–506.

Johansson, M. A. *et al*. 2021. "SARS-CoV-2 transmission from people without COVID-19 symptoms." *JAMA Netw Open* 4.1:e2035057.

Liotta, E. M., Batra, A., Clark, J. R., Shlobin, N. A., Hoffman, S. C., Orban, Z. S. and Koralnik, I. J. 2020. "Frequent neurologic manifestations and encephalopathy-associated morbidity in Covid-19 patients." *Annals of Clinical and Translational Neurology*. doi: 10.1002/acn3.51210.

López Barreda, R., Robertson-Preidler, J. and García, P. B. 2019. "Health assessment and the capability approach." *Global Bioethics* 39.1: 19–27.

Malaney, P., Spielman, A. and Sachs, J. 2004. "The malaria gap." *American Journal of Tropical Medicine and Hygiene* 71: 141–146.

Médecins Sans Frontières. n.d. *Strategies to secure access to generic hepatitis C medicine*. www. msfaccess.org/content/strategies-secure-access-generic-hepatitis-c-medicines. Accessed 13 November 2016.

Medicines for Malaria Venture. 2015. *Annual Report 2014*. Geneva: Medicines for Malaria Venture.

Newby, G., Bennett, A., Larson, E., Cotter, C., Shretta, R., Phillips, A. A. and Feachem, R. G. A. 2016. "The path to eradication: a progress report on the malaria-eliminating countries." *The Lancet* 387: 1775–1784.

Nussbaum, M. C. 2000. *Women and Human Development. The Capabilities Approach*. New York: Cambridge University Press.

Nussbaum, M. C. 2003. "Capabilities as fundamental entitlements: Sen and social justice." *Feminist Economics* 9: 33–59.

Nussbaum, M. C. 2005. "Women's bodies: violence, security, capabilities." *Journal of Human Development* 6.2: 167–183.

Nussbaum, M. C. 2011. "Capabilities, entitlements, rights: supplementation and critique." *Journal of Human Development and Capabilities* 12: 23–37.

Nussbaum, M. C. and Dixon, R. 2012. *Children's Rights and a Capabilities Approach: the Question of Special Priority*. Chicago, IL: University of Chicago Law School.

Observatorio de Mortalidad Materna en México. n.d. www.omm.org.mx. Accessed 13 November 2016.

Olney, D., Kariger, P., Stoltzfus, R., Khalfan, S., Ali, N., Tielsch, J., Sazawal, S., Black, R. E., Allen, L. and Pollitt, E. 2013. "Developmental effects of micronutrient supplementation and malaria in Zanzibari children." *Early Human Development* 89: 667–674.

Ondoa, P. *et al.* 2020. "COVID-19 testing in Africa: lessons learnt." *Microbe* 1 (July): e103–e104.

Physicians For Human Rights. n.d. *The Principle of Medical Neutrality*. www.physiciansforhumanrights. org/issues/persecution-of-health-workers/medical-neutrality/. Accessed 13 November 2016.

Richardson, S. *et al.* 2020. "Presenting characteristics, comorbidities, and outcomes among 5700 patients hospitalized with COVID-19 in the New York City area." *JAMA* 323.20: 2052–2059.

Roberton, T. *et al.* 2020. "Early estimates of the indirect effects of the COVID-19 pandemic on maternal and child mortality in low-income and middle-income countries: a modelling study." *Lancet Global Health* 8: e901–08.

Saracci, R. 1997. "The World Health Organisation needs to reconsider its definition of health." *British Medical Journal* 314: 1409.

Sen, A. 2009. *The Idea of Justice*. Cambridge, MA: The Belknap Press of Harvard University Press.

Seytre B. 2020. "Erroneous communication messages on COVID-19 in Africa." *Am J Trop Med Hyg* 103.2: 587–589.

SIAPS – ETHIOPIA PMI/AMDM Program. 2014. Technical report: availability, price, and affordability of artemisinin-based combination therapies (ACTs) and other antimalarial drugs in Oromia regional state of Ethiopia: implications on universal access to malarial treatments, June 2014. Arlington, VA: Management Sciences for Health.

Smith, M., Shannon, S. and Vickery, K. 2015. *Health Actions for Women. Practical Strategies to Mobilize for Change*. Berkeley, CA: Hesperian Health Guides.

Strathdee, S. A. and Beyrer, C. 2015. "Threading the needle – how to stop the HIV outbreak in rural Indiana." *New England Journal of Medicine* 373: 397–399.

Susser, M. 1974. "Ethical components in the definition of health." *International Journal of Health Services* 4: 539–548.

Tan, W. *et al.* 2020. "A novel coronavirus genome identified in a cluster of pneumonia cases – Wuhan, China 2019–2020." *China CDC Weekly* 2.4: 61–62.

Taylor L. 2020. "Covid-19 misinformation sparks threats and violence against doctors in Latin America." *BMJ* 370:m3088. 11 August.

Thaddeus, S. and Maine, D. 1994. "Too far to walk: maternal mortality in context." *Social Science and Medicine* 38: 1091–1110.

United Nations. 1966. International Covenant on Economic, Social, and Cultural Rights. New York, NY: United Nations.

United Nations. 1990. Convention on the Rights of the Child. New York, NY: United Nations.

United Nations General Assembly. Human Rights Council. 2012. Technical guidance on the application of a human rights-based approach to the implementation of policies and programmes to reduce preventable maternal morbidity and mortality. *Report of the Office of the United Nations High Commissioner for Human Rights*. New York, NY: United Nations.

Utzinger, J., Tozan, Y., Doumani, F. and Singer, B. H. 2002. "The economic payoffs of integrated malaria control in the Zambian copperbelt between 1930 and 1950." *Tropical Medicine and International Health* 7: 657–677.

Webster, D. P., Klenerman, P. and Dusheiko, G. M. 2015. "Hepatitis C." *The Lancet* 385: 1124–1135.

World Health Organization. n.d. "COVID Dashboard." www.covid19.who.int/table. Accessed 18 January 2021.

World Health Organization. 2014a. *Egypt steps up efforts against Hepatitis C*. www.who.int/features/2014/egypt-campaign-hepatitisc/en/. Accessed 13 November 2016.

World Health Organization. 2014b. Trends in maternal mortality: 1990 to 2013. Estimates by WHO, UNICEF, UNFPA, The World Bank and the United Nations Population Division. Geneva: World Health Organization.

World Health Organization. 2015. *WHO moves to improve access to lifesaving medicines for hepatitis C, drug-resistant TB and cancers*. www.who.int/mediacentre/news/releases/2015/new-essential-medicines-list/en/. Accessed 13 November 2016.

World Health Organization. 2019a. Trends in maternal mortality: 2000 to 2017: estimates by WHO, UNICEF, UNFPA, World Bank Group and the United Nations Population Division. Geneva: World Health Organization. Licence: CC-BY-NC-SA 3.0 IGO.

World Health Organization. 2019b. WHO Global Malaria Program. World Malaria Report 2019. Geneva: World Health Organization.

World Health Organization. 2020a World Malaria Report 2020: 20 years of global progress and challenges. Geneva: World Health Organization; 2020. Licence: CC BY-NC-SA 3.0 IGO.

World Health Organization. 2020b. Hepatitis C Fact sheet. Updated July 2020. Geneva: World Health Organization. www.who.int/en/news-room/fact-sheets/detail/hepatitis-c. Accessed 19 December 2020.

Wu, Z. and McGoogan J. M. 2020. "Characteristics of and important lessons from the coronavirus disease 2019 (COVID-19) outbreak in China." *JAMA* 323.13: 1239–1242.

Yamin, A. E. 2013. "From ideals to tools: applying human rights to maternal health." *PLoS Medicine* 10.

Zeuzem, S. *et al.* 2018. "Glecaprevir-pibrentasvir for 8 or 12 weeks in HCV genotype 1 or 3 infection." *New England Journal of Medicine* 378: 354–369.

# 5  Geographical and spatial poverty

*Benjamin Curtis*

## Learning objectives

- Explain why tropical areas of the planet are more likely to be poor than temperate areas.
- Explain why landlocked and mountainous places are more likely to be poor.
- Summarize what remoteness has to do with poverty, and how integration can promote human and economic development.
- Describe the connection between spatial poverty and capabilities.
- Identify polices that can counteract the geographical and spatial aspects of poverty.

## Introduction

Look at the map of countries classified by the World Bank's income groups, shown in Figure 5.1. Two things immediately stand out: low-income countries are for the most part clustered in a band around the equator, while the high-income countries tend to fall in the higher latitudes, whether in the northern or the southern hemispheres. Notice also that many lower income countries are landlocked. A map of countries by their Human Development Index score similarly shows that nearly all the highest-scoring countries are located outside of the planet's tropical zone (Figure 5.2).

A mere glance at a map is of course not enough to ascertain whether location on the globe has anything to do with the level of economic or human development. Dig deeper, though, and a number of surprising facts present themselves. Consider this: of the 30 countries in the world with the highest per capita gross domestic product (GDP) purchasing power parity (PPP), only three – Hong Kong, Brunei, and Singapore – lie completely within the tropics. According to one analysis, tropical countries have on average a third of the income of countries located in the temperate zone. Astoundingly, a small group of countries in the temperate zone, encompassing only eight percent of the planet's total land and 22 percent of the total population, accounted for approximately 52 percent of the world's gross national product (GNP). Life expectancies for people living in tropical countries were also seven years below those for people in temperate countries, even when factoring out the effects of overall income level and female education (Hausmann 2001).

The relationship between geography and poverty does not just pertain to the tropics. There are a number of other spatial factors that impact a person's poverty status – in fact, the 2009 World Development Report declared that "Place is the most important correlate of a person's welfare" (WDR 2009: 1). This chapter will examine several key

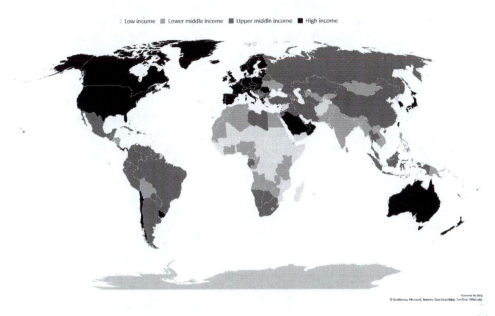

*Figure 5.1* Countries by World Bank income group classification

Source: World Bank data. Created by the author. Powered by Bing. © GeoNames, Microsoft, Navinfo, OpenStreeMap, TomTom, Wikipedia.

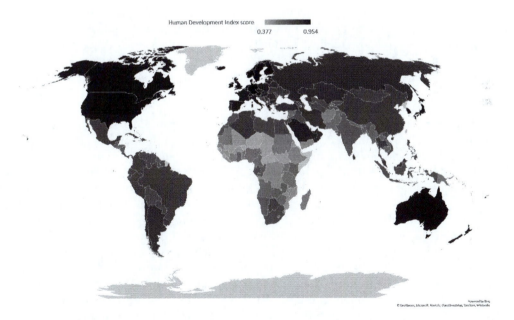

*Figure 5.2* Countries by Human Development Index score 2018

Source: UNDP data, http://hdr.undp.org/en/data#. Created by the author. Powered by Bing. © GeoNames, Microsoft, Navinfo, OpenStreeMap, TomTom, Wikipedia.

characteristics of places that are detrimental to human and economic development at the country, regional, local, and individual level. Some characteristics – the prevalence of disease, a lack of agricultural endowments such as soil quality and rainfall, a remote or rugged location – have *direct* poverty effects by influencing individuals' health, food security, livelihoods, and political rights. Other characteristics – such as the longer-term impact between environmental geography and institutions – can have *indirect* poverty effects (Nunn and Puga 2012).Taken together, such disadvantages of place can create poverty traps. Simply put, certain geographical and spatial factors make it more likely that a person is poor, and make it harder for that person to escape poverty (see i.a. Jalan and Ravallion 1997, Minot *et al.* 2006, Ravallion and Wodon 1999 ).This is a problem in terms of long-run factors that explain development, but also because around a billion people today live in such geographical "poverty hotspots" (Cohen *et al.* 2019).

We will explore how geographical and spatial factors can become a poverty trap, and survey policy responses to remedy such problems. But we must begin with definitions: what is the distinction between "geographical" and "spatial" poverty? There is a great deal of conceptual overlap between these two terms. Geography can be studied in many different ways; as an academic discipline, there are branches of physical geography, economic geography, cultural geography, and political geography, to name a few. As we use the term in this chapter, though, "geography" has two main applications: environmental geography and relative geography. Environmental geography refers to how humans interact with the attributes of the natural world characterizing a particular place on the planet, such as climate, latitude, biodiversity, the extent of rivers and coastline, and topographical features such as mountains and plains. These environmental attributes, as we will see, can have a variety of both beneficial and detrimental effects on a society's human and economic development. Relative geography, as its name implies, has to do with how certain geographical units – such as countries and their markets, but also regions within a country – relate to each other. The easiest way of thinking about relative geography is as "neighbor geography." Just as in any city or town, the neighbors who live next to you can impact your wellbeing. In explaining poverty, the relative geography between neighboring countries or regions can have a significant effect.

The term "spatial" refers to the characteristics of a particular space or place. It subsumes the environmental and relative factors above but also adds in other characteristics including the availability of infrastructure and public services (Kanbur and Venables 2005). A spatial perspective pays attention to things that may not be thought of as "geographical," such as the locational impact of institutions, markets, politics, and culture on individuals' capabilities or economic opportunities.The spatial perspective thus considers the *interactions* between features of environmental and relative geography with those institutions, markets, etc., as well as the *distribution* of factors that contribute to poverty. This is vital because such factors are often concentrated in particular places rather than being evenly spread throughout a territory. Hence applying a spatial framework sheds light on inequality, and why some areas within a country can remain mired in multiple deprivations even as other areas experience strong economic growth (Chronic Poverty 2005: 26).This chapter takes an expansive approach to analyze the characteristics of places that contribute to such deprivations, and will generally use the term "spatial poverty" to embrace the various geographical, political, and other factors.

## The disease burden

To begin with, one environmental characteristic of certain places can have a powerful impact on poverty, namely conditions in which diseases and parasites flourish. Places with warmer temperatures, in particular, provide the perfect breeding grounds for parasites such as the malaria virus. The problem of health and poverty is treated in a separate chapter, so at present our goal is simply to demonstrate that this burden does have a pronounced geographic connection. Look at Figure 5.3, showing the areas of the planet with the highest malaria incidence. Some 200 million people per year are infected with malaria, primarily in the tropics. Malaria is only one of the various debilitating afflictions in such regions; dengue fever is another, with around 100 million cases per year (WHO 2020). Besides the climate and biological conditions that lend themselves to disease, these areas also often suffer from poor food production, which in turn leads to poor nutrition. If a person is undernourished, she is also more susceptible to disease; children and the elderly are in general most susceptible. Further, poverty itself makes it harder for people to resist diseases, because they are more likely to be illiterate and lack access to adequate medical care and sanitation. Studies have shown that when income is factored out of the equation, infant mortality and life expectancy are worse in the tropics than in temperate zones (Sachs 2001). It is on average simply less healthy to live in a tropical area.

The disease burden of such areas can increase poverty in a variety of ways. First, there are several direct, human effects. These effects often reduce a person's capabilities. For instance, if a person is unhealthy, he is less likely to be able to work productively to support himself or his family. Diseases can reduce not only physical capacity but cognitive capacity as well, whether by stunting a person's brain development or simply because it is harder to attend school if you are sick. Additionally, in places with high rates of disease-related mortality, fertility rates are likely to be higher, which can result in more mouths to feed with continually limited resources, thus depressing household incomes. As discussed in Chapter 4 on health and poverty, if you are sick, you are more likely to be poor, and if you are poor you are more likely to be sick. Disease negatively impacts quality of life and thereby makes people more capability poor. It also reduces a person's chance to earn an adequate income.

There are a number of additional, indirect economic effects of the disease burden. Foreign investment to highly disease-prone regions may be reduced because the labor force is less productive or more costly. Other forms of trade can also be disrupted by disease outbreaks. Tourism takes a major hit in epidemics such as bird flu or Covid-19. As just two examples, serious economic damages have been calculated from the costs of the SARS outbreak in 2003 (estimated at USD 40 billion worldwide), and the H1N1 influenza in Mexico in 2009 (USD 2.9 billion) (Smith *et al.* 2019). Sadly, the high disease burden in tropical regions, especially in Sub-Saharan Africa, amounts to a poverty trap: countries that most urgently need treatment and public health measures against rampant malaria are often too poor to afford them, but untreated malaria is also a cause of poverty in those countries.

## Temperature, agriculture, and natural resource endowments

The next element in spatial and geographical poverty might be summed up as a person's ability to earn a productive livelihood given environmental constraints. Temperature is the simplest aspect: in hot climates, it can be harder to work hard. Higher temperatures are

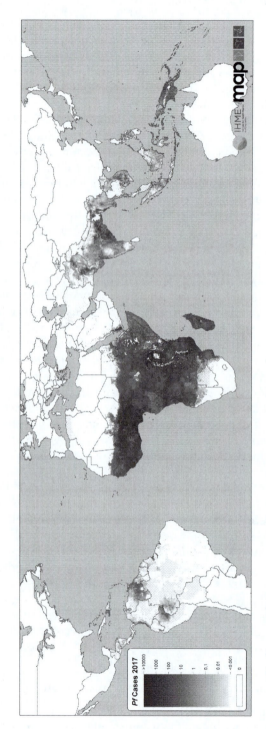

*Figure 5.3* Malaria (*Plasmodium falciparum*) clinical cases in all groups in 2017

Source: Malaria Atlas Project, https://malariaatlas.org/trends/region/MAP/GLOBAL.

associated with lower productivity, such that countries were on average 8.5 percent poorer per-capita per 1°C warmer (Dell *et al.* 2014; see also Castells-Quintana *et al.* 2017). The quality of the land on which a person lives also makes an enormous difference. Certain parts of the world have less fertile land and a dearth of natural resources. Many people in lower income countries live from agriculture, and where the land is not particularly fertile, that limits a family's economic potential. These problems affect many: 500 million people in the developing world live in arid areas with very limited irrigation, and some 400 million live on lands with poor soils (Chronic Poverty 2005: 31). At the country level, territory that is primarily desert, and lacks exportable natural resources such as minerals or oil, can impede economic growth. It is true that the natural resource "curse" can undermine development and democracy, as we discuss in Chapter 7 on institutions. Yet having no natural resources can also be bad. One example is coal: relatively few tropical countries have significant reserves of coal, which may have negatively impacted their potential for energy production to provide power for people and the economy.

Deficient agricultural endowments can increase poverty in four main ways: (1) via the prevalence of pests and parasites; (2) soil quality; (3) water availability; and (4) lower plant growth rates. The problem of pests and parasites is related to the disease burden. But whereas the disease burden exacerbates poverty through its effects on humans, pests and parasites can harm crops or livestock. Again, tropical areas in particular suffer from the warm conditions that foster rampant growth of pests, and those pests can wipe out plants or animals that people depend on for food or trade. The contrast is with locations in higher latitudes, and particularly those areas that experience a winter frost. Frost tends to kill pests and parasites, so they are less likely to damage agriculture in temperate areas. Winter frost plays a role in soil quality as well. In areas with winter frost, soil tends to build up for long periods of time, thereby becoming richer and more fertile. In tropical areas, soil often does not build up but is instead washed away by the heavy rains common to this climate zone. Moreover, due to the unique nature of tropical climatic conditions, most of the rich minerals exist not in soils but in the plant biomass above the ground. If those plants are cleared to make way for a farmer's field, their minerals are often lost rather than returning to the soil. The problem of poor soils is not exclusively a tropical condition: agriculture is more difficult anywhere with unfertile soil, and some tropical areas are highly productive (Barrett and Bevis 2015).

The problem of water availability refers above all to irrigation for crops. The optimal condition for agricultural production is a fairly steady supply of precipitation throughout the year. Areas that are especially arid, or where precipitation is very heavy in certain months but very light in others, make agriculture more difficult. In some areas in the tropics, for instance, there is a particular rainy season of the year, during which intense downpours occur most days. Not only do such downpours have the effect of eroding soils, but they can also flood fields and make storage and accumulation of grains more problematic. In the months of the dry season, conversely, precipitation can be too sparse. Some parts of the world are more prone to drought or wild year-to-year fluctuations in the amount of precipitation. In rugged, mountainous areas, both soil erosion and irrigation can make agriculture overall less productive. Finally, all of the above factors can affect plant growth rates. In the tropics, the intense, short downpours can be too much for plants to absorb, and the typical high temperatures mean that the excess water often evaporates quickly. Thus, water can actually be scarce in some tropical areas.

Again, these problems are not all unique to the tropics, and it can be difficult for a person to earn a livelihood anywhere with extreme heat, poor soils, or insufficient precipitation. However, these various disadvantages of agricultural endowments do tend to coalesce in certain areas, contributing to spatial poverty. Much of Africa suffers from several of these problems, such as the prevalence of pests and parasites, soil insufficiencies, and feast-or-famine with water availability. To understand how these conditions impact individuals' lives, imagine a small subsistence farm in the landlocked West African country of Burkina Faso. The northern part of the country belongs to the Sahel, the semi-arid transition zone between the Sahara desert and the savannas farther south. The modest mud houses are surrounded by small fields of reddish soil, acacia trees, and grassland. Here most of the local villages literally live for the rainy season: with few other sources of irrigation, families depend on the approximately 50 days a year when it rains. When the rains come, in August for example, the precipitation is usually short and intense.

Farmers in this part of Burkina Faso have to contend not only with soil erosion from such rainstorms, but also with expanding desertification and the many droughts that have plagued their region over the past several decades. Farmers who wanted to leave behind these problems of poor soils and drought have often migrated to the more verdant south of the country. Even there, though, they have to avoid settling near a river – despite its promise of better soil and ample water – because in such areas their cattle would be prey to the tsetse fly, and the farmers themselves would be more likely to come into contact with the parasite that causes onchocerciasis, otherwise known as African river blindness. Though this latter affliction has been greatly reduced in recent decades, the combination of problems such as these in Burkina Faso helps explain why agricultural productivity throughout Africa tends to be low in comparison to other parts of the developing world. The environmental disadvantages of much of sub-Saharan Africa, and tropical areas in particular, are an important reason that agriculture in these regions can be some 30 to 50 percent less productive than agriculture in temperate zones, even when controlling for the impact of tractors, fertilizer, and irrigation (see Forum for Agricultural Research in Africa 2006, Gallup *et al.* 1999).

## Remoteness and integration

The idea of remoteness incorporates a number of features that can exacerbate poverty, while integration is generally held to promote economic and human development. Remoteness means being located far from markets, political centers, or public services such as health care and education. There are three typical situations that can make a household, region, or country more remote: being landlocked, or otherwise far from the sea or navigable rivers; being mountainous, or having rugged terrain such as jungle; and being surrounded by poor neighboring countries. Remoteness and isolation can be the product of both physical distance (measured as miles/kilometers or travel time) and socio-cultural distance (if a group of people comes from a culture that is different from the dominant culture). Multiple studies have shown that physical remoteness is associated with higher rates of poverty (Chomitz 2007, Jalan and Ravallion 2002). As one example of socio-cultural distance, minority ethnic groups in Vietnam were more likely to live in remote villages and rugged areas, and were more likely to suffer from poverty (Epprecht *et al.* 2011). In general, people living in remote areas are more likely to have insecure economic livelihoods, poor quality housing, very limited access to banking and credit, less productive land, and nutrition deficits (Bird *et al.* 2002). These problems of remoteness and integration affect a very large number of people: some 1.8 billion according to one analysis (Chronic Poverty 2005).

## Box 5.1 Challenges of farming in semi-arid areas, by Andrew Gorvetzian

When I first met Naidu, he smiled and immediately asked, "When are you coming to my farm?" We exchanged telephone numbers and he explained how he believed in organic farming not only because it was more sustainable, but also because of how it offered a fulfilling lifestyle. By no means would a small farmer gain extraordinary wealth, but organic farming offered a lifestyle that provided many positive outcomes. His goal in life was to share this knowledge with as many people as possible.

On the day we went to his farm, I immediately saw that Naidu's farm was a veritable paradise among the barren and rocky land that surrounded it. The semi-arid climate and sandy soils of this region of India's Telangana state require a lot of work to become viable farmland. Naidu's 30 years of hard toil in such conditions were clear when I saw his huge trees that swayed lazily in the breeze. The 12 acres before us were covered in not just trees, but crops and flowers in which 15 varieties of dragonflies and butterflies lived. In the nearby field, four workers hunched over the rows of newly planted mango trees, working the earth with well-worn tools to usher the creeping irrigation water down the rows. Naidu showed me around the farm, pointing out tomatoes, brinjal, wheat, mangoes, papayas, bitter gourd, banana, Bird of Paradise flowers, tamarind, coconut, coffee beans, black pepper, allspice, teakwood trees, a honeycomb, and more. I gaped in wonder.

Visiting Naidu's farm offered the chance to witness the potential of organic farming practices for small farmers in the face of so many obstacles. Naidu's farm is an oasis, yet the details of his daily routine are hardly anyone's idea of paradise. The Telangana state government could only provide three hours of power per day and one hour of water, a severe constraining factor for small farmers in a semi-arid environment. Naidu owned no vehicle yet transported thousands of pounds of produce per year using public transit on overcrowded buses. Climate change compounds these constraints as weather patterns become increasingly erratic. Yet he and his workers persevere, without complaint, despite these obstacles. To witness the effort behind the beauty of Naidu's farm revealed a glimpse into the daily struggles a farmer faces. It also engenders an appreciation for the scope of the challenges that agriculture faces in India, where too many small and marginal farmers are living at or below the USD 2 a day threshold.

Glaring problems are not solved with easy solutions, but rather hard work and creative solutions. Naidu has been able to create a beautiful and successful farm using organic techniques, including a focus on maintaining biodiversity through cultivating many different crop types. This diversity of crops, trees, flowers, and herbs creates a healthy ecosystem that eliminates the need for expensive and harmful chemical fertilizers and pesticides. For many small farmers in India, maintaining biodiversity on farms is a potential key for reducing reliance upon expensive chemical inputs that can reduce soil fertility with no guarantee of higher yields.

However, the ability to cultivate biodiversity is coming under threat from restrictive intellectual property rights used by large agricultural corporations. These corporations identify and develop lucrative varieties and traits and then restrict others from accessing those seeds without paying large royalties. Furthermore, farmers may have to return to the market to buy seeds from year to year, because the patents do not allow farmers to resow their seeds. The problems are exacerbated by a lack of institutional credit available to provide small farmers with loans to buy such inputs. This forces them to rely on middlemen who are providers of both loans and physical inputs, ensnaring small farmers in debt traps from which escape is almost impossible. These practices have led to an alarming reduction in the diversity of seeds available to farmers who are strapped for cash, threatening biodiversity that is so crucial to sustainable farming systems. When you are living on only USD 2 a day, it can be very hard to afford seeds at market prices.

The Open Source Seed Initiative seeks to protect the rights of farmers and plant breeders to have access to seeds whose use is not restricted by patents. With an open source framework, farmers and breeders would have access to seeds in a protected open access commons, to which entry is guaranteed to those who promise to share openly the varieties that are developed from sources within the protected commons. This framework seeks to avoid the restrictions of agricultural patents and foster an ethic of sharing of seeds between farmers and breeders with legal protection against proprietary forces. Through open access plant breeding, many are hoping that resilient and locally adapted seeds can withstand the challenges of climate change and inefficient governments.

Naidu's farm was visible proof of the ability of organic farming to maintain a healthy ecosystem that provides biodiversity and productive fields while also providing a more secure stream of income. With innovative solutions like the Open Source Seed Initiative, the development and improvement of diverse varieties of crops that can withstand the challenges of agriculture in India becomes more feasible. The socio–economic dimension of poverty is obvious, but what is not so obvious is the ecological aspect. With creative initiatives such as open source seed, perhaps both of these dimensions of poverty can be alleviated for small farmers in India.

Remote areas' difficulties with transportation can exacerbate both economic and capability poverty. Mountainous terrain means that building infrastructure such as roads or rail lines is significantly more expensive than in flat topography, and therefore mountainous places particularly in lower income countries are more likely to have deficient transportation infrastructure and to be remote from markets. Studies consistently find that low access to roads or other transportation infrastructure is associated with higher rates of poverty. In Tanzania, for example, households located within 100 meters of a gravel road passable 12 months of the year, with bus service, had incomes a third higher than the rural average (Bird *et al.* 2010: 5). Even where roads exist, they can be of poor quality, which limits the mobility of people and goods. Bad roads mean that it can take hours to travel relatively short distances, making people and villages more isolated. Bad roads also drive up transport costs, which can make travel unaffordable for people, reducing their access to markets and public services. Higher transport costs hinder economic development by making it more difficult for goods to reach distant markets. Thus being landlocked can raise shipping costs as much as 50 percent over shipping costs for coastal countries (Henderson *et al.* 2001).

People living in remote areas also typically have less access to public goods such as clean water, sanitation, and health care. One study found that rural areas in over 90 percent of countries had reduced access to sanitation and clean water, and 100 percent of rural areas had less access to primary health care (IFAD 2000). The quality of services such as health care and education in remote areas also tends to be worse, in part because it can be harder to attract experienced medical professionals or teachers to those areas. This is another aspect of the relationship between spatial factors and institutions: remote areas may well suffer from neglect by government officials, and/or the costs of bringing public services to those areas may be prohibitive. The potentially beneficial effects of pro–poor policies may thus not reach poor people in the remotest areas.

Another public good that can be in shorter supply in remote areas is security from crime and conflict. Though it is not always the case, there are numerous examples from around the world (such as Madagascar, India, Zimbabwe, and Sri Lanka) where crime rates were higher in rural and other areas more distant from law enforcement (Fafchamps and Moser 2003). Besides remoteness, spatial factors play a role in crime and security through regional inequalities, especially where these overlap with ethnic cleavages. For example, if an ethnic group is concentrated in a particular region, and the group's members share a sense of grievance about unequal political or economic opportunities compared to another group or within the state as a whole, tensions can erupt into armed conflict (Buhaug *et al.* 2011, Østby *et al.* 2009). Areas with rugged geography such as mountains or tropical jungles can also be associated with a higher risk of terrorism and illegal activities such as drug production and trafficking (Abadie 2004). And once conflict has broken out, geographical factors complicate conflict resolution. It is more difficult for the central state to root out criminal activity and violent rebel groups in remote and rugged areas. An extensive literature has also shown how climate shocks such as less rainfall are associated with increased conflict and political instability (see Dell *et al.* 2014 for a review).

The deleterious political dimensions of remoteness combine to isolate regions or people from centers of decision making and influence. In this way, integration problems due to geography can increase capability poverty by marginalizing people economically, politically, and even socially. People remote from political and economic centers may be more likely to suffer from exclusion that prevents them from fully exercising their rights or maximizing their economic livelihoods. As but one example, consider the case of villagers from minority ethnic groups in Cambodia's far northeastern province of Ratanakiri. Jeremy Ironside (2009) has documented how these villagers' relative remoteness from the capital made them neglected and often powerless. Villages in this province consistently had worse health indicators such as malnutrition and infant mortality, and some were too far from schools for their children to get an education. Villagers in the region were rarely consulted on Cambodia's development projects, such as road building or policies to convert local agriculture to cash crops that may be less traditional, such as cashews. There is even evidence of open discrimination by individuals and government officials from the Khmer majority, since in some cases minority villages have lost their communal land to expropriation or illegal sales by outsiders.

There are a number of very specific economic aspects of remoteness as well (see i.a. Bosker and Garretsen 2012). Countries that are poorly connected with world markets will have difficulty developing the industries that would help them integrate to those markets, and which would in turn help them become more prosperous. Paul Krugman and Anthony Venables (1995) have shown how agglomeration effects accrue to places that are able to integrate into producing for world markets. What this means is that companies will choose to locate near each other in somewhere like Vietnam, even if wages are higher there than in Tanzania, because moving to where wages are lowest can impose additional costs through the transportation and other difficulties of being farther from world markets. Therefore, assembly and manufacturing jobs have "agglomerated" in certain Asian countries, often bypassing low-wage but less integrated Africa, at least for now. It has also been shown that being landlocked can reduce a country's growth rate by 0.6 percent compared to a country that is not landlocked (cited in Hausmann 2001: 46). Coastal areas, and/or those with good transportation infrastructure, in general have a better chance of consistent economic development, while landlocked, poorly integrated, and remote areas are more likely to remain poor.

### The problem of neighbors

In addition to difficult terrain and a landlocked location, neighboring countries also can have an impact on poverty status. This is the issue of *relative geography* mentioned at the beginning of the chapter. Countries' economies and politics have an identifiable impact on nearby countries. In terms of economies, a country that is surrounded by poor countries is itself more likely to be poor. This happens for several reasons. First, take the example of a landlocked country such as Chad. For this country to reach international markets, it must depend on the transportation infrastructure of the countries that surround it, including Sudan, Cameroon, and Nigeria. Unfortunately, these are countries with seriously deficient transportation systems and histories of occasional conflict. Thus, even if Chad had a reasonably well-functioning economy and stable politics, it would still be a "hostage to its neighbors" (in a phrase from Collier 2008) because it would have to depend on other countries to reach the sea. As Limão and Venables (2001) have explained, being landlocked is not a death sentence. Switzerland and Austria are landlocked and rich, for instance, but they can depend on rich neighbors with excellent infrastructure – such as Germany – to reach wider markets. As one interesting example of Africa's disadvantages, an analysis by Redding and Venables (2004) concluded that Zimbabwe's GDP per capita would be 24 percent higher if it had a seacoast, and 80 percent higher if it were located in central Europe.

Paul Collier's research (2008) has added another aspect to how neighbors can be a problem. The difficulty is not solely with infrastructure; countries also must depend on their neighbors as markets for their own goods. Switzerland and Austria have rich neighbors with big markets, such as Germany, Italy, and France, and that has helped Switzerland and Austria grow rich themselves. Unfortunately for Chad, neighbors such as Sudan, Niger, and the Central African Republic are poor countries with small markets. All of these countries have weak economic growth, which makes it much harder for Chad to develop a thriving economy. Weak regional economies, and country borders, also inhibit labor migration that can help pull people out of poverty. In the case of Mexico, the huge, high-wage economy of the United States provides an abundant source of jobs to Mexicans who come north looking for work, and who often send part of their wages home. Chad does not benefit from that kind of regional magnet economy. In sum, being landlocked and having to cross borders can impose high costs on a country's potential economic development.

Political problems associated with neighbors can also have distinct, though related, negative effects. The essence of this problem is that countries must deal with each other to coordinate their efforts on issues such as infrastructure, particularly if they are landlocked. Chad, even if it had the resources to build a fast rail line to reach the sea, cannot easily do so: it would have to work with the governments of Cameroon or Sudan in order to build any such link. In Switzerland's case, such a hurdle is not so high, since France and

Germany have stable governments. Chad, though, lives in a "bad neighborhood." Sudan and the Central African Republic have experienced bouts of serious instability and conflict. This is where the relative geography of neighbors is an especially serious problem.

Political instability in one country can impose all kinds of costs on a neighboring country, such as causing the second country to increase military expenditures, or cope with refugees fleeing conflict, or bring waves of disease from mass population movements. Further, the "bad neighborhood effect" can result in one country financing rebels in the second country. Alternatively, investors can be scared off because they associate (rightly or wrongly) the first country's corrupt institutions with the institutions in the second country (Bosker and Garretsen 2009). All these setbacks mean that a landlocked country in Africa has much more serious impediments to its economic growth than does a landlocked country in Europe. And unfortunately, Sub-Saharan Africa has an unusually large number of landlocked countries.

In fact, all of the above problems of remoteness and integration plague Sub-Saharan Africa especially (though not exclusively). Studies have repeatedly found that Sub-Saharan Africa's geography helps account for the lower levels of trade both on world markets and even among African countries, when compared to the levels for Asian or Latin American countries (see i.a. Faye *et al.* 2004, Limão and Venables 2001). Especially compared to some Asian countries, many African countries, because of their geography, have been hindered in exploiting their low labor costs to break into the market for assembling goods. The assembly of such goods, such as clothing or electronics, is something that has helped reduce poverty in a number of Asian countries such as Taiwan, Vietnam, or China. However, the Asian countries that have managed to use their low labor costs to their advantage all benefited from coastal locations, which meant that their transport costs were relatively low and integration into the world economy was relatively easy. Sub-Saharan Africa's number of landlocked countries also means more borders between countries, which makes shipping goods across borders more expensive because of tolls and customs fees. None of these difficulties are insurmountable, but they require particular policies to help overcome Sub-Saharan Africa's geographical disadvantages.

## Geography and institutions

How geography can impact poverty through institutions can be a controversial topic; here we will cover it briefly, including a scholarly debate it has provoked. Deficient institutions and governance often have a spatial dimension strongly associated with poverty. Areas where very poor people are concentrated tend to have a weaker civil society, less responsive government, and less involvement by NGOs (Chronic Poverty 2005: 33). Those concentrations of poverty may even arise as a *result* of state institutions and government. Areas that are politically marginalized typically have less government investment in projects for human and economic development. The reasons for that neglect can include a high proportion of people from a minority ethnic group living in an area, an area being a stronghold of an opposition political party, and distance from the capital or other centers of political power. It is thus possible that institutional neglect can make a place more remote, less integrated, and therefore poorer – though it can be difficult to isolate such factors' causal contribution to spatial poverty (Burke and Jayne 2010).

The scholarly debate concerns the relative importance of geography or institutions for explaining human and economic development. Writers such as Acemoglu *et al.* (2001) have claimed that geography exerts only an *indirect* influence on economic development by helping shape the kind of institutions that arose in a given territory. Acemoglu *et al.* claim that certain geographical factors induced European settlers to create either (1) "extractive institutions" that subjugated local populations and concentrated power and wealth in a small minority, or (2) more egalitarian, democratic institutions that fostered more widely shared prosperity. The key geographical factors were the disease burden (principally the incidence of malaria), the prevalence of natural endowments such as good soils and/or mineral wealth, and indigenous population densities sufficient to provide a large pool of labor. Where the disease burden was high, where there were abundant minerals such as gold, and where there was a large indigenous population, Europeans set up extractive institutions.

This thesis attempts to explain specifically how the geographical endowments in much of Latin America helped shape the undemocratic governance of colonialism. In Latin America, and eventually in Africa, Europeans created a social and political structure designed to protect the interests of the small, wealthy landowning class from the interests of the larger population. The contrast is with places such as North America, Australia, or New Zealand, which had low disease burdens and low indigenous population densities. More Europeans settled there, land ownership was broader based, and a more egalitarian rule of law was implemented. In short, institutions created under certain geographical conditions depended on undemocratic power concentration, while those created under other conditions were for the most part democratic.

The position held by Acemoglu *et al.* (2001), Rodrik *et al.* (2002), and Easterly and Levine (2003), that geography affects economic growth only through its impact on institutions, has been widely criticized (see i.a. Auer 2013, Carstensen and Grundlach 2006). One target of criticism is the way that these scholars have conducted their econometric analyses of the relative effects of geography and institutions. Critics of these analyses say that the causal relationships between geography, income levels, and institutions are extremely difficult to separate. For example, geography does impact institutions and institutions impact income levels, but geography also impacts income and institutions can impact geographical attributes (good governments can eradicate malaria, for example). Moreover, geographical disadvantages encompass a number of different potential effects on poverty, as we have seen. Though malaria and the disease burden are an important one, there are the additional factors of temperature, soil quality, precipitation, landlocked location, and potentially even such long-term influences as biodiversity and diffusion of technologies. These latter factors are typically glossed over by many of the strongest proponents of the institutions thesis.

It is important to remember that geography's effect on institutions presupposes direct effects on human health, environmental stability, and the productivity of economic systems (Sachs 2003). In terms of relative geography, evidence suggests that a country surrounded by neighbors with good institutions is more likely to trade with them and the rest of the world (Bosker and Garretsen 2009). There are also many different aspects of institutions. For example, markets are an institution that can be debilitated by spatial/geographical factors. Where terrain is difficult, individuals' access to markets can be impaired by a lack of adequate roads or otherwise high transportation costs. Where population densities are low, similarly, markets may be underdeveloped and access reduced. It may therefore be difficult for people to earn money by selling what they produce, or to trade for desired goods. Such conditions can contribute to income poverty as well as capability poverty, since deficient access to markets can limit the capability to earn a livelihood. Though the debate over the relative importance of geography or institutions for explaining poverty has not been definitively settled, in a sense the debate does not need to be resolved. Both spatial/geographical factors and institutions explain poverty levels, and they both affect each other.

## Spatial poverty and capabilities

Spatial/geographical factors can impact capabilities in a variety of ways, some obvious and some less so. To begin with, remoteness and isolation can deprive people of basic capabilities in health and education. The reason is that people living in remote and isolated places may have less access to health services and school opportunities. Reduced access to other public services can also undermine capabilities: lack of clean water and sanitation can be bad for a person's health, and lack of electricity can limit a person's ability to read and study at night, among many other possible effects. Peripheral areas, particularly isolated ones with minority ethnic groups, also can suffer from deprivations in political capabilities. People in peripheral areas may not be able to make their voices heard to distant policymakers. The deprivations here can be the result of both neglect (when political elites ignore people in remote or isolated places) and discrimination (when political elites purposefully deprive people of their rights). Such discrimination can lead to exclusion along a variety of dimensions (cultural, economic, political), which cripples both people's capabilities and functionings. To the extent that remote areas suffer from increased criminality or conflict, capabilities in basic personal security also suffer. Living in fear from banditry, terrorism, or other forms of crime can sharply reduce a person's quality of life.

Digging deeper, we see that spatial/geographical factors can weaken capabilities in a number of other ways. Having adequate food security and nutrition is a basic human entitlement, but this can be hard to achieve in places with low agricultural productivity due to poor soils. A place prone to famine can be seriously detrimental to a person's basic capabilities. Having adequate shelter is also typically considered a basic capability, in part for its influence on health and security. Some places make having adequate shelter much more difficult. A dwelling in a place prone to floods, landslides, epidemics, heavy pollution, or a host of other problems may well violate the right to adequate shelter. People who are forced to live in such places typically suffer from multiple overlapping deprivations. If they have to live in marginal areas, they are very likely victims of discrimination, with few economic and educational opportunities, unable to exercise political rights, and possibly afflicted with health problems as a result of their dwelling's location.

Remoteness and isolation in themselves can potentially deprive people of basic capabilities. Remember that the capabilities approach prioritizes "the actual freedom of choice a person has over alternative lives that he or she can live" (Sen 1990: 114). Living in an isolated area can reduce a person's freedom of choice. Depending on how severe the remoteness and lack of integration, a person may have reduced choice over her profession, over where she lives, over how and when she participates in her society, in short, over the life that she wants. For example, one of Nussbaum's basic capabilities is access to information (Nussbaum 2011). The idea is that everyone should have the ability to learn from a variety of sources that he or she chooses, so that choice is not unfairly restricted either by governments or other external circumstances. Living in a remote area, however, can restrict a person's access to information. Remote and rural areas in the developing world often lack access to landline telephones, television, and the internet. Media sources may also be limited, with inadequate access to newspapers or radio stations, or perhaps monopoly control over the supply of news (whether by a government or a single, dominant media outlet). In areas where the access to information is restricted, the free flow of ideas is limited, which amounts to a deprivation in both capabilities and functionings.

The capabilities approach primarily focuses on the individual as the main unit of analysis, that is, what can this person be and do? The rationale is that individuals' lives are the proper focus for our moral concern. However, the geographical disadvantages discussed in this chapter also point to the relevance of what are known as *collective capabilities* (see i.a. Alkire 2008, Ballet *et al.* 2007, Murphy 2014, Thorp *et al.* 2005). These are the capabilities that adhere to groups. Those groups could be village councils, women's clubs, unions, minority ethnic groups, or other kinds of communities. Groups can have a major impact on an individual's capabilities because groups help constitute what people value. For instance, a group's cultural norms of what is "good" influence what an individual wants for herself. Moreover, an individual's opportunity to attain what she values often depends on a group. The possibility to act together with others who share similar values gives rise to a collective agency that can benefit both the individual and the group (Evans 2002, Ibrahim 2006). Individual and collective capabilities are part of broader social structures and relationships, and the particular dynamic of concentrated spatial poverty demonstrates this interrelationship.

The disease burden, deficient agricultural endowments, and remoteness have distinct place-based natures, which means that everyone living in such a place is potentially negatively affected. This is the concentration effect of spatial poverty: in an area with geographical disadvantages, what individuals and groups can achieve can be seriously limited. *Both* the individual's capabilities and the group's suffer. Refer again to the example of the villagers in the Cambodian province of Ratanakiri, cited earlier. These villagers were so remote from centers of power that they were often neglected or ignored by political authorities. The village itself suffered from worse outcomes in health and education, and both individually and collectively the villagers were discriminated against by members of the majority Khmer ethnic group. This is a concentration of disadvantage that undermines the group's freedoms, not just the individual's. It is a good illustration of how what an individual can be and do often depends on the collectivity's opportunities.

Strengthening the group's opportunities thus can help expand the individual's opportunities, since they are often mutually interdependent. The possibility of collective action is the reason the group can be important for expanding the individual's capabilities. Individuals almost always have to organize in order to make broader societal change. Collective action is a vital organizational strategy to bargain, to share resources, to increase economic opportunities, to use democratic structures to press one's interests. Acting together, individuals can often achieve more than by acting alone. Acting together will also likely have more success at changing *un*democratic power structures and righting injustices. Collective action in this sense supports not just an individual's self-interest (to realize individual capabilities and functionings), but helps achieve a social good that can expand the group's capabilities and functionings as well.

The idea of collective capabilities is especially relevant for people living in poverty, who typically must organize to improve their situation since individual action is less likely to lead to change for the group beyond the individual. The concentration of multiple, overlapping geographical disadvantages makes individual efforts at escaping poverty much more difficult. In Ratanakiri, one individual might improve her situation by leaving the village, but even if she expands her capabilities that way, what she could be and do might still be limited if she is obviously from a minority group and hence could be subject to discrimination. Thus, because her capabilities depend in part on her collective membership, collective action is ultimately a more robust way of combating her individual and group-based capability deprivations.

It must be said that not all groups support an individual's capabilities, since some groups are exclusionary or repressive. Sen himself is also dubious that groups per se have capabilities beyond the sum total of individual capabilities (Davis 2015). Whether collective capabilities add that much to our understanding of an individual's freedoms is a question worth debating – and there are a number of other applications of the capabilities approach to spatial poverty that likewise merit discussion. Often the question comes down to whether a capability should count as "basic," such that its deprivation equates to poverty. One example is with mobility. As we have seen, remote and rugged areas have weaker road networks and higher transportation costs, hence people in such areas in lower income countries often have less mobility. Is this a problem? What would be the basic level of mobility to which everyone is entitled, so that we could ascertain when there is a fundamental capability deprivation in this area? Similarly, Nussbaum cites sociability and affiliation as aspects of basic capabilities. Here the idea is that people should have the freedom to choose their social relations, affiliating with the individuals and groups they want. However, isolation in some remote mountain village may limit a person's capabilities and functionings in this regard. If your social relations are limited to people from your own kinship group in your far-flung village, is that a fundamental capability deprivation? Finally, what should be the standard for basic capabilities in market access and earning a livelihood? Again, as we have seen, people in remote areas often have reduced access to markets and reduced choices for their livelihoods. In such geographical and spatial conditions, people's freedoms are definitely constrained, but it may be debatable as to whether those limitations constitute poverty.

The difficult geography discussed in this chapter does not automatically translate to capability deprivations. Obviously, it is possible to live in a far-flung, rugged, tropical place and still enjoy the full range of basic capabilities. The challenge with difficult geography is that it can make it harder to enjoy that full range. Recall Sen's insistence that a person's freedom must include some perspective on the quality, quantity, and diversity of her opportunities (Sen 1985, 1983). At its root, the problem of disadvantageous geography is that it often limits opportunities. It is not impossible to have adequate basic nutrition from farming in an arid place, but it is much harder. It is not impossible to gain an adequate education when living in a remote mountain village, but it is much harder. It is not impossible to earn a sustainable livelihood as a trader when you live far from roads, but it is much harder. Geographical factors can disadvantage a person's agency, that is, her actual freedom to make valuable choices for herself. People who live in areas with difficult geography are often already marginalized: if given a real choice, few would elect to live in the malarial swamp distant from roads, electricity, and health clinics. Therefore, individuals and groups who live with the geographical disadvantages that undermine basic capabilities may have already been deprived of the freedom to choose to live somewhere *without* those geographical disadvantages.

## Policy solutions

A key lesson from this chapter is that poverty can not only be caused or worsened by spatial/geographical factors, but also that poor people can be concentrated in certain areas, which then deserve more attention for policies to reduce poverty. One of the difficult aspects of spatial effects and poverty, however, is that those effects are often overlapping.

This means that the deprivations associated with living in a certain area can be multiple and reinforcing. Some "hotspots" have few roads, a high disease burden, poor soils, weak market opportunities, and/or deficient access to public services such as health clinics or sanitation. With such multiple disadvantages, it can be very difficult for an individual, family, or community to escape chronic poverty. Hence policies to reduce poverty associated with spatial factors should themselves be multifaceted to address the various deprivations. Altering geography might seem a Herculean task. In order to help poor people afflicted with spatial disadvantages, is it necessary to level mountains, make dry places rain, and give landlocked places access to the sea?

Certainly major investments can be required to overcome spatial and geographical disadvantages. But there are also smaller-scale policies that can help. We will first consider projects focused primarily on benefiting households and regions, and then turn to country-level policies. To begin with, extending access to public services for remote areas is a common and essential approach to reducing spatial poverty. Doing so can support both individual and collective capabilities. Rural areas in developing countries tend to have less access to clean water and sanitation. Similarly, building roads in rural areas should improve potential mobility for people and goods. One difficulty with such policies is that costs to expand public goods in remote areas are often high. Building roads through mountainous areas is very expensive, and extending the reach of water, sanitation, electricity or health services may bring remote areas onto the grid but may not serve many people in areas where population densities are low. Inadequate access to public services is not just a problem for rural areas, however. Remember that poverty can be spatially concentrated in urban areas too: slums or other marginalized settlements may often be deprived of clean water or sanitation.

Regionally targeted development programs have been tried in a number of countries. Ghana, for instance, devoted special attention to creating successful secondary schools in the more remote and impoverished northern part of the country. In China, breakneck economic growth has led to enormous income disparities between the richer eastern coastal regions and the poorer interior provinces. Several programs for the poorer areas attempted to ameliorate these disparities, such as subsidized loans for households and enterprises, food-for-work programs, and grants to governments to spur investment in disadvantaged areas (Higgins *et al.* 2010). Vietnam invested massively in expanding electricity access; in 1990, only 14 percent of the population had electricity, but by 2010, 97 percent did (Scott and Greenhill 2014). For places with deficient agricultural endowments there are a number of strategies. Increasing farmers' access to fertilizers can improve soil health. Irrigation projects such as pumps, wells, and large- or small-scale dams can help areas where managing water for agriculture is a problem (Sachs 2004). As noted in Box 5.1, supplying farmers with specially-bred seeds is another way of increasing productivity. An innovative service in Kenya provides accurate market price information by phone or online for agricultural goods such as maize and beans, which has helped farmers negotiate and make more money (Bird 2019).

Because the disease burden disproportionately affects some places and is severely detrimental to basic capabilities, it is a particular focus for policies to promote human development. Though international efforts to combat malaria are perhaps the most prominent example, there are programs for other parasites and diseases endemic to tropical areas. Such programs can involve aspects of infrastructure to improve a population's health status, such as building delivery systems for clean water or sanitary sewage systems. One such project that involved providing safe water, larvicide, and health education has helped drastically reduce the toll of guinea worm disease. Cases of this disease fell from 3.5 million people infected in 1986 to fewer than 11,000 20 years later (see Levine 2004). Reducing the disease burden is often linked to technological assistance to lessen lower-income countries' gap with the rich world, particularly with vaccines. Strategies to improve health in places with a high disease burden are essential not only to help people live lives that they value, but also to fight economic poverty by reducing disease's toll on productivity.

Policies to address the spatial dimensions of poverty should also take into account collective capabilities, since minority groups can disproportionately suffer from remoteness, exclusion, and attendant deprivations. Because some groups can be more deprived than others, there is a strong argument that they deserve additional resources from poverty reduction programs. Such an approach might target regions where people from minority groups are concentrated, and/or target minority group households even in a region where most people are from another group and better off. The idea is to reduce inequalities not just between regions but between people, and to promote social inclusion of people who may often be discriminated against or disproportionately disadvantaged in some other way. One example is a program in Laos that relocated entire ethnic minority villages in an effort to improve their access to markets and the range of public services. While this strategy may bring some benefits, it also shows the difficulties of trying to help minority groups suffering from multiple deprivations, since moving entire villages raises questions about coerced displacement and disruption of the villagers' cultural traditions and distinctness (Bechstedt *et al.* 2007). Besides steps to improve people's economic wellbeing and reduce capability deprivations, policies for social inclusion can also have as a goal promoting cross-cultural understanding and tolerance among groups through multilingual education (Epprecht *et al.* 2011). Such programs can decrease cultural distance between groups, and value minority groups' cultures.

Increasing trade can play a vital role in reducing income poverty at both the household and the country levels. There are a number of ways to reduce remoteness, increase integration, and foster more trade for poor countries. The first is to lower trade barriers by reducing tariffs and trade quotas. Establishing free trade zones and reforming customs and border protocols can help increase trade for landlocked countries whose goods must often traverse multiple borders to reach world markets. With reduced customs restrictions, the hope is that trade between neighbors will improve, bringing "spillover effects" of economic growth that can raise people's incomes. Another strategy for increasing trade is Collier's (2008) suggestion that a country can become a "haven" in a particular regional sector. The idea is that a country can strive to have noticeably better, more transparent policies in one industry such as finance, thereby becoming the center of finance for its region. Free trade does not always benefit the poor, but as a general principle most economists would agree that increasing poor countries' participation in world markets has overall positive outcomes (see i.a. Buys *et al.* 2006, IMF 2007, World Bank 2007).

Investing in infrastructure is another policy strategy relevant both to overcoming various spatial disadvantages as well as promoting trade. Better transportation infrastructure – whether roads, rail lines, or port facilities – can make trade easier and more cost effective. A key goal is to improve access to the coast for landlocked countries. For Chad, improving transportation links to the sea via Cameroon could be an important boost to the economy of both countries, again through spillover effects. Part of what makes such infrastructure improvements difficult, though, is that they typically do depend on the cooperation and coordination between neighboring countries. Nonetheless, such regionally focused projects should be a priority for their potential to benefit several countries at once.

If we examine the opposite side of the coin from spatial/geographic *dis*advantages, we can see which spatial/geographic factors are actually beneficial for economic growth. Contemporary thinking on this question has echoed and provided empirical support for the theories that Adam Smith proposed in his epochal work *The Wealth of Nations* in 1776. As Smith said, countries that have good harbors on the seacoast, or that have sea-navigable rivers, are more likely to be prosperous. In our terms, those countries are likely to be less remote from world markets, and may find it easier to integrate into those markets. In fact, Bloom, Canning and Sevilla (2003) have found that the percentage of a country's land that is within 100 kilometers of the coast is a good predictor of that country's income level. The other key variables in Bloom *et al.*'s analysis are measurements of a country's maximum average monthly temperature, average monthly rainfall, and the distribution of rainfall over the months of the year. They claim that these four variables account for 60 percent of cross-country comparisons of income per capita. There are a few other factors that are also associated with higher incomes. These include a low average elevation (thereby obviating the problem of difficult, mountainous terrain), and neighboring countries with good institutions and sizeable markets.

The good news is that the international development community has acknowledged the need to help countries address geographical disadvantages. Infrastructure projects such as building dams, power plants, airports, phone and broadband networks, as well as roads, rail lines and ports, have been an objective for several decades. Countries such as Rwanda have benefited from assistance to construct a fiber optic network to improve communications within the country and the rest of the world, reducing this land-locked country's remoteness. The Philippines has received aid to improve port facilities and thereby boost trade, and Sri Lanka has been assisted with building expressways to improve transportation, as two further examples. Likewise, programs to develop vaccines for diseases prevalent in the lower-income countries are receiving increasing attention. For instance, countries such as Canada, Norway, and Italy, along with private donors such as the Gates Foundation, have committed more than a billion dollars to incentivize the development of vaccines for malaria, polio, rotavirus, and meningitis.

## Conclusion

Imagine that you live in a rural area of Papua New Guinea. You most likely live in a rugged place: over half of that country is mountainous or hilly. Like most rural people in the country, you live on and partly from the land. However, the land you live on is not very good. It is steep, with bad soil, has heavy rainfall, and is prone to flooding; in fact, nearly 60 percent of the land in Papua New Guinea is considered to be "low" or "very low" in quality (Allen *et al.* 2005). With land like that, it is no wonder you would have trouble growing enough food for yourself and your family. You therefore probably suffer from health problems due to protein and other nutrient deficiencies, and your children's growth will be stunted. Why not just buy better food? Living in such an area, you certainly would not be able to earn much of a living from agriculture, but there are few other jobs.

Even if you owned enough land that you had surplus crops to sell, your income would likely be limited by the very bad roads, which make it difficult to get your crops to market. The infrastructure throughout much of Papua New Guinea is compromised not only by mountain ranges but also by big rivers and swamps. Mobility is not easy in this country. That means that if you need any serious health care, you probably have a long journey, if you can afford it at all. To top it off, parts of the country have significant risk of earthquakes and volcanoes, which means that your house, your livelihood and indeed your life are less secure (Allen *et al.* 2001). If you lived in such a place, then, you would find it much harder to earn a respectable income. Your opportunities to choose a different life for yourself would also most likely be limited. In such a place, you would see first-hand how spatial and geographical disadvantages can worsen capability poverty by limiting opportunities in health, education, political rights, and livelihoods.

These overlapping disadvantages affect not just you but many others in your community. Economic opportunities in a locality or a region may be limited because transportation of goods is more expensive in landlocked or rugged terrain than it is along the coast. Likewise, a high disease burden typically reduces worker productivity, potentially impairing your own ability to earn money as well as economic growth for your whole region. These factors amplify each other and add up over time, so that a country that is landlocked, with a high disease burden and poor soils, will almost certainly have lower growth rates historically than a country without these disadvantages. According to Henderson *et al.* (2018), geographical variables explain about half of worldwide economic activity. This is why geographical difficulties have been termed a "tax on development" (Woods 2004). Think of it this way: economic growth has been like a race. The countries with more difficult spatial and geographic conditions do not start out the race even with other countries, and they have more hurdles to jump. Because productivity, technological innovation, and economic growth have mutually reinforcing effects, those countries that start out ahead have also found it easier to lengthen their lead on the geographically disadvantaged countries (McCord and Sachs 2013).

Does this mean that spatial and geographic problems condemn some countries or people to poverty forever? Absolutely not – there is no geographical determinism. Being landlocked, mountainous, remote, tropical, or with a high disease burden does not preclude human flourishing. Such features are only some of the many that can contribute to poverty. And while spatial disadvantages can overlap and worsen poverty, they are only part of an explanation for why individuals are poor. It is easy to think of places that share some of these disadvantages but that are nonetheless prosperous, such as landlocked Switzerland or tropical zone Singapore. Moreover, quite a few countries outside the temperate zone have made great strides in malaria eradication, including Paraguay, Costa Rica, and Malaysia – even Papua New Guinea has significantly reduced malaria incidence in recent years through the provision of insecticide-treated bed nets and better diagnostic and surveillance tools. Nonetheless, it has been estimated that geographical "hotspots" will account for most of the world's extreme poverty by 2030 (Cohen *et al.* 2019). Overcoming spatial deprivations will require coordinated effort at the global and national levels to support basic capabilities in health and education, promote market opportunities through access, integration, and information, and reform state institutions to make them more effective.

## Discussion questions

1 How do geographical disadvantages negatively impact individual and collective capabilities? How should programs to combat those disadvantages understand the relationship between individual and collective capabilities?

2    In what ways can geographical and spatial factors be a poverty trap?
3    What are the dangers of assuming a "geographical determinism"?
4    What are the limits of geographical/spatial explanations? What can they *not* explain in terms of why places or people are poor? Do geographical/spatial factors do a better job of explaining why some places get rich or why some places remain poor?
5    What should be the top global priority to ameliorate the geographical disadvantages that can exacerbate poverty? What is your rationale?
6    Some development experts, as in the 2009 World Development Report, have said that spatial inequalities are inevitable, and that economic growth will always be uneven. According to this perspective, the key to economic development is to promote population density, urbanization, and infrastructure projects in the areas that are most economically promising and suffer least from geographical disadvantages. Critics of this perspective say that it will only promote further divergence and inequality of opportunities. What do you think?

## Online resources

- Explore Worldmapper to see what you can learn about the global spatial distribution of various indicators related to poverty and inequality: https://worldmapper.org/
- The Global Infrastructure Connectivity Alliance has many different data visualizations relevant to human and economic development: http://gica.global/key-maps-search
- A wide range of poverty maps is hosted at NASA's Socioeconomic Data and Applications Center: https://sedac.ciesin.columbia.edu/data/collection/povmap/maps/gallery/search

## Further reading

Bird, Kate. 2019. "Addressing Spatial Poverty Traps." *Chronic Poverty Advisory Network*, Overseas Development Institute, February.
Diamond, Jared. 2005. *Guns, Germs, and Steel: The Fates of Human Societies*. New York: W.W. Norton.
Kanbur, Ravi, and Anthony J. Venables, eds. 2005. *Spatial Inequality and Development*. Oxford: Oxford University Press.
Sachs, Jeffrey D., Andrew D. Mellinger and John L. Gallup. 2001. "The Geography of Poverty and Wealth." *Scientific American* (March): 70–75.
Woods, Dwayne. 2003. "Bringing Geography Back In: Civilizations, Wealth, and Poverty." *International Studies Review* 5: 343–354.

## Works cited

Abadie, Alberto. 2004. "Poverty, Political Freedom, and the Roots of Terrorism," National Bureau of Economic Research Working Paper No. 10859, October.
Acemoglu, Daron, Simon Johnson and James A. Robinson. 2001. "The colonial origins of comparative development: an empirical investigation." *American Economic Review* 91.5: 1369–1401.
Alkire, S. 2008. "Using the Capability Approach: Prospective and Evaluative Analyses," in Comim, Flavio, Mozaffar Qizilbash and Sabina Alkire, eds. *The Capability Approach: Concepts, Measures and Application*. Cambridge, UK: Cambridge University Press.
Allen, Bryant, R. Michael Bourke and John Gibson. 2005. "Poor rural places in Papua New Guinea." *Asia Pacific Viewpoint* 46.2: 201–217.
Allen, Bryant, R. Michael Bourke and Luke Hanson. 2001. "Dimensions of PNG village agriculture," in *Food security for Papua New Guinea: Proceedings of the Papua New Guinea food and nutrition 2000 conference*. Australian Centre for International Agricultural Research, Canberra.

Auer, Raphael A. 2013. "Geography, institutions, and the making of comparative development." *Journal of Economic Growth* 18.2: 179–215.

Ballet, Jérôme, Jean-Luc Dubois and François-Régis Mahieu. 2007. "Responsibility for each other's freedom: agency as the source of collective capability." *Journal of Human Development* 8.2: 185–201.

Barrett, Christopher B., and Leah EM Bevis. 2015. "The self-reinforcing feedback between low soil fertility and chronic poverty." *Nature Geoscience* 8.12: 907–912.

Bechstedt, Hans-Dieter, V. Gilbos and O. Souksavat. 2007. "Impact of Public Expenditures on Ethnic groups and Women–Lao PDR, Phase 2." Poverty and Social Impact Assessment (PSIA) Final Report. Part 1.

Bird, Kate. 2019. "Addressing Spatial Poverty Traps." Chronic Poverty Advisory Network, Overseas Development Institute, February.

Bird, Kate, Andy McKay and Isaac Shinyekwa. 2010. "Isolation and poverty: the relationship between spatially differentiated access to goods and services and poverty." Overseas Development Institute Working Paper 322, December.

Bird, Kate, David Hulme, Karen Moore and Andrew Shepherd. 2002. "Chronic poverty and remote rural areas." Chronic Poverty Research Centre Working Paper 13.

Bloom, David E., David Canning and Jaypee Sevilla. 2003. "Geography and poverty traps." *Journal of Economic Growth* 8.4: 355–378.

Bosker, Maarten, and Harry Garretsen. 2009. "Economic development and the geography of institutions." *Journal of Economic Geography* 9: 295–328.

Bosker, Maarten, and Harry Garretsen. 2012. "Economic geography and economic development in Sub-Saharan Africa." *The World Bank Economic Review* 26.3: 443–485.

Buhaug, Halvard *et al.* 2011. "It's the local economy, stupid! Geographic wealth dispersion and conflict outbreak location." *Journal of Conflict Resolution* 55.5: 814–840.

Burke, William J., and Thom S. Jayne. 2010. "Spatial disadvantages or spatial poverty traps: Household evidence from rural Kenya." Overseas Development Institute Working Paper 327, December.

Buys, Piet, Uwe Deichmann and David Wheeler. 2006. *Road Network Upgrading and Overland Trade Expansion in Sub-Saharan Africa.* Vol. 4097. Washington, DC: World Bank.

Carstensen, Kai, and Erich Gundlach. 2006. "The Primacy of Institutions Reconsidered: Direct Income Effect of Malaria Presence." *The World Bank Economic Review* 20.3: 309–339.

Castells-Quintana, David, Maria del Pilar Lopez-Uribe and Thomas K.J. McDermott. 2017. "Geography, institutions and development: a review of the long-run impacts of climate change." *Climate and Development* 9.5: 452–470.

Chomitz, Kenneth. 2007. *At Loggerheads? Agricultural Expansion, Poverty Reduction, and Environment in the Tropical Forests.* Washington, DC: World Bank.

Chronic Poverty Research Center. 2005. *The Chronic Poverty Report 2004–05*, Chapter 3: 'Where do chronically poor people live?' Manchester: Chronic Poverty Research Center.

Cohen, Jennifer L., Raj M. Desai, Homi Kharas. 2019. "Spatial Targeting of Poverty Hotspots," in Homi Kharas, John W. McArthur and Izumi Ohno, eds. *Leave No One Behind: Time for Specifics on the Sustainable Development Goals.* Washington, DC: Brookings Institution Press.

Collier, Paul. 2008. *The Bottom Billion: Why the Poorest Countries Are Failing and What Can Be Done About It.* New York: Oxford University Press.

Davis, John B. 2015. "Agency and the Process Aspect of Capability Development: Individual Capabilities, Collective Capabilities, and Collective Intentions." (1 July 1. *Filosofía de la Economía*, forthcoming. http://ssrn.com/abstract=2625673

Dell, Melissa, Benjamin F. Jones, and Benjamin A. Olken. 2014. "What do we learn from the weather? The new climate-economy literature." *Journal of Economic Literature* 52.3: 740–798.

Easterly, William, and Ross Levine. 2003. "Tropics, germs, and crops: how endowments influence economic development." *Journal of Monetary Economics* 50.1: 3–39.

Epprecht, Michael, Daniel Müller and Nicholas Minot. 2011. "How remote are Vietnam's ethnic minorities? An analysis of spatial patterns of poverty and inequality." *The Annals of Regional Science* 46.2: 349–368.

Evans, Peter. 2002. "Collective capabilities, culture, and Amartya Sen's *Development as Freedom.*" *Studies in Comparative International Development* 37.2: 54–60.

Fafchamps, Marcel, and Christine Moser. 2003. "Crime, isolation and law enforcement." *Journal of African Economies* 12.4: 625–671.

Faye, Michael, John W. McArthur, Jeffrey Sachs and Thomas Snow. 2004. "The challenges facing landlocked developing countries." *Journal of Human Development* 5.1: 31–68.

Forum for Agricultural Research in Africa. 2006. *Framework for African Agricultural Productivity.* Accra, Ghana: Forum for Agricultural Research in Africa.

Gallup, John Luke, Jeffrey D. Sachs and Andrew Mellinger. 1999. "Geography and Economic Development." Center for International Development Working Paper No. 1, March.

Hausmannn, Ricardo. 2001. "Prisoners of geography." *Foreign Policy* 122.1: 44–53.

Henderson, J. Vernon, Tim Squires, Adam Storeygard, and David Weil. 2018. "The Global Spatial Distribution of Economic Activity: Nature, History, and the Role of Trade." *Quarterly Journal of Economics* 133.1: 357–406.

Henderson, J. Vernon, Zmarak Shalizi and Anthony J. Venables. 2001. "Geography and development." *Journal of Economic Geography* 1: 81–105.

Higgins, Kate, Kate Bird and Dan Harris. 2010. "Policy responses to the spatial dimensions of poverty." Overseas Development Institute Working Paper 328, December.

Ibrahim, Solava S. 2006. "From individual to collective capabilities: the capability approach as a conceptual framework for self-help." *Journal of Human Development* 7.3: 397–416.

International Fund for Agricultural Development (IFAD). 2000. *Annual Report 2000: Working with the Rural Poor.* Rome: IFAD.

International Monetary Fund. 2007. *Regional Economic Outlook: Sub-Saharan Africa.* Washington, DC: IMF.

Ironside, Jeremy. 2009. "Development – in whose name? Cambodia's economic development and its indigenous communities – from self-reliance to uncertainty," in Peter J. Hammer, ed. *Living on the Margins: Minorities and Borderlines in Cambodia and Southeast Asia.* Detroit, MI: Wayne State University, Center for Khmer Studies.

Jalan, Jyotsna and Martin Ravallion. 1997. "Spatial Poverty Traps." Policy Research Working Paper 1862. Washington, DC: World Bank, December.

Jalan, Jyotsna and Martin Ravallion. 2002. "Geographic poverty traps? A micro model of consumption growth in rural China." *Journal of Applied Econometrics* 17: 329–346.

Kanbur, Ravi, and Anthony J. Venables, eds. 2005. *Spatial Inequality and Development.* Oxford: Oxford University Press.

Krugman, Paul and Anthony J. Venables. 1995. "Globalization and the Inequality of Nations." *The Quarterly Journal of Economics* 110.4: 857–880.

Levine, Ruth, ed. 2004. *Millions Saved: Proven Successes in Global Health.* Vol. 3. No. 3. Washington, DC: Peterson Institute.

Limão, Nuno, and Anthony J. Venables. 2001. "Infrastructure, geographical disadvantage, transport costs, and trade." *The World Bank Economic Review* 15.3: 451–479.

McCord, Gordon C. and Jeffrey D. Sachs. 2013. *Development, Structure, and Transformation: Some Evidence on Comparative Economic Growth.* No. w19512. National Bureau of Economic Research.

Minot, Nicholas, Bob Baulch and Michael Epprecht. 2006. *Poverty and Inequality in Vietnam: Spatial Patterns and Geographic Determinants.* Washington, DC: International Food Policy Research Institute.

Murphy, Michael. 2014. "Self-determination as a collective capability: the case of indigenous peoples." *Journal of Human Development and Capabilities* 15.4: 320–334.

Nunn, Nathan, and Diego Puga. 2012. "Ruggedness: the blessing of bad geography in Africa." *Review of Economics and Statistics* 94.1: 20–36.

Nussbaum, Martha. 2011. *Creating Capabilities: The human development approach.* Boston, MA: Harvard University Press.

Østby, Gudrun, Ragnhild Nordås and Jan Ketil Rød. 2009. "Regional inequalities and civil conflict in sub-Saharan Africa." *International Studies Quarterly* 53.2: 301–324.

Ravallion, Martin, and Quentin Wodon. 1999. "Poor areas, or only poor people?" *Journal of Regional Science* 39.4: 689–711.

Redding, Stephen, and Anthony J. Venables. 2004. "Economic geography and international inequality." *Journal of International Economics* 62.1: 53–82.

Rodrik, Dani, Francesco Trebbi and Arvind Subramanian. 2002. *Institutions Rule: The Primacy of Institutions Over Integration and Geography in Economic Development.* Washington, DC: IMF.

Sachs, Jeffrey. 2001. "Tropical Underdevelopment." NBER Working Paper No. 8119. National Bureau of Economic Research, Cambridge, MA.

Sachs, Jeffrey. 2003. "Institutions Don't Rule: Direct Effects of Geography on Per Capita Income," National Bureau of Economic Research Working Paper No. 9490, February.

Sachs, Jeffrey *et al.* 2004. "Ending Africa's poverty trap." *Brookings papers on economic activity* 1: 117–240.

Scott, A. and Greenhill, R. 2014. *Turning the Lights on Sustainable Energy and Development in Viet Nam.* Development Progress, Environment Case Study. London: Overseas Development Institute.

Sen, Amartya. 1983. "Poor, relatively speaking." *Oxford Economic Papers*, New Series 35.2: 153–169.

Sen, Amartya. 1985. "A sociological approach to the measurement of poverty: a reply to Professor Peter Townsend." *Oxford Economic Papers*, New Series 37.4: 669–676.

Sen, Amartya. 1990. "Justice: means versus freedoms." *Philosophy and Public Affairs* 19: 111–121.

Smith, K. M., Machalaba, C. C., Seifman, R., Feferholtz, Y., Karesh, W. B. 2019. "Infectious disease and economics: The case for considering multi-sectoral impacts." *One Health* 7: 100080.

Thorp, Rosemary, Frances Stewart and Amrik Heyer. 2005. "When and how far is group formation a route out of chronic poverty?" *World Development* 33.6: 907–920.

Woods, Dwayne. 2004. "Latitude or rectitude: geographical or institutional determinants of development." *Third World Quarterly* 25.8: 1405.

World Bank. 2007. *Accelerating Development Outcomes in Africa-Progress and Change in the Africa Action Plan.* Washington, DC: World Bank.

World Development Report. 2009. *Reshaping Economic Geography.* Washington, DC: World Bank.

World Health Organization. "Fact sheet on vector-borne diseases." 2020. http://who.int/newsroom/fact-sheets/detail/vector-borne-diseases. Accessed March 2020.

# 6    Race, class, gender, and poverty

*Serena Cosgrove*

## Learning objectives

- Familiarize yourself with the basic concepts of social difference, including race, ethnicity, social class, gender, and sexuality.
- Understand how forms of social difference – race, ethnicity, social class, gender, among others – affect people's capabilities and can contribute to poverty.
- Analyse how multiple forms of social difference interact to exacerbate poverty.
- Consider how people on the margins are uniquely positioned to use their oppositional knowledge to create change and promote inclusion.

## Vignette 6.1

*Gladis is a young indigenous woman from Sololá, Guatemala (see Figure 6.1). In Central America, Guatemala still experiences high levels of violence even though the 30-year civil war ended in 1996. Guatemala enjoys a fairly high level of economic development at the aggregate level, but income inequality and poverty are severe for the country's majority Maya, comprised of over 20 different indigenous groups, most with their own languages. From an early age Gladis observed that her women relatives and women in her community suffered a lot, often in silence. Women were expected to have as many children as they could. Women were expected to do all the unpaid domestic work but simultaneously had to generate income because even if male partners or other relatives had jobs, it was often not enough to ensure the family could eat. According to Gladis, their culture says that men are better, that men are the only ones who have the right to study. Women only serve to work, to cook. Gladis saw how her women family members also did so much for their communities: active in church events, charity and service activities, and always stepped up to take care of the community when there was a crisis due to drought, bad weather, or political crisis. Women work around the clock and seldom get to have fun or time off.*

*Gladis began to ask why women suffer so much. Why is it women's role to work so hard and suffer so much? How could it be that her culture dictates that women must suffer? Then Gladis had a flash of insight: culture is not something that exists outside of us. We re-create culture through our actions. The point is not to continue suffering but to transform these oppressive practices. So, Gladis began to talk to other young women in her community about their dreams. They wanted to study; they wanted to become professionals and serve their communities in new and more impactful ways. They wanted to be social workers, teachers, nurses, and lawyers. They wanted to choose when they would marry and have children. They wanted to know about their legal rights, and they wanted to know more about their bodies because many did not know how women actually get pregnant or why they have their periods.*

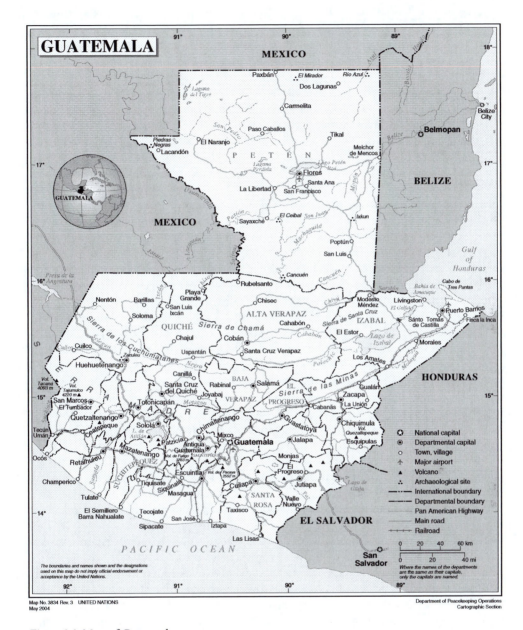

*Figure 6.1* Map of Guatemala
Source: Map No. 3834 Rev. 3 UNITED NATIONS May 2004.

*These conversations led Gladis and this group of young women to form an organization. First, they sought out mentors from women's organizations to teach them the topics they wanted to know. Then they developed training materials which they take to the schools where they teach girls and boys about the rights of young women and men; and they teach basic sexual education. In this process, Gladis and her young women's group have begun to transform their own lives and the lives of others. They are transforming the very cultural limitations put on them. Through conversations with their elders, they are in active conversation about what aspects of their culture are vital for the community, such as values and practices around the importance of nature, community and family and speaking their own language. Today, Gladis continues to run this organization and each year a new cohort of young women take up teaching in the schools and supporting each other's dreams. Gladis is now finishing law school, working towards her career goal of defending women's and indigenous rights. Gladis not only found a way to earn a law degree, but she decided to bring along other young women in her community, showing them that change is possible.*

## Introduction

Like Gladis, who is a young, poor and Indigenous woman from the highlands of rural Guatemala, many people around the world face poverty and discrimination due to social difference. Gladis faces obstacles because she is Indigenous in a country that preferences mixed race or Ladino Guatemalans over the Indigenous groups who comprise 40 percent of the population; this racial hierarchy privileges those of mixed or European descent over those of Indigenous heritage and makes it harder if you are Indigenous to earn a living, get an education, and get access to healthcare. Gladis also faces obstacles because she is a woman in a patriarchal society, including Guatemala, in general, and her community, in particular. Gladis faces obstacles because she is poor and comes from a rural community: around the world, the worst poverty can be found in the countryside where public services often do not reach remote communities. Gladis also faces obstacles because she is young and power is held by adult men in her community. Nonetheless, Gladis, like many people who face obstacles due to social difference that limit their capabilities/contribute to capability poverty, decided to do something about her marginalization and poverty by working with others to create change. Agency and activism from the margins is a common theme in this chapter.

Forms of social exclusion such as race, ethnicity, gender, sexuality, and social class are embedded in societies: this means that people accept and reproduce these differences as "normal" and "the way things are." This, in turn, creates opportunities and disadvantages between people and can lead to discrimination and capability deprivation for subaltern or subordinate groups. Privilege, "the right to benefits or immunity granted to specific people or groups" (Lindsey 2021: 19) is accorded to some and gives some groups advantages in society. For example, men from patriarchal societies benefit from control over resources and access to opportunities and decision-making positions while women, girls, and gender minorities often do not. In societies where racial differences are used to determine access to resources or opportunities, the outcomes are seldom positive for the other group(s). We see this in the United States where a history of slavery and discrimination against African Americans makes it much harder for African Americans to achieve wellbeing than for whites. Furthermore, ethnic differences have been used to justify genocide, sexual violence, and discrimination as illustrated by multiple examples from around the world. There is the treatment of Native Americans by the United States government or how Indigenous communities around the world have been dispossessed and oppressed by European colonial powers in the past and subjected to the ongoing pressures of settler incursion in the present. During the Rwandan genocide in 1994, for example, the Hutu-led government killed 850,000 Tutsis and moderate Hutus in 100 days.

Differences due to social class and economic stratification also privilege some and exclude many others. For instance, income inequality – as measured by the Gini Index (see Chapter 3) – is high in countries where a rich minority has much more income than the majority poor. Income alone is not the only economic factor that contributes to class-based exclusion; social capital – the networks, contacts, friends, and access to certain opportunities – that people have are also disproportionately affected by social class: wealthy people often have more contacts that will help them generate wealth and wellbeing than poorer people with limited access to resources.

This chapter is about how forms of social difference can limit people's capabilities and cause poverty. Obviously, there are many forms of social difference that we cannot cover adequately in this chapter, such as ability, citizenship and migration status, religion, to mention a few; please see the further reading section at the end of the chapter for additional sources if you want to learn more. Leadership from the margins is key; it is very important to understand the ways in which people who are minoritized or marginalized can simultaneously be key contributors to their communities, not just at home, but within their wider communities and across the countries where they live. Like Gladis, people on the margins are often the ones to volunteer on community development projects or set up soup kitchens and lead advocacy efforts during economic or political crisis (Cosgrove 2010). Furthermore, people on the margins often leverage their oppositional knowledge (Hill Collins 2014) to organize and fight against the structural manifestations of difference that affect their communities.

This chapter begins with defining race and ethnicity, social class, and gender and sexuality and how these forms of difference can contribute to exclusion and poverty. Then, the chapter looks more deeply at the differences between men and women (and often people with minority gender identities as well) and how gender affects capabilities. Women and gender minorities – as well as people who are excluded due to their sexuality, race/ethnicity, abilities, and other forms of social difference – are not just more likely to earn less income than men or those who benefit from heterosexist societies, racial and ethnic hierarchies, ableist ideologies, and so on; they are also more likely to face discrimination and harassment and suffer diminished capabilities and functionings. Unpacking the connection between social difference and poverty will lead us to an analysis of how the agency, empowerment and participation of people on the margins can benefit all in countries around the world.

## Understanding race and ethnicity

Definitions of race and ethnicity vary by epoch and place and have deep historical roots in discrimination, exclusion, poverty, and the preservation of elite power and control over resources and opportunities, or what Ijeoma Oluo describes as "the profit and comfort of the white race, specifically, rich white men" in reference to the United States (2018: 32).[1] Race generally refers to the unitary, socially-imposed hierarchy that separates people into different groups often dependent on how they are perceived. Classifications into racial groups are theoretically based on differences in the biophysical traits (Smedley 1998: 693), but these differences get translated into political, economic, and social advantages for some to the detriment of others, who I will refer to as subordinate or subaltern groups. This is racism or "a prejudice against someone based on race, when those prejudices are reinforced by systems of power" (Oluo 2018: 27). Though different from country to country, the institutionalization and assumptions that "this is how things are" mean that many people are raised in societies that assign certain meanings to some perceived physical variations and this is called "race." "Race is frequently a hegemonic discourse, and race appears to be part of the natural order of things; i.e., both dominant and subordinate peoples take for granted the idea that social divisions have a biological basis" (Hangen 2005: 51). Perceived racial and ethnic differences are used to stratify social groups: certain races or ethnicities use their power and status in society to elevate themselves at the cost of groups who are treated as inferior.

In the United States, for example, racial and ethnic differences have been used historically to discriminate against African Americans and Native Americans as well as other people of color and immigrant groups. Seldom, though, is the past just in the past: ongoing discrimination against certain racial or ethnic groups becomes structural; it is institutionalized and supported by legal frameworks and the branches of government at the local, regional, and national levels. These structures, rules, and scripts are supported by the status quo and often go unchallenged. Many "studies have concentrated on how the concept of race, crafted by a dominant group, operates as a discourse to categorize and exclude groups from political and economic power" (Hangen 2005: 51). Nonetheless, race and ethnicity can also serve as a powerful form of identification for subaltern or marginalized groups and "in some form…has been and continues to be a salient basis for survival, resistance and opposition" (Hangen 2005: 51). Many oppositional movements around the world – comprised of people who are discriminated against and their allies – have emerged to demand change and inclusion; exclusion can serve as a rallying point for challenging injustice.

Ethnicity, on the other hand, can be similar to exclusionary racial categories such as in Guatemala where European descended and mixed race Ladinos hold more power than the Indigenous Maya and other Indigenous groups in the country. Ethnicity can also apply to the multiplicity of groups – either cultural, linguistic, or locational – with which people identify themselves. Sociologist Dalton Conley describes the ethnic complexities people have to negotiate in the following anecdote:

> I have a friend who was born in Korea to Korean parents, but as an infant, she was adopted by an Italian family in Italy. Ethnically, she feels Italian: she eats Italian food, she speaks Italian, she knows Italian history and culture. She knows nothing about Korean history and culture. But when she comes to the United States, she's treated racially as Asian.

(2003)

I am sure this story resonates with a number of readers: either many of us have multiple ethnic identities ourselves, we know people who do, or we have seen examples of when someone is assigned to a particular group because of how they are perceived, not necessarily how they self-identify. Racial and ethnic categories are social constructions – and by this I mean that they get reproduced by members of a particular culture to the extent that they are normalized and institutionalized – and are often used to justify discriminatory treatment of people as well as used by people themselves as a sense of identification and community.

Interestingly, race has not always been a category that held significance for societies, especially those that emerged from around the Mediterranean. As anthropologist Audrey Smedley explains in her history of the concept of race, "Historically biological variation did not have significant social meaning" (1998: 693). In ancient times, racial categories often did not serve to identify or separate different groups. What made someone a citizen or elite member of a society was not their race as much as the place where they were from, their social class, language group, kinship, occupation, and/or religion. Yes, difference and extreme disparities between people existed in ancient times, but seldom due to perceived racial differences: elites and slaves could be from any nation or place.

Racial hierarchies developed in the US colonies, for example, as a strategy to keep disadvantaged and marginalized groups separate. Bacon's Rebellion, the 1676 uprising in Virginia, was carried out by white frontiersmen, indentured servants, and African slaves concerned by the lack of support from local authorities for safety, security, and the excesses of local elites; together they rose up against their employers which led colonial authorities to implement measures to keep these groups separated through miscegenation laws (laws prohibiting interracial marriages), prohibitions against travel without authorization, and a passport system requiring anyone traveling from one place to another to show papers demonstrating their freedom to travel. It is at this point that race as a socially constructed hierarchy solidifies: we begin to see "[r]ace as social status is in the eye of the beholder" (Smedley 1998: 697). Howard Zinn argues that racism in the United States owes its existence not to the innate differences between whites, African Americans, or Native Americans but to a conscious move on the part of white elites to protect their interests at the expense of all other peoples (1980). Based on the racist ideologies against African Americans and Native Americans, the United States has a long history of xenophobic treatment of people perceived as being racially or ethnically different. "Xenophobia literally means fear and hatred of foreigners…characterized as individual prejudice, animosity, or bias towards foreigners" (Lee 2019: 7). Similar to how racism becomes institutionalized, xenophobia manifests itself in legal frameworks, immigration policies, and even civil society efforts, which took the form of prejudice against the arrival to the United States of Catholic Irish and Italian, Chinese, Japanese, Jewish, Mexican, and Central American peoples, among others, from the eighteenth century to the present day. Some groups overcome prejudice – like the Irish or Italian immigrants of the eighteenth and nineteenth centuries – because ultimately their "whiteness" trumped their religion or class status. But other groups continued to experience prejudice through the twentieth centuries and up until present day as evidenced by the incarceration of Japanese and Japanese Americans during the Second World War or the islamophobia against Muslims or the racist treatment of Mexican and Central American immigrants and Asian Americans today.

In the preceding paragraph, I mentioned how groups like the Irish Americans or Italian Americans overcame prejudice and "became white." There is a fascinating academic literature about how some early immigrant groups to the United States were able to change social status or by "today's terminology, it should be read that these European groups changed their ethnicities to become part of whites, or more precisely they were racialized to become white" (Yang and Koshy 2016: 16). This literature, notwithstanding, the racial hierarchy in the United States remained one that benefited white people and discriminated against people of color, such as African Americans, Native Americans, Latinx communities, to mention a few. In the case of Guatemala where Gladis is from, there is pressure on Indigenous people to "Ladinizarse" or become Ladinos, people of mixed race. This is why many Indigenous people feel pressure to stop speaking their native languages, not teach their children their language, stop wearing their *guipiles* and other traditional clothing, or leave communities of origin for bigger cities.

Though people often choose to identify as one race or another, the institutionalization of racial exclusion by governments and elites has more to do with who is benefitting from it than who is described by it. "Today scholars are beginning to realize that 'race' is nothing more and nothing less than a social invention" (Smedley 1998: 698) with severe ramifications, nevertheless, for the capabilities of people who are discriminated against, targeted, and excluded for their racial and ethnic identities. To underscore this further, let us consider the capability deprivation facing Indigenous people in Guatemala (see Table 6.1) where we will see how racism unfolds along ethnic lines.

*Table 6.1* Capability deprivation

| Categories | Indicators for Indigenous people in Guatemala |
| --- | --- |
| Health and reproductive health | • One of the major challenges for health service delivery in Guatemala – particularly for health promotion – is monolingualism, especially among Mayan women, who speak their Mayan mother tongue but not Spanish, the official language. This is a real challenge, because most service providers are also monolingual and speak only Spanish.<br>• 46.5 percent of children under 5 had stunting…Such prevalence in this age group reflects a failure to meet basic dietary and health needs due to deficient social, economic, and environmental conditions. Prevalence rates are higher in indigenous (58 percent) than nonindigenous groups (34.2 percent).<br>• Maternal mortality has remained high, although it has fallen in recent years. In 2013, the MMR was 113.4 per 100,000 live births, derived from 452 deaths, leaving 1,394 orphans. Of these deaths, 68.4 percent of the women were indigenous, 42 percent were illiterate, 41 percent had had some degree of primary education, and 43 percent had died at home or on the way to some health care facility. Rural departments inaccessible to the health services and with larger indigenous populations have the highest MMR values. The country did not reach the MDG target of an MMR of 55 per 100,000 live births. |
| Economy | • The extreme poverty rate in the indigenous population was 39.8 percent in 2014, versus 12.8 percent in the nonindigenous population, and 35.3 percent in the rural population, versus 11.2 percent in the urban population.<br>• The incidence of poverty is systematically higher in indigenous populations. The National Employment and Income Survey of 2014 found that the poverty rate in the indigenous population (79.2 percent) was 1.7 times higher than that of the nonindigenous population (46.6 percent). Poverty has likewise been historically higher in rural areas than in urban areas, although the gap has been narrowing: in 2000, the rural poverty rate was 74.5 percent, or 2.7 times higher than the urban rate, while in 2014, the rate (76.1 percent) was 1.8 times higher than the urban rate (42.1 percent).<br>• The National Employment and Income Survey of 2014 found that 65.8 percent of people were working in the informal sector. This percentage was 80.3 percent for indigenous people, in contrast to just 57.7 percent for nonindigenous people. |
| Education | In 2014, the National Survey of Living Conditions (ENCOVI, for its Spanish acronym) reported a literacy rate of 79.1 percent in the population aged 15 and over (84.8 percent in men and 74.0 percent in women; 86.1 percent in urban dwellers and 71.4 percent in rural dwellers). Literacy among rural women was 64.7 percent. Indigenous women, with a literacy rate of 57.6 percent, were the most disadvantaged in terms of access to education. |

Sources: "Guatemala" The Pan-American Health Organization: www.paho.org/salud-en-las-americas-2017/?p=3338.

## Understanding social class

Similar to how race and ethnicity can affect people's capabilities or ability to choose the lives they want to live, social class or socio-economic status also marks people's lives. Since the late nineteenth century, class differences have been the scholarly focus of early sociologists such as Karl Marx and Max Weber. "Yet feminists have clearly critiqued these theories for their failure to address the processes through which class is produced on the gendered and raced bodies of its subjects in ways that assure the perpetuation of systems of stratification and domination" (Adair 2002: 452). I propose using a definition of social class that facilitates understanding how stratification by income and social class can lead to inequalities and discrimination for those at the bottom, especially for those who experience multiple forms of social difference. These divisions form distinct cultural subsystems that inform consciousness, organize perceptions, define priorities, and influence forms of behavior (Rose 1997: 463) and are even inscribed on poor people's bodies (Adair 2002), which means that social class organizes people into cultural groupings with accompanying expectations, behaviors, and customs. The socio-economic class structure has evolved in many industrialized economies to include an upper class, an upper-middle class, a middle class, a working class, and a lower class or marginalized sector of society. However, stratification is not solely based on income. For instance, access to certain elite clubs is not solely dependent on income but often on such concepts as social capital, cultural knowledge, and status that do not inherently accrue to the holder with money. Someone with a very low income is not necessarily as hard off as their neighbor if education, family, and contacts can generate opportunities.

In many high- and middle-income countries, a sizable middle class has emerged which can serve as a stabilizing force: the middle class serves wealthier interests, uses the labor of the working classes and the poor, and yet, making it into the middle class often remains elusive for the lower classes. The professional middle class brings with it a new set of values and goals, most significantly its emphasis on rationality and rejection of arbitrary authority. It creates new forms of hierarchy based on merit, educational attainment, and rational regulation by experts (Rose 1997: 465). Cultural myths about "pulling oneself up by one's bootstraps" support the notion that every individual just needs to apply hard work and commitment to move up socially and economically. But in societies where there are institutionalized barriers to choosing the life you want to live, this belief is often no more than an illusory dream and not a real possibility. Similar to other forms of difference, social class does not just mean that some people earn more money than others. Class gets used to exclude and shame poor people; these forms of discrimination, in turn, reinforce and perpetuate difference, making it hard for people to get out of poverty. For example, in the United States, many scholars (see Adair 2002 for a summary of this literature) have documented how women and children who receive welfare and other benefits from the government are trapped in "systems of power that produce and patrol poverty through the reproduction of both social and bodily markers" (Adair 2002: 452). What does this mean? It means that when a poor, single mother cannot afford to take her child to the doctor, for example, the child is often left debilitated, scarred, or otherwise marked. It can also mean that when a poor mother has lost housing and is living in her car, her children may come to school unwashed or without clean clothes or hungry. They may have difficulty focusing in school. They are made fun of by peers and reprimanded by teachers and the cycle continues.

In under-resourced or low-income countries, one can often identify class structures as in the industrialized world such as elites and marginalized, poorer groups. Often, economic exclusion and low wages contribute to limiting the size of the middle class and increasing the number of poor people in a country. This, in turn, can be exacerbated by macro-level policies implemented by multilateral and bilateral agencies. Let us take the example of neo-liberal structural adjustment policies imposed on countries by the International Monetary Fund and other financial intermediaries in the late twentieth century.

> Such was the case with the structural adjustment and macroeconomic stabilization policies of the 1980s, which suggested that countries caught in a debt spiral with severe balance of payment problems should reduce price subsidies and infrastructure investment; cut back spending on education, health, and public services; liberalize trade and capital accounts; and privatize public enterprises.
>
> (Nallari and Griffith 2011: 15)

These draconian policies often translated as cuts to state spending on social welfare and job loss for government functionaries and working class laborers whose jobs have been cut due to privatization and restructuring; these policies also had gendered consequences for women and other care providers and led to greater poverty and exclusion.

Not all countries around the world have developed along the lines of industrialized economies; one can identify other cultural formations that entail alternative sources of power and status than socio-economic positioning. Traditional leaders of tribal communities, lineages, or ethnic groups, leaders with cultural or environmental knowledge such as healers, midwives, witches or sorcerers, leaders of social movements, and directors of non-governmental organizations, for example, may exercise power and have status that allow them access to opportunities and resources that others of an otherwise similar background might not enjoy.

Research points to the fact that "socioeconomic status is a fundamental cause of variation in well-being and that the social resources associated with socioeconomic status constitute the fundamental cause of variation in well-being" (Roxburgh 2009: 357). Not only can poor and marginalized groups seldom afford the costs associated with good quality nutrition, shelter, and recreation, but often they are denied access to the opportunities represented by education, healthcare, and access to credit so they can overcome adversity and enjoy the life they would like to have. Abundant research documents the relationship between higher socio-economic class and better health outcomes (Bowleg 2012: 1269). Medical sociologists have long argued that society's poorer and less privileged members live in worse health and die much younger than the rich and more privileged ones (Link and Phelan 1995). Table 6.1 above shows specific health, economic, and education indicators for how Indigenous people in Guatemala experience capability poverty; similar trends are true for poor people in comparison to wealthier counterparts: they often earn their living in the informal sector without access to public services, face greater inequalities in terms of health and education, and have less access to other capabilities like recreation, political participation, to name a few. As I describe below, the restrictions of socio-economic poverty are frequently compounded when they collide with other forms of discrimination.

## Understanding gender and sexuality

According to Linda L. Lindsey, gender and sexuality like class, race, and ethnicity are "concepts used to collectively categorize people…[they] do not exist objectively, but unfold through a socially constructed process" (2021: 14), or what some call a "sexual system" (Rupp 1999) or "gender order" (Connell 2011). Different cultures have different systems; this includes cultural authorities in the fields of health, law, and education and frameworks for identifying practices around and responses to gender and sexual conformity and non-conformity. To understand how this happens and identify ways to address gender discrimination, it is important to look at the differences between men and women – as well as gender minorities[2] – and examine the gendered messages or social scripts of the gender system that reinforce difference and institutionalize exclusion. Gender is often presented as a binary, which refers to how males and females are organized into two distinct groups (Lindsey 2021: 601). However, in reality, gender is significantly more fluid than these two categories allow, with a lot of variability, especially in global perspective, making it important to define the term in a way that does not simply reaffirm the gender binary. Gender is an organizing set of categories for human experience; in patriarchal societies, it has been defined as the culturally ascribed roles for masculine and feminine behaviour (Russo and Pirlott 2006), but the existence of a range of gender identities as well as cultures around the world with more than two genders encourage us to look beyond the gender binary. Though socially constructed, gender also includes people's embodied experiences and by this I am referring to the way people's bodies inform their lived, gendered lives. There is vast diversity across social, biological, neurological, endocrinological, emotional, and psychological factors when it comes to human gender identities and sexualities. It is worthwhile to take O'Brien's invitation "to be mindful of the wide range of [gender] behavioral possibilities and expressions, especially when disconnected from unexamined assumptions…" (2016: 19), which pushes us to reflect on our own biases and beliefs about gender – as well as how we each "do gender" – when considering how gender plays out in our societies and others different from our own. To help unpack assumptions about gender, O'Brien suggests using the metaphor of a box of multi-colored, multi-shaped blocks to understand gender better.

---

**Box 6.1  Gender as a box of blocks**

Imagine you had a box of blocks with at least five or more shapes and you were required to sort them all into two piles. What would you do? Most likely you would find a particular characteristic and use that as your sorting rule. Perhaps some of the shapes look more roundish to you and some seem squarish. You can sort them into two piles of roundish and squarish, but you will still see the variation within each pile. For instance, where did you decide to place the star-shaped block? Over time, and the more you emphasize the binary you have created, the more likely you will come to see it that way (and to overlook the variation). You may even forget that you originally determined this categorical scheme yourself and come to see it is something "natural." Similarly, the historical practice has been to shoehorn potential gender variation in the one of two gender boxes (O'Brien 2017: 3).

---

In many countries, understandings of gender and sexuality are expanding due to breakthroughs in research, the growing acceptance of a gender continuum and different sexualities, and coverage of transgender people in the media. Furthermore, there are many indigenous cultures and other communities around the world with multiple genders, such as two spirit people in many Native American communities in North America, the Muxe, among others, in Mexico, the Hijra in India, and the Sambia in Papua New Guinea, to name a few. The diversity of gender identities confirms that the gender binary is, in fact, often used to discriminate against the non-dominant, that is, women, and difference, that is, gender minorities. "When binary categories are imposed, not only is scientific understanding distorted, but such usage is a disservice to multitudes of people… who identify as gender variant" (Lindsey 2021: 7). Gender identities include people who identify as men and women as well as people who do not and identify instead as gender non-conforming, a-gender, or as transgender, "an umbrella term from transgender studies to include persons who identify as transgender, trans, trans women, trans men, gender nonbinary, gender queer, gender variant, and a range of related possibilities" (O'Brien 2016: 21). These options are expressions of gender fluidity: the shifting of gender identity and its presentation according to various contexts (Lindsey 2021: 54).

Before moving to analyse how gender identities affect people's capabilities, it is germane to define sexuality given how it is often associated with gender and can also contribute to exclusion. Gender studies and sexuality studies overlap because many societies expect certain genders to be sexual in certain ways. Gender refers to roles and expectations – often informed by the gender binary – while sexuality has to do with how people experience and embody sexual identities through sexual orientation and desire (Bashford and Levine 2010: 174). Who are you attracted to? Connected to the gender binary, heterosexuality is the expected sexuality in patriarchal societies. "Heteronormative scripts mark heterosexuality as the proper sexual orientation and sustain power differences between women and men, and between players who may define themselves in one or more LGBTQ [lesbian, gay, bisexual, transgender, queer] categories" (Lindsey 2021: 15). Sexual minorities can be "identified and grouped according to three separate criteria: 1. People who describe themselves using sexual minority terminology. 2. People whose sexual partners are the same gender, or a minority gender. 3. People who experience attraction to individuals of the same or a minority gender" (Park 2016: 9). Commonly used terms for sexual identities are summarized in Table 6.2.

In patriarchal societies, gender and sexuality provide privilege to men and people who identify as heterosexual; however, on a global level, these categories also serve to limit people's capabilities who occupy non-dominant identities, such as women, gender minorities, and people who do not identify as heterosexual. The gender binary – or gender order or gender system – includes social relations, in which women (Moser 1993: 3, Russo and Pirlott 2006) and gender minorities are subordinated to men and have

*Table 6.2* Sexuality identities

| Category | Description |
| --- | --- |
| Heterosexual | sexual preference for and erotic attraction to those of the other gender |
| Homosexual / Gay / Lesbian | sexual preference for and erotic attraction to those of their own gender |
| Asexual, celibate | a lack of sexual attraction combined with one's definition as asexual (Chasin 2013: 405) |
| Bisexual | sexual orientations may shift and are sexually responsive to either gender |
| Pansexual | attracted to all sexes and genders of people (Jakubowski 2014) |

Source: Most definitions taken from Linda Lindsey 2021: 59, others marked individually.

less power, privilege, and resources. In patriarchal cultures where fathers and male relatives exercise power, women, girls, and people with non-dominant gender identities are often not allowed to make basic decisions that affect their lives. This means that often they do not get to choose how to spend income they earn; they do not get to choose whether they get to continue school or have to get married; and they do not get to decide when and if they will have children. They are also more vulnerable to sexual and gender-based violence. As the gender system in a particular place informs the societal expectations placed on how people should "do gender," sexuality also simultaneously manifests at the individual level and responds to structures in society:

> What I have been calling the 'sexual system' is closely connected to large scale eco-nomic social and political development. Although in everyday life we tend to think of sexuality as something personal, historians of sexuality see it as a complex product of individual desires, group activities and ideas, and societal forces as the country grew up, the ways people express their love and desire changed.
>
> (Rupp 1999: 40)

Sexual and gender minorities face multiple forms of exclusion in their respective societies that puts multiple demands on them, such as pressure to be and/or pass as heterosexual or occupy a gender identity that fits with dominant gender and sexual beliefs. "A global view also reveals the persistent inclination to blame other people from other countries or class or racial others within a society for sexual desires and behaviors denounced as deviant" (Rupp 2009: 8). Pressure can be societal but it can also be punitive, leading to criminal-ization, or medical, leading to forced conversion therapies: all of which are harmful and limit people's capabilities. This is a place where the "capabilities approach helps us avoid creating cultural preferences for specific kinds of identities. It does not pre-determine the kind of identity, sexuality, or gender one should adopt. Therefore, the young trans-gender man's identity is just as valuable as that of the young woman who wants to live according to traditional gender roles" (Park 2016: 45). When the discriminatory actions of societies penalize or punish people with non-conforming gender and sexuality iden-tities, their capabilities and functionalities are limited. All of these demands "contribute to poor health outcomes which limit full human development" (Park 2016: 10). The perils associated with these challenges against sexual minorities, however, cannot be dismissed. LGBTQ rights are under assault in places where, for centuries, enactments of accepted gender-variant roles contributed to community betterment and individual survival. "Today legal rights awarded to gender variant people do little to guarantee their safety. In many developing world regions, fear of reprisal drives gender [and sexual] minor-ities underground. Violence is often sanctioned and ignored for third-gender people who breach gender binaries in traditional communities" (Lindsey 2021: 62). Often the discrim-ination and reprisals that transgender people face is even more dire than those of other gender minorities: "While the global transgender community receives frequent mention as the 'T' under the umbrella of so-called LGBT rights, the international call for increased prevention of rights abuses against transgender persons, promotion of transgender rights, and protection of transgender communities pales in comparison to the similar call for the global LGB population" (Kritz 2014: 2). This is corroborated by the numbers of trans-gender people who have been assassinated in recent years (Kritz 2014: 3).

To sum up, this means that often women and gender and sexual minorities are denied access to basic capabilities, assets and income opportunities necessary for their wellbeing and agency: gender inequalities mean increased risk of poverty for people who are disadvantaged due to their gender identity, such as women, girls, and gender and sexual minorities, and the family members who depend upon them for their wellbeing. The gender equality aspiration "hasn't sufficiently overcome the brutal reality for millions of women and gender minorities in the world who suffer sexual and domestic violence, lack access to essential prerequisites for health and safety, or are denied basic human rights and control over their own bodies" (Clark and Horton 2019: 2368). Obviously, gender and sexuality are not the sole factors explaining differences between people, because their lives are not determined solely by these roles but by other forms of difference as well.

## Women and girls, poverty and capabilities

In no way denying the discrimination, vulnerability to violence, and capability poverty that affects gender and sexual minorities, this section will focus on women and girls due to the fact that women and children comprise 70 percent of the world's poor[3] and that there have been many international commitments from the United Nations, international agencies, and governments to end discrimination against women and girls along with the vast scholarship available on the topic. Given that women can appear privileged according to certain indicators – such as length of life – when compared to men and given that people with non-dominant gender identities can suffer from discrimination and exclusion even more than women, a commitment to addressing gender inequality thus necessarily entails a careful review of which capabilities are essential so that inequality does not get invisibilized (see Robeyns 2003 for a robust exploration of this topic).

Other academics influenced by the capabilities approach have studied how accepted gendered expectations become habitual – accepted as normal by many, including those themselves whose options are limited (Khader 2011, Klasen 2004). This explains why many people may not even be aware they are discriminated against and do not find their situations problematic: they have had no other experience of how life might be. These "adaptive preferences" mean that they have adapted their outlooks to their circumstances and do not question that men receive better treatment than they do in their societies. Adaptive preferences, according to Serene Khader, are "formed in response to unjust social arrangements that are incompatible with a person's basic wellbeing" (2012: 303) and thereby limit that person's capabilities and functionings. Careful distinction needs to be applied here: just because a person may "seem to acquiesce to their own deprivation" (Khader 2011: 4) does not mean that the person lacks agency or has been brainwashed. Rather, they have had to find a way to survive as best they can given the unjust social conditions they face. There is a vast amount of research about how people negotiate, challenge, and subvert limitations that are placed on their behaviour. Many capabilities scholars such as Amartya Sen, Marth Nussbaum and others argue that the discrimination and gender bias people face have to be addressed by more than a call for cultural change, which can take generations, but has to be led by governments and institutions that can implement laws so that capabilities become achieved functionings. For this reason, many programs focus on the accountability of governments to enforce laws and protect rights. This is also why there is a push to get more women and people with non-dominant gender identities into political leadership positions and security forces: more people in these roles will mean that it is that much easier to increase their inclusion.

There are hidden aspects of the discrimination that women and gender minority caretakers face such as having to work a double day – income generation and family responsibilities (Klasen 2004) – or a triple day – income generation, unpaid care work (UNIFEM 2005), and community activism (see Cosgrove 2010: 10–11, Chant 2006: 206–207, 214). This *triple burden* (Craske 2003: 67) means that women from poor communities are often working around the clock to guarantee their families' survival. Women's triple work day is a useful analytical lens for bringing attention to how hard women are working, but it does divide women's activities into separate categories. Many women, for example, carry out their responsibilities simultaneously or in an interspersed manner rather than separately. This multi-layered, simultaneous and dense set of activities includes taking care of family members, generating income and even leading a group of people to achieve a certain goal.

---

**Box 6.2 Unpaid care work**

The term "unpaid care work" is used to refer to the provision of services within households for other household and community members. It avoids the ambiguities of other terms, including "domestic labor," which can refer both to unpaid care work and the work of paid domestic workers; "unpaid labor," which can refer to unpaid care work as well as unpaid work in the family business; "reproductive work," which can refer to unpaid care work as well as giving birth and breastfeeding; and "home work," which can refer to paid work done in the home on subcontract basis from an employer. Each word in the term "unpaid care work" is important:

- "UNPAID" means that the person doing the activity does not receive a wage for it.
- "CARE" means that the activity serves people and their wellbeing.
- "WORK" means that the activity has a cost in terms of time and energy and arises out of a social or contractual obligation, such as marriage or less formal social relationships.

(Summarized from UNIFEM 2005)

---

In addition to working around the clock because of the gendered expectations that inform their lives, women also face gender discrimination in the workplaces of their societies. Women make up the majority of those who generate their income in the informal sector, earning income as marketers, itinerant saleswomen and service providers (childcare, cleaning, cooking, and so on) without receiving benefits or state protections. When women do get formal sector jobs, they comprise the majority of service sector jobs where employees earn less than in other sectors (see Nallari and Griffith 2011 for an in-depth exploration of this topic). Women predominate in sectors that are associated with women's caretaking roles in the family, working in fields such as education, nursing, and social work, which often are remunerated less than occupations where men predominate. Though exact ratios are debated, there is agreement that when women do enter the labor force in sectors where men predominate, they are paid less than men.

## Box 6.3 Women and the economy

### Introduction

Expanding women's participation in the workforce is not just something that shows off a company's commitment to diversity. It has powerful, positive and measurable results. Academics, policy makers and business leaders assert that long-term economic growth requires the expanded participation of women in the workforce. "Greater representation of women in senior leadership positions within governments and financial institutions is vital not only to find solutions to the current economic turmoil, but to stave off such crises in the future," says Klaus Schwab, Founder and Executive Chairman of the World Economic Forum.

### Economic force

The economic benefits of investing in women are self-evident when you consider that women reinvest 90 percent of their income in their families and communities compared to men who reinvest only 30 to 40 percent.

### Occupational and wage disparities

Despite their obvious potential, women do not enjoy the full benefits of participation in the workforce. In 2005, women accounted for roughly 40 percent of the world's economically active population. But in most developing countries, women in the labor force work longer hours than men, earn significantly less when doing so, and spend more time on unpaid tasks such as household work.

### Critical mass

"From supporting micro-enterprise in the Global South to assuring gender parity in the executive suite, investing in women is the smartest economic venture that the corporate world can undertake," says The White House Project's Marie Wilson. "Decades of research have proven that adding women to the leadership mix not only begets creative solutions and a focus on long-term results, but also higher profits. Advancing women is more than a powerful tool for advancing communities alone; it is also a critical tool for advancing the bottom line."

(Summarized from Ernst and Young 2009)

These economic and employment discrepancies are institutionalized into society and perpetuated by legal frameworks and political institutions that allow this to continue. Though the rates of women in ministerial positions and legislatures are on the rise, men still predominate, comprising 75 percent of legislators worldwide, with notable exceptions like Rwanda (61 percent women legislators) and parity of women and men in a couple of Latin American and European countries (World Bank 2020). The discrimination and exclusion of women continues, in part, because there is still an education gap for women and girls as well as for vocational training and education for women. If women cannot get educations, then they cannot get jobs and improve their lives. The status quo of gender discrimination gets reinforced by widely held beliefs that women are different from men when it comes to doing certain things, and women exist to serve their families and their men. These cultural constructs – ideas that are reproduced by groups of people – can change, but this takes time and sustained effort. Today, many of you reading this text may have been raised by mothers and fathers who both worked, or you have been raised by your dads, or you have been given role models that reinforce non-traditional gender roles. But for many girls and young women in the developing world or in less-resourced families in the developed world, they do not have a lot of freedom to challenge oppressive gender roles: this can lead to their discrimination, but also limits their agency or ability to chart their actions, life choices, and goals. As you continue reading this chapter, think about what life might be like for a young woman from a country ranked low in terms of human development: will she even be able to go to school? Will she have to get married young and drop out of school if she was able to go to school? Will she be able to work outside of the house when she is an adult? What would the challenges look like for gender and sexual minorities?

In addition to the gender discrimination and subordination that can restrict women and girls in their livelihoods, gender-based violence has been defined as "any act that results in, or is likely to result in physical, sexual, or psychological harm or suffering to women [and gender minorities], including threats of such acts, coercion or arbitrary deprivation of liberty, whether occurring in public or private life" (Russo and Pirlott 2006: 181). As a result of the pervasive nature of this phenomenon, one in three women worldwide will face abuse or sexual violence in her lifetime. This is not a problem just for women in the developing or developed worlds: many women in most societies face threats of violence at home or out in the world. In the United States one in four (or 25.9 percent) of women, on average, will experience nonconsensual sexual contact while at college, according to a recent study commissioned by the Association of American Universities (AAU 2020: ix). Also in the United States, 25 percent of women will be affected by domestic violence in their families. The situation is also very serious for women in less-resourced regions. In addition to high rates of risk of sexual assault and domestic violence, gender-based violence also manifests itself in such actions as female gender mutilation and high rates of abortion of girls while in utero compared to boys. In his work on capabilities, Amartya Sen was one of the first to use the term "missing women" in which he quantified how selective abortions were leading to increased rates of births of males in places in the world where boy children are preferred over girls.

---

**Box 6.4 Missing women**

To get an idea of the numbers of people involved in the ratios of women to men, we can estimate the number of "missing women" in a country, say, China or India, by calculating the number of extra women who would have been in China or India if these countries had the same ratio of women to men as calculated in areas of the world in which they receive similar care. In China alone this amounts to 50 million "missing women," taking 1.05 as the benchmark ratio. When that number is added to those in South Asia, West Asia and North Africa, a great many more than 100 million women are "missing." These numbers tell us, quietly, a terrible story of inequality and neglect leading to the excess mortality of women.

(Sen 1999, 1990)

---

Another gender-based practice that leads to acts of violence enacted on women's bodies is female genital mutilation (FGM). This coming-of-age practice involves the full or partial removal of girls' external genitalia. Ending FGM will not be achieved solely by decrying its practitioners as barbaric, nor will the behaviors simply be changed because the law changes to make it illegal in a particular country. Though legal frameworks and the implementation of laws are very important, there must be buy-in from local communities. Long-term change resides in supporting the efforts of local leaders and communities to create new cultural forms to replace the old ones. In many societies, FGM emerged as a cultural practice acknowledging women were of the age to marry; the practice also served to control women's sexuality and assure their fidelity, but today, it may not be as relevant to lines of succession and property rights as it may once have been. FGM is performed on girls by traditional circumcisers, often older women; in countries where FGM is practiced, it is a rite of passage for girls, a form of employment for those who practice the ritual, and women are expected to have this when they marry. Stopping FGM will require addressing all these aspects through the formation of new cultural practices for girls' rite of passage into adulthood, income generation for the women who perform the operation, and cultural change from societies where women are not considered marriageable without it. For this reason, transforming harmful culture practices requires a long-term view and must have a bottom-up approach; change is seldom accepted and acted upon just because another country or institution says something should be done differently.

### Women, girls, and international development efforts

At the international level, development efforts have evolved over the past decades in how they have targeted women and gender inequality. In the 1960s and 1970s, as social scientists began to carry out research about women's discrimination and how it contributed to poverty, new programming was designed to address the situation. The Women in Development agenda was created to ensure women also benefited from modernization and development efforts (Rai 2011). The focus was on supporting women's participation in society through women's income-generation projects, for example, but not on transforming gender relations between men and women. Women in Development proponents advocated for legal and economic reform, believing that unjust gender relations would change automatically as women become income earners. Though many of these projects were successful in the short term, increased income does not mean that women have control over the income or increased agency in society.

Critiques of the Women in Development approach led international agencies, particularly the agencies of the United Nations, to focus on gender relations (Rai 2011). Development efforts that focus on gender relations are often referred to as "gender and development" initiatives and include a broad range of local, national, and international strategies aimed at transforming oppressive gender roles and increasing women's agency and participation, not just wellbeing. These efforts focused on the gender differences and expectations for women at home and in the labor force, access to and control over resources, and the material and social rewards that men and women receive in different contexts (Rai 2011). "There is now an international consensus that 'men are both part of the problem and part of the solution' for achieving gender justice and equality" (Wanner and Wadham 2015: 28). Men – who are often in a position to facilitate access for women, be it at home, in the workplace or in society at large – need to be included in gender-sensitive development efforts – particularly training and consciousness-raising efforts – for a number of reasons: (1) when men and boys know about (and have sensitivity towards) women's rights, they are in a position to advocate for women's rights, and (2) men's privileged position in society means they have more access to positions of power; so if they see themselves as partners in women's empowerment, they can help change the structural and institutional barriers to women's advancement.

Pressure is being applied to international development efforts, especially gender and development programs, to include men in gender-sensitization efforts and development programming as well (Wanner and Wadham 2015). Empowering women and not training men as well can lead to dire consequences for women who go home armed with knowledge about their rights but with few other resources to protect themselves against violence. Supporting women in productive projects without opportunities for men can reinforce messages that men are failures and not good providers. This lack of programming can reinforce gender messages that women can do it all. In fact, there is some concern that because of economic crises and uneven economic development, there is actually a crisis of masculinity in which men – unable to fulfil their role as providers – have lost self-esteem and decreased their abilities to help their families (Cosgrove 2010, Chant 2006). For all of these reasons, it is important to work with men and women, girls and boys, as well as all sectors of society, to ensure the basic capabilities and functionings of women as well as those of men are fulfilled.

"Gender and development" efforts also received criticism because they focused on gender relations as separate from other development priorities. This led to gender mainstreaming, in which international agencies and even governments are expected to integrate a gender perspective into all policies and programming (Prugl and Lustgarten 2006). The UN Economic and Social Council described it as "the process of assessing the implication for women and men of any planned action, including legislation, policies or programs, in any area and at all levels" (cited in Prugl and Lustgarten 2006). Though many agree that it is important to carry out gender analysis in institutions, not just in target communities, mainstreaming has led to assumptions that a gender perspective is now cross-cutting. The problem is that there is uneven implementation of mainstreaming efforts across institutions due to differences in funding, leadership, training, and commitment. Where once there may have been a gender office in a particular agency, now there have been trainings of staff and the gender experts have been spread across the organizations.

These different approaches have attempted to include women and address unequal gender relations. Academic research and impact assessments about the effectiveness of programming targeting women or transforming unequal gender relations have led to a robust literature in which quantitative and qualitative research is being used to improve programming. From the randomized control trials of the Massachusetts Institute of Technology's Poverty Action Lab in which the impact of microcredit or health projects on poor women are investigated to in-depth impact assessments over time in communities, there are more data about what works and does not work, which can lead to improved efficiency and effectiveness of programming. However, given the complexity of transforming gender relations and cultural messages that place limits on women (and gender minorities), it is also important to work with institutions such as the media, the business sector, and political leaders to reinforce new messages. These changes, in turn, must be supported by changes in legal frameworks, laws, enforcement, and resource allocation so that they protect discriminated groups and their capabilities, on one hand, and help level the playing field and open up leadership positions. These cultural and political transformations will only be sustained if there are economic changes so that women and gender minorities can participate in the labor force, so that they receive equitable reimbursement for their work, are not consigned to the informal sector or only certain types of formal sector jobs, and have local opportunities so they are not pushed to leave their own countries.

## Interlocking identities and capabilities

In this chapter so far, multiple forms of social difference, such as race, ethnicity, social class, gender, and sexuality, have been defined and analysed in global perspective, attempting to trace the ways that difference can privilege or benefit groups of people and how it can lead to exclusion, discrimination, and capability deprivation. However, not all members of groups separated by difference such as gender, race, ethnicity, or class are discriminated against equally: some will have advantages through education, socioeconomic status and gender that others do not. Often, actions and choices are informed by multiple forms of social difference such as sexual orientation, life events and circumstances, race, ethnicity, education, socio-economic class, ability, and political activism, to mention a few. This is why the sociological concept of *intersectionality* is a useful theoretical framework for analysing the impact of race and gender, for example. Intersectionality is "(1) an approach to understanding human life and behavior rooted in the experiences and struggles of disenfranchised people; and (2) an important tool linking theory with practice that can aid in the empowerment of communities and individuals" (Hill Collins and Bilge 2016: 36). This concept explains the compounding interaction of sexism and racism, as well as explaining how "multiple social identities…intersect at the micro level…to reflect interlocking systems of privilege and oppression…at the macro social-structural level" (Bowleg 2012: 1267).

As a sociological theory, intersectionality has its roots in early Black feminist leaders such as Sojourner Smith who "challenged the notion that being a woman (i.e. gender) and Black (i.e. race) are mutually exclusive: 'That man over there says that women need to be helped into carriages, and lifted over ditches, and to have the best place everywhere. Nobody ever helps me into carriages, or over mud-puddles, or gives me any best place! Ain't I a woman?'" (Bowleg 2012 citing Sojourner Smith: 1268). Kimberlé Crenshaw, a Black feminist legal scholar, coined the term in 1991, and it was further developed by Patricia Hill Collins (2014), and by others, such as Grzanka and contributors (2014) and Hill Collins and Bilge (2016) along with other scholars. Initially, Black feminist scholars used the term to describe the compounding challenges that Black women face in the United States due to the combined and mutually reinforcing effects of racism and sexism, arguing that Black women faced a set of challenges that was distinct from the sexism faced by white women or the racism that affects Black men due to the "interactive effects of race and gender discrimination" (Crenshaw 2000: 1). Black women face greater challenges than either white women or Black men because their exclusion is due to multiple forms of discrimination which "interact with preexisting vulnerabilities to create a distinct dimension of disempowerment" (Crenshaw 2000: 5).

Crenshaw (2000) applied intersectionality globally advocating for increased attention by United Nations agencies to how "the conjoining of multiple systems of subordination has been described as compound discrimination, multiple burdens, or double or triple discrimination" (2000: 8) around the world. Today intersectionality is used consistently by many activists and engaged scholars globally trying to understand and address the compounding effects of multiple forms of social difference on marginalized groups in global perspective (Cosgrove *et al.* 2021, Kagal and Latchford 2020, Cosgrove 2019, Radcliff 2015, Cosgrove 2010, Crenshaw 2000).

Intersectionality is a dual-purpose concept that simultaneously explains how unequal structures disempower and marginalize, referred to as "structural intersectionality," and how experiences of compounded difference can ignite agency, leadership, and resistance, referred to as "political intersectionality" (Grzanka 2014: 16). On the one hand, *structural intersectionality* explains the oppression and exclusion that accompanies multiple forms of social difference or division. *Political intersectionality*, on the other hand, explains why oppressed and discriminated groups often resist the forces aligned against them, using their "powerful oppositional knowledge" (Hill Collins 2014) "to challenge the conditions of their lives" (Crenshaw 2000: 13). When it is clear that one has been left out of the social contract of the broader society, the contradiction between societal values versus the treatment of one's own people becomes evident. In my research about women's civil society leadership in Argentina, Chile, and El Salvador (2010), I argued that those who had the most reasons to despair and do nothing (mothers with disappeared children; Indigenous women in Chile after generations of genocidal state practices; militant feminists in neoliberal El Salvador; working-class women in peri-urban Buenos Aires) were, in fact, the most active: turning hard experiences into action so others would not have to face the repression and exclusion that they had experienced. People on the margins often use the meanings, beliefs, and practices they have to fight back whether it is simply making it through the day, renewing a cultural practice that might have been abandoned, or destroying a private property sign that settlers have put up on communal land.

When multiple forms of difference intersect to place someone at a disadvantaged position, the results can lead to extreme limitations of capabilities and functionings, suffering, and oppression. For example, "the poorest women from disadvantaged ethnic groups are being left behind. In 11 of 16 countries with data, they have the fewest average years of education. In 14 of 16 countries with data, they have the highest share of child deaths" (Lenhardt and Samman 2015: 6). Rural Indigenous women in Guatemala, like Gladis and the women with whom she works, are discriminated against by the broader Guatemalan society and the government. Often these women comprise the poorest of the poor, and they have to contend with gender discrimination within their families and communities as well. They are discriminated against because they are Indigenous and because they are young women. This phenomenon can be seen in numerous countries around the world; the most vulnerable sectors of society are also most often those with the least participation, representation, and opportunities to change their situations. Research shows that "people who belong to one or more disadvantaged groups experience outcomes that are significantly below the average" (Lenhardt and Samman 2015: 7). This is why it is so important to address social discrimination and support the efforts of people themselves when they do become aware of their rights and seek fair redress for their situations or opportunities for education, health care, and advancement.

## Vignette 6.2

*Many experts, peacebuilders and women's rights activists claim that the Democratic Republic of the Congo is the worst place to be a woman (Figure 6.2). In Congo the civil war of the 1990s and ensuing regional war led to the extensive practice of sexual assault by army soldiers and rebel groups who were ordered to rape and sexually assault women, girls, boys, and some men to prove local leaders could not protect their own. It is in the cities – as well as displaced people's camps and marginalized urban communities – where people have arrived fleeing violence in the countryside that sexual assault, molestation and sexual harassment are still on the rise. Young women – often minors as well as from poor communities or refugee camps or non-dominant tribal groups – are raped or coerced into having sex in exchange for food or household goods and then find themselves pregnant. Patriarchal values that reinforce sex only in the context of marriage are used against these young women by their families, communities and institutions, and they are shunned, ostracized from society and forced to deal with their situations on their own as best they can.*

*At a local non-governmental organization in Goma, a city in eastern Congo, young mothers come together for vocational training and training in human and women's rights. In turn, these women are able to earn a living; and even more telling, they take what they have learned and visit schools, displaced people's camps and other institutions to talk with girls, boys, young women, and young men about health, hygiene, and birth control. These young women, who have been shunned by their own families and societies, find empowerment through trying to change the very circumstances that have led to their ill treatment. Marie said, "The camp where we went to make our presentations is calling us to come back and teach others." Others echoed her sentiments: "Many people don't know about these subjects and are thirsty for knowledge," "I went to the school and got permission to talk with the students about family planning," "I have kept track of who I've talked with; each of us talks with 90 people every month," "It is very important for us to work to bring awareness to as many people as possible given how important the messages are that we have to share." These young women have decided that education and knowledge are the way to transform the way young women are treated, and they're raising awareness about these issues. (Adapted from Cosgrove 2016)*

This example from the Democratic Republic of the Congo depicts how a group of teen mothers – marginalized by their young age, gender, citizen status, social class, and non-dominant tribal group identities – are educating other teens about gender-based violence, women's reproductive health, and other related topics in Democratic Republic of the Congo. Not only are they trying to help other girls not get pregnant, they are working with young men to transform their assumptions about women. Even more, these women are giving workshops in local schools and other public institutions and demanding that their government enforce the laws which exist on paper to protect women's rights. Even though gender-based violence and gender inequality are deeply rooted and pernicious, there is so much that can be done to transform the problems with programing that empowers survivors and gives them the knowledge and skills to change their own lives and those of others as well as advocate and demand accountability from their governments. Non-governmental organizations with a gender equity focus like the one that provided the Congolese teen mothers with training and support can help address the challenges that women face. An empowerment focus deviates from the "victim" narrative and generalization in order to create a more inclusive and positive support system based on strengths, differences, and capabilities of women. At the national and international levels, social movements in the form of women's and LGBTQ and other inclusion movements and other like-minded organizations, such as self-help groups and community associations, can coordinate actions, advocate for change, and even carry out projects together.

At an international level, international agencies and non-governmental organizations need to promote a more holistic analysis of gender-based violence, for example, that avoids seeing violence as an isolated problem in programing and funding. "More often than not, programs and projects in INGOs are split into programmatic siloes, with funding limited to particular thematic areas or specific forms of VAWG [violence against women and

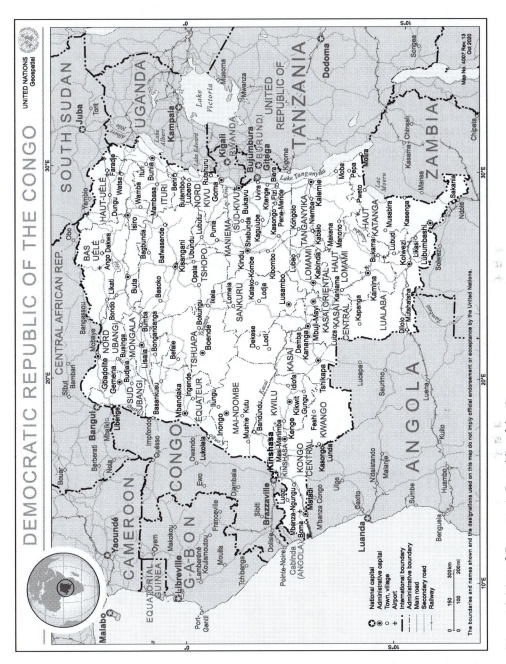

*Figure 6.2* Map of Democratic Republic of the Congo
Source: Map No. 4007 Rev. 11 UNITED NATIONS May 2016.

girls]" (Kagal and Latchford 2020: 17). They can provide funding and facilitate training to support locally led programs that empower and train local leaders and the organizations they run. International efforts can support the capacity building of public sector efforts to address these problems. Together, international efforts and government programing – such as affirmative action policies in employment and education, quotas for the political participation of women and other minorities, and access to credit for business loans – can promote increased participation, income generation and leadership opportunities.

## Conclusion

When people on the margins gain knowledge about their rights, receive an education so they can read and write, and obtain the tools to generate income, they are able to employ themselves and support their families and meet their obligations towards their children and families. For example, research shows that women invest 90 percent of their earnings back into their families while men only bring home 40 percent (Ernst and Young 2009). It makes good sense to invest in the empowerment of women and gender minorities, but it also makes good sense to invest in increasing men's awareness of how their decisions and their privilege affect their partners and children. Long-term change requires transforming gender roles and expectations, racist ideologies, and classist exclusions so people can flourish and choose the lives they want to live, feeling agency in their lives, communities, and societies. This can happen through the efforts of people themselves to achieve change, education and training, the support of governments and international agencies, and long-term sustained cultural change.

This chapter began with the story of Gladis, a young Indigenous woman in Guatemala, who has grown up seeing that women's lot in life is suffering. Indigenous women in Guatemala face discrimination for their ethnicity, thereby limiting their economic, educational, and social opportunities. Women have little control over their bodies and sexuality, leading to high rates of teenage pregnancy and vulnerability to sexual violence. We read about a similar dynamic for poor young women in Democratic Republic of the Congo. In both cases, we read about young, poor, marginalized women advocating for change; they are not just waiting for governments and organizations to assure their protection. They believe their lives can be different and organize together to achieve that change.

## Discussion questions

1   How would you compare and contrast the challenges and opportunities that women have in low-income and high-income countries? Girls? Transgender people? Women with additional minoritized identities?
2   How does the concept of intersectionality support a more nuanced understanding of the dynamics around social difference and poverty? How is that experiences of marginalization can also serve as powerful oppositional knowledges?
3   Why has there been a move to consider "gender" and not just "women," which includes some of the reasons for talking about "non-dominant gender and sexual identities" as well as "men and masculinities"?
4   Gender and race relations that lead to discrimination often have their roots in cultural, historical, economic, and political institutions that have evolved over long periods of time. Whose responsibility is it to address this unfair treatment? Governments? International organizations? Local organizations?

5   Gender activity: Get out a piece of paper and write a line down the middle of the page. On the left side write down characteristics of what it means to be a good man in the place where you are from. On the right side, write down what it means to be a good woman. Then, next to each point, describe where that message comes from: media/TV, family, school, and so on. Then reflect on how you embody or challenge the messages you receive.

## Online resources

- Resources, blogs, and publications from World Bank on Social Inclusion: www. worldbank.org/en/topic/social-inclusion
- Human Rights Watch has a number of resources about disability rights www.hrw. org/topic/disability-rights# as well as resources about other forms of difference which can be found under the tab "Topics" at: www.hrw.org/
- The Social Institutions and Gender Index measures discrimination against women across 180 countries: www.genderindex.org/
- The Women's Power Index ranks countries on their progress toward gender parity in political representation: www.cfr.org/article/womens-power-index.

## Notes

1  In this chapter, I will draw multiple examples from the United States. I do this for a couple of reasons: (1) poverty and exclusion happen in all parts of the world not just in less resourced regions; and (2) racism in the United States has global implications, not just because of how the United States participated in the Atlantic Slave trade and allowed slavery to exist until 1865 with the passing of the 13th amendment to the constitution, but also because of the role that the United States has played (and continues to play) in the world with its foreign policy, economic interests, and spread of US communications and media, which often have content that reinforces discrimination and exclusion.
2  Gender minorities can be identified and grouped according to any one of three different criteria: (1) People whose inner self-identity does not match gender assigned at birth. (2) People whose gender expression (or socially assigned gender) does not match gender assigned at birth. (3) People whose social expression does not conform to relevant cultural norms and expectations of gender.
3  Since the 1990s, many international development agencies and experts have claimed that 70 percent of the world's poor are women and children (see Chant 2006, Klasen 2004) due to systemic discrimination and violence against women. Though the actual statistic is debated, there is a consensus – corroborated by UN Women (the United Nations Entity for Gender Equality and the Empowerment of Women), UN Women affiliated agencies, and other international development agencies – that women often face greater deprivation than men in regard to income and economic participation, education, certain health-related issues, and political representation.

## Further reading

Abu-Lughod, L. 2013. *Do Muslim Women Need Saving?* Cambridge, MA: Harvard University Press.
Adichie, Chimamanda Ngozi. 2003. *Purple Hibiscus: A Novel.* New York City: Anchor Books.
Adichie, Chimamanda Ngozi. 2015. *We Should All Be Feminists.* New York City: Anchor Books.
Bulawayo, NoViolet. 2013. *We Need New Names.* London: Chatto & Windus.
Cosgrove, Serena, José Idiáquez, Leonard Joseph Bent, and Andrew Gorvetzian. 2021. *Surviving the Americas: Garifuna Persistence from Nicaragua to New York City.* Cincinnati, OH: University of Cincinnati Press.

Danticat, Edwidge.1994. *Breath, Eyes, Memory*. New York: Vintage Books.

Devandas-Aguilar, Catalina. 2020. *Report of the Special Rapporteur on the rights of persons with disabilities* (20 July). www.undocs.org/en/A/75/186

Ehrenreich, Barbara and Arlie Russell Hochschild, eds. 2004. *Global Woman: Nannies, Maids, and Sex Workers in the New Economy*. New York City: Henry Holt.

Fausto-Sterling, Anne. 2013. *Sex/Gender: Biology in a Social World*. New York: Routledge.

Hill Collins, Patricia and Bilge, Sirma. 2016. *Intersectionality. (Key Concepts)*. Chichester: Wiley.

Kristof, Nicholas and Sheryl WuDunn. 2009. *Half the Sky: Turning Oppression into Opportunity for Women Worldwide*. New York: Random House.

Lee, Erika. 2019. *America for Americans: A History of Xenophobia in the United States*. New York: Basic Books.

Menchu, Rigoberta.1984. *I, Rigoberta Menchu: An Indian Woman in Guatemala*. New York City: Verso.

Thomas, Deborah. 2019. *Political Life in the Wake of the Plantation: Sovereignty, Witnessing, Repair*. Durham, NC: Duke University Press.

## Works cited

Adair, Vivyan C. 2002. "Branded with Infamy: Inscriptions of Poverty and Class in the United States." *Signs: Journal of Women in Culture and Society* 27.2: 451–471.

Association of American Universities. 2020. "Report on the AAU Campus Climate Survey on Sexual Assault and Misconduct," revised 17 January 2020. www.aau.edu/sites/default/files/AAU-Files/Key-Issues/Campus-Safety/Revised%20Aggregate%20report%20%20and%20appendices%201-7_(01-16-2020_FINAL).pdf. Accessed 12 January 2021.

Bashford, A. and Levine, Philippa. 2010. *The Oxford Handbook of the History of Eugenics (Oxford Handbooks)*. New York: Oxford University Press.

Bowleg, Lisa. 2012. "The Problem with the Phrase 'Women and Minorities': Intersectionality – an Important Theoretical Framework for Public Health." *American Journal of Public Health*. 102.7: 1267–1273.

Chant, Sylvia. 2006. "Rethinking the 'Feminization of Poverty' in relation to aggregate gender indices." *Journal of Human Development* 7.2: 201–220.

Chasin, C. J. DeLuzio. 2013. "Reconsidering Asexuality and Its Radical Potential." *Feminist Studies* 39.2: 405–426.

Clark, Jocalyn and Richard Horton. 2019. "A Coming of Age for Gender in Global Health." *The Lancet* 393.10189: 2367–2369.

Conley, Dalton. 2003. "Race: The Power of an Illusion." *Ask the Experts*. Public Broadcasting Service (PBS). www.pbs.org/race/000_About/002_04-experts-03-02.htm. Accessed 14 April 2021.

Connell, Raewyn. 2011. *Confronting Equality: Gender, Knowledge and Global Change* . Malden, MA: Polity Press.

Cosgrove, Serena. 2010. *Leadership from the Margins: Women and Civil Society Organizations in Argentina, Chile, and El Salvador*. New Brunswick, NJ: Rutgers University Press.

Cosgrove, Serena. 2016. "The Absent State: Teen Mothers and New Patriarchal Forms of Gender Subordination in Democratic Republic of Congo," in Sanford, Victoria, Katerina Stefatos and Cecilia Salvi, eds. *The State and Gender Violence*. New Brunswick, NJ: Rutgers University Press.

Cosgrove, Serena. 2019. "Who will use my loom when I am gone? An Intersectional Analysis of Mapuche Women's Progress in Twenty-First Century Chile," in Olena Hankivsky and Julia Jordan-Zachery, eds. *The Palgrave Handbook of Intersectionality in Public Policy*, New York: Palgrave Macmillan.

Cosgrove, Serena, José Idiáquez, Leonard Joseph Bent and Andrew Gorvetzian. 2021. *Surviving the Americas: Garifuna Persistence from Nicaragua to New York City*. Cincinnati, OH: University of Cincinnati Press.

Craske, Nikki. 2003. "Gender, Poverty, and Social Movements," in Sylvia Chant, ed. with Nikki Craske. *Gender in Latin America*, 46–70. New Brunswick, NJ: Rutgers University Press.

Crenshaw, Kimberlé. 1991. "Mapping the margins: intersectionality, identity politics, and violence against women of color." *Stanford Law Review* 43.6: 1241–1299.

Crenshaw, Kimberlé. 2000. *Background Paper for the Expert Meeting on the Gender-Related Aspects of Race Discrimination.* United Nations.

Ernst and Young. 2009. Groundbreakers: Using the strength of women to rebuild the world economy. www.vitalvoices.org/sites/default/files/uploads/Groundbreakers.pdf. Accessed 29 October 2016.

Grzanka, Patrick R., ed. 2014. *Intersectionality: A Foundations and Frontiers Reader.* Boulder, CO: Westview Press.

Hangen, Susan. 2005. "Race and the politics of identity in Nepal." *Ethnology* 44.1: 49–64.

Hill Collins, Patricia. 2014. *Black Feminist Thought: Knowledge, Consciousness, and the Politics of Empowerment* (2nd ed.). New York: Routledge.

Hill Collins, Patricia and Sirma Bilge. 2016. *Intersectionality.* Malden, MA: Polity Press.

Jakubowski, Kaylee. 2014. "Pansexuality 101: It's More Than 'Just Another Letter'" Everyday Feminism: 12 November. www.everydayfeminism.com/2014/11/pansexuality-101/

Khader, Serene. 2011. *Adaptive Preferences and Women's Empowerment.* New York: Oxford University Press.

Khader, Serene. 2012. "Must theorising about adaptive preferences deny women's agency?" *Journal of Applied Philosophy* 29.4: 302–317.

Klasen, Stephan. 2004. *Gender-Related Indicators of Well-Being.* Discussion Papers/Universität Göttingen, Ibero-Amerika-Institut für Wirtschaftsforschung, No. 102. www.econstor.eu/handle/10419/23863. Accessed 26 April 2015.

Kritz, Brian. 2014. "The global transgender population and the International Criminal Court." *Yale Human Rights & Development Law Journal* 17.1: 1–39. www.digitalcommons.law.yale.edu/yhrdlj/vol17/iss1/1.

Lee, Erika. 2019. *America for Americans: A History of Xenophobia in the United States.* New York: Basic Books.

Lenhardt, Amanda and Emma Samman. 2015. "In quest of inclusive progress: Exploring intersecting inequalities in human development." London: Overseas Development Institute. www.developmentprogress.org.

Lindsey, Linda L. 2021. *Gender: Sociological Perspectives* (seventh edn). New York: Routledge.

Link, Bruce G. and Jo C. Phelan. 1995. "Social conditions as fundamental causes of disease." *Journal of Health and Social Behavior Extra Issue*: 80–94.

Moser, Caroline O. N.1993. *Gender Planning and Development: Theory, Practice and Training.* New York: Routledge.

Nallari, Raj and Breda Griffith. 2011. *Gender and Macroeconomic Policy.* Washington DC.: The World Bank.

O'Brien, Jodi. 2016. "Seeing agnes: notes on a transgender biocultural ethnomethodology." *Symbolic Interaction* 39: 306–329.

O'Brien, Jodi. 2017. "Introduction: Where is Gender?" in O'Brien, Jodi and Arlene Stein, eds. *Gender, Sexuality, and Intimacy: A Contexts Reader.* Newbury Park, CA: Sage.

Oluo, Ijeoma. 2018. *So You Want to Talk about Race.* New York: Seal Press Book.

Park, Andrew. 2016. "A Development Agenda for Sexual and Gender Minorities," International Programs, The Williams Institute, UCLA School of Law: June. www.williamsinstitute.law.ucla.edu/wp-content/uploads/Development-Agenda-SGM-Jul-2016.pdf. Accessed 23 December 2020.

Prugl, Elisabeth, and Audrey Lustgarten. 2006. "Mainstreaming Gender in International Organizations," in Jaquette, Jane S. and Gale Summerfield, eds. *Women and Gender Equity in Development Theory and Practice: Institutions, resources, and mobilization.* Durham, NC: Duke University Press.

Radcliffe, Sarah A. 2015. *Dilemmas of Difference: Indigenous Women and the Limits of Postcolonial Development Policy*. Durham, NC: Duke University Press.

Rai, Shirin M. 2011. "Gender and Development: Theoretical Perspectives," in *The Women, Gender and Development Reader* (2nd edn). London: Zed Books.

Robeyns, Ingrid. 2003. "Sen's capability approach and gender inequality: selecting relevant capabilities." *Feminist Economics* 9.2–3: 61–92.

Rose, Fred. 1997. "Toward a class-cultural theory of social movements: reinterpreting new social movements." *Sociological Forum* 12.3: 461–494.

Roxburgh, Susan. 2009. "Untangling inequalities: gender, race, and socioeconomic differences in depression." *Sociological Forum* 24.2: 357–381.

Rupp, Leila J. 1999. *A Desired Past: A Short History of Same-sex Love in America*. Chicago, IL: University of Chicago Press.

Rupp, Leila J. 2009. *Sapphistries: A Global History of Love Between Women*. New York City: New York University Press.

Russo, Nancy Felipe, and Angela Pirlott. 2006. "Gender-based violence." *Annals of the New York Academy of Sciences* 1087.1: 178–205.

Sen, Amartya. 1990. "More than 100 Million Women are Missing." *New York Review of Books*. www.nybooks.com/articles/archives/1990/dec/20/more-than-100-million-women-are-missing/. Accessed 26 April 2015.

Sen, Amartya. 1999. *Development as Freedom*. New York: Anchor Books.

Smedley, Audrey. 1998. "'Race' and the construction of human identity." *American Anthropologist* 100.3: 690–702.

United Nations Development Fund for Women (UNIFEM). 2005. "Progress of the world's women: Women, work, and poverty." www.un-ngls.org/orf/women-2005.pdf. Accessed 8 April 2017.

Wanner, Thomas, and Ben Wadham. 2015. "Men and masculinities in international development: 'menstreaming' gender and development?" *Development Policy Review* 33.1: 15–32.

World Bank. 2020. "Proportion of seats held by women in national parliaments (%)" *Data*. www.data.worldbank.org/indicator/SG.GEN.PARL.ZS?most_recent_value_desc=false. Accessed 12 January 2020.

Yang, Philip Q. and Koshy, Kavitha. 2016. "The "Becoming White Thesis" Revisited." *Journal of Public and Professional Sociology* 8.1, 1–27. www.digitalcommons.kennesaw.edu/cgi/viewcontent.cgi?referer=https://scholar.google.com/&httpsredir=1&article=1096&context=jpps. Accessed 22 January 2021.

Zinn, Howard. 1980. *A People's History of the United States*. New York: Harper Perennial Modern Classics.

# 7 State institutions, governance, and poverty

*Benjamin Curtis*

## Learning objectives

- Define "governance" and "institutions."
- Explain how governance and institutions contribute to poverty.
- Analyze why bad or inadequate governance/institutions occur.
- Describe policies to promote better governance and institutions that can contribute to human development.

## Vignette 7.1

*As we drove up to the intersection, an electronic sign indicated that there were four seconds left before the traffic lights would turn. We slowed, the light turned to yellow, and we stopped. A traffic cop stood on one of the corners and nodded at us pleasantly. Our driver nodded back and said to us, "You don't have to fear the police. You can always ask them a question or ask for help if you need it." For many of us raised in high-income countries, this anecdote seems so commonplace as not to warrant recounting, much less inclusion in a book on causes and solutions to global poverty. But this event did not occur in some comfortable, affluent suburb in the rich world – it occurred in Rwanda, where in 1994 the extremist Hutu government, militias, and paramilitary groups perpetrated a genocide that killed around 850,000 Tutsis and moderate Hutus.*

*The government that took power after the genocide was headed by President Paul Kagame, the leader of the rebel forces that fought the Hutu extremists. Though much of what state institutions provide – laws, law enforcement, courts, public services, and infrastructure – had been destroyed during the genocide, President Kagame vowed to rebuild the country and make it an example of the type of development and prosperity African countries can achieve. From utter calamity in 1994, Rwanda has made significant progress, in 2019 ranking 157 out of 189 countries rated on the Human Development Index and 51 out of 180 on the Corruption Perceptions Index. Needless to say, Rwanda is still a low-income country, but it is definitely not a failed state. From functioning traffic lights to police who can be trusted, our research trip to Rwanda operated quite smoothly. Even when leaving the capital to drive to the border with the Democratic Republic of the Congo, we were happy to find good, paved roads that reached out across the country. When work was being done on the road, highway workers organized the traffic so everyone could get to their destination promptly and in an orderly fashion.*

*This picture changed dramatically when we walked across the border to the Congolese city of Goma. With one million inhabitants, Goma is the largest city in the Eastern Congo, a region ravaged by war since 1994. Our all-wheel drive vehicle rocked and bucked as it attempted to make its way around the city, traversing potholed roads strewn with volcanic rock that had not been cleared since the 2002 eruption of nearby Mount Nyiragongo. Here there were no functioning traffic lights, but there were a few traffic police in evidence. Mostly, they acted as human traffic lights, waving one line of vehicles through an intersection at a time. In other cases, they stood on the side of the road, motioning drivers around particularly deep potholes. As we commented on the more chaotic traffic situation in Goma, our driver said, "Don't trust the police or the soldiers." And both times we were stopped during our trip there, soldiers asked for bribes even though we had all vehicle papers in order and had committed no traffic infractions.*

*Given how poor the Congo is (with a very low HDI score), you might assume that the government has prioritized health, education, security, and poverty over such things as road maintenance and traffic police. But that would assume that there is a functioning government with adequate resources to fund its priorities. In fact, doctors, teachers, and other state employees often seek employment outside of their regular jobs because the government is seldom able to pay them. It has not been government police that managed to improve the security situation around Goma, but rather the peace-enforcing troops of the United Nations. When we visited camps outside of Goma for people displaced by the conflict, we were overwhelmed by the poverty and need of those living there. Without access to any form of housing that would be considered dignified, families sleep on the rocky ground under tattered tarps. Disease, malnutrition, violence, and unemployment keep these families dependent on handouts from UN agencies and international non-governmental organizations. After a long day visiting community leaders in the camps, we drove back into the city and invited our hosts out to dinner. They declined, saying, "It's best you be in for the night by 6pm because it's just not safe once it's dark."*

## Introduction

What a difference a border can make. But what is the difference, precisely? This anecdote comparing Rwanda with the Eastern Congo reveals a lot about the relationship between state institutions, governance, and poverty. When institutions and governance function reasonably well, as in Rwanda, people's wellbeing can be demonstrably improved. When institutions and governance do not function well, as in the Congo, then governments cannot pay their employees, control their territories, uphold laws, or prevent violence; citizens lack basic services and democratic public institutions that respond to their needs; and people may fear for their very lives. In the worst case, when institutions completely collapse, a society risks falling into anarchy, as in Rwanda in 1994 or Somalia more recently, and human development is tragically compromised.

Over the past several decades, state institutions and governance have increasingly been recognized as crucial for good development outcomes. The World Bank and many other international bodies have enshrined "good governance" as a programmatic goal for promoting economic growth. But there are still some major uncertainties about the relationship between institutions, governance, and poverty. Those uncertainties can perhaps best be summed up by this question: Do countries get rich because they have good institutions, or do they have good institutions because they get rich? This chapter will explore answers to that question, explaining what "institutions" are, how they relate to poverty, and how they can be improved for the purposes of poverty reduction.

## Definitions and measures

The scholarly literature offers many different attempts to define institutions, and a consistent criticism of the institutional approach to studying poverty and development is that these definitions are too vague or multifarious (see i.a. Gisselquist 2012, Hydén and Court 2002, Sáez 2012, Van Doeveren 2011, Williams and Siddique 2008). Douglass North provides probably the most commonly-cited definition of institutions as "the rules of the game in society, or the humanly devised constraints that shape human interaction" (North 1990: 3). What does this mean? Institutions are sets of formal and informal rules that determine how humans behave in society. Informal rules include norms, traditions, religion or culture most broadly; their relationship to poverty is discussed in Chapter 6 on social difference. The present chapter is primarily concerned with formal institutions such as laws, the judiciary, the bureaucracy, and electoral systems, in other words, state institutions. These state institutions are what provide basic services such as education, health care, and other forms of infrastructure, including roads and electricity, as well as law enforcement and protection of public order. They also, as per the North definition, shape human interaction: laws obviously help determine how we behave in society, and institutions such as the judicial system or the representative assemblies of government deeply impact how society functions. So, for example, property rights are an institution, as are the laws laying out business regulation, or who can run for political office.

Governance can be thought of as a specific aspect of institutions, which is why these two concepts are combined in this chapter. "Governance" is also subject to a dizzying variety of definitions, but its key components include: how citizens and groups express their interests and exercise their rights; how officials are selected; how policies are formulated and implemented; and how public services are managed. Governance thus refers not only to how governments are elected by and respond to citizens, but also to how public policies are designed and carried out. So, governance encompasses *what* is done (i.e. specific policies) but also *how* it is done (i.e. the processes for making policies), and it operates at multiple levels (local, regional, national, and international). Governance grows out of institutions such as the constitution, the electoral system, the bureaucracy, and other administrative systems that manage a country's affairs. If institutions are the "rules of the game," then governance can be thought of as "how the game is played," that is, how those formal state institutions are used in practice (Williamson 2000). Governance (and political elites) can also change institutions, such as by passing laws that then become "the rules."

More concretely, institutions such as the constitution, the courts and bureaucratic/administrative offices can all determine how elections are run or what economic policies are adopted, and governance is the actual running of elections and the implementation of economic policies. Think of state institutions as structures, and governance as the particular policies implemented within those structures. In the United States, the Internal Revenue Service is an institution, but tax policies are examples of governance. Likewise in, say, Algeria, the Ministry of Education is a governmental institution, but the policies it adopts and services it provides depend upon the governance, namely the interaction of citizens, political elites, civil society groups, and other actors. Hence governance can determine the extent to which people have access to institutions and the services they provide. For example, policies relating to school fees affect whether poor families can send their children to school. Decisions on where to locate medical clinics influence whether poor families have access to health care. Henceforth, to avoid unwieldy language, most of the time when "institutions" are mentioned in this chapter the concept of governance will be included, unless otherwise noted.

These basic definitions of institutions and governance have generally avoided normative claims, that is, what state institutions and governance *should* be. Such normative prescriptions for institutions are commonplace, however. The United Nations has proposed that "good" institutions operate according to these principles: equity, transparency, participation, responsiveness, efficiency, accountability and the rule of law (United Nations 2012). The idea is that good institutions treat everyone equitably, are reliably transparent, promote citizen participation, and are both responsive and accountable to those citizens. Further, good institutions operate efficiently and according to the rule of law.

Similarly, as soon as one examines the typical indicators or measures used to evaluate governance quality, normative assumptions enter. A number of different evaluative schemes exist, such as the Polity Project or the Quality of Government Institute; two data sets more accessible to non-specialists are Freedom House's Freedom in the World Survey, or the World Bank's Worldwide Governance Indicators (WGI). The World Bank's system, while often criticized, is also highly influential, so this chapter draws heavily from it (for critiques see i.a. Apaza 2009, Fukuyama 2013, Hickey 2012). The WGI defines governance as "the traditions and institutions by which authority in a country is exercised. This includes (a) the process by which governments are selected, monitored and replaced; (b) the capacity of the government to effectively formulate and implement sound policies; and (c) and the respect of citizens and the state for the institutions that govern economic and social interactions among them" (Kaufmann *et al.* 2010: 4). Six different indicators each relate to one of these three areas (see Box 7.1).

---

**Box 7.1 The World Bank's Worldwide Governance Indicators**

1    The process by which governments are selected, monitored and replaced:

    a    **Voice and Accountability:** capturing perceptions of the extent to which a country's citizens are able to participate in selecting their government, as well as freedom of expression, freedom of association and a free media.

    b    **Political Stability and Absence of Violence/Terrorism:** capturing perceptions of the likelihood that the government will be destabilized or overthrown by unconstitutional or violent means, including politically-motivated violence and terrorism.

2    The capacity of the government to effectively formulate and implement sound policies:

    a    **Government Effectiveness:** capturing perceptions of the quality of public services, the quality of the civil service and the degree of its independence from political pressures, the quality of policy formulation and implementation, and the credibility of the government's commitment to such policies.

    b    **Regulatory Quality:** capturing perceptions of the ability of the government to formulate and implement sound policies and regulations that permit and promote private sector development.

3    The respect of citizens and the state for the institutions that govern economic and social interactions among them:

a　**Rule of Law:** capturing perceptions of the extent to which agents have confidence in and abide by the rules of society, and in particular the quality of contract enforcement, property rights, the police and the courts, as well as the likelihood of crime and violence.

b　**Control of Corruption:** capturing perceptions of the extent to which public power is exercised for private gain, including both petty and grand forms of corruption, as well as "capture" of the state by elites and private interests.

Source: Kaufmann *et al.* (2010)

Voice and accountability, because they relate to freedom of expression and assembly, involve basic freedoms without which a government may be unresponsive to citizens. Moreover, a denial of these basic freedoms is also an infringement of an individual's basic capabilities, as we will discuss later. Political stability and the absence of violence is fairly self-explanatory, since problems in these areas impact basic human security (see Chapter 8 on conflict). Government effectiveness attempts to gauge how well a government fulfils the requirements of providing basic services for human development such as education and health. One element of this indicator, the quality of the civil service, has major influence on the quality of government services. Regulatory quality is another compound of measures related to "market-unfriendly policies" such as price controls and excessive government regulations on business.

Rule of law refers to a collection of concepts such as security of property rights, contract enforcement, and incidence of crime. The rationale for this indicator is that such legal guarantees are essential to protect not only rights but also investments and the incentive for economic gain. For example, if property rights are not protected, such that political elites can come along at any time and expropriate a businesswoman's enterprise that she built up over years, then the individual drive for economic development will be undermined. The control of corruption is generally measured by *perceptions* of corruption in a given country (since actual corruption is usually illegal, and hence often hidden). Corruption's definition as "the exercise of public power for private gain" can refer to government officials engaging in graft, embezzlement, or taking bribes in order to enrich themselves. Though corruption exists to varying degrees in almost every society, where it is frequent it represents a breakdown of law that amounts to a fundamental failure of both institutions and governance. Tables 7.1, 7.2, and 7.3 give lists of the countries that rank best and worst on several of these indicators.

## How institutions impact poverty and development

When state institutions break down or do not operate well, they make people's lives worse. Think of the example of the Congo and Rwanda at the beginning of this chapter: local government did very little for the displaced people in the camps outside Goma, so it was up to international institutions to provide relief. Or refer to the case of Nigeria: official corruption results in persecution and human rights abuses against the disempowered in particular (see Box 7.2). These examples suggest that institutions can have a profound impact on both economic and human development. The theory behind the Worldwide Governance Indicators is that good institutions make economic growth possible. Good

*Table 7.1* Countries ranked according to voice and accountability score

| Best | Worst |
|------|-------|
| Norway | North Korea |
| New Zealand | Eritrea |
| Switzerland | Turkmenistan |
| Finland | South Sudan |
| Denmark | Syria |
| Sweden | Equatorial Guinea |
| Netherlands | Sudan |
| Luxembourg | Somalia |
| Canada | Yemen |
| Australia | Laos |

*Table 7.2* Countries ranked according to government effectiveness score

| Best | Worst |
|------|-------|
| Singapore | Somalia |
| Switzerland | South Sudan |
| Finland | Yemen |
| Andorra | Somalia |
| Hong Kong | Haiti |
| Norway | Libya |
| Denmark | Eritrea |
| Netherlands | Central African Republic |
| Sweden | Syria |
| Luxembourg | Comoros |

*Table 7.3* Countries ranked according to rule of law score

| Best | Worst |
|------|-------|
| Finland | Venezuela |
| Norway | Somalia |
| Switzerland | Syria |
| Sweden | South Sudan |
| New Zealand | Yemen |
| Austria | Libya |
| Singapore | DR Congo |
| Denmark | Iraq |
| Netherlands | Central African Republic |
| Luxembourg | Afghanistan |

Source: World Bank World Governance Indicators, 2018 data.

institutions protect property rights, which bolster individuals' incentives to work for gain. When people work hard and are rewarded appropriately for their labor, their incomes should rise. There are some serious methodological difficulties that complicate teasing out how much good institutions contribute to economic growth, and how much economic growth leads to good institutions. Therefore, though there are many studies claiming that good institutions promote economic growth, there are also many that deny a clear relationship (see i.a. Glaeser *et al.* 2004, Perera and Lee 2013, Rodrik *et al.* 2004).

---

**Box 7.2 Corruption and poverty in Nigeria**

Nigeria has a regrettable but well-founded reputation for high levels of corruption; the country ranked 146 out of 180 in Transparency International's 2019 Perceptions of Corruption Index. Many Nigerians can tell a story of extortion at the hands of a police officer. At traffic checkpoints, police routinely demand bribes for invented reasons. There are even reports of police simply pulling guns on people and demanding money, which is robbery as much as corruption. Police officers have admitted to targeting women sellers at markets because they are so vulnerable: they have to sell in order to make a living, so they will pay anything to stop the police from arresting them. Sometimes when the women do not have money, the police demand sex as payment. Resistance to such techniques can be costly in many ways. Police may round up a group of people for detention, which forces the people to pay for their freedom. One man in such a roundup described what happened when he refused to pay: "Two of them started to beat me. They used their guns to hit me on my face and body. […] The police said I was an armed robber and that they would kill me." When police officers demand even a small bribe equivalent to a few US dollars, it can represent a frighteningly large sum to a poor person. The poor are also less likely to have the knowledge, time, money, or personal connections to use the legal system for redress against corrupt officials. Judges and lawyers in Nigeria have confirmed that anyone who brings a criminal complaint might first have to pay for the complaint to be investigated. Corruption cases such as these fundamentally compromise the rule of law and constitute a human rights abuse. There are also very large crimes: embezzlement at upper levels of government has been unfortunately common. According to one estimate, in the 40 years after 1960, USD 380 billion was lost to graft and mismanagement. As a single example, a governor of one of Nigeria's oil-producing states was convicted of stealing USD 55 million, though he was later (controversially) pardoned. The theft of such large sums of money prevents the funds from potentially being spent on projects that would benefit the public. Corruption also seriously undermines the equitable distribution of economic development and its benefits.

Sources: Human Rights Watch (2011, 2010); US State Department (2012)

---

Nonetheless, there are several specific aspects of institutions/governance that have been reliably shown to boost economic growth. Those aspects can include protecting property rights, providing adequate security, and upholding the law in general. Corruption, for example, has often been highlighted as impeding economic growth and exacerbating poverty (see Herrera *et al.* 2007, Méon and Sekkat 2005, Tebaldi and Mohan 2010). Tebaldi and Mohan call institutions a "deep factor" impacting prosperity and poverty, that is, a factor with both long- and short-term implications that can influence various other causes of poverty. For example, meritocratic bureaucracies have been associated with economic growth, and higher levels of corruption deter economic growth. Similarly, countries with more stable governance and institutions have also been found to have experienced more growth (Soubbotina and Sheram 2000). Countries with better institutions as measured by the World Bank's indicators also do better in terms of health outcomes such as lower infant mortality, education outcomes such as higher literacy rates, and food security (Sacks and Levi 2010, UNDP 2011).

Evidence is strong overall that better institutions can limit poverty (Chong and Calderón 2000). They do so in part by determining who benefits from economic growth, which in turn helps determine who exercises political power (Bastiaensen *et al.* 2005, Rodrik 2000). Some institutional arrangements such as tax policies allow political elites disproportionately to capture the benefits of economic growth. This is the problem whereby, say, the top one percent of the population holds 40 percent of a country's wealth, as has happened in the United States in recent years. Institutions and governance can thereby produce income inequality, but income inequality can also reinforce weak or bad institutions (Chong and Gradstein 2007). "Bad" or "predatory" institutions means that they are used consciously by political elites to reinforce inequality, or otherwise where institutions intentionally disadvantage the poor. "Weak" institutions disadvantage the poor not through intention but by being inadequate through lack of funds, competency, planning, and so on.

Institutional failures can come about through intentional and unintentional means (Rotberg 2003). Sometimes people in power (whether in political office, or with major economic or political influence) use institutions and governance to pursue policies that create poverty. For example, Omar al-Bashir, the former president of Sudan, was charged by the International Criminal Court with waging genocide in Darfur for his own political ends. Elites in many lands' colonial regimes structured institutions so that rights and economic benefits accrued to very small segments of the population. Institutional arrangements that allow political elites to neglect public services to the poor, or in which government is so weak that it cannot provide those services, are another way that institutions contribute to poverty. In intentional cases, institutions, governance, and politics are all designed to benefit certain groups or individuals while disadvantaging others.

Unintentional institutional deficiencies can arise in concert with intentional ones, but sometimes separately. Inadequate basic services such as clean water or sanitation are not always the outcome of insidious elites. Sometimes governments and people in power have the will to provide such services, but they do not have the means. Likewise, weak legal systems, lack of security for life and property, and inequitable economic development can exist despite efforts against them; institutional change, as we will see, can be very difficult. It is not uncommon that countries may adopt policies with the intention of aiding the poor, but the country's institutions are too weak to implement those policies effectively. There is a poverty trap here: bad or weak institutions can make poverty worse, but poverty also can make institutions worse (Bowles 2006).

## Institutions and capabilities

Whatever their exact relationship with economic growth, state institutions' impact on poverty must also be considered from the capability perspective. We will consider four main areas in which institutions can either diminish or expand human freedom: (1) basic human security; (2) basic public services; (3) economic development with equity; and (4) basic civil rights such as political participation and free speech. Failures and inadequacies of institutions in these areas create capability and income poverty. They limit what people are able to do and to be; they unjustly constrain the choices people are able to make to live a life that they have reason to value.

Basic human security refers to the most fundamental facts of daily safety (for more on human security, see Chapter 8). Are we afraid of being killed at any moment? Of someone stealing our property or otherwise hurting us? When we fear for the most elemental protection of our bodies and our lives, we are living in a kind of unfreedom, namely to live without constant fear. In a violent society such as that famously described by the seventeenth-century philosopher Thomas Hobbes – the "war of all against all," where life is "solitary, poor, nasty, brutish, and short" – institutions are so deficient that basic security is threatened. Such an unsafe society does not support human flourishing. Institutions to guarantee basic bodily and property security include a police force, laws that are clear and apply equally to everyone, and a court system that aids in the enforcement of those laws. Fragile and failed states such as the Democratic Republic of the Congo, and other states experiencing conflict such as Rwanda in 1994 or Syria more recently, often have serious deficiencies to meet this basic criterion of adequate human life.

Basic public services refers to clean water, sanitation, education, health care, and infrastructure such as roads. In some countries, government programs supply needy people with housing, food subsidies, fuel such as kerosene, seeds for planting, relief during natural disasters, or pensions for widows and the disabled. Institutions impact capabilities by the provision of such public services. For instance, are people able to read and write? That often depends on whether there was a school in their community that they were able to attend. State institutions are vital here because private markets are less likely to supply these public goods, or at any rate unlikely to supply them in a way that would assure equitable access to the services for people who do not have the money to acquire them. Educational and health deficiencies exacerbate poverty, but institutions partly account for why those deficiencies exist, and who suffers the most from them. Besides excluding the poor, institutions can also exclude people from minority or marginalized backgrounds, such that the benefits of functioning institutions are not shared equitably across a country's population.

The level at which a government should supply public services can vary and may be disputed – to how much health care are we entitled in order to meet "basic" levels, for instance? Those basic minimum threshold levels can be societally specific. However, we can affirm that it is the job of state institutions to provide access to these services, especially for people who would not otherwise be able to afford them. There is a long and powerful tradition in ethical philosophy holding that one of the foremost jobs of government is to assist the poorest and neediest in a society. The reason is that without such governmental assistance, the poorest and neediest would continually fall below the minimum thresholds of an adequate human life. Government assistance is supposed to help them over the minimum threshold and ensure that they are not perpetually deprived and disadvantaged. Thus, government must have some preference for the poor to assure the attainment of the minimum capabilities, otherwise it will fail to meet basic standards of justice. When institutions are so weak or bad that government cannot perform this function, then they help create or perpetuate poverty.

Institutions that promote economic development with equity will usually be attentive to this preference for the poor and the need to assure the attainment of basic capabilities. As we have seen, most scholars agree that certain institutional features are beneficial for economic development, including the aforementioned rule of law, low levels of corruption, and bureaucratic effectiveness. When these features are not present – in other words, when you have a government in which corruption is rampant, that does not protect property rights, that does not provide roads and other infrastructure – the absence of such features can retard economic growth. On an individual, human level, state institutions impact capabilities by setting the rules of earning a livelihood. For instance, are people able to own land without fear of expropriation, and invest in that land to make it more productive and help support themselves or their family? This often depends upon legal frameworks that recognize rights and ensure equal enforcement of laws. Hence bad or weak institutions contribute to conditions in which people are likely to live in material and income poverty. Beyond this, institutional arrangements including laws, the electoral system and the judicial system can influence who benefits from economic growth, sometimes concentrating wealth and power in the hands of a small minority, as mentioned earlier. Such institutions disproportionately distribute and exacerbate poverty by disadvantaging people economically and politically.

The fourth area in which institutions can contribute to poverty is through basic civil rights. In accordance with the Universal Declaration of Human Rights, every human being is entitled to freedom of expression, of association and assembly, of religious exercise, and other fundamental rights guaranteeing political participation and freedom from unwarranted search and seizure. These rights equate to capabilities: we should all have the capability to reason for ourselves, to express our political opinions, to associate with the individuals or groups we choose, and to exercise some control over our political officials. Put simply, the absence of such rights and capabilities is a form of poverty, since we are all entitled to them as human beings. Institutions that infringe upon such rights therefore create or increase poverty. Regimes that arrest democratic protestors, for instance, or that crack down on speech criticizing the government, or that uphold discriminatory laws against people of particular minority groups whether religious, ethnic, or sexual, all exacerbate forms of poverty. There is a deeper issue beyond the authoritarian regimes that curtail civil rights freedoms, however. The absence of political participatory rights can mire people in poverty because, without those rights, how are people going to articulate their political interests and hold leaders accountable?

It is clear that institutional deficiencies disproportionately disadvantage the poor. This is first of all because poor people are more likely to depend upon public goods that the state should provide (since they often cannot afford private schools, private health care, their own cars for transportation, and so on). When institutions are weak, then public goods are probably in short supply, and the possibilities for poverty reduction are seriously limited. A very common complaint of poor people is that public services do not reach them, or that they are denied access to existing public services. "Poor people have no access to the police station, bank, government offices, and the judge of the village court," a villager in Bangladesh reported. "The rich people dominate these institutions" (Narayan *et al.* 2000a: 200). A respondent from a participatory poverty assessment in Madagascar lamented, "The state is simply absent from people's lives and strategies for securing their needs" (Narayan *et al.* 2000b: 67). "Only God listens to us," a respondent in Egypt said (Narayan *et al.* 2000a: 200).

Poor people often rate state institutions very low on responsiveness, trust, accountability, respect, honesty, and fairness. Indeed, research from the *Voices of the Poor* series found that poor people rate state institutions as overwhelmingly ineffective (Narayan *et al.* 2000a). They reported that the services themselves were often shoddy: wells or other water schemes did not work, hospital care was substandard or unavailable, teachers did not show up for school, subsidies for farming did not arrive or did not help. "We keep hearing about money that the government allocates for projects, and nothing happens on the ground," according to one respondent in South Africa (Narayan *et al.* 2000b: 67). Access problems are also very common. Poor people often complained that because of corruption and maltreatment on the part of government officials, they found their inter- action with state institutions to be humiliating. Respondents said that they would rather not go to a police station to report a crime because the police would extort money from them; that hospital workers would ignore them, harass them, or demand bribes; or that when they went to government assistance offices, they were made to feel stupid and greedy for asking for help. In short, institutions sometimes fail poor people by robbing them of their dignity.

### The importance of democracy in institutions and governance

The discussion of basic civil rights alludes to the relationship between democracy, institutions, and governance. Is democracy essential for human development? Interestingly, it is not essential for *economic* development. Scholars dispute whether democratic govern- ment promotes stronger economic growth. Some studies have found that democratization increases GDP per capita (Acemoglu *et al.* 2019). Others have dismissed such findings, however – and there are certainly historical examples of authoritarian governments achieving significant economic growth, such as in South Korea, Taiwan, Singapore, or China (Gerring *et al.* 2011). It has even been claimed that democracy has no necessary association with the quality of government (Rothstein and Tannenberg 2015). Despite these contrary perspectives, democracy should still be an ideal for every society, for two reasons. The first is that poor people themselves often see undemocratic governance as contributing to their poverty (Leavy and Howard 2013). The second is that democratic practices are fundamental to the expansion of capabilities.

To avoid the imprecision of loose understandings of "democracy," it must be defined. Robert Dahl's influential criteria of democracy include free and fair elections in which officials are chosen, and inclusive suffrage in those elections so that the vast proportion of the adult population has the right to vote and run for office. Further, democracy presumes freedom of expression, such as to criticize political officials without fear of punishment, and what in American terms is often referred to as freedom of assembly, that is, the right to form independent associations or organizations, whether political parties, non- governmental organizations (NGOs), or interest groups. Dahl also adds the component of "alternative information," such that citizens have the right to sources of information that are not controlled by the government or any one political group (Dahl 2000). These various practices and arrangements help assure that citizens can challenge their govern- ment and other sources of power (such as large corporations), and that these sources of power remain accountable to citizens. Finally, democracy entails that citizens have legal means of redress against each other, against government and against corporations; this again is part of the equitable rule of law.

The capabilities approach explores more specifically why these democratic rights and practices help bring people out of poverty. As Sen (2000) proclaimed, development is about expanding the scope of human freedoms. So, the denial of basic political freedoms is a kind of poverty. Deficits in democracy therefore lead to capability poverty. Such deficits can take many forms, as indicated in Table 7.4.

One way that people can be empowered, that poverty can be eliminated, is by elimin- ating these democratic deficits. Democratic institutions help ensure that people have the

*Table 7.4* Forms of democratic deficits

| In formal constitutional and political arrangements | In substance or practices of power |
|---|---|
| • Poorly protected civil and political rights<br>• Access to legal and administrative systems skewed against minorities, the unorganized, the poor<br>• Lack of free and fair elections<br>• Electoral systems that distort outcomes or disenfranchise minorities<br>• Weak constitutional checks and balances<br>• Rule of law absent or weak<br>• Lack of governmental transparency<br>• Weak democratic control of military, police, and intelligence bodies<br>• Key decisions made by international bodies (IMF, World Bank, UN and its agencies, etc.) not by national governments | • Major societal inequities (on basis of class, gender, region, religion, ethnicity, etc.)<br>• De facto disenfranchisement of the poor due to lack of resources and organization<br>• Uncivil society: cultures of intolerance, lack of respect for difference<br>• Violence, intimidation, especially against marginalized groups<br>• Electorates offered little effective choice between alternative political programs<br>• Few autonomous, effective, broadly-based civil society groups to challenge the government and vested interests<br>• Political processes weakened and social capital destroyed through violent conflict<br>• Patrimonial politics: government manipulation via patronage, ethnicity, etc.<br>• Endemic corruption<br>• Political processes suborned by elite economic and social interests<br>• Judiciary weak or coopted<br>• Weak opposition parties<br>• Media lacking in independence<br>• Hegemony of international firms |

Source: Luckham *et al.* (2000: 24).

agency to decide collectively about matters that concern their communities. Similarly, democratic processes enhance people's influence over decisions that may impact their capabilities (Drydyk 2005). Political participation cannot be reduced merely to elections. It needs to be both deeper and more expansive. The kind of democratic participation that the capabilities approach envisions promises that every adult should have a participatory role in discussions and deliberation (Alkire 2002, Crocker 2007). Reasoning, for both private and public matters, is one of Nussbaum's central capabilities. True democracy means that all individuals should be equipped so that they can realize the functionings of their rights to deliberation, discussion, and political decision making. Thus through democratic practices, individuals collectively construct their own social realities, and together define their societal priorities and values (Bonvin and Laruffa 2018).

This commitment to democracy must operate in both high politics and "deep politics" in order to expand people's capabilities. High politics refers to the state-level institutions such as electoral systems and representative government. It can also refer to a "high" level of civil society beyond that of the nation-state. Democratic politics that give people agency must apply to the institutions of governance at the state level, but should also operate above the state, at a supranational or global level. International institutions that ignore, discriminate, devalue, or marginalize people or societies from lower income countries can be undemocratic, just as dictators within a country can. Hence global civil society must have the same respect for agency, deliberation, and participation as nation states. "Deep politics" is a term used by Luckham *et al.* (2000) to denote the micro level of political interactions at a quotidian, often individual level. Democratic deep politics embrace the rights, voice, and agency of women, the poor, and other marginalized groups to give them their due influence in institutions and on governance. Much as institutions created to entrench particular individuals' or groups' power are harmful to democratic government, so too are persistent inequities of power at the micro level, in homes, schools, markets, places of worship, or local governmental offices. From the capabilities perspective, democratic politics affirms that all people are entitled to participate not just at the most visible levels of voting and freedom to speak out against rulers, but also with decision making and freedom of expression at the household, village, and international levels.

Democracy is an elusive goal – even the vaunted democracies in the West such as the United States or Britain have to work at (and often fall short of) including marginalized and excluded groups, and equalizing political power. So, in many regards democratic institutions and governance are an *aspiration*, but one that all societies should strive for in order to maximize human development. Democracy is the best way of respecting human dignity and providing a space wherein people can express their interests and decide collectively on the public good. Even in countries with relatively good institutions, democratic governance must battle against corruption, bureaucratic inefficiencies, and unequal distributions of power. Indeed, democratic institutions are no guarantee of democratic politics, since political elites and/or wealthy people are adept at manipulating those institutions to serve their interests. Thus, throughout the world poor people have difficulty driving pro-poor policies. Besides the way the wealthy are able to engineer policies that favor themselves, poor people face an additional hurdle in that they may lack the education, social capital, and security that would enable them to mobilize more effectively so that the government is responsive to their needs and interests. When it works as it should, however, democracy means that the poor have equitable access to and control over institutions that enhance capabilities such as schools, hospitals, and government bodies. By exercising that control, people are empowered, their agency is strengthened, and they are free to develop both their aspirations as well as their opportunities to lead a life that they value (Sen 2009).

## What shapes institutions and governance?

The necessity of correcting institutional deficiencies points to the need to understand how institutions develop. Most simply, how do you get "good" institutions rather than "bad" ones? We will devote most of our attention to factors influencing institutional development in the shorter term, roughly since the Second World War. However, there is an expansive scholarly literature analyzing the long-term factors, roughly over the last 500 years (for reviews, see Lloyd and Lee 2018, Nunn 2009). These long-term factors can include the impacts of the slave trade, the legal system of the colonizing country, and how much the colonizing country invested in public goods such as education. Some colonizers set up "extractive" institutions with lasting, unequal power structures that have impeded economic development over many years (Acemoglu *et al.* 2001, 2004, 2006; Engerman and Sokoloff 1997, 2003). Not all the long-term factors are tied to colonialism, however. Other research shows how societal cultural traits such as family structures, moral attitudes, and levels of trust and individualism have impacted institutions (Alesina and Giuliano 2015). Institutions and cultural attributes that existed in Africa before the European colonizers arrived also influenced how different tribal groups developed, quite apart from colonial or national borders (Michalopoulous and Papaioannou 2013, 2014). In general, high levels of ethnic/linguistic heterogeneity have been found to be historically problematic for the development of good institutions (Johnson and Koyama 2017).

The long-term legacy of undemocratic institutions has promoted both income and capability poverty by helping keep the rich, rich, and the poor, poor. However, these historical "deep determinants" of institutional development can be very difficult to change; institutional arrangements exhibit a high degree of inertia and persistence. For this reason, we focus on the shorter-term factors, which may be more amenable to improvement. The less pernicious short-term factors include an inadequate tax base and a dearth of qualified civil servants. In especially poor countries, there may be relatively little taxable wealth, and hence fewer resources for governments to provide services to the population. For example, whatever Haiti's other institutional and governance problems, the society as a whole is so poor that it limits what funds a government could raise to build things such as hospitals, highways, schools, and ports. A shortage of highly-trained and competent bureaucrats can also hamper government effectiveness. Any program, municipality, or region is not likely to be well administered if the people responsible have little experience or know-how. Sometimes weak governance in the developing world is due to a scarcity of qualified managers.

The more malign deficiencies relate to politics. As mentioned previously, it is not at all uncommon that institutions remain unequal, and governance inadequate, by intention. If political elites regard sharing power, protecting civil rights, promoting equitable economic development, or ensuring widespread access to basic services as undermining their own powers or privileges, then concentrated power and wealth will persist. Perhaps the most famous example of elites insidiously manipulating governance is the "resource curse" (for reviews, see Ross 2015, van der Ploeg 2011). Dependence on natural resources, such as oil in countries like Venezuela, Nigeria, Chad, or Iraq, has had pronounced negative impacts on institutions and governance. Scholars have shown that autocratic governments are more common in countries where the economy is dominated by natural resources: leaders try to control the resource revenues, clamping down on political competition to ensure that they do (Humphreys *et al.* 2007, Mehlum *et al.* 2006, Robinson *et al.* 2006). Obviously, dictatorships do not arise in every country where natural resources are important to a country's economy; Norway is a major oil producer, for instance, yet remains a sturdy democracy. But Norway already had strong institutions before its oil sector grew, unlike many low- and middle-income countries.

Whether with oil, diamonds, copper, cocoa, or some other commodity, revenues from natural resources are relatively easy for political elites to capture, compared to economic sectors based on manufacturing or services. State-owned oil companies are ripe for corruption and authoritarian control in a way that, say, the technology sector would not be. If a dictator attempted to capture Silicon Valley, he would kill the goose that laid the golden egg, whereas oil wells will probably keep pumping even if they are not managed in a perspicacious fashion. Besides how they lend themselves to authoritarian control, natural resource revenues can warp institutions and governance in another way as well. Such revenues reduce the need to tax, which weakens accountability for leaders. If your government is flush with money by selling diamonds from the mines you control, then you have less motivation to tax your population. Once you start taxing the population, you become more beholden to the citizenry. Hence natural resource revenues mean that leaders can derive money for government functions without a strong tie to citizens' consent through taxes. By attenuating the bond between government and populace, natural resource revenues can corrupt the institutions that are supposed to serve the people, again making government a preserve of the elite. In short, the resource curse incentivizes political elites to manipulate institutions in a way that serves the few rather than the many.

Several final short-term factors further undermine institutions and governance. Political calculations and the resource curse can play another role through the corruption of bureaucratic administration. Bureaucracies that are not staffed by qualified people are sometimes an intentional strategy of political elites. When people in power give civil service jobs as a reward to their supporters, it creates a system of patronage. Patrons generate support by doling out such rewards at the local, regional, or national level. The result is that a society's bureaucratic administration is not meritocratic and there truly to serve the society, but rather to serve the interests of the patrons and their supporters (known as "clients"). The resource curse acts here in that elites can use resource revenues to buy support through patronage (such as by paying for roads, subsidies for consumer products, or other giveaways) rather than through electoral competition. So not only does a society end up with an ineffective institution in the form of a bureaucracy that cannot adequately administer, it also is saddled with autocratic institutions that are less responsive to citizen interests and less respectful of citizen rights.

The resource curse can also impact capabilities by harming basic human security, since resource-rich countries are sometimes more prone to conflict. The Democratic Republic of the Congo is again a paradigmatic case: the unaccountable official government has long warred with various paramilitaries and other states such as Rwanda, the fighting spurred in part by a contest to control the Congo's rich resources in diamonds and minerals. Economic development with equity is damaged by the resource curse because countries that are heavily dependent on natural resources tend to have lower economic growth. When a developing country's economy depends heavily on oil, diamonds, or minerals, it will probably lack productive investment in other economic sectors that could boost the country's competitiveness. Indeed, the resource curse has been shown to make other economic sectors less competitive, leaving the country even more dependent on the problematic natural resource. Low levels of economic development are usually associated with weak institutions, which in turn are associated with inadequate public services and civil rights, thereby contributing to poverty.

## Critiques of the institutions/governance perspective

Though weak or bad institutions can certainly worsen poverty, it is important to remember that the relationships between particular institutions and economic development are not always clear. There are enough questions or criticisms of the institutions literature that caution is necessary in drawing too firm conclusions about how institutions impact economic development. Some scholars such as Sachs *et al.* (2004), for instance, say that bad governance is not really a powerful explanation for underdevelopment. Others have noted that many of the concepts, definitions, and operationalization of variables in studies of institutions are vague at best and faulty at worst. The methodology of some studies that have claimed positive relationships between institutional quality and economic development have later been found problematic. Again, causality can be hard to isolate given that indicators such as rule of law, corruption, accountability, government effectiveness and so on are often intertwined. What is the relative impact of corruption versus faulty rule of law versus a lack of accountability in explaining poverty in, say, Myanmar? As yet, there are few definitive answers to that question.

Another caution is not to privilege Western models of institutions unduly. The typical definition of what constitutes "good" institutions is derived primarily from the Western experience and examples. There is some justification for this practice, but one must not go too far and conclude that Western models in their idealized form are appropriate for every society around the world (Hickey 2012, Unsworth 2010). For example, Ha-Joon Chang (2005) has criticized economists' fixation on property rights, alleging that this is an obsession too unquestioningly derived from Anglo-American examples, and that even the notion of "property rights" itself is a bundle of many other institutional arrangements such as land law, tax law, contract law, and intellectual property law. The point is that what works in Western societies, which have grown to depend on formal institutions, may not work so well elsewhere, such as in much of Sub-Saharan Africa where informal institutions may still predominate (Hydén 2007). One must beware of adopting a "one size fits all" approach to institutions and governance, assuming that what works in one high income country will work everywhere.

Two things should be kept in mind about this dispute over the importance of institutions. The first is that the dispute above all concerns institutions' role in economic development. The problems of causality and conceptual application are trickiest there. Much more confidence can hold for the role of institutions in human development. Certainly there are potential causality problems here too, in that relationships between health, education, and other forms of measurable wellbeing operate in a feedback loop with institutional development. Nonetheless, good institutions are essential for the capability approach by virtue of protecting political rights and helping to assure the equitable distribution of other rights and resources in a society. The second important thing to keep in mind from critiques of the institutions literature is that such critiques make policy prescriptions more difficult. Given that the precise impact of institutions on economic development is still questioned, what policies should countries in the global south implement to promote development? What do the cautions not to impose "one size fits all" Western-derived institutions mean for trying to cultivate some of the benefits of such institutions in countries that currently lack them?

## What works to get better institutions and governance

The preceding two questions are vital as we turn to policies that can reduce poverty. The difficulties alluded to in these two questions remind us that easy, prescriptive lists of how developing countries must reform governance are unlikely to be helpful. Because there is no one right path for achieving good institutions, different contexts and societies demand an array of different responses – an array far too vast to cover in depth here. Rather than provide prescriptions for multiple different scenarios, this section will examine some general principles for governance reform and zoom in on a few applications of specific reforms.

First off, reforms to improve governance and institutions are daunting in complexity. As Merilee Grindle has written:

> Getting good governance calls for improvements that touch virtually all aspects of the public sector – from institutions that set the rules of the game for economic and political interaction, to organizations that manage administrative systems and deliver goods and services to citizens, to human resources that staff government bureaucracies, to the interface of officials and citizens in political and bureaucratic arenas. Getting

good governance at times implies changes in political organization, the representation of interests, and processes for public debate and policy decision-making.

(Grindle 2002: 1)

Additionally, these reforms often have to take place in very poor countries, where institutions are deeply deficient, and/or in societies that are plagued by violent conflict and tremendous inequities. This means that the countries that most urgently need better institutions will have the most difficulties in carrying out reform. For this reason, it is unrealistic to expect that merely "transplanting" Denmark's institutions to South Sudan will be successful.

Instead, the more pragmatic approach is to work within the (sometimes severe) local constraints, and aim for incremental improvements. Brian Levy (2014) calls this "working with the grain," and it can lead to what Merilee Grindle (2002, 2007, 2011) dubbed "good enough governance." Governance that is "good enough" insists that reforms should "fit" the particular society. Achieving "fit" should start with locally-nominated problems (rather than blueprints from outside), then search for innovative solutions; these can incorporate what practitioners have learned from reforms in other countries, but be adapted to build a specific state's capacities (Andrews *et al*. 2017). From the perspective of poverty reduction, a guiding question should be how institutions can expand human capabilities. They can do so by emphasizing equity (so that the most disadvantaged get special attention), participation, and empowerment (so that people have the freedom and agency to make their own choices).

We will discuss how these values can be applied to three broad areas of institutional reform: administration, participation, and legal frameworks (Deolalikar *et al*. 2002). Reforms to administration deal principally with improving the bureaucracy to make the state more efficient and effective, which should in turn help guarantee the public services that poor people depend on. There are a number of ways this reform can be accomplished, including technical capacity building by training competent civil service workers. More competent people in administration should provide better public services. Making the bureaucracy more meritocratic (rather than a preserve of patronage) is an important step in the right direction. Adequate fiscal resources are necessary to fund those services, which means that another critical institution is an effective and legitimate system of taxation. (If large numbers of people evade taxes, where is the money supposed to come from for schools, hospitals, roads, and sanitation?) A more efficient state administration can also foster economic growth by reducing regulatory hindrances to private enterprise and by increasing transparency, which can help reduce corruption. Part of the rationale for transparency is to improve the administration of public finances through strengthened protocols of auditing and monitoring budgets. Better budget management can make even scarce fiscal resources more efficient.

Reforms to participation involve ensuring regular, free, and fair elections, guaranteeing freedom of expression and assembly, and the right to run for office. Assistance to poor or other non-dominant sectors of society to form political parties, interest groups or other means of articulating and advancing their interests can boost participation and enhance democracy. If institutions and governance incorporate broader citizen involvement, then they should be more responsive to citizens' needs and desires. Increased citizen engagement can make governments more transparent and accountable, which helps foster good governance. For the purposes of poverty reduction, such reforms should pay special attention to boosting participation and civic engagement for the poor and marginalized.

Recall that part of the definition of poverty is the denial of the basic civil rights that political participation presumes. Thus, institutional reforms to boost participation are a critical method for empowering the poor. When they are more civically engaged, poor people have more ability to influence policy, and thereby to support politicians and programs that are working to reduce poverty (Holmes *et al.* 2000). At the level of basic capabilities, these institutional reforms support items from Nussbaum's list such as "senses, imagination and thought," "practical reason," and "affiliation."

All of these participatory reforms are also ways of strengthening civil society. A robust civil society will probably have more success in changing unequal structures of political power that reinforce bad institutions. Note, too, that this recommendation for institutional reform applies not just to national governments but also to international organizations and NGOs. Incorporating local participation should help ensure that poverty-reduction programs genuinely serve a community's needs, and that those programs are accountable to the community.

Finally, institutional reform of the legal framework refers to strengthening the rule of law and judicial systems. Improved legal institutions enhance law enforcement, help combat corruption, and encourage investment and political/economic stability. A strong legal regime to guarantee order and public safety is a vital step towards reducing one source of poverty, particularly in societies that have experienced conflict. The legal regime must protect bodily integrity and the basic capability to live a life of a normal human length, and it is also essential for ensuring economic development with equity. Reforms should therefore support the equitable protection of civil and human rights, in part by expanding the access that poor people have to the judicial system. Reformed legal frameworks contribute to strengthening checks and balances between levels of government as well. A concrete policy example in this area is land reform, which can involve making sure that poor people have secure title rights to their land, and instituting a system that resolves land disputes fairly (Deolalikar *et al.* 2002). The importance of land reform is that people who own and cultivate their land are more productive than tenant farmers, which leads to productivity growth and (ideally) poverty reduction.

Two specific facets of poverty reduction give an idea of how the above areas of institutional reform overlap. First, one of the indispensable functions state institutions must fulfil is to protect basic human security, whether from corruption, crime, violence, or economic shocks. Security from corruption, crime, and violence comes from fair, impartial, and easily accessible law enforcement whether from police or courts, which depend on adequate legal frameworks as well as efficient government bodies to uphold the laws. Institutions that are more democratic, accountable, and transparent may also help avoid the kind of violence engendered by domestic and international conflicts. Reforms to protect against economic shocks target the very high vulnerability of poor people to sudden changes in their physical or financial assets. Such reforms can include legal statutes to protect the property rights of poor people, social insurance to cushion the blow of job loss, and vocational training to build marketable skills. All of these programs depend on basically functional governance and institutions.

Second, another essential aspect of reducing poverty is providing economic opportunities to the poor. Reforms can institute/enforce laws and rules to prevent discrimination against poor people in markets for land, labor, and credit. Economic opportunities can also be enhanced by making it easier to start a business, instituting anti-monopoly laws to prevent harmful concentrations of market (and attendant political) power, and assuring access to loans for poor people – all of which require effective institutions (Holmes *et al.* 2000).

## Box 7.3 Strengthening independent judiciaries, by Alexander Ozkan

What is an independent judiciary, and why is it so often considered an important part of institutional reform? The United States Agency for International Development (USAID) claims that "Judicial independence lies at the heart of a well-functioning judiciary and is the cornerstone of a democratic, market-based society based on the rule of law." An independent judiciary is one where judges render impartial rulings, are not manipulated by politicians, have the power to regulate the government's behavior, and interpret the constitution and laws from a neutral perspective. According to this definition, three main tenets must hold for a judiciary to be independent: insularity, impartiality, and legitimacy. First, the judges must be insulated and protected from manipulation. Second, judges must be impartial and unbiased when making decisions. Third, the judiciary should have enough legitimacy and power to be respected by elites and the general population.

Studies have found that countries with established independent judiciaries have a number of benefits for human and economic development. Independent judiciaries can help prevent democracies from regressing into authoritarian regimes. They can help ensure a separation of powers and act as an essential check to the power of the executive branch of government. Independent judiciaries are also associated with stronger protection of citizens' political rights and rule of law, which in turn can promote economic growth. Thus, independent judiciaries have an important role to play in protecting basic human security and civil rights, and in encouraging equitable economic development. However, a familiar problem arises in trying to ascertain causal relationships: it may be that independent judiciaries contribute relatively little to such benefits, and that other factors are more important.

Nevertheless, policies to create an independent judiciary are common in the developing world, even if many countries struggle with implementing the long list of suggested reforms. That list includes depoliticized appointment systems, objective criteria for career advancement, constitutionally codified powers of judicial review for the highest court, continuing legal education for judges and judicial staff, formal ethics codes, and public access to judicial proceedings. Two of the most common policies to insulate judges from political interference are security of tenure and of salary. If politicians have the ability to punish judges for their decisions, either by means of job termination or by reducing their salaries, then judicial independence is compromised. To keep judges impartial, many countries forbid their judges from participating in political activity or engaging in economic activity besides writing or teaching. The idea is that a judge who works in some way for the timber industry cannot be impartial when hearing a case on deforestation. Policies such as minimum education or professional requirements for judges, and publication of rulings, are designed to increase legitimacy as well as the public's access to the judiciary. While these reforms can strengthen a country's institutions in a variety of ways, as with many other such reforms, scholarship is not yet clear on how they should be optimally prioritized.

Sources: Gibler and Randazzo (2011), Howard and Carey (2004),
Larkins (1996), Sousa (2007), USAID (2002)

There are several final points to keep in mind when considering how governance reform can be made most effective for poverty reduction. Countries at different levels of institutional development should focus on different things. For example, in some fragile or collapsed states such as the Democratic Republic of the Congo or Somalia, institutional deficiencies are so acute that it makes sense to focus on protecting basic security and personal safety. In countries with an existing if weak institutional structure, such as Burkina Faso or Honduras, reforms can support the expansion of public services, reducing corruption, and formalized rules for political succession. In countries with more established institutions such as India, Thailand, and Mexico, the focus can be on boosting participation, making administrative structures more efficient, and encouraging government transparency, accountability, and responsiveness (Grindle 2007). Lastly, it is not enough merely to change laws or policies: what matters is whether the law or policy is effectively implemented.

Institutional reforms, like most projects for societal change, can take decades to show results. For many countries in the global south, it will take a complex constellation of factors, including technological change, economic growth, and support from international bodies to surmount the considerable hurdles to institutional reform. Remember that there is a poverty trap here. Low-resource societies typically have deficient institutions; one reason that governance is weak in places such as Niger or Nepal is because those places lack the financial and human capital to have good governance. Despite such difficulties, reducing poverty depends fundamentally (though not exclusively) on governance systems that do not undermine human capabilities, and that can carry out policies to *expand* capabilities. Amartya Sen reminds us that institutions are central to poverty reduction and, in particular, to the expansion of human freedoms: "Our opportunities and prospects depend crucially on what institutions exist and how they function" (Sen 1999: 142).

---

**Box 7.4 Examples of governance reform programs**

**Mexico**

A goal for many countries is to strengthen state capacity by hiring more highly-qualified people into the bureaucracy. An evaluation by the Poverty Action Lab confirmed that in Mexico, raising salaries attracted more talented people to enter the civil service. Higher pay could also induce them to live in less desirable locations where the government's effectiveness might otherwise be weaker.

**Indonesia**

Seeking to combat corruption, an initiative focused on the village governance level, specifically on the misuse of public funds to build local roads. Audits of government accounts were increased, actual incidents of corruption were more widely publicized when they were uncovered, and community members were more consistently invited to open meetings on corruption. These measures helped decrease the misuse of public funds and strengthened community–government engagement as well.

**Ethiopia**

The World Bank and other donors have pursued a program called the Protection of Basic Services. Besides supporting services in health, water, agriculture, education, and other areas, the program sought to increase governmental accountability for those services. Donors wanted to avoid giving money to the central government because of its lapses in democracy, so instead funding was decentralized to regional and district governments, which had to follow strict transparency regulations.

## Peru

Natural resources account for a very large proportion of Peru's export economy, but the country has implemented measures to prevent corruption and ensure good governance. There are laws on transparency and access to information to strengthen monitoring and accountability. Peru also became the first Latin American country fully compliant with the Extractive Industries Transparency Initiative, which advances a global standard for resource governance.

## Tajikistan

The Global Partnership for Social Accountability has overseen a program to improve management and transparency of water service providers. Citizens (and particularly women) have been assisted to form oversight boards for those providers. The boards have made the providers more responsive to people's needs and boosted people's willingness to pay the fees for the water they use. This is an example of how civil society and state institutions can work together to improve public services and increase trust in government.

For more information, see the websites of the Poverty Action Lab (Indonesia, Mexico), the World Bank (Ethiopia), the Extractive Industries Transparency Initiative (Peru), and the Global Partnership for Social Accountability (Tajikistan).

## Conclusion

Deficient institutions are a major reason why people are poor. Ill health, illiteracy, and insecure economic livelihoods often exist or persist because of institutional failings. State institutions have a major responsibility for protecting basic personal security, providing essential public services, guaranteeing key rights of expression, speech, and participation, and ensuring that economic benefits are fairly distributed. When they fail to do these things, institutions increase poverty. Institutions can also rob people of the dignity to which they are entitled. "Dysfunctional institutions do not just fail to deliver services," Narayan explains. "They disempower – and even silence – the poor through patterns of humiliation, exclusion and corruption. The process is further compounded by legal and other formal barriers that prevent the poor from trading or gaining access to benefits. Thus, those at society's margins are further excluded and alienated" (Narayan *et al.* 2000b: 85). When state institutions (or the government officials behind them) are disempowering and shaming people in this way, they are fundamentally impeding a person's right to live a life that she has reason to value.

Development practitioners have staked a lot on the proposition that building better institutions and reforming governance in poorer countries will improve people's lives. The bad news is that institutional change can be a very long and difficult road. Indeed, according to an analysis by Pritchett *et al.* (2010), many developing countries may *never* attain the high quality of institutions such as in Singapore. For instance, at the average rate with which countries improved their bureaucratic administration between 1985 and 2009, it would take Côte d'Ivoire 503 years, Paraguay 377 years, and Cameroon 314 years to reach Singapore-level institutions. However, because many of these countries over this time period exhibited a *negative* rate of improvement (i.e. the quality of their bureaucratic administration actually worsened), if that rate continued then they simply could not reach Singapore's level. That discouraging conclusion applies also for the opportunity of almost all the countries in the survey to make progress along another dimension of institutional quality, lack of corruption: most of them will never attain Singapore's low levels.

The good news is that institutions are human creations and so *can* be changed. Indeed, institutions are an essential means for responding to other causes of poverty that are not outcomes of human action. For instance, the inherent conditions associated with geography, such as being landlocked or in an area with a high disease burden, require institutions to address them. To improve institutions, reforms may have to be incremental and country-specific. But all such reforms should seek to secure basic human capabilities, encompassing personal security, public services, participation, and economic opportunities. In both the long run and the short term, without functioning institutions – whether an effective police force, adequate health and education programs, democratic means of ensuring citizens' power and politicians' accountability, or legal systems that equitably protect individuals' economic gains – probably no society will be able to escape poverty.

## Discussion questions

1   How would you answer this question: Do countries get rich because they have good institutions, or do they have good institutions because they get rich?
2   Give examples of state institutions and/or governance that can impact poverty. What role do capabilities play?
3   How do the examples of governance reform programs in Box 7.4 reduce poverty and/or support capabilities?
4   Investigate how countries score using the following measurement tools. What patterns do you see, if any? What stands out to you?
    a   The World Bank's Worldwide Governance Indicators. Pick a country and see how it scores according to the six indicators, and then compare countries by indicator.
    b   The Bertelsmann Transformation Index. This is a complex but informative tool to measure countries' institutions. What are the indicators, and how might they relate to poverty? Go to Country Reports, pick a country, and see how it scores.
    c   Transparency International's Corruption Perceptions Index
5   Examine Sustainable Development Goal number 16 ("Promote just, peaceful, and inclusive societies"). What does it have to do with institutions? What are the targets for this goal? How can you measure those targets?
6   What do you see as the pros and cons of the following proposal? Some analysts have suggested that foreigners be installed as the governing power in fragile states. Doing so could break the common cycle of warlords capturing political power in such states, and instead allow democratic institutions to be built up.
7   Assume that a benevolent dictator takes over a developing country. He or she promotes peace, good governance, and economic and human development in the country. However, institutions are not democratic. Can this situation be justified? What do you see as the pros and cons?

## Online resources

- The Legatum Prosperity Index ranks countries on several factors, including safety and security, personal freedom, governance, and social capital: www.prosperity.com/
- The Sustainable Governance Indicators are an example of metrics for institutional quality for OECD countries: www.sgi–network.org/
- The Freedom in the World Report assesses political rights and civil liberties in most countries: www.freedomhouse.org/report/freedom-world

## Further reading

Acemoglu, Daron and James Robinson. 2013. *Why Nations Fail: The Origins of Power, Prosperity, and Poverty*. New York: Crown Business.

Bonvin, Jean-Michel, and Francesco Laruffa. 2018. "Deliberative democracy in the real world, the contribution of the capability approach." *International Review of Sociology* 28.2: 216–233.

Carothers, Thomas and Diane de Gramont. 2011. *Aiding Governance in Developing Countries*. Carnegie Endowment for International Peace, Washington, DC, November.

Gisselquist, Rachel and Danielle Resnick. 2014. "Aiding government effectiveness in developing countries." *Public Administration and Development* 34.3: 141–148.

Grindle, Merilee S. 2010. *Good Governance: The Inflation of an Idea*. HKS Faculty Research Working Paper Series, RWP10–023, John F. Kennedy School of Government, Harvard University.

## Works cited

Acemoglu, Daron, James A. Robinson. 2006. *Economic Origins of Dictatorship and Democracy*. New York: Cambridge University Press.

Acemoglu, Daron *et al*. 2019. "Democracy does cause growth." *Journal of Political Economy* 127.1: 47–100.

Acemoglu, Daron, Simon Johnson and James A. Robinson. 2001. "The colonial origins of comparative development: an empirical investigation." *American Economic Review* 91.5: 1369–1401.

Acemoglu, Daron, Simon Johnson and James A. Robinson. 2004. "Institutions as the Fundamental Cause of Long-Run Growth," NBER Working Paper 10481. Cambridge: National Bureau of Economic Research.

Alesina, Alberto, and Paola Giuliano. 2015. "Culture and institutions." *Journal of Economic Literature* 53.4: 898–944.

Alkire, Sabina. 2002. *Valuing Freedoms: Sen's Capability Approach and Poverty Reduction*. Oxford: Oxford University Press.

Andrews, Matt; Pritchett, Lant; Woolcock, Michael. 2017. Building State Capability: Evidence, Analysis, Action. Oxford: Oxford University Press.

Apaza, Carmen R. 2009. "Measuring governance and corruption through the worldwide governance indicators: Critiques, responses, and ongoing scholarly discussion." *PS: Political Science & Politics* 42.01: 139–143.

Bastiaensen, Johan, Tom De Herdt and Ben D'Exelle. 2005. "Poverty reduction as a local institutional process." *World Development* 33.6: 979–993.

Bonvin, Jean-Michel, and Francesco Laruffa. 2018. "Deliberative democracy in the real world, the contribution of the capability approach." *International Review of Sociology* 28.2: 216–233.

Bowles, Samuel. 2006. "Institutional Poverty Traps," in Bowles, Samuel, Steven N. Durlauf and Karla Hoff, eds. *Poverty Traps*. Princeton, NJ: Princeton University Press.

Chang, Ha-Joon. 2005. "Understanding the Relationship between Institutions and Economic Development: Some Key Theoretical Issues," paper presented at the WIDER Jubilee conference, June.

Chong, Alberto, and César Calderón. 2000. "Institutional quality and poverty measures in a cross-section of countries." *Economics of Governance*, 1.2: 123–135.

Chong, Alberto, and Mark Gradstein. 2007. "Inequality and Institutions." *The Review of Economics and Statistics*, 89.3: 454–465.

Crocker, David A. 2007. "Deliberative participation in local development." *Journal of Human Development*, 8.3: 431–455.

Dahl, Robert. 2000. *On Democracy*. New Haven, CT: Yale University Press.

Deolalikar, Anil B., Alex B. Brillantes Jr., Raghav Gaiha, Ernesto M. Pernia and Mary Racelis. 2002. "Poverty Reduction and the Role of Institutions in Developing Asia." ERD Working Paper No. 10. Asian Development Bank. May.

Drydyk, Jay. 2005. "When is development more democratic?" *Journal of Human Development*, 6.2: 247–267.

Engerman, Stanley L. and Kenneth L. Sokoloff. 1997. "Factor Endowments, Institutions and Differential Paths of Growth Among New World Economies: A View from Economic Historians of the United States," in Stephen Haber, ed. *How Latin America Fell Behind*. Stanford, CA: Stanford University Press.

Engerman, Stanley L. and Kenneth L. Sokoloff. 2003. "Institutions and Non-Institutional Explanations of Economic Differences," NBER Working Paper 9989. Cambridge: National Bureau of Economic Research.

Fukuyama, Francis. 2013. "What Is Governance?" Center for Global Development Working Paper 314, January.

Gerring, John, Peter Kingstone, Matthew Lange and Aseema Sinha. 2011. "Democracy, history, and economic performance: a case-study approach." *World Development* 39.10: 1735–1748.

Gibler, Douglas M. and Kirk A. Randazzo. 2011. "Testing the effects of independent judiciaries on the likelihood of democratic backsliding." *American Journal of Political Science* 55.3: 696–709.

Gisselquist, Rachel. 2012. Good Governance as a Concept, and Why This Matters for Development Policy. WIDER Working Paper No. 2012/30.

Glaeser, Edward L., Rafael La Porta, Florencio Lopez-de-Silane and Andrei Shleifer. 2004. "Do Institutions Cause Growth?" NBER Working Papers 10568,. Cambridge: National Bureau of Economic Research.

Grindle, Merilee S. 2002. "Good Enough Governance: Poverty Reduction and Reform in Developing Countries," World Bank Poverty Reduction Paper, November.

Grindle, Merilee S. 2007. "Good enough governance revisited." *Development Policy Review* 25.5: 553–574.

Grindle, Merilee S. 2011. "Governance reform: the new analytics of next steps." *Governance* 24.3: 415–418.

Herrera, Javier, Mireille Razafindrakoto and François Roubaud. 2007. "Governance, democracy and poverty reduction: lessons drawn from household surveys in sub-Saharan Africa and Latin America." *International Statistical Review* 75.1: 70–95.

Hickey, Sam. 2012. "Turning governance thinking upside-down? Insights from 'the politics of what works.'" *Third World Quarterly* 33.7: 1231–1247.

Holmes, M., S. Knack, N. Manning, R. Messick and J. Rinne. 2000. "Governance and Poverty Reduction," World Bank, April.

Howard, Robert M. and Henry F. Carey. 2004. "Is an independent judiciary necessary for democracy?" *Judicature* 87.6: 284–290.

Human Rights Watch. 2010. "Everyone's in on the Game: Corruption and Human Rights Abuses by the Nigeria Police Force." August.

Human Rights Watch. 2011. "Corruption on Trial? The Record of Nigeria's Economic and Financial Crimes Commission." August.

Humphreys, Macartan, Jeffrey D. Sachs and Joseph E. Stiglitz, eds. 2007. *Escaping the Resource Curse*. New York: Columbia University Press.

Hydén, Göran. 2007. "Governance and poverty reduction in Africa." *PNAS 104*.43: 16751–16756.

Hydén, Göran and Julius Court. 2002. "Governance and Development," World Governance Survey Discussion Paper 1, United Nations University, August.

Johnson, Noel D., and Mark Koyama. 2017. "States and economic growth: Capacity and constraints." *Explorations in Economic History* 64: 1–20.

Kaufmann, Daniel, Aart Kraay and Massimo Mastruzzi. 2010. "The Worldwide Governance Indicators: Methodology and Analytical Issues," World Bank Policy Research Working Paper 5430, September.

Larkins, Christopher M. 1996. "Judicial independence and democratization: a theoretical and conceptual analysis." *The American Journal of Comparative Law* 44.4: 605–626.

Leavy, Jennifer et al. 2013. *What Matters Most? Evidence from 84 Participatory Studies with Those Living with Extreme Poverty and Marginalisation.* Brighton: Institute for Development Studies.

Levy, Brian. 2014. *Working with the Grain: Integrating Governance and Growth in Development Strategies.* Oxford: Oxford University Press.

Lloyd, Peter, and Cassey Lee. 2018. "A review of the recent literature on the institutional economics analysis of the long-run performance of nations." *Journal of Economic Surveys* 32.1: 1–22.

Luckham, Robin, Anne Marie Goetz, Mary Kaldor, Alison Ayers, Sunil Bastian, Emmanuel Gyimah-Boadi, Shireen Hassim and Zarko Puhovski. 2000. "Democratic Institutions and Politics in Contexts of Inequality, Poverty, and Conflict: A Conceptual Framework." Institute of Development Studies Working Paper 104.

Mehlum, Halvor, Karl Moene and Ragnar Torvik. 2006. "Institutions and the resource curse." *The Economic Journal*, 116.508: 1–20.

Méon, Pierre-Guillaume, and Khalid Sekkat. 2005. "Does corruption grease or sand the wheels of growth?" *Public Choice* 122.1–2: 69–97.

Michalopoulos, Stelios, and Elias Papaioannou. 2013. "Pre-colonial ethnic institutions and contemporary African development." *Econometrica* 81.1: 113–152.

Michalopoulos, Stelios, and Elias Papaioannou. 2014. "National institutions and subnational development in Africa." *The Quarterly Journal of Economics* 129.1: 151–213.

Narayan, Deepa, Robert Chambers, Meera Kaul Shah and Patti Petesch. 2000a. *Voices of the Poor: Crying Out For Change.* New York: Oxford University Press.

Narayan, Deepa, with Raj Patel, Kai Schafft, Anne Rademacher and Sarah Koch-Schulte. 2000b. *Voices of the Poor: Can Anyone Hear Us?* New York: Oxford University Press.

North, Douglass. 1990. *Institutions, Institutional Change and Economic Performance.* Cambridge: Cambridge University Press.

Nunn, Nathan. 2009. "The importance of history for economic development." *Annual Review of Economics* 1.1: 65–92.

Perera, Liyanage Devangi H., and Grace H.Y. Lee. 2013. "Have economic growth and institutional quality contributed to poverty and inequality reduction in Asia?" *Journal of Asian Economics* 27: 71–86.

Pritchett, Lant, Michael Woolcock and Matt Andrews. 2010. "Capability Traps? The Mechanisms of Persistent Implementation Failure," Center for Global Development Working Paper 234, December.

Robinson, James A., Ragnar Torvik and Thierry Verdier. 2006. "Political foundations of the resource curse." *Journal of Development Economics* 79.2: 447–468.

Rodrik, Dani. 2000. "Institutions for high-quality growth: what they are and how to acquire them." *Studies in International Development* 35.3: 3–31.

Rodrik, Dani, Arvind Subramanian and Francesco Trebbi. 2004. "Institutions rule: the primacy of institutions over geography and integration in economic development." *Journal of Economic Growth* 9.2: 131–165.

Ross, Michael L. 2015. "What have we learned about the resource curse?" *Annual Review of Political Science* 18: 239–259.

Rotberg, Robert, ed. 2003. *When States Fail: Causes and Consequences.* Princeton, NJ: Princeton University Press.

Rothstein, Bo and Marcus Tannenberg. 2015. "Making Development Work: The Quality of Government Approach," EBA Report 2015: 07.

Sachs, Jeffrey, John W. McArthur, Guido Schmidt-Traub, Margaret Kruk, Chandrika Bahadur, Michael Faye and Gordon McCord. 2004. "Ending Africa's Poverty Trap." *Brookings Papers on Economic Activity* 1: 117–240.

Sacks, Audrey and Margaret Levi. 2010. "Measuring government effectiveness and its consequences for social welfare in sub-Saharan African countries." *Social Forces* 88.5: 2325–2351.

Sen, Amartya. 1999. *Development as Freedom*. New York: Oxford University Press.

Sen, Amartya. 2000. "Democracy: the only way out of poverty." *New Perspectives Quarterly* 17.1: 28–30.

Sen, Amartya. 2009. *The Idea of Justice*. Cambridge, MA: Harvard University Press.

Soubbotina, Tatyana P., and Katherine Sheram. 2000. *Beyond Economic Growth: Meeting the Challenges of Global Development*. Washington, DC: World Bank.

Sousa, Mariana. 2007. "A Brief Overview of Judicial Reform in Latin America," in Eduardo Lora, ed. *The State of State Reform in Latin America*. New York: The Inter-American Development Bank.

Tebaldi, Edinaldo and Ramesh Mohan. 2010. "Institutions and poverty." *Journal of Development Studies* 46.6: 1047–1066.

United Nations Development Programme (UNDP). 2011. *Human Development Report 2011: Sustainability and Equity: A Better Future For All*. New York: UNDP.

United Nations System Task Team on the Post-2015 UN Development Agenda. 2012. "Governance and Development: Thematic Think Piece." UNDESA, UNDP, UNESCO. May.

United States Agency for International Development, Office of Democracy and Governance. 2002. "Guidance for Promoting Judicial Independence and Impartiality," January.

United States State Department, Bureau of Democracy, Human Rights, and Labor. 2012. *Country Reports on Human Rights Practices for 2012: Nigeria*. www.state.gov/j/drl/rls/hrrpt/humanrightsreport/index.htm?year=2012&dlid=204153. Accessed December 2013.

Unsworth, Sue. 2010. *An Upside Down View of Governance*. University of Sussex Brighton: Institute of Development Studies.

Van der Ploeg, Frederick. 2011. "Natural resources: curse or blessing?" *Journal of Economic Literature* 49.2: 366–420.

Van Doeveren, Veerle. 2011. "Rethinking good governance: identifying common principles." *Public Integrity* 13.4: 301–318.

Williams, Andrew, and Abu Siddique. 2008. "The use (and abuse) of governance indicators in economics: a review." *Economics of Governance* 9.2: 131–175.

Williamson, Oliver E. 2000. "The new institutional economics: taking stock, looking ahead." *Journal of Economic Literature* 38.3: 595–613.

World Bank. 2018. Worldwide Governance Indicators data. Available at: www.info.worldbank.org/governance/wgi/. Accessed April 2021.

# 8 Conflict and poverty

*Serena Cosgrove*

## Learning objectives

- Understand the relationship between poverty and armed conflict and how poverty can cause conflict and war and vice versa
- Analyze the effects of armed conflict on individuals, communities, and countries
- Explain how war and conflict can be considered a trap
- Discuss strategies that can promote reconstruction, recovery, and reconciliation after a war
- Apply the capabilities and human security approaches to conflict and post-conflict situations
- Consider how social difference, such as race, ethnicity, and gender, affects capability poverty in conflict and post-conflict situations

## Vignette 8.1

*I came of age in a war zone. From 1986 to 1988 I worked with the ecumenical organization Witness for Peace, living in an active war zone in northern Nicaragua (Figure 8.1) where I was a witness to the war between the Sandinista Army – the armed forces of the Nicaraguan government – and the US-backed rebels – the Contras or counter-revolutionaries. What does it mean to be a witness? My role was to live with civilian communities located in the war zones and document the effects of the war on their lives. I took testimony from farmers whose crops, livestock, houses, and barns had been destroyed by nearby fighting or looting. I visited civilians in clinics and field hospitals who had been injured by crossfire, attacks, or land and anti-personnel mines. I accompanied women who had lost family members due to conflict or had to flee their homes for the resettlement community of San José de Bocay, the small town where I was based in the department of Jinotega.*

*While living in Bocay, I was approached by a group of women who wanted to form a sewing cooperative and learn a new skill that would occupy their time and help them generate income. They argued that my help was more important than documenting the war: "Help us build something positive", they urged me. Mercedes, the town baker, was also a seamstress and agreed to teach the women if I could raise funds for the sewing machines and other materials. Even though I enjoyed starting to get to know the women as they met with Mercedes for classes, my focus was on finding three sewing machines, fabric, thread, zippers, and buttons. This was not an easy feat when there were no sewing supplies in town, the roads to bigger towns were mined, and once I made it to a city, sewing supplies were limited due to the US trade embargo against Nicaragua. I took advantage of an annual trip home to the United States to talk about*

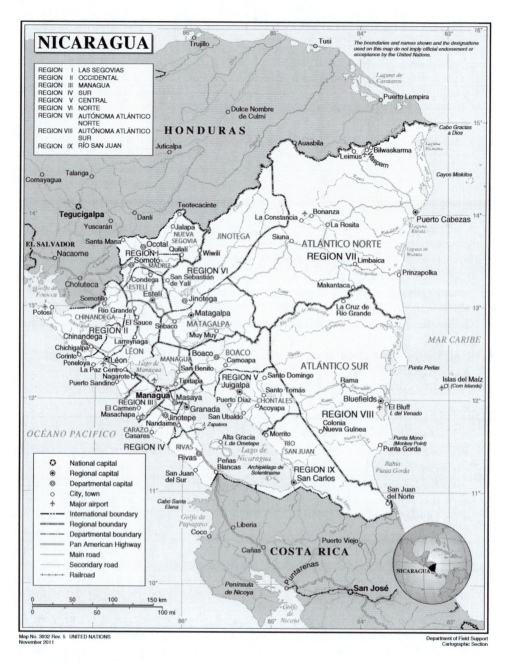

*Figure 8.1* Map of Nicaragua[3]
Source: Map No. 3932 Rev. 5 UNITED NATIONS November 2011.

*Nicaraguan farming women and how hard it is for them to generate income while a war is going on. I raised the money to purchase the machines. And slowly but surely the women began to sew: first for themselves and then family and community members as they mastered their new craft.*

*Each woman had strong motivation to learn to sew: Valeria and Eugenia wanted to have a way to generate income for when their boyfriends came back from fighting. Four other women were single moms – widowed by the war – and they desperately needed income for food for their children. And there was Violeta, whose husband was with the Contras, but she did not talk too much about him given the town was held by the Sandinista army. She was 24 years old and had never been to school. A small woman, she had a permanent expression of dismay on her face: she was accustomed to bad news. Violeta had three children: a girl age ten and two little boys. When the counter-revolution attacked the town of Bocay, her husband was killed in combat. Suddenly she was widowed, with three children to feed, with no pension because her husband had fought on the wrong side, and with no family in town to help her because they were spread out across the country having fled the fighting themselves. She lived in a makeshift house of bamboo with a dirt floor and no electricity or access to potable water. Her children were always hungry and frequently ill. When Violeta's husband died, the cooperative was just getting started, and the members were still learning, not generating income yet. Then Violeta's daughter, Jasmine, died of dehydration. Her health had been compromised by lack of food, preventable diseases, and diarrhea. She just could not resist any more.*

*The members of the cooperative and I went to the wake the night before the funeral, all of us sensing that things would never be the same. As dusk fell, I watched Jasmine's body. She lay on the table with her one nice dress on, flowers tucked all around her, her hair plaited, her nostrils stuffed with cotton. Her skin looked yellow in the wavering light of the small kerosene lamps. The next day a group carried the little coffin to the cemetery. As the coffin disappeared into the ground, I looked up at the verdant mountains surrounding us; I listened to the river rushing by; I adjusted my glasses against the tropical sun. How could there be so much suffering and death in such a lush and beautiful place?*

*Soon after Jasmine's death, Violeta left Bocay for Managua, hoping relatives living in a shantytown in the capital would take her in. One by one the other women abandoned the cooperative: most of the group followed Violeta, leaving Bocay for other towns or cities away from the fighting. Valeria stayed in town but said her fiancé did not want her working outside the home. And then Mercedes, our teacher, told me she had stored away the sewing machines and our few remaining supplies in the health center. She had decided to close the bakery and move south to Jinotega City where she had a small house on the edge of the city. "It's just too dangerous and sad here," she told me guiltily. "I have to think about my children."*

## Introduction

War and other forms of armed conflict can be devastating for people, whether they are combatants or civilians. But as Violeta's story demonstrates, militarized violence and poverty interact in deep and complicated ways leaving families separated, traumatized by loss, and without any possibility of earning a living. Certainly, conflict can cause or contribute to poverty. The turmoil in which Violeta lived made it even harder for her to provide her daughter Jasmine with food and protect her from illness. Moreover, the fighting rendered very difficult any opportunity to learn new skills and earn a livelihood, and hence the sewing cooperative collapsed. These effects were writ large across the Nicaraguan countryside in the 1980s: villages scattered, people killed, bridges blown up, houses, schools, and health clinics bombed. Thus, conflict can destroy the economic and physical capital that a country needs to grow economically. However, what makes the poverty–conflict relationship so complex is that poverty can also contribute to violence. There is a very strong correlation between low per capita incomes and a higher likelihood for civil war.

But does this mean that poverty can *cause* violent conflict? If so, how frequent or powerful an explanation is poverty for why wars erupt? And if conflict causes poverty and poverty causes conflict, what are the ways out of this conflict–poverty trap?

The conflict–poverty nexus is not just complicated: it is common. According to a World Bank estimate, over two billion people routinely suffer from extreme violence. A third of all countries in the world have endured a civil war, and more than half the countries in Africa have experienced conflict in the last few decades. Oxfam (2007) calculated that Africa had lost more than 284 billion USD to armed conflict since 1990; yet, it is also important to keep in mind that "the impact of conflict depends on its intensity, with more intense conflicts leading to greater destruction of human and physical capital and implying larger and more persistent economic costs" (IMF 2019). More than a quarter of the world's population of people in extreme poverty live in fragile, conflict-ridden states. Those states account for one-third of children's deaths. UNICEF estimates that some 300,000 child soldiers are currently exploited in conflicts worldwide, six million children have been severely injured or disabled, 11 million are living as refugees, and an additional 17 million have been displaced within their own countries due to conflict. As one final, sad fact, around 68 percent of the global arms trade goes to developing countries (Grimmett 2012). Conflict, then, has been a major, all too frequent contributor to poverty.

These statistics are a reminder that wars are seldom waged solely between combatants (Kinsella 2011). Since the mid-twentieth century, there have been ten civilian deaths on average per single combatant death in conflicts around the world.[1] Though there is debate about the exact ratio because some conflicts with very high civilian casualties can skew the average, the point remains: it is generally agreed that over the past 60 years, it is more dangerous to be a civilian in a war zone than a soldier (Slim 2003). This is because often armed groups – be they government forces (the army, the police, the national guard, and so on), paramilitary groups affiliated with government forces, rebel groups and terrorists – intentionally target not only each other but also civilians. Street by street or community by community, warfare has affected many in the developing world, such as in Sierra Leone, Liberia, Guatemala, El Salvador, and Vietnam. Terrorism similarly targets soldiers and non-combatants to kill, demoralize, and destroy infrastructure and livelihoods needed by civilian populations for survival.

Militarized violence can be divided into the broad categories of intra- and inter-state conflicts. Intra-state conflicts are the most common: they are internal within a country's national borders, such as civil wars or coups. Civil wars are a specific phenomenon that entails a rebel group or multiple rebel groups fighting a central government for control over the country. Coups, on the other hand, involve actors within the state challenging each other for dominance, that is, one faction of the army trying to wrest control from a president of another faction. Though internal conflicts are often distinguished by barbarism and intimacy due to proximity and familiarity (Kalyvas 2006), wars between countries extend the numbers of peoples affected directly and indirectly. These inter-state conflicts can range from conflict between neighboring states to world wars, and also include imperial and anticolonial wars (Dimah 2009). The scope of the suffering increases exponentially as additional countries – and their resources – are committed to the fighting and the spillover effects of traumatized refugees, political instability, and economic stagnation spread to neighboring countries not even participating in the fighting. Though there are useful distinctions to be drawn between these two broad categories, the dynamics behind intra- and interstate wars can be similar (Wimmer and Min 2006). There are also other forms of violent conflict such as rampant crime, genocide, and terrorism that are not necessarily captured by these two categories. "Many current conflicts do not fit neatly into the traditional categories of international and non-international armed conflict" (Waszink 2011: 5). In reality, the differences can become fuzzy, and often an intra-state war can become an interstate war or vice versa.

The purpose of this chapter is not to provide a precise typology of wars but rather to study the commonalities in how armed conflicts affect human lives. Conflicts, no matter the definition, often have similar impacts at the level of individuals, households, and communities. This chapter takes a broad perspective on how militarized violence of various kinds damages human development. The objective is to untangle the complex relationships between conflict and poverty and suggest how human development can be promoted even in conflict and post-conflict societies. The first section explores how poverty can cause conflict, while the second examines how conflict causes poverty at the macro level. The third section deepens the analysis by looking at conflict's micro-level impact on capabilities. The final section employs the human security framework to review some strategies to protect wellbeing during conflicts and to help societies rebuild once the fighting has stopped.

## How poverty causes conflict

Poverty according to both economic and other definitions can and does cause conflict, though the dynamic is multifaceted and complex. This makes poverty eradication programs an important component of peacemaking efforts. One of the most solid scholarly findings is that poverty conceived as low GDP per capita is a good predictor of when civil wars will erupt (Blattman and Miguel 2010). Slow economic growth rates, economic shocks, low crop yields due to drought or other causes, and vertical (between individuals) and horizontal (between groups) income inequality (Stewart 2016) can also spark conflict, since if people are poor enough, the opportunity risks of violence will diminish, and conflict will appear a better survival strategy than extreme poverty. Economic motivations for war can sometimes be lumped under the term "greed": the idea is that people start fighting in order to capture wealth through loot or plunder (Collier and Hoeffler 2000). However, this motivation does not apply just to poor people, since even those who are reasonably well off can be motivated by greed to seize assets. Some regional leaders in various Sub-Saharan African countries such as Liberia or Congo serve as an example: they may come from the elite, but they want to capture diamond mines or oil wells partly to enrich themselves.

Horizontal inequality – inequality among groups including ethnic, racial, political, religious, and class dimensions – is argued by some theorists (Langer 2005 and Stewart 2000 and 2016) to contribute to creating inter-group conflict: as inequality and poverty increase for some groups in a society in comparison to other groups, so does the risk of conflict. Interestingly, horizontal inequality is not just about income inequality between groups but also inequality across capabilities – political participation, citizenship status, access to health, education and other public services, and cultural entitlements – as well. Stewart (2000) argues that when groups mobilize violently, they do so out of group motivations, not just individual desires. Sometimes the mobilization occurs along ethnic lines, religious differences, or class dissimilarities. In an analysis of the Ivory Coast, Langer (2005) proposes that ethnic inequalities at the level of societal elites combined with socio-economic inequalities at the level of the majority poor can combine in explosive ways. Disenfranchised elites can become leaders of poor people along ethnic lines protesting unequal treatment. It can be an interesting exercise to examine a war or conflict from the perspective of horizontal inequality indicators at the beginning of hostilities: to what extent were there differences between groups that were later used by group leaders to foment violence? Certainly, a number of examples used in this chapter lend themselves to this analysis.

"Grievance" is a related factor that can spark conflict. It means that people start fighting because of anger over historical injustices or inter-group inequalities (Buhaug *et al.* 2013). The poverty in this case can be relative deprivation in access to economic opportunities, political rights, or other basic entitlements. Economic or political disparities between social classes or ethnic groups can become grievances that motivate leaders to form rebel groups, army officers to lead coups, or even collective violent responses from the population that lead to internal or regional wars. Where grievances overlap with ethnic fragmentation, some scholars claim that conflict is more likely (Gurr 1993, Stewart 2011) due to the prejudice and discrimination that minorities face (Green and Seher 2003). As but two examples: the Tamil Tigers in Sri Lanka and Basque separatists in Spain both launched campaigns of violence based on claims that as minority ethnic groups they were disadvantaged economically and politically.

While there is some empirical support for all of the above factors, there are also disputes over their relative impacts (Justino *et al.* 2013). Ethnic fragmentation by no means always leads to conflict. There are plenty of peaceful multi-ethnic societies such as Zambia or Indonesia. Likewise, effectively every society has some inequalities between people and groups, but that does not always mean that people are fighting. Though most civil wars occur in places with extreme poverty, not all extremely poor countries fall into conflict. These explanatory frameworks are all broad generalizations, but sometimes conflict can occur because of idiosyncratic reasons endogenous to that region or country such as a particularly despotic ruler or a drought, for example (Justino 2009 and 2010) or the complex interaction of multiple causal factors (Bara 2014). Moreover, such generalizations at the societal level should be unpacked to examine the micro level of factors that spur individual decisions to fight. For instance, a person who has no job might join an armed group because it provides a kind of work. Or a person might have a job, but regard joining an armed group as providing a chance to earn more. Or a person might join an armed group as self-protection and the only way to protect family, especially if the government is seen as unable or unwilling to do so. Any of these motivations *could* impel someone to take up arms, but whether they actually do so will depend on individual motivations.

There are of course other potential factors besides poverty associated with conflict (Arnson and Zartman 2005, Demmers 2012, and Levy and Thompson 2011). States' strategic interests, or weak states that are not able to provide services, security, or rule of law to all or parts of their territory, can be powerful explanations. Also with a role are neighboring countries experiencing conflict, or mountainous territory where rebel groups can easily form and hide from the national government or international observers. Even where common motivators for conflict exist, when violence actually breaks out can be influenced by variables such as the level of technology and resources available to any armed group and/or the intensity and nature of a group's ideological beliefs (Justino 2011). The takeaway is that "greed and grievance" and the factors they subsume (weak economic growth, income inequality, injustices of various kinds) *can* lead to conflict – but beyond these general principles, understanding how poverty sparks violence requires a more detailed examination of individual societies, such as the Democratic Republic of Congo (Box 8.1).

## Box 8.1 Conflict in the Democratic Republic of the Congo, by Sophia Sanders

The Democratic Republic of the Congo (DRC) is Africa's largest country and host to the deadliest conflict in the continent's modern history. The First and Second Congo Wars, also called the Great African War, began in 1996. As the names suggest, the fighting was concentrated in one country; however, it engulfed much of Sub-Saharan Africa, blurring the line between interstate war and intra-state conflict. The bloody and brutal fighting has killed over five million people (Stearns 2011: 4) and as of 2020, has displaced over five and a half million Congolese. Wars are rarely fought over a single issue, resulting instead from an escalation of several factors. Congo is no different, but what has made its conflict so deadly and so prolonged are the staggering amounts of armed groups, variety of state actors supporting the various sides, and ever-shifting alliances. When compounded by high poverty, inequality, landlessness, a vicious colonial legacy, and ineffective governance, Congo was and unfortunately continues to be little more than a staging ground for imported conflict.

The official start of the conflict can be traced back to the aftermath of the Rwandan genocide in 1994, though Congo was already an unstable and weak state, vulnerable to this spillover for a multitude of reasons. After the Tutsis succeeded in overthrowing the Hutu government and ending the Rwandan genocide, over two million Hutus fled into the eastern part of the DRC (Prunier 2009). Hutu militiamen responsible for genocidal crimes formed new groups and the Congolese Tutsi population suddenly became the victims of escalating violence at the hands of these militias. Rwanda, looking to prevent the Hutus from establishing a stronghold so close to its borders, began to encourage and support Tutsi militias in eastern Congo. Eventually a Rwandan and Ugandan invasion of Congo sparked the First Congo War and led to the ousting of the Congolese government. However, the new government was just as incapable of stopping the violence in the east or disarming the many warring militias. This instability was once more intolerable to Rwanda and, with the support of Burundi and Uganda, it again invaded the DRC, beginning the Second Congo War. At the height of the conflict there were nine countries fighting each other on Congolese soil, including Angola, Chad, Namibia, and Zimbabwe. Though the official war technically ended in 2003 with a peace agreement, eastern DRC remains plagued with armed conflict carried out by proxy militias supported by various regional countries, despite the most expensive and longest-running UN peacekeeping mission in history.

As the militias continue to vie for power and resources, civilians suffer deeply, with few options for escaping starvation, moving out of poverty, receiving an education or being sheltered from the violence. Young men are relatively easy recruits for armed rebel groups because most militias offer some food, wages, and protection that the state does not. It is not a difficult decision to move from civilian to combatant when faced with unending starvation and destitution. This is just one example of how poverty and conflict reinforce each other in the Congo. Until these issues are addressed through effective governance, at the national as well as the provincial levels, the Congolese of eastern DRC will continue to suffer in this vicious, self-perpetuating cycle.

It would be too simplistic to say that the Congo's recent wars are due only to the spillover of ethnic fragmentation, as this ignores historical factors that first crippled the country, making it so vulnerable to violence in the first place. Land inequality, colonial rule, illogically drawn borders, corrupt dictators, and lack of public services have impeded economic and human development since the early 1900s and particularly after it gained independence in 1960. Issues of land inequality began under Belgian colonial rule when white settlers declared vacant land to be property of the colonial state. Congolese land owners were heavily taxed, often forced to give up their property. Once independent, DRC was ruled and robbed by a corrupt dictator who rewarded loyalty by giving away large swathes of land, further entrenching land inequality and food insecurity. Today

> since the start of the Congolese war, land has turned from a "source" of conflict into a "resource" of conflict … Rebel leaders … have turned land into an asset to be distributed among their members. These practices are both based on inclusion and exclusion: those belonging to the ethnic network in control are granted free access to land; those not belonging to it become the main victims.
>
> (Vlassenroot and Huggins 2004: 2)

Among the many tragic consequences of the continued violence (beyond the devastating loss of life) is that the largest country in the region, which has the capacity to feed the entire continent with its arable land, cannot even feed a majority of its own people.

Apart from land, perhaps Congo's greatest vulnerability is its abundance of natural resources including copper, diamonds, minerals, uranium, and oil. These mineral and energy deposits have the potential to fuel significant economic growth and provide the Congolese with basic human services. Instead, the vast resources have been plundered and exploited to line the coffers of high-ranking government officials and militia groups who sell them to the highest bidder to fund their attacks. Many well-known US companies, such as Party City (the makers of My Little Pony toys among other household names) and Apple, have found conflict minerals from Congo in their supply chains (Browning 2015). And while they profit from cheap access to these minerals, it is the Congolese who pay the real price. According to the United Nations World Food Programme, 21.8 million Congolese are acutely food insecure, and the country has the highest rate of extreme poverty in the world, more than 80 percent of the population living on less than USD 1.25 a day (United Nations World Food Programme 2019). Is it the continuation of armed conflict that entrenches these conditions or is it the prevalence of these problems that make the country a magnet for conflict? Autesserre (2010) argues that regional wars – and the Congolese conflict exemplifies this – cannot be explained solely by regional or national narratives such as minerals or political elites but also has to include local tensions and stakeholders, what Kalyvas (2006) refers to as the macro-level, the meso-level, and intra-community dynamics.

Sources: Browning 2015, Prunier 2009, Soderlund *et al.* 2013,
United Nations World Food Programme 2019,
Vlassenroot and Huggins 2004

## How conflict causes poverty at the macro level

Conflict can create or worsen poverty at both the macro and micro levels. "Macro" in this case refers to effects that are society-wide, national, or regional in scope. The "micro" level centers on the individual but includes the household, the group, and the local community. At the macro level we focus primarily on various forms of capital, while at the micro level we study conflict's effects on people's capabilities and functionings. We will also note both short-term and long-term effects. In reality, the macro and micro levels are difficult to separate: effects at the societal level can obviously have an impact at the individual level, and vice versa. Similarly, economic and capability poverty are deeply intertwined here as in many other areas.

To begin with, conflict can severely retard economic growth (Collier 1999, 2007). This is not surprising since fighting often destroys key infrastructure such as roads, bridges, markets, and factories. War typically disrupts agriculture, industry, and traditional crafts and skills. Through its economic effects, conflict can become a poverty trap, since it can exacerbate factors that lead to conflict in the first place, such as low incomes, stagnant economies, weak states, and limited economic opportunities for youth (Blattman and Miguel 2010). A country that has had a civil war has roughly double the chance of relapsing into conflict (Collier *et al.* 2003). However, conflict is not *always* an economic poverty trap since, in the long run, war-torn countries' economies can rebound. There is some evidence that at least in the case of civil wars, countries can recover a significant portion of economic growth relatively quickly (Cerra *et al.* 2008), and somewhere in the middle lie countries that do not relapse into conflict but still cannot regain their economic footing, like Mozambique for example (Hanlon 2010).

Examining conflict's effects on different kinds of capital is a useful way of clarifying poverty relationships at the macro level. All of the kinds of capital we discuss can help support human wellbeing (see Table 8.1), so when they are destroyed, economic and human development are both undermined (Goodhand 2001).

Physical capital includes the bridges, roads, and so on mentioned above, but also buildings and even people's houses – their destruction will obviously affect people in many ways. The loss of the materials and products that arrive on roads and are transported over bridges can lead to market shocks at a tremendous cost to economic growth and livelihoods. If products cannot be imported and exported, business stagnates, and markets shut down. Conflict can also destroy environmental capital as people's access to natural resources such as forests, fields, rivers, and air is impaired by bombing, shooting, chemical

*Table 8.1* Types of capital

| Types of capital | |
| --- | --- |
| Physical | Infrastructure such as bridges and roads, and buildings, including housing |
| Financial | Loans, investments, banks, and markets |
| Political | Necessary institutions, and relationships and trust for participation and governance |
| Human | Skills, training, and experience of population and health services |
| Social | Vertical and horizontal relationships between people |
| Environmental | Natural resources |

weapons, and/or land mines. If fields are mined, or fighting makes it unsafe to work them, then agricultural production plummets. Fearful of attack and displacement, farmers will not plant, which raises the risk of famine. As one example of how conflict can destroy environmental capital, in the Vietnam War the United States dropped millions of liters of the defoliant Agent Orange on forests, creating vast swathes of barren territory.

Conflict can damage financial capital by destroying financial institutions and/or inhibiting access to investment, credit, and markets. Foreign investors are extremely unlikely to invest in a country in conflict, and when violence erupts, investors often pull out their capital. For example, during Angola's civil war (1975–2002), capital flight in financial terms totaled upwards of USD 40 billion, one of the highest rates in Africa. Violence damages political capital by weakening states and the public goods they provide, by eroding the rule of law and democratic political processes (see Box 8.2). Schools and training programs flounder as students and their families choose the immediacy of survival rather than attending classes and investing in the future. Health services are hindered as clinics and hospitals are destroyed and public health campaigns cancelled. Human capital is thereby retarded as young people miss out on an education, or a population loses access to healthcare, including mental healthcare. If you have limited amounts of anesthesia in the local hospital, for example, who do you prioritize? The child soldier? The civilian mother? Or do you resell it for a higher price? Long-term, sustainable economic development, and participative forms of governance are extremely difficult to implement in war-affected areas because education, health services, other governmental services, local markets, and local production cease or decrease when conflict occurs, not to mention the destruction to environmental capital, the natural resources necessary for local communities and national economic interests to flourish.

---

**Box 8.2  Effects of conflict on the rule of law**

1  Erosion of checks and balances on government powers
2  Increasing corruption
3  Decline in order and security
4  Violations of fundamental rights
5  Lack of open government
6  Inadequate regulatory enforcement
7  Inadequate access to civil justice
8  Ineffective criminal justice system

(Adapted from Haugen and Boutros 2014).

---

Conflict can also be particularly injurious to social capital (Aghajanian 2012). Social capital is a term that encompasses the vertical and horizontal relationships between people; these links help guarantee the survival of all members in the community. Most societies are hierarchically organized, whether by social class, gender, ethnicity, roles in institutions important to the community, or traditional forms of leadership such as chiefs and local healers. This means that the people you know above and below you in your society's social hierarchy can help you to gain the necessary goods to provide for your family. Horizontal relationships can include peers, agemates, and siblings: these are important allies for surviving and thriving. Social capital also includes the connections that an individual has with others placed in important institutions such as schools, government offices, and so on. The importance of social capital is not just one individual's connections but the extensive network of relationships that sustains a community.

In times of war, social capital suffers as families and communities are disrupted and separated, neighbors inform against neighbors, institutions cease to function, and communities scatter (Ghobarah *et al.* 2003). After spending time in the eastern part of the Democratic Republic of Congo, Jones discusses how in wartime, social capital dissolves, exemplified by how "the durability of extended family ties, the allegiance of kinfolk, the pleasant give-and-take of hospitality … all fade and fracture" (2010: 162). Trust is another factor necessary for human cooperation that can diminish during times of violent conflict. Given the fear, suffering, and deprivation of war, the horizon of trust relationships can shrink. This, in turn, leads to the dissolution of social norms employed by the community for their survival, and the wealth of wisdom and knowledge that informs the ways of life of the group, including food production, marriage, and the raising of children, is eroded. Stearns comments that "Mass violence does not just affect the families of the dead. It tears at the fabric of society and lodges in the minds of the witnesses and perpetrators alike" (2011: 261). The collapse of social capital, trust, and mores further weakens poor communities' chances for survival. This analysis is useful when studying particular countries such as El Salvador (see Box 8.3).

---

**Box 8.3 Case study on El Salvador and intra-state conflict**

El Salvador, a small Central American country the size of Connecticut, exemplifies many of the challenges associated with intra-state conflicts (Table 8.1 and Box 8.2). El Salvador experienced a civil war from 1980 to 1992, during which over 75,000 people were killed, 7,000 were "disappeared" and 500,000 civilians were internally displaced or became refugees fleeing to Honduras and other countries (see Cosgrove 2010, Silber 2010). The guerrillas proclaimed they were fighting to protect the civilian population that was being targeted by the repressive government. After the assassination of six Jesuit Catholic priests, their housekeeper, and her daughter by the Salvadoran Army in November of 1989, towards the end of the war, international opinion turned against the Salvadoran government, and it found itself obliged to negotiate. In January 1992, the guerrillas (the Farabundo Martí National Liberation Front, known as the FMLN) and the Salvadoran government ended their armed conflict and agreed that the FMLN would become a legally-inscribed political party. By 2009, the FMLN had won presidential elections, ending an 18-year run of presidents from the far-right. Sadly though, El Salvador is not a lot better off today than it was in 1980 when the civil war started. The FMLN negotiated a political settlement to the war and many commanders received government jobs or multiple turns in the National Assembly, but the majority of the country remains in poverty, with unemployment high, which has only been exacerbated by Covid-19. The minimum wage of USD 10 a day cannot meet the basic needs of a family of four. Gangs, whose membership increases as Salvadoran-American gang members are deported from the United States, have become the de facto leaders in many urban and rural communities where the government has little control. Over the past decades, there have been as many homicides as during the war, as organized crime and urban gangs fight for dominance in the arms and drug trades. Impunity still reigns as the police forces struggle to contain the violence and bring perpetrators to justice, which has only been worsened due to the draconian measures taken by the president and army during the Covid-19 pandemic.

The Salvadoran case exemplifies a number of common themes that trap countries emerging from civil war in ongoing conflict. These challenges include the reintegration of displaced populations within the country and refugees outside the country; the reactivation of the economy, and distributive policies that guarantee a basic living for all; the reconstruction of destroyed infrastructure; the demobilization, retraining, and reintegration of combatants into civilian life and the economy; the purging of human rights abusers from the military, former guerrillas, and security forces; and the reconciliation of a country that has suffered so much death, torture, and fear over an extended period of time. El Salvador has high levels of violence past and present, impunity for human rights abuses committed during the war as well as violent acts perpetuated today, and high income inequality. As a result, the majority of Salvadorans are not able to enjoy their basic capabilities, including the ability to support themselves and their families, to access education and health services, to live in communities that are safe and secure, and to have a judicial system that enforces laws, investigates crimes, protects vulnerable groups, and takes cases to court so that justice can be served (Cosgrove 2010, Lovato 2015, Silber 2010).

## How conflict causes poverty at the micro level

As important as they are, the macro-level effects of conflict are too general and abstract unless you drill down to the micro level to understand how mass violence actually impacts individuals, families, and communities. War and conflict lead to unfreedom and poverty by limiting people's most central capabilities and functionings, particularly their entitlements to earn a living, to live free of fear, to receive an education, and to live free of disease. Under the best of circumstances, these capabilities of poor people are vulnerable. Not only are their opportunities typically limited – which is one thing that defines poverty – but even the opportunities they do have may be insecure. Imagine that a poor woman does have the right to vote in her society, but on election day the road to the nearest polling place is blocked by a rebel group. She does not have the time or money to get to the polls any other way, so she has effectively lost the capability freedom to vote. Conflict is in many ways the *worst* of circumstances, which means that it pervasively threatens already vulnerable capabilities and functionings, and thereby creates and/or intensifies deprivation, inequality, and suffering.

Violent conflict has short-term, long-term, and direct and indirect consequences, all of which relate to both temporary and chronic poverty. Most broadly, violence involves coercion, often leading to states of unfreedom. Rebel groups, and even governmental forces, frequently maim children – including forced sterilization of boys and rape of girls and boys – and compel women, the elderly, and children to feed and house their troops. When the troops move on, they often coerce civilians into joining them, either as new recruits, cooks and other support roles, or to provide combatants with sexual services. Civilians are not given choices: they are ordered to comply or be killed. Sadly enough, such attacks on non-combatants are not just collateral damage to achieve a military goal but the purposeful destruction of civilian communities believed to support or harbor "the enemy." Sometimes, the troops do not take civilians with them but instead subject them to violence and torture to send a message to their enemies. These tactics mean unarmed

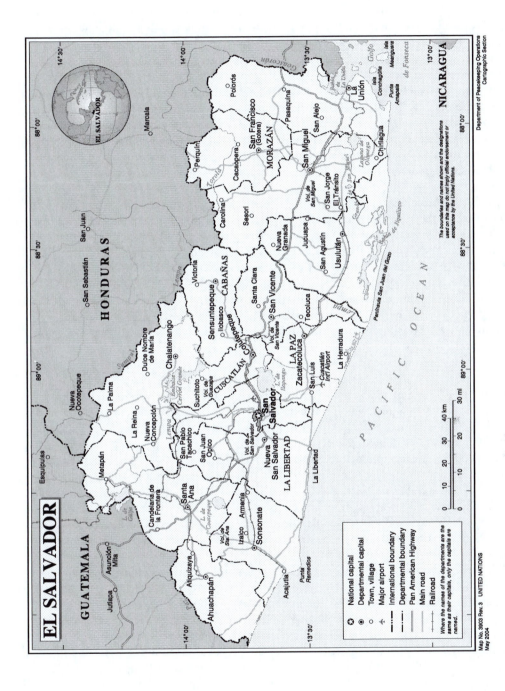

*Figure 8.2* Map of El Salvador

Source: Map No. 3903 Rev. 3 UNITED NATIONS May 2004.

civilians have few means of protecting themselves and little recourse to recovering what has been taken from them. This is one of the reasons why today's wars create so many internally displaced people and refugees who seek safety outside of the country. Take the example of Syria. In 2015, the Economist claimed that "The latest UN figures obtained by this newspaper…show that Syria's population has shrunk to just 16.6m, down from a pre-war level of around 22m." As we prepare the second edition of this book, over 50,000 refugees – according to the UNHCR – have fled into Sudan from Ethiopia escaping escalating conflict there.

Examining conflict's effects on several central capabilities from Nussbaum's list, some points are obvious (Nussbaum 2005). To begin with the capability of *life*, violence causes the premature death of over 500,000 people per year, roughly one person a minute.[2] Conflict also has massive effects on the capabilities of *bodily health* and *bodily integrity*. Soldiers and non-combatants alike sustain injuries: crippled or missing limbs, blindness, and/or damaged internal organs. Conflict further impacts health through the spread of disease, famine, and the destruction of public health services. People may not be able to go to the health center for emergencies or check-ups because the actual building has been destroyed, or they fear the dangers that might lie on the way to the clinic. Illnesses that could have been easily prevented turn lethal. This phenomenon has many manifestations as infectious diseases proliferate: children already weakened by diarrhea catch more fatal illnesses; regular complications of birth mean increased risk for mothers and infants; the flu becomes pneumonia; and cuts and abrasions get infected and turn gangrenous. Public health campaigns are cancelled: children do not get immunized and insect-treated bed nets do not get distributed. The disease burden increases as more people contract malaria, typhoid, tuberculosis, and sexually transmitted diseases, such as HIV/AIDS transmission (Iqbal and Zorn 2010).

In fact, many civilian deaths in wartime are due to illness rather than combat. Malnutrition that people suffer during wartime can kill as well as have long-run and macro effects. For example, in both Zimbabwe and Burundi, children who were malnourished are shorter as adults, which can reduce their lifetime labor productivity (Alderman *et al.* 2006, Bundervoet *et al.* 2009). Furthermore, bodily integrity is threatened also not just by injuries but through the mass sexual violence often practiced against women, children, gender and sexual minorities, and men as well (Albutt *et al.* 2016, Kiss *et al.* 2020, and Stearns 2011). Those violations often seriously damage mental health, leading to depression, anxiety, and despair (Kiss *et al.* 2020). A common tactic in war is to attack mental health by sowing fear. Through violence against civilians, the objective is to demoralize enemy combatants and entire populations. Finally, bodily integrity in Nussbaum's formulation also involves the capability for mobility, which is restricted if it is too unsafe to move freely from place to place.

Violence also undercuts the capabilities for practical reason and affiliation. Education fits in here as one of the main ways every person can cultivate practical reason and expand their opportunities. When the public good of schools is destroyed, however, this basic building block of human wellbeing collapses. Unfortunately, attacks on schools are a depressingly common tactic in conflict: they have been directly targeted in Nigeria, Afghanistan, and Syria among many other places (Global Coalition 2014). Schools are also a vital community gathering point where children, parents, and teachers interact and coordinate actions for the best of the children and the community. Education can also be interrupted when people have to flee fighting, or when it becomes too unsafe to travel to wherever the learning institution is located. A study in Tajikistan showed how girls whose homes were destroyed in that country's civil war were less likely to get a secondary education, reducing both wages and life chances in the long term (Shemyakina 2006). In terms of affiliation, if you live in a war zone, you may not be able to speak freely, or join any group you want (particularly if the local leader views the group as dangerous), or participate in politics. War also often means that newspapers do not go to press, radio stations are not on the air, and local people do not have reliable access to information about what is transpiring or how to avoid conflict and dangerous areas. Access to information is an important entitlement so people can make informed decisions about how to maximize their options.

Losing the capabilities to free speech, political participation, and affiliation relate to how conflict can cripple the basic capability of control over one's environment. This refers partly to environmental assets: in conflict, people might use such resources unsustainably because their urgent need for survival induces them to think with extremely short timeframes. For example, because people in Afghanistan have been so worried about immediate survival, they have in some places exploited scarce water and grazing land in such a way that degrades the long-term potential use of those assets (Goodhand 2001). Nussbaum includes employment under the heading of control over one's environment, and conflict can certainly damage livelihoods. Service providers such as masons, cobblers, and seamstresses have to abandon their businesses and may no longer be able to generate an income. Farming families lose crops and animals. Discussed further in Chapter 12, informal sector employment – under-the-table jobs that are outside of state control – suffers as well. The marketwoman or salesperson who walks around selling goods loses their livelihoods in times of conflict as well as their access to loans, bartering, and the promise of future payments. In Mozambique's 15–year-long civil war, people lost 80 percent of their cattle, a key part of rural households' economic livelihood (Brück 1996).

Conflict's impact on capabilities also has a specific gendered dimension. High levels of sexual violence often happen in war zones. Commanders order soldiers to rape as a way of subjugating the local population, or soldiers carry out sexual violence as a part of pillage and looting. Since 1998, over 200,000 women have been raped in eastern part of the Democratic Republic of Congo and a large part of the female population has experienced some form of sexual violence (Cockburn 2004, Stearns 2011). Women, gender minorities, girls, and boys are raped often by multiple soldiers and by multiple objects being introduced into their bodies. Women, children, and other vulnerable groups, such as gender minorities, are sometimes forced to watch the torture and assault of their own family or community members. Parents very well may have witnessed the deaths of their children. Orders to rape and pillage can also shape men's lasting habits, and so conflict can lead to the increased violent masculinization of society. The contributions of survivors of sexual violence to society are thereby minimized and their subjugation exaggerated, leading to an increased risk of physical, emotional, and sexual abuse (Ghobarah *et al.* 2003). Furthermore, survivors of sexual violence are often shunned by their partners, families, and communities exacerbated by the social impact of gender discrimination (Albutt *et al.* 2017, Cosgrove 2016). All of these gendered effects can seriously reduce survivors' freedom to live a life that they value. More research has been carried out about how sexual and gender-based violence affects women and girls leaving a gap in the advocacy, development, and scholarly literatures about "the health of men, boys, and lesbian, gay, bisexual, transgender (LGBT) and other non-binary people exposed to sexual violence in conflict…" (Kiss *et al* 2020: 2). Calling for more research, Kiss *et al.* argue violence against LGBT people gets exacerbated in war: "Violence against LGBT people in conflict settings has been recognized by the United Nations as a form of gender-based violence (GBV) that is often motivated by homophobic and transphobic attitudes and directed at those perceived as defying hegemonic gender norms. In post–conflict settings, LGBT people often experience harassment and need to hide their sexual orientation or gender identity" (2020: 2).

The micro-level effects mentioned above are frequent realities for people living in war zones. They are often long-lasting: each of the above tragedies, when they do not lead to death, can lead to physical and/or emotional scarring. Soldiers and civilians alike suffer from the emotional and psychological effects of conflict, but for civilian populations the effects can be even more extreme because of sustained feelings of uncertainty and lack of control over many of life's basic decisions (Waszink 2011). The disruption of being forced from your home, the fear of getting caught in crossfire or falling into the hands of combatants who will treat you like the enemy, the hunger and thirst of not knowing where you will get your next meal or find potable water, the grief of having lost family members, and the trauma of having witnessed atrocities – all these conditions create stressors which can cause anxiety and panic attacks, insomnia, nightmares, flashbacks, antisocial behaviors, violent behaviors, and increased susceptibility to abuse of drugs and alcohol. These symptoms often manifest themselves both during times of conflict and long after hostilities have ceased. Addressing the physical, psychological, and social side effects of war is one of the biggest challenges countries face after fighting has ceased.

Conflict's micro-level effects on capabilities are intensely overlapping. When conflict directly harms capabilities in health, bodily integrity, and so on, it indirectly undermines capabilities in many other areas. This means that conflict seriously increases the vulnerability of capability freedom. One of the defining characteristics of poor people's vulnerability is that they may not be able to substitute one asset or capability for another (Dubois *et al.* 2007). If pests destroy the harvest you were planning to use to earn income and feed your family, then you might not have money and food to survive. In the case of conflict, if fighting makes roads impassable (directly destroying the capability for mobility), then you might not be able to get your goods to market (indirectly destroying the capability to earn a livelihood). Conflict typically threatens poor people's survival strategies more fundamentally than do environmental or economic shocks (De Waal 1997). Also, let us not forget the concept of intersectionality that was introduced in Chapter 6: exclusion can be particularly exacerbated in times of conflict, especially for people with multiple minoritized identities. In times of war, it is often the most vulnerable people who will suffer disproportionately: women, gender and sexual minorities, and children are raped; ethnic minorities are at greater risk as are people with disabilities; children go hungry; and the elderly may be abandoned. By making it harder for poor and marginalized people to cope, conflict renders their capabilities even more fragile.

That said, there are some surprising ways that conflict can actually expand opportunities (Justino 2011 and 2013). For example, some people will take advantage of violence to begin looting assets. The turmoil of conflict can increase some groups' political empowerment and enjoyment of civil rights, particularly if they were formerly oppressed. It is also possible that population movements can have an upside for livelihoods and economic opportunities. Some individuals may find more freedom when they take up arms. For example, there is research about women as combatants and participants in violence against civilians. In Latin American civil wars, women participated as combatants in significant numbers in El Salvador and Cuba, for example, which led to changing gender roles (Shayne 2004), and in Sierra Leone and Liberia, researchers such as Coulter

(2008 and 2009) and Cohen (2013) document women's participation as combatants and even perpetrators of sexual violence. Obviously, these effects are not always positive, and expanding one person's capabilities at the expense of another's is not moral. However, the point is that though conflict can exacerbate capability poverty in many ways, it can also have some unexpected (if perhaps rare) upsides. As one last example, some research has shown that experiences of violence made individuals' and groups' behavior more altruistic and fair (Bauer *et al.* 2014, Voors *et al.* 2012).

## Protecting people in conflict

Because of the many ways that conflict can harm basic capabilities, it is obviously essential to ask how those effects can be prevented or mitigated. There is a huge literature on humanitarian intervention, peacebuilding and post-conflict reconstruction (see i.a. Addison and Brück 2009, Call and Cousens 2008, Lambourne 2000, Ware 2014, Weinstein 2007, Zartman 2007). This chapter section focuses primarily on how such interventions can preserve or restore human security and the fundamental entitlements to wellbeing that it presumes. Human security is a specific theoretical tradition that serves as a component to human development (Fukuda-Parr and Messineo 2012, Gasper and Truong 2005). According to one prominent definition, "the objective of human security is to safeguard the vital core of all human lives from critical pervasive threats, in a way that is consistent with long-term human fulfillment" (Alkire 2003: 2). This refers not just to security from violence, but to any condition that can threaten an individual's ability to secure "what is humanly central," which can be defined as fundamental freedoms (Gasper 2005: 222). The capabilities approach is foremost concerned with "freedom to" (i.e. positive liberties, what an individual can be and do). In a complementary way, human security emphasizes "freedom from" (i.e. negative liberties, what robs an individual of the basic components of a decent human life). The negative liberties include freedom from fear, want, and indignity. Human security's perspective is multidimensional, encompassing threats to these freedoms that come from economic, food, health, environmental, and other crises (Owen 2004). Violent conflict, as we have shown, can create crises in all these areas, threatening the essential components of wellbeing and compromising a person's right to live a life that they value.

What is the "vital core" of human security that must be protected? Adapting Alkire's (2003) formulation, it is defined by a limited set of central capabilities necessary for basic survival, dignity, and access to a livelihood. They are the essential capabilities so that people have security during shocks and emergencies. These capabilities embrace political and civil liberties as well as economic, social, and cultural rights. However, much as in the question of what constitutes the universal central capabilities, Alkire shies away from offering a definitive, precise list for the vital core, insisting that its contents need to be context specific, and should be elaborated in a democratic fashion. This is a sensible strategy because the actual operationalization of human security can depend on specific circumstances. In other words, in any given conflict situation, how do you know when central "vital core" capabilities have been violated? Ideally, the people whose security is endangered should be consulted on their situation, which is one reason why operationalization is context dependent.

It is nonetheless essential to establish a few general parameters on which fundamental human entitlements must be prioritized for protection in an armed conflict. Johan Galtung, one of the founders of peace research, claims that human security entails the fulfilment of basic human rights that are in turn the fulfilment of basic human needs, which we can equate with capabilities in the vital core (Galtung 2005). Therefore, internationally-valorized, human rights guarantees suggest an outline for the vital core at the global level. Human security most broadly presumes a "right to survive," and the Universal Declaration of Human Rights (UDHR) enumerates several guarantees relevant to that right. Article 3 of the UDHR states that "everyone has the right to life, liberty, and security of person." Article 5 states that "no one shall be subjected to torture or to cruel, inhuman or degrading treatment or punishment." Article 9 concerns freedom from arbitrary arrest or detention, and Article 13 the freedom of movement. Additionally, the International Covenant on Economic, Social, and Cultural Rights includes a right to adequate food in its Article 11 and a right to physical and mental health in Article 12. Hayden (2004) even goes so far as to assert that there should be a fundamental human right to peace. These guarantees are admittedly often abstract, so context is again vital to ascertain exactly what amounts to "inhuman treatment" or a lack of freedom of movement.

For conflict situations, a legal framework has been elaborated for humanitarian treatment in war that makes abstract guarantees more specific. United Nations policies, the Geneva Conventions, and the 1977 Additional Protocols comprise the key components of this legal framework that regulate behavior in war. States, rebel groups, and combatants and their commanders – regardless of whether they are actual signatories to particular treaties – are today bound by these rules on treatment of civilians, captured enemy soldiers, and the wounded. They are expected to implement a broad range of measures to pro-tect civilians from conflict's effects. This means distinguishing between military objectives and risks to civilians, analyzing the extent to which civilians may be affected by military objectives, and taking precautions to avoid undue impacts on civilians and civilian objects. Unfortunately, the gap between international agreement and enforcement on the ground is often wide: these legal norms are routinely violated in actual conflict situations.

---

**Box 8.4 International human rights organizations and the different offices of the United Nations that monitor human rights abuses in conflict-affected areas and provide services to affected populations**

- International Red Cross
- Amnesty International
- Human Rights Watch
- Doctors without Borders
- International Rescue Committee (IRC)
- United Nations High Commissioner on Refugees (UNHCR)

---

International humanitarian law provides both a legal justification and concrete policy areas relevant to human security. In practice, human security translates first of all to prevention and protection, namely, to stop or mitigate threats to the vital core. It focuses mostly on shorter-term needs, such as peacekeeping in a conflict situation or humanitarian aid in a disaster. However, protecting the vital core is not sufficient for adequate human fulfil-ment, which is why human security must go along with human development. Human development is concerned with an individual's ability to flourish, with a long-term focus to ensure improvement in wellbeing over months and years. Both human security and

*Table 8.2* Elements of human security protection and human development promotion

| Public safety | Humanitarian relief | Rehabilitation and reconstruction | Reconciliation and coexistence | Governance and empowerment |
|---|---|---|---|---|
| Control armed elements (enforce cease-fire, disarm, demobilize) | Facilitate return of conflict-affected people to places of origin or new settlements (refugees and internally displaced) | Integrate conflict-affected people (refugees, internally displaced, former combatants) | End impunity (accountability, support, and technical assistance so government offices can resume functions) | Establish rule of law (through judicial, legal, legislative institutions) |
| Protect civilians (rule of law, removing landmines and small arms) | Assure food security (adequate nutrition for the vulnerable) | Rebuild or rehabilitate infrastructure (roads, housing, power, etc.) | Establish truth (through truth commissions set up tribunals, use traditional justice processes) | Initiate political reform (focus on democratic processes and institutions) |
| Build national security institutions (police, military, other security forces) | Ensure health security (access to basic healthcare for all) | Promote social protections (employment, education, shelter, health, etc.) | Announce amnesties (immunity for lesser crimes, reparation for victims) | Strengthen civil society (through participation, accountability, and funding) |
| Enforce external security (combat illegal trafficking in weapons, drugs and people) | Establish emergency safety net for people at risk (women, children, elderly, indigenous, disabled) | Dismantle war economy (fight criminal networks, re-establish markets) | Promote coexistence (rebuild social capital) | Promote access to information (through independent media and transparency) |

Source: adapted from Ogata and Sen (2003).

human development are necessary to preserve and promote people's basic capabilities and help societies recover from conflict. Table 8.2 presents an overview of steps that societies in conflict need to undertake to further human security and human development.

Like any effort for poverty reduction, achieving success in protecting human security can be very difficult. Conflict situations have particularly complex and dangerous dynamics. When war ravages communities, people have to flee their homes and communities to seek refuge in other regions or countries. Large groups of refugees lead to enormous logistical and security concerns: how to guarantee the safety of and access to food, health, and sanitation necessary to sustain the refugee populations? If active fighting is going on, this can make it difficult for humanitarian organizations to get support to refugees or other threatened people. Sometimes rebel groups set up check points and "tax" organizations serving civilian populations, requisitioning supplies from aid workers for troops or profit. In her book about the contradictions of international humanitarian aid, Linda Polman (2010) shows how easily humanitarian workers get bullied or face obstacles to their work because of intimidation by military forces and armed groups.

These tactics put humanitarian workers in an ethical bind: should they share goods with rebels in order to reach civilian populations or not? The ethical and practical dilemmas of protecting people during conflict are just the first part of the story – promoting human development in post-conflict societies comes with its own challenges.

### Reconstruction, recovery, and reconciliation

*War Is Not Over When It's Over* is the title of Ann Jones' 2010 book on how war affects women and children even after the formal fighting has ended. As present-day homicide rates in Guatemala and El Salvador demonstrate, post-conflict societies can often be as dangerous as wartime conditions for multiple reasons (Lovato 2015, Manz 2008, Silber 2010). These reasons include the fact that international attention formerly focused on the unfolding drama of the war turns instead to other parts of the world. Or state institutions, including the judicial system, may remain ineffectual, debilitated, or dominated by elite interests and cannot enforce the rule of law. A cessation in armed hostilities does not mean that the physical, cultural, health, and education systems of a country are magically reinstated. In post-conflict periods, people's capabilities often remain deeply insecure. Just because warring parties have signed a cease-fire or even a peace accord, there is no guarantee that it will immediately be embraced by all. There is also the issue of impunity: how will the perpetrators of human rights abuses and destruction of infrastructure make reparations and be judged for their actions? And even if soldiers have demobilized for the time being, there is always the possibility that they will return to fighting or seek violent and/or illegal options for income generation.

For a post-conflict period to become a time of peace and reconstruction, a country must have an institutional commitment and the necessary resources to address human rights abuses (see Lake 2014), return to a system of laws and civil behavior, get government services back up and running, rebuild the infrastructure of the country, and activate the economy. It is no simple challenge to accomplish these tasks. Culturally sensitive responses and economic development are needed for large segments of a population suffering various maladies associated with post-traumatic stress but who are also struggling to earn their livings after the fighting has ceased (Herman 1997). If neighbors have killed or denounced neighbors, if government forces have perpetrated human rights abuses against civilians, if rebel forces have participated in atrocities, then national programs have to be implemented to hold abusers accountable and promote reconciliation. Disagreements have to be resolved legally, illegal activities have to be punished according to law, and those who commit crimes must be apprehended and held accountable for their crimes in court. This means that governmental offices and functionaries have to resume their work, or new staff has to be hired and trained. Police forces need training and support to carry out their jobs in an effective and lawful manner. Once the players are in place, the crimes of human rights abuses, torture, and mistreatment of civilians have to be addressed and a plan for reconciliation implemented.

Peacekeeping efforts and commitments to transitional justice are based on the idea that long-term peace has to involve addressing the past violence and weakness of state institutions (Doyle and Sambanis 2000, Leebaw 2008). The overall objectives of transitional justice are promoting national reconciliation and conflict resolution but, to achieve this, transitional justice lawyers and advocates first must create the truth commissions and criminal tribunals to document what has happened during the war, gathering testimony from survivors and witnesses. Then they can assure that those guilty of the worst abuses are prosecuted. Transitional justice involves tensions: to what extent does the truth of what happened have to be clarified so a society can move on? And who leads these processes? Leebaw argues that "in evaluating the political role of transitional justice institutions, more attention should be given to the ways in which their efforts to expose, remember and understand political violence are in tension with their role as tools for establishing stability and legitimating transitional compromises" (2008: 97). Part of the tension is that combatants may be reluctant to turn in their arms if they know that they will be held accountable for their actions, but civilians may be reluctant to trust peace if those who have perpetrated abuses against them do not have to face justice.

In the case of El Salvador, the Truth Commission was part of the United Nations peacekeeping efforts. It gathered testimony from survivors, officially documenting the atrocities of the war, while other UN agencies supported the creation and training of a new police force. When a population that has suffered extreme trauma in times of war has the opportunity to provide testimony to their suffering, the possibility of healing can emerge. Advocating for the importance of telling survivor stories, be it by civilians or former combatants, psychiatrist Jonathan Shay stresses "that healing from trauma depends upon communalization of the trauma – being able to safely tell the story to someone who is listening and who can be trusted to retell it truthfully to others in the community" (1994: 4). Also, if not handled appropriately, survivors can be retraumatized by having to share their stories. Attention to survivors has to be culturally sensitive and integrated with physical and mental health services, community development, and vocational training. Though telling one's story can be an important part of the reconciliation process, it remains incomplete if perpetrators are not held accountable in some form.

After the Rwandan genocide in which 850,000 Rwandans (mostly Tutsis and moderate Hutus) were killed in 1994, the new government instituted a country-wide program called Gacaca Courts ('Justice among the Grass' Courts) in which local communities held outdoor tribunals based on traditional justice practices to hear the cases of violent perpetrators in the communities. The reinstatement of civil authorities and rule of law, a country-wide attempt to gather testimony of what happened, and some efforts of accountability are all vital for promoting healing, reconciliation, and a resumption of normal life after conflict. Sadly enough, many fighting forces negotiate amnesty before ceasing hostilities, which creates challenges for justice to be served. There has to be recognition worldwide that the worst human rights perpetrators will be tried and punished for their abuses. However, those promoting peace and reconciliation activities often face funding and time limitations, as well as the difficult balance between justice and reconciliation.

Reactivating the economy, creating productive options for all citizens, and rebuilding destroyed infrastructure requires massive investments and sustained commitment from a variety of stakeholders, national and international. If citizens cannot earn a living, they will not be able to heal and embrace peace. Citizens at all levels of society need to feel that they can generate enough income to support themselves and their families and achieve their goals. This requires training programs, access to credit, and economic development that creates the necessary forward and backward linkages so that produce, products, and goods created by people have markets. Income generation can also help empower women, but this often requires accompaniment and non-traditional vocational training programs so that women can acquire higher-earning trades. Countries need integrated development plans in which local production feeds into national and international markets. Former combatants need training and support to reintegrate into civilian life.

The reconstruction of destroyed infrastructure will support economic development: road and bridge construction will facilitate transportation; the re-establishment of electrical lines, sewer systems, and potable water will provide the necessary inputs for industry and other types of businesses to resume production and support basic needs; and the rebuilding and staffing of schools, hospitals, and health centers will support the basic capabilities and functionings necessary for human development. In areas of the country that were active war zones, entire communities have to be reconstructed, from housing to marketplaces. Governments have to prioritize the needs of the majority of the country, not solely the needs of urban political and economic elites.

Social norms – the habits of a people to guarantee the survival of the group – often get perverted in times of war. Belligerent forces have grown used to using violence to feed, clothe, and take care of themselves, but former soldiers who have participated in violent practices during the conflict must abandon these practices during peace. Perversion and abuse may have been ordered or condoned by their commanders. Some may have been coerced to participate in violent acts. Violence and sexual abuse can become normalized, so much so that men will continue wartime practices of rape into the post–conflict "peace." In peace and reconciliation processes, it is imperative that practices related to the hyper-masculinization of war be addressed and eradicated through social services and the judicial system, often with the support of non-governmental organizations (NGOs). Doing so will require effective state institutions, national media campaigns, the collaboration of leadership from local to national levels, the involvement of civil society organizations – especially women's and minority-rights organizations – and consequences for those who continue to use violence in this way (Cosgrove 2016). If authorities do not punish crime, they become complicit with criminals, creating a "culture of impunity," a society in which the strong can continue to brutalize the weak (Jones 2010). To prevent such abuses in post-conflict societies, it is extremely important that government institutions charged with implementing justice and protecting vulnerable groups receive sufficient capacity building and support to carry out their mandates. The case of Bosnia-Herzegovina (see Box 8.5) exemplifies a number of these challenges.

---

**Box 8.5 Case study of post-conflict peacebuilding in Bosnia-Herzegovina**

The war in Bosnia-Herzegovina (see Figure 8.3) lasted from 1992 to 1995. More than two million people were displaced, approximately 100,000 people died and tens of thousands of women were raped. The Dayton Peace Accords put an end to the shooting, but created a political system that essentially institutionalized the ethnic cleansing committed by the three warring groups (Bosniaks, Serbs, and Croats). Fashioning a stable country with an operational justice system in the post-conflict period has been extremely difficult, since political elites are barely accountable and can stoke up nationalist passions to remain in power. In some ways, Bosnia is a lesson in how *not* to conduct peacebuilding at the state level, though at the civil society level efforts have been more successful. According to the schema of peacebuilding proposed by Paffenholz and Spurk (2010), Bosnia has made progress in some areas while it lags in others. The first element in peacebuilding is *protection*, which refers to protecting people from the state and other armed actors. National, international, and civil society actors should create safe zones, provide humanitarian aid and peacekeeping troops to ensure the vital core of human security. In Bosnia, international troops often failed their protection duties during the war. The saddest example is when UN peacekeeping forces stood idly by as Serbian extremists massacred 8,000 Bosniak men and boys at Srebrenica in 1995. Since the war, though, a strong international presence has helped guarantee public safety and that most basic needs are met.

One essential element of protection in most post–conflict societies is disarmament, demobilization, and reintegration (DDR). In Bosnia, 300,000 soldiers had to be demobilized after the war. A few state-level programs to reintegrate former combatants into civilian society provided financial and job search assistance, vocational training, and a basic civics course. However, a more profound effort has been made by the Centre for Nonviolent Action (CNA), a pioneering NGO that works to promote reconciliation among war veterans. As part of its work, CNA brings together men from the three nationalities in small groups so that they learn how to "deal with the past." Though they may have previously tried to kill each other, through CNA's method the men confront their prejudices, hate, and fear associated with the other ethnic groups. They work to establish trust, which promotes emotional healing, which in turn can radiate out from the former soldiers to their families and communities. Kenan, one of CNA's peace trainers, lamented that many former soldiers are stuck in a feeling of victimization tied to their ethnic identity. But despite Bosnia's many divisions, he insisted that "everyone wants the same version of peace."

A second step in the peacebuilding process is *monitoring*, which involves tracking and reporting on human rights abuses. It is a critical part of democratization to hold governments accountable and promote rule of law. The Balkan Investigative Reporting Network (BIRN) conducts exemplary monitoring work in Bosnia. BIRN is an NGO that covers many issues relevant to peacebuilding, such as war crimes trials held both in Bosnia and at the International Criminal Tribunal for the former Yugoslavia (ICTY) in The Hague. BIRN and the ICTY form part of Bosnia's efforts for transitional justice. Daniel, one of BIRN's journalists, identified four pillars of transitional justice: justice itself (e.g. bringing war criminals to trial), the right to truth, institutional reform, and the right of reparations. In his view, Bosnia has focused mostly on the first of these, and has seriously neglected truth: the country never set up a truth commission to establish the facts of the war, like El Salvador, for example. Institutional reform and reparations have also made little progress. Even justice itself, Daniel said, is "failing spectacularly," since so few of the criminal cases have been prosecuted at the national level. The process is moving so slowly that many of the perpetrators will never be tried. Many have already died of old age or will die within a decade.

Paffenholz and Spurk's peacebuilding schema also depends on *inter-group social cohesion*, which involves restoring social capital, trust, civic engagement, and ties between groups. This has been an extremely fraught process in Bosnia. Where before the war Croats, Serbs, and Bosniaks lived peacefully side by side, now they often live in ethnically homogeneous towns, interact relatively little with people from another ethnic group, and have dramatically divergent views on what happened during the conflict. Intolerant attitudes are prevalent even among young people who did not experience the war. That is not surprising since in many parts of the country the school system has been divided: Croat children learn one version of history, Bosniak children another. Evidence from the leading Bosnian social psychologist Sabina Čehajić-Clancy shows that dehumanizing attitudes are still widespread. People from one ethnic group attribute less complex emotions to people from other groups, and continue to deny that people from their ethnic group have committed war crimes. As a result, Bosnia is a long way from reconciliation.

Nonetheless, some organizations have done courageous work to promote inter-group social cohesion. One is the network of Nansen Dialogue Centres throughout the country. These centers have brought together young people from the different ethnicities for joint activities outside of their divided schools. According to Čehajić-Clancy's research, over time such inter-group contact can help people take the perspective of others. They learn to appreciate that multiple groups were both perpetrators and victims, and realize that all Bosnians still share much in common.

Sources: Čehajić-Clancy (2012), Kostic (2008), Moratti and Sabic-El-Rayess (2009), Paffenholz and Spurk (2010), and field research by the authors

Peacebuilding is a demanding process that requires cooperation, funding, sustained commitment, and a new vision for society. To avoid a return to violence, people's basic capabilities and functionings have to be respected: there have to be opportunities for all to education, health, income generation, and participation in the co-creation of the polity. State institutions and civil society organizations have to work together in the five areas of public safety, humanitarian relief, rehabilitation and reconstruction, reconciliation and coexistence, and governance and empowerment. Paul Lederach, who has worked as a mediator and peacebuilder around the world, writes, "Transcending violence is forged by the capacity to generate, mobilize, and build the moral imagination" (2005: 5). This means envisioning a society where together the survivors – combatants and civilians alike – construct new opportunities and responsibilities for what it means to be citizens and what it means to be a state accountable to its citizens.

## Conclusion

Poverty and armed violence form a complex, vicious cycle. Both economic poverty and relative deprivation (including in areas relevant to capabilities, such as political rights) can spark conflict. And conflict, as we have shown, often creates or exacerbates many dimensions of poverty. Access to safety and security, education, health, generating income, and freedom from discrimination are typically curtailed during periods of war. Economies are ruined, infrastructure destroyed, environmental assets degraded, and institutions damaged. These losses can spread poverty as children who have not received proper nutrition, education, and access to health services may be affected for the rest of their lives. The most severe effects of war are often the least visible to the human eye – the spread of famine and disease, loss of social capital and traditions, psychological symptoms from trauma – and continue to be felt decades after the hostilities have ceased. This is why "war is not over when it's over": poverty effects often persist long into the post-conflict period.

The way that poverty and violence can reinforce each other is one reason why this relationship is so complex. This is also why post-conflict peacebuilding is so very difficult, and rarely completely successful. Where some aspects of human security may be stronger – such as a reduction in violence and increased rule of law – other elements may be weak. Rwanda, for instance, has made strides in economic and human development and the inclusion of women in political leadership at the national level, but it is considered by many to be an authoritarian state, lacking a robust civil society, and where

*Figure 8.3* Map of Bosnia-Herzegovina
Source: Map No. 3729 Rev. 6 UNITED NATIONS March 2007.

women still face barriers to gender equity at the local level. In Bosnia, civil society, civil liberties, and basic needs are more secure, but problems of impunity, access to truth, and lack of social cohesion fester. In El Salvador, basic human security is still seriously threatened. Though this picture can seem bleak, these societies and global society cannot give up on peacebuilding. Accountable governments, international coordination, citizen participation, and economic and human development are all essential to promote reconstruction and reconciliation after periods of conflict.

Another part of the complexity is the blurred lines that conflict can create. Though civilians die at higher rates than combatants, sometimes civilians are complicit in the violence either through denunciations or support to one armed group or another. Though women are often disproportionately affected by war because of their cultural roles as mothers and caretakers, there are cases of women serving as combatants and even participating in human rights abuses in conflicts around the world. And though conflict does deepen poverty in all kinds of ways, it can sometimes reduce it, as new power structures rise, corrupt leaders are deposed, and individuals find their opportunities expanded.

Finally, this complexity is why the poverty–conflict dynamic is such a major challenge for economic and human development. Besides the way violence can violate the essential components of a decent human life, it can have ripple effects around the globe. Chauvet and Collier (2005) have estimated that fragile states prone to conflict can cost USD 100 billion, a number that imposes costs on many people even far away from the conflict zone, and which is larger than typical budgets for international development aid. Indeed, the danger from violence, the intertwining causes and effects, and the intense misery that the poverty–conflict dynamic can create make this one of the thorniest of all development challenges. The negative effects on human lives are severe, pervasive, and all too common around the world. In order to help people secure their basic capabilities and live a valued life, however, this is a challenge those working for poverty reduction cannot shirk. A number of testimonials, memoirs, and novels written by people who have lived through or researched war provide powerful, very human reminders of why this issue matters – see the list of further reading.

## Discussion questions

1    In what ways does armed conflict contribute to poverty? In what ways does poverty contribute to armed conflict?
2    What are the relationships between capabilities, functionings, and conflict?
3    What can happen to the culture – values, ways of living, habits, roles – of a people during and after a conflict?
4    What does it mean to say that "war is not over when it's over"?
5    From the elements of protecting human security and promoting human development in Table 8.1, which seem the most important and why? How might you prioritize them in a conflict or post-conflict situation?
6    Imagine you are a humanitarian aid worker taking food and medicine to civilians in an area where there is frequent fighting between rebels and the national army. You get stopped at a military check point by a rebel group. In order to let you on your way, they request half of your load, telling you it is a road tax. What would you do?

## Online resources

- The Small Arms Survey has a variety of resources related to conflict, including the Global Violent Deaths data, which tracks the number of violent deaths in every country: www.smallarmssurvey.org/gbav

- The Fragile States Index measures risk and vulnerability, showing which countries are stable and sustainable and which are most prone to conflict: www.fragilestatesindex. org/
- The Vision of Humanity site offers several interesting pieces of analysis such as the Global Terrorism Index and the Global Peace Index, which shows the world's most peaceful societies: www.visionofhumanity.org/resources/

## Notes

1 "Civilians have borne the brunt of modern warfare, with ten civilians dying for every soldier in wars fought since the mid-twentieth century, compared with nine soldiers killed for every civilian in World War I, according to a 2001 study by the International Committee of the Red Cross." *New York Times*, 10 October 2010.
2 Geneva Declaration, Global Burden of Armed Violence 2015.
3 Since this map was produced, Nicaragua has changed the names of the regions on the Caribbean coast.

## Further reading

Adichie, Chimamanda Ngozi. 2006. *Half of a Yellow Sun*. New York City: Anchor Books.

Beah, Ishmael. 2007. *A Long Way Gone: Memoirs of a Boy Soldier*. New York City: Sarah Crichton Books.

Cain, Kenneth, Heidi Postlewait and Andrew Thomson. 2006. *Emergency Sex (and Other Desperate Measures): True Stories From a War Zone*. London: Ebury Press.

Demick, Barbara. 2012. *Logavina Street: Life and Death in a Sarajevo Neighborhood*. New York City: Spiegel & Grau.

Gavilán Sánchez, Lurgio. 2015. *When Rains Become Floods*. Durham, NC: Duke University Press.

Gourevitch, Philip. 1998. *We Wish to Inform You that Tomorrow We Will Be Killed with Our Families: Stories from Rwanda*. New York City: Picador USA.

Households in Conflict Network research: www.hicn.org

Marra, Anthony. 2013. *A Constellation of Vital Phenomena: A Novel*. New York City: Hogarth.

Menchu, Rigoberta. 1984. *I, Rigoberta Menchu: An Indian Woman in Guatemala*. New York City: Verso.

Moore, Adam. 2013. *Peacebuilding in Practice: Local Experience in two Bosnian Towns*. Ithaca, NY: Cornell University Press.

## Works cited

Addison, Tony and Tilman Brück, eds. 2009. *Making Peace Work: The Challenges of Social and Economic Reconstruction*. Houndmills, Basingstoke: Palgrave Macmillan.

Aghajanian, Alia. 2012. "Social Capital and Conflict." Households in Conflict Network Working Paper 134, November.

Albutt, Katherine, Kelly, Jocelyn, Kabanga, Justin, and VanRooyen, Michael. 2016. "Stigmatisation and Rejection of Survivors of Sexual Violence in Eastern Democratic Republic of the Congo." *Disasters* 41.2: 211–227.

Alderman, Harold, John Hoddinott and Bill Kinsey. 2006. "Long term consequences of early childhood malnutrition." *Oxford Economic Papers* 58.3: 450–474.

Alkire, Sabina. 2003. *A Conceptual Framework for Human Security*. Center for Research on Inequality, Human Security, and Ethnicity, University of Oxford.

Arnson, Cynthia J., and I. William Zartman, eds. 2005. *Rethinking the Economics of War: The Intersection of Need, Creed, and Greed*. Baltimore, MD: Johns Hopkins University Press.

Autesserre, Séverine. 2010. *The Trouble with the Congo: Local Violence and the Failure of International Peacebuilding*. New York City: Cambridge University Press.

Bara, Corrine. 2014. "Incentives and opportunities: A complexity-oriented explanation of violent ethnic conflict." *Journal of Peace Research* 51(6): 696–710. doi: 10.1177/0022343314534458.

Bauer, Michal, Alessandra Cassar, Julie Chytilová and Joseph Henrich. 2014. "War's enduring effects on the development of egalitarian motivations and in-group biases." *Psychological Science* 25.1: 47–57.

Blattman, Christopher, and Edward Miguel. 2010. "Civil war." *Journal of Economic Literature* 48.1: 3–57.

Browning, Lynnley. 2015. "Companies Struggle to Comply With Rules On Conflict Minerals." *The New York Times*. www.nytimes.com/2015/09/08/business/dealbook/companies-struggle-to-comply-with-conflict-minerals-rule.html?_r=0. Accessed 25 May 2017.

Brück, Tilman. 1996. *The Economic Effects of War*. Diss. University of Oxford.

Buhaug, Halvard, Lars-Erik Cederman and Kristian Skrede Gleditsch. 2013. "Square pegs in round holes: inequalities, grievances, and civil war." *International Studies Quarterly* 58.2: 418–431.

Bundervoet, Tom, Philip Verwimp and Richard Akresh. 2009. "Health and civil war in rural Burundi." *Journal of Human Resources* 44.2: 536–563.

Call, C. T. and E. M. Cousens. 2008. "Ending wars and building peace: international responses to war-torn societies." *International Studies Perspectives* 9: 1–21.

Čehajić-Clancy, Sabina. 2012. "Coming to Terms with the Past Marked by Collective Crimes: Collective Moral Responsibility and Reconciliation," in Olivera Simić, Zala Volčič and Catherine R. Philpot, eds. *Peace Psychology in the Balkans*. New York City: Springer.

Cerra, Valerie, Meenakshi Rishi and Sweta C. Saxena. 2008. "Robbing the riches: capital flight, institutions and debt." *The Journal of Development Studies* 44.8: 1190–1213.

Chauvet, Lisa and Paul Collier. 2005. "Policy turnarounds in Fragile States." Oxford: CSAE. www.cgdev.org/doc/event%20docs/MADS/Chauvet%20and%20Collier%20-%20Policy%20Turnarounds%20in%20Failing%20States.pdf. Accessed 8 April 2017.

Cockburn, Cynthia. 2004. "Continuums of Violence," in Wenona Giles and Jennifer Hyndman, eds. *Sites of Violence: Gender and Conflict Zones*, 24–44. Berkeley: University of California Press. www.ebookcentral.proquest.com/lib/seattleu/detail.action?docID=223959.

Cohen, Dara Kay. 2013. "Female combatants and the perpetration of violence wartime rape in the Sierra Leone civil war." *World Politics* 65.3: 383–415.

Collier, Paul. 1999. "On the economic consequences of civil war." *Oxford Economic Papers* 51.1: 168–183.

Collier, Paul. 2007. *The Bottom Billion: Why the Poorest Countries Are Failing and What Can Be Done About It*. New York City: Oxford University Press.

Collier, Paul and Hoeffler, Anke. 2000. *Greed and Grievance in Civil War* (May 2000). www.ssrn.com/abstract=630727.

Collier, Paul, Lani Elliot, Håvard Hegre, Anke Hoeffler, Marta Reynal-Querol and Nicholas Sambanis. 2003. *Breaking the Conflict Trap. Civil War and Development Policy*. Oxford: Oxford University Press.

Cosgrove, Serena. 2010. *Leadership from the Margins: Women and Civil Society Organizations in Argentina, Chile, and El Salvador*. New Brunswick, NJ: Rutgers University Press.

Cosgrove, Serena. 2016. "The Absent State: An Analysis of Teen Mothers' Vulnerability in Goma, the Democratic Republic of the Congo," in Victoria Sanford, Katerina Stefatos and Cecilia M. Salvi, eds. *Gender Violence in Peace and War*. New Brunswick, NJ: Rutgers University Press.

Coulter, Chris. 2008. "Female fighters in the Sierra Leone War: Challenging the assumptions?" *Feminist Review* 88: 54–73.

Coulter, Chris. 2009. *Bush Wives and Girl Soldiers: Women's Lives Through War and Peace in Sierra Leone*. Ithaca, NY: Cornell University Press.

Demmers, Jolle. 2012. *Theories of Violent Conflict: An Introduction*. New York City: Routledge.

De Waal, Alexander. 1997. *Famine Crimes: Politics and the Disaster Relief Industry in Africa.* Bloomington: Indiana University Press.

Dimah, Agber. 2009. "The roots of African conflicts: the causes and costs." *Africa Today* 55.4: 129–134.

Doyle, Michael W. and Nicholas Sambanis. 2000. "International peacebuilding: a theoretical and quantitative analysis." *The American Political Science Review* 94.4: 779–801.

Dubois, Jean-Luc, Patricia Huyghebaert and Anne-Sophie Brouillet. 2007. "Fragile States: An Analysis from the capability approach perspective." Paper presented at the 'Ideas Changing History' Conference, September.

Economist. 2015. "Syria's drained population." *The Economist.* www.economist.com/graphic-detail/2015/09/30/syrias-drained-population. Accessed 23 December 2020.

Fukuda-Parr, Sakiko, and Carol Messineo. 2012. "Human Security: A Critical Review of the Literature." Centre for Research on Peace and Development (CRPD) Working Paper 11.

Galtung, Johan. 2005. "Meeting Basic Needs: Peace and Development," in Felicia Huppert, Nick Baylis and Barry Keverne, eds. *The Science of Well-Being.* Oxford: Oxford University Press.

Gasper, Des. 2005. "Securing humanity: situating 'human security' as concept and discourse." *Journal of Human Development* 6.2: 221–245.

Gasper, Des, and Thanh-Dam Truong. 2005. "Deepening development ethics: from economism to human development to human security." *The European Journal of Development Research* 17.3: 372–384.

Ghobarah, Hazem Adam, Paul Huth and Bruce Russett. 2003. "Civil wars kill and maim people long after the shooting stops." *The American Political Science Review* 97: 189–202.

Global Coalition to Protect Education from Attack. 2014. *Education under Attack* 2014. Report.

Goodhand, Jonathan. 2001. "Violent Conflict, Poverty and Chronic Poverty," Chronic Poverty Research Center Working Paper 6, May.

Green, Donald, and Seher, Rachel. 2003. "What role does prejudice play in ethnic conflict?" *Annual Review of Political Science.* 19085642. 509–531.

Grimmett, Richard. 2012. "Conventional Arms Transfers to Developing Nations, 2004–2011." *Congressional Research Service* 7–5700. www.crs.govR42678.

Gurr, Ted R. 1993. "Why minorities rebel: a global analysis of communal mobilization and conflict since 1945." *International Political Science Review* 14.2: 161–201.

Hanlon, Joseph. 2010. "Mozambique: 'the war ended 17 years ago, but we are still poor'." *Conflict, Security & Development* 10.1: 77–102. doi: 10.1080/14678800903553902.

Haugen, Gary A., and Victor Boutros. 2014. *The Locust Effect: Why the End of Poverty Requires the End of Violence.* Oxford: Oxford University Press.

Hayden, Patrick. 2004. "Constraining war: human security and the human right to peace." *Human Rights Review* 6.1: 35–55.

Herman, Judith. 1997. *Trauma and Recovery: The Aftermath of Violence – From Domestic Abuse to Political Terror.* New York City: Basic Books.

International Monetary Fund. 2019. Regional economic outlook. Sub-Saharan Africa: recovery amid elevated uncertainty. Other titles: Sub-Saharan Africa: recovery amid elevated uncertainty. | World economic and financial surveys| World economic and financial surveys. Washington, DC: International Monetary Fund. www.elibrary.imf.org/doc/IMF086/25761-9781484396865/25761-9781484396865/Other_formats/Source_PDF/25761-9781498304139.pdf?redirect=true. Accessed 23 December 2020.

Iqbal, Zaryab, and Zorn, Christopher. 2010. "Violent conflict and the spread of HIV/AIDS in Africa." *The Journal of Politics* 72: 149–162. 10.1017/S0022381609990533.

Jones, Ann. 2010. *War Is Not Over When It's Over.* New York City: Henry Holt.

Justino, Patricia. 2013. "Research and Policy Implications from a Micro-Level Perspective on the Dynamics of Conflict, Violence and Development." Households in Conflict Network Working Paper 139, January.

Justino, Patricia. 2009. "Poverty and violent conflict: a micro-level perspective on the causes and duration of warfare." *Journal of Peace Research* 46.3: 315–333.

Justino, Patricia. 2010. "War and Poverty." MICROCON Research Working Paper 32.

Justino, Patricia. 2011. "Poverty and Violent Conflict: A Micro-Level Perspective on the Causes and Duration of Warfare." IDS Working Paper No. 385, December.

Justino, Patricia, Tilman Brück and Philip Verwimp, eds. 2013. *A Micro-Level Perspective on the Dynamics of Conflict, Violence, and Development*. Oxford: Oxford University Press.

Kalyvas, Stathis N. 2006. *The Logic of Violence in Civil War*. New York City: Cambridge University Press.

Kinsella, Helen. 2011. *The Image before the Weapon: A Critical History of the Distinction Between Combatant and Civilian*. Ithaca, NY: Cornell University Press.

Kiss, Ligia., Quinlan-Davidson, Meaghen, Pasquero, Laura, Ollé Tejero, Patricia, Hogg, Charu, Theis, Joachim, Park, Andrew, Zimmerman, Cathy, and Hossain, Mazeda. 2020. "Male and LGBT survivors of sexual violence in conflict situations: a realist review of health interventions in low-and middle-income countries." *Conflict and Health* 14.11: 1–26. www.doi.org/10.1186/s13031-020-0254-5.

Kostic, Roland. 2008. "Nationbuilding as an instrument of peace? Exploring local attitudes towards international nationbuilding and reconciliation in Bosnia and Herzegovina." *Civil Wars* 10.4: 384–412.

Lake, Milli. 2014. "Organizing hypocrisy: providing legal accountability for human rights violations in areas of limited statehood." *International Studies Quarterly* 58.3: 515–526

Lambourne, Wendy. 2000. "Post-conflict peacebuilding." *Security Dialogue* 31: 357–381.

Langer, Arnim. 2005. "Horizontal inequalities and violent group mobilization in Côte d'Ivoire." *Oxford Development Studies* 33.1: 25–45.

Lederach, John Paul. 2005. *The Moral Imagination: The Art and Soul of Building Peace*. New York City: Oxford University Press.

Leebaw, Bronwyn Anne. 2008. "The irreconcilable goals of transitional justice." *Human Rights Quarterly* 30.1: 95–118.

Levy, Jack S. and William R. Thompson. 2011. *Causes of War*. New York City: John Wiley & Sons.

Lovato, Roberto. 2015. "El Salvador's gang violence: the continuation of civil war by other means." *The Nation*, 8 June.

Manz, Beatriz. 2008. "The continuum of violence in post-war Guatemala." *Social Analysis* 52.2: 151–164.

Moratti, Massimo, and Amra Sabic-El-Rayess. 2009. "Transitional Justice and DDR: The Case of Bosnia and Herzegovina." International Center for Transitional Justice Research Unit, June.

Nussbaum, Martha C. 2005. "Women's bodies: violence, security, capabilities." *Journal of Human Development* 6.2: 167–183.

Ogata, Sadako and Sen, Amartya, co-chairs. 2003. Human Security Now! New York: Commission on Human Security. www.reliefweb.int/sites/reliefweb.int/files/resources/91BAEEDBA50C6907C1256D19006A9353-chs-security-may03.pdf. Accessed 29 January 2021.

Owen, Taylor. 2004. "Human security, conflict, critique and consensus: colloquium remarks and a proposal for a threshold-based definition." *Security Dialogue* 35.3: 373–387.

Oxfam Briefing Report 107. 2007. "Africa's Missing Billionsk," August.

Paffenholz, Thania, and Christopher Spurk. 2010. "A Comprehensive Analytical Framework," in Thania Paffenholz, ed. *Civil Society and Peacebuilding: A Critical Assessment*. Boulder, CO: Lynne Rienner.

Polman, Linda. 2010. *The Crisis Caravan: What's Wrong With Humanitarian Aid?* New York City: Metropolitan Books.

Prunier, Gérard. 2009. *Africa's World War: Congo, the Rwandan Genocide, and the Making of a Continental Catastrophe*. Oxford: Oxford University Press.

Shay, Jonathan. 1994. *Achilles in Vietnam: Combat Trauma and the Undoing of Character.* New York City: Scribner.

Shayne, Julie. 2004. *The Revolution Question: Feminisms in El Salvador, Chile, and Cuba.* New Brunswick, NJ: Rutgers University Press.

Shemyakina, Olga. 2006. "The Effect of Armed Conflict on Accumulation of Schooling: Results from Tajikistan." Households in Conflict Network Working Paper 12.

Silber, Irina Carlota. 2010. *Every Day Revolutionaries: Gender, Violence, and Disillusionment in Postwar El Salvador.* New Brunswick, NJ: Rutgers University Press.

Slim, Hugo. 2003. "Why protect civilians? Innocence, immunity and enmity in war." *International Affairs* 79.3: 481–501.

Soderlund, W., E. Donald Briggs, Tom Pierre Najem and Blake Roberts. 2013. *Africa's Deadliest Conflict: Media Coverage of the Humanitarian Disaster in the Congo and the United Nations Response, 1997–2008.* Waterloo, ON: Wilfrid Laurier University Press.

Stearns, Jason. 2011. *Dancing in the Glory of Monsters: The Collapse of the Congo and the Great War of Africa.* New York City: Public Affairs.

Stewart, Frances. 2011. 'Religion versus Ethnicity as a Source of Mobilisation: Are There Differences?' in Yvan Guichaoua, ed. *Understanding Collective Political Violence.* Houndmills, Basingstoke: Palgrave Macmillan.

Stewart, Frances. 2016. "Changing perspectives on inequality and development." *Studies in Comparative International Development* 51: 60–80.

Stewart, Frances. 2000. "Crisis prevention: tackling horizontal inequalities." *Oxford Development Studies* 28.3: 245–262.

United Nations World Food Programme. 2019. "Congo, Democratic Republic of." World Food Programme USA. www.wfp.org/countries/democratic-republic-congo. Accessed 28 January 2021.

Vlassenroot, Koen, and Chris Huggins. 2004. "Land, migration and conflict in Eastern D.R. Congo." *Eco-Conflicts, African Centre for Technology Studies* 3.4: 1–4.

Voors, Maarten, Eleonora Nillesen, Philip Verwimp, Erwin Bulte, Robert Lensink and Daan van Soest. 2012. "Violent conflict and behavior? Evidence from field experiments in Burundi." *American Economic Review* 102.2: 941–964.

Ware, Anthony, ed. 2014. *Development in Difficult Sociopolitical Contexts: Fragile, Failed, Pariah.* Houndmills, Basingstoke: Palgrave Macmillan.

Waszink, Camilla. 2011. "Protection of Civilians under International Humanitarian Law: Trends and Challenges." *NOREF Report,* August. Norwegian Peacebuilding Resource Centre (NOREF).

Weinstein, Jeremy. 2007. *Inside Rebellion: The Politics of Insurgent Violence.* Cambridge, UK: Cambridge University Press.

Wimmer, Andreas, and Brian Min. 2006. "From empire to nation-state: explaining wars in the modern world, 1816–2001." *American Sociological Review* 71.6: 867–897.

Zartman, I. William, ed. 2007. *Peacemaking in International Conflict: Methods and Techniques.* Washington, DC: US Institute of Peace Press.

# 9 Migration and poverty reduction

## Balancing human security and national security

*Audrey Hudgins*

## Learning objectives

- Understand the relationship between poverty and migration.
- Appreciate the connections between migration and capabilities.
- Articulate the intersections between migration and human development.
- Know the reasons people migrate.
- Articulate the contemporary state of global frameworks governing migration.
- Convey the key aspects of the migration policy debate.

## Vignette: Human security and national security along the United States–Mexico Border[1]

I sit across from 23-year-old Carlos, a young man from Chiapas, Mexico who has just been deported from the United States. The look of determination on his face is at odds with the sense of defeat his body communicates. As a volunteer on the border in Nogales, Sonora, Mexico with the bi-national NGO Kino Border Initiative,[2] my job is to welcome him, register him, and orient him to the services Kino provides. The intake interview starts with basic demographic questions then proceeds to the meatier queries: *What was your principal reason for leaving your hometown? Did you just cross the border or were you living in the US? Were you separated from anyone or were you harmed by anyone in the deportation process?*

In one hand he clutches his repatriation certification, an official Mexican government paper that documents the stark reality of his situation. With it he can eat, sleep, and receive support services for a few days at several area shelters while deciding his next move.

His other hand rests on a clear plastic bag stamped with "Department of Homeland Security" (see Figure 9.1). The small bag contains his possessions. Carlos is lucky: many arrive without the things collected from them when apprehended – identification, cell phone, family photos, and the like. The who, where, and why of the human condition.

Like many others, he left Chiapas for a variety of reasons, the threats of local gangs, the absence of work, the grinding poverty, the need to support his family, and the dogged pursuit of the "American dream," a colorful yet misleading myth that masks settler colonialism. He does not yet know if he will return home or try to cross again.

This experience causes me to question the presence and purpose of borders. The United States and other (mostly White) countries spend billions of dollars in the name of national security, yet millions of economic migrants and those forcibly displaced by conflict, violence, and climate change are on the move in search of human security. Should one trump the other? While official US government rhetoric welcomes the tired, poor,

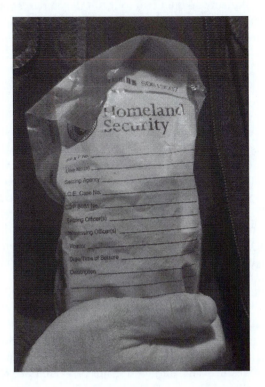

*Figure 9.1* Department of Homeland Security bag

huddled masses, the historical reality is marked by laws and policies such as the Chinese Exclusion Act,[3] the Bracero program,[4] and the present-day erosion of the United States as a haven for asylum seekers and refugees.[5]

Instead of economic and social mobility, what Carlos and other migrants get from their journey to the United States is an object lesson in structural violence[6] and I meet its human consequences every day here in Nogales. On this day, Carlos shares his experience with three souls who have also been deported from the United States, all of whom are barred from reentry:

> There's Ines from Mexico who has lived in the US for 20 years. A single mother, she works, pays taxes, volunteers in her community, goes to church, and has never committed a crime. She weighs her options from Nogales while caring neighbors look after her two US citizen teenage girls back in the United States.

> Jorge, born in Mexico, has lived in the United States since his parents brought him there when he was four years old. Like many, he did not apply for Deferred Action for Childhood Arrivals (DACA) status because of the amount of personal information the government required of him and the risk that the program would be rescinded. He is "American" by any standard by which you might judge him, which may make it difficult to navigate a country he hardly knows.

Edgar, from Mexico, served in the US Army and did two tours in Afghanistan before being honorably discharged. Despite the path to citizenship he was promised upon enlistment, he has been deported to Mexico.

You might recognize them. They might have visited the same park to enjoy a lovely summer's day, volunteered alongside you at a local food bank, or shopped at the same grocery store. These folks and hundreds of others just like them seek entry to the United States daily. Most did not want to leave their homes; they left because they wanted better lives for their families, just like Carlos. Who wouldn't?

Yet structural violence is everywhere, driving migration from its source, accompanying Carlos and other migrants on the journey. At a global level, the north's perpetuation of structural violence complicates the challenges experienced by the south. In the Americas, one might argue that the United States is reaping the seeds sown in its own national self-interest. A history of US interventions – fighting or supporting several proxy wars and interfering in elections and the functioning of governments – continues to plague many countries into the twenty-first century through varied progress in human development.

None of this matters to Carlos. He just remains hopeful for a better future made possible by the simple act of migration.

## Introduction

What is the relationship between poverty and migration? The opening vignette shines a light on several facets of this multi-dimensional connection. Throughout this chapter we will meet others who left their homes in search of a better life or livelihood. You may be reading this chapter as an undergraduate student who left home to go to college. What led you to where you are at this moment? In one sense, this is a form of migration. Like you, every person who migrates has a story that illuminates the numbers and statistics.

*Monetary poverty* can drive migration. If a person is economically poor like Carlos, he may move to find a job so can provide for his family. Imagine yourself in the months after graduating from school. The education you just completed strengthened your capabilities, yet you may need to relocate to put them to use. If the only job offer you receive is in an unfamiliar city, do you take it?

One might migrate to escape poverty, but migration can also be a remedy for the poverty your family faces back home. Remittances – monies sent home by migrants – give origin communities the means to put food on the table, fund school fees, build adequate housing, and meet many other needs. Carlos may feel immense pressure to be successful in his journey due to his own expectations and those of his family in Chiapas. Drawn by the possibility of high wages and the resultant value of expanding opportunities, Carlos accepts the painful challenges of being away from his family.

*Capabilities poverty* can also drive migration. Carlos faces an impossible choice – join a gang or be killed for rejecting the invitation. If a person is deprived among one or more dimensions of wellbeing, they might migrate to access capabilities or activate functionings such as control over one's environment and affiliation. Capabilities – opportunities, choices, and freedoms – create the potential to live a life one can value (Sen 1990).

This chapter explores the relationship between poverty and migration through the lens of the capabilities approach to human development. It will first define migration and explore the questions *Who is a migrant?* and *Why migrate?* Several theories capture the range of reasons people move, and these transitions bring a migrant's personal and social identities into stark relief against a backdrop of political, legal, social, cultural, economic, and environmental realities. Second, it will chart the history of migration and the global frameworks that govern migration today. In this section, we will explore the seismic shifts in migration and the resultant impacts, from increased anti-immigrant sentiment and xenophobia across the globe to innovations in cooperation and regularization within and among countries. In the third and final section, we will attend to the intersections of migration and human development, exploring case studies and policies that sharpen our understanding of the complexities.

Migration alters the human experience, often challenging one's capacity for agency, and placing limits on the conversion of capabilities into functionings, as we see with Carlos in the opening vignette. At the same time, one's agency may be expanded in ways that support the flourishing of human potential (Gasper and Truong 2010). As states cycle through periods of global cooperation and competition, the migrant becomes the rope in a tug of war. Stretched between national security and human security, the migrant's life and livelihood hang in the balance.

## The vocabulary of migration

*Migration* is a "change of residency across administrative borders" (de Haas *et al.* 2020: 21). Historically, a preference for national security over human security[7] – privileging the security of the state over the individual – dominates in states with significant immigrant or transit populations despite the existence of international human rights regimes. The state plays a powerful role in determining who may reside within its boundaries, the status of migrants, their attendant rights, and mechanisms for societal participation. Before we can consider the myriad complexities of migration, we must first learn its vocabulary.

### Who is a migrant?

*Who is a migrant?* The answer is complicated by the absence of a recognized definition under international law. The United Nations defines a migrant as "a person who moves away from his or her place of usual residence, whether within a country or across an international border, temporarily or permanently, and for a variety of reasons" (International Organization for Migration [IOM] 2019: 132). Using this broad definition, you would be considered a migrant if you study in another city or if you work in another country – with or without documents. Yet complexities abound; for example, the United Nations (UN) Department of Economic and Social Affairs (DESA) excludes temporary movements abroad due to "recreation, holiday, visits to friends and relatives, business, medical treatment or religious pilgrimages" (1998: 9). An umbrella term, migrant includes a variety of legally defined categories and generally accepted groupings, with those relevant to the themes covered in this book presented in Table 9.1.

### Four key categories

While the "undocumented" dominate the news cycle, many migrants are documented in one form or another, are in search of asylum due to fear of persecution at home, or are internally displaced due to conflicts and other factors. Four key categories of migrants will frame our discussion throughout the chapter. The first is international migrant:

*Table 9.1* Categories of migrants

| Category | Short Definition | Source and Further information |
|---|---|---|
| **Asylum seeker** | An individual who is seeking international protection, typically someone whose claim has not yet been finally decided on by the country in which he or she has requested protection. Not every asylum seeker will ultimately be recognized as a refugee, but every recognized refugee is initially an asylum seeker. | United Nations High Commissioner for Refugees, Master Glossary of Terms (2006). |
| **Internal migrant** | Any person who moves from her home or place of usual residence within the borders of the state. | International Organization for Migration (IOM), International Migration Law: Glossary on Migration (no. 34), p. 108. |
| **Internally displaced person** | Any person who has been forced or obliged to flee from their home to another location within the borders of the state due to conflict, violence, disaster, or human rights violations. | UN Guiding Principles on Internal Displacement, UN Doc E/CN.4/1998/53/ Add.2, 6. |
| **International migrant** | Any person who changes his or her country of usual residence. | UN DESA, Recommendations on Statistics of International Migration, Revision 1 (1998) para. 32. |
| **Irregular migrant** | Any person who crosses a border in an unauthorized way as determined by the destination state pursuant to its own laws and to international agreements to which that state is a party. | International Convention on the Protection of the Rights of All Migrant Workers and Members of Their Families 2220 UNTS 3, Art. 5. |
| **Migrant worker** | Any person who is to be engaged, is engaged or has been engaged in a remunerated activity in a state of which he or she is not a national. | International Convention on the Protection of the Rights of All Migrant Workers and Members of Their Families 2220 UNTS 3, Art. 2(1). |
| **Refugee** | Any person who is outside his or her country of nationality or habitual residence; has a well-founded fear of being persecuted because of his or her race, religion, nationality, membership of a particular social group or political opinion; and is unable or unwilling to avail him or herself of the protection of that country, or to return there, for fear of persecution. | UN Convention Relating to the Status of Refugees, 1951, Article 1A(2). |
| **Regular migrant** | Any person who crosses a border in an authorized way as determined by the destination state pursuant to its own laws and to international agreements to which that state is a party. | International Convention on the Protection of the Rights of All Migrant Workers and Members of Their Families 2220 UNTS 3, Art. 5. |

*Table 9.1* Cont.

| Category | Short Definition | Source and Further information |
|---|---|---|
| **Smuggled migrant** | Any person who is or has been the object of the crime of smuggling, which is an agreed–upon transaction between a migrant and a smuggler. | United Nations Office on Drugs and Crime, Model Law Against Smuggling of Migrants, (2010) p. 19. |
| **Trafficked migrant** | Any person subject to trafficking in human beings. | Council of Europe Convention on Action Against Trafficking in Human Beings CETS No. 197, Art. 4(e). |

> Any person who is outside a State of which he or she is a citizen or national, or, in the case of a stateless person, his or her State of birth or habitual residence. The term includes migrants who intend to move permanently or temporarily, and those who move in a regular or documented manner as well as migrants in irregular situations.
>
> (International Organization for Migration [IOM] 2019: 112)

As the definition suggests, an international migrant can be regular and irregular (Koser 2016). The former typically possesses a valid document such as a visa or work permit yet may revert to an irregular status if she stays in the country after her document expires. Parallel terms such as illegal, unauthorized, and undocumented are often employed rhetorically by states and the media to advance a particular perspective, often critical of immigrants (de Haas *et al.* 2020). While human acts can be considered unlawful, human beings can never be illegal (IOM 2019), so in our choice of vocabulary we must remain conscious of othering discourses that seek to exploit differences in identity, culture, or religion to sow seeds of division in societies (de Haas *et al.* 2020).

The second term is refugee, which the 1951 United Nations Convention Relating to the Status of Refugees, defines as a person who fears returning home due to a well-founded fear of persecution (see Table 9.1 for the full definition). As former IOM Director General Swing has observed, "all refugees are migrants, but not every migrant is a refugee" (Carling 2017). A third, closely related term is asylum seeker, a temporary status for those who have applied for refugee status and await a decision from the destination country or agencies such as the UNHCR. We all possess the fundamental right to cross borders to seek protection from persecution and non–refoulment, a foundational principle inscribed in international refugee law, protects the asylum seeker from being returned to a country due a fear of persecution. While the principle is well defined, it is not matched by clear or widely accepted regulations and countries vary in their approaches. For example, the European Union's perspectives on asylum and refugee status have been challenged by mass migration across the Mediterranean, a sea transformed into "a cemetery without graves" (FitzGerald 2019: 264) for the nearly 20,000 migrants who have died on that treacherous journey since 2014 (IOM 2020b).

The fourth and final term is internal (or domestic) migrant, which includes a special category of migrant called internally displaced person or internal refugee (de Haas *et al.* 2020). An internal migrant is one who exercises her agency to move from a rural to an urban area within the same country in search of a job or better opportunities, such as movement to metropolitan Manila from the rural provinces of the Philippines, for example. In contrast, an internally displaced person (IDP) or internal refugee moves within his country in response to conflict, violence, disaster, or human rights violations – an obligatory or forced movement like the 2008 displacement of thousands of Yemenis due to a drought in the mountainous regions of the country (The New Humanitarian 2008). Because these migrants remain inside their country's borders, they presumably retain the same rights and guarantees, yet the UN Guiding Principles on Internal Displacement are not legally binding, which results in varying state responses to forced displacement.

*Useful distinctions in the vocabulary of migration*

Using these four terms as a foundation, we can now consider key distinctions that will deepen our understanding of the intersections of migration and poverty.

The migrant persona might be more easily understood when juxtaposed with the image of the citizen. A migrant in transit across borders, depending on her regular or irregular status, moves through spaces of inclusion and exclusion defined largely by the nation-state; in turn, this governs the migrants' capabilities and conversion into functionings. For example, when considering the capability of affiliation, an undocumented migrant youth brought to the United States by her parents may assimilate into the new nation's culture, generating feelings of inclusion. However, she might remain excluded by the state, unable to become a citizen, perhaps at most gaining DACA status, which comes with limited rights. In the alternative, a migrant who lived for decades in the United States might regularize his status and become a citizen yet remain closely connected to his home country, limiting acculturation in his newly adopted country. In both cases, these human beings might experience social, political, economic, and/ or cultural exclusion within the state and across its communities. Yet we all have some rights by virtue of our humanity; our agency hangs in the balance, affecting our capacity to activate our capabilities and covert them to functionings, both within and beyond the state.

Ultimately, we can acknowledge that our humanity is bound up in the idea that all of us should be able to access and exercise our capabilities to live a fulfilled life. One might experience a variety of deprivations that may only be overcome through the act of migration. Yet limitations on capabilities in origin countries are often matched by constraints in destination countries. For example, a young man unable to find work in The Gambia due to pervasive poverty in his village might make the dangerous journey across the Mediterranean to Italy only to be unsuccessful in finding work. As Van Hear *et al.* (2009) suggest, labor migration for the survival of one's family is not so different from asylum migration when considered from the perspective of poorer households. Who should be denied this opportunity?

Many states are unable to reconcile domestic and international legal structures with the current realities of human mobility. For example, humanitarian protection is historically embedded in ethnic, religious, or political persecution, yet violation of one's economic or environmental rights does not warrant asylum or refugee status. Economic deprivations, when complicated by generalized violence and social disorder, can become life-threatening over time (Suro 2019). *Survival migration* – mobility in response to an existential threat to which the migrant has "no access to a domestic remedy or resolution" (Betts 2010: 361) – calls us to acknowledge the reality of mixed motives for migration as well as the limitations of our present legal and political frameworks for humanitarian protection. Let us consider the example of migration from impoverished, autocratic Zimbabwe to middle-income, democratic South Africa. Is the impoverished young man who migrates in search of work to feed his family less deserving of humanitarian recognition than the failed opposition party candidate from the political elite who seeks protection from political persecution?

We might well think of migration as a *process* because its realities are far more fluid (de Haas *et al.* 2020). For example, a migrant who crosses a border transforms from an internal migrant into an international migrant as she moves from an origin – usually her country of birth or habitual residence – to a destination country, perhaps through one or more transit countries on her journey. Migrants might also be classified as permanent or temporary (alternatively, short-term or long-term), labels that highlight state concerns over sovereignty and policies of inclusion, as is the case with Somali refugees who have lived in Dadaab Refugee Complex in Kenya for more than 20 years (United Nations High Commissioner for Refugees [UNHCR] n.d.). This example also highlights the difference between voluntary and forced movement, which contrasts the international and internal migrant from the asylum seeker, refugee, and internally displaced person (Koser 2016). Van Hear *et al.* (2009: 29) invite us to consider the blurred distinction between voluntary and forced migrants:

> motivations may be mixed at the point of making the decision to move, which involves varying combinations of choice and compulsion; people may travel with others in mixed migratory flows; motivations may change en route; and people may find themselves in mixed communities during their journeys or at their destination.
>
> (p. 26)

This complexity invites us to think of migration as a continuum ranging from force to choice (see Van Hear 2011), within which many migrants crossing the boundaries of the state "combine characteristics, responding to economic, social and political pressures over which they have little control, but exercising a limited degree of choice in the selection of destinations and the timing of their movements" (Richmond 1994: 61).

### Why migrate?

*Why migrate*? Money, love, and fear demonstrate three points along Van Hear's (2011) continuum. Founding director of the Pew Hispanic Center Roberto Suro (2018) offers this simple framework for describing migration motives. The first, money, is shorthand for labor or economic migration, a key factor driving both migration and government policy. Whether low- or high-skilled, migrants play an important role in both advanced and emerging economies by meeting labor demand in destination countries and sending remittances home to origin countries. Globalization and the shift to neoliberal policies have expanded demand for high-skilled workers while increasing the precarity of low-skilled workers, whose capabilities are restricted by limited legal pathways for work authorization and labor market segmentation, an increasingly common marker of sectors offering dirty, dangerous, and demanding work with little pay, status, or security in jobs that are often rejected by native workers. Economic migration contributes to poverty reduction through remittances and other forms of investment, as well as the transfer of skills, ideas, knowledge, and technology. Manuel's story in Box 9.1 highlights this phenomenon.

---

**Box 9.1 Economic migration from El Salvador**

21-year-old Manuel dreamed of opening his own business and building a life for himself near his family in El Salvador. Like many Central Americans, he needed to migrate to the United States to work and save money to accomplish his goals, for there was simply no way to do that in his home country. While living with relatives in Colorado and Los Angeles, Manuel earned 12,000 USD over five years, then returned to El Salvador to make his dream a reality (B. Johnson, personal communication, August 28, 2020).

---

Love serves as a proxy for a variety of migration forms that are inherently social such as family reunification and marriage. A parent who migrates to provide for his family might earn money for the transit of his spouse and children. Increasingly, these flows may be initiated by women rather than men or as whole family units, reflecting economic necessity, labor demand, or a desire to end family separation. In some cases, unaccompanied minor children will undertake an often-dangerous journey to reunite with their parents.[8] These movements, characterized as network migration, create links that are then used by extended family and friends; the accumulated knowledge of the process and the access to additional resources for transit smooths the process for those who follow and has the potential to alter one's relationship with poverty as well.

Finally, fear captures a variety of motivations that force one to flee from civil war, political persecution, genocide, domestic violence, and environmental disaster, to name a few. The resulting deprivations limit one's capacity to live a good life and can drive the decision to migrate. María's story underscores the challenges migrants face.

---

**Box 9.2 Forced migration from Honduras**

María, a single mother with a nine-year-old boy, lives in a small town outside Tegucigalpa, Honduras and earns a meager living in a grocery store. The local gang warns María they intend to recruit her son when he turns ten, so she flees with the financial support of her local church. Her hope is to receive asylum in the United States because she fears returning to the gang violence in her home country (B. Johnson, personal communication, August 28, 2020).

---

A fourth point on Van Hear's (2011) continuum might be development disparities due to increasing globalization, climate change, population growth, structural inequality, and shoddy or failed governance (Koser 2016). Poor countries are often the most challenged due to limitations in the rule of law, extensive corruption, overpopulation, and/or fragile governance and economic structures. People in all countries experience limitations in capabilities, whether challenged by inequality, hunger, illiteracy, ill health, access to clean water, or inadequate sanitation. Yet these limitations are commonplace in much of the global south and the differentials between countries create powerful incentives to migrate.

*The aspirations–capabilities framework*

The foregoing motives for migration are fundamental categories in a complex array of migration theories. What were called push–pull factors (Passaris 1989) are now problematized as drivers of migration, reflective of a more nuanced and intersectional understanding (see Carling & Collins 2018, Van Hear *et al.* 2018). Conventional wisdom holds that international migration is driven by global differences in wealth and human development, and that by boosting development in poor countries we can reduce international migration. The latter proposition is problematic because it presumes a priori that a reduction in migration is good or even possible (de Haas *et al.* 2020), but more critically, development has been shown to drive migration. The two share a unique relationship theorized by de Haas (2014, 2009) and others, based on the work of Sen (1999).

Why would we choose to migrate when development happens at home? Migration can enhance and be enhanced by one's social, economic, and human capital. Thus, we can migrate when development happens because we increasingly have access to the capabilities to do so. Drawing on Sen (1999) and the discussion of the capabilities approach in Chapter 1, we know that our *capabilities* reflect our freedom to choose a life we value. In applying this approach to human mobility, de Haas (2014) offers the aspirations–capabilities framework.

- *Aspirations* are a function of one's life goals and perceptions of opportunities beyond one's home.
- *Capabilities* rely on positive and negative liberties.[9]

Imagine that the government builds a road near your village that reduces travel time to the capital city from weeks to days. This development may enhance your capability to migrate in search of higher wages, and these earnings and experiences may build your capabilities in the process. In turn, your aspirations may expand through your awareness of new opportunities and resources – whether you decide to stay or go – and can be described in two dimensions, instrumental and intrinsic (de Haas 2009, 2014). In seeking a better life or access to better opportunities, migration can be instrumental to achieving one's goals, while intrinsic describes the accompanying wellbeing derived from the freedom of expanded opportunities.

Remember from Chapter 1 that unfreedom describes the deprivation of freedoms necessary to lead a fulfilled life. In the context of migration, one can also exercise their freedom by choosing to stay. In other words, just because one can go elsewhere does not mean they must do so to achieve their own conception of a fulfilled life. It only matters that one has the liberty to make the choice. Yet aspiring migrants must have the resources to make the journey and much of one's capability for safe, legal, and regular migration is tied to money (Flahaux and de Haas 2016).

As the aspirations–capabilities framework suggests, in low-income countries, development contributes to expanded capabilities and aspirations to migrate. With increasing levels of development, middle-income countries are shown to have the highest rates of emigration. Examples can be found in countries as diverse as South Korea, Turkey, the Philippines, and Brazil (see Clemens 2014, DeWind *et al.* 2012). As we look to the future, this theory suggests that Sub-Saharan Africa will be the source of the next major wave of migration.

Through this discussion we might imagine a variety of possible combinations within the aspirations–capabilities framework. Table 9.2 depicts these relationships and can help our thinking on the interactions between migration and capabilities poverty. The typology distinguishes between voluntary and involuntary mobility as well as movement and non-movement:

- The young man who does not possess resources to flee his country may be trapped by involuntary immobility as he rejects repeated invitations to affiliate with local gangs.
- Most migration can be described as voluntary mobility, meaning one has the desire (aspiration) and resources (capability) to move to from a rural town to an industrialized city to work.
- Acquiescent immobility characterizes the impoverished single mother with three children who may choose to stay close to her supportive extended family because she sees that the benefits of the familial network outweigh the risks and costs of a move.
- High capability combined with low aspirations – voluntary immobility – explains the high school graduate who chooses to go to college in her hometown despite receiving an offer from a college in another state.
- A politically-active woman of means fighting against an authoritarian regime may be forced to flee for her life due to political persecution, a case of involuntary mobility.

As with Nussbaum's list of central capabilities, a crucial point is the freedom to exercise the capability, not the exercise itself. Thus, human mobility is grounded in the freedom to move or to stay, two sides of the freedom-of-mobility coin (de Haas 2014).

## Other key paradigms and theories of migration

From the perspective of capabilities poverty, several key migration theories can be analyzed through the lens of migrant agency. Theories of migration are historically rooted in two paradigms, functionalist and historical-structural, both of which view migration as a response to poverty, inequality, and development challenges (de Haas *et al.* 2020). Functionalist approaches view society as a system in which migration optimizes markets and development, and the individual as one motivated by maximizing income. Neoclassical migration theory, like Rostow's modernization theory,[10] posits labor supply and demand differences between rural and urban sectors as encouragement for mobility (see Borjas 1989, Todaro 1969). Neither approach fully acknowledges the migrant's agency, instead

*Table 9.2* Migration aspirations–capabilities framework (adapted from de Haas 2014: 32)

| | | Migration capabilities | |
| --- | --- | --- | --- |
| | | Low | High |
| **Migration aspirations** (intrinsic and/or instrumental) | *High* | **Involuntary immobility** (Carling 2002) (feeling 'trapped') | **Voluntary mobility** (most forms of migration) |
| | *Low* | **Acquiescent immobility** (Schewel 2015) | **Voluntary immobility** *and* **Involuntary mobility** (e.g. refugees) |

portraying migration as an individualized passive response to external factors (de Haas *et al.* 2020).

The second paradigm recognizes structural constraints on migration decision making. Historical-structural approaches emphasize the unequal distribution of economic power. In a migration context, dependency theory[11] and world systems theory suggest that migration away from developing countries contributes to underdevelopment through the economic domination of the global north. From these theories emerged globalization theory, akin to Chapter 2's discussion of neoliberalism, which paints liberalized economic and social processes as imperialism, reinforcing structural inequalities (see Petras and Veltmayer 2000, Weiss 1997). As with the functionalist view, human agency in the historical-structural paradigm is also limited, with migrants characterized as victims of an exploitative capitalist system (de Haas *et al.* 2020).

The theory of cumulative causation instead centers migrant agency and focuses on the reproduction of mobility through changes in social and economic structures (Massey 1990). The resultant development of social capital and agency within migrant networks drives an industry to serve related needs, both legal and illegal. For example, travel experience makes follow-on journeys less costly while labor brokers, smugglers, and remittance agencies provide support services for transit of people and money (Curran 2016). More recently, migration transition theories have emerged as a counterpoint to the functionalist and historical-structural approaches due to the advent of empirical research demonstrating that development processes and migration patterns share a complex relationship and change over time (see de Haas 2010, Hatton and Williamson 1998, Skeldon 1997, Zelinsky 1971). These theories also embrace migrant agency.

It should be clear from this discussion that the drivers of migration are myriad and that migration requires an individual to have both the agency to convert the capability of mobility into the functioning of movement as well as the aspiration to do so. It follows that one's migration might be due to a range of factors, both within and outside one's control. There is no one simple description of today's migrant, with many taking part in what scholars and policymakers alike increasingly recognize as mixed migration, a concept that captures the reality of myriad drivers of and motivations for mobility (Van Hear *et al.* 2009). In combination with the emergent reality of transnationalism – both as a phenomenon to describe migrants' attachments to cross-border communities as well as the institutional efforts to manage increasing global mobility – the stage is set for societal transformation on an unprecedented scale (Vertovec 1999). As de Haas explains, "to understand society is to understand migration, and to understand migration is to better understand society" (2014: 16). We now turn to the evolution of migration over time.

## The emergent realities of migration

From the Rift Valley in Africa to Europe to other continents around the world, we have migrated since the birth of our species. In ancient empires – Mesopotamia, Inca, Shang, Indus Valley – migration supported expansion. Later, forced migration of slaves and voluntary and involuntary transit of indentured servants, laborers, and settlers fueled the growth of European and American empires. This predominately north–north migratory flow shifted following the Second World War to an emerging pattern of south–south migration (Curran 2016, UNDESA Population Division 2014). While North America today remains the fastest growing destination, labor migration has grown and shifted toward Asia and the Gulf states.

In this section we will review the main patterns and trends that affect migration today, then consider some of the significant regimes and agreements that govern human mobility.

### What are the key migration trends and patterns?

Today, almost 272 million people, approximately 3.5 percent of the world's population, are international migrants (McAuliffe & Khadria 2019). Since 1960, the increase in international migration keeps pace with world population growth, fluctuating around 3 percent annually (de Haas *et al.* 2020). Yet popular media portrays migration as an uncontrollable crisis. Why? As a proportion, growing numbers of asylum seekers, refugees, and irregular migrants – fleeing conflict, persecution, disaster, or pursuing enhanced capabilities – signal increased humanitarian and development needs throughout the world (McAuliffe and Khadria 2019).

Migration is a process, far from uniform and shaped by myriad factors that have evolved over many years. Four emerging patterns and trends – economic, geographic, demographic, and political – help contextualize this ever-changing ecosystem and the increasing salience of migration across the world.

### Economic patterns and trends

Large movements of people contribute to and are a result of globalization. Improvements in communication and transportation infrastructure facilitate migration, trends that diversify destinations through language, culture, and ethnicity. Migration corridors, created through colonial, economic, or social processes, smooth the transition of countless persons and support the flow of experience, ideas, contacts, and money. Remittances make an increasingly important contribution to poverty reduction, enhanced access to capabilities, and development in general. In fact, a significant collection of studies suggest that remittances reduce poverty (see Adams & Page 2005, Ajayi *et al.* 2009, Anyanwu & Erghijakpor 2010, Fajnzylber & Lopez 2007, Gupta *et al.* 2007). Remittances have grown from an estimated 126 billion USD in 2000 to 689 billion USD in 2020; they account for more than three times the amount of official development assistance (ODA) and foreign direct investment (FDI) combined (McAuliffe and Khadria 2019). Not included in these figures are informal remittance networks, where migrants carry cash themselves or send it with friends and relatives returning home. A well-developed example of this can be found in the Somali *hawala* system (see e.g. Ismail 2007).

However, the remittance–development relationship is complex. At the national level, remittances form an increasingly significant part of gross domestic product (GDP) in some countries and are often larger than foreign exchange reserves (IOM 2019). In Haiti, for example, the World Bank (2019) estimates that remittances account for more than 25 percent of GDP. A powerful contributor to the economic health of many countries, remittance dependence may fuel economic insecurity and inequality, slow necessary government economic reforms, and discourage foreign investment (see Ahmed 2012, Agunias 2006, Amuedo-Dorantes 2014, Ratha *et al.* 2011).

At the community level, remittances diversify a family's income and serve as insurance against risk, while spending on education and health care enhance capabilities (see Stark 1991). In turn, the community may benefit directly or indirectly through the establishment of local businesses or investment in community development projects (Koser 2016). Through hometown associations, a cooperative form of support for home communities through the pooling of remittances, migrants can enable the collective exercise of power with local officials to support a variety of needs, such as the construction of roads and schools as well as the installation of electric, water, and sewer services. However, these infusions of cash into the local economy also can have limited or counter-productive effects. For example, cars, televisions, and appliances are consumer goods whose purchase benefits the local economy and enhances quality of life, but they can also create disparities between households and increase economic and social inequality within and across communities.

The impact of these economic patterns and trends on development is mixed. As de Haas notes, "[i]nstead of being a development 'game changer', migration tends to reinforce already existing trends of social, economic and political change – whether these are negative or positive – of which migration is an intrinsic part" (2014: 20). Increasingly, development creates linkages between international and internal migration (Curran 2016). As developing countries improve income, education, and infrastructure, the resulting economic transformation triggers migration, and de Haas (2014) and others have shown that a rise in internal (rural-to-urban) migration is then followed by an increase international migration. Once more developed, these countries experience a reduction in emigration and growth in immigration, with higher general levels of mobility and migration at increasing levels of wealth.

*Geographic patterns and trends*

A second trend is apparent in the geography of migrant origins and destinations, which has shifted over the years. Traditional distinctions between origin, transit, and destination countries have merged, such that nearly every country serves all three functions (Koser 2016). Intercontinental migration has grown rapidly, from 38 percent of global migration in 1960 to 55 percent in 2017 as a percentage of total migration (de Haas *et al.* 2020); while outward flows from a wider array of origin countries continue, destinations are concentrated among countries with robust economic and employment opportunities.

Today, the largest numbers of migrants living abroad come from India, Mexico, and China, who head to countries with robust or growing economies such the United States, France, the Russian Federation, the United Arab Emirates and Saudi Arabia (McAuliffe and Khadria 2019). Well-worn migration corridors develop and strengthen over time, making the journey easier and cheaper for those who follow. The United States remains the top destination country with 50.7 million international migrants, yet as a share of national population, the highest immigration levels can be found in Singapore (2.1 million/37 percent), Hong Kong (2.9 million/40 percent), and the United Arab Emirates (8.6 million/ 87 percent) (McAuliffe and Khadria 2019).

Many countries are both origin and destination countries, with flows concentrated in industrialized countries and emerging industrial countries. The emergent pattern of south–south migration is characterized by social connectedness factors such as cultural similarity and geographic proximity, which play an important role in destination choices (Ponce 2016).

Significantly, most migration is *internal*, characterized by movements from rural to urban areas, and is rising faster than international migration (McAuliffe and Khadria 2019). In China alone, Li and Wang (2015) estimate that 250 million people have moved internally, a figure close to the total number of international migrants worldwide. A Gallup poll by Esipova *et al.* (2013) suggests that eight percent of the world's adult population is estimated to be internal migrants, and the inclusion of children doubles this proportion (Curran 2016). We also expect climate change to further alter these geographical trends.

### Demographic patterns and trends

The demographics of migrant flows have shifted; mobility patterns have traditionally been shaped through state control of male migration in relation to its labor needs, yet growing demand in gender-selective jobs, such as those in the service and health care industries, supports female participation in the labor force (Koser 2016). Often referred to as the feminization of migration, this dynamic is supported by a concurrent relaxation of gender roles that enable agency for mobility. In fact, increasing numbers of women migrate independently and serve as the primary breadwinners in their families (Koser 2016). While scholars note that female migrants have been an enduring characteristic of flows, women now represent nearly half (48 percent) of international migrants and 42 percent of migrant workers (McAuliffe and Khadria 2019). These labor statistics likely undercount the high participation of women in the informal sector (de Haas *et al.* 2020).[12]

Exploitation is another persistent feature of labor migration patterns, particularly of women. From the maid trade (domestic work) and gender-segmented forms of precarious work (insecure and exploitative working conditions) to human and sex trafficking, women pay a steeper price for their mobility (de Haas *et al.* 2020). From an intersectional perspective, women are subject to interlocking forms of exploitation by their often-precarious undocumented status working in the informal sector, when subjected to gendered assumptions about their family role, and via persistent racial and ethnic stereotypes (de Haas *et al.* 2020). With the increasing diversity of gender and sexual identity among migrant populations, scholars have called for the collection of data variables to enhance our understanding of the range of migrant experiences and vulnerabilities (IOM 2020a).

Increasing levels of education among migrants are associated with increasing levels of development, yet legal migration opportunities are most often the prerogative of the privileged who have access to the necessary credentials and capital. Over time, this can result in the "reproduction of global privilege" among elites that both concentrates social, economic, and political power and can contribute to brain drain as emigrant elites search for a higher quality of life (de Haas 2014: 10). Those at the margins must resort to irregular forms of migration as they search for the same, a prospect often stymied by a lack of educational credentials or skills and the increasing segmentation of labor markets.

### Political patterns and trends

Higher levels of productivity and development are possible through the act of migration, bringing enhanced capabilities to an ever-wider range of people, which in turn can strengthen communities and the state. Simultaneously, these movements promote diversity, catalyzing societal change – social, cultural, economic, and political – in origin and destination countries (de Haas *et al.* 2020). Yet increasing diversity is often portrayed as a threat to state sovereignty and security in developed and developing countries alike, making international migration further politicized and securitized (Koser 2016, Hansen and Papademetriou 2014). Paradoxically, these efforts at securitization drive irregular migration, in turn fueling a progressively lucrative smuggling industry and immigration–industrial complex (Ghosh 2000). In fact, irregular migration is estimated to be greater than regular migration, driven by migrant labor availability and employer needs (Massey *et al.* 1998). Increasing barriers and obstacles along borders contribute to a reduction in circular and return migration as migrants choose to stay rather than risk the challenge presented by the journey home (de Haas 2007, Portes 2007). The United States–Mexico border is an oft-cited example, but similar strategies are at play across the globe, notably in the waters off the coasts of Australia, Spain, and Myanmar.

The concurrent rise of nationalism, xenophobia, and racism exacts its toll on migrants and refugees across the globe, an othering through both policy channels and societal conduct. Today, from the nativist policies of authoritarian regimes in Eastern Europe to the outright refusal of migrant landings on the shores of Italy and Australia, these restrictionist perspectives arise, in part, from a poorly distributed burden of responsibility for new arrivals and resettlement within and across states (Bhabha 2018). The concentration of diverse others, a result of migration corridors and historic resettlement programs, can threaten majority groups who often wield power in society. The state's resultant pursuit of migrant criminalization – often called crimmigration (Stumpf 2006) – out of concern for public safety and/or national security is matched by discourse labeling migrants as criminals, rapists, and the like. This reinforces a dehumanizing narrative in which governments are granted license to violate rights and perpetuate indignities while citizens are freed of moral culpability. Kubal and Olayo-Méndez (2020) offer an example in the Operation Streamline hearings in Arizona, where lines of chained detainees recall an historic system of slavery than a modern system of justice. A guilty-before-innocent approach pairs well with nationalism and anti-immigrant sentiment across the globe.

Much of this intense debate can be traced to the increasing limitations of the strict definitions and frameworks that have emerged over the last half century. The sharp historical divide between migrants "worthy of protection" and those who are not complicates scholarly and policy efforts to address mixed migration. For example, you might be unemployed and forced from your home due to violence or conflict and wish to settle in a country where you have family and support. You cross one or more borders – with or without documents – to be with them, but some governments might reject your claim of asylum because they perceive you as attempting to abuse the system.

On balance, migrants are negatively impacted by exclusionary, discriminatory, and racist immigration policies imposed by destination countries. The response of origin states has ranged from ambivalent to complacent, often driven by the necessities of diplomatic or economic relations. A long-standing preference for *national security* prevails in countries and regions of immigration and transit despite the presence of long-held international declarations and conventions to the contrary. Can we reconcile our national security interests with our moral demand for human security? This debate has raged unabated since the birth of international migration governance framework in the wake of the Second World War, the subject to which we now turn.

### What are the key regimes and agreements that govern migration?

The global migration trends and patterns discussed in the prior section inform the present-day system of migration governance, which emerged primarily from the experiences of the First and Second World Wars. This loose framework of international laws and norms is heavily focused on refugees, a small fraction of the population of international migrants.

Despite the signing of two historic agreements in 2018 – the Global Compact for Safe, Orderly and Regular Migration and the Global Compact on Refugees – an enduring tension between international cooperation and national sovereignty continues to complicate efforts at global governance. Migrants on the margins pay the price with their lives and livelihoods.

*Human rights accords*

Any discussion of global migration regimes must start with human rights, specifically, the 1948 Universal Declaration of Human Rights (UDHR).[13] The structure of international protection of human rights is also codified in the International Covenant on Civil and Political Rights and the International Covenant on Economic, Social, and Cultural Rights. Together, these three are known as the international bill of rights.

Refugees, forced to flee because of a threat of persecution, access a robust – if inadequately enforced – set of rights formally enshrined in the 1951 Convention Relating to the Status of Refugees and its 1967 Protocol, which establish that a person has,

- the right to leave and return to their country,
- the right not to be punished for illegal entry into the territory of signatory states,
- the right not to be returned to their own country forcibly (non–refoulment),
- the right to full economic and social rights, and
- the responsibility to abide by the laws and regulations of their country of asylum.

Under this convention a UN member state has an express obligation to protect the refugee, even if that refugee crossed a border in violation of that state's immigration laws (Bustamante 2002). Bustamante (2011) further notes that the protection and promotion of human rights within the state are often contradictory in application. Whereas most states' constitutions distinguish nationals and foreigners, states affirming the UDHR acknowledge that both groups have equal access to these rights by virtue of international law. Yet in practice, "the vulnerability of immigrants is equal to a virtual disempowerment of their human rights" (Bustamante 2002: 352). An example analysis is presented in Box 9.3.

---

**Box 9.3 Migration, capabilities, and human rights in the Mediterranean**

A Nigerian family is forced from their home and migrates through war-torn Libya to cross the Mediterranean for Italy. Under the Universal Declaration of Human Rights, the family has the right to leave their country (Article 13) and the right to seek protection from persecution in other countries (Article 14). During the journey, the boat springs a leak, placing the family in grave danger. A nearby coastal patrol discovers the sinking boat, triggering a duty to rescue the family to save their lives (Article 3). The rescuers are further bound by the 1951 Refugee Convention, specifically Article 33, which codifies the principle of non-refoulment, and Article 14, which calls for the rescuers not to return the family to a place where life or freedom may be threatened (Cogolati *et al.* 2015).

In practice, asylum systems in many countries are increasingly discriminatory, leaving many with unresolved yet rightful claims. FitzGerald (2019) describes remote-control patterns that have emerged to prevent asylum seekers from reaching refuge through legal means.

At the heart of discourse on the intersections of migration and capabilities is the question *Should we not have reason to value the same rights in all places?* When we are at home, for example, we are generally free to go to the library to check out a book or visit our local polling station to cast our ballot in an election. We take for granted this capability for movement. Similarly, Gasper and Truong posit that Sen's perspective on capability theory is based on an assumed notion of one's locality as self-evident. "Migration, by contrast, concerns movement between localities; and cross-border migration concerns movement also between polities" (2010: 340). We might conclude then that just as migrants travel, so should their rights.

The absence of a comprehensive legal framework for migrant and refugee rights is the driving force behind the International Migrants Bill of Rights, as well as the Inter-American Principles on the Human Rights of all Migrants, Refugees, Stateless Persons and Victims of Human Trafficking. The former articulates a state's obligations and the latter's rights-based approach can inform other regional architectures (Kysel 2016, 2020).

## The Sustainable Development Goals and the Global Compacts

Migration or mobility is a feature of 11 out of 17 Sustainable Development Goals, reflected most directly in target 10.7 to facilitate orderly, safe, regular, and responsible migration and mobility of people through the implementation of planned and well-managed migration policies. These aspirations have taken tangible form in the 2018 Global Compact for Safe, Orderly and Regular Migration and the Global Compact on Refugees, the most comprehensive effort to date to collaborate internationally on migration. Their primary achievements:

- creates the United Nations Network on Migration, bringing together 38 UN entities;
- commits to the incorporation of development-oriented approaches;
- acknowledges the important role of refugees and host communities in designing accessible and inclusive responses;
- improves migration data, migrant documentation and services, and remittance processes;
- lays the groundwork for better border management and migration procedures;
- pledges to expand legal pathways for migrants and cooperation on return and reintegration;
- clarifies goals around reducing migration drivers, vulnerabilities, and discrimination, while enhancing migrant social inclusion and cohesion.

As with most international agreements, the future of the global compacts will depend heavily on the willingness of signatory states to invest in their implementation. Critics charge the compacts do not go far enough. Climate change is an area in which agreement was elusive. Of great concern is failure to address mixed migration, an increasingly common pattern in which forced migration may transform into migration for economic or livelihood reasons (Van Hear *et al.* 2009), which places substantial limitations on migrants' capabilities to achieve a fulfilled life.

*Labor migration accords*

More than 90 percent of international migrants move for primarily economic reasons, yet the corresponding global frameworks are the least robust. The 1990 International Convention on the Protection of the Rights of All Migrant Workers and their Families has been ratified by only 55 states, all of which are migrant origin countries. In parallel, labor laws advanced by the International Labor Organization (ILO) codify protections in such categories as migration for employment (ILO 97 in 1949), migrant workers (ILO 143 in 1975), and domestic workers (ILO 1989 in 2011), yet ratifications similarly low, with 50, 25, and 29 states acceding, respectively. Those on the margins bear the greatest burden.

The UN High Commissioner for Human Rights offers powerful examples of the impact on capabilities of migrant workers and their families:

> The rights of migrant workers are frequently, indeed routinely, violated. They work in dangerous or harmful conditions, with high incidences of injury, death and sickness; receive wages far under the minimum baseline; and are subjected to fraudulent practices, excessive working hours and even illegal confinement by their employers, as well as sexual harassment, threats and intimidation. Their families are also vulnerable to human rights abuses in other contexts. These abuses of migrants are intensified when their immigration status is irregular. Not only are they often denied even the most basic labour protections, personal security, due process guarantees, healthcare and, in the case of their children, education; they may also face abuses at international borders, including prolonged detention or ill-treatment. And in some cases they risk being trafficked, enslaved, sexually assaulted or murdered.
>
> (Hussein 2015: paras 4–5)

Across the globe, labor exploitation is particularly problematic for vulnerable groups such as women, the undocumented, and people of color, which result in deprivations of fundamental dignity and rights. These deprivations can inform labor and other policy responses targeting the intersections of migration and human development, the subject to which we now turn.

## The intersections of migration and human development

In the first section of the chapter, we charted the vocabulary of migration, building a foundation for the second section in which we explored frameworks for thinking about the emergent realities of migration. In this final section, we will investigate the intersections of migration and human development by focusing on two case studies that strike at the heart of the matter. We will then survey two policy areas that highlight efforts to make inroads on these issues.

### *How might we contextualize migration and capabilities?*

Analyses of migration often begin by considering the economic and political causes and effects, yet a more comprehensive accounting investigates this global phenomenon through a human lens as well. Curran (2016) describes migration as broadly transformative; encompassing individuals, communities, and institutions; affecting migrants and non-migrants alike; and spanning origin, transit, and destination societies. Such a multi-dimensional perspective can be used as an analytical framework to consider emergent realities of migration and development by examining the tensions between:

- individuals and society (decision making, incorporation, reintegration)
- behavior of people in groups (networks, transnational communities, diasporas, enclaves)
- dynamics of structure and action (laws and policies influencing and being influenced by migrant behavior)

The case studies presented below offer different views of the intersections of capabilities and two forms of migration relevant to the study of poverty. As you study both, consider this analytical framework. If you were a policymaker, what structural changes would you encourage your government to make?

*Garifuna mixed migration and capabilities*[14]

Migration can emerge from a deprivation of opportunities, showing us there is more to migration than escaping poverty. In this case study, we meet the Garifuna, a people confronted with the twin forces of colonial domination and racial discrimination.[15]

---

**Box 9.4 Mixed migration and capabilities among the Garifuna in Central America and the United States**

The Garifuna are an Afro-indigenous group who live along the Caribbean coast of Central America, spread across Honduras, Belize, Guatemala, and Nicaragua. Their history began on a sinking slave ship, whose survivors ended up on the island of San Vicente, where they thrived until their violent expulsion at the hands of British colonial forces in 1797. Forced to resettle in the northern Honduran island of Roatán, the Garifuna later migrated along the rest of the Caribbean Coast.

In the mid-twentieth century, in response to racial discrimination, territorial dispossession, and unemployment, Garifuna migration reached the United States. Mirtha, a member of the Garifuna diaspora, characterized its shifting nature: "[w]e haven't had the same forced migration like that of our ancestors from St. Vincent, but our migration is forced because we are always looking for economic stability."

Today, the Garifuna maintain a robust transnational network and Garifuna migration has led to the accumulation of immense social and economic capital across the Americas. Through transnational organizations such as the Black Fraternal Organization of Honduras (OFRANEH), the Garifuna work to protect various interests and rights in Honduras, for example:

- *Economic.* Garifuna Coalition, United States, a New York-based organization that helps immigrants develop entrepreneurial skills, supports the flourishing of human capital, which in turn increases remittances that fund the construction of new homes, businesses, and schools.
- *Cultural.* A Garifuna Language Academy at the National Autonomous University of Honduras preserves the Garifuna's increasingly transnational culture.
- *Territorial.* The Garifuna's pristine lands and beaches along the Caribbean coast are a target for Honduran business interests bent on their development for a burgeoning tourism industry.

This case highlights the complex ecosystem of Garifuna migration, and mixed migration in general, as an aspirational search for capabilities and quality of life. In applying our three-tiered analytical framework, we can see the tension on the first level between individuals and society; in Honduras, human and territorial rights violations and discrimination coupled with steep unemployment shape migration flows. The Garifuna began migrating due to the deprivation of freedom, and the phenomenon continues in pursuit of educational and economic opportunities, providing new capabilities that enable freedom and self-actualization.

At the group level, the diaspora serves as insulation against disintegration of collective capabilities, at home and abroad. Like many transnational migrant networks across the globe, Garifuna communities in Honduras have greatly benefitted from the organized efforts of diaspora organizations such as OFRANEH, which by working to represent the interests and secure the rights of the Garifuna diaspora community, helps strengthen their collective capabilities.[16] Through collective action, these organizations help protect vulnerable people in a way that individual action has less power to accomplish.

At the structural level, the case reveals a tension between ethnic nations and nation-states, further challenging the concept of sovereignty. The experience of the Garifuna highlights the possibilities and complexities of government policy and legal pathways in addressing the drivers of mixed migration and the protection of vulnerable communities. Honduras, while officially acknowledging the rights of its indigenous communities, has pursued policies of territorial dispossession in the name of development (Brondo 2018). In 2015, Garifuna activists were successful in their petition to the Inter-American Court on Human Rights that the Honduran government was in violation of the free exercise of the Garifuna's collective property rights under the international Indigenous and Tribal Peoples Convention (ILO 169). This legal victory opens the possibilities for other indigenous groups to use legal pathways to advance their rights (Agudelo 2019). Yet continuing territorial dispossession, the related shift out of agricultural livelihoods, and increasing security-oriented impediments to circular migration make Garifuna migration more permanent than cyclical (Brondo 2008).

*Labor migration and the unfreedom of migrant workers[17]*

Manuel and Yvonne's story illustrates the potential benefits and risks at the intersection of economic migration and capabilities. Drawn by the higher wages and the resultant value of expanding their family's opportunities, Manuel and Yvonne accept the painful challenges of being away from their relatives.

---

### Box 9.5 Labor migration and the unfreedom of migrant workers in the United States and Mexico

39-year-old Manuel and his wife Yvonne, both originally from Mexico, are undocumented immigrants living for over two decades in suburban Long Island, New York. Together, they are raising their three young US-born children, one of whom receives regular specialized care for a critical health condition. Like clockwork, they would send money home to their families in Mexico, providing a lifeline of support amidst grinding poverty.

On an early weekday morning in 2018, US Immigration and Customs Enforcement (ICE) agents detained Manuel outside his apartment as he was leaving for his construction job. A poor driving record – which Manuel confesses was the result of drinking too much – had ultimately harmed no one physically yet placed him at greater risk of deportation. Taken to a detention center in New Jersey, Manuel was deported the next year to Mexico, a country he barely knows.

Without the medical infrastructure in Mexico to support his critically ill child, Manuel's family remains in New York, eking out an existence on Yvonne's minimum wage salary. Manuel, without access to supportive social networks in a country confronting drug violence, is wracked with guilt for being unable to provide for his family, barely making enough to eat in his low-wage job in agriculture in rural Puebla.

At the individual level in our analytical framework, Manuel and Yvonne live a precarious life as undocumented immigrants under near-constant fear of deportation. Numerous capabilities, including control over one's environment, bodily integrity, and over time, bodily health, are at issue. For half their lives, migration initially created opportunities for a more fulfilled life, yet the deportation of a wage-earning family member introduces added stressors.

At the group level, Manuel's deportation affects him and his immediate family through separation, affecting the capabilities of emotion and play. The family network extending into Mexico is also affected. Manuel and Yvonne migrated to New York in search of work, and the money they sent home to Mexico supported relatives by diversifying family income and funding education and health care expenses. Strengthened social and economic capabilities emerged from this financial lifeline at both the individual and group levels.

At the structural level, we can posit the limitations emplaced by their undocumented status on Manuel and Yvonne's employment situations. Employers can exploit workers in situations where labor laws are absent or laxly enforced. Neither earned more than minimum wage and had little expectation of promotion or benefits due to their status; they are likely constrained by labor market segmentation. Similarly, migrant farm workers who move with the seasons are in an ever-more precarious situation, with enhanced border security making circular migration more challenging. Most states do not offer robust visa programs for low-skilled migrants, whose work in low-wage occupations is often essential; the Covid-19 pandemic heightened global awareness of this inequity. The US government's visa system preferences high-skilled workers, driving many like Manuel and Yvonne to undocumented work, a precarious situation that increases their vulnerability.

In both of these case studies, migration policies in origin and destination countries, or the lack thereof, contributed to the experiences of migrants and their concurrent capacity to convert capabilities into functionings. If policymakers were to view migration as a fundamental and inescapable aspect of our global reality, our world and migration governance structures might look very different from their present form. We will now turn to an overview of two policy areas that attempt to address the complex intersection of migration and poverty.

## What are the key policies at the intersection of migration and capabilities?

Migration policies encompass rules, laws, regulations, processes, measures, and procedures that states use to manage the flow, origin, direction, and composition of migration (Czaika and de Haas 2013). An empirical study by Czaika *et al.* (2018) demonstrated that since 1945 migration policies have overall become more liberal at the global level, despite increasing restrictions in particular migration corridors such as between the United States and Mexico or the European Union and Morocco. At times, these changes do not always have their intended effect or elicit the opposite of what was intended. For example, scholars have shown that restrictive border policies in destination countries disrupt the sought-after responsiveness of migration to economic variations, and greater limitations on movement reduce return and circular migratory patterns (de Haas *et al.* 2019). The policy challenges are many, as are the policy prescriptions. Two policy areas highlight both the possibilities and complexities at the intersection of migration and capabilities, with profound implications for the human security of migrants.

### Policy area: Improving human mobility and capabilities through enhanced labor migration management

International migration is primarily driven by global demand for labor, the policies and regulations for which are often exploitative and inadequately regulated (de Haas *et al.* 2020). Scholars and policymakers alike view migration as a means to promote economic growth and reduce poverty – called the migration–development nexus – yet challenges remain in balancing labor market needs with immigration policy (see Faist 2008, Nyberg-Sørensen *et al.* 2002, Vammen & Brønden 2012).

Preibisch *et al.* (2016: 12) note that "[s]tructural barriers and interests within the global political economy that benefit from cheap, insecure migrant labour need to be exposed for their role in perpetuating and entrenching the 'unfreedoms' of migrant workers." The present-day surplus in global labor keeps commodity prices low, a powerful incentive for the status quo. Ultimately, origin and destination countries have opposing interests. Origin states favor liberal regimes that provide for free movement while destination states prefer to retain control over who enters and works (de Haas *et al.* 2020).

Calls for centering the migrant worker alongside economic growth in global policy discussions have largely gone unheeded (Bhabha 2018). Government policies are most robust for highly skilled workers while no- or low-skilled worker visas are limited and force many into vulnerable situations that are both illegal and ripe for exploitation (Papademetriou 2014). Sen's (1985) conception of capabilities extends to human mobility, and many who have good cause to migrate may not be able to afford a passport and visa or a smuggler. An inconvenient truth can be found in the choices irregular labor migrants make to enter into exploitative relationships with employers and smugglers precisely because they see a long-term benefit, which calls us to consider more deeply the relationship between exploitation and consent or agency (de Haas *et al.* 2020).

Focused policy changes can dramatically alter this counterproductive reality and four examples highlight the possibilities that enhance the fulfillment of capabilities:

- At the start of free movement across Europe in 1995 – called the Schengen area – many feared being overwhelmed by migration from poorer to richer countries within the European Union, a result that failed to materialize.

- Economic Community of West African States (ECOWAS) agreements provide for the free movement of persons, goods, and services across all 15 member states and include cooperation on labor rights, irregular migration, and refugees. While obstacles to full implementation remain, these mechanisms can prove instructive in other regions across the world (Awumbila *et al.* 2014) and offer signs of the progress that may come as aging populations alter workforce composition in some regions (de Haas *et al.* 2020).
- Efforts to lower the costs of remittances extend the reach of money migrant workers send home. In 2014, the G20 agreed to implement National Remittance Plans that support effective remittance flows and reduce transfer costs (Global Partnership for Financial Inclusion 2020). When paired with policies in origin communities that focus on improving infrastructure, accountability, and strengthening of institutions that enable economic growth, greater opportunities exist for migrants to invest at home (de Haas *et al.* 2020, Curran 2016).
- *Temporary migration programs* in destination countries have grown in number since the turn of the century (see Castles 2006, Martin *et al.* 2006, Plewa and Miller 2005), yet labor market segmentation remains a challenge and many systematically exclude and discriminate against them (de Haas *et al.* 2019). Transnational movements advance protections for labor migrants; for example, a partnership between the General Federation of Nepalese Trade Unions and the Korean Confederation of Trade Unions coordinates protection of Nepali migrant workers' rights in South Korea (Gordon 2009, 2011).

*Policy area: Improving human mobility and capabilities through enhancements to the international refugee regime*

Refugees comprise less than 10 percent of the migrant population, yet many experience profound limitations on their capabilities as well as pervasive poverty due to their displacement. Their life choices are wholly focused on survival, on life rather than quality of life. Historic definitions such as refugee no longer well-characterize those forcibly displaced and risk dehumanizing the migrant; in fact, only five million of the 100 million forcibly displaced were granted asylum protections in 2019 (UNHCR 2019). A consequence is that "more displaced persons are being assisted by more actors in more ways than at any time in history" (Aleinikoff and Zamore 2019: 106).

Since the signing of the 1951 Convention on Refugees, progress can be seen in four key areas, which Aleinikoff and Zamore (2019) have labeled the arc of protection:

- the classes of protected persons covered by the international refugee regime have expanded beyond their geographical and temporal limits;
- increasingly robust protection activities – identity and travel documents, education and health programs, support for especially vulnerable populations, refugee rights advocacy – have been undertaken by UNHCR and other international non-governmental organizations;
- a broader array of refugee rights has been enshrined in human rights conventions protecting women, children, and migrant workers, among others;
- displacement intervention operations have become more central to the work of development agencies and the private sector.

While the signing of the Global Compact on Refugees ostensibly advances the arc of protection, challenges remain. Three examples illuminate the possibilities for change:

- If granted asylum, most recipients are practically confined to their country of first asylum, unable to return home and barred from moving elsewhere. Many have education, skills, and credentials that are not accepted by the host country, limiting their economic prospects or delaying their workplace reintegration due to retraining or recredentialing requirements. Legal frameworks for third country movement would enable capabilities and enhance economic capacity (Aleinikoff and Zamore 2019).
- Through the Nairobi Declaration, the Intergovernmental Authority for Development (IGAD), a subregional body of eight African states, agreed to concrete steps to address the decades-long plight of Somali refugees. Tenets include voluntary repatriation, development-oriented responses to drought conditions plaguing the region, workforce training and education, and calls for international cooperation and facilitation of development initiatives in Somalia through debt relief, financial assistance, and other programs (Aleinikoff and Zamore 2019).
- The European Parliament labor market integration policy recommendations include language training, skills assessment, integration counseling and mentoring, job search assistance, and schemes for recognition of foreign credentials and assessment of informal learning and work experiences (Konle-Seidl and Bolits 2016). Complementary civic integration programs can support refugee adjustment to civil society, which can be demanding in the face of myriad personal, social, and economic deprivations most have faced since fleeing their home country. Sweden, Norway, Germany, the UK, Slovenia, and Portugal each offer examples of integration infrastructure that can serve as models for expansion in states with less integration experience, yet challenges remain. Strong disagreement exists on benefits and minimum wage levels. That said, labor market integration policies in Europe will enhance the capabilities of refugees and can serve to inform other regional efforts, perhaps even seeding a discussion of protections for economic migrants over the long term.

## Conclusion

Migration is a cause and consequence of human development as well as an effect and end. While globalization enables greater diversity among those who migrate and extends their reach, the ratio of international migrants to the world population has remained generally stable since the mid-twentieth century. What has changed is the direction and destination of flows and the role of women.

With greater diversity comes the potential for the weaponization of migration policy to counter the perceived threat posed by migrants and refugees to national security and cultural identity, although this phenomenon primarily affects migrants who lack certain skills required by destination societies, money, or advanced degrees, reinforcing ever-present structural inequalities across societies. For those with the means for mobility, movement from origin to destination for the purpose of expanding capabilities can also have counterproductive effects through social, cultural, and political discrimination and exclusion.

The increasingly selective approach to migration management – limiting skilled or wealthy migrants and regional citizens while restricting pathways for asylum and the low-skilled – might be thought of as a filter rather than as a tap in altering migrant flows (de Haas *et al.* 2019). Using travel visas to moderate entry, governments can exercise some degree of administrative control. In fact, 73 percent of bilateral migration corridors require a visa (Czaika *et al.* 2018) and most migrants travel legally in this way (Flahaux and de Haas 2016). Yet those who overstay are the dominant source of the undocumented globally, eclipsing unauthorized border crossers.

As the adage goes, "where you stand is based on where you sit," and perspectives on global migration are no different. For example, from a global north point of view, international refugee flows appear to have reached crisis proportions, yet 85 percent of refugees live in the global south and Western societies receive comparatively low numbers of refugees (UNHCR 2017). Meanwhile, refugee flows represent a small slice of global mobility compared to labor and family migrants (Hatton 2009).

Migration is a natural process, driven by a complex set of intersecting factors connected to the levels of development in sending countries. In fact, most migration happens between middle-income and high-income countries and most migrants from low-income countries belong to middle-income groups (Czaika 2012, Mahendra 2014). Absolute poverty is associated with lower emigration levels, as resource constraints deprive people of the capability to emigrate (de Haas *et al.* 2019). As Van Hear *et al.* note:

> It is clearly not fair that someone who is better resourced in terms of money or networks should receive better quality protection than someone with just as strong a case for protection but with fewer resources and less developed networks. It cannot be right that protection is accorded differentially according to resources.
>
> (2009: 30)

Were we to consider policies that achieve a greater balance between national security and human security, would all benefit? Greater global cooperation requires ceding or reimagining national sovereignty, a tall order with the rife contradictions in policy choices at the national, regional, and international levels.

## Discussion questions

- What are the reasons people migrate?
- How does poverty contribute to migration?
- How does migration relate to capabilities?
- What are the social, economic, political, and cultural rights of migrants in your home country?
- What rights would you want access to if you were to move to another country?
- Where is migration evident in your own community? Do migrants in your community have the same capabilities as you?
- How can you and your university community contribute to studying and making visible violations of migrants' rights?
- What policy areas resonate the most with you and what advocacy efforts could you undertake?

## Online resources

- See the global trends and report produced by the United Nations High Commissioner for Refugees: www.unhcr.org/

- Very useful is the International Organization for Migration (www.iom.int/) and its Global Migration Data Portal (www.migrationdataportal.org) and annual World Migration Report (www.iom.int/wmr/)
- The site www.iamamigrant.org/ has many personal stories that help put a human face on the issues of migration.
- The Internal Displacement Monitoring Centre has several focus areas including climate- and disaster-related displacement, with a wealth of data and research: www.internal-displacement.org/
- The International Migrants Bill of Rights Initiative is an example of cutting-edge policy and legal work: www.law.georgetown.edu/human-rights-institute/our-work/international-migrants-bill-of-rights-initiative/
- Two sources for raw data are the World Bank Global Bilateral Migration Database (www.datacatalog.worldbank.org/dataset/global-bilateral-migration-database) and United Nations Population Division, DESA, Trends in International Migration (www.un.org/en/development/desa/population/migration/data/index.asp)

**Acknowledgments:** Thanks to Serena Cosgrove and Ben Curtis for the opportunity to contribute to a book I love to teach. With deep appreciation to the many students I have learned with and from, who have helped me think more deeply about the intersections of migration and poverty. Special gratitude to Guillermo Yrizar Barbosa, Andy Gorvetzian, and Brinkley Johnson for their contributions to the chapter and to these students for their thoughtful commentary on its final draft: Brennan Hart, Nate Nollan, Hannah Macias, Sarah Bueter, Janae Theodore, and Ruth Zekariase.

## Notes

1  Photo courtesy of Leidiry Peña Andrades.
2  For more information on the work of the Kino Border Initiative, visit www.kinoborderinitiative.org/.
3  See Erika Lee. 2019. *America for Americans*. New York: Basic Books.
4  See Kitty Calavita. 2010. *Inside the state: The Bracero Program, immigration, and the INS*. New Orleans: Quid Pro Books.
5  See Michael Kagan. 2020. *The Battle to Stay in America*. Reno: University of Nevada Press.
6  See Chapter 1 for a discussion of structural violence.
7  See Chapter 8 for a fuller explanation of human security.
8  See, for example, Sonia Nazario's *Enrique's Journey*.
9  See Chapter 1 for a full discussion of positive and negative liberties and their relationship to capabilities.
10  See Chapter 2 for a discussion of modernization theory.
11  See Chapter 2 for a discussion of dependency theory.
12  See Chapter 1 for a discussion of this concept.
13  See Chapter 1.
14  Vignette courtesy of Andy Gorvetzian, co-author of *Surviving the Americas: Garifuna Persistence from Nicaragua to New York City*.
15  See Cosgrove *et al.* (2020).
16  See Chapters 5 and 11 for more on collective capabilities from the perspectives of geography and environment, respectively.
17  Adapted from Yrizar Barbosa (2020).

# Further reading

Bastia, T. and Skeldon, R. (eds.). 2020. *Routledge Handbook of Migration and Development*. New York: Routledge.

Bhabha, J. 2018. *Can We Solve the Migration Crisis?* Cambridge: John Wiley & Sons.

Curran, S. R. 2016. "Migration and development: Virtuous and vicious cycles." *The Sociology of Development Handbook*, 311–339.

de Haas, H. 2008. *Migration and development – a theoretical perspective*, Working Paper 9, International Migration Institute, Oxford.

de Haas, H., Miller, M. J. and Castles, S. 2020. *The Age of Migration: International Population Movements in the Modern World*. New York: Red Globe Press.

Truong, T.-D. and Gasper, D. (eds.) 2011. *Transnational Migration and Human Security: The Migration-Development-Security Nexus* (Vol. 6). Berlin: Springer.

# Works cited

Adams Jr, R. H. and Page, J. 2005. "Do international migration and remittances reduce poverty in developing countries?" *World development* 33.10: 1645–1669.

Agudelo, C. 2019. "The Garífuna community of Triunfo de la Cruz versus the State of Honduras: territory and the possibilities and limits of the Inter-American Court of human rights verdict." *Latin American and Caribbean Ethnic Studies* 14.3: 318–333, doi:10.1080/17442222.2019.1673069

Agunias, D. R. 2006. *Remittances and Development: Trends, Impacts, and Policy Options: A Review of the Literature*. Migration Policy Institute.

Ahmed, F. 2012. "The perils of unearned foreign income: aid, remittances, and government survival." *The American Political Science Review* 106.1: 146–165. doi:10.2307/23275367

Ajayi, M. A., Ijaiya, M. A., Ijaiya, G. T., Bello, R. A., Ijaiya, M. A. and Adeyemi, S. L. 2009. "International remittances and well-being in sub-Saharan Africa." *Journal of Economics and International Finance* 1.3: 078–084.

Aleinikoff, T. A. and Zamore, L. (2019). *The Arc of Protection: Reforming the International Refugee Regime*. Stanford: Stanford University Press.

Amuedo-Dorantes, C. 2014. *The Good and the Bad in Remittance Flows*. IZA World of Labor.

Anyanwu, J. and Erghijakpor, A. 2010. "Do Remittances Affect Poverty in Africa?" *African Development Review* 22.1: 51–91.

Awumbila, M., Y. Bennah, J. Kofi Teye, and G. Atiim. 2014. *Across Artificial Borders: An Assessment of Labour Migration in the ECOWAS Region*. Ref: ACPOBS/2014/RRS05. ACP Observatory on Migration.

Betts, A. 2010. "Survival migration: A new protection framework." *Global Governance: A Review of Multilateralism and International Organizations* 16.3: 361–382.

Bhabha, J. 2018. *Can We Solve the Migration Crisis?* Cambridge: John Wiley & Sons.

Borjas, G. J. 1989. "Economic theory and international migration." *International migration review* 23.3: 457–485.

Brondo, K. V. 2008. "Land loss and Garifuna women's activism on Honduras' north coast." *Journal of International Women's Studies* 9.1: 99–116.

Brondo, K. V. 2018. "A dot on a map: cartographies of erasure in Garifuna territory." *PoLAR: Political & Legal Anthropology Review* 41.2: 185–200.

Bustamante, J. A. 2002. "Immigrants' vulnerability as subjects of human rights." *International Migration Review* 36.2: 333–354.

Bustamante, J. A. 2011. "Extreme vulnerability of migrants: The cases of the United States and Mexico." Migraciones Internacionales 6.1: 97–118.

Carling, J. 2017. www.meaningofmigrants.org.

Carling, J. and Collins, F. L. 2018. "Aspiration, desire and the drivers of migration." *Journal of Ethnic and Migration Studies* 44.6: 909–926.

Castles, S. 2006. "Guestworkers in Europe: A resurrection?" *International migration review* 40.4: 741–766.

Clemens, M. A. 2014. *Does Development Reduce Migration?* Washington, DC: Center for Global Development.

Cogolati, S., Verlinden, N. and Schmitt, P. 2015. *Migrants in the Mediterranean: Protecting Human Rights.* European Parliament Committee on Subcommittee on Human Rights.

Cosgrove, S., Idiaquez, J., Bent, L. and Gorvetzian, A. 2020. *Surviving the Americas: Garifuna Persistence from Nicaragua to New York City.* Cincinnati: University of Cincinnati Press.

Curran, S. R. 2016. "Migration and development: virtuous and vicious cycles." *The Sociology of Development Handbook.* Oakland: The University of California Press.

Czaika, M. 2012. "Internal versus international migration and the role of multiple deprivation." *Asian Population Studies* 8.2: 125–149.

Czaika, M. and De Haas, H. 2013. "The effectiveness of immigration policies." *Population and Development Review* 39.3: 487–508.

Czaika, M., de Haas, H. and Villares-Varela, M. 2018. "The global evolution of travel visa regimes." *Population and Development Review* 44.3: 589.

de Haas, H. 2007. *Remittances, Migration and Social Development. A Conceptual Review of the Literature.* United Nations Research Institute for Social Development.

de Haas, H. 2009. *Mobility and Human Development,* Working Paper 14, Oxford: International Migration Institute.

de Haas, H. 2010. Migration transitions: A theoretical and empirical inquiry in the development drivers of international migration. *IMI working paper 24.*

de Haas, H. 2014. Migration Theory: Quo Vadis? DEMIG project paper 24, International Migration Institute Working Paper 100, Oxford.

de Haas, H., Castles, S. and Miller, M. J. 2020. *The Age of Migration: International Population Movements in the Modern World* (6th edn). New York: Red Globe Press.

de Haas, H., Czaika, M., Flahaux, M. L., Mahendra, E., Natter, K., Vezzoli, S. and Villares-Varela, M. 2019. "International migration: Trends, determinants, and policy effects." *Population and Development Review* 45.4: 885–922.

DeWind, J., Kim, E. M., Skeldon, R. and Yoon, I. J. 2012. "Korean development and migration." *Journal of Ethnic and Migration Studies* 38.3: 371–388.

Esipova, N., Pugliese, A. and Ray, J. 2013. "The demographics of global internal migration." *Migration Policy Practice* 3.2: 3–5.

Faist, T. 2008. "Migrants as transnational development agents: an inquiry into the newest round of the migration–development nexus." *Population, space and place* 14.1: 21–42.

Fajnzylber, P. and Humberto, L. J. 2007. *Close to Home: The Development Impact of Remittances in Latin America* (No. 48911, pp. 1–89). Washington, DC: The World Bank.

FitzGerald, D. S. 2019. *Refuge Beyond Reach: How Rich Democracies Repel Asylum Seekers.* Oxford: Oxford University Press.

Flahaux, M. L. and de Haas, H. 2016. "African migration: trends, patterns, drivers." *Comparative Migration Studies* 4.1: 1.

Gasper, D. and Truong, T.-D. 2010. "Movements of the 'We': International and Transnational Migration and the Capabilities Approach." *Journal of Human Development and Capabilities* 11.2: 339–357, doi:10.1080/19452821003677319

Ghosh, B. (ed.). 2000. *Managing Migration: Time for a New International Regime?.* Oxford: Oxford University Press.

Global Partnership for Financial Inclusion [GPFI]. 2020. 2020 Update to Leaders on Progress Towards the G20 Remittance Target.

Gordon, J. 2009. *Towards Transnational Labor Citizenship: Restructuring Labor Migration to Reinforce Workers Rights.* www.papers.ssrn.com/sol3/papers.cfm?abstract_id=1348064.

Gordon, J. 2011. "Citizens of the global economy: A proposal to universalize the rights of trans-national labor." *New Labor Forum* 20.1: 57–64.

Gupta, S., Pattillo, C. and Wagh, S. 2007. "Making remittances work for Africa." *Finance and Development* 44.2: 1–8.

Hansen, R. and Papademetriou, D. G. 2014. "Securing borders: The intended, unintended, and perverse consequences." Migration Policy institute Working Papers series.

Hatton, T. J. 2009. "The rise and fall of asylum: What happened and why?" *The Economic Journal* 119.535: 183–213.

Hatton, T. J. and Williamson, J. G. 1998. *The Age of Mass Migration: Causes and Economic Impact.* Oxford University Press on Demand.

Hussein, Z. 2015. Opening Statement by Mr. Zeid Ra'ad Al Hussein, United Nations High Commissioner for Human Rights. Geneva: Office of the United Nations High Commissioner for Human Rights. www.ohchr.org/EN/NewsEvents/Pages/DisplayNews.aspx?NewsID=163 97&LangID=E#sthash.u8i9PL32.dpuf.

International Organization for Migration (IOM). 2019. *International Migration Law: Glossary on Migration* (no. 34). Geneva: IOM.

International Organization for Migration (IOM). 2020a. *Migration Data Portal: Gender and migration.* www.migrationdataportal.org/themes/gender-and-migration.

International Organization for Migration (IOM). 2020b. *Missing Migrants Project: Spotlight on the Mediterranean.* www.missingmigrants.iom.int/region/mediterranean.

Ismail, A. A. 2007. "Lawlessness and economic governance: the case of hawala system in Somalia." *International Journal of Development Issues* 6.2: 168–185.

Konle-Seidl, R. and Bolits, G. 2016. *Labour Market Integration of Refugees: Strategies and Good Practices: Study.* European Parliament.

Koser, K. 2016. *International Migration: A Very Short Introduction.* 2nd edn. Oxford: Oxford University Press.

Kubal, A. and Olayo-Méndez, A. 2020. *Mirrors of Justice? Undocumented Immigrants in the United States and Russia.* New York: Fordham University Press.

Kysel, I. M. 2016. "Promoting the recognition and protection of the rights of all migrants using a soft-law International Migrants Bill of Rights." *Journal on Migration and Human Security* 4.2: 29–44.

Kysel. I. M. 2020. *Could a Migrants' Bill of Rights Provide a Blueprint for Migration Policy in the Americas?* Just Security. www.justsecurity.org/73776/could-a-migrants-bill-of-rights-provide-a-blueprint-for-migration-policy-in-the-americas/.

Li, X. and Wang, D. 2015. "The impacts of rural–urban migrants' remittances on the urban economy." *Annals of Regional Science* 54: 591–603.

Mahendra, E. 2014. "Financial Constraints, Social Policy and Migration: Evidence from Indonesia." *International Migration Institute, IMI/DEMIG Working Paper 101/25.*

Martin, P., Abella, M. and Kuptsch, C. 2006. *Managing Labor Migration in the Twenty-First Century.* New Haven: Yale University Press.

Massey, D. 1990. "Social structure, household strategies, and the cumulative causation of migration." *Population Index* 56: 3–26.

Massey D., Arango, J., Hugo, G., Kouaouci, A., Pellegrino, A. and Taylor, J. 1998. *Worlds in Motion: International Migration at the End of the Millennium.* Oxford: Oxford University Press.

McAuliffe, M. and Khadria, B. 2019. *World Migration Report 2020.* Geneva: International Organization for Migration.

New Humanitarian (formerly IRIN News). 2008. *Yemen: Drought displaces thousands in mountainous northwest.* www.thenewhumanitarian.org/news/2008/05/05/drought-displaces-thousands-mountainous-northwest.

Nyberg–Sørensen, N., Van Hear, N. and Engberg–Pedersen, P. 2002. "The migration–development nexus evidence and policy options state–of–the–art overview." *International migration* 40.5: 3–47.

Papademetriou, D. G. 2014. Curbing the Influence of "Bad Actors" in International Migration (Transatlantic Council Statement). Migration Policy Institute. www.migrationpolicy.org/research/curbing-influence-bad-actors-international-migration.

Passaris, C. 1989. "Immigration and the evolution of economic theory." *International migration* 27.4: 525–542.

Petras, J. and Veltmeyer, H. 2000. "Globalisation or imperialism?" *Cambridge Review of International Affairs* 14.1: 32–48.

Plewa, P. and Miller, M. J. 2005. "Postwar and post-Cold War generations of European temporary foreign worker policies: implications from Spain." *Migraciones internacionales* 3.2: 58–83.

Ponce, A. 2016. "From Macrostructural Forces to Social Connectedness: Uncovering the Determinants of South–South Migration." *International Journal of Sociology* 46.2: 85–113.

Portes, A. 2007. "Migration, Development and Segmented Assimilation: A Conceptual Review of the Evidence." *Annals of the American Academy of Political and Social Science* 610: 73–97.

Preibisch, K., Dodd, W. and Su, Y. 2016. "Pursuing the capabilities approach within the migration–development nexus." *Journal of Ethnic and Migration Studies* 42.13:, 2111–2127.

Ratha, D., Mohapatra, S. and Scheja, E. 2011. "Impact of Migration on Economic and Social Development: A Review of Evidence and Emerging Issues." Policy Research working paper, no. WPS 5558. World Bank. www.openknowledge.worldbank.org/handle/10986/3328.

Richmond, Anthony. 1994. *Global Apartheid: Refugees, Racism, and the New World Order.* Oxford: Oxford University Press.

Sen, A. 1985. "A sociological approach to the measurement of poverty: A reply to Professor Peter Townsend." *Oxford Economic Papers, New Series* 37.4: 669–676.

Sen, A. 1990. "Justice: means versus freedoms." *Philosophy and Public Affairs* 19: 111–121.

Sen, A. 1999. *Development as Freedom.* Oxford: Oxford University Press.

Skeldon, R. 1997. *Migration and Development: A Global Perspective.* Harlow: Addison Wesley Longman.

Stark, O. 1991. *The Migration of Labor.* Cambridge and Oxford: Blackwell.

Stumpf, Juliet P., 2006. "The Crimmigration Crisis: Immigrants, Crime, and Sovereign Power." *American University Law Review* 56: 367. Lewis & Clark Law School Legal Studies Research Paper No. 2007-2. www.ssrn.com/abstract=935547

Suro, R. 2018. "We Need to Offer More Than Asylum." *New York Times* Opinion Section, July 14.

Suro, R. 2019. "The Flight of Women and Children from the Northern Triangle and Its Antecedents," in Suarez-Orozco, M. (ed.). *Humanitarianism and Mass Migration: Confronting the World Crisis.* Oakland: The University of California Press.

Todaro, M. P. 1969. "A model of labor migration and urban unemployment in less developed countries." *The American economic review* 59.1: 138–148.

United Nations Department of Economic and Social Affairs [UNDESA]. 1998. *Recommendations on Statistics of International Migration,* Revision 1.

UNDESA Population Division. 2014. Trends in International Migrant Stock: The 2013 Revision–Migrants by Destination and Origin. CD-ROM documentation. www.un.org/en/development/desa/population/publications/index.shtml.

United Nations High Commissioner for Refugees [UNHCR]. n.d. Horn of Africa Somalia Situation. www.data2.unhcr.org/en/situations/horn.

UNHCR 2019. Global Trends: Forced Displacement in 2019. www.unhcr.org/5ee200e37.pdf.

UNHCR 2017. Left behind: Refugee education in crisis. www.unhcr.org/left-behind/.

Vammen, I. M. and Brønden, B. M. 2012. "Donor-Country Responses to the Migration–Development Buzz: From Ambiguous Concepts to Ambitious Policies?" *International Migration* 50.3: 26–42.

Van Hear, N. 2011. *Mixed Migration: Policy Challenges.* Oxford: Migration Observatory, University of Oxford.

Van Hear, N., Bakewell, O. and Long, K. 2018. Push–pull plus: reconsidering the drivers of migration. *Journal of Ethnic and Migration Studies* 44.6: 927–944.

Van Hear, N., Brubaker, R. and Bessa, T. 2009. "Managing mobility for human development: The growing salience of mixed migration." United Nations Development Programme Human Development Reports Research Paper 2009/20.

Vertovec, S. 1999. "Conceiving and researching transnationalism." *Ethnic and Racial Studies* 22: 445–462.

Weiss, L. 1997. "Globalization and the Myth of the Powerless State." *New left review*: 3–27.

World Bank. 2019. "Money sent home by workers now largest source of external financing in low- and middle-income countries (excluding China)." *World Bank Blog.*

Yrizar Barbosa, G. 2020. "Paper, places, and familias: Tracing the social mobility of Mexicans in New York" (2020). PhD dissertation, Sociology. Graduate Center, City University of New York. CUNY Academic Works.

Zelinsky, W. 1971. "The hypothesis of the mobility transition." *Geographical review*: 219–249.

# 10 Education as poverty reduction

*Benjamin Curtis*

## Learning objectives

- Explain why educational deficiencies are a form of poverty.
- Summarize how educational access and outcomes are measured, and which parts of the world have the biggest deficiencies in these areas.
- Interpret the capabilities perspective on education and development.
- Characterize different policies and programs that reduce education poverty by improving access and outcomes.

## Introduction

A lack of an adequate education is one of the definitions of poverty. If a person is illiterate, he is almost certainly poor along one or more dimensions. He is quite probably poor according to economic measures: it is unlikely that a person lacking basic literacy or numeracy will have a livelihood that brings in a generous income. If a person lacks an education, he is also probably deprived along all sorts of other dimensions of wellbeing. He is more likely to have health infirmities, and less likely to be able to protect his political rights. Moreover, a deficient education is a kind of poverty trap. Families that are economically poor are less likely to send their children to school, which means the children may remain illiterate and innumerate, and hence poor. But even for children in the developing world who do manage to attend school, there are other ways that poverty can affect their education. Going to primary school in a low-income country is often a very different experience from that in a high-income country. The school may not have walls, or a roof, or toilets. Schools often lack many other resources that students in rich countries take for granted, such as textbooks, desks, paper, and pencils. As a specific example, a World Bank study of Vietnam in the 1990s found that in one region, 39 percent of primary school classrooms did not even have blackboards (Glewwe and Kremer 2005). In Malawi around 2015, the average primary school class had 126 students (World Bank 2018a).

A lack of an adequate education is a cause and definition of poverty – but education can also be an essential remedy for poverty. Thomas Awiapo's story is an excellent illustration of this complex interrelationship. Thomas grew up in the northern part of Ghana, in one of the country's poorest areas. Both of his parents died when he was a little boy, and two of his brothers died from malnutrition. Thomas had to find a way to survive, but he lacked marketable skills, almost any physical assets, and the maturity to figure out how to cope with his situation. Because he and his surviving brothers often did not have enough to eat, Thomas began attending a nearby school run by the Catholic Church, just because it offered a daily meal. At the outset, he would come for the food but not stay for the instruction. One of the teachers nonetheless gradually encouraged him to attend school regularly. Thomas came to find that he liked and was good at learning. He completed primary school, then secondary, and proved such an excellent student that he received a scholarship to attend university. His dedication and intelligence then secured him another scholarship, this time to attend graduate school in the United States. After he finished his Master's degree, Thomas returned to the northern region of Ghana to work in development. He became a global ambassador for Catholic Relief Services, and his experience demonstrates both how poverty can hinder access to education, and how education can be a way out of poverty.

This chapter explores these relationships, focusing on some of the most promising ways in which education can reduce poverty. It begins by surveying the common problems with educational access and learning outcomes in the developing world. After a consideration of the capabilities approach to education and development, the chapter then details several programs that have proven effective for boosting access and outcomes. An understanding of the challenges and benefits of education in the global south is absolutely essential to grasp why, from the capabilities perspective, people are poor. This is also one of the biggest policy challenges in human development today. Some 85 percent of the world's children – around two billion people in total – live in low and middle income countries, and too many of them are forced to deal with the problems of inadequate education every day.

Fortunately, there is good news to report on education as a development priority. Between 2000 and 2018, the number of children of primary school age who were not attending school fell by nearly 40 million. Children in low-income countries enroll in primary school at nearly the same rate as in high-income countries (UNICEF Data on Primary Education n.d.). In the 60 years from 1950 to 2010, the average years of schooling for people in the developing world grew from 2.0 to 7.2 years (Beatty and Pritchett 2012). And the ratio of girls to boys in primary and secondary school has reached near parity; as recently 1991, only 84 girls were enrolled for every 100 boys (World Bank 2011). Nonetheless, much remains to be done to guarantee an adequate education to children everywhere, and to prevent educational deficiencies from being a cause of poverty.

## Problems with access

One of the persistent problems with education in low- and middle income countries is that of access, such that many children who should be in school are not. There are still some 59 million primary school-aged children out of school. Many of them live in the poorest countries or in fragile states. According to recent data, in Liberia 57.3 percent of primary-aged children were not in school, with Chad at 49.7, Mali at 48.1, Senegal at 36.6, and Afghanistan at 36.4. In Pakistan, 38.1 percent of primary-aged children were not in school (UNICEF Data on Primary Education 2020). For every 100 out-of-school children of primary age, roughly 20 will never start school, 45 will start late, and 35 have dropped out. These children also come disproportionately from the poorest families, or from areas suffering from conflict or natural disasters. On the whole, schooling levels are still lowest in Sub-Saharan Africa, where 32 million children are out of primary school, which accounts for roughly half of the total number worldwide. And while increasing primary school enrolment has been the internationally valorized goal, secondary enrolment not surprisingly lags. Around 62 million children who should be in secondary school are not. Educational deficiencies are not just a concern for children: some 750 million adults worldwide lack basic literacy (UNESCO Institute of Statistics n.d.). Another troubling fact to keep in mind is that even while enrolment rates have risen, merely enrolling in school does not mean that a child attends regularly.

The single best predictor of children's school attendance is their parents' level of education: the more educated the parents, the more likely the kids are to get educated. What other reasons do children who are of school age not attend? The most common answers are financial costs, opportunity costs, life disruptions, and systematic discrimination. In terms of financial costs, even though fees to attend primary school have been eliminated in many countries, families often still have to pay for uniforms, pencils, paper, books, or transportation to the school. Because such costs can add up to well over 100 USD annually, some families simply cannot afford to send their children even to supposedly "free" schools. Opportunity costs can also be high: sending a child to school often means that he cannot work to help support his family. Such was the situation of Ernesto, a shoe-shine boy I met in the town of Chichicastenango in Guatemala. Ernesto was about 12 years old, but he was far behind in his education because he so often missed school. His parents routinely expected him to walk the five miles into town to make money for the family. The more school Ernesto missed, the more likely it became that he would fail his classes and drop out. Sadly, having to earn an income for the short-term support of his family was depriving Ernesto of the opportunity to gain skills and develop capabilities that might improve his long-term chances for a prosperous and healthy life. To his credit, Ernesto was not unaware of this unfortunate compromise, but he had to obey his parents' wishes and contribute to his family's immediate survival.

Time spent in school can also take away from children's time doing household duties such as cleaning, cooking, or tending to the familial fields. This problem particularly affects girls. Various disruptions in life also prevent children from attending school. Besides shocks such as war and natural disasters, cyclical duties such as agricultural work can impede school attendance. In countries with pronounced wet and dry seasons, families can need children to help out in the fields during the rainy period. During the dry period, food and incomes can be sharply reduced, which not only hinders the family's ability to pay school costs, but also can lead to children's malnutrition, which hinders their progress if they do attend school. As Thomas's story illustrates, the death of parents is another life disruption that impacts school attendance, since children often have to fend for themselves. According to one study from the Central African Republic, school enrolment for children who had both parents living was almost twice that for children whose parents had died (Durston and Nashire 2001).

Systematic discrimination inhibits school attendance for people from various groups. The most obvious is discrimination against girls (see i.a. Cameron 2012, Unterhalter 2012). The worst effects here are in Sub-Saharan Africa and West and South Asia, which make up three-quarters of the approximately 62 million girls not in primary or secondary school. Poverty compounds the problem, such that in low-income countries, only 25 percent of the poorest girls complete primary school (UNESCO Institute of Statistics n.d.). The same cultural norms that discriminate against girls getting an education can disadvantage people from minority groups; in fact, almost 70 percent of the girls worldwide who are not in school are members of discriminated groups. This exclusion affects cultural minorities such as indigenous girls in Guatemala, only 26 percent of whom completed primary school (compared to 62 percent of non-indigenous Guatemalan girls) according to one study. Similarly, girls from hill tribes in rural Laos received on average two years of school, compared to five years for girls from the majority ethnicity (Lewis and Lockheed 2006). Such exclusion does not just affect women, of course. People from groups such as the Dalit in India, rural tribes in Pakistan, Berbers in the Middle East and North Africa, or the Roma in Eastern Europe often suffer from major educational disadvantages. Part of the problem is school curricula that do not accommodate them. Very often, members of these groups may find that teaching is not in the language they speak at home, but rather in the majority language. For example, the indigenous Guatemalan girls may be most comfortable in K'iche', and the fact that their schooling is in Spanish can pose problems for them. Similarly, it can happen that school systems throughout the developing world are designed by elites for elites. The education a child in rural Senegal receives may have little relevance to her if the curriculum centers on the lives of urban Senegalese.

## Problems with outcomes

Enrolment rates are only one, narrow view of educational inadequacies that can be caused by and contribute to poverty. At least as serious are inadequate learning outcomes for the children who *do* attend school. In Ghana and Malawi, for instance, more than 80 percent of students finishing grade two could not read simple words such as "the" (Gove and Cvelich 2011). In parts of India, half of grade 5 students could not read text from the grade 2 curriculum (ASER Centre 2017). In Peru, only about half of second graders could read anything. In Brazil and Botswana, two solidly middle-income countries, 66 and 63 percent of people were found to be functionally illiterate (Hanushek and Wößmann 2007). When it comes to mathematics, proficiency levels are often depressingly low. In Mali, only seven percent of assessed students rated proficient; in Nicaragua, 30 percent, and in the Philippines, 34 percent (World Bank 2018a). In Tanzania, of children who finished grade seven, only 21 percent passed a benchmark language test and only 19 percent passed the math test (Levine and Birdsall 2005). In Pakistan, half of third graders could not answer the most basic multiplication questions (World Bank 2011). On international tests that compare learning outcomes for a range of high- and middle-income countries, results showed that the average math ability of Brazilian students would put them in the bottom two percent of students in Denmark (Kenny 2010). Here again, poverty and other factors such as gender or disability combine. For instance, in Cameroon, only five percent of girls from the poorest families had learned enough in primary school to advance to secondary school, compared to 76 percent of girls from the richest families (World Bank 2016).

The evidence is painfully clear that many students are not being well served by their school systems. There are myriad reasons for that failure, but two of them include problems with both teachers and school management. Teachers are too often absent from work: in an influential study by Chaudhury *et al.* (2006), 11 percent of teachers were absent on the average day in Peru, 16 percent in Bangladesh, 20 percent in Kenya, 25 percent in India and 27 percent in Uganda. Another study in Africa found that 40 percent of teachers were absent either from school or their classrooms on a day when random inspections were carried out (Bold *et al.* 2013). Additionally, too many teachers lack adequate qualification for their jobs. They may lack knowledge: studies in Africa found that many primary school math teachers were barely numerate, and that a majority of third grade teachers in South Africa could not pass a literacy test for sixth graders (Kenny 2010). Or they may lack training: only 69 percent of secondary school teachers in the developing world had adequate training, according to one study (Glewwe and Kremer 2005). Evidence from Latin America also suggests that people who pursue teaching are academically weaker than others in higher education (Bruns and Luque 2015). One result is that teachers may be unaware of the most effective pedagogical strategies to help students learn. The problems with school management are similar. Good school leadership is associated with improved student outcomes, but poorer communities tend to have both less effective school managers *and* less capacity for effective oversight by parents (Bloom *et al.* 2015).

## Education as a development strategy

These are not the sum total of all the problems of education in low-resource societies, nor are they an exhaustive list of reasons why such education is often inadequate. But they should give an unmistakable picture that many people in developing countries are not receiving the basic quality of education that we might wish. Why should everyone be entitled to a quality education? The answers are to some extent obvious – but they need to be empirically grounded, and linked to poverty reduction. To begin with, education has been recognized as a basic human right in the Universal Declaration of Human Rights. The reason it is a basic right is that an education is absolutely essential to so many things in human life, such as earning an income, enjoying decent health, thinking for oneself, and participating fully as an autonomous adult and citizen. Education also has a particular connection to the rights of children. According to the Convention on the Rights of Children, young people have specific entitlements not only to education per se, but to aspects of a decent human life relevant to their educational process such as freedom of expression, freedom from child labor, and access to information (see UNICEF 2004).

Beyond the argument for education from basic rights, a great deal of research over the years has shown that education is associated with improved agricultural productivity, technological adaptation, higher wages, better nutrition, reduced female fertility and infant mortality. More educated people cope better with economic shocks (such as depressions or other crises) and environmental adversity (such as extreme weather events). A number of scholars have also claimed that having more educated people in a society tends to go along with more democracy, including higher rates of voting, improved governance, and more tolerance for diversity (see i.a. Campante and Chor 2012, Glaeser *et al.* 2007). One reason is that schooling helps educate people on their political rights and duties, empowering them as citizens.

The health benefits of education are particularly pronounced: mothers who have more education are more likely to have healthier children, thanks to being aware of better basic health practices such as elementary hygiene and the necessity of vaccinations. They will also likely have fewer children. In fact, educating girls is one of the surest ways of combating various forms of poverty, since it means that girls usually have fewer children and take better care of the ones they do have. Admittedly, the causal relationships here can be murky. A greater number of educated girls alters norms about what girls are entitled to, but it is also partially a result of other cultural changes in society that are already empowering women. In any case, healthier children are more likely to stay in school, which leads to better learning outcomes (UNESCO 2014b). Thus, it is not always possible to say that education *causes* improved health outcomes and women's empowerment, but it is definitely part of a valuable feedback loop leading to progress in these areas.

Education has long been considered essential for creating "human capital" that contributes to a society's economic growth. It does so by boosting people's skills and labor productivity. Education is also associated with the potential for economic innovation because it facilitates the acquisition of new technologies, skills, and other sorts of new knowledge (Hanushek and Wößmann 2007). At the individual level, education is clearly associated with higher earnings and more secure livelihoods. A minor debate in the scholarly literature has been fought by a few scholars who say that education mostly provides private returns, that is, individual outcomes such as higher wages. These scholars claim that education makes only a negligible contribution to social returns, that is, the "spillover effects" that improve society as a whole. The preponderance of the scholarship, however, holds that education does benefit societies as well as individuals, through such things as reduced crime, reduced fertility and infant mortality, and improved economic productivity. The reason this debate is relevant is because it raises the question of education's benefits beyond the economics-based human capital approach (Robeyns 2006).

Simply stated, regardless of economic benefits, education is still indispensable because of its relationship to human capabilities. Besides helping people attain a livelihood and generate income, education builds many different skills and abilities – and this range of skills, habits, knowledge, and personal growth can empower people to live lives that they value. The positive economic effects associated with educational attainment are typically the easiest to measure. The other positive effects may be more difficult to quantify, such as empowering women and men to make decisions for themselves, to adopt more open-minded and reflective intellectual attitudes, to become more aware of the world and one's own rights, and to expand their opportunities. Such changes might not even lead to higher incomes. But they give individuals greater agency over their own lives. So though the human capital approach and its economic orientation have their merits, education is best conceived as expanding individuals' capabilities and hopefully helping them to realize their functionings (see Chiappero-Martinetti and Sabadash 2014, Saito 2003). In Amartya Sen's view, the capabilities approach is a vital supplement to human capital understandings of education, since the attainment of individual wellbeing and freedom will have indirect effects on economic production (Hart 2014).

Education is thus central to human development, both in the specialized sense of that term as a counterpart to economic development, and for the crucial meaning of development itself as growth, burgeoning, change. As a World Bank education report has noted, "The human mind makes possible all other development achievements, from health advances to agricultural innovation to infrastructure construction and private sector growth." And there is "no better tool" for unleashing the potential of the human mind than education (World Bank 2011). Education promotes change and, ideally, improvement in human beings. This is one reason why education has a special relevance to the wellbeing of children: it helps young people develop their own capabilities, which then helps them develop into adults who can enjoy a full complement of capabilities and functionings (Comim *et al.* 2011). Education therefore *is* development, as Sen has remarked (Sen 1999). Conversely, lack of an adequate education *is* poverty.

Sen has pointed to three ways that education expands capabilities and can thereby reduce poverty. These three ways are grounded on ideas of what constitutes justice in regards to education. Through promoting literacy, education makes possible public debate and dialogue about social structures and politics, about the way society should be. Every person should be able to participate in that dialogue. Education also helps people to acquire the analytical and practical tools to make reasoned decisions for themselves, for their families and for their communities. Every person is entitled to make such decisions. Lastly, in Sen's framework, education has a special role in empowering marginalized and excluded people to both of the above functions. Once they are empowered in this way, they should hopefully gain leverage to reduce the conditions that contribute to their marginalization and exclusion (Unterhalter 2009). Furthermore, without an adequate education a person may be denied basic capabilities that Nussbaum (2011) has identified as fundamental to human life, including health (because of the relationships between education and better health); senses, imagination and thought (which in Nussbaum's formulation explicitly depend on intellectual training); practical reason (such as the ability to make decisions for oneself, which can be better informed through education); and control over one's environment (since education can be positively associated with political participation and democratic traditions of free speech).

Because education is central to development, it is critical to improve education especially for those people who experience the most serious deficiencies described earlier, and who therefore face the most serious threats to their basic capabilities. Children again deserve a special focus here since they are often disproportionately represented among poor populations. Moreover, poor children typically suffer from severe capability deprivations that can have long-lasting impacts on their own development and on the poverty status of their families (Biggeri and Mehrotra 2011). A difficult question when thinking about how to help such children is this: in applying the capabilities approach to poverty reduction through education, what is the minimum adequate threshold? In other words, what counts as the basic level of educational attainment and quality to which everyone is entitled?

The Millennium Development Goals pre-2015, and the Sustainable Development Goals post-2015, have both proposed answers to this question. The MDGs focused on universal primary enrolment, but paid very little attention to learning outcomes. In contrast, SDG number 4 has goals that by 2030 every child will be able to complete early childhood, primary, and secondary education; that all young people and adults should be fully literate; and that education should be adequately financed and governed, with transparency and community participation. This SDG includes both greater attention to learning outcomes, and to equity for disadvantaged groups such as poor people and girls. However, the SDGs' definition of education quality and equity have been questioned. While the SDG does attempt to address various kinds of disadvantage such as disability status, poverty status, and rural/urban divides, a more profound perspective on equity would try to undo structures of discrimination and oppression that operate at all levels of schooling, including within the classroom and among school management (Unterhalter 2019). Likewise, an understanding of "quality" should involve not just students' scores on learning assessments, but also metrics to gauge their participation and empowerment in school, as well as their graduation and employment rates post-school (Hart and Brando 2018). Ideally, quality education should embrace inclusion, sustainability, and support for personal development among school staff as well, including teachers (Tao 2016).

The problem of assuring a minimum standard of education for everyone can be usefully conceived with the terminology of capabilities and functionings. The goal of universal primary enrolment envisions giving everyone the capability of going to school, though it says little about what capabilities come from being well educated. Moreover, it ignores the issue of how individuals can convert the capability of going to school to the functionings of actually using the capabilities that come from education. Different children will need different resources to be able to attend school, to be able to participate and understand, and then to complete learning successfully (Vaughan 2007). For example, if a child is hungry, or speaks a different language at home than at school, or fears for bodily safety at school because of her identity, gender, or disability status, then that child will need extra help to succeed in education. This is the equity issue: the poorest people may need additional resources to convert educational capabilities (such as the ability to attend school) to educational functionings (such as actually being able to read and reason) (Hart 2019).

The capabilities approach does not propose a universally agreed-upon set of indicators to gauge basic educational capabilities. However, there are various useful principles for thinking about what constitutes a minimum standard of educational quality. The EdQual Research Program, which focused on improving quality in low-income countries, offered this definition:

> A good quality education is one that enables all learners to realize the capabilities they require to become economically productive, develop sustainable livelihoods, contribute to peaceful and democratic societies and enhance wellbeing. The learning outcomes that are required vary according to the context but at the end of the basic education cycle must include threshold levels of literacy and numeracy and life skills including awareness and prevention of disease.
>
> (Tikly 2010)

This definition leaves open the possibility for societies to decide their own outcomes beyond the minimum basic level. But the implication is that an adequate education must ensure that people have certain skills. These skills must include "functional life skills" such as being able to provide shelter and assure sufficient nutrition for oneself and/or one's family. Every person must have certain minimum cognitive skills, too, which are not just literacy and numeracy but also the ability to access new information (Young 2009). Many of these skills – including social skills to live in harmony with one's community – are subsumed into Lorella Terzi's (2007) proposed list of specific "basic capabilities for educational functionings." (See Box 10.1) This list is certainly open to debate as to what it includes and how it could be measured and operationalized. The importance, however, is to consider how programs to improve education relate to these proposed fundamental entitlements. The ultimate goal, as Terzi says, is that everyone should be able "to participate in society as equals" (Terzi 2014: 9).

---

**Box 10.1  Basic capabilities for education**

- **Literacy**: being able to read, write, and use language
- **Numeracy**: being able to count, measure, and solve mathematical questions
- **Sociality and participation**: being able to establish positive relationships with others and participate in social activities without shame
- **Learning dispositions**: being able to concentrate, pursue interests, complete educational tasks
- **Physical activities**: being able to exercise and engage in sports activities
- **Science and technology**: being able to understand natural phenomena and use technological tools
- **Practical reason**: being able to relate means and ends and reflect critically on one's and others' actions

Source: adapted from Terzi (2007).

## What works to improve education?

While there are a number of specific programs that have demonstrated successes in improving education and reducing poverty, there is no "one size fits all" policy. Some programs do a better job of increasing access to schooling, helping to meet the goal of universal enrolment. Other programs are more relevant to improving learning outcomes, so that the quality of the education children receive is adequate. Many times, these goals do not overlap, so that improvements in access do not necessarily translate to improvements in quality. Therefore, programs must be selected for their fit to an individual society's conditions – blanket recommendations are of little utility. Moreover, many scholars who have studied the challenges of education in lower income countries affirm that simply putting more financial resources into existing systems will not produce markedly better outcomes. For instance, increasing teachers' salaries does not automatically translate to more student learning. To achieve real improvement, educational systems must often be reformed, including how teachers are trained, how schools are managed and held accountable, and how data on student progress are gathered. Because there is no magic bullet to ensure optimal poverty reduction through education, we will focus on just a few promising strategies, programs whose positive outcomes have been most convincingly demonstrated.

The past several decades' impressive gains in primary enrolment have come thanks to a variety of initiatives to expand access to children whose backgrounds might previously have hindered them from attending school. Building schools has been a logical first step in expanding access, and while rural and marginalized areas may sometimes still lack adequate school facilities, development policy now increasingly focuses on other means of ensuring that children attend and stay in school. Reducing the costs of attendance is a consistent objective that can be met by providing uniforms and textbooks (so families do not have to pay for them), or eliminating school fees. After school fees were eliminated, primary enrolment jumped by 307.4 percent in Ethiopia, 95.5 percent in Tanzania, 68 percent in Uganda and 49 percent in Malawi (see Bentaouet-Kattan 2006, Morgan *et al.* 2014). One of the most effective models worldwide for reducing costs and incentivizing school attendance are conditional cash transfers (CCTs). These programs give low-income families money conditioned upon the family meeting certain goals, such as ensuring that daughters regularly attend school. The amount of money families receive is usually fairly small, around ten percent of the household's consumption level. CCTs have been implemented in some 28 countries, including nearly all countries in Latin America, plus a handful in Africa, Asia, and the Middle East.

The most famous CCT program is Mexico's Prospera, formerly known by several other names. It works by specifically targeting poor families (at first in rural areas, now in urban areas too), and mothers and daughters: the subsidies families receive for keeping their children in school are higher for girls. The payments typically start in the third grade, and their amount varies – including, for example, a grant to buy food – but the total can sometimes equal what one of the parents earns in a month from work. The money is given directly to the families rather than channeling it through a local intermediary, which reduces the potential for corruption. Besides regular school attendance, the conditions also include routine visits to a health clinic, where the children are vaccinated, weighed, and given vitamins. Mothers have to attend basic health classes covering issues such as nutrition and sanitation. Studies have repeatedly documented this program's positive effects. It increased school enrolment on average by 3.5 percent, with larger effects in increasing enrolment in grade six, which improved by 11.1 percent (Schultz 2004). Boys who participated in Prospera starting at age nine completed a year more of schooling than boys not in the program. Girls who began participating at early ages received 0.7 more years of schooling. Child labor for boys decreased, though not for girls (Behrman *et al.* 2011).

Studies of CCTs in other countries have found even larger effects. In Nicaragua, time in school increased 18 percent for children aged 7–13. In Bangladesh, time in school increased by 27 percent for girls aged 11–18, and in Pakistan the increase was 38 percent for primary school girls (Orazem 2012). The CCT in Ecuador decreased child labor by 17 percent in addition to increasing school enrolments by ten percent (Schady and Araujo 2006). In Malawi, a CCT helped girls add the equivalent to one-sixth of a year of schooling and increased their test scores; daily attendance also rose by eight percentage points (Baird *et al.* 2011). A scholarship program for girls in Cambodia worked similarly to a CCT, giving awards equivalent to 45 USD each to families whose daughters had good attendance and good grades in school. This program led to significant increases in enrolment for girls from the poorest households, whose enrolment actually surpassed girls from the richest households (Filmer and Schady 2006, 2014). Other indicators of child and family wellbeing also improved, such as increased health-care visits, better nutrition, and vaccinations.

While CCTs have achieved some excellent results in getting children in school and encouraging them to stay there, such programs do have limitations. They have been shown mostly to improve access, sometimes to have health benefits, but not consistently to improve learning outcomes. So, though they help get kids in school, CCTs do not necessarily ensure quality learning. CCTs are relatively expensive, since in large countries such as Mexico they can involve monetary transfers to millions of families. CCTs also require a reasonably effective government administrative system to manage them. For these reasons, they have been more commonly implemented in middle-income countries that have greater financial resources and greater governmental capacity. Though CCTs are often beneficial, there are other programs to improve access that may be more cost effective for low-income countries.

One widely useful, often highly cost-effective policy that can improve access and outcomes begins before formal schooling. Early childhood development (ECD) programs can bring very positive benefits for children such as boosting cognitive skills, nutrition and health status, and levels of school attainment. This is particularly important because deficiencies in these areas contribute to early grade repetition, dropping out, and delayed intellectual development. Strong ECD has also been associated with gains in lifetime earnings (see i.a. Anderson *et al.* 2003, Barnett 1995, Heckman 2006). A program in the Philippines aimed specifically at disadvantaged families provides an example of what ECD can accomplish. Day-care centers were set up to serve as pre-schools and provide health services including micronutrient supplements. Participants in the program were visited in their homes by health workers who delivered immunizations among other services. Parents were educated about best practices in raising their children. Schools were also involved through workshops for teachers and administrators to train them in better skills relevant to ECD. An analysis of the program's results showed that over six years, children displayed satisfactory physical and cognitive development, and as students their test scores improved by 12–15 points (Armecin *et al.* 2006, Yamauchi and Liu 2012). This Philippine ECD program thus successfully managed to improve children's access to school via improved health and nutrition, as well as their learning outcomes.

Whether separately or as part of such ECD programs, health interventions in general can address both access and learning problems. Providing meals at school is often beneficial especially in areas with high food insecurity. In various countries it has boosted both attendance and learning outcomes. The program in Guyana even had wider societal benefits by stimulating community ownership of the program's implementation, and requiring schools to purchase produce for meals from local farmers (Snilstveit *et al.* 2016). Other health programs such as deworming or anti-malaria prophylaxis are quite common and often inexpensive. Deworming, for instance, can cost as little as 50 cents per child per year (Orazem 2012). There is some evidence for the positive effects of these kinds of interventions, but the results vary widely depending on the context, so as yet consensus is lacking on how best to utilize them. Nonetheless, because good health is essential for children to attend school and learn, such initiatives may be promising particularly for the poorest populations in a given country.

Obviously, even if children manage to attend school, they will not learn very much unless a teacher is also present. Indeed, studies in countries such as the United States and China have pointed to teacher quality as the single most important in-school factor for explaining students' achievement (see i.a. Akiba *et al.* 2007, Hanushek and Rivkin 2006, Rockoff 2004). Given the problems in many countries with teachers' absenteeism and inadequate professional preparation, how can programs support teachers to do their job better and hold them more accountable for student learning outcomes? Merely raising teachers' salaries may help improve morale and attract more able people to the profession, but is not always effective. As an example, Kenya instituted a bonus pay scheme so that teachers would be rewarded as their students' test scores improved, but an analysis found that teachers focused on preparing their students mostly to do better on the test, at the expense of other lessons (Kremer and Holla 2008).

Instead, the most promising strategies to improve teaching generally involve giving teachers the materials and skills they need to cope with diverse learners in sometimes challenging learning environments. In terms of materials, providing curriculum appropriately geared for its setting is key: it is not uncommon that a teacher in a rural African village might be using books or pedagogical materials too advanced or irrelevant for learners. A program in Kenya showed a better way, supplying content in both Kiswahili and English, training teachers in how to carry out lessons optimally, then supervising and coaching teachers on an ongoing basis (Piper *et al.* 2014). Other initiatives that have proven beneficial include more practice teaching incorporated into teacher education programs; ongoing professional development trainings to make curriculum more appropriate for multilingual learners and inclusive for students from disadvantaged backgrounds; and courses for headteachers to help them improve pedagogy in their schools (Barrett *et al.* 2007, Tikly and Barrett 2011, UNESCO 2014a).

Altering the structure of learning environments can also aid both teachers and students. One way is through what is sometimes called "teaching at the right level." Unless they are trained differently, teachers have a tendency to teach to the brightest students in a classroom, neglecting the students who are struggling. In contrast, teachers who were trained to do more effective diagnostics of their students, and given additional materials, saw better results in programs in both Liberia and Malawi (Bolyard 2003, Piper and Korda 2011). The Liberia program involved a week-long intensive teacher training, followed by teacher coaches visiting schools at least once a month. Teachers were given scripted lessons, sequential curriculum resources including assessments, and instructions for report cards for students. The teachers themselves also received feedback on their performance.

The whole scheme led to increases of up to 150 percent in students' literacy tasks (Piper and Korda 2011). Another aspect of teaching at the right level is grouping students by their learning level, for example, weaker students together, more advanced students together. Though this practice is sometimes controversial, it has had positive results in India and Kenya (World Bank 2018a). One of the most admired education NGOs in the world is Pratham in India, which has successfully implemented ability grouping, remedial tutoring, and classes outside the formal schooling system (see Banerjee *et al.* 2016, and Box 10.2).

Several other ideas have been repeatedly tested but did not consistently manage to improve education in low-resource contexts; these are worth noting because though they have many advocates, the evidence base for their benefits is lacking. Technology interventions are a prime example, as with the "One Laptop Per Child" programs in Peru and Uruguay. These programs showed no positive impacts, and indeed many other computer-assisted learning strategies have not been effective (Cristia *et al.* 2017, Snilstveit *et al.* 2016). While there are a few successful examples – as with a software program in India that provided personalized instruction and boosted students' math and language scores – there is no clear guidance at present for "what works" with education technology in developing world classrooms (Muralidharan *et al.* 2016). The story is much the same with high-profile initiatives directed at school management and accountability. School-based management is a strategy to decentralize decision-making to teachers, parents, and school leaders. The theory behind it is appealing – give local people more control over their schools – but, so far, results are widely variable. Community-based monitoring similarly seeks to increase local authority over schools by instituting steering committees made up of parents and other stakeholders. Again, the hope is that when communities take ownership of educational provision, they may be able to drive quality improvements. However, the evidence to this point suggests that poorer communities simply do not have the resources or expertise to make school-based management or community-based monitoring consistently effective (World Bank 2018a).

---

**Box 10.2 Pratham**

I followed a narrow lane hemmed in by closely-crowded little buildings made of concrete, bricks, cinder blocks, and often whatever other materials were at hand. These sometimes slapdash structures rose two or three stories above the lane, pressed so tightly together that I could glimpse only fragments of the hazy sky above. Also overhead, electricity and other cables skeined from house to house, their thick, coiled masses jerry-rigged and a little threatening. The footpath itself was made of broken bits of stone or concrete, the heavy rains leaving frequent puddles of dirty standing water – or sometimes the puddles may have been undrained sewage, judging from their foul smell. My guide was leading me into one of Mumbai's poorest neighborhoods, where she acted as a local coordinator for Pratham's activities. Inside the densely-packed houses, in tiny, often dark rooms, people ran businesses, cooked meals, sold necessities, tended to children, listened to the radio, lived their lives. Somewhere in that labyrinth of lanes, we headed to a modest room that Pratham rented to provide educational services to the residents of the neighborhood. Since most of the residents were Muslim, the class I observed was conducted in the Urdu language: several children around eight or nine years of age sat on the floor and listened to their teacher explain concepts of basic math. The children were attentive and appreciative as they performed exercises with rulers and other tools to learn their measurements. A bright, smiling woman probably in her middle 20s taught them. Though her training as a teacher mostly came from the short preparation courses of a few weeks' duration that Pratham offered, I could see that she was a natural, and my guide told me that this teacher was reputed to be one of Pratham's best in Mumbai. The class she was teaching that morning was non-formal and supplemental for the children, since they would attend regular government schools in the afternoon.

Pratham is the largest non-governmental organization in India. Its programs are wide-ranging, including vocational skills training for young adults, English instruction for both children and adults, urban learning centers such as I visited, and other initiatives such as household surveys throughout many communities in India. I also visited two of Pratham's early childhood education centers elsewhere in Mumbai. Since most Indian children, especially from poor backgrounds, do not have access to pre-school, Pratham's programs are important for boosting children's school readiness. I observed as one of Pratham's teachers led very young children in recitations in English of things like the numbers and months. In another center, as the youngest children were taught in one part of the room, several girls who were a little older sat quietly in a corner and read from books. After a while, a teacher would come over to discuss what they had read. The energetic coordinator of this center told me that Pratham's programs helped not only the children who studied in them, but also the local women who taught there. These women were usually volunteers, sometimes receiving a modest salary, but they reportedly enjoyed the work because it employed people from the community and helped to ensure that girls got an education. These hard-working teachers had clearly decided that the diverse educational opportunities Pratham provided could help them better their lives and the lives of others.

## Conclusion

Significant progress has been made in improving education as a poverty reduction strategy, though of course much remains to be done. This progress has come in part from the push for universal primary education per Millennium Development Goal 2, which did much to provide school facilities and basic learning opportunities to children around the world. As we have seen, conditional cash transfers are one generally successful means of encouraging enrolment and school progression. Going forward, policymakers must devote even more attention to interventions that can keep children in school and help them learn. Expanding school feeding and early childhood development programs should give children the physical wellbeing necessary for adequate intellectual development. More resources should be directed at effective programs to ensure that teachers are appropriately prepared, with the skills and pedagogical materials to help students learn most effectively. Prioritizing an expanded notion of education quality to develop thorough metrics for equity and inclusion also belongs on the international policy community's agenda.

From the accepted goal of universal, quality primary education, the focus must also now move to expanding access and learning at the secondary and tertiary levels. Primary education has been the agreed-upon minimum floor, but it cannot become a ceiling; as more people in low and middle income countries attain that minimum requirement, they must then be assured a quality secondary education as well. Secondary education is the minimum threshold in high-income countries, and that guarantee should not be denied to people elsewhere. This next frontier of expanding educational access and outcomes poses a major challenge, since resources for poverty reduction are finite. Therefore, it has to be carefully decided which development initiatives to promote at the regional, country, and global levels. A compelling case can be made that education should be a consistent top priority. Education *is* development. It builds human capabilities along multiple dimensions. It contributes to wage increases, productivity growth, health improvements, and cognitive gains, which are all essential to escaping poverty and helping people live lives that they have reason to value. Though certainly other strategies are useful in targeting particular facets of poverty, education's importance lies in its very broad effects.

Admittedly, achieving large-scale educational improvements is a difficult task. Progress may be slow. The increases in enrolment that have brought some developing countries near to universal primary enrolment have often taken 30 years to accomplish. Improving learning outcomes may take even longer. According to one analysis, though it may take a few lower-income countries around 25 years to approach the averages on international tests attained by students in higher-income OECD countries, the prognosis for many other countries is much worse. At realistic rates of progress, it could take countries in southern and eastern Africa around 150 years to equal current test score averages in OECD countries (Beatty and Pritchett 2012). Finally, the parts of the world where people are most educationally deprived tend to be the weak and fragile states. Such states are typically too dysfunctional and/or corrupt to expect effective transformation of governmental education provision. Tragically, people caught in conflict and state failure are also prone to see education as not worth the investment, since those societies are so troubled that skills gained through education are often not economically rewarded except via emigration.

---

### Box 10.3 Case study: Indonesia

Indonesia (Figure 10.1) is a lower middle-income country that has seen significant advancements in economic and human development since the 1970s. One reason for its progress has been investments in education: the country has the fourth largest education system in the world (behind China, India, and the United States). Indonesia's record is illustrative of both the promises and pitfalls of policies to improve educational access and outcomes. Between 1973 and 1978 the Indonesian government constructed more than 61,000 primary schools, and primary enrolment rates for children aged seven to 12 increased from 60 percent in the early 1970s to 94 percent by 1984. Universal primary enrolment has been achieved, and roughly 98 percent of children go on to complete primary education. This major commitment to increasing school access contributed not only to increased years of schooling for the average child, but also to increases in wages. On the whole, poverty defined as low incomes and educational and health deficits declined significantly into the first decades of the twenty-first century. For example, the proportion of people living below the poverty line has fallen by half since 1999, to 9.4 percent of the population in 2019. Women's literacy grew from 47 percent in 1970 to 94 percent most recently. The increased education of women also lowered Indonesia's fertility rates, as more women entered the labor force and were empowered to exercise greater control over their reproductive lives.

Despite this positive picture, Indonesia faces ongoing challenges in both educational access and outcomes. With universal primary enrolment achieved, the access goal shifted in the 1990s to a minimum standard of nine years basic education for everyone. This standard has been difficult to attain because of impediments such as school fees, the costs of uniforms, and significant numbers of students dropping out. According to analyses from the World Bank, 55 percent of Indonesian students who completed their education were still functionally illiterate, and nearly half could not correctly answer basic math questions. Similarly, Indonesia tends to score near the bottom of reading, math, and science results on the Program on International Student Assessment (PISA) test. Educational disparities also remain a problem. Outside urban areas, and especially outside the higher-income cities on the main Indonesian island of Java, access to schooling beyond primary is often deficient, and quality low. As elsewhere in the world, children from the poorest households are the most likely to be out of school: 53 percent of secondary school-age children from the poorest households were not attending school, compared to 19 percent of children from the richest households. Quality of teaching has also often lagged, with inadequate teacher preparation and excessive emphasis on rote learning.

Given that education has already played such an important role in reducing poverty in Indonesia, it is encouraging that policymakers there continue to devote attention to improving the weak spots in access and quality. A number of non-formal educational delivery programs seek to reach rural areas or adults who may never have received adequate schooling. Programs to eradicate illiteracy have been broadcast over the radio and television, for instance, or classes have been created to help people with literacy and job-related skill-building. An ambitious law was passed in 2005 to reform teaching, including provisions to improve teacher preparation and accountability. Most ambitiously of all, the Indonesian government pledged to devote 20 percent of the entire national budget to education. Critics question how realistic or efficient that particular goal may be. But it is nonetheless a clear signal of education's acknowledged contribution both to easily-measured improvements in economic development, as well as to less easily-measured but equally valuable improvements in human development.

Sources: Chang *et al.* (2012), Duflo (2001), EDPC (2018), Maralani (2008), Oswald and Cummings (2007), World Bank (2018b)

None of these problems negates the value of education as a poverty reduction strategy. One thing that policymakers as well as students of development must not forget is that the persistent inadequacies of education in poorer countries are an affront to justice. There is no reason the world should accept the unfortunate fact that a year of schooling in Togo is so blatantly unequal in its human and economic development effects to a year of schooling in Finland. We have an ethical imperative to ameliorate these egregious disparities in educational outcomes between high- and low-income countries. Perhaps the difficulties of education as a development strategy only reaffirm the necessity to focus improvements on the people who need them the most, namely the poorest. Reducing the poverty disproportionately experienced by excluded people should be a priority for educational policies. Scholarships for girls and people from traditionally underserved groups can encourage enrolment. Recruiting more teachers who are women or from minority

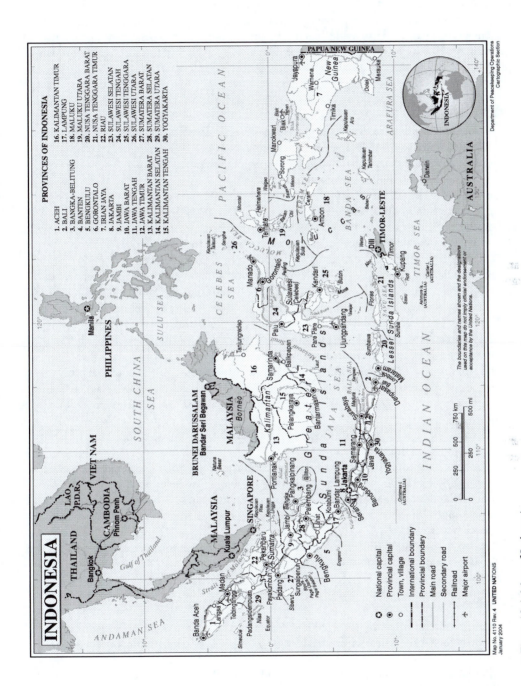

*Figure 10.1* Map of Indonesia

Source: Map No.4110 Rev. 4 UNITED NATIONS January 2004.

groups could further boost enrolment and possibly lead to better learning outcomes. Tutoring, remedial programs, and other non-formal options for schooling can also open up learning opportunities for those who have otherwise been deprived. Once again, the potential avenues of combating poverty through education are numerous. The ongoing challenge is to identify what works best, and then to implement expanded, well-designed programs so that no person in the world is denied full development of his or her human capabilities because of educational disadvantages.

## Discussion questions

1   What does being illiterate or innumerate have to do with being poor? How can getting an education help a person to escape poverty?
2   If, as some scholars have claimed, education's economic benefits to a society are negligible, is it a worthwhile development strategy?
3   Explore the World Inequality Database on Education (www.education-inequalities.org) to research educational deprivations. Pick a country and examine along which educational indicators it has the severest disparities. Pick an indicator and examine which countries experience the severest disparities in that area.
4   Explore the UNESCO eAtlas of Out-of-School Children (http://uis.unesco.org/apps/visualisations/oosci-data-tool/index-en.html#en/intro) for information on worldwide trends of educational deficiencies. Where are the most children denied their right to education? Where are the most severe gender disparities? Choose a country and read its profile to see how it rates in international comparison.
5   In accordance with the capabilities approach, what do you think should be the minimum threshold of educational attainment to which every human is entitled? How do you measure that threshold? How does your answer relate to the potential problem of "adaptive preference," whereby a group of poor, rural children might say that their highest educational aspiration is primary school because that is all that seems realistic to them?
6   How do the specific programs mentioned in this chapter relate to the ideas of basic capabilities for education?
7   Consider the problems of improving education in fragile or failing states. What are those problems? Do you agree that these problems undermine the potential for improving educational outcomes in fragile or failing states? What are some counterarguments to the idea that educational investments in such states are unlikely to bring major benefits?
8   Examine the Sustainable Development Goals for education. What strengths and weaknesses do you see in those goals?

## Online resources

- This website summarizes key facts and trends in education around the world through themes including access, equity, learning, and quality: www.education-progress.org/en
- The World Bank is the largest financer of education projects in the developing world, and this site has a wealth of related information: www.worldbank.org/en/topic/education

## Further reading

Global Education Monitoring Reports. www.en.unesco.org/gem-report/

Kremer, Michael, Conner Brannen and Rachel Glennerster. 2013. "The challenge of education and learning in the developing world." *Science* 340.6130: 297–300.

Snilstveit, Birte, Stevenson, Jennifer, Menon, Radikha, Phillips, Daniel, Gallagher, Emma, Geleen, Maisie, Jobse, Hannah, Schmidt, Tanja and Jimenez, Emmanuel. 2016. *The Impact of Education Programmes on Learning and School Participation in Low- and Middle-Income Countries* (Systematic Review Summary 7). London: International Initiative for Impact Evaluation (3ie).

Tikly, Leon and Angeline M. Barrett, eds. 2013. *Education Quality and Social Justice in the Global South: Challenges for Policy, Practice and Research.* London: Routledge.

Unterhalter, Elaine, Rosie Vaughan and Melanie Walker. 2007. "The capability approach and education." *Prospero* 13.3.

## Works cited

Akiba, Motoko, Gerald K. LeTendre and Jay P. Scribner. 2007. "Teacher quality, opportunity gap, and national achievement in 46 countries." *Educational Researcher* 36.7: 369–387.

Anderson, Laurie M. *et al.* 2003. "The effectiveness of early childhood development programs: a systematic review." *American Journal of Preventive Medicine* 24.3: 32–46.

Armecin, Graeme, Jere R. Behrman, Paulita Duazo, Sharon Ghuman, Socorro Gultiano, Elizabeth M. King and Nanette Lee. 2006. "Early Childhood Development through an Integrated Program: Evidence from the Philippines." World Bank Policy Research Working Paper 3922, May.

ASER Centre. 2017. *Annual Status of Education Report (Rural) 2016.* New Delhi: ASER Centre. www.img.asercentre.org/docs/Publications/ASER%20Reports/ASER%202016/aser_2016. pdf. Accessed February 2020.

Baird, Sarah, Craig McIntosh and Berk Ozler. 2011. "Cash or condition? Evidence from a cash transfer experiment." *Quarterly Journal of Economics* 26.4: 1709–1753.

Banerjee, Abhijit Vinayak *et al.* 2016. "Mainstreaming an Effective Intervention: Evidence from Randomized Evaluations of 'Teaching at the Right Level' in India." NBER Working Paper 22746, National Bureau of Economic Research, Cambridge, MA.

Barnett, W. Steven. 1995. "Long-term effects of early childhood programs on cognitive and school outcomes." *The Future of Children* 5.3: 25–50.

Barrett, Angeline, Sajid Ali, John Clegg, J. Enrique Hinostroza, John Lowe, Jutta Nikel, Mario Novelli, George Oduro, Mario Pillay, Leon Tikly and Guoxing Yu. 2007. *Initiatives to improve the quality of teaching and learning: A review of recent literature.* Background paper for the Global Monitoring Report 2008, EdQual working paper no. 11.

Beatty, Amanda, and Lant Pritchett. 2012. "From Schooling Goals to Learning Goals: How Fast Can Student Learning Improve?" Center for Global Development Policy Paper 012, September.

Behrman, Jere R., Susan W. Parker and Petra E. Todd. 2011. "Do conditional cash transfers for schooling generate lasting benefits? A five-year followup of PROGRESA/Oportunidades." *Journal of Human Resources* 46.1: 93–122.

Bentaouet-Kattan, Raja. 2006. *Implementation of Free Basic Education Policy.* Washington, DC: World Bank.

Biggeri, Mario, and Santosh Mehrotra. 2011. "Child Poverty as Capability Deprivation: How to Choose Domains of Child Well-being and Poverty," in Mario Biggeri, Jérôme Ballet and Flavio Comim, eds. *Children and the Capability Approach.* Basingstoke: Palgrave Macmillan.

Bloom, Nicholas, Renata Lemos, Raffaella Sadun, and John Van Reenen. 2015. "Does Management Matter in Schools?" *Economic Journal* 125.584: 647–74.

Bold, Tessa, Mwangi Kimenyi, Germano Mwabu, Alice Ng'ang'a, and Justin Sandefur. 2013. "Scaling Up What Works: Experimental Evidence on External Validity in Kenyan Education." Working Paper 321, Center for Global Development, Washington, DC.

Bolyard, K. J. 2003. "Linking Continuous Assessment and Teacher Development: Evaluating a Model of Continuous Assessment for Primary Schools in Malawi." EQUIP1 Continuous Assessment, Educational Quality Improvement Program, U.S. Agency for International Development, Washington, DC.

Bruns, Barbara, and Javier Luque. 2015. *Great Teachers: How to Raise Student Learning in Latin America and the Caribbean*. With Soledad De Gregorio, David K. Evans, Marco Fernández, Martin Moreno, Jessica Rodriguez, Guillermo Toral, and Noah Yarrow. Latin American Development Forum Series. Washington, DC: World Bank.

Cameron, John. 2012. "Capabilities and the global challenges of girls' school enrolment and women's literacy." *Cambridge Journal of Education* 42.3: 297–306.

Campante, Filipe R., and Davin Chor. 2012. "Schooling, Political Participation, and the Economy." *Review of Economics and Statistics* 94.4: 841–59.

Chang, Mae Chu, Sheldon Shaeffer, Andy Ragatz, Joppe de Ree, Ritchie Stevenson, Susiana Iskandar and Samer Al-Samarai. 2012. "Teacher Reform in Indonesia: The Role of Politics and Evidence-Based Policymaking: A Preview," World Bank Report No. 73624-ID, November.

Chaudhury, Nazmul, Jeffrey Hammer, Michael Kremer, Karthik Muralidharan and F. Halsey Rogers. 2006. "Missing in action: teacher and health worker absence in developing countries." *Journal of Economic Perspectives* 20.1: 91–116.

Chiappero-Martinetti, Enrica, and Anna Sabadash. 2014. "Integrating Human Capital and Human Capabilities in Understanding the Value of Education," in Solava Ibrahim and Meera Tiwari, eds. *The Capability Approach: From theory to practice*. Houndmills, Basingstoke: Palgrave Macmillan.

Comim, Flavio, Jérôme Ballet, Mario Biggeri and Vittorio Iervese. 2011. "Introduction," in Mario Biggeri, Jérôme Ballet and Flavio Comim, eds. *Children and the Capability Approach: From Theory to Practice.*. Houndmills, Basingstoke: Palgrave Macmillan.

Cristia, Julián, Pablo Ibarrarán, Santiago Cueto, Ana Santiago, and Eugenio Severín. 2017. "Technology and Child Development: Evidence from the One Laptop Per Child Program." *American Economic Journal: Applied Economics* 9.3: 295–320.

Duflo, Esther. 2001. "Schooling and Labor Market Consequences of School Construction in Indonesia: Evidence from an Unusual Policy Experiment." The American Economic Review 91.4: 795–813.

Durston, Susan, and Nice Nashire. 2001. "Rethinking poverty and education: an attempt by an education programme in Malawi to have an impact on poverty." *Compare* 31.1: 75–91.

Education Policy Data Center. 2018. "Indonesia: National Education Profile." www.epdc.org/education-data-research/indonesia-national-education-profile-2018. Accessed February 2020.

Filmer, Deon, and Norbert Schady. 2006. "Getting Girls into School: Evidence from a Scholarship Program in Cambodia." World Bank Policy Research Working Paper 3910, May.

Filmer, Deon, and Norbert Schady. 2014. "The medium-term effects of scholarships in a low-income country." *Journal of Human Resources* 49.3: 663–694.

Glaeser, Edward, Giacomo Ponzetto and Andrei Shleifer. 2007. "Why does democracy need education?" *Journal of Economic Growth* 12.2: 77–99.

Glewwe, Paul, and Michael Kremer. 2005. "Schools, Teachers, and Educational Outcomes in Developing Countries," in *Handbook on the Economics of Education*. Amsterdam: Elsevier.

Gove, Amber, and Peter Cvelich. 2011. *Early Reading, Igniting Education for All: A Report by the Early Grade Learning Community of Practice*. Rev. ed. Research Triangle Park, NC: Research Triangle Institute.

Hanushek, Eric A., and Ludger Wößmann. 2007. "The Role of Education Quality in Economic Growth," World Bank Policy Research Working Paper 4122, February.

Hanushek, Eric A., and Steven G. Rivkin. 2006. "Teacher quality." *Handbook of the Economics of Education* 2: 1051–1078.

Hart, Caroline Sarojini. 2014. "The Capability Approach and Educational Research," in Caroline Sarojini Hart, Mario Biggeri and Bernhard Babic, eds. *Agency and Participation in Childhood and Youth: International Applications of the Capability Approach in Schools and Beyond*. London: Bloomsbury.

Hart, Caroline Sarojini. 2019. "Education, inequality and social justice: A critical analysis applying the Sen-Bourdieu Analytical Framework." *Policy Futures in Education* 17.5: 582–598.

Hart, Caroline Sarojini, and Nicolás Brando. 2018. "A capability approach to children's well-being, agency and participatory rights in education." *European Journal of Education* 53.3: 293–309.

Heckman, James J. 2006. "Skill formation and the economics of investing in disadvantaged children." *Science* 312.5782: 1900–1902.

Kenny, Charles. 2010. "Learning about Schools in Development," Center for Global Development Working Paper 236, December.

Kremer, Michael, and Alaka Holla. 2008. "Improving Education in the Developing World: What Have We Learned From Randomized Evaluations?" mimeo, November.

Levine, Ruth, and Nancy Birdsall. 2005. "On the Road to Universal Primary Education," Center for Global Development CGD Brief, February.

Lewis, Maureen A., and Marlaine E. Lockheed. 2006. *Inexcusable Absence: Why 60 Million Girls Still Aren't in School and What To Do About It.* Washington, DC: Center for Global Development.

Maralani, Vida. 2008. "The changing relationship between family size and educational attainment over the course of socioeconomic development: evidence from Indonesia." *Demography* 45.3: 693–717.

Morgan, Claire, Anthony Petrosino and Trevor Fronius. 2014. "Eliminating school fees in low-income countries: a systematic review." *Journal of MultiDisciplinary Evaluation* 10.23: 26–43.

Muralidharan, Karthik, Abhijeet Singh, and Alejandro Ganimian. 2016. "Disrupting Education? Experimental Evidence on Technology-Aided Instruction in India." NBER Working Paper 22923, National Bureau of Economic Research, Cambridge, MA.

Nussbaum, Martha. 2011. *Creating Capabilities: The Human Development Approach.* Boston, MA: Harvard University Press.

Orazem, Peter F. 2012. "The Case for Improving School Quality and Student Health as a Development Strategy." Copenhagen Consensus Paper, April.

Oswald Christano, Rita, and William K. Cummings. 2007. "Schooling in Indonesia," in Gerard A. Postiglione and Jason Tan, eds. *Going to School in East Asia.* Westport, CT: Greenwood Press.

Piper, Benjamin, Zuilkowski, Stephanie and Mugenda, Abel. 2014. "Improving reading outcomes in Kenya: First-year effects of the PRIMR initiative." *International Journal of Educational Development* 37: 11–21.

Piper, Benjamin, and Medina Korda. 2011. *EGRA Plus: Liberia. Program Evaluation Report.* RTI International.

Robeyns, Ingrid. 2006. "Three models of education Rights, capabilities and human capital." *Theory and Research in Education* 4.1: 69–84.

Rockoff, Jonah E. 2004. "The impact of individual teachers on student achievement: evidence from panel data." *American Economic Review* 94.2: 247–252.

Saito, Madoka. 2003. "Amartya Sen's capability approach to education: a critical exploration." *Journal of Philosophy of Education* 37.1: 17–33.

Schady, Norbert, and María Caridad Araujo. 2006. "Cash Transfers, Conditions, School Enrollment, and Child Work: Evidence from a Randomized Experiment in Ecuador." World Bank Policy Research Working Paper 3930, June.

Schultz, T. Paul. 2004. "School subsidies for the poor: evaluating the Mexican Progresa poverty program." *Journal of Development Economics* 74.1: 199–250.

Sen, Amartya. 1999. *Development as Freedom.* New York: Knopf.

Snilstveit, B., Stevenson, J., Menon, R., Phillips, D., Gallagher, E., Geleen, M., Jobse, H., Schmidt, T. and Jimenez, E. 2016. *The Impact of Education Programmes on Learning and School Participation in Low- and Middle-Income Countries* (Systematic Review Summary 7). London: International Initiative for Impact Evaluation (3ie).

Tao, Sharon. 2016. *Transforming teacher quality in the Global South: Using capabilities and causality to re-examine teacher performance.* New York: Palgrave Macmillan.

Terzi, Lorella. 2007. "The Capability to Be Educated," in Melanie Walker and Elaine Unterhalter, eds. *Amartya Sen's Capability Approach and Social Justice in Education.* New York: Palgrave Macmillan.

Terzi, Lorella. 2014. "Reframing inclusive education: Educational equality as capability equality." *Cambridge Journal of Education* 44.4: 479–493.

Tikly, Leon. 2010. "Towards a Framework for Understanding the Quality of Education." EdQual Working Paper No. 27. November. EdQual Research Programme on Implementing Education Quality in Low Income Countries.

Tikly, Leon, and Angeline M. Barrett. 2011. "Social justice, capabilities and the quality of education in low income countries." *International Journal of Educational Development* 31.1: 3–14.

UNESCO Institute of Statistics. n.d. www.uis.unesco.org/EDUCATION/Pages/default.aspx. Accessed February 2020.

UNESCO. 2014a. "Teaching and Learning: Achieving Quality for All." Education for All Global Monitoring Report 2013/4.

UNESCO. 2014b. "Sustainable Development Begins with Education: How education can contribute to the proposed post-2015 goals." Paris: UNESCO.

UNICEF Data on Primary Education. n.d. www.data.unicef.org/education/primary, accessed February 2020.

UNICEF. 2004. *Childhood under Threat: The State of the World's Children 2005*. New York, NY: UNICEF.

Unterhalter, Elaine. 2009. "Education," in Séverine Deneulin and Lila Shahani, eds. *An Introduction to the Human Development and Capability Approach*. London: Earthscan.

Unterhalter, Elaine. 2012. "Inequality, capabilities and poverty in four African countries: girls' voice, schooling, and strategies for institutional change." *Cambridge Journal of Education* 42.3: 307–325.

Unterhalter, Elaine. 2019. "The many meanings of quality education: politics of targets and indicators in SDG 4." *Global Policy* 10: 39–51.

Vaughan, Rosie. 2007. "Measuring Capabilities: An Example from Girls' Schooling" in Melanie Walker and Elaine Unterhalter, eds. *Amartya Sen's Capability Approach and Social Justice in Education*. New York: Palgrave Macmillan.

World Bank. 2018a. *World Development Report 2018: Learning to Realize Education's Promise*. Washington, DC: World Bank.

World Bank. 2018b. *Indonesia Economic Quarterly: Learning more, growing faster*. Washington, DC: World Bank, June.

World Bank. 2016. *Francophone Africa Results Monitor: Basic Education (Multiple Countries)*. World Bank, Washington, DC. www.documents.worldbank.org/curated/en/docsearch/projects/P156307.

World Bank Group Education Strategy. 2011. *Learning for All: Investing in People's Knowledge, and Skills to Promote Development*. Washington, DC: World Bank.

Yamauchi, F. and Liu, Y. 2012. School quality, labor markets and human capital investments: long-term impacts of an early stage education intervention in the Philippines. Washington, DC: World Bank.

Young, Marion. 2009. "Basic capabilities, basic learning outcomes and thresholds of learning." *Journal of Human Development and Capabilities* 10.2: 259–277.

# 11 The environment and poverty reduction

*Benjamin Curtis*

## Learning objectives

- Describe the relationships between environmental conditions and poverty.
- Explain what environmental assets and ecosystem services are.
- Analyze how capabilities relate to environmental entitlements and wellbeing.
- Summarize initiatives that can help communities pursue sustainable development.

## Vignette 11.1

*We first met Chita and Rosa at a small roadside shack in northern Costa Rica (Figure 11.1). Sitting in a simple structure with a thatched roof and no walls, they were selling artisan products such as elaborately painted, hard-carved wooden masks, gourds carved with intricate designs, and colorful weavings. This was some of the traditional art of their culture: Chita and Rosa both belong to the Maleku indigenous group, a people numbering less than 700 who live in a lush but isolated area of Costa Rica. "I grew up here in the community so poor that I had to tie my hair up with blades of grass before going to school," Chita said. She is a mother of four who sells her art to make a living. Describing the poverty that older generations of Maleku people faced, she told us: "My grandmother died giving birth to my mother, so she was raised by another relative and didn't get the opportunities she might have had her mother survived. We were so poor that I only made it through third grade." Because of Chita's childhood poverty, when she was a teenager she left the community with the first non-indigenous man she met who promised her a better life.*

*"We grew up poor too," agreed Rosa, "but in my case, we had an extended family network and everyone pulled together to survive. I grew up proud of being Maleku because my grandmother spent the evenings telling us stories about Maleku myths and customs. We didn't even miss the fact that we didn't have electricity in the house because she told stories every night about our community and its history." Rosa and Chita both sit on the local school board, and one day they and other community leaders described for us the unique situation of the three Maleku palenques (villages) outside the town of San Rafael Guatuso. Some of the men remembered how when they grew up, poverty was intense: their families did not have potable water, a decent road to the community, access to credit, or even shoes. Teachers came from outside the community and did not respect Maleku ways.*

*The Maleku school leaders we interviewed agreed that their community faces different challenges today than did their parents and grandparents. Though they have made great strides teaching the younger generation about important values of the community – love of nature, respect for elders*

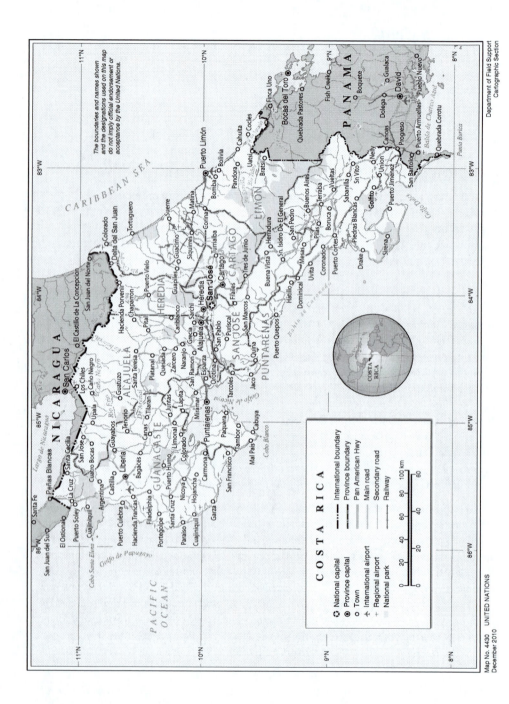

*Figure 11.1* Map of Costa Rica
Source: Map No. 4430 UNITED NATIONS December 2010.

*and the importance of preserving the stories that have been handed down – today young people find themselves chafing for more opportunities than the area can offer. Farming, ecotourism, and teaching are the few options available for motivated youth, so many of them leave.*

*The difficulty of making a living on the lands the Maleku call home points to the complex interrelationships between poverty, capabilities, and the natural environment for this community. Farming often generates only a meagre income for Maleku people – and roughly a quarter of all Maleku do not own any land, which means that they cannot grow their own food, and have to find other sources of income. The Maleku have actually been deprived of their land: though they live on a reservation where their land rights are supposed to be legally protected, there are many non-indigenous property owners living on the reserve, such that the Maleku own only 20 percent of their own reservation. The Maleku teachers we spoke with explained that many of the better-off homes we observed in the area belonged to non-Malekus who moved into the villages over the generations; some of those newcomers even self-identify as Maleku to obtain access to opportunities reserved for indigenous people. The Maleku have also been denied hunting and fishing rights in nearby areas that their people had used for centuries. Beyond land deprivation and scarce economic opportunities, environmental degradation has made it harder to maintain some of the Malekus' cultural traditions. For example, certain plants that were traditionally used in spiritual ceremonies, and wood for the traditional palenque structures, are now very difficult to obtain.*

*The Malekus' story is not unusual. Indigenous peoples throughout the world often face major difficulties in protecting traditional relationships with their natural ecosystem. As colonial powers infringed on indigenous lands, and incipient states expanded their control after independence, indigenous groups in Latin America like the Maleku found their livelihoods, traditions, and values in danger of extinction. The Maleku were able to gain title to a small portion of the land they had inhabited prior to the arrival of the Spanish, but poverty in the early twentieth century forced many of them to sell their property to speculators and wealthier, non-indigenous neighbors. Thus, land that the Maleku had typically used for communal farming and other household needs was divvied up to private owners. The size of many indigenous groups has been greatly reduced since the colonial era, yet their continued presence raises complex questions about environmental justice: how should people be guaranteed access to land and other environmental assets that are essential to their quality of life?*

## Introduction

We begin this chapter with the example of the Maleku of Costa Rica because discussions about the environment and the capabilities approach involve acknowledging the range of capabilities that are affected by environmental changes, particularly for indigenous people and other marginalized groups, including the poor. Many indigenous groups around the world experience unfreedom when they are deprived of the opportunity to manage community natural resources, whether for economic aims or for traditional cultural and spiritual practices (Duraiappah 2002 and 2004).

It may seem surprising that the Maleku have such challenges in Costa Rica, a country known worldwide for its efforts to protect the environment and promote sustainable development. It is particularly famous for its reforestation and conservation efforts, protecting roughly 30 percent of its territory. Costa Rica is a high human development country according to the Human Development Index (HDI), with a score of .794 that is above average for Latin America. It has also done very well on multiple different indicators: it ranked as the highest Latin American country on the Where-To-Be-Born Index (30th out of 80 countries, above several European countries), and until 2014 it ranked in the top ten of all countries according to the Environmental Performance Index (EPI). Three times Costa Rica has topped the Happy Planet Index, a composite of indicators for ecological footprint, life expectancy, and subjective wellbeing. However, most recently Costa Rica has fallen in the EPI because of failures in treating wastewater and responding to climate change. As the example of Chita, Rosa, and the Maleku suggests, even in relatively successful developing countries such as Costa Rica, there are many challenges to ensuring that ecosystem management promotes human wellbeing and capabilities.

Environmental conditions and resources are crucial to every person's life, but poor people and indigenous groups typically depend even more on the natural environment than do the non-poor. This chapter investigates the links between environmental conditions and poverty, and how programs can reduce poverty by targeting those conditions. Costa Rica is our empirical focus: it is a useful model for how countries can address the ecosystemic factors that contribute to poverty. Thus, despite the challenges the Maleku are facing, there is hope. At the end of the chapter we will return to the Maleku to consider some lessons about environmental factors and capabilities. First, however, the chapter will provide a global overview of how environmental conditions impact poverty. Then it will consider the relationship between the environment, poverty, and capabilities. Finally, three case studies will explore how environmentally sustainable initiatives have promoted human and economic development in Costa Rica.

## Understanding key concepts

It is important at the outset to provide definitional clarity for several key concepts. The "environment" means the living (biodiversity) and non-living (soil, rocks, atmosphere, etc.) components of the natural world, whose interactions are essential for life on earth. The environment provides natural resources and various ecosystem services that in turn supply food, energy, medicine and incomes (DFID *et al.* 2002). "Ecosystem services" is a specialized term; "ecosystems" include forests, grasslands, rivers, lakes, the ocean, coral reefs, etc., as well as the biological organisms (such as plants and animals) that live in them. According to the influential analysis of the Millennium Ecosystem Assessment, ecosystems provide four categories of "services": provisioning, regulating, cultural, and supporting (Millennium Ecosystem Assessment 2005). Provisioning services include food, fresh water, wood, and fuel. Regulating services include how ecosystems purify air and water, mitigate floods and droughts, stabilize the climate, and reduce disease. Cultural services encompass recreation and ecotourism, but also spiritual and scientific/educational uses. Underlying the previous three categories are "supporting services," which refer to environmental factors with an indirect impact on humans such as systems of soil formation, nutrient and water cycling, and oxygen production (see Alcamo and Bennett 2003).

Ecosystem services are essential for economic and social functions, and for wellbeing. They form part of complex "social-ecological systems" in which human use of ecosystem resources feeds back into the health of the resources themselves (McGinnis and Ostrom 2014, Ostrom 2009). Though all life depends on ecosystem services, because of their vulnerability and marginalization poor people are often more dependent on "environmental assets." Environmental assets can include a coral reef, a river, soil, wildlife, a watershed, air, a coal deposit, a forest, and many other things. These assets contribute a very wide range of services to the poor, such as food, water, fuel, shelter, health, livelihoods, and cultural practices. Whether it is a lake to fish in, a field to farm, a hillside on which to graze animals, or a forest to harvest for fuelwood or building materials, poor people in rural areas need environmental resources as a basic support to life, including fertile land, water, crop diversity, forest products (for fuel, food, medicines, etc.), and protein sources such as fish and wild meat.

Poor people in urban areas also depend on environmental resources including water (for drinking and washing), energy, sanitation, and drainage (DFID *et al.* 2002). However, many of the environmental assets the poor depend on they do not privately own – they may be owned collectively (by the local community), publicly (as with national forests), or really by no one (e.g. the ozone layer). This means that poor people's access to such resources can easily be threatened by depletion, degradation, or deprivation, and it is harder for poor people to assert their rights of access. A particular characteristic of environmental assets relevant to the poor is that those assets are often difficult to substitute. For example, if a forest is cut down or a lake polluted, then the poor may have few or no alternatives for their wood or water (Pearce 2005).

The ultimate goal in protecting ecosystem services and environmental assets for the purposes of poverty reduction is to promote sustainable development. Much ink has been spilled debating what this term means; see the further reading at the end of the chapter to pursue those debates. For the purposes of this chapter, though, sustainable development means expanding the substantive freedoms (capabilities) of people today while making reasonable efforts to avoid seriously compromising those of future generations (UNDP 2011: 2, see also Sen 2013). In other words, sustainable development is meeting the needs of today while guaranteeing that our grandchildren will have their needs met. Intergenerational justice is a critical aspect of sustainability. What this means is that future generations should not have less freedom than people today – indeed, if the present generation despoils the environment, its impact on people in the future is arguably little different than depriving people of their rights now (Ballet *et al.* 2013, UNDP 2011). The non-negotiable minimum for justice and sustainability is capabilities: every generation must have the right to develop the same basic capabilities. We will return to the relationships between capabilities, the environment, and poverty below but, for now, consider this provocative claim: it may not be necessary that future generations attain today's level of resource use or quality of life as long as the minimal requirements for a good life – as defined by the basic capabilities – are fulfilled (Burger and Christen 2011).

## Poverty–environment relationships

Deficiencies in ecosystem services and environmental assets are widespread, contributing to poverty around the world. Poor people tend to live on "marginal lands." Around 1.6 billion people live in areas that are relatively unproductive or ecologically highly vulnerable because of poor soil quality, low rainfall, or otherwise difficult terrain (Barbier and Hochard 2018a). About a third of this number are the rural poor – but hundreds of millions of more poor people live on land that is not quite so marginal (Barbier 2010). The incidence of marginal lands is increasing. According to one estimate, 40 percent of land on the planet has been degraded by soil erosion or overgrazing (UNDP 2011). Deforestation is a major global problem that impacts how poor people live. Around a billion people on the planet depend on forests for subsistence or income. However, 30 percent of global forest cover has already been lost, and between 2000 and 2010 an area the size of England was cleared every year (World Resource Institute 2014).

Desertification is another global problem that can make land marginal. It is estimated that the livelihoods of one billion people are threatened by desertification. Already, about 25 percent of the Earth's territory is desertified, and every year roughly 12 million hectares of land are lost to further degradation (IFAD 2010). Moreover, approximately 1.8 billion people will likely suffer from water scarcity by 2025 (UNDP 2011). Women and girls can be more starkly affected than men, since in rural areas of lower-income countries, it is often women's job to collect water. As water sources become degraded or depleted, women have to walk farther and farther to get the water, sometimes eating up a significant portion of time they could devote to other activities such as education, generating income, or working in the home. Problems such as deforestation, desertification, and water scarcity will likely increase food prices by 30 to 50 percent, which will affect everyone on the planet, but hurt the poor the most by making food increasingly unaffordable (UNDP 2011).

Environmental conditions also have a huge impact on health. "Environmental health" is a term denoting "aspects of human health, including quality of life, that are determined by chemical, physical, biological, social and psychosocial factors in the environment" (PEP 2008: 10). As one example of the environment's impact on health, every year diseases related to environmental conditions such as respiratory infections and diarrhea kill at least three million children under the age of five. Some of these conditions, such as unsafe water or lack of sanitation, count among the top ten leading causes of disease worldwide (UNDP 2011). Overall, it has been estimated that 24 percent of the global disease burden and 23 percent of all deaths are associated with environmental conditions (Prüss-Üstün and Corvalán 2006). Many of these problems may be worsened by climate change (WHO 2018). For instance, rising temperatures increase the risks from vector-borne diseases such as malaria and dengue fever. Diarrheal diseases are also projected to increase, especially in poorer areas (Smith *et al.* 2014).

There are other impacts of climate change beyond health. Around 40 percent of economically active people in the world work in agriculture, fishing, forestry, or hunting and gathering – and most of these people are in lower-income countries (UNDP 2011). Because the poor usually depend disproportionately on environmental resources, they are more likely to be negatively impacted by climate change and its effects on those resources (for reviews, see Carleton and Hsiang 2016, Castells-Quintana *et al.* 2017, Leichenko and Silva 2014). Those effects include reductions in freshwater availability and crop productivity, and increasing sea levels and extreme weather events. Rising sea levels could render islands and low-lying terrain (including much of Bangladesh) uninhabitable, displacing millions of people. Extreme weather events such as droughts, floods, and storms can deprive people of their livelihoods, displace them, or kill them. In many cases, hotter areas of the world will get hotter and dryer, leading to increased problems with agriculture and food security (Livelihoods and Climate Change 2003). According to projections, loss of fertile topsoil could reduce agricultural productivity by 50 percent in some areas, so that climate change may produce more malnutrition (UNDP 2011). In sum, not only are the poor generally more exposed to the stresses from climate change, they often lack resources from family, community, or governments to cope and adapt (Hallegatte *et al.* 2016). Hence climate change in most cases will worsen poverty.

Environmental conditions also have a relationship with politics, not surprisingly (Adger *et al.* 2014). Competition over land, water, and other ecosystem resources can spark conflict, as in Rwanda in 1994, Kenya in 2008, or repeatedly in Sudan and the Democratic Republic of the Congo. Furthermore, environmental change – such as temperature rises and increasing water scarcity – have been associated with the likelihood of civil wars (UNEP 2009). As discussed in Chapter 8 on conflict and poverty, conflict is a poverty trap; its particular environmental dimension is a Catch-22 in which "environmental degradation fuels conflict, and conflict degrades the environment" (UNDP 2011: 58). Evidence also suggests that more democratic political systems (as measured by literacy, political rights, and civil liberties) have superior environmental quality such as clean water and sanitation (Gallagher and Thacker 2008). Where inequality of political power is greater, environmental degradation such as pollution is also greater, and services such as access to clean water less (Torras 2006). For poor people, a significant part of the problem is institutions that do not respect their interests with regard to environmental resources. Where people are powerless to stop it, industries or other powerful actors can degrade environmental resources with relative impunity. Poor communities often lack the capacity or institutions to deal with the risks of depletion, degradation, and deprivation.

High vulnerability to depletion, degradation, or deprivation of the environmental resources on which they depend is one of the factors that make people poor. In some cases, those resources can be further depleted via a "poverty-environment trap" (Barbier and Hochard 2018a). The trap is a vicious cycle in which dependence on environmental resources actually depletes those resources. A good example would be with forests. A family needs fuel for cooking, yet if they are poor, they may have no choice but to chop down trees for fuel. However, unless managed in a sustainable way, felling trees can deplete the very resource on which the family depends. Research suggests that, above all, it is poor families lacking other assets who can fall into such traps. Often, however, the poverty–environment relationship is much more complex than this vicious cycle (Barbier and Hochard 2018b, Rai 2019). Again, a social–ecological system is at work in which resources, governance systems, and the people who use the resources all interact. A variety of factors, including whether a poor person has other income opportunities, access to markets for land, labor, and credit, and the variety/quality of environmental resources available will influence the interaction (Barbier 2010). Sometimes, poor communities are able to come together to manage their resources more sustainably to prevent depletion and degradation. It is also important to note that on a global scale, rich people are most responsible for the unsustainable exploitation of environmental resources; the most serious overconsumption and depletion, which affects the entire planet, happens in high-income countries.

---

### Box 11.1 Environmental degradation, health, and poverty

- **Indoor air pollution:** Half of the earth's population still uses biomass fuels (such as wood or dung) for heating and cooking. These fuels typically produce smoke that can cause respiratory infections, lung cancer, cardiovascular disease, low birth weight, and carbon monoxide poisoning. Indoor smoke contributes to nearly four million deaths a year, especially in poorer countries, most affecting women and children.
- **Outdoor air pollution:** Caused by sources such as industry, transportation, fires, or dust storms, outdoor air pollution has many of the same health effects as above. Again, it is the poorest communities that are disproportionately exposed to outdoor air pollution and most susceptible to its ill effects.

- **Water and sanitation:** Dirty water and inadequate sanitation are an enormous problem, contributing to ill health, disability, and early death. They lead to malnutrition, parasites, hepatitis, typhoid, malaria, and polio, among many other maladies. In countries with low human development, 65 percent of people do not have adequate sanitation, and 38 percent lack clean water.
- **Waste:** Whether from industrial, municipal, or household sources, inadequate waste disposal has a variety of negative effects on environmental health. Waste can be a breeding ground for vermin and insects. It can contaminate surface water, groundwater, and soil. Toxic waste in landfills can lead to cancer, anemia, mental retardation, and various birth defects. Poor people are much more likely to be exposed to these effects because they often live in marginal, disadvantaged areas.

Sources: Pearce 2005, PEP 2008, Prüss-Üstün
and Corvalán 2006, UNDP 2011

Overconsumption of resources on a global or local scale leads to degradation of the natural environment. Degradation means that the quality of the environmental assets on which poor people depend is reduced. Air pollution is an example of how contaminants can degrade an environmental resource – air – which humans and so many other living things need to survive. Pollution can also affect water and land, both of which can cause people to become sick. Poor people are again most vulnerable here, since they often will not have the resources to, say, buy bottled drinking water if their stream or well becomes polluted. Nor, if the land on which they live is degraded, can they necessarily just move; they may not have the money or the opportunity to find shelter somewhere else. Deprivation comes about when poor people cannot use environmental assets on which they depend. They are most commonly denied use of those assets by people who are more powerful because of wealth or politics. Poor people often lack legal title to their land, which makes it too easy for them to be forced off it.

The 2011 United Nations Human Development Report used the Multidimensional Poverty Index to examine three areas of environmental assets whose deprivation not only undermined basic capabilities but also constituted "major violations of human rights" (UNDP 2011: 5). Access to modern cooking fuel, clean water, and basic sanitation are conceived as absolute and fundamental entitlements, and therefore as essential to human development. Unfortunately, deprivation in these three areas was found to be very common: 60 percent of people in developing countries had at least one of these environmental deprivations, and 40 percent were deprived in two or more. This means that deprivations overlap, intensifying poverty. According to the UNDP's analysis, 29 percent of people in 109 countries were deprived in *all three* of these areas. The people who were most intensely poor along multiple dimensions were found in rural areas. 97 percent of the rural poor were deprived in at least one environmental area, compared to 75 percent of poor people in urban areas. Globally, too, multiple environmental deprivations vary, with Sub-Saharan Africa the worst affected: 60 percent of poor people there were deprived across all three dimensions, compared to 18 percent of poor people in South Asia. In both these regions, the most consistent deprivation was modern cooking fuel, followed by improved sanitation. Overall, environmental deprivations are one of the most powerful reasons why people are poor according to the MPI.

## Capabilities and environmental conditions

From the capabilities perspective, environmental conditions are important because they directly impact the opportunities available to people (see i.a. Ballet *et al.* 2018, Lehtonen 2004, Polishchuk and Rauschmayer 2012, Sen 2009, Voget-Kleschin 2013). In fact, environmental conditions amount to a "meta-capability" according to Holland (2008). These conditions help make a range of basic capabilities and functionings possible; they are a "pre-condition for all the capabilities that Nussbaum defines as necessary for living a good human life" (Holland 2014: 112). For example, human life (the first basic capability on Nussbaum's list) depends fundamentally on the natural environment for food, water, air, and energy. The natural environment is thus crucial to the meta-capability of "sustainable ecological capacity" that supports most of the other basic capabilities – but which recognizes that the current generation's utilization of environmental services must not unduly disadvantage future generations. Because of the way they underlie and support so many basic capabilities, we should conceive of "certain environmental entitlements as a matter of basic justice" (Holland 2008: 320).

What then are the minimum environmental entitlements that constitute basic justice, and whose absence can define poverty? Duraiappah (2002, 2004) has specified ten key relationships between ecosystems and wellbeing. These are the capabilities that ecosystems support; if people fall below minimum thresholds in these ten areas, they are in poverty, failing to benefit from the ecosystem(s) as they are entitled. Note that there are many interrelationships between the ten areas listed below. The distinct ecosystem services are often interdependent, and combine to support wellbeing.

1   "Being able to be adequately nourished." Certain ecosystems provide food, whether through agriculture or hunting and gathering. The rural poor especially depend on ecosystem services for nourishment, so droughts, pests, other ecological disasters, or being forced off their land can fatally compromise their capability to feed themselves.

2   "Being able to be free from avoidable disease." As we have seen, environmental conditions have a very large impact on health. No one should have to live in conditions that promote heightened morbidity. When such conditions threaten basic entitlements to health, then people are deprived of basic ecosystem services.

3   "Being able to live in an environmentally clean and safe shelter." Certain conditions in the ecosystem will also jeopardize this entitlement: pollution, high susceptibility to disease, poor drainage, insecure or marginal terrain, even unacceptable levels of noise. Depletion, degradation, and deprivation can all mean that people do not have adequate shelter.

4   "Being able to have adequate and clean drinking water." Clean water is obviously essential to basic health, which in turn is essential to an enormous range of other capabilities and functionings.

5   "Being able to have clean air." Likewise, clean air is essential to adequate health and capabilities. Poor people, however, are often deprived of this entitlement. The environmental conditions in which they live – with indoor pollution because they lack access to cleaner cooking fuels, or outdoor pollution because they live in degraded, marginal areas – mean that too often poor people's access to ecosystem services is compromised.

6   "Being able to have energy to keep warm and to cook." Energy is essential to several other basic capabilities, such as adequate shelter (that provides warmth in cold

environments) and nourishment (for preparing food). When an ecosystem does not provide resources to meet this basic entitlement, and people cannot meet it any other way, then they are fundamentally deprived and poor.

7   "Being able to use traditional medicine." Many poor people depend on traditional medicine since they often lack access to modern, Western health care for cost and other reasons. Many traditional remedies used by indigenous groups come from eco-system sources, so when those are compromised, so too are poor people's traditional health care and health status.

8   "Being able to continue using natural elements found in ecosystems for trad-itional cultural and spiritual practices." This relates to several basic capabilities from Nussbaum's list, such as senses, imagination, thought and emotion. For many people around the world, ecosystems are essential for cultural enjoyment and inspiration, as well as for spiritual practice. When ecosystems are degraded, people's entitlements in this area can be infringed, especially if their cultures are informed by a close relation-ship with nature.

9   "Being able to cope with extreme natural events including floods, tropical storms and landslides." Poor people are typically the most vulnerable to such extreme events, and the least able to cope with them. Ecosystem degradation can make such events more likely, thereby disproportionately harming the poor. Healthy ecosystems are essential for adaptation and resilience to extreme events.

10  "Being able to make sustainable management decisions that respect natural resources and enable the achievement of a sustainable livelihood." People have a fundamental right to participate in management of ecosystem resources that will affect them. If they are deprived of that right, it can be a cause of poverty. And, unfortunately, too often poor people have been denied participation in such management, and been forced into unsustainable resource use that contributes to depletion and degradation.

One of the ways that all of the relationships above affect poor people is that the poor often have few choices. Hence from the capabilities perspective, a key aspect in the poverty–environment relationship is unfreedom in terms of which environmental assets you depend on, and how you depend on them (Ballet *et al.* 2013). If your land becomes degraded, you cannot necessarily just go find another field to farm, or move to a new house that is not sitting on land polluted by toxic waste. This is vulnerability because of a lack of opportunity – in other words, the inability to choose something different beyond the (possibly compromised) environmental resources on which your life depends.

Three particular themes from the research on capabilities and the environment will play out in the case studies below: vulnerability clusters, recognition, and collective cap-abilities. First, as this chapter has shown, the distribution of environmental resources, and the benefits of ecosystem services, disproportionately disadvantage the poor. Indeed, that disadvantageous distribution is one reason why people are poor: it creates clusters of vulnerability (Wolff and de-Shalit 2007). In such vulnerability clusters – think of people living on infertile land prone to drought, far from markets, lacking health and educa-tion services, with deficient infrastructure such as roads and electricity – a weakness in one capability area is likely to undermine many others. Why do some communities end up in such vulnerability clusters? One reason is a lack of recognition, namely of every individual's entitlement to fundamental standards of social justice, including enjoying the full complement of basic capabilities (Fraser 1997, Young 2011). Recognition operates along multiple dimensions (legal, institutional, social) and prevents political, economic, and cultural exclusion. Since individuals' entitlements are often bound to their group membership, some groups, such as ethnic or religious minorities, frequently suffer from a lack of recognition that leads to an unjust distribution of environmental advantages and disadvantages (Schlosberg 2012).

When individuals' capabilities are undermined by disadvantageous environmental conditions, collective capabilities are as well (Schlosberg and Carruthers 2010). Collective capabilities adhere to an entire community, and help determine what the group is able to do and to be. Group membership impacts an individual's opportunity to attain what she values, so exclusion/discrimination based on a lack of recognition limits capabilities at both the group *and* individual level. One reason that collective capabilities are important is because they embody the opportunity for collective agency to improve a group's situation (Evans 2002, Ibrahim 2006). In particular, collective capabilities are relevant to people organizing for more sustainable management of environmental resources (Pelenc *et al.* 2015). Throughout this book we follow Nussbaum in primarily focusing on individual capabilities. However, the particular dynamic of vulnerability clusters, recognition, and environmental conditions provides a useful lens for considering how collective capabilities can contribute to wellbeing.

## Case studies

Our three case studies explore examples of how communities in Costa Rica have worked to promote sustainable development and poverty reduction by managing their environmental assets. The projects each community has undertaken have sought to secure some of the ten freedoms outlined above. The first case study centers on democratic management of a particular ecosystem service, namely water. The second is about how a community with severe environmental disadvantages can ameliorate some of them to reduce poverty. The third discusses how conservation of ecosystem resources can promote sustainable livelihoods.

### Case study 11.1 The community water systems of Costa Rica

"The best inheritance I can leave future generations is water," explained Guillermo, the elderly man whose job it is to make sure that the potable water stays crystal clear day after day for his semi-rural community. As he said this, we were high up on the Poás Volcano above his little town of San Roque, visiting the multiple springs that produce the water for his town. Surrounded by dancing blue Morpho butterflies in the dense rain forest near his water source, he told us that potable water for his great-great grandchildren depends on protecting the springs and watershed. That in turn requires involving the whole community in water management and environmental conservation. Ninety-five percent of the citizens of Costa Rica enjoy clean water in their homes, more than most other countries in Central and South America. You can just turn on the tap and drink the water (something people take for granted in high-income countries), but this is a basic environmental entitlement that many people throughout the world do not enjoy. Because it is very difficult to have adequate health without access to clean water, Costa Rica has recognized the importance of this entitlement and set up a structure to manage the environmental resources that assure water for today *and* tomorrow.

A state-run company, Aqueducts and Sewage Systems (known as AyA, its Spanish acronym), installs community water systems across the country, but the communities themselves run these systems by forming cooperatives. These cooperatives bring together the citizens from the local area who want water from the community system; they pay for their water usage but also collectively govern the cooperative that oversees the system. Across Costa Rica, there are 80,000 community-managed water systems that provide 20 to 40 percent of the rural and semi-rural population with water; the denser urban areas are provided water by local municipalities. We had the opportunity to visit three communities at different altitudes up the Poás Volcano of central Costa Rica: Barrio Latino, San Miguel, and San Roque. Each community and its water system employees emphasized the importance of local buy-in for protecting water and watersheds for sustainable local water consumption.

Barrio Latino is an urban community in the small city of Grecia, just up from the Pan-American Highway that connects Costa Rica to its northern neighbor Nicaragua and southern neighbor Panama. Many years ago, the community's water only arrived in a slow trickle from 11pm to 3am due to a municipal water system that privileged more centralized neighborhoods over Barrio Latino. Carol Muñoz, the treasurer for the water system, told the story of how Don Freddy Chacón, a community elder, convened the community, proposing that they find their own water source and get the support of AyA to help them build the infrastructure so that they would have water around the clock. Carol recalled:

> Don Freddy remembered that the town used to get its water from a nearby wooded valley, and he started digging in this abandoned valley. He dug and dug and didn't find anything, and then he lay down his shovel and asked God to show him water. Suddenly the water broke through. We have enough water to serve today's 730 families for the next 20 years, including population growth. People identify with the community water system because it's *their* water. So they call when they see there's a leak or if they taste too much chlorine. Furthermore, we're working to educate people about taking care of the water, not just the spring but waste water too. We're encouraging people to recycle cooking oil and not pour it down the drain. We recycle it into bio-diesel. People can drop off their used oil at our office. But there are dangers to our spring: above us on the volcano there are sugar cane farmers who use a lot of fertilizers which can get into the water table. The older farmers – like Don Freddy – have environmental awareness, but sometimes their children have gone to school in the cities and just want to make money from the land. They just see the money. Agriculture in harmony with the environment like their parents did it isn't profitable, and so the younger generation chooses to plant crops that require fertilizers or too much water. This is why it's so important to educate the entire surrounding area about protecting watersheds and buying land around our springs.

Eager to learn more about how neighboring communities had worked together to assure their right to water, we headed up the volcano to the springs that supply water to San Miguel, a semi-rural community above Grecia. There, leaders have worked closely with a local landowner whose holdings include the springs that provide water for the community. The community water system has educated the landowner about the importance of keeping cattle away from the springs and farming sustainably so that the springs remain uncontaminated. It is particularly important that animals do not contaminate springs, but also vital that ground water run-off not contain harmful pesticides which can poison the natural springs that communities rely on for potable water. The community organization that runs the water system for San Miguel has also worked closely with the local schools to educate young people about the importance of protecting water. Evidence for the effort to involve the younger generation in taking care of the watershed are the signs – around the springs and throughout the community – that encourage disposing of garbage properly and not contaminating water sources. The community itself has participated in work days to help protect the springs and guarantee that at the point of capture the water is potable and safe.

Even higher up on the Poás Volcano where the community of San Roque draws its water, we visited a rainforest where the community has been purchasing and reforesting ever-widening swaths of land around their springs. With only two water system employees, the community has worked hard to reforest these properties with native plants, efforts that are also very important for the preservation efforts of the nearby national park. Community awareness, commitment, and resources are essential for the continuity of potable water resources. The community water system is run by its members who elect delegates to provide oversight and hire employees. In the case of San Roque, the community raised thousands of dollars to buy the land adjoining their springs, and followed up by donating thousands of volunteer hours to reforest and preserve the property. It is true that not every community's cooperative has that kind of money or is as efficient as the ones we visited. Nonetheless, this model of state–civil society partnership via cooperatives has worked throughout Costa Rica – in communities rich, poor, and in between.

This case is an excellent example of sustainable community management of critical natural capital (Pelenc and Ballet 2015), namely the vital resource of clean water. The sustainability ethos is clear from Guillermo's words about leaving an inheritance for future generations. The resource itself supports several of the relationships between ecosystems and wellbeing from Duraiappah's list: being able to be free from avoidable disease, being able to have adequate and clean drinking water, and being able to make sustainable management decisions. In turn, those relationships underlie some basic capabilities such as bodily health and affiliation. The connection to affiliation may seem surprising, but that is actually one of the most notable achievements of these communities' self-management. The water cooperatives exemplify participatory planning for a critical resource, and this kind of self-management empowers communities to manage additional resources and work together for collective goals. This in turn helps strengthen capabilities.

In other words, these water cooperatives are examples of collective action that supports wellbeing in ways far beyond sustainable resource management. They secure collective capabilities in a way that individuals acting alone probably could not. Moreover, from the capabilities perspective, there is a benefit in the community coming together to decide democratically on what functionings (such as being healthy and managing joint resources) are valuable. This democratic form of self-organization builds capability freedoms, strengthening individuals' and the collective's agency and social capital. Particularly favorable contextual factors benefit the Costa Rican cooperatives' self-organization, specifically the distinctive institutional arrangement of the state–civil society partnership with AyA. AyA facilitates both the infrastructural build-out of the clean water system and the sustainable management via citizen participation. As the next case shows, contextual factors are not always so favorable in mediating wellbeing–environment relationships.

### Case study 11.2 The urban settlement of La Carpio

In the 1990s, thousands of Nicaraguans came to Costa Rica, fleeing violence, poverty, and political unrest in their home country. Many of these refugees settled in San José, the capital city, occupying a piece of land that was owned by the Carpio family. This land was marginal, with many environmental disadvantages: the area is sandwiched between two deep river canyons and an airport. It is prone to landslides and flooding. Open sewage from a nearby neighborhood runs directly into the river canyons, and flows right by the houses that Nicaraguan emigrants constructed. The poorest people could build only the most insecure structures: dirt floors, recycled tin roofs, walls made of scavenged cardboard and other materials. In the early years, residents of the area told us, the roads of their neighborhood were muddy and filthy, strewn with trash and sometimes dead dogs. This neighborhood is called La Carpio. Its population is around 35,000, and it is perhaps the best-known marginalized community in the largest city in Costa Rica.

In 2002, the Costa Rican government decided to construct a garbage dump right next to the neighborhood. Naturally, the people living there protested: no one wants to live next to a landfill. However, the government insisted, threatening the people of La Carpio that they could be deported (since most were undocumented Nicaraguans), but also offering them a deal of improved public services if they would drop their opposition to the dump. In the end, the dump was constructed, and now some 200 garbage trucks pass through the neighborhood daily, carrying hundreds of tons of trash each day. Worse, an enormous pile of garbage rises just on the edge of where people live. The dump has already surpassed its mandated lifespan as well as regulations about how high the pile can rise, yet the rules were rewritten so that the garbage trucks can keep coming. On some days, when the wind blows a certain way, the smell is unbearable. Without proper treatment, the dump can be a breeding ground for rats, insects, and other pests. It can also lead to contamination of the water people drink. To cap off the neighborhood's environmental disadvantages, a sewage treatment plant was also subsequently built next door.

In a way, none of this is surprising. As so often throughout the world, poor people have no choice but to live on the worst land. In La Carpio, poverty across a variety of dimensions is very common. More than half the population lives below the national income poverty line. Few people have legal title to their land, which means that some of their most important physical assets such as their house are insecure. Moreover, many of the lots on which people have constructed their houses are smaller than the minimum required by law. A fair portion of those houses have been constructed in places where they can be swept away by floods. In general, Nicaraguans in Costa Rica experience higher rates of poverty than do native-born Costa Ricans. They tend to have less educational attainment, higher unemployment, higher fertility rates, and worse health outcomes including low birth weight, more malnutrition, and inadequate immunizations (see Funkhouser *et al.* 2002, Marquette 2006, Sandoval *et al.* 2010). Nicaraguans, too, are often subject to discrimination by native-born Costa Ricans. All of these conditions apply in La Carpio. It is a stigmatized area, both by negative popular stereotypes against Nicaraguans and by public policy that has disproportionately concentrated undesirable facilities in the neighborhood such as the dump or high-voltage electrical cables that pass very close to houses.

La Carpio, then, is a severe case of a vulnerability cluster. The neighborhood's geographical, social, and political circumstances combine to threaten many fundamental entitlements. In particular, the open sewage and omnipresence of garbage can make it harder to be free from avoidable disease. Pollution, the marginal terrain, and even the noise from the nearby airport can compromise being able to live in a clean and safe shelter. Being able to have clean air is obviously threatened by the dump. Basic human security is jeopardized by the higher levels of crime, the hazards to bodily health, and the area's susceptibility to flooding and landslides. And a key reason for these multiple disadvantages is a lack of recognition. Because the population of La Carpio is heavily Nicaraguan, hence sometimes undocumented and with insecure legal rights, it is more likely to be disempowered. All these disadvantages combine to undercut the collective capabilities that would help the community exercise effective management of environmental conditions.

In particular, the contextual factors of La Carpio shed a stark light on the importance of conversion factors. Conversion factors are what enable individuals and groups to convert capabilities (i.e. opportunities) to functionings (i.e. actual achievements) (Pelenc *et al.* 2015). For example, too many residents of La Carpio lack the resources (such as financial capital) to build adequate shelters, which impedes key functionings in bodily health. Many other external conversion factors also work against them, such as the political and institutional contexts that hinder undocumented immigrants from actualizing legal rights. This is where discrimination, power relationships, and a lack of recognition stand in the way of the basic capability of control over one's environment. There are also deficiencies with internal conversion factors; these are things such as health, education, and psychological states. If you are sick because you do not have clean water, or barely literate because you haven't been able to complete your education, or continually stressed by the pressure to feed your family, then it can be much more difficult to mobilize to address the environmental conditions undermining your capabilities. In comparison to the communities from the preceding case study that have been successfully managing their water resources, people in La Carpio have many more barriers to securing their collective capabilities.

There is good news, however. In roughly the last 20 years, government, the private sector, and the community itself have undertaken a variety of steps that have reduced poverty in the neighborhood and made environmental entitlements more secure (Solano 2012). These initiatives correspond to several best-practice measures on environmental contributors to poverty in urban areas (Satterthwaite 2003). For instance, municipal services now provide the infrastructure for sanitation and clean water. The housing stock has also been improved for most people. Most dwellings are now made of brick or concrete, a major upgrade from the days of living in unsafe constructions of cardboard and tin. Now that there is electricity in La Carpio, residents do not have to rely on unclean household fuels for cooking and light. Transport options are also much improved: nearly all roads are paved, and the neighborhood is connected to the rest of the city by frequent public buses. Paved roads also help with storm and surface water drainage, a step up from the muddy roads of the past, which were more likely to spread waste and excrement.

Community management of its own affairs is also much stronger (Alvarado 2020). The neighborhood has a number of civil society organizations such as churches and a few non-governmental organizations. These organizations contribute significantly to social capital, providing specific programs such as sex education for young people and inclusion for older people. Self-government is also more robust in the form of several neighborhood councils. Finally, there is a health clinic in the neighborhood now, funded by the government, which has helped reduce though not eliminate problems of malnutrition and maternal health. The garbage dump, though still an assault on the eyes and the nose, has been reasonably well run: the garbage pile is usually covered up, with pest control and treatment to prevent leakage into water supplies. The company that runs the dump even makes some gestures at corporate social responsibility by providing funds to community organizations within La Carpio.

Not all of La Carpio's problems have been resolved, of course. Though there is a primary school in the neighborhood, to attend high school young people must take a bus elsewhere, which they cannot always afford. Employment opportunities are lacking, average incomes are generally low, and this remains marginalized land. Vulnerability clusters persist, particularly for the people who live in the most insecure dwellings down by the river, where female-headed households, larger families with more children, malnutrition, and lower incomes are more common. Nonetheless, La Carpio has shown how community organizations, public services such as water, health and electricity, and negotiation between civil society, government, and the private sector can mitigate environmental disadvantages. Indeed, because the people of La Carpio have been at least somewhat empowered to demand transparent and responsive government, they have been able to adapt to those disadvantages and make some progress on securing their basic capabilities.

### Case study 11.3 Sustainable development in Monteverde

In Costa Rica, the strong laws protecting national parks – which overall are beneficial – nonetheless sometimes have unintended consequences, such as alienating local communities who are denied possibilities for sustainably using the forests and other environmental assets. It can be difficult for rural communities near national parks and conservation areas to preserve ecosystems while also developing sustainable livelihoods that generate enough income to meet their needs. (See Adams *et al.* 2004 for a summary of academic research on the challenges of conservation and poverty reduction.) One notable exception is the community of Monteverde. In the midst of Costa Rica's central mountains at almost 5000 feet above sea level and set within a cloud forest, Monteverde is one of Costa Rica's prime tourist destinations. Today Monteverde is a lesson in sustainable development for Costa Rica and beyond. The community has transitioned from agriculture to ecotourism, and while there are substantial environmental challenges in both of those economic and social models, on the whole the people of Monteverde have done an admirable job trying to protect their ecosystem while also furthering development (see i.a. Baez *et al.* 1996, Davis 2007, Farrell and Marion 2001, Koens *et al.* 2009).

For decades, the relationship of humans to the ecosystem in Monteverde was based in agriculture. Though people had been farming in the area for years, a major change came in 1951, when 12 Quaker families from the United States bought 3800 acres of mountainous terrain from a Costa Rican mining company. Fleeing the military draft in the United States because of their pacifist beliefs, this group of Quakers chose Costa Rica because it had dissolved its army in the 1940s and promised respite from warmongering and Cold War politics. The Quaker community negotiated with the few local farming families and bought many of them out as well. Given the favorable conditions in the area for raising milk cows, the community founded the Monteverde dairy factory (Productores Monteverde in Spanish) in 1954, which purchased local milk production and created a wide selection of cheeses. At its height, the company was a major economic engine, employing 200 local people and buying milk from 500 members. Many of the landowners preserved the cloud forest rather than cutting it down, knowing that it was necessary to protect watersheds. Thus, back to the 1950s there was an effort to manage ecosystem resources sustainably and grow the dairy business with a commitment to a triple bottom line: environment, community, and profits.

However, the community also learned that it had to adapt in order to have truly sustainable livelihoods. For example, over time, milk and milk products from bigger companies began to flood the market. According to Sarah Stuckey, a former board member of the company, it was harder for the Monteverde dairy to remain competitive unless it became very big and more industrialized, or very small and artisanal. In the end, the community decided to sell the dairy, and now it employs about 50 people. Yet interestingly enough, this was not an economic disaster. The Quaker families from the United States had not remained isolated in their mountain hamlet. They welcomed Costa Rican farming families into the community when land came up for sale, and they continued to educate residents about the importance of conservation efforts and sustainable development, making sure that these messages were prominent in school and community initiatives. They inculcated their values of sustainability and social justice in the community, even founding a local bilingual school whose pedagogy was informed by the importance of environmental stewardship. Though the dairy factory was sold, the community had grown and diversified. Young people from nearby and newcomers drawn by the area's beauty, connection to the environment, and pacifist values wanted more income-generating activities than farming and cattle. Those same values drew many other people to visit Monteverde, and the area grew into an ecotourism hub.

Ecotourism has been defined as "responsible travel to natural areas that conserves the environment, sustains the wellbeing of the local people, and involves interpretation and education" (TIES 2015). Monteverde mostly succeeds in these three areas. Tourism has given the area's distinctive ecosystem a significant economic value, which incentivizes the preservation of that ecosystem. As the tourist business has grown, it has also provided many people with an income; some 90 percent of the population now depends on tourism for a living. A few people do still raise cattle and produce milk for local and national consumption, but now there is a new generation of green entrepreneurs who run hotels, restaurants, shops, adventure sports, and other attractions. These businesses generate income, create employment opportunities, increase environmental awareness in the tourists who come to visit, and continue the tradition of protecting the cloud forests. Education has long been a priority for Monteverde. Besides the bilingual school the Quakers built, there is also a state secondary school that offers vocational training in tourism, and the Monteverde Institute, which offers a variety of programs for research, place-based education, and community engagement.

Though most locals think that on balance the tourism boom has been positive, the area's popularity has had some problematic environmental impacts. The building of hotels, shopping areas and other facilities has disturbed wildlife and done some damage to vegetation. The influx of new people coming to live and work in the area has weakened some aspects of the traditional culture as well as the traditions of self-governance. And with all the new people, there is more vehicle traffic, more garbage, and more sewage, which Monteverde's infrastructure is not always equipped to handle. The community is actively working to mitigate these negative environmental impacts. Local councils strive to make better plans for growth, for example. It is a major benefit that much of the money spent by visitors stays in the area, rather than benefiting international chains or absentee owners. Similarly, many of the local taxes gathered stay local, which helps fund social services such as a health clinic.

As Monteverde's residents have learned, being sustainable means learning how to adapt. With climate change, many communities around the world will be forced to adapt in the coming years. Monteverde's experience points to some key conditions that support adaptation, and these also relate to conversion factors. This is a community with notably strong resources including income, financial capital, human capital, and physical capital (since all the dairy farming infrastructure counts as an important asset). The way it was able to cooperate and transition shows that Monteverde has admirably healthy social capital as well. These resources undergirded internal conversion factors such as good health, and technical and organizational skills, which together enabled people to move from one livelihood to another. The internal conversion factors then helped the community to manage external conversion factors such as the political, economic, and infrastructural contexts that could impact on adaptation from agriculture to ecotourism. In comparison to La Carpio, Monteverde is quite a wealthy community, with secure basic capabilities at both the individual and collective levels. Because vulnerability in Monteverde was so low, adaption to new circumstances has been much easier than it would have been in a community with fewer resources.

Monteverde also provides many lessons on how the range of ecosystem services support human wellbeing. The forests help provide water, the fields provide grazing land for cows that provide food, and the biodiversity provides cultural opportunities for tourism that in turn supports livelihoods. Monteverde's environment is also critical to the basic capabilities from Nussbaum's list of play (which embraces recreational activities) and being able to live in harmonious relation to other species. So in many ways, Monteverde embodies the "green trademark" that Costa Rica has claimed for itself. This community's survival – economically, socially, biologically, and otherwise – depends on the wealth of its environmental assets. Shrouded in mists much of the year, isolated up in the mountains, with sometimes rough roads connecting it to the outside world, Monteverde could be little more than a remote village trying to escape poverty. But its residents have recognized that their environmental assets are what bring prosperity, and therefore that they have to manage those assets in the most perspicacious and sustainable way possible.

## Conclusion

As these case studies suggest, when communities have the agency and support to manage their ecosystem resources sustainably, that is one of the best ways of strengthening capabilities and countering poverty–environment dynamics. Much the same is true in the case of Costa Rica's Maleku people. Over the years, a number of their environmental entitlements have been threatened, including being adequately nourished, having clean water, participating in the management of their own environmental assets, and using traditional medicine and other natural elements for cultural and spiritual practices. In Costa Rica, like many other parts of the world, indigenous people are too often forced to live on the margins of their societies, suffering major capability deprivations as their ecosystems are degraded. As Schlosberg and Carruthers (2010: 29) have written, indigenous struggles are not only about land and political rights; they are struggles "for the health of the environment, the protection of traditional village economies, respect for sacred sites, and the preservation of native religion, culture, and practices." These are ultimately struggles for both individual and collective capabilities – and part of an ongoing effort for indigenous groups to achieve recognition, overcome vulnerability, and secure functionings.

The Maleku have made significant progress, despite difficulties in keeping their lands, preserving their culture, and finding adequate economic opportunities. Maleku leaders we talked to affirmed that their communities are healthier now than they were in previous generations. The Maleku people were in danger of dying out completely in the early twentieth century, but since then their numbers have grown. They now have some powers for self-government and management of their ecosystem resources. For example, the local school board to which Chita and Rosa belong helps ensure that Maleku culture and language are passed on through education. There is a local cooperative to promote economic development, a few NGOs working on land rights and conservation, and the Maleku sit on the national-level organization that protects indigenous interests. Public services have also demonstrably helped reduce poverty in the area. Health centers provide medical care, including programs combating malnutrition. The community has generally secure access to clean water and reliable electricity. The teachers specifically mentioned that the Maleku do not suffer from information poverty, since they had ample access to cell phones and the internet. The Maleku teachers we talked to affirmed, "We are not poor."

Elders do still worry about how many young people leave the community, and how to maintain the culture if the young are not interested. Young people are often more attracted to global youth culture and learning English than Maleku. When they migrate to the cities in search of work, it is difficult to keep their Maleku identity alive. Nonetheless, sometimes those who leave do return: Chita came back to her village, brought her children, and now works to strengthen the community. "My mother was indigenous, and we grew up around here. For the past 15 years, I've been back here in the community with my new common-law husband," she said proudly. Rosa's family, too, actively promotes Maleku rights and culture. Her brother, sisters, mother and father, and grandkids all live together in separate houses on the ancestral property. Though her mother does not have strong Maleku ancestry and her father is only half Maleku, both grew up following the traditional customs and speaking the language:

> My grandmother had a particular bond with my brother, and she planted a lot of her wisdom in him. Today he is an advocate for our culture and travels widely sharing the stories and customs of our people. But all of my sisters have remained here in the community, and this is where we are raising our children to be good Malekus.

Just as the Maleku have been empowered to exercise more control over their own environment, vulnerable people around the world could benefit from a number of initiatives to reduce poverty and strengthen capabilities (see i.a. Barbier 2010, Castells-Quintana *et al.* 2018, Hallegatte *et al.* 2016). A necessary first step is often vulnerability mapping, to pinpoint communities such as La Carpio that suffer from multiple, overlapping deprivations in their environmental conditions. With better information on people and places in the most fragile conditions, programs such as crop/weather insurance or cash transfers (as part of a safety net) can be targeted to reduce insecurity. Infrastructure projects for sanitation, irrigation, energy, and transport can support basic capabilities as well as livelihoods, such as by reducing negative environmental impacts on health or improving agricultural productivity. In particularly fragile areas, diversification of livelihoods can help people find other income-generating activities, such as by teaching farmers how to grow new crops, or other training so that people gain new skills to depend less on scarce ecosystem resources. Many communities can also benefit from better land use planning, and some will come to depend on improved information and warning systems for severe weather events such as droughts or storms. Given that such events are likely to increase with climate change, a range of initiatives are going to be necessary to help people adapt.

Adaptation at the local level should go along with empowerment on a global scale, since people in the poorest countries have very little ability to stop environmental degradation caused by people in the richest countries. One could point to many different statistics to demonstrate how consumption of resources is not only vastly higher in rich countries, but inequitable and unsustainable. For example, according to a United Nations analysis, countries with high scores on the HDI had a per capita water consumption of 425 liters per day, compared to 67 liters per day in countries with low HDI scores (UNDP 2011). People in the richest countries like the United States and Canada were responsible for 30 times the carbon dioxide emissions of people in countries with low human development.

Such facts pose two unavoidable challenges for everyone reading this book. First, what are we doing to assure that consumption levels for the poor are minimally adequate to secure basic quality of life and equality of opportunities with the rich? Second, are consumption levels in rich countries so high that they are unjust from the perspective of causing negative environmental impacts that harm the quality of life and opportunities of future generations? That environmental conditions at local and global levels are often worsening poses a fundamental problem of justice because people in low-income countries have usually done the least to contribute to the worsening conditions, yet they will suffer the most from those changes. This means that all of us who wish to be ethical global citizens – both in lower income and higher income countries – must deeply consider the choices we make, the environmental consequences of those choices, and those consequences' impacts on the poor and vulnerable everywhere.

## Discussion questions

1　Using the above three case studies and the Maleku vignette, describe the opportunities and challenges of the sustainable management of ecosystem resources. Summarize the role that vulnerability clusters, recognition, and collective capabilities play.
2　Which environmental conditions would you judge to have the strongest negative impact on capabilities, and why?
3　Examine the Environmental Performance Index (https://epi.yale.edu/). What exactly does it purport to measure? How do different countries rank? What connections do you see with poverty?
4　What is your reaction to the claims of intergenerational justice with environmental sustainability, such as that overconsumption today equates to oppression of people in the future, or that what matters for people in the future is not equality of resources but equality of basic capabilities?
5　Imagine a scenario where the world has depleted petroleum resources and now only uses what today are called alternative energy sources such as solar energy, wind power, and hydro power. In this future world, your grandchildren may have less mobility than you do. Will their capabilities be less, more, or equal to yours? What are the justice considerations in this scenario?

## Online resources

- The United Nations Environment Programme has a wealth of resources, including information on the relationships between the environment and gender, education, conflict, technology, etc.: www.unep.org/
- The Notre Dame Global Adaptation Initiative focuses on the risks of the changing climate and includes a ranking of countries based on the readiness to adapt: www.gain.nd.edu/

## Further reading

Barbier, E. 2013. "Environmental Sustainability and Poverty Eradication in Developing Countries," in Eva Paus, ed.. *Getting Development Right: Structural transformation, inclusion, and sustainability in the post-crisis era*. New York: Palgrave Macmillan: 173–194.

Biggeri, M. and Ferrannini, A. 2014. *Sustainable Human Development: A New Territorial and People-Centred Perspective*. New York: Palgrave Macmillan.

Hallegatte, S., Bangalore, M., Bonzanigo, L., Fay, M., Kane, T., Narloch, U., Rozenberg, J., Treguer, D., Vogt-Schilb, A. 2016. *Shock Waves: Managing the Impacts of Climate Change on Poverty*. Washington, DC: World Bank.

Hopwood, B., Mellor, M. and O'Brien, G. 2005. "Sustainable development: mapping different approaches." *Sustainable Development* 13.1: 38–52.

Lessmann, O. and Rauschmeyer, F., eds. 2014. *The Capability Approach and Sustainability*. London: Routledge.

World Health Organization. 2018. OP24 Special Report: Health and Climate Change. Geneva: WHO.

## Works cited

Adams, W., Aveling, R., Brockington, D., Dickson, B., Elliott, J., Hutton, J., Roe, D., Vira, B. and Wolmer, W. 2004. "Biodiversity conservation and the eradication of poverty." *Science* 306: 1146–1149.

Adger, W. N., Pulhin, J. M., Barnett, J., Dabelko, G. D., Hovelsrud, G. K., Levy, M., Oswald Spring, Ú. and Vogel, C. H. 2014. "Human security," in Field, C. B., Barros, V. R., Dokken, D. J., Mach, K. J., Mastrandrea, M. D., Bilir, T. E., Chatterjee, M., Ebi, K. L., Estrada, Y. O., Genova, R. C., Girma, B., Kissel, E. S., Levy, A. N., MacCracken, S., Mastrandrea, P. R., and White, L. L., eds. *Climate Change 2014: Impacts, Adaptation, and Vulnerability*. Part A: Global and Sectoral Aspects. Contribution of Working Group II to the Fifth Assessment Report of the Intergovernmental Panel on Climate Change. Cambridge, UK and New York: Cambridge University Press, pp. 755–791.

Alcamo, J. and Bennett, E. M., eds. 2003. *Ecosystems and Human Well-Being: A Framework for Assessment*. Washington, DC: Island Press.

Alvarado, N. A. 2020. "Migrant Politics in the Urban Global South: The Political Work of Nicaraguan Migrants to Acquire Urban Services in Costa Rica." *Geopolitics*: 1–25.

Baez, A. L., Price, M. F. and Smith, V. L. 1996. "Learning from experience in the Monteverde Cloud forest, Costa Rica." *People and Tourism in Fragile Environment*: 109–122.

Ballet, J., Koffi, J.-M. and Pelenc, J. 2013. "Environment, justice and the capability approach." *Ecological Economics* 85: 28–34.

Ballet, J., Marchand, L., Pelenc, J. and Vos, R. 2018. "Capabilities, identity, aspirations and ecosystem services: an integrated framework." *Ecological Economics* 147: 21–28.

Barbier, E. B. 2010. "Poverty, development, and environment." *Environment and Development Economics*: 635–660.

Barbier, E. B. and Hochard, J. P. 2018a. "The impacts of climate change on the poor in disadvantaged regions." *Review of Environmental Economics and Policy* 12.1: 26–47.

Barbier, E. B. and Hochard, J. P. 2018b. "Land degradation and poverty." *Nature Sustainability*, 1.11: 623–631.

Burger, P. and Christen, M. 2011. "Towards a capability approach of sustainability." *Journal of Cleaner Production* 19.8: 787–795.

Carleton, T. A., and Hsiang, S. M. 2016. "Social and economic impacts of climate." *Science* 353.6304: aad9837.

Castells-Quintana, D., del Pilar Lopez-Uribe, M. and McDermott, T. K. J. 2017. "Geography, institutions and development: a review of the long-run impacts of climate change." *Climate and Development* 9.5: 452–470.

Castells-Quintana, D., del Pilar Lopez-Uribe, M. and McDermott, T. K. J. 2018. "Adaptation to climate change: A review through a development economics lens." *World Development* 104:183–196.

Davis, J. 2007. *Evolution of Protected Area Conservation in Monteverde, Costa Rica.* Diss. University of Florida.

Department for International Development (DFID), European Commission Directorate General for Development, United Nations Development Programme and The World Bank. 2002. "Linking Poverty Reduction and Environmental Management." July.

Duraiappah, A. K. 2002. *"Poverty and ecosystems: a conceptual framework."* UNEP Division of Policy and Law Paper. UNEP Nairobi.

Duraiappah, A. K. 2004. *Exploring the Links: the United Nations Environment Programme 2004: Human Well-being, Poverty & Ecosystem Services.* Nairobi: United Nations Environment Programme; Winnipeg: International Institute for Sustainable Development.

Evans, P. 2002. "Collective capabilities, culture, and Amartya Sen's *Development as Freedom.*" *Studies in Comparative International Development* 37.2: 54–60.

Farrell, T. A., and Marion, J. L. 2001. "Identifying and assessing ecotourism visitor impacts at eight protected areas in Costa Rica and Belize." *Environmental Conservation* 28.03: 215–225.

Fraser, N. 1997. *Justice Interruptus: Critical Reflections on the "Postsocialist" Condition.* New York: Routledge.

Funkhouser, E., Pérez Sáinz, J. P. and Sojo, C. 2002. "Social Exclusion of Nicaraguans in the Urban Metropolitan Area of San José, Costa Rica." *Inter-American Development Bank Research Network Working paper #R-437* (April).

Gallagher, K. P. and Thacker, St. 2008. "Democracy, Income, and Environmental Quality." Working Paper 164. University of Massachusetts, Amherst, Political Economy Research Institute, Amherst, MA.

Hallegatte, S., Bangalore, M., Bonzanigo, L., Fay, M., Kane, T., Narloch, U., Rozenberg, J., Treguer, D. and Vogt-Schilb, A. 2016. *Shock Waves: Managing the Impacts of Climate Change on Poverty.* Washington, DC: World Bank.

Holland, B. 2008. "Justice and the environment in Nussbaum's capabilities approach: why sustainable ecological capacity is a meta-capability." *Political Research Quarterly* 61.2: 319–332.

Holland, B. 2014. *Allocating the Earth: A Distributional Framework for Protecting Capabilities in Environmental Law and Policy.* Oxford: Oxford University Press.

Ibrahim, S. S. 2006. "From individual to collective capabilities: the capability approach as a conceptual framework for self-help." *Journal of Human Development* 7.3: 397–416.

International Ecotourism Society, The (TIES). www.ecotourism.org/. Accessed April 2015.

International Fund for Agricultural Development. 2010. "Desertification" fact sheet. August.

Koens, J. F., Dieperink, C. and Miranda, M. 2009. "Ecotourism as a development strategy: experiences from Costa Rica." *Environment, Development and Sustainability* 11.6: 1225–1237.

Lehtonen, M. 2004. "The environmental–social interface of sustainable development: capabilities, social capital, institutions." *Ecological Economics* 49.2: 199–214.

Leichenko, R. and Silva, J. A. 2014. "Climate change and poverty: vulnerability, impacts, and alleviation strategies." *Wiley Interdisciplinary Reviews: Climate Change* 5.4: 539–556.

Livelihoods and Climate Change. 2003. "Conceptual framework paper prepared by the Task Force on Climate Change, Vulnerable Communities, and Adaptation." *The International Institute for Sustainable Development.*

Marquette, C. M. 2006. "Nicaraguan migrants in Costa Rica." *Población y Salud en Mesoamérica* 4.1.

McGinnis, M. D. and Ostrom, E. 2014. "Social-ecological system framework: initial changes and continuing challenges." *Ecology and Society* 19.2: 30.

Millennium Ecosystem Assessment. 2005. *Ecosystems and Human Wellbeing.* Washington, DC: Island Press.

Ostrom, E. 2009. "A general framework for analyzing sustainability of social-ecological systems." *Science* 325.5939: 419–422.

Pearce, D. W. 2005. "Investing in Environmental Wealth for Poverty Reduction." Poverty-Environment Partnership. September.

Pelenc, J. and Ballet, J. 2015. "Strong sustainability, critical natural capital and the capability approach." *Ecological Economics* 112: 36–44.

Pelenc, J., Bazile, D. and Ceruti, C. 2015. "Collective capability and collective agency for sustainability: A case study." *Ecological Economics* 118: 226–239.

Polishchuk, Y. and Rauschmayer, F. 2012. "Beyond 'benefits'? Looking at ecosystem services through the capability approach." *Ecological Economics* 81: 103–111.

Poverty-Environment Partnership (PEP). 2008. "Poverty, Health and Environment: Placing Environmental Health on Countries' Development Agendas." Joint Agency Paper, June.

Prüss-Üstün, A. and Corvalán, C. 2006. *Preventing Disease Through Healthy Environments.* Geneva: World Health Organization.

Rai, J. 2019. "Understanding poverty-environment relationship from sustainable development Perspectives." *Journal of Geography, Environment and Earth Science International* 19.1: 1–19.

Sandoval, C., Brenes, M., Paniagua, L. and Masís Fernández, K. 2010. *Un país fragmentado. La Carpio: comunidad, cultura y política.* San José: Editorial Universidad de Costa Rica.

Satterthwaite, D. 2003. "The links between poverty and the environment in urban areas of Africa, Asia, and Latin America." *The Annals of the American Academy of Political and Social Science* 590.1: 73–92.

Schlosberg, D. 2012. "Climate justice and capabilities: A framework for adaptation policy." *Ethics & International Affairs* 26.4: 445–461.

Schlosberg, D. and Carruthers, D. 2010. "Indigenous struggles, environmental justice, and community capabilities." *Global Environmental Politics* 10.4: 12–35.

Sen, A. 2009. *The Idea of Justice.* Cambridge, MA: Belknap Press.

Sen, A. 2013. "The ends and means of sustainability." *Journal of Human Development and Capabilities: A Multi-Disciplinary Journal for People-Centered Development* 14.1: 6–20.

Smith, K. R., Woodward, A., Campbell-Lendrum, D., Chadee, D. D., Honda, Y., Liu, Q., Olwoch, J. M., Revich, B. and Sauerborn, R. 2014. "Human health: impacts, adaptation, and co-benefits," in Field, C. B., Barros, V. R., Dokken, D. J., Mach, K. J., Mastrandrea, M. D., Bilir, T. E., Chatterjee, M., Ebi, K. L., Estrada, Y. O., Genova, R. C., Girma, B., Kissel, E. S., Levy, A. N., MacCracken, S., Mastrandrea, P. R. and White, L. L., eds. *Climate Change 2014: Impacts, Adaptation, and Vulnerability.* Part A: Global and Sectoral Aspects. Contribution of Working Group II to the Fifth Assessment Report of the Intergovernmental Panel on Climate Change. Cambridge, UK and New York: Cambridge University Press, pp. 709–754.

Solano, S. V. 2012. "Acción colectiva y ciclos de protesta: experiencias de participación política en La Carpio, 1993–2013." *Anuario Centro de Investigación y Estudios Políticos* 3: 91–125.

Torras, M. 2006. "The impact of power equality, income, and the environment on human health: some inter-country comparisons." *International Review of Applied Economics* 20.1: 1–20.

UNDP. 2011. *Human Development Report 2011. Sustainability and Equity: A better future for all.* New York: United Nations Development Programme.

UNEP. 2009. *From Conflict to Peacebuilding: The role of natural resources and the environment.* Nairobi: United Nations Environment Programme.

Voget-Kleschin, L. 2013. "Using the capability approach to conceptualize sustainable development." *Greifswald Environmental Ethics Papers*, no. 4, February.

Wolff, J. and De-Shalit, A. 2007. *Disadvantage.* Oxford: Oxford University Press.

World Health Organization. 2018. *OP24 Special Report: Health and Climate Change.* Geneva: WHO.

World Resource Institute. 2014. www.wri.org/our-work/topics/forests. Accessed 24 December.

Young, I. M. 2011. *Justice and the Politics of Difference.* Princeton, NJ: Princeton University Press.

# 12 Financial services for the poor

*Serena Cosgrove*

## Learning objectives

- Understand why microfinance programs have become so popular with development agencies
- Comprehend how financial services – such as credit, savings, and insurance – can be so important for microentrepreneurs, marketers, and others who earn their income outside of the formal economy
- Consider how the use of mobile phones and the internet can help facilitate access to financial services, especially for low-income people
- Be able to explain the major debates about microfinance
- Apply concepts from other chapters to explain why most clients of financial services are women
- Analyze the evidence about microfinance's effectiveness as a poverty reduction strategy

## Introduction

"I've been able to increase my sales and diversify what I sell thanks to the small loan and training I got from Lumana here in our town," said Mary, a Ghanaian microentrepreneur who sells salted fish and now dry goods from her home in Anloga, a small town near the ocean. "And even though I don't know how to read or write, we received business training that taught us how to figure out whether we're making a profit or not, by using small stones to count with," she said proudly. The fact that a low-income, rural woman considers herself better off thanks to the microfinance institution that provided her with business training and a small loan speaks to the possibilities inherent in a range of financial and non-financial services often referred to as microfinance. In countries around the world, many poor women like Mary have received small loans, to expand their businesses and build relationships with other microentrepreneurs.

In the mid-1990s, the success of Muhammad Yunus' Grameen Bank in Bangladesh began attracting a great deal of attention: impoverished women in Bangladesh were emerging from poverty and gender oppression through access to small loans and obligatory savings programs, *and* they were repaying their loans at the rate of 97 percent, a higher rate than rich men on Wall Street. Referred to as microfinance or microcredit, such programs provide low-income microentrepreneurs with small loans, savings, and other services from rotating credit funds. These funds can be used for microenterprise development, acquisition of technologies and other assets, land purchase, farming, and housing construction and improvement. In the years since Yunus won the 2006 Nobel Peace Prize, however, microfinance has also attracted less favorable attention. Critics have claimed that such programs take advantage of poor people, do little to help them escape poverty, and siphon off development funds from more effective uses. There was even a rash of suicides by people in India and other countries who became heavily indebted through microfinance.

Given such controversies, what is the real utility of programs that promise financial services for poor people? There are certainly good reasons to believe that microfinance *could* be a valuable poverty reduction strategy. In many developing countries a large proportion of the economically active population works in the informal sector, which means that their income-generating activities tend to happen outside of state control, that is, their businesses do not operate according to regulations on taxation or labor. Many of these income-generating activities are run by women, their average income is low, and their businesses are oriented towards survival, not savings or business growth (Le and Raven 2015). These microentrepreneurs, marketers, and craftspeople have little to no recourse to legal protections, employment laws, and security from illegal behavior such as gang-related activities and drugs and arms trafficking. Historically, they have also rarely had access to the services of the formal banking system (loans, savings, retirement accounts) and other financial services (insurance, pension plans), let alone access to formal education, vocational training, and specifically business training opportunities.

The theory behind microfinance is that with access to financial services, poor people may be able to develop income-earning businesses that will lift them and their families out of poverty. For its proponents, part of the appeal of microfinance is often as a "bottom-up" solution to development, that it can empower people, who are excluded from access to formal financial services, to help themselves. Due to the preponderance of women marketers and microentrepreneurs in the informal sector throughout the developing world, microfinance has predominantly targeted women. Microfinance institutions typically see women as good credit risks because they are regarded as more likely to repay loans due to socialized traits such as obedience and selflessness, often associated with women's caretaking roles. In turn, because of their roles in the family and their communities as mothers and caretakers, increased income for women can translate into improved economic conditions and wellbeing for them as well as their children and communities. Thus, another rationale for microfinance is that it has the potential to contribute to human and economic development by empowering women, especially.

This chapter examines the theory and rationale for microfinance, comparing them to the evidence for this strategy's impacts on poor people. It centers on the debates that have arisen around microfinance's implementation, impact, and empowerment potential. The chapter first describes the practicalities of receiving services through a microfinance program, explaining the methodologies, concepts, and values behind this type of programming, exploring typical financial services and non-financial services delivered by microfinance institutions (MFIs), as well as conditional and direct cash transfers, and the use of technology for opening up access to financial services. It then considers the poverty reduction potential of microfinance through the lens of the capabilities approach. In the final section, the chapter investigates a number of the debates in this area, including the different modes of microfinance (credit-only versus credit-plus), who implements microfinance programming, and the goals and ideological assumptions of such programs. Most importantly, the chapter surveys the evidence on microfinance's effectiveness as a poverty reduction strategy, including whether it does consistently empower women. The chapter's conclusions are based on field research in El Salvador in the 1990s, Zambia in

2011, Ghana in 2012, and Nicaragua 2017 as well as a review of recent academic work in many other countries. Ultimately, though such research does sometimes show increased incomes and other positive effects for microfinance clients, additional programming and structural change are often necessary to catalyze longer-term processes of empowerment and development.

## Microfinance: examples and definitions

Microfinance typically targets microenterprises, which are characterized by little to no capital invested in the businesses, and a maximum of two to three employees. Francisca's cheese stall, or Mari, José, and Rosa Elba's vegetable stalls in El Salvador (described below in Box 12.1) are all examples of microenterprises. Microenterprises cover a wide spectrum of income-generating activities in urban and rural areas: in El Salvador, for example, these businesses included making tortillas; working leather for belts, purses, and satchels; selling fruit juices, cheese, milk, soft drinks, fruits and vegetables, shoes, underwear, and cosmetics; preparing and selling food; or raising animals for slaughter or resale. Sometimes these businesses were small stores or *tiendas* run from the microentrepreneurs' homes, serving the needs of their immediate neighbors. The small loans that MFIs provide are often intended for use for investment in the microentrepreneurs' businesses: for repairs, expansion, diversification, inventory acquisition, or to acquire such assets as corn mills, a computer, or even access to water or electricity for a business run from the home. These loans can also translate into housing improvements when the business or part of it is located in the borrower's place of residence. Some loan programs do not require that microentrepreneurs invest directly in their businesses because they understand that what might be most useful to the client is paying for her children's schooling or other costs. In addition to loans, sometimes clients choose to work with MFIs because they have savings programs for personal or business investment goals as well as insurance programs that help clients access health insurance or insurance against crop failures.

---

### Box 12.1  Becoming a microfinance client in El Salvador

54-year-old Francisca is a cheese seller in the marketplace of Apopa, El Salvador, a small city on the outskirts of the Salvadoran capital, San Salvador. Francisca is also a natural leader, a hard worker, and a creative microentrepreneur. Though illiterate, she supports her family by selling cheese at an open-air stall near the Apopa municipal market. I met her for the first time when she brought three other marketers – Mari and José, a married couple, and their sister, Rosa Elba – who sell fruits and vegetables near her to attend an orientation meeting at the Apopa office of the non-governmental organization (NGO) FUSAI (Fundación Salvadoreña de Apoyo Integral – Salvadoran Foundation for Integral Support). My initial impression of Francisca was her determination. She did not hesitate to ask Roberto, the FUSAI promoter, questions about FUSAI's microfinance program when something was not clear; often women do not ask clarifying questions of men, especially educated men seen as belonging to a higher status group, such as professionals.

Francisca had been financing her microenterprise with high-interest loans from one of the many moneylenders working in the Apopa market. Paying an exorbitant interest rate of ten percent per day (compared to three percent per month with

FUSAI), low-income market vendors end up *dándole de comer al gordo* (feeding the fat man) instead of feeding their own kids, as Francisca explained. Francisca accurately conveyed the consensus of the group: "We want a break. We want out from under the loan shark." So, Francisca and the three others applied to become a communal bank and receive loans from FUSAI.

My next meeting with Francisca was accompanying Roberto, the FUSAI promoter, as he checked out the businesses of the potential communal bank members and helped them fill out the application forms. Outside of an already bustling market building, sellers set up boxes and baskets occupying the streets in their allotted areas under black pieces of plastic that had been strung up to protect vendors and shoppers from both sun and rain. It is like entering a different world: a thriving center of commerce under black plastic. First, I walked past Elba and her vegetable stand, then past Mari and José with their vegetables before I saw Francisca, waving a fly swatter over a metal box filled with *cuajada* (farmers' cheese) and little plastic bags of *crema* (sour cream).

Little over a week later, the loans were ready for disbursement. Gathered at the FUSAI office in Apopa, José, Mari, Elba and Francisca prepared to sign the contracts and take their checks for USD 100–150 to the local bank around the corner to be cashed. Francisca turned to me and told me she was getting a headache. Francisca cannot read or write; she has received no formal education. She can just barely write her initials, but that does not qualify as a signature in El Salvador. In Salvadoran banks, a check is not valid to be cashed unless it has been signed. Francisca had to ask one of the other members of her communal bank to accompany her to sign the check for her. Holding her head in her hands, she said to me, "This is my father's fault. He used to say that it made no sense to send a girl to school just so she could learn to write letters to a boyfriend." She went on, "It just hurts my head to know that I cannot sign my own name." Francisca got Mari to help her sign the check, and thus she received her first loan from a microfinance institution.

Francisca gets up at 5am and catches a bus to the outlying municipality of Aguilares where she walks out into the countryside to buy the cheese. By 9am, she is back at the Apopa market selling cheese; she stays at the market until she has sold everything she has, returning home in the mid-afternoon. Slowly, as we got to know each other under the black plastic, Francisca let me take responsibility for the fly swatter, waving it over the cheese and, as the weeks went by, I joined her in singing out the many qualities of the cheese for sale that day in order to entice buyers to visit the stall. By the end of my fieldwork stint, Francisca began to talk about the problematic relationship with her common-law husband. She no longer shares a bed with him. He does not contribute financially to the household anymore. She would just put his things out in the street, but his name is on the title to the house. Recently, he got angry at her and slammed her hand in the door, injuring her fingers. "What can I do to leave him?" she asked me. Francisca is also concerned about her three teenage sons. Trying to keep them occupied after school so they do not get into trouble, she has apprenticed them to a baker. They earn some money, get job experience, and keep their distance from the gangs.

As the income-earner for her family, Francisca struggles to make ends meet and provide a home for her sons. Though beset by a number of problems – from the abusive husband to gang activity in her community – not only did her income increase during her loan period, but she was able to increase her inventory by 15 percent. As I followed her progress after the loan disbursement, she told me that sales were up, she had increased the amount of cheese she was buying for resale and felt she had increased the amount of money she took home at the end of the day. "I feel rested working with FUSAI," she said explaining how she felt less economic stress now that she was not depending on the loan shark. "I was drowning working with the loan shark."

(Adapted from Cosgrove 1999a and 1999b)

Throughout this chapter, and the development literature in general, the terms microfinance, microcredit, and microenterprise lending are often used interchangeably, but in strict rigor, the umbrella term is microfinance. Microfinance encompasses a range of financial and non-financial services including microcredit or small loans, savings, insurance, money transfers, other business opportunities such as access to technologies, and sometimes training and accompaniment. Whereas microfinance refers to numerous financial services for clients, microcredit and microenterprise lending are the terms used to refer specifically to the loans (or credit) that clients will pay back with interest to the MFI. Frequently managed by local MFIs (often NGOs), microfinance institutions use a rotating credit fund from which they distribute small loans (typically 100–500 USD), collect savings from clients/entrepreneurs, recover the loans with interest, and then expand the number of clients served as the credit fund grows. MFIs often target a particular city or neighborhood, letting community leaders know about their services. With input and recommendations from local leaders, microfinance promoters from the MFI will begin to build networks of contacts in the community. After an orientation and site visit from the promoter, borrowers are encouraged to form groups with people they know and vouch for, and soon they can access their loans.

In order to minimize administrative costs and increase the commitment of clients to the process, MFIs often use a peer group method for distributing and recovering the loans. There are two different models that MFIs around the world use to provide credit: the communal bank and the solidarity group. The communal bank, as we will see in Francisca's case, is a small group of borrowers – from five to 20 depending on the program – who apply together for loans, receive training or orientation together, and then commit to the same repayment schedule. In the case of the communal bank model, individuals each put up some form of collateral, be it a television, a refrigerator, or simply the income-generating potential of their microenterprise. The solidarity group – or the peer lending group as it is also called – is used for borrowers who have no assets to put up for collateral. In this case, a group of clients (the group size can vary) commits to covering each other should one of them not be able to make a repayment. Group pressure, and the social bonds that connect the borrowers, keep members repaying their loans on time. The solidarity group model often includes an obligatory savings program which can be used to repay delinquent accounts. In cases where borrowers may not have immediate access to funds, they often take extraordinary measures to find the payment to avoid the shame of defaulting, even for one payment. Since women predominate in the informal sector, most microfinance clients are women. And because of culturally-coded messages about the caretaking and maternal responsibilities of being a woman as well as the class-coded messages about respect for authority, women tend to be very responsible loan clients. In fact, they repay their loans better than men and usually invest more of their profits in the health and welfare of their families.

Many microfinance programs focus solely on providing credit, and they are referred to as credit-only programs. Some programs include obligatory savings of five to ten per cent on the amount loaned. However, given the need of clients for basic financial services, MFIs have begun to offer additional financial services such as different savings programs, health insurance, and insurance in case of personal, familial emergencies, or crop failures (Zeller and Sharma 2000). There are a number of programs providing additional services other than financial ones, especially when targeting low-income women; these programs are often referred to as credit-plus and can include health-related trainings or medicine, vocational training, business skills enhancement (business basics, marketing or entrepreneurship, for example), gender awareness workshops, or specific workshops on best practices for particular kinds of microenterprises (Table 12.1).

Microfinance programs exist around the globe and, not surprisingly, there can be a lot of variation in how the programs work. The most well-known microfinance model is the Grameen Bank in Bangladesh, whose solidarity group model has loaned more than USD 17 billion for self-employment purposes, with repayment rates approaching 100 percent (Grameen Bank 2015).

*Table 12.1* Types of microfinance and associated services

| Microfinance and associated services | | | |
|---|---|---|---|
| **Financial services** | | **Related services, also referred to as credit-plus** | |
| *Financial services* | *Importance for entrepreneurs served* | *Additional services* | *Importance for entrepreneurs served* |
| Credit-only: microcredit or small loans<br><br>Savings programs | Clients, like Francisca mentioned above, who just want loans<br><br>Many programs include savings programs for clients so they can begin to build their own capital for their businesses or other personal and family-related needs | Business skills and strategies training<br>Entrepreneurship and community engagement training | Provides clients with knowledge for managing their businesses better<br>Training for how clients' businesses can expand or diversify and contribute to development in their communities |
| Insurance (health, life, disaster) and pensions | Because so many clients are not employed in formal sector jobs with benefits and often do not meet prerequisites to be served by the formal banking sector, they find these services useful for unexpected illnesses in the family, weather shocks that affect crops, and long-term planning | Training and programming related to clients' other capabilities such as women's empowerment and rights, health and hygiene, citizen participation and advocacy, and green technology | Serves to connect clients' individual businesses to address bigger challenges that limit their capabilities and contribute to poverty |

---

**Box 12.2 The Grameen Bank**

As of 2013, the Grameen Bank in Bangladesh had almost USD 129 million in capital, 22,000 employees, 8.5 million borrowers and 2500 branches. The Grameen Foundation has its headquarters in Washington DC, and it works to replicate the Grameen model around the world. (Data taken from the Grameen Bank and Foundation websites.)

---

**Box 12.3 The importance of an array of financial services, by Julian Fellerman**

The expansion of financial services beyond microcredit has been a major focus for the microfinance sector in recent years. Savings and insurance products tailored to the needs of the world's unbanked have been at the forefront of this expansion.

Emblematic of this larger trend is MiCredito, a Nicaraguan MFI that has developed an array of savings and insurance products into its core microcredit offerings. When a new client takes out a microloan with MiCredito, they automatically enroll in a life-insurance plan funded by a small percentage of their loan repayments to the MFI. MiCredito has also partnered with Banco de America Central (BAC), a larger regional bank, to begin offering new and existing clients a syndicated debit card option. These saving and insurance products serve a dual purpose: in the case of insurance, the product serves to create a stronger "future-orientation" among clients wherein long-term financial planning is literally built into the loan repayment plan. The debit card is one of the most fundamental tools in the financial inclusion arsenal; specifically, access to a savings account with no required minimum balance improves MiCredito's clients' ability to manage repayments by reducing transaction costs associated with storing and moving money. Most importantly, though, is the role of the MFI savings account as a pre-requisite step in the client's journey towards banking with a formal financial sector institution.

I had the opportunity to witness the transformative power of savings in action during a field visit to Maribel, one of MiCredito's clients in Rivas, Nicaragua, located about 20 miles north of the Costa Rican border. Maribel relocated to Rivas after spending most of her life living on the outskirts of the colonial city of Leon. After much of her family fell victim to the counter-revolutionary forces during the Nicaraguan civil war of the 1980s, she was forced to relocate to this economic hub in southern Nicaragua. "I escaped from there with nothing in terms of money. We had a few family friends down here (in Rivas) where we stayed for a few years trying to rebuild," she comments. Maribel began to realize her homemade tortillas were gaining popularity in her new community. This led her to start an artisanal tortilla enterprise she now operates out of her home. She has taken out multiple microloans from MiCredito to fund the expansion of her increasingly popular business, with a small percentage of each loan repayment depositing into her savings account. When I asked her about her experience as a MiCredito client, she expressed particular gratitude for the savings account option: "This has really changed things for me. As small business owners, we want a safe place to store our money – however, because many of our businesses are so small, our options for a formal savings account are often limited."

According to Maribel, this savings cushion has also come in handy as a means of smoothing out her personal consumption during lulls in the business. She says she has greater peace of mind because of the increased preparedness she feels in the event of a financial emergency. This peace of mind from something so seemingly basic as a savings account has fundamentally changed the outlook of this budding entrepreneur.

Bangladesh is also the home of two other important microfinance institutions, the Building Resources Across Communities (BRAC) and the Proshika Human Development Centre. According to Lamia Karim's research, there are over 21 million women in a country of 140 million being served by MFIs in Bangladesh (2011). The work of ACCION International in the Americas includes the ACCION NGO-credit network and the commercially successful, credit-only institution BancoSol. Also active in Latin America, with many national affiliates, is FINCA International. In Central America, governmental offices, NGOs, and private sector credit associations provide credit throughout the region from rotating credit funds that are managed by the communities themselves, NGOs, or governmental institutions. In Indonesia, the country-wide program Bankya Rakyat's Unit Desa System has been successfully implemented by the government (Boomgard and Angell 1994). Interestingly, Bankya Rakyat Indonesia requires that clients buy life insurance so that their loans can be repaid in the case of illness or death (Zeller and Sharma 2000).

Many of the bigger MFIs – such as Grameen and BRAC – focus on small loans and if they have a savings program, it is an obligatory one, serving more as "a down-payment on a loan and a screening device" (Zeller and Sharma 2000: 159) than as a flexible savings account tailored to the borrower's accumulation needs. Catholic Relief Services and other international NGOs, such as CARE and Caritas, have promoted models of lending and saving in the developing world that are built with capital from a group of women themselves: women organize as a group and pool their own savings and then loan it out to group members. This way they do not have to rely on an outside source for their capital. These models are called SILCs (savings and internal lending communities) and ROSCAs (rotating credit and savings associations). Microfinance efforts can also be found in the developed world: there are successful MFIs in the United States, such as the Working Capital model in Boston and Ventures in Seattle, a non-profit that provides microloans at graduated levels and individual development accounts, matching client savings 2:1.

A financial service that is not a loan deserves mention here. Conditional Cash Transfers (CCTs) – or cash dividends from governments to low-income citizens – is a redistributive program that is being taken up by governments in multiple regions of the world from Latin America to Africa and even in Asia (Pérez-Muñoz 2017). (See Chapter 10 "Education as poverty reduction" for more information on CCTs and education.) Cash transfer "programs provide noncontributory cash grants to selected beneficiaries to satisfy minimum consumption needs" (Garcia and Moore 2012: 32–33). The money is generally dispersed to families on the condition they meet certain health or nutritional or educational requirements for children in the home by encouraging investments in the human development of family members, particularly children. According to a survey of research on the effectiveness of these programs, "CCTs have positive effects on the health and education of recipients' children as well as in terms of poverty reduction" (Pérez-Muñoz

2017: 443). According to Garcia and Moore, "[e]valuations of unconditional programs have found significant impacts on household food consumption … nonfood consumption; and children's nutrition and education" (2012: 23).

Though rooted in good intentions (see Cookson 2018), one of the main critiques of CCTs is not about the effectiveness of the program, but how the enforcement of the conditions or requirements could be "potentially both intrusive and stigmatizing" (Pérez-Muñoz 2017: 445). Cookson goes even further saying, "One of the appeals of conditional aid is its alleged efficiency, but in practice CCTs are efficient only if women's time and unpaid labor is worth nothing" (2018: 148). The concern here is that women's time is not taken into account when considering the real costs of CCTs.

In the case of people who are extremely poor, direct cash transfers or asset transfers, such as a pig, chickens, or a cow, for example, can catalyze income–generation and help beneficiaries start microenterprises. Many impact assessments speak positively about the potential for this type of programming. The results of research that looks for patterns in a large number of cases – often referred to as "large-n" research – and quantitatively assesses the impacts of cash transfers and business training for ultra–poor women in rural northern Kenya found that, "[a]fter one year, this program has a positive and statistically significant impact on income (31%), savings (131%), asset accumulation (35%), and, less clearly, on livestock (12%)" (Gobin *et al.* 2017: 1363–1364). The advantage of direct cash transfer for a microenterprise is that it allows the beneficiary to start their business without debt, and for people who are very poor, this can be a very impactful investment for them and their families.

Assessing the impact of the international NGO, GiveDirectly (www.givedirectly. org), and their distribution of cash across Kenya, Haushaufer and Shapiro start by saying that "[c]ompared to in-kind transfers, UCTs [unconditional cash transfers] are attractive because cash is fungible and thus cannot be extramarginal and distortionary; households with heterogeneous needs may be better able to turn cash into long–run welfare improvements than transfers of livestock or skills" (2016: 1974). These same authors conclude that cash transfers can facilitate economic and psychological wellbeing. A critique of direct cash transfers is that they constantly require new sources of cash for investment. Traditional microfinance rotating credit funds are sustainable if managed efficiently: as loans are returned with interest, more money can be loaned out.

---

### Box 12.4 Microfinance and business training in Ghana

Lumana is an MFI in Ghana (Figure 12.1) that operates on a credit–plus model with small communal bank groups. Once they are approved for a loan, but before they receive any money, these groups attend a three–day business training in the local language. This training includes basic accounting appropriate even for illiterate clients, as well as instruction in personal savings. Obligatory micro–savings are built into Lumana's model to help clients with goal setting, such as saving for children's education or home repairs. Once they have completed the training, Lumana sets up a bank account for each group, and each member gets the equivalent of about USD 60 for their first loan. Lumana charges an interest rate of 24 percent, compared to 30 to 90 percent that other banks or MFIs offer. If clients successfully repay in six months (with a two–month grace period), they become eligible for larger loan amounts. At the time of research, Lumana's repayment rate was 94 percent.

To assess impacts, Lumana administers a "Progress Out of Poverty" survey every year to each client, which is based on a Grameen Foundation instrument adapted for Ghana. It asks questions about the total family size, the highest grade level completed by the female head of the household, the construction material of the roof, the main source of drinking water for the household, and whether the household owns a working stove, radio, and/or other household goods. Besides gathering some additional items of financial data, Lumana also employs people from the local community to act as case managers. These managers are mostly recent university graduates whose local contacts and knowledge of the language are essential for understanding clients' lives and maintaining good community relationships.

In the little seaside village of Dzita we met one of Lumana's clients, Alice, a very sharp, friendly woman who has a number of income-generating activities. Alice buys fresh fish, smokes it, then sells it. She also has a store, sells corn, and regularly travels to the nearby country of Benin to buy small crabs that she can resell in Ghana's capital of Accra. The day we met her; Alice was sitting alongside her mother smoking shrimp on a big pan over a fire. She said that she learned you have to have multiple business strategies to survive, since if sales are not good in one area, you can compensate with another. Women who had taken loans just for their shrimp business have had trouble repaying, she noticed.

Alice is in a communal bank group with four other women, and she has taken out four loans from Lumana. She had very positive things to say about her experience with microfinance: "you can take in a big amount and pay back small." She found Lumana's business training useful because "it tells you what to do with your money," and "how to attract customers and market yourself." If she had not had that training, Alice told us, she would not know how to spend better and save. She noticed how some women spent their loans on personal or family needs and had trouble repaying, but she was determined to use her loans to invest in her businesses so she could bring in more income. She wants to use her next loan to increase her family's farming productivity so they can have more beans, corn, and groundnuts to sell, especially in the off-season when they fetch a higher price. With her savings, Alice has already bought a refrigerator for the house, and her next goals include saving for her children's university education and to buy land for a guest house to rent out.

On a market day, Alice wakes up as early as 3am to smoke fish so that she is done by 7am. She also has to get her store ready and her kids off to school by the time she leaves for the market, usually before 8am. She spends the entire day selling, while her mother minds the store and takes care of the younger kids. Alice usually gets home after 7pm, when she cleans up, spends a little time with her children, then goes to sleep so she can get up early and start again the next day. Her family lives in her husband's house, but he works at a hospital in Accra, a few hours away. Alice's husband comes home only a few times per month, and she says she does not really miss him, though she does like it when he is home. They make their decisions on finances and family matters together. Alice is obviously a hard worker: she developed her businesses while she was raising three small children. Though her life is by no means easy, it is more secure and comfortable in part, she thinks, because of microfinance.

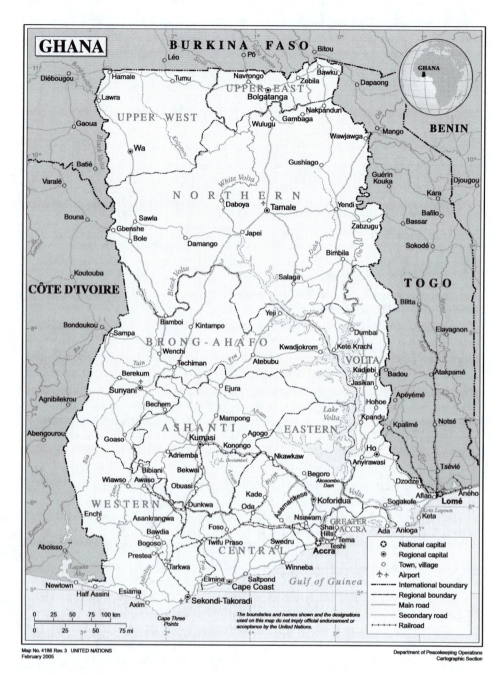

*Figure 12.1* Map of Ghana

Source : Map No. 4186 Rev. 3 UNITED NATIONS February 2005.

## Microfinance and technology

An expanded use of credit and debit cards and cellphone usage around the world has helped increase poor people's access to financial services with some notable impacts in capabilities. Often referred to as "mobile money," technology is helping expand access to financial services, cash transfers, and remittances from relatives in other countries. "At the most basic level, mobile money is the provision of financial services through a mobile device" (Donovan 2012: 61).

Mobile money is also referred to as mobile banking, "a global behavioral phenom-enon, or more accurately...the result of significant behavioral changes that have been occurring all over the world since the introduction of the Internet and the World Wide Web" (Krishnan 2014: 24–25). Expanding access to financial services (mobile phone-based money transfers, payments, and small loans) through technology has been led by companies like M-PESA, which was "started [in 2007] in Kenya and is now operational in six countries; it has 20 million users who transferred $500 million a month during 2011" (Donovan 2012: 61).

---

### Box 12.5  Mobile phones and mobile money

"Mobile phones are multifunctional devices that allow for a variety of commu-nication methods. These range from ubiquitous voice and SMS channels to more sophisticated means such as software applications or web browsers. To be a viable solution for mobile money, the channel should ideally be universally available (including the cheapest mobile phones) and must be secure. In practice, this require-ment largely limits mobile money to using a standard network service, such as USSD (Unstructured Supplementary Service Data) or SMS (short message system), or an application preloaded on a unique SIM card. Since mobile operators con-trol both of these channels, they remain essential gatekeepers in deploying mobile money" (Donovan 2012: 62).

---

The application of technology and the internet to financial services has benefited people around the world in resourced countries as well as under-resourced countries. However, these developments have created opportunities for the unbanked and underbanked, in particular. And by this, I am talking about the extremely poor and poor, many of whom have mobile phones (Owens 2013: 271). In turn, this means that MFIs and banks are better able to reach and serve their clients, especially those in remote or difficult to reach places. "The adoption of mobile technology enables MFIs to efficiently provide financial services to their clients, in particular to those who live in remote areas, and thereby to achieve their bottom line of poverty alleviation" (Dorfleitner *et al.* 2019: 356). The use of mobile banking or digital financial services has a number of impacts, including "con-venient access, flexible and real-time services...Mobile financial services can also be more convenient and affordable compared to traditional banking, which can help users manage their money on a daily basis, especially women as financial controllers in their families who tend to plan for the future, compare financial products and keep them informed" (Soekarno and Setiawati 2020: 48). Furthermore, mobile money is contributing to the important capability of increased safety and security of people because it contributes to less muggings due to less cash being in circulation.

## Microfinance and capabilities

From an economic development perspective, how microcredit and related financial services could help lift people out of poverty should be clear. In theory, these programs can help people generate income, but also smooth consumption so that they are less vulnerable to economic shocks. Economic shocks can include major spending events such as illnesses, weddings, funerals, or natural disasters (drought, floods, hurricanes) that affect a family's ability to generate income or produce food for consumption. Smoothing consumption means, for example, helping poor people get the same amount of food every month, so that they do not go hungry in a month when they have had an emergency or otherwise run out of money. Though small loans can help, it is more often other financial services such as savings and insurance that provide important resources, so clients can survive hard times which plague vulnerable and poor people (Zeller and Sharma 2000). From the capabilities perspective, all of these potential effects could reduce risk and vulnerability for the poor. This is why Tseng says that microfinance could be a "shock absorber": by helping people to cope with emergencies or other sudden shortfalls in consumption, microfinance can bring financial stability, without which people may not be able to realize their goals or valued capabilities in health, education, empowerment, or other life plans (2011: 244). Therefore, microfinance's economic effects should give people more agency to live the life they choose.

The capabilities approach adds a further theoretical perspective for analyzing how microfinance could reduce poverty. By strengthening the ability of poor people to manage their money, and by raising their incomes, microfinance can actually promote freedom (Roodman 2012). It can do so in several different ways. First, higher incomes and more secure finances can expand a variety of other life opportunities. Very simply, more money often opens up more possibilities. As mentioned above, financial security helps people withstand shocks that can limit what they can do with their lives. Second, and more concretely, with higher incomes, poor people may be able to invest more in their health and education and the health and education of family members. This is money as a means to an end: not just the end of more physical assets or growing one's business, but the end of achieving more robust human development (Zeller and Sharma 2000). Third, by expanding economic opportunities, microfinance may also expand various other social and political opportunities. The reason here is that with more secure finances, poor people may be less vulnerable to corrupt officials, or they may be able to escape restrictive social/cultural situations that limit their choices. This latter idea relates directly to the fourth way that microfinance may promote freedom, specifically by empowering women.

Think again of Francisca: her loan helped her actualize the capability to earn a living. The microfinance institution FUSAI helps people such as Francisca break barriers preventing them from accessing financial services because of restrictive eligibility requirements like not being able to sign one's own name. Giving the loan to Francisca, which helped her grow her business, ultimately put more money in her pocket, and gave her the power to make more of her own financial decisions. In the big picture, Gilardone *et al.* argue that microfinance can "increase women's incomes and facilitate their financial independence, stabilize their entrepreneurship activity notably by training, but also, and maybe especially, improve their status within the family and strengthen the respect of themselves, and finally, favor their capacities of auto-organization and thus, their capacities of expression and claiming" (2014: 245). This is the theory of how microfinance can enhance capabilities, and it does have some empirical support, as we will see below.

However, even in Francisca's case, there are a number of reasons for caution. Yes, she is doing better with her business thanks to the loan and mutual support from her communal bank, but does she have more freedom and options to choose the life she wants, given that she faces gendered and structural limitations imposed by poverty, including oppressive gender roles, a lack of education, and high levels of insecurity due to gang violence? Moreover, how much has microfinance helped with other contributors to Francisca's poverty, such as personal safety? In fact, there are some ways that a small loan may *reduce* clients' freedoms. For example, it does undeniably lock people into sometimes severe contracts and potentially lead them into debt spirals. It is also possible that solidarity groups can actually be coercive, disempowering at least as much as they empower. For example, if you are a member of a solidarity group and you cannot repay your loan, the group may seize your belongings, leaving you worse off than before you joined. This potentially disempowering aspect of microfinance suggests that the feel-good stories one often encounters on promotional websites can have a dark side – and it points the way to the many debates about this poverty reduction strategy.

## Microfinance debates

There is no denying microfinance's powerful, intuitive appeal: reduce the limitations around credit, savings, and insurance for poor people, and they will be able to build or expand businesses, increase their incomes, and escape cycles of indebtedness from high-interest loans. It may even be an impressive vehicle for women's empowerment. Furthermore, because of the mounting criticism of bilateral aid (large aid flows from one government to another), microfinance is often seen as a decentralized, bottom-up strategy that does not rely on big aid commitments making it to the local level: once an MFI has established a rotating credit fund either through donations, an investment, or a loan itself, it can grow to serve more borrowers if it is managed efficiently. There is no shortage of cases such as Mary's, Francisca's, or Alice's where a microfinance client is able to make her business more lucrative and attain greater control over her life in the process.

Nonetheless, there are also many analysts who disagree with microfinance proponents' claims about its effectiveness. In fact, there are a number of contentious debates that swirl around the utility of microfinance as a poverty reduction strategy. I will examine four specific areas of debate: (1) the arguments about the most effective models for providing microfinance to clients; (2) the critiques that arise from examining the worldviews or underlying ideologies of microfinance programs; (3) the discussions about whether or not microfinance "empowers" its clients, especially impoverished women, or places them under more pressure as they have to repay loans or risk being shamed in their communities; and (4) the long-term effectiveness and impact assessment of microfinance programs on loan clients, their communities, and developing world economies in general. Through studying these debates, we will examine the best research on the outcomes of microfinance to understand the pros and cons of this strategy. Given that there is no "magic bullet" to reduce global poverty, the essential question is this: under what conditions can microfinance most benefit its clients and contribute to the expansion of their capabilities?

### Credit-only or credit-plus?

A familiar debate in the sector has been whether financially-sustainable, credit-only programs are preferable to a broader array of services including savings and insurance or more expensive credit-plus programming in which borrowers access financial services and educational opportunities. Some MFIs have promoted a credit-only model in part because it can be easier for financial institutions to manage since it does not include the range of training, solidarity, and other development inputs with which they may not have experience or resources. This minimalist model or credit-only approach emphasizes the financial sustainability of the program's loan portfolio via the expansion of borrowers served. The focus is simply on providing credit to a population that needs it. As Muhammad Yunus himself said, "[t]he fact that the poor are alive is clear proof of their ability … So rather than wasting our time teaching them new skills, we try to make maximum use of their existing skills" (1999: 135). The credit-only model is attractive to certain donors because of the focus on loan portfolios' financial sustainability, and the ability to serve larger numbers of borrowers resulting from the relatively limited services provided.

However, critics allege that other sustainability concerns, such as the long-term sustainability of borrowers' businesses and communities, are more likely to be neglected by the credit-only approach. Zeller and Sharma (2000) argue that the poor and near-poor need savings and insurance more than they need credit. Advocates of credit-plus approaches insist that when little attention is given to the cultural, economic, institutional, and political factors that contribute to poverty and a lack of social protections for clients, their families, and communities, individual borrowers may see an increase in consumption, but other contributors to poverty will persist. Models using the credit-plus approach, while more costly, aim at promoting human development for greater economic and non-economic sustainability in the long term. There is evidence from around the world about the impact of additional financial services and training programs in conjunction with business training. In Peru, women borrowers increased their business knowledge and demonstrated likelihood to stay with the MFI offering the training compared to a control group without training who demonstrated lower levels of retention (Karlan and Valdivia 2011). In Vietnam, business training did increase business performance overall, and the heterogeneity of women microentrepreneurs explains why some – such as isolated rural entrepreneurs – showed more satisfaction with the training than those in the lowlands (Le and Raven 2015).

Though it generated much discussion in the 1990s and 2000s, the ongoing relevance of the credit-only versus credit-plus debate is as a reminder that programming must respond to the needs of the clients and their cultural context. One of the risks with a one-size-fits-all model is that it does not have the flexibility to respond to clients' specific needs. If cultural practices and gender systems mean that women are not supposed to touch money, then programming will have to focus on cultural change and consciousness raising among women *and* men. If the community faces significant violence – such as gang violence and/or gender-based violence – it would be important to have an alternative to saving money at home and possibly gender sensitivity training for clients, their spouses, and family members before simply giving women money. However, if the clients have years of experience selling in markets and other places, but credit constraints prevent them from growing their businesses, then a program restricted to small loans with a low interest rate might be appropriate.

The issue of credit–only versus credit–plus is also related to the question of which organizations should implement microfinance programming. Presently, there is a range of different institutions running such programs. Initially, NGOs and mission–driven, for-profit institutions like the Grameen Bank, which only serve impoverished borrowers, were the primary providers of microfinance. But as time went by and governmental agencies and the formal banking sector saw that microfinance was profitable and addressed an important need in their communities, new actors joined the ranks. The pros and cons are multiple. When government agencies run microlending programs, they can assure that programming fits into local, regional, and national development plans, and coordinate ways to leverage the resources of all government agencies working in those communities. However, governments should not use microfinance projects as an excuse to decrease programming that provides citizens with basic social protections. Other MFIs also need to make sure that their efforts fit into broader development goals when instituting a microlending program. For instance, in the Salvadoran town of Nejapa, local NGOs and the municipal government worked together efficiently towards common goals. As NGOs provided microentrepreneurs with loans and business skills and knowledge, the mayor raised money to rebuild the municipal market building. By the time the building was finished, many marketers had expanded their businesses and were happy to relocate to the new building (Cosgrove 1999a and 2002).

When established financial institutions develop programming for low-income clients, they are meeting a need in the community by expanding services they already provide. Banks do not have to go through an intensive learning curve about the financial management of a loan fund, though they do have to develop client-sensitive materials and services. Because some microentrepreneurs do not read or write, banks need to understand that they cannot require microentrepreneurs to sign or fill out extensive forms as we learned when reading about Francisca earlier in this chapter; they need to streamline requirements. When an NGO, on the other hand, decides to include microlending as part of their programming, they often have to train staff and establish the necessary systems to manage the fund efficiently. But the NGO is probably better suited to administering additional services clients may need such as education, vocational training, health workshops, and consciousness-raising groups. And finally, NGOs play an important role in the strengthening of civil society and its ability to monitor government fulfilment of rights and obligations. If an NGO manages a microfinance program well, it can generate additional resources for other kinds of programming, thus serving clients and the community better.

### Ideological disputes around microfinance

The credit–only versus credit–plus debate, along with the issue of which organizations should operate which kinds of microfinance programs, are mostly practical in nature. Another contentious area with microfinance as a poverty reduction strategy deals more with ideology and competing worldviews. No matter the development strategy, it is always important to assess the worldview of its proponents. A particular worldview does not necessarily render a poverty reduction strategy ineffective; rather, the imperative is to understand the motivations behind actions as well as the long-term vision for the future. Microfinance, like virtually any other strategy, is not free of politics. The politics come in choosing this approach over other interventions; in promoting individual businesses over collective enterprises; in starting small and scaling-up programs and client numbers. We should not simplistically presume that increasing the assets and income of poor microentrepreneurs is good for communities, and that incorporating this sector of society into the broader economy can thereby promote development. The reason is that microfinance may not only be about getting microentrepreneurs capital to build their businesses at fair interest rates.

To the contrary, critics raise concerns about how ideological assumptions and political views of neo-liberal development inform much of the popularity of microfinance. For example, Isserles (2003) contends that microfinance facilitates devolving state responsibilities of welfare and development to MFIs, thereby putting poor communities' social protections at risk. The potential problem with doing so is that it avoids the structural problems confronting a country by enforcing a bootstrap ideology in which poor people must generate their own opportunities and their governments are let off the hook for fulfilling their social contract. The microcredit revolution hit the front pages of newspapers as bilateral aid agencies were requiring that the governments of developing countries implement structural adjustment programs to qualify for additional grants and loans. In order to make governments more streamlined and foster increased economic competition, structural adjustment policies compelled governments to privatize state businesses, cut spending, lay off state employees, eliminate subsidies for basic food items, and decrease social protections and welfare programs. Expecting state employees who have been laid off to start microenterprises to make ends meet is deeply problematic. How realistic is it to assume that almost anyone can earn a living by running their own business? Moreover, for those already stuck in poverty, the price increase of basic food goods often associated with structural adjustment strained any possibility they had of moving out of poverty. How much help can a small loan provide in these circumstances?

Also, because women – often the most subordinated members of societies – make up the majority of microlending borrowers, it is important to consider how they might be affected differently than male borrowers. For instance, in her feminist critique of microfinance, Isserles suggests that targeting women because they repay loans and invest more in families is actually idealizing women and lowering expectations of men: "This instrumental approach to women as conduits for credit ... plays on, and reinforces, traditional cultural notions of womanhood, with women seen as moral guardians of the household and policers of recalcitrant men" (2003: 48). Thus, while focusing on women for microfinance programs has the potential of empowering them, it also has the potential of saddling them with new debt, new responsibilities, and new problems as they challenge traditional norms around women handling money and running businesses.

Many critics of microfinance also criticize how the managers of the credit funds charge interest to borrowers. They ask how it can be considered "development" to charge poor people for services. For instance, Karim's research (2011) in Bangladesh has raised concerns that the contradictory impulses of making profit get entangled with helping the poor. Furthermore, microfinance periodically attracts controversy over usurious interest rates that new players – particularly the formal banking system – are charging clients (MacFarquhar 2010). For many in the sector, especially the mission-driven NGOs, interest rates hover at roughly 1–3 percent per month (12 to 36 percent per year), but the new players from the banking system and for-profit companies are charging interest sometimes above 75 percent annual average rate. However, these rates are still less than what moneylenders charge, which stands at 120 percent annual average in Bangladesh, for example (Karim 2011).

This debate over interest rates is not new. Many microfinance proponents – including Muhammad Yunus – as well as critics of microfinance chastise banks and companies that charge excessively high interest rates. This argument applies to both the formal banking system and MFIs. For the formal banking system and for-profit businesses investing in microfinance, critics again ask if something that enriches investors and stockholders should be considered "development" for poor people. For the NGOs and municipal programs that charge the more moderate 12 to 36 percent annual interest rates, on the other hand, interest provides them with an important income stream for improving and expanding programming, especially for their clients. First, these rates are not exorbitant compared to what other moneylenders charge. Second, microloans can generate higher costs for lending organizations than bigger loans do for banks. It seems fair that micro-credit organizations be able to cover their costs with the interest generated. The issue is complicated because when microcredit organizations make a profit, they may put it to the service of their mission. As in the case of FUSAI, the organization that gave Francisca a loan, the organization was able to support difficult-to-fund development programming from the profits of the microcredit fund. Is this usurious? I would argue that it is not.

### Debates about empowerment

The claim that microfinance empowers women is contentious in part because of differing definitions of "empowerment." There can be an economic dimension to empowerment when women have more money to spend and more power within the household to influence decisions over how to spend that money. However, even if they are earning a higher income, women may not have control over their income if they live in a patri-archal culture where financial decisions are made by fathers, older brothers, husbands, or sons. Empowerment can also be social, such as through strengthening a woman's social capital, normative influence, and social cooperation (Sanyal 2009). Social capital refers to kinship and other social networks, connections that can help people in all kinds of ways. Normative influence refers to the ability to influence not just financial but other decisions, practices, and values. Social cooperation is related to the idea of soli-darity, women helping and supporting each other. Moser (1993) offers a useful, sum-mative definition of empowerment as women increasing their capacity for self-reliance, their right to determine choices, and their ability to influence the direction of change by gaining control over material and non-material resources. In theory, microfinance can empower women by giving them control over income, strengthening their community relationships and influence, and breaking down restrictive cultural norms about gender roles. What, however, does the evidence show – does microfinance truly and consistently empower women?

There is a wide range of qualitative studies and stories that affirm microfinance's empowering effects (see Duvendack *et al.* 2011, Sanyal 2009 for a review). These studies typically find, for instance, that the perception of women within their communities does change because of their participation in microfinance. Women have reported improved feelings of self-worth and a sense of increased agency. They have secured ownership over household assets and acquired financial management skills. There is also evidence that participation in microfinance increases mobility, trust, social capital, and women's ability to organize for positive community change. As an example, in Sanyal's research, groups of women that had come together via microfinance began intervening to stop domestic vio-lence and underage marriages. Increased social capital for women can thus lead to positive outcomes for the whole community, in addition to the benefits of generosity, a safety net, and mutual support for the women microfinance clients themselves. A big caveat is necessary for all these findings, however: most of these qualitative studies focus on individual programs in particular places and have been criticized for their generalizability to other programs in other places. This means that conclusions about empowering effects for microfinance may be too highly contextualized, or insufficiently rigorous, to enable us to say broadly and definitively that microfinance does empower.

In fact, according to quantitative and more generalizable evidence, microfinance does not consistently empower women. One reason is that though a woman may be the microfinance client, she may not actually end up controlling the money she receives (whether as a loan or as income from her enterprise). In various studies, women attained only limited control over household finances. Women in Bangladesh, for instance, often gave their loans to their male relatives, assuming the debt, but not the ability to decide how the money gets spent (Karim 2011; see also Banerjee *et al.* 2013, Goetz and Sen Gupta 1996). According to some researchers, women can even be disempowered by microfinance. Karim (2011) argues that credit makes women more dependent on men, exposes them to shaming and dishonor if they do not repay, and puts them into debt. Evidence from one study even found that women microfinance clients suffered increased violence from the men in their lives (Schuler *et al.* 1998). The solidarity group lending model can also potentially have negative effects. Such groups can exclude new entrants, stifle innovation ("this is how we have always done it"), and exclude women along ethnic, political, religious and other forms of difference (Mayoux 2001).

As with the qualitative research mentioned above, here too a caveat is necessary. In large-n, quantitative studies, a likely reason that empowering effects of microfinance have not consistently appeared is because of the research design. Few studies have been able to isolate when empowerment effects are due to the microfinance program itself, or due to other aspects of the program (such as education for literacy, numeracy, or about gender norms). Even when women do attain increased spending capacity, that does not necessarily mean increased ability to chart the future, to participate in decisions that affect their bodies and lives, and to work at the community or collective level towards mutual goals.

What then to conclude from this debate? Think of microfinance's empowerment potential in terms of capabilities. It is certainly conceivable that microfinance could enhance a woman's capabilities, for instance by increasing her income, raising her social status, or strengthening her decision-making power. All three of these areas could support a woman's capability to live a life that she values. Microfinance programs have the potential to contribute to valuable freedoms, to empower women to have greater agency. However, there is no rigorous, generalizable evidence that microfinance programs consistently do so (Tseng 2011; see also Lewis 2004, Selinger 2009). They may do so in some cases, but even then, it is not clear that the empowering effects come from the actual financial services of the program (the loan, micro-savings, and/or insurance) or the non-financial services such as training or programming related to other community needs such as health or women's rights. In reality, the empowerment effects most probably come from the non-financial aspects, such as increased access to training, and attention to gender issues, health, and hygiene, all of which are more likely to help women address the challenges they and their communities face.

Earlier in this chapter we read about Francisca and her market stall in El Salvador. For her, there was no business training, technical assistance, or attention to social issues affecting the loan clients. Low-interest loans can help some clients increase income simply by cutting the amount they pay for loans from moneylenders, but Francisca had difficulties at home in terms of an abusive partner and a community plagued by gang violence. The loan helped Francisca get out of the vicious cycle of the moneylenders, but she still cannot read or write, nor was she empowered to address the domestic or community challenges. For reasons such as these, microfinance programs ought to emphasize the "credit-plus" model, with specific gender-focused programs to promote human development. Many players in the microfinance sector have recognized this concern. As one example, Global Partnerships, a Seattle-based international NGO, raises money for investment in credit-plus MFIs in Latin America, to offer both training and credit to support long-term empowerment and sustainable development in the region.

A last facet of the empowerment issue is that borrowers may very well not escape from the moneylenders or the indebtedness trap because they have the opportunity to take out multiple loans from different MFIs to pay off pending loans. Until the rise of microenterprise lending in the early 1990s, Salvadoran marketers, for example, could only turn to local moneylenders for their credit needs, but now they have many MFIs competing to give them loans. Yet, there are valid concerns that women have traded the trap of the moneylenders for the trap of microfinance, borrowing loans to repay loans. This is why other impact assessment questions are so important: are borrowers actually increasing profits and assets? Are they investing profits in their families or using loans to pay for shocks and then having to take out loans to repay the initial loan? Though these questions, too, are debated, a close look at the evidence will provide the most reliable answers.

## Microfinance's impacts at the micro and macro levels

Research about the impacts of microfinance programs has evolved significantly over the last three decades. It has moved from analyzing the financial performance of MFIs and sharing anecdotes of client success stories to more systematic quantitative and qualitative research approaches which attempt to measure whether microfinance efforts increased the incomes and capabilities of participants. Contradictory conclusions about the impact of programs often stem from different research methodologies as well as different time, geographic, and cultural settings where studies have been carried out. There is a growing application, though, of large-n quantitative methods using randomized controlled trials in which treatment groups, that is, microfinance beneficiaries, are compared with control groups, that is, people with similar characteristics who have not received loans (see Chapter 3, Box 3.5 "Measuring outcomes with randomized controlled trails" for an in-depth description of this type of research). These studies measure whether clients have increased their income, businesses, and assets by comparing their progress to a control group of similar standing who did not receive loans. The Poverty Action Lab at the Massachusetts Institute of Technology was one of the first to carry out this kind of research for microfinance. In 2005, researchers began a baseline study in 104 marginalized neighborhoods in Hyderabad, India and then the Indian MFI, Spandana, formed lending groups and dispersed loans to eligible women in 52 of the 104 neighborhoods (Banerjee *et al.* 2013). After 12 to 18 months, researchers resurveyed households across the 104 neighborhoods to see if there were differences between the credit-receiving neighborhoods and the control neighborhoods.

What did they find? According to this influential study, the positive effects of microfinance are modest at best. There was no rise in overall average monthly expenditures for the microcredit neighborhoods, but there was an increase in expenditures on durable goods – assets such as refrigerators, televisions, carts, sewing machines etc. – and new businesses increased by one-third. Such findings contrast with the many inspiring stories one reads on the websites of particular microfinance programs. Ultimately, the different research methods, and the sometimes contradictory findings, mean we must become educated interpreters of data. What is being compared? What indicators are used to make comparisons? What are the cultural mores that could influence how borrowers use their loans? How honestly will the borrower participate in a survey or a conversation when interviewed by a local researcher or foreigner? Keeping these questions in mind, we will carefully survey the research on micro- and macro-level impacts, with a focus on capabilities. Micro-level impacts refer to the effects on individuals and families. This is where, according to the theory behind microfinance, we would expect to see the strongest effects in poverty reduction and enhancement of capabilities.

In reality, microfinance's theoretical positive effects are only sporadically confirmed: impacts tend to be mixed. Sometimes microfinance does lead to business creation or growth, but it does not consistently lead to increased or "smoother" consumption (see Banerjee 2013, Bateman 2011, Chowdhury 2009, Dichter 2006, Milana and Ashta 2012). A few of the studies that Van Rooyen et al. (2012) deem most rigorous do find that microfinance increased incomes, but many of the studies they examine reject that finding, and one even found that microfinance decreased incomes in some cases. On the other hand, micro-savings do sometimes have positive economic effects by helping poor people increase their assets (Adjei et al. 2009, Barnes et al. 2001a). This evidence is promising because microsavings does not come with the freedom-reducing potential downside of debt and the harsh consequences of default. Microsavings may not boost people's incomes or consumption in the short term in the way a microloan can, but there is evidence that microsavings may actually contribute more to developing microenterprises than microloans do (Dupas and Robinson 2009). Microfinance has also, in a number of cases, helped families to have more secure housing. People became more likely to own their home, to make improvements to it, and even to acquire rental units for additional income (Barnes et al. 2001a, Brannen 2010, Lacalle Calderón et al. 2008). This means that microfinance has supported the capability to have more secure shelter.

Another area of generally positive impact is health, where several large studies have found that microfinance strengthens capabilities. When coupled with education and training on health practices, microfinance programs reduced the incidence of diarrhea and encouraged the use of mosquito nets and contraception. People in these programs also saw reductions in the number of days they were unable to work due to sickness, and the total number of episodes of sickness (Van Rooyen et al. 2012). Similarly, there is evidence that microfinance programs can support improved food quality and nutrition, though the research consensus is not strong here. For example, in Tanzania and Rwanda, microfinance clients saw increases in meal quality, and in Zimbabwe the poorest clients began consuming more nutritious food (Barnes et al. 2001b, Brannen 2010, Lacalle Calderón et al. 2008). A key reason for improvements in health and nutrition is that microfinance can (though it does not always) lead to increased control for women over household expenditures (Duflo 2003).

In contrast, microfinance programs do not appear consistently to promote human development in the area of education. The research actually shows contradictory impacts. Sometimes microfinance is associated with higher household expenditure on education and increased school enrolment for children. In other cases or places, however, those positive effects are absent. Sometimes, in fact, microfinance has negative impacts on education.

In both Malawi and Uganda, for example, children's school attendance declined: boys had to repeat primary grades, fewer girls entered school, and families were unable to pay their school fees (Barnes *et al.* 2001a, Shimamura and Lastarria-Cornhiel 2010). There are even some suggestions that microfinance contributed to a higher incidence of child labor as families put their children to work in the family business (Tseng 2011).

Turning to the macro level, most of the research cited above focuses solely on the impact of the loans on individual clients; relatively fewer studies examine the macro-economic impact of the programs. At first, this could be explained by the fact that many microfinance efforts were restricted to target areas of individual NGOs. However, some-times participative development plans in which loan clients, MFIs, and municipal councils work together to increase local economic activity can lead to economic growth for the municipality (Cosgrove 2002). As an illustration, for the municipality of Nejapa (a 30-minute trip from the capital of San Salvador, El Salvador), microfinance tied to infra-structure development was a successful strategy for catalyzing the local economy. Wary of the motives of the Salvadoran private sector and international companies, the mayor of Nejapa concentrated economic development planning on increasing local production – agriculture, animal husbandry, petty commodity production, and the buying and selling of products by local people. As marketers strengthened their businesses with microcredit and technical assistance, the municipal government designed and built a new market building for them. Now, Nejapa is a destination for those seeking *pupusas* and other traditional dishes at lunch time and on national holidays.

This research points to the potential for municipal-level impacts of successful microfinance models, though its small scale limits its generalizability. Other researchers have examined impacts at the regional level since many formal banks and other commercial lenders have joined NGOs in the field of microfinance. This is what Nargiza Maksudova (2010) calls integration with national financial systems. Because the microfinance industry is no longer a marginal actor, can it act as a "locomotive for economic growth" (ibid: 5)? In a number of countries, Maksudova saw a positive relationship between microfinance and economic growth, but this trend decreases when there is credit saturation, that is, competition between MFIs for clients.

Maksudova's research raises another important macro question, namely who is actually benefiting from microfinance. Globally, MFIs show an increase in loan amounts but not new clients. This means that instead of reaching out to the traditionally "unbankable," efforts are focused on growing businesses that are already doing well. If this is the case, then how many people have been lifted out of poverty? Is microfinance really responding to the experiences, concerns, and hopes of the poor? In a study about the impact of microfinance in Bolivia, Mosley (2001) argues that yes, income increased for clients and, in fact, between ten and 20 percent of clients surveyed passed over the poverty line. Nonetheless, he acknowledges that those in extreme poverty, especially the rural poor, did not have access to credit. This claim – that the poorest of the poor are getting left out of the potential benefits of microfinance – has been corroborated by Karim (2011), who notes that in Bangladesh MFIs are increasingly targeting middle-class borrowers with a better chance of repayment than women in extreme poverty.

Looking over all of this evidence, what are the key takeaways? Microfinance *can* have positive effects in boosting incomes, supporting entrepreneurship, acquiring durable goods, smoothing consumption, improving health, and helping people have more sustainable livelihoods (Terberger 2013). All of these things can help expand people's freedoms, con-tributing to economic and human development at the national and household levels, and supporting capabilities at the individual level. However, relatively few of the microfinance programs analyzed around the world reliably do have these effects. Microfinance does not typically help the poorest of the poor. Nor is micro-savings in itself a sufficient strategy to reduce poverty: how can poor people save if their incomes do not adequately cover consumption to begin with? And microfinance does sometimes have negative impacts, whether through encouraging deeper debts or reduced expenditures on education (Barnes *et al.* 2001a, Waelde 2011).

As one further element in this mixed bag, remember that microfinance does appear to have respectable macro effects, contributing to a society's financial system in a variety of ways that go beyond poverty reduction. MFIs can help small and medium-sized enterprises that previously had limited access to banking services, and the mushroom-like growth of MFIs worldwide has provided jobs and professional financial training for many employees. Should microfinance be pursued as a poverty reduction strategy? The answer is yes, but programs must be carefully adapted to their societal context and have realistic expectations. They should also be transparent, flexible, and rigorously evaluated, and they must be designed to minimize harm. These recommendations obviously apply to any poverty reduction program. Additional financial services and credit-plus programs do have the most potential to enhance people's capabilities through trainings, health interventions, and a conscious focus on multiple aspects of empowerment for women. Ultimately, what may help the poor more than loans is cash grants or conditional cash transfers. (See Fiszbein *et al.* 2009 and the discussion of CCTs in this book's Chapter 10 on education.)

## Conclusion

Microfinance's potential is more limited than its most ardent proponents would like us to believe. It is certainly not ineffective, but its objectives must be realistic: if development efforts seek to promote increased capabilities and functionings for all, microfinance can play a role, but those efforts must address the structural roots of poverty and lack of social protections for the most vulnerable in society. The inclusion of low-income people requires access to financial services as well as important social services. This requires integrated, participative community development as well as community, municipal, and state funding. It requires participative development planning with an intersectional perspective that takes social difference into account and awareness about how other forms of social difference exclude people. Poor people in developing countries, especially women and those marginalized by gender, sexuality, race, ethnicity, ability, religion, geographic location, and class, face a rough road to reach empowerment. Income generation can be a piece of that project, but so is eradicating discriminatory practices and endemic structures that keep people and their communities in poverty. Microfinance can help women and their families increase income, savings, and assets, but unless they have control over how their increased income gets spent, and their empowerment is part of an integrated plan of human development, these achievements will only help them get by, surviving from one day to the next. Increased survival chances are a good thing, but empowerment means being able to make choices over one's life and contributions to one's community.

Even if microfinance does not always live up to its inspiring reputation as a means of poverty reduction, it does have a lot to teach us about the development sector more broadly. It shows how ideologies play into poverty reduction strategies. Microfinance has a particular appeal to those who believe in the bootstrap ideology of giving individuals the economic tools to lift themselves out of poverty. Microfinance also shows how rigorous evaluation methods have been introduced through research using randomized controlled trials and produced more conclusive evidence for impact assessment. In this way, it is a test case for the push towards more intensive assessment of development program outcomes and measurement. However, microfinance also shows how conflicts over evaluation methodologies can play out, namely through disputes over the relative limitations and strengths of qualitative and quantitative evidence that pit individual empowerment stories on the one hand against large-n, quantitative studies on the other.

The debates around microfinance also point to larger conflicts over what really matters in poverty reduction: is it increasing incomes, empowerment however defined, improving health or education, or securing basic capabilities? These goals are not mutually exclusive, but which to emphasize does involve hard choices. Making those hard choices requires a systematic, careful study of what clients or participants want, what works, as well as transparency in methodology, epistemology, and ideology. The sometimes inconclusive results of such research illustrate the need for caution even with the question of "what works to reduce poverty?" What works in some cases may not work in others. Similarly, programs may work according to some definitions of success but not others – and those definitions can again depend on the goals and the stakeholders. There is no one-size-fits-all poverty reduction strategy, as we emphasize throughout this book.

Microfinance and its associated debates remind us that addressing and eradicating poverty is hard, contentious, riven by competing interests, and rarely clear-cut. In the end, a fundamental question to ask is whom anti-poverty programs such as microfinance actually help. It can happen – and has sometimes happened, in the case of microfinance – that big players have become involved, and their interests have eclipsed the interests and priorities of poor people. Nonetheless, the lives of poor people must always remain in the center, and poverty reduction should focus on helping the poor to have a life that they value. Francisca in El Salvador, and Mary and Alice in Ghana, all see some value in microfinance. But each of them would also say that microloans and other financial services are only one small part of ending poverty in their communities.

## Discussion questions

1   In what areas (income, consumption, education, health, etc.), does microfinance have the most consistently positive effects? In what areas does it have few consistently positive effects, or actually cause harm?

2   What might be the circumstances when a microfinance program would not be appropriate for a given situation or group of people?

3   How would you define "empowerment" for a marketwoman or microentrepreneur in the developing world? For a small business owner in a high-income country? For yourself? How do capability considerations play into your definitions?

4   What do you see as the pros and cons of having local, NGOs manage microfinance programs versus government agencies or for-profit companies?

5   If you were to carry out a research project to measure the impact of a microfinance program, what indicators would you choose to measure and what kinds of research methods would you use? Justify your answer.

6   Microfinance activity: depending on the size of the group, divide into three sub-groups (a credit committee, a communal bank group comprised of individual microentrepreneurs seeking loans, and an outside assessment team). Let the entire group know the total amount available for loans and the maximum amount for an individual loan. Then, give each sub-group 15 minutes to prepare. The credit committee will need to agree on what criteria are necessary to make a loan. The

members of the communal bank group will select their individual business ideas and ideal loan amounts based on their real experiences and skills. The outside assessment team will consider what indicators would need to be assessed to measure the effectiveness of increasing income for college students. For the next 15 minutes, the different potential members of the communal bank will present on their proposed business ideas and credit needs. Then the credit committee will interview the potential communal bank members: weeding out risky investments and announcing loans. The members of the assessment group will comment on the challenges of assessing the impact of the loans.

7    Data analysis activity: spend some time analyzing the data available about microfinance efforts around the world on www.themix.org/mix-market and consider checking out the resources below as well.

## Online resources

- The Global Financial Inclusion Database provides 850+ country-level indicators of financial inclusion summarized for all adults and disaggregated by key demographic characteristics – gender, age, education, income, employment status and rural residence. Covering more than 140 economies, the indicators of financial inclusion measure how people save, borrow, make payments, and manage risk: www.datacatalog. worldbank.org/dataset/global-financial-inclusion-global-findex-database
- The Group of Twenty (G20) recognizes the key role of financial inclusion in the realization that financial inclusion is a key enabling element in the fight against poverty and the pursuit of inclusive development is leading to an increasing focus on financial inclusion policies and initiatives. Reliable data covering the major components of sustainable financial inclusion development is critical to inform these policies and to monitor the effect of initiatives. Data also provides a starting point on which to base ambitious financial inclusion targets: www.gpfi.org/news/ g20-financial-inclusion-indicators

## Further reading

Banerjee, Abhijit, and Esther Duflo. 2012. *Poor Economics: A Radical Rethinking of the Way to Fight Global Poverty*. Philadelphia, PA: Public Affairs.

Bornstein, David. 1996. *The Price of a Dream: The Story of the Grameen Bank and the Idea that is Helping the Poor to Change Their Lives*. New York: Simon & Schuster.

Collins, Daryl, Jonathan Morduch, Stuart Rutherford and Orlanda Ruthven. 2009. *Portfolios of the Poor: How the World's Poor Live on $2 a Day*. Princeton, NJ: Princeton University Press.

McKinsey Co. 2015. "How digital finance could boost growth in emerging economies." www. mckinsey.com/featured-insights/employment-and-growth/how-digital-finance-could-boost-growth-in-emerging-economies#

Robinson, Marguerite. 2001. *The Microfinance Revolution: Sustainable Finance for the Poor*. Washington DC: World Bank.

Yunus, Muhammad. 1999. *Banker to the Poor*. New York: Public Affairs.

## Works cited

Adjei, Joseph Kimos, Thankom Arun and Farhad Hossain. 2009. *The Role of Microfinance in Asset-Building and Poverty Reduction: The Case of Sinapi Aba Trust of Ghana*. Manchester: University of Manchester.

Banerjee, Abhijit Vinayak. 2013. "Microcredit under the microscope: what have we learned in the past two decades, and what do we need to know?" *Annual Review of Economics* 5.1: 487–519.

Banerjee, Abhijit, Esther Duflo, Rachel Glennester and Cynthia Kinnan. 2013. "The miracle of microfinance? Evidence from a randomized evaluation." National Bureau of Economic Research Working Paper 13–09, April.

Barnes, Carolyn, Gary Gaile and Richard Kibombo. 2001a. "The impact of three microfinance programs in Uganda." Development Experience Clearinghouse, USAID, Washington, DC.

Barnes, Carolyn, Erica Keogh and Nontokozo Nemarundwe. 2001b. "Microfinance program clients and impact: An assessment of Zambuko Trust, Zimbabwe." Washington, DC: Management Systems International.

Bateman, Milford. 2011 "Microfinance as a development and poverty reduction policy: is it everything it's cracked up to be?" Overseas Development Institute Background Note, March.

Boomgard, James J., and Kenneth J. Angell. 1994. "Bank Rakyat Indonesia"s Unit Desa System: Achievements and Replicability", in María Otero and Elisabeth Rhyne, eds., *The New World of Micro-Enterprise Finance: Building Healthy Financial Institutions for the Poor.* West Hartford, CT: Kumarian Press. 206–228.

Brannen, Conner. 2010. *An Impact Study of the Village Savings and Loan Association (VSLA) Program in Zanzibar, Tanzania.* Diss. Wesleyan University.

Chowdhury, Anis. 2009. "Microfinance as a poverty reduction tool-a critical assessment." United Nations, Department of Economic and Social Affairs (DESA) working paper 89.

Cookson, Tara Patricia. 2018. *Unjust Conditions Women"s Work and the Hidden Cost of Cash Transfer Programs,* Oakland, CA: University of California Press.

Cosgrove, Serena. 1999a. *Give Them the Credit They Deserve: Marketwomen and the Impact of Microenterprise Lending in the Municipalities of Apopa and Nejapa, El Salvador.* PhD Dissertation, Northeastern University.

Cosgrove, Serena. 1999b. "Engendering Finance: A Comparison of Two Micro-Finance Models in El Salvador," in Kavita Datta and Gareth Jones, eds., *Housing, Finance, and Gender in Developing Countries.* London: Routledge.

Cosgrove, Serena. 2002. "Levels of empowerment: marketers and microenterprise-lending NGOs in Apopa and Nejapa, El Salvador." *Latin American Perspectives* 29.5: 48–65.

Dichter, Thomas. 2006. "Hype and hope: the worrisome state of the microcredit movement." *The Microfinance Gateway.* Prepared by the QED Group, LLC, and International Resources Group for review by the United States Agency for International Development.

Donovan, Kevin. 2012. "Chapter Four: Mobile Money for Financial Inclusion," *2012 Information and Communications for Development.* The World Bank.

Dorfleitner, Gregor, Nguyen, Quynh Anh, and Röhe, Michaela. 2019. "Microfinance institutions and the provision of mobile financial services: First empirical evidence." *Finance Research Letters,* 31.

Duflo, Esther. 2003. "Grandmothers and granddaughters: old-age pensions and intrahousehold allocation in South Africa." *The World Bank Economic Review* 17.1: 1–25.

Dupas, Pascaline, and Jonathan Robinson. 2009. "Savings constraints and microenterprise development: evidence from a field experiment in Kenya." No. w14693. National Bureau of Economic Research.

Duvendack, Maren, Richard Palmer-Jones, James G. Copestake, Lee Hooper, Yoon Loke and Nitya Rao. 2011. *What is the Evidence of the Impact of Microfinance on the Well-Being of Poor People?* London: EPPI-Centre, Social Science Research Unit, Institute of Education, University of London,.

Fiszbein, Ariel, Norbert Rüdiger Schady and Francisco H. G. Ferreira. 2009. *Conditional Cash Transfers: Reducing Present and Future Poverty.* Washington, DC: World Bank.

Garcia, Marito and Moore, Charity G. 2012. *The Cash Dividend: The Rise of Cash Transfer Programs in Sub-Saharan Africa,* Washington, D.C.: World Bank.

Gilardone, Muriel, Isabelle Guérin and Jane Palier. 2014. "The weight of institutions on women's capabilities: how far can microfinance help?", in Flavio Comim and Martha C. Nussbaum, eds. *Capabilities, Gender, Equality: Towards Fundamental Entitlements.* Cambridge: Cambridge University Press.

Gobin, Vilas J, Santos, Paulo, and Toth, Russell. 2017. "No longer trapped? Promoting entrepreneurship through cash transfers to ultra-poor women in Northern Kenya." *American Journal of Agricultural Economics* 99.5: 1362–1383.

Goetz, Anne Marie, and Rina Sen Gupta. 1996. "Who takes the credit? Gender, power, and control over loan use in rural credit programs in Bangladesh." *World Development* 24.1: 45–63.

Grameen Bank, Historical Data from June 2015, www.grameen-info.org/monthly-reports-06–2015/. Accessed June 2015.

Haushofer, Johannes, and Shapiro, Jeremy. 2016. "The short-term impact of unconditional cash transfers to the poor: experimental evidence from Kenya." *Quarterly Journal of Economics* 131.4: 1973–2042.

Isserles, Robin. 2003. "Microcredit: the rhetoric of empowerment, the reality of 'development as usual'." *Women's Studies Quarterly* 31.3/4: 38–57.

Karim, Lamia. 2011. *Microfinance and its Discontents: Women in Debt in Bangladesh.* Minneapolis, MN: University of Minnesota Press.

Karlan, Dean, and Martin Valdivia. 2011. "Teaching entrepreneurship: impact of business training on microfinance clients and institutions". *The Review of Economics and Statistics* 93.2: 510–527.

Krishnan, Sankar. 2014. *The Power of Mobile Banking: How to Profit from the Revolution in Retail Financial Series?* (1st edn). Hoboken, NJ: Wiley.

Lacalle Calderón, Maricruz, Silvia Rico Garrido and Jaime Durán Navarro. 2008. "Estudio piloto de evaluación de impacto del programa de microcréditos de Cruz Roja Española en Ruanda." *Revista de Economía Mundial* 19: 83–104.

Le, Quan, and Peter Raven. 2015. "Teaching business skills to women: impact of business training on women's microenterprise owners in Vietnam." *International Journal of Entrepreneurial Behavior and Research* 21.4.

Lewis, Cindy. 2004. "Microfinance from the point of view of women with disabilities: lessons from Zambia and Zimbabwe." *Gender and Development* 12.1: 28–39.

MacFarquhar, Neil. 2010. "Banks Making Big Profits from Tiny Loans." *The New York Times*, 3 April.

Maksudova, Nargiza. 2010. "Macroeconomics of Microfinance: How Do the Channels Work?" (1 October). CERGE-EI Working Paper Series No. 423. www.ssrn.com/abstract=1699982. Accessed 28 November 2010.

Mayoux, Linda. 2001. "Tackling the down side: social capital, women's empowerment and micro-finance in Cameroon." *Development and Change* 32.3: 435–464.

Milana, Carlo, and Arvind Ashta. 2012. "Developing microfinance: a survey of the literature." *Strategic Change* 21.7–8: 299–330.

Moser, Caroline. 1993. *Gender Planning and Development.* London: Routledge.

Mosley, Paul. 2001. "Microfinance and poverty in Bolivia." *The Journal of Development Studies* 37.4: 101–132.

Owens, John. 2013. "Offering digital financial services to promote financial inclusion: lessons we've learned." *Innovations* 8.1–2: 271–282.

Pérez-Muñoz, Christian. 2017. "What is wrong with conditional cash transfer programs?" *Journal of social philosophy* 48.4: 440–460.

Roodman, David. 2012. *Due Diligence: An Impertinent Inquiry into Microfinance.* Washington, DC: Center for Global Development.

Sanyal, Paromita. 2009. "From credit to collective action: the role of microfinance in promoting women's social capital and normative influence." *American Sociological Review* 74.4: 529–550.

Schuler, Sidney Ruth, Syed M. Hashemi and Shamsul Huda Badal. 1998. "Men's violence against women in rural Bangladesh: undermined or exacerbated by microcredit programs?" *Development in Practice* 8.2: 148–157.

Selinger, Evan. 2009. "Does Microcredit 'Empower'? Reflections on the Grameen Bank Debate." *Human Studies* 31.1: 27–41.

Shimamura, Yasuharu, and Susana Lastarria-Cornhiel. 2010. "Credit program participation and child schooling in rural Malawi." *World Development* 38.4: 567–580.

Soekarno, Subiakto, and Setiawati, Marla. 2020. "Women and digital financial inclusion in Indonesia as emerging market." *International Review of Management and Marketing* 10.5: 46–49.

Terberger, Eva. 2013. "The Microfinance Approach: Does It Deliver on Its Promise?", in Doris Köhn, ed. *Microfinance 3.0. Reconciling Sustainability with Social Outreach and Responsible Delivery.* Heidelberg: Springer.

Tseng, Chuan Chia. 2011. *Microfinance and Amartya Sen's Capability Approach.* Diss. University of Birmingham.

Van Rooyen, Carina, Ruth Stewart and Thea de Wet. 2012. "The impact of microfinance in sub-Saharan Africa: a systematic review of the evidence." *World Development* 40.11: 2249–2262.

Waelde, Helke. 2011. "Demasking the impact of microfinance," Gutenberg School of Management and Economics, University of Mainz, Germany. www.macro.economics.unimainz.de/RePEc/pdf/Discussion_Paper_1115.pdf. Accessed 3 October 2016.

Yunus, Muhammad. 1999. *Banker to the Poor.* New York: Public Affairs.

Zeller, Manfred, and Manohar Sharma. 2000. "Many borrow, more save, and all insure: implications for food and micro-finance policy." *Food Policy* 25.2: 143–167.

# Conclusion

## Ethics and action – What should you do about global poverty?

*Benjamin Curtis and Serena Cosgrove*

### Learning objectives

- Summarize some important ethical principles in relation to reducing poverty.
- Compare and critique prominent arguments for why we should or should not work to reduce poverty.
- Evaluate concrete actions you can take to fight poverty at home and abroad.

### Introduction

If you are reading this book, you are most likely privileged and probably live in a high-income country. You hopefully have never experienced the deprivations of basic capabilities that constitute absolute poverty. But what kind of world would you want to live in if you *didn't* have a comfortable life? What would you think the world's moral obligations should be towards those living in poverty if you yourself were poor? The philosopher John Rawls (1999) famously proposed that we should evaluate standards of justice from the perspective of a "veil of ignorance." This perspective asks us to consider what kind of society we would want to be born into if we did not know what kinds of advantages we would have. If you did not know what your class, race, gender, sexual orientation, disability status, and income were going to be, then what societal arrangements would you insist on? How would you want rights and resources to be distributed?

Though the veil of ignorance test is typically applied to think about what justice might look like in a particular society, it can also fruitfully be applied on a worldwide level to consider standards of *global* justice. It is too easy for people living well in rich countries to disregard the ethical implications of poverty. If I have enough to eat, decent health, a middle-class income, and secure civil rights, how likely am I to sympathize with the plight of people who do not have those things? If we live comfortably, we may be ignorant or dismissive of the needs of the poor. Therefore, we need to think very carefully about our ethical duties in this world with widespread poverty and massive inequities. This topic has for decades provoked debates among philosophers, politicians, and development professionals. The debates, however, are not purely theoretical. They have a direct relevance to all sorts of poverty reduction policies, whether to alleviate a famine, to end a genocide, to intervene in a war, or to pursue projects that may alter a way of life.

It is essential to think through issues such as the veil of ignorance: considering how to reduce poverty also requires considering ethics. This book is founded upon a sometimes implicit, sometimes explicit ethics. Though we of course think it is imperative that everyone who reads this book – and everyone around the world – should work to reduce poverty, that perspective is complicated in terms of what one should do. There are so many questions to ask, such as: What do we owe people at a minimum? What do we owe people *beyond* the minimum? Who is the "we" that owes? When do we stop owing – is it when people have attained sufficiency or equality and, if so, of what? Of outcomes or opportunities? Such questions are considered in depth by development ethics, a subfield of development studies. Here we will examine only a few provocative issues and thinkers in this subfield, and provide few definitive answers, so further investigation is certainly warranted (see i.a. Crocker 2008, Drydyk and Keleher 2018, Gasper 2004). The chapter begins with an analysis of a number of ethical principles relevant to poverty reduction, then examines several debates about what individual and global ethical obligations should be. Finally, the chapter translates principles into action, suggesting what you personally can do to help reduce poverty.

## Ethical principles

Though development ethics is vital for helping to think through why and how we should work to reduce poverty, it does not always provide easy answers. Some of the answers, including a few we consider in this section, are challenging. But that is to be expected when the questions are themselves very difficult. One text on development ethics actually defines the field in terms of the questions it asks: development ethics "seeks to engage in debates around basic ethical questions: what are the costs of change and who bears them? How can we decide when costs are outweighed by gains? Who has the right to intervene, by what procedures, and to promote what ends? What is social improvement? What fundamental changes are desirable or undesirable?" (Penz *et al.* 2011: 36). Do not expect that any one of those questions will have a single right answer – what is "right" in any given situation may sometimes depend on the situation. However, some general principles should guide thinking on those questions. According to Penz *et al.*, "ethically responsible development" depends on seven essential values: human wellbeing and human security, equitable development, empowerment, cultural freedom (such as with the rights of indigenous peoples), environmental sustainability, human rights, and anti-corruption practices. These values have guided many of the topics and much of the discussion in this book, and we have explored their application to most of the poverty reduction programs we have highlighted.

However, these values are admittedly broad, and by no means exhaustive. An ethical consideration of the rationale for reducing poverty must plumb deeper to some basic principles of ethical action. We must ask, why do most people in high-income countries not care very much about the wellbeing of children in low-income countries? It is difficult to deny that this is the normal state of affairs. According to World Health Organization statistics, some 14,000 children die every day from causes related to poverty, which translates to ten children every minute. Why are more people not outraged by that fact? Were you aware of that number before you read this book? If you were not, then why not? If you read that statistic now and do not resolve to do something about it, why not? One simple answer to these questions is that it is often hard to care about people you do not know. We tend to feel few or no obligations to faceless people. This is a deeply rooted psychological reason for why more people are not outraged by the statistics on child mortality.

There is a more powerful reason, however, which relates to ethics: most people do not regard human lives as equal. Most people will regard the lives of children in their immediate community as more worth saving than the life of a child in some far-off, poverty-stricken country, with all the stereotypes that image provokes. Therefore, a bed-rock ethical principle in relation to poverty is that all people truly are equal, that their lives have equal value; call this "humanist egalitarianism" (Gilabert 2012: 9). An ethical global citizen recognizes the humanity of all people around the world and acknowledges the implications of equally valuing all humans' lives. One of those implications is that principles of global justice extend across humanity and bind all people to certain respon-sibilities. Where there is injustice, where there are people whose lives are being threatened by extreme poverty, then those who can help must help.

This global, moral responsibility to help people who are suffering can be motivated by two further principles: assistance and restitution. The assistance principle insists that because wealthier people around the world have the means, and poor people around the world have the need, the wealthy have a duty to help the poor (see Barry and Øverland 2009, Chatterjee 2004). The restitution principle asserts that wealthier people are actually doing things that harm poor people and exacerbate poverty, and therefore they have a duty to help those in need. The rationale and application of both these principles will be explored in greater detail below.

Global justice, whether impelled by the assistance or restitution principles, demands an effort to reduce poverty. In order for that effort to be ethical, in turn, it must involve three more principles: solidarity, non–elite participation, and decent sufficiency for all. These three principles were espoused by Dennis Goulet (2006), one of the founders of development ethics; they have also threaded throughout this entire book, and continue to play out in the discussion which follows. Solidarity means recognizing the equal value of all human lives, that the wellbeing of any one person is interdependent on the good of all people. In her scholarship on solidarity with Central America, Serena Cosgrove (forth-coming) writes, "solidarity involves listening to those who are oppressed, learning from them, and accompanying them in their struggle, which means doing everything possible to raise awareness and support a positive resolution of their grievances."

Practicing true solidarity entails a genuine and possibly difficult commitment (per the assistance principle) on the part of those who are well off. It means operationalizing and "institutionalizing the principle that the world's wealth belongs to all its inhabitants, on the basis of priority needs, not on geographical accident or on different technological abilities to extract or exploit resources that some groups enjoy over others" (Goulet 2006: 166–167). This amounts to a redistribution of global resources, such that those in high–income countries may have to give up some of their luxuries to ensure that the poor have equitable access to food, education, health care, and other basic entitlements. The implication of this principle is that the richest societies, and the people in those societies, may have to go on an austerity diet: we may have to accept reductions in our standard of living in order to raise the standard for the poor.

The next of Goulet's principles, "non–elite participation," means that reducing poverty involves empowering poor people. The participation of poor people must be sought not just to help guide development projects. They must be able to make decisions for their own societies, families, and bodies; they must be fully empowered so that they can choose a life that they have reason to value. Recall that one of the definitions of poverty is lacking that power in certain key areas. It follows, then, that a fundamental ethical principle is for poor people to participate in efforts to address their own poverty. The poor must never be mere objects of poverty reduction programs: they must be *subjects* in those programs, with their own agency and voice included. It is not just about having the basic resources one needs to survive: it is also about participation and access to power. Finally, "decent suffi-ciency" entails that everyone will have equitable access to the resources that can ensure human wellbeing such as food, shelter, medicine, etc. This principle entails a minimum threshold of resources so that no one is poor, and a minimum threshold of rights and/or capabilities. A world where everyone has enough of the resources essential for a dignified human life is a world where no one is denied basic capabilities to live the life they choose. It is also a world, in Goulet's framing, whose inhabitants will live more sustainably, so that resources and opportunities will be adequately guaranteed not just for this generation but for future ones as well.

These principles ground the fundamental claim that people in poverty must be assisted, that injustice must be righted. How, though, should justice and injustice be defined? One powerful way is via human rights. International humanitarian law and the Universal Declaration of Human Rights lay out the different civil, political, social, cultural, and eco-nomic rights to which all people are entitled. These include familiar civil and political rights such as the freedoms of speech and assembly, prohibitions against torture, and the right to vote. As we mentioned in Chapter 1 and have suggested throughout this book, there are other guarantees besides, including rights to education, shelter, health care, and access to employment. When countries sign the international treaties framing human rights and join the United Nations (which has certain human rights guarantees as part of its charter), they are obligated to respect and protect those rights within their own boundaries. Human rights thus involve a substantial body of agreed-upon norms as well as various international institutions to promote those rights (Nickel 2007). Ensuring that everyone enjoys the "decent sufficiency" of basic human rights is a vital way of defining global justice.

Human rights are not merely legal provisions, however, nor do the relevant obligations fall solely on countries. Human rights have a moral force beyond any formal legal commitments. This goes back to the idea of the fundamental equality of all human beings. Basic morality insists that we not torture, that we not let people starve, that we not deprive them of political agency, dignity, or the possibilities of earning a livelihood. Because of this inherent moral force of human rights, individuals have a duty to respect and protect them. Thus, a just society, and a just person, works to uphold human rights – and injustice means violating those rights. In many ways, as this book has argued, poverty violates basic human rights. Therefore, we *all* have a duty to fight poverty.

## Debates about ethical obligations

It might seem easy to acknowledge that duty in an abstract, non-committal way: sure, extreme poverty and gross inequality are deplorable, and we should do something about them. But the admonishment to "do something" is far too vague. We need to move beyond lazy slogans. Anyone reading this book should aspire to think more deeply about both their obligations to reduce poverty and the actions they can take to that end. Thinking more deeply requires considering arguments and counter-arguments about those obligations. This section surveys several relevant debates without, however, offering final adjudications on which perspectives are "right." Though some arguments here are stronger than others, readers should think through their own evaluation of the contending perspectives.

To begin with, Peter Singer (2019) has posed a famous thought problem about a drowning toddler, which forces us to interrogate our commitment to the ethic of assistance. This is the scenario: you have just bought a pair of very expensive shoes, and you are out for a walk in the park. You come across a toddler drowning in a pond, and you are the only person around who can save the child. Getting to him in time means you run into the water and ruin your new shoes. Probably everyone will say yes, they would save the toddler rather than their new shoes. That is the morally justifiable answer. However, Singer claims that almost everyone in the rich world every day chooses to save their shoes. His point is that for the amount of money we spend on a luxury item such as designer shoes, or a nice restaurant, or an expensive vacation, we could easily save a poor child's life. And yet very few of us will give up that vacation or new pair of shoes or fancy phone.

The fact that so many people in high-income countries shirk the ethic of assistance has led Singer to propose a reasonable "giving scale." This standard calculates how much money you should give to reduce poverty, based on your total annual income. While most people in affluent countries can afford to give something, Singer insists that the richest need to give the most and, if they did, they could easily provide enough money to end extreme poverty around the world. For example, according to Singer's calculations, if the top ten percent of income earners in the United States gave away just one percent of their income, it would raise hundreds of billions of dollars, enough to end extreme poverty globally. While it is easy for those who are not rich to claim that wealthy individuals need to pitch in more than they do, even those of moderate incomes are not off the hook. If we could skimp on some of the indulgences we enjoy in order to help the poor but we choose not to, then "we are doing something wrong" Singer says (2019: 48). Singer's basic principle is that we have a duty to reduce suffering when we can do so at a minimal cost to ourselves.

If Singer's ideas compel us to consider more deeply our obligations to assist those in poverty, Thomas Pogge (2008) pushes even further with an argument relying on reparations or what he calls "the restitution principle," which holds that we have a duty to reduce poverty because we are responsible for creating it. Pogge sees poverty as a human rights violation in which nearly everyone living in high-income countries is complicit. As Pogge explains, "we are *harming* the poor if and insofar as we collaborate in imposing an *unjust* global institutional order upon them. And this institutional order is definitely unjust if and insofar as it foreseeably perpetuates large-scale human rights deficits that would be reasonably avoidable through feasible institutional modifications" (Pogge 2005a: 5). Pogge argues that there are hundreds of millions of people who are being denied basic rights, living in conditions below what a fair, proportional distribution of resources among the world's population should be. Why do some have so much and others have so little? It relates back to the idea of structural violence mentioned in Chapter 1. Pogge argues that global institutions have been designed to benefit the rich (which includes all of us who live in high-income countries) and disadvantage the poor.

Pogge bases his argument that the richer countries have systematically impoverished the global south on several points. First, rich countries are rich in part because of massive historical injustices such as colonialism, which made many exploited parts of the world poorer, such as Sub-Saharan Africa and other former colonies. Second, history aside, rich countries are harming poor people right now. They do so through the institutional economic order that reproduces the "radical inequality" in the global distribution of resources (Pogge 2005a: 4). The rich countries largely control the World Trade Organization (WTO), which enforces protectionist trade barriers including tariffs, quotas, anti-dumping mandates, and subsidies to domestic producers that favor rich countries. WTO rules also limit poorer countries' access to drugs, software, seeds, and biological technologies that could reduce poverty. Global institutions create trade relations disadvantageous to poorer countries by compelling them to open up their markets to rich countries' exports, while doing much less to open rich countries' markets to poorer countries' exports.

In Pogge's view, the global economic order is structured through international negotiations "in which our governments enjoy a crushing advantage in bargaining power and expertise" over poorer countries (Pogge 2007: 27). According to McNeill and St. Clair (2009), organizations such as the WTO and the World Bank actively resist arrangements more favorable to poorer countries because the powerful northern elite that controls those organizations wants to protect its own interests. Finally, Pogge alleges that the antidemocratic and corrupting effects of the resource curse are in large part the fault of rich countries. The economies of rich countries consume resources from low-income countries, but payments for those resources rarely benefit the poorest people in those countries. Instead, payments typically just benefit local elites, and rich countries care very little whether rulers in those countries are democratic. Rulers in countries whose economies are highly dependent on natural resources sometimes oppress their people, which in turn creates situations where the people have to resist with force, leading to armed conflict that exacerbates poverty.

We should not assume that only distant international institutions are guilty: the guilt also falls on us because we in the rich world are partly responsible for the policies that our national governments take. Pogge explains that "the fact that we choose to remain ignorant, choose to allow important structural features of the world economy to be shaped by unknown bureaucrats in secret negotiations cannot negate our responsibility for the harms that our governments inflict upon the innocent" (Pogge 2005b: 79). Therefore, we have a duty to influence our national governments and to lobby international organizations to create a global institutional order that is more just for the poor. While we should work for institutions that do not violate human rights, we must also provide financial compensation for the harm we have caused. This means that governments in the global north should provide restitution to countries in the global south. Individuals, too, have a duty here. Pogge does not go as far as Singer in specifying the amounts that people must contribute, but he claims that it should be easy to raise the roughly USD 300 billion he calculates it would take to eradicate extreme poverty.

Pogge's perspective is certainly provocative, and not surprisingly it has attracted a fair amount of criticism (Jaggar 2010, Schweickart 2008, Vizard 2006). For example, critics retort that Pogge does not make a meaningful distinction between when global institutions actively harm the poor, or when they simply fail to reduce poverty adequately. The idea is that a failure to reduce poverty is not morally equivalent to actively causing poverty. Another criticism holds that Pogge puts too much blame on countries in the global north, failing to hold countries in the global south accountable for good governance. Pogge, though, explains that problem through the metaphor of a "strong headwind" in which "national policies and institutions are indeed often quite bad; but the fact that they are can be traced to global policies and institutions" (Pogge 2008: 149). As another means of questioning this perspective, remember the debate on foreign aid in Chapter 2. It is possible that the idea to raise USD 300 billion for poverty eradication is not the best option because aid money may be spent inefficiently.

Some thinkers would counter Pogge by rejecting both the ethics of assistance and restitution. Among the most famous cases in development ethics is the debate Garrett Hardin waged in the 1970s with Peter Singer (among others) over "lifeboat ethics." Hardin (1974) insisted that we have a duty *not* to help the poor because doing so will only increase suffering. Hardin constructed a metaphor in which rich countries are like lifeboats, and swimming in the sea around the lifeboats, trying to get in, are the poor people of the world. What should the lifeboat passengers do in this situation? The way Hardin sets up the problem is to stipulate that the lifeboat can only carry 60 people, and it already has 50 people inside. There are a hundred people swimming in the sea. If you could only save ten of them, how would you choose which people to save? In Hardin's view, any choice you make will be problematic. If you try to let too many people crowd onto your lifeboat, they will overwhelm the carrying capacity, and you will all drown. According to Hardin, the most defensible choice is to keep only the 50 people in the boat and let no more in, since that will give the best possibility of survival for those already in the boats. If you feel guilty about not helping those poor people swimming in the sea, then Hardin says you need to get out of the lifeboat: give up your place to one of the swimmers, and go swim yourself.

Hardin referred specifically to food aid, though his argument is relevant to poverty reduction efforts more generally. In his view, countries such as Bangladesh were overpopulated and needed to bring their populations down. Every new mouth to feed in countries with weak economies and high rates of population growth means that there are fewer resources for the people already alive. This assumes that available resources are not expanding quickly enough to meet the needs of the growing population. The growing population makes everyone's life worse, and therefore the population needs to stop growing. Famine (i.e. letting people die) could halt that growth, resulting in a sustainable population size. Aid, in contrast, would only worsen the situation by keeping people alive who would be dependent on handouts, which moreover would encourage poor people to continue having children, resulting in yet more mouths that they could not adequately feed. His conclusion was that rich countries should not undertake aid projects that only put further pressure on limited resources, thereby threatening to sink the existing lifeboats.

Hardin also denies the ethic of restitution by claiming that we do not have intergenerational obligations for past injustices. Even if our ancestors may have perpetrated colonialism, that does not mean that people today owe restitution. "We are all the descendants of thieves," Hardin claims, and "we cannot remake the past." Given those facts, and that the world's resources have been fundamentally inequitably distributed, "we must begin the journey to tomorrow from the point where we are today. […] We cannot safely divide the wealth equitably among all peoples so long as people reproduce at different rates. To do so would guarantee that our grandchildren and everyone else's grandchildren would have only a ruined world to inhabit" (1974). Thus, Hardin makes a surprising argument relating to sustainability: the wellbeing of future generations depends upon *not* helping the poor today.

Since he wrote his essay on lifeboat ethics, many of Hardin's assumptions have been proven wrong, though his questioning of obligations to fight global poverty still resonates for some. Bangladesh's population is actually larger now than it was in the 1970s, yet it is not experiencing a famine.[1] In contrast to Hardin's prediction, aid did not worsen the situation. Nonetheless, there are still people, such as acolytes of the philosopher Ayn Rand, who insist that helping the poor simply makes them dependent, thereby perpetuating poverty. In this view, because charitable assistance can do more harm than good, it is not a moral duty. A different strain within political philosophy claims that redistribution and justice are only relevant within a state – so the duty to help the poor applies within your own country, but not globally (see Blake and Smith 2013, Nagel 2005).

These last two perspectives clash with one final argument we will consider, which justifies action on global poverty based on self-interest rather than ethics. Paul Collier has argued that the wellbeing of people in richer countries is threatened by a situation in which hundreds of millions of people worldwide live in extreme poverty. The rich world is threatened by fragile states that can harbor terrorists, such as in Afghanistan; threatened by armed conflict that spills over borders, breeding destruction, political and economic instability; threatened by outbreaks of disease in countries lacking the resources to deal with them, such as Ebola in Sierra Leone; and threatened by massive population movements spurred by climate shocks, war, or economic migration. The problem of global poverty matters, Collier writes, "and not just to the billion people who are living and dying in fourteenth-century conditions. It matters to us. The twenty-first century world of material comfort, global travel, and economic interdependence will become increasingly vulnerable to these large islands of chaos" (Collier 2007: 4–5). According to this argument, poverty, its discontents, and the bad institutions associated with it will increasingly put at risk even those of us living complacently in the rich world. Therefore, to help ourselves, we must help those in poverty.

## What should you do?

Whether you find most compelling the arguments about the ethics of assistance or restitution, or the self-interest motivation, they all urge us to take action to reduce poverty. Indeed, libertarian or social Darwinist perspectives of Hardin's ilk notwithstanding, it is very difficult to deny the moral imperative to help people who are in extreme poverty. Is it not a basic humanitarian duty to aid those who are desperate? If you accept that we all have moral obligations here, then how can you do your part to reduce global poverty? There are actually many different things you can do, and some of them are easy enough that it is hard to justify doing nothing. Our list proceeds on a scale from a relatively simple engagement to actions that demand a deeper, ongoing commitment to promoting global justice. You should determine what you will do based on your own resources, values, aspirations, and conscience.

### *Give money*

This is the easiest, most common recommendation for helping to reduce poverty, and it is a reasonable place to start. Giving money to an organization working either in your home country or abroad is something that almost everyone can afford to do. For example, if a few times a week you go to Starbucks or eat out for lunch, consider skipping one of those times and putting the money aside to donate. Over a month, giving up one coffee a week will add up, and over a year, it could add up to a respectable donation. Peter Singer urges everyone to give *at least* 1 percent of their annual net income to charities, though those with higher incomes should give more. The website www.thelifeyoucansave.org/take-the-pledge has a calculator for how much you should donate to charity based on your income. Besides your individual giving, you can also form a giving circle and/or motivate other people in your network to give. A giving circle is a group of people who agree to donate to a common cause. Giving circles help to raise larger donations for an organization, and they can strengthen the donors' commitment both to the cause and to making regular donations. You can also encourage other people to give just by talking about the organizations you believe in and why you think it is important to donate. You do not have to be aggressive: people are often swayed by example, so if you donate regularly and generously and are open about it, you can influence other people to be more generous as well.

---

**Box 13.1 Poverty and basic humanity**

In Chapter 1, we promised to return to two fundamental questions in the Conclusion. The first was the question of what counts as the basic minimum capabilities necessary for an adequate human life. The second was the question of what it means to be a human living in poverty. Most of the chapters have considered these questions in one way or another, and though we would not pretend to arrive at conclusive answers to such big and fundamental issues, we can offer a few final thoughts.

If you have read all the preceding chapters, does it seem like there are, could be, or should be basic capabilities with minimum universal standards? Would it be possible for the world to agree upon such standards? It is possible that the answer is "no," that ideas of an adequate human life simply differ too much from culture to culture, society to society, ever to allow for universal definitions. Note, however, that some universal standards *have* been adopted. Take the Universal Declaration on Human Rights, for instance: dozens of countries around the world have ratified the core provisions of this declaration, though there are indeed countries that have abstained or agreed to only some of the rights in the list. Nonetheless, the valorized body of international human rights law suggests substantial agreement on basic entitlements that no human being should be deprived of.

If human rights seem too abstract to serve as measures for poverty reduction, then consider the Sustainable Development Goals. The detailed lists of very specific indicators have also been agreed upon by nearly all of the world's countries. This means, for example, that there is an effectively universal belief at the global level that everyone should attain a minimum of food consumption, that everyone should complete primary school, that all children should be able to be immunized against measles, that everyone who has HIV/AIDS should have access to treatment, and that everyone should have access to safe drinking water. The Multidimensional Poverty Index is another widely respected measurement tool based upon minimum thresholds, and it was directly inspired by ideas of fundamental entitlements that can support basic capabilities.

Inevitably there will be disputes about which capabilities are "basic." In many countries around the world there is disagreement about whether women should have reproductive rights including access to birth control and abortion. Certainly, in practice, many societies do not guarantee freedoms of speech, association, or religion. And within reason, minimum standards can be societally specific. However, in our view, there are incontrovertibly some capabilities that every human being must be guaranteed, so that no one falls below minimum thresholds in key areas such as health, education, and political rights. The world has already agreed on many of these areas and many of the indicators. Although there is still room for debate on some details, societally specific variation should not be an excuse to resist minimum guarantees for all human beings.

The reason is that, despite cultural differences, there is also broad agreement on what constitutes basic humanity. Qizilbash emphasizes that "there is some notion of a distinctly *human* life, which crosses culture and time, and this must guide us in formulating the precise standards for what is basic to any human flourishing" (1998: 12). Philosophers have of course argued for millennia over what defines a human life. But one powerful idea is that humanity depends in part on dignity. Dignity is something inherent to all human beings, something we all want for ourselves, something that makes our life precious (Bernardini 2010). It is a worth we all have simply by virtue of being human. For Nussbaum, dignity means "being endowed with capacities for activity and striving" (2008). It means being able to enjoy certain fundamental freedoms of action, key opportunities to shape one's own life.

To be a human living in poverty, then, means that you are denied basic capabilities to which every human being is entitled. Living in poverty often means a denial of your dignity, since dignity includes being able to exercise agency and freedom. And when your dignity is denied, so too is your humanity, since being human means having dignity. In this way, poverty is an affront to the very definition of being human. This is not to imply that people in poverty are in any way "less human." Quite the contrary: the poor are human beings just like the rest of us, they are our brothers and sisters, but they are deprived of the opportunities to realize a fully flourishing human life that everyone should enjoy. Every human's life is equal, and predicated on a fundamental dignity, which means having the basic capabilities to live a valued life. Poverty deprives us of those capabilities, of that dignity, and therefore robs us of an important aspect of our humanity.

How can you find a good organization to give to? We recommend that you first identify an issue that you really care about. Perhaps from reading this book you have latched on to the issue of global health, or women's rights, or education. Whatever the issue might be, think about what you are most committed to, and then identify the organizations that work on that issue. We have mentioned many commendable organizations in this book, from Pratham to Catholic Relief Services to PATH. You should research any organization you are interested in to find out more about its activities. That research can be as in-depth as you want it to be, such as exploring the details of the organization's website including its annual reports, or it can be relatively easy. A simple way of evaluating an organization is to check out its listing at sites such as www.givewell.org, www.charitynavigator.org, or www.guidestar.org. Such sites offer ratings systems partly inspired by the trend of "effective altruism," which seeks to create evidence-based strategies to evaluate the most impactful ways of improving the world (Singer 2015). You should be aware of critics' claims that such ratings systems overemphasize how much organizations spend for programs versus administrative or fundraising costs. Nonetheless, the three sites listed above are all reputable and useful. Finally, if you have no strong preference as to an issue or organization, then consult the list of recommended organizations at www.thelifeyoucansave.org and www.givewell.org.

### Make different choices

You can also help fight poverty by making different choices in your daily life about how you consume. Remember that people in high-income countries consume planetary resources at a drastically more intensive rate than do people in lower-income countries.

We thereby contribute to the radical inequities in the distribution of those resources. Hence, we need to change how we consume. To begin with, pollution from humans' carbon consumption is partially responsible for climate change; therefore, drive less, if possible. Take public transportation more. Also, make sure that you recycle and re-use. Many communities now have respectable recycling programs. Encourage your friends, family, school, and/or workplace to participate in those programs. Better yet, work to expand those programs. Does your community separate yard waste and food scraps from other trash for use as compost? Doing so is another way of reducing the amount of garbage that goes to landfills and, hopefully, consuming more sustainably. Consuming more sustainably also means making other choices, such as eating less meat. Huge industrial cattle, pig, and chicken farms are often responsible for heavy water use and pollution, not to mention cruel conditions for the animals. If everyone in the world ate as much beef as North Americans do, the strain on the planet's resources would be unsupportable. Even if you do not go full vegan, eating a more plant-based diet has many positive impacts, for others and yourself. You can consider working in other ways, too, for a more just and sustainable food system. Get involved with a community garden, for instance, to help support more local agriculture and food sources.

When you shop, seek out fair trade products. Fair trade is a standard promoting greater equity in international trade by improving conditions for marginalized producers and workers in the global south particularly. Look for products that are labelled fair trade, whether coffee, bananas, chocolate, flowers, or many others. Ten Thousand Villages is a fair trade retailer with shops throughout North America, as well as an online portal where you can buy many different fair trade-certified items such as jewelry, clothes, and furniture. You may also consider buying from companies that operate on a "buy one, give one" business model. The idea behind this model – whose most famous exponents include Toms Shoes and Warby Parker eyewear – is that for every purchase you make, the company donates a product to a needy person or community. While this strategy can be beneficial, it has also drawn much criticism, so you should research the particular company you are buying from and its donation practices. Finally, consider consuming less by doing a "buy nothing" day (or week), once a year or even more often. Encourage other people in your social network to consume less. It is true that your consumption choices may not immediately better the lives of poor people. However, the point is to adopt practices that make you a more considerate global citizen, aware of and committed to acting in the interests of the poor at home and around the world. Working for a more just society really can start with something as simple as eating less meat and dairy.

### Volunteer

While giving money is something nearly everyone can do, giving time involves a deeper commitment. Active work to reduce poverty and promote social justice has the power to make more visible change – not just for the poor, but for you too. Volunteering for an organization can help it reach its goals of improving people's lives. Volunteering can also give you experience and skills, and the transformative experience of working for the benefit of others. For this reason, we believe that if you possibly can, you should *always* volunteer. As with many of our recommendations, you can strive to make this a lifelong habit. The admonition to "think globally, act locally" fits in here. You might not be able to work to reduce poverty in some far-off country on a regular basis. However, you can routinely give your time and energy to an organization with projects abroad. Or you can give your time and energy to an organization that works to fight poverty in your own community.

Volunteering can be relatively uncomplicated, such as working an hour or two a week at a local soup kitchen, or tutoring kids at a high-needs school a few times a month. Your commitment can go much deeper, too, such as by helping an organization with whatever basic, unglamorous tasks it consistently needs like cleaning or maintenance; by contributing specialized skills you might have, such as accounting, marketing, or social media; or by contributing expertise (and usually fundraising assistance) through serving on an organization's advisory board. How do you find worthy volunteer opportunities? Often a university will have a community service office to partner with organizations that need volunteers. Alternatively, United Way is a community network operating throughout North America; consult your local branch's website for its list of local organizations with volunteer opportunities. Idealist.org is another site with many searchable, localized volunteer opportunities. Or if you are interested in volunteering abroad, www.volunteerinternational.org is a good place to start.

### Study programs

If you are reading this book, you may already be embarked upon a study program connected to poverty or global development. Regardless, we hope that this book is only a beginning for your engagement with these issues. Keep learning about poverty, what causes it, and how to reduce it. Consider pursuing a major relevant to international development, social work, sociology, or another topic that can lead to a career working for justice. Besides a formal course of study, keep learning by reading reputable news sources such as the *New York Times* or the *Economist* – follow the news outside of your home country, pay attention to events in the global south, read articles that deal with poverty and injustice. Follow a good blog or Twitter feed of organizations such as CARE, Oxfam, or the Center for Global Development. Look at the "Online resources" and "Further reading" suggestions in the chapters throughout this book to continue exploring the topics that most interest you. Go to lectures at your local university or sponsored by other organizations in your community. Many cities in the United States have a World Affairs Council, for instance, which routinely feature interesting speakers knowledgeable about global development topics.

It is also extremely important to study global poverty by spending time in a developing country, if you can. There is no substitute for talking with people who have endured poverty, and learning first-hand about their lives, troubles, successes, and aspirations. Particularly if you want to pursue a career in international development, you must develop intercultural competencies, that is, working across difference, and gain international experience. Consider learning a second or third language. You should study abroad, whether in formal university courses or by doing an international internship. Generally speaking, the more time you spend abroad, the more you will learn. However, there are also shorter-term opportunities. Many universities offer short, intensive courses that take students abroad to engage in issues central to this book. Global Brigades is a large, student-led sustainable development organization that offers valuable study and service-learning programs doing international development work. Global Visionaries is an organization with programs in Central America for high-school and gap-year students, and there are many similar outfits. You could also consider the "reality tours" offered by

Global Exchange, which are open to a wide age range and focus on specific issues such as human rights in the countries visited.

### Pursue a career

It may be that, as a result of your studies, volunteering experiences, and lifestyle choices you feel a calling to work professionally to reduce poverty. While many of our recommendations in this section are focused on actions you can take in the short and medium terms, pursuing a relevant career is a long-term strategy. Keep in mind that anti-poverty work does not necessarily mean being on the "front lines" ministering to destitute mothers and children. Because poverty is multi-dimensional, jobs in many different sectors – law, health, education, politics, science, social services, business, or finance, to name a few – can contribute to poverty reduction. For instance, people with a law degree can work to secure voting rights, or to craft legislation that supports the capabilities of people from marginalized minority groups. People who want to combine business with anti-poverty work might look into social enterprise, that is, entrepreneurial activities that can both turn a profit but also produce positive social impacts. If you are interested in biology or chemistry, consider how you can contribute to combatting neglected diseases that primarily affect people in lower-income countries. Careers in the more "traditional" anti-poverty areas of public health, education, or social work are certainly important, but it is worth thinking creatively about how you can combine your professional life with efforts to promote social justice. The possibilities are wide-ranging; what we suggest is to decide which professional opportunities you find most engaging, then research potentially relevant social impact jobs.

If you are in a stage of life where you are considering career possibilities, one of the best things you can do is to network with people who actually have jobs you might be interested in. Talk to friends, family, or professors to see if they can introduce you to someone. Search on LinkedIn for any connections to people or organizations that might agree to do an informational interview with you about job opportunities. Universities typically have careers offices that would be glad to help you, and alumni networks can provide useful connections. The Appendix to this book features advice for those considering careers specifically in international development. We interviewed a number of professionals with long experience in development and/or humanitarian assistance to get their perspectives on work in their fields. They offer insights on the kinds of skills you should acquire, study programs worth pursuing, trends to be aware of, and pitfalls to avoid.

### Educate

If you have devoted real energy to learning about global poverty – by reading this book, by taking various classes, by doing development work abroad, or by whatever other means – then another way you can work to combat poverty is by educating others. Talk to your family, your friends, your co-workers, any community groups you belong to. What do you tell them? Open with what you find compelling. Explain to them that poverty is best conceived as the deprivation of fundamental freedoms, the denial of basic capabilities to which we are all entitled. Explain how poverty is multi-dimensional and needs to be measured not just by income but by a range of other indicators in health, education, and civil rights. Talk about what good development looks like, and examples of effective poverty reduction programs. Mention why empowering women, girls, and others on the margins is so important for reducing poverty, and how that can be accomplished. Give the rationales from this chapter for why we all have a responsibility to reduce poverty – encourage people in your social networks to think about their own ethical obligations in relation to suffering and injustice around the globe. Combat the common misunderstandings that one hears so often when uninformed people talk about poverty. People are not poor just because they are lazy, assistance does not merely make them dependent, poverty is not mainly a result of cultural pathologies, foreign aid does not always go down a rat hole, people cannot just lift themselves up by their own bootstraps to get out of poverty, and so on. Remind people that there are universal human rights and basic capabilities that are violated not only abroad but at home, too.

Educating others about poverty does not mean that you have to become a professional teacher, though that would certainly be a commendable career ambition. Nor does it mean that you have to be a hectoring nuisance who annoys everyone by bringing up poverty at every family meal. Be informed, judicious, and strategic. If in conversation friends or family are expressing ignorant things about poverty, share examples with them from this book or your own reading and experience. Be prepared to provide a compelling argument and evidence for your more informed perspective. Suggest an article or book that people might read – or share an article when you come across a good one. Every so often, instead of watching an entertaining but shallow popcorn movie with a group, watch something that actually deals with issues related to global poverty, whether it is a documentary or fiction, and then spark a discussion about those issues. Demonstrate leadership and organize a documentary or speaker event at your school, workplace, or community group. The objective is to give other people the chance to learn some of the same things that you have learned about global poverty, and there are many ways to accomplish that goal.

### Advocate

If you are ready to push your engagement with poverty issues to a still deeper level, then you need to start talking to people in power. Educate public officials about poverty and what you think should be done about it. For all the outsize role that rich donors play particularly in American politics, many politicians will still listen to you even if you are not rich, especially if you are a voter in their district. Do a search to determine which politicians represent your local area. You can focus on the municipal level, the state/provincial/regional level, and/or the national level. Call or visit your politicians' offices, send them an email or a letter. Sending a personal email or letter (i.e. not a form letter) is most likely to get attention. Go to city hall meetings or other public forums where policy that can impact poverty is being discussed. Then speak up! It is not hard to make your voice heard, and you truly can make an impact even as one individual.

What should you tell your politicians? At the most general level, you could urge them to increase funding to support anti-poverty programs worldwide. The United States, in particular, is a laggard here. In a 2015 poll, Americans guessed that 26 percent of the federal budget goes to foreign aid.[2] That guess is wildly inaccurate; the correct answer is less than one percent. Shamefully, most wealthy countries fall far below the internationally valorized target of spending 0.7 percent of their gross national income on development assistance. The United States only spends 0.17 percent, far below the UK (at 0.7), or Norway and Sweden, which give over 0.9 percent.[3] Beyond increasing funding, you can get more specific with your advocacy. Tell politicians to decrease subsidies for agribusiness, which are often grossly unfair to farmers in the global south. As one famous example, it was estimated that thanks to subsidies the average cow in the European Union earned around USD 2.20 a day, which meant that European cows were earning more than one billion human beings living on less than two dollars a day.[4] Similarly outrageous stories could be told about agricultural policies throughout most high-income countries. Advocate not just for more funding for health and education programs abroad, but remember the needs of people in your own community and country. Push for equitable education funding for children in disadvantaged areas, mental health programs, shelters, and low-income housing for the homeless, vocational training to help those who are unemployed. Oxfam is an organization that often does excellent advocacy work – pay attention to its campaigns and get involved when you can.

### *Agitate*

If you are willing to educate and advocate for global justice, then you may be willing to agitate for it as well. Agitating means not just learning, not just caring, not just speaking up. It means working actively to make a positive change. It means taking some risks, challenging entrenched and complacent power structures. It means making a more profound, lasting commitment to change. It means taking on leadership roles and building coalitions for collective impact. Agitating means protesting against forms of injustice whether in your own backyard or far away. You might participate in a march for human rights or stage a rally against unethical corporations. You might launch a campaign to encourage your university to divest from fossil fuel industries. You might lead protests against income inequality or for immigration reform or racial justice. You might join an existing organization such as Oxfam, RESULTS, One.org or InterAction and work in their campaigns. You might create a new group that focuses on a specific poverty issue that you care deeply about. You might start a social enterprise that can respond to a carefully determined community need. You might spend a period of time living in solidarity with people marginalized by poverty or discrimination. Doing this kind of work to promote justice means that you must think deeply about what really matters to you, and what kind of life you want to live. There are many different ways you can be a "changemaker," and though none of them may be easy, probably nothing else in life is more rewarding than when you give yourself and your energies to help other people.

What do you agitate for? Besides whatever specific issue(s) to which you might dedicate your activism, we urge you to remember that reducing poverty ultimately depends on supporting people to gain their freedoms. These are the fundamental freedoms of the basic capabilities, all of which lead to the most important freedom, which is the freedom to live a life that one has reason to value. Because we are human beings, we are all entitled to basic rights such as minimum standards of housing, health, education, control over our own bodies, and political agency. These capabilities are basic because they make all sorts of other valuable choices possible. Take just one example: girls' education. Education, remember, promotes better health outcomes. It helps people have more secure economic livelihoods. It leads to greater support for democracy and tolerance for diversity. Education combats ignorance, which is a form of poverty. Education empowers – it helps support a girl's freedom to choose a life for herself.

What are other actions you might consider? With whom might you join forces? It is worthwhile to reflect on your privilege and how you can give back. Maybe your spiritual or religious community – temple, church, synagogue, mosque, etc. – has activities to generate compassion and service. Maybe your workplace has an anti-poverty program you can join or support. However you get involved, anti-poverty work requires changes in both the discourse about poverty and in practical policy approaches. These changes are happening in many places. For example, about half the countries in the world have a right to health care in their constitutions. Some, such as South Africa, even have constitutional rights regarding basic shelter. The US Constitution recognizes neither of these rights. Among many politicians as well as the general public, this change in discourse and policy practice has yet to occur. They have not learned that global justice insists that whatever basic rights we want for ourselves we must guarantee to everyone around the world, and vice versa. Our objective as a moral community of human beings must be that no one anywhere lives in the absolute poverty defined by the deprivation of those basic rights and capabilities.

## Conclusion

Studying global poverty, it is possibly unavoidable and probably essential to consider global justice. Any sincere effort to think about how to reduce poverty requires an ethical framework. That ethical framework can provide the fundamental motivation for poverty reduction, even if there are different and not always congruent ethical perspectives on this issue. As we have seen, some writers argue from the assistance ethic: in effect, people around the world who are suffering from poverty are part of our human family and, as such, we should do for them what we would do for a family member who is suffering. Other writers emphasize the restitution ethic. The former colonial powers and the leading countries of the global north have benefited so much from the global south – through cheap primary commodities, cheap labor, and cheap products – that they have structured the international system to preserve their own advantages, which actually creates poverty. There is also the legal and moral framework of human rights treaties that commit our governments (and urge us as individuals) to prevent violations to those rights posed by poverty and suffering. Finally, the self-interest argument holds that if you live comfortably in a high-income country, and you want to continue to enjoy that life, then you must work to reduce global poverty. Otherwise, conflict, terrorism, disease outbreaks, and mass migrations from poorer countries will put your lifestyle at risk.

These are all big, broad arguments for why we should work to reduce poverty, but they give us relatively little ethical guidance for *how* to reduce it. For that guidance, we must rely on the principles of solidarity, non-elite participation, and decent sufficiency for all. These principles underlie ethically responsible development, which in turn must be based on standards of equity, empowerment, cultural freedom, environmental sustainability, and human wellbeing. Even with all these ideas in mind, we should remember that doing poverty reduction and development work is hard. This is one reason why some writers insist that intervention will only prolong suffering, especially because northern countries sometimes get it wrong. It is important to acknowledge this perspective too. Well-intentioned but naïve meddling in people's lives, helping them to eat for one day while failing to address long-term structural causes of poverty, is a stopgap solution that does not remove systemic barriers. Nonetheless, we prefer to err on the side of action rather than inaction. All human lives are equal, and the ethos of humanist egalitarianism demands that we try to prevent avoidable suffering. Where human rights are being violated, where people are being denied basic capabilities to lead lives that they value, then we have a responsibility to act.

You of course must make your own choices, even if it is to do nothing, to remain complacent. What you should not do is *not* decide. You should ask yourself: what am I going to do? Given the massive injustices in the world, at home and abroad, what are you going to do about them? Whatever you decide, you should make a commitment. Write down what you are going to do. Do not be vague – be specific as to exactly what you will do. Plan for how you will accomplish whatever you have written down. If you write it down, you are more likely to commit, and more likely to follow through. After you have written it down, then tell someone else about your commitment. Make your commitment public. Decide to take action, and then carry it out. Fanciful as it may seem, it is true that one person can make a difference. You do not have to change the world; perhaps all you have to do is change yourself. Ultimately, we can all be part of a solution to global poverty, and if we are good global citizens, we all have an obligation to do so.

## Discussion questions

1   What are some ethical, moral, and political reasons for fighting poverty? Choose a particular issue relevant to poverty and develop a set of arguments you would use to persuade someone about the importance of this goal. What counter-arguments can you anticipate?
2   What are some different potential meanings of "global justice" that you take from this chapter?
3   What would you do in Hardin's lifeboat scenario? What is your reaction to this line of argument? What are the limitations of his scenario?
4   What is your evaluation of Pogge's perspective? Would you agree with his critics that a failure to reduce poverty is not morally equivalent to actively causing poverty, and therefore entails different obligations?
5   If you were given a billion dollars to end global poverty, what specifically would you do and why? Would your answer change if you only had a thousand dollars to spend? If so, what does that difference tell you about strategies for poverty reduction?
6   Go to this site: www.givingwhatwecan.org. Look for the section "How rich am I?" Enter your or your parents' annual income. What are the results? What else can you learn from the facts on this page, and how do they impact your understanding of yourself and your obligations in relation to global poverty?
7   At www.givingwhatwecan.org, how are charities evaluated, what recommendations are there for donors, and what do you think about the suggestions for getting involved?

## Online resources

- www.thelifeyoucansave.org and www.givewell.org both have lists of rigorously evaluated charities working to reduce poverty and promote human development.
- In this TED Talk, Peter Singer explains the why and how of effective altruism: www. ted.com/talks/peter_singer_the_why_and_how_of_effective_altruism?language=en
- This site is a good resource to learn more about effective altruism: www. effectivealtruism.org/
- This site offers excellent advice on how to have a career that maximizes positive social impact: www.80000hours.org/

## Notes

1  Famines rarely happen because of a lack of food, and more typically because of a lack of democratic political structures (Sen 1981).
2  Kaiser Family Foundation, January 2015, www.kff.org/global-health-policy/poll-finding/data-note-americans-views-on-the-u-s-role-in-global-health/.
3  OECD data, 2018, www.oecd.org/dac/financing-sustainable-development/development-finance-data/ODA-2018-complete-data-tables.pdf.
4  Oxfam, December 2008, www.oxfamblogs.org/fp2p/killer-facts-a-users-guide/.

## Further reading

Deneulin, Séverine. 2014. *Wellbeing, Justice and Development Ethics*. New York: Routledge.
Effective Altruism, "Take Action." www.effectivealtruism.org/get-involved/.
Illich, Ivan. 1968. "To hell with good intentions." An Address to the Conference on InterAmerican Student Projects (CIASP) in Cuernavaca, Mexico, on 20 April.
Pogge, Thomas. 2005. "World poverty and human rights." *Ethics & International Affairs* 19.1: 1–7.
Satz, Debra. 2005. "What do we owe the global poor?" *Ethics & International Affairs* 19.1: 47–54.
Singer, Peter. 2019. *The Life You Can Save: How to Do Your Part to End World Poverty*. Bainbridge Island, WA: The Life You Can Save. www.thelifeyoucansave.org.

## Works cited

Barry, Christian, and Gerhard Øverland. 2009. "Responding to global poverty: review essay of Peter Singer, The Life You Can Save." *Journal of Bioethical Inquiry* 6.2: 239–247.
Bernardini, Paola. 2010. "Human dignity and human capabilities in Martha C. Nussbaum." *Iustum Aequum Salutare* 6: 45–51.
Blake, Michael, and Patrick Taylor Smith. 2013. "International distributive justice," in Edward N. Zalta, ed. *The Stanford encyclopedia of philosophy* (Winter 2013 edn). www.plato.stanford.edu/archives/win2013/entries/international-justice/. Accessed October 2020.
Chatterjee, Deen K., ed. 2004. *The Ethics of Assistance: Morality and the Distant Needy*. Cambridge: Cambridge University Press.
Collier, Paul. 2007. *The Bottom Billion: Why the Poorest Countries Are Failing and What Can Be Done About It*. Oxford: Oxford University Press.
Cosgrove, Serena. (Forthcoming). "Chapter 9: Nicaraguan Solidarity 3.0 and University Partnerships" from *University under Fire: Higher Education, Repression, and the Neoliberal Turn in Nicaragua*. New York: Routledge.
Crocker, David A. 2008. *Ethics of Global Development: Agency, Capability, and Deliberative Democracy*. Cambridge: Cambridge University Press.
Drydyk, Jay, and Lori Keleher, eds. 2018. *Routledge Handbook of Development Ethics*. London: Routledge.
Gasper, Des. 2004. *The Ethics of Development: From Economism to Human Development*. Edinburgh, UK: Edinburgh University Press.
Gilabert, Pablo. 2012. *From Global Poverty to Global Equality: A Philosophical Exploration*. Oxford: Oxford University Press.
Goulet, Denis. 2006. *Development Ethics at Work: Explorations 1960–2002*. London: Routledge.
Hardin, Garrett. 1974. "Lifeboat ethics: the case against helping the poor." *Psychology Today*, September. www.garretthardinsociety.org/articles/art_lifeboat_ethics_case_against_helping_poor.html. Accessed May 2015.
Jaggar, Alison, ed. 2010. *Thomas Pogge and His Critics*. Cambridge, UK: Polity Press.
McNeill, Desmond, and Asunción Lera St. Clair. 2009. *Global Poverty, Ethics and Human Rights: The Role of Multilateral Organisations*. London: Routledge.

Nagel, Thomas. 2005. "The problem of global justice." *Philosophy & Public Affairs*, 33.2: 113–147.

Nickel, James W. 2007. *Making Sense of Human Rights* (2nd edn). Malden, MA: Blackwell.

Nussbaum, Martha. 2008. "Human Dignity and Political Entitlements," in M. Nussbaum, ed. *Human Dignity and Bioethics: Essays commissioned by the President's Council on Bioethics*. Washington, DC. www.bioethicsarchive.georgetown.edu/pcbe/reports/human_dignity/chapter14.html. Accessed August 2015.

Penz, Peter, Jay Drydyk and Pablo S. Bose. 2011. *Displacement by Development: Ethics, Rights and Responsibilities*. Cambridge, UK: Cambridge University Press.

Pogge, Thomas. 2005a. "World poverty and human rights." *Ethics & International Affairs* 19.1: 1–7.

Pogge, Thomas. 2005b. "Severe poverty as a violation of negative duties." *Ethics & International Affairs* 19.1: 55–83.

Pogge, Thomas. 2007. "Severe poverty as a human rights violation," in T. Pogge, ed. *Freedom from Poverty as a Human Right: Who Owes What to the Very Poor*. Paris: UNESCO. 11–53.

Pogge, Thomas. 2008. *World Poverty and Human Rights: Cosmopolitan Responsibilities and Reforms* (2nd edn). Cambridge: Polity Press.

Qizilbash, Mozaffar. 1998. "Poverty: Concept and Measurement." Research Report Series #12. Sustainable Development Policy Institute.

Rawls, John. 1999. *A Theory of Justice*. Cambridge, MA: Harvard University Press.

Schweickart, David. 2008. "Global poverty: alternative perspectives on what we should do – and why." *Journal of Social Philosophy* 39.4: 471–491.

Sen, Amartya. 1981. *Poverty and Famines: An Essay on Entitlement and Deprivation*. Oxford: Oxford University Press.

Singer, Peter. 2015. *The Most Good You Can Do: How Effective Altruism Is Changing Ideas About Living Ethically*. New Haven, CT: Yale University Press.

Singer, Peter. 2019. *The Life You Can Save: How to Do Your Part to End World Poverty*. Bainbridge Island, WA: The Life You Can Save.

Vizard, Polly. 2006. "Pogge vs. Sen on global poverty and human rights." *Éthique et économique/Ethics and Economics* 3.2: 1–22.

# Appendix

## Careers in international development

This appendix offers insights about careers in international development and humanitarian assistance from professionals in these fields. We interviewed nine people with a variety of specializations, asking questions that should interest anyone thinking about similar work. We have also supplemented the interviews with information based on our own personal experiences from working on development projects. The respondents' answers represent only their personal views, not an official position of any organization with which they are affiliated. Biographies are at the end of the appendix.

### *What skills do you think are most important for someone entering the field of international development to have?*

Our respondents' answers to this question broke down into three categories: technical skills, personal skills, and personal qualities.

**Technical skills:** Several respondents agreed that project management is one of the most important technical skills. It opens up so many opportunities, and will help you do your job better, regardless of what your job is. Project management skills specifically relevant to development projects – such as dealing with large budgets, constructing logframes, writing donor reports etc. – may be difficult to come by until you actually have a job. However, there are some formal project management training programs such as PRINCE2 that may be helpful.

Two other overarching skill areas can also be useful regardless of your specific job. The first is being a good communicator. Jennifer Anderson, a consultant on democracy and civil society projects, discussed how it is very important to be able to communicate with people who are involved at all levels of programs you are working on. Writing skills are one aspect of this, but more generally you should be able to explain effectively what your programs are about and why they matter.

The second widely-applicable area is quantitative skills. Having some grounding in statistics and data science is becoming increasingly useful in the development sector. If you have good quantitative skills, more opportunities will open to you. Even if carrying out complicated econometric analyses is not a primary feature of your job, understanding those methods, and having strong facility with Microsoft Excel, will be beneficial.

Beyond those two overarching skill areas, almost any kind of specialized skill can be useful, depending on the kind of work you are doing. It might be a language, computer programming, agricultural science, behavioral change, monitoring and evaluation, or something else. Robin Bush, who has led many development projects in Southeast Asia, said that the important thing is to have some specialized expertise.

**Personal skills:** Several of the respondents mentioned the importance of "soft skills" including interpersonal skills and cross-cultural communication. Kizzy Gandy, who has worked with Australian and British development agencies, said that these skills help you understand contexts where you are working, to read between the lines and adapt. Much development work is fundamentally about stakeholder management, so being attuned to context and culture will help you understand what is practicable and possible, who the decision makers are, and who is going to work with you. Soft skills help you navigate difficult situations, get people on board, and ultimately get things done. Similarly, Jessica Olney, a researcher in Bangladesh, described interpersonal skills as essential for learning to build trust, especially if you are working in a community where you are an outsider.

Soft skills include emotional intelligence, which will help you in any career or situation. Besides how you understand other people, this relates to how you understand yourself: emotional self-regulation is absolutely critical to good professional practice and broader personal wellbeing. Additionally, having an analytical and self-reflective attitude is important. This is how you solve problems, learn from your own mistakes or other things that went wrong, and improve.

**Personal qualities:** Our respondents were nearly unanimous that people wanting to work in the development and humanitarian sectors should have two fundamental qualities: empathy and humility. Empathy is about understanding what people need, what their challenges are, and how they are vulnerable. David Holiday of the Open Society Foundations said that the best development practitioners he has known can identify with the average person: this helps them understand the situation, get beyond abstract models, try to fit into the community, and sense what the real problems are. Merit Hietanen, an expert on refugee and women's rights issues, cautioned that striking the right balance between professional detachment (so that you can get your job done and maintain your own wellbeing) and empathy can be difficult, but that it is right to err on the side of empathy.

Humility means approaching situations with an open mind, an open heart, and an interest to learn. Ciaran O'Toole of Conciliation Resources put it this way: Assume as an outsider that you "just don't know." Do not assume that you understand the intricacies of whatever society you are working in. If you presume you know, you are not curious enough, you are not consulting the locals enough, you are not really trying to understand the people and the local contexts. You need to be able to sit and just listen. Humility goes along with careful self-awareness. A development professional should understand their own position in the environment where they are working. Think about these things: How do people perceive you; how do they judge you, how aware are you of those judgments and how do you react to them? Ciaran also suggested that you should always be comfortable with difference.

### *Do you have any particular recommendations for education, degrees, or courses of study that you think are important for a career in international development?*

Several of the respondents suggested that degrees in anthropology, economics, geography, or political economy are useful because they can provide an understanding of historical and cultural contexts. In general, though, you can get a job in development from a wide range of educational backgrounds. At some point, you will almost certainly need to do a Master's degree because employers typically expect that for career advancement. Graduate school is where it makes sense to specialize, whether in law, health, governance, or whatever area particularly interests you. If you can, it is good to gain technical skills (such as in data, statistics, IT, or languages) in your graduate program, though not all include this as part of the curriculum. Merit praised Fordham University's humanitarian studies course for incorporating practical training.

Once you have decided in what more specialized area you would like to pursue your graduate degree, then it is helpful to try to get into the best university you can. Having a degree from a little-known school or program is not a fatal disadvantage, but a pedigree from a famous program definitely opens doors. Do research on the highest-rated schools for what you want to study; for development studies in particular, the universities of Sussex, Oxford, and the London School of Economics often top the rankings in the United Kingdom, while Harvard, Berkeley, and Stanford usually lead in the United States.

### What do you know now that you wish you would have known when you were starting out in this field?

Respondents offered a wide range of useful advice in this area. Jessica mentioned that she would have gotten more technical preparation, such as project management certifications, learning how to build out a logframe, manage budgets, and other such operational skills that donors typically require of development/humanitarian programs.

Ciaran said that he really had to do some hard work to understand his power and privilege as a white male. He thought that if he had studied anthropology more directly, it would have helped him in that regard. He had to learn to be aware of his own power because of how people perceive him.

Andrew Russell of UNDP mentioned that he had to learn how to improvise. Sometimes you just have to dive right into whatever you are working on, get your hands dirty, and start learning. You cannot assume that you will be able to figure everything out in advance and know all the rules; you might have to learn by doing. He also said that you should never ignore your own self-care. You will not be able to sustain your social change work if you do not look after yourself, your family, and your community first.

Jennifer suggested that it is very important to invest time building relationships with other organizations working in your geographic area so that you can complement (and not duplicate) each other's work. Those kinds of relationships should help whatever work you are trying to do, but could also further your career down the line.

Arturo Aguilar of the Rockefeller Brothers Fund wishes that he had known that everything is connected. He said that if you are trying to make change happen, you have to do it in an integrated way. That means you need legal, financial, political, and communications resources, knowledge, and contacts. You have to leverage multiple areas and disciplines in order to make a real impact: your chances of success will be much better with an integrated vision and an interdisciplinary approach.

Kizzy's advice was to recognize that when you are in your 20s, you probably will not need as many luxuries in life, but that will change as you get older. Past your 30s, you might be less interested in some of the hardships that can go along with a posting in some low- or middle-income countries. Other constraints in life, such as family, may also make it harder to spend long periods of time in the field. So she suggested that it can be worthwhile developing significant in-country geographical expertise when you are younger because it can be harder to accomplish later.

Merit echoed Kizzy's points about how what sounds exciting in your 20s might not be so appealing when you are older. She added a particular complication: in your 20s, you might have to take roles that would not be your first choice. As your career goes on, you will get more appealing opportunities, but they may come when you are wanting to start a family. She noted that women in particular often drop out of the sector right as they are starting to develop significant expertise. Therefore, women should think very carefully about how their personal life might relate to development/humanitarian work, and whether they think they will want to have children. These considerations can really change what your career will look like.

A last piece of advice is that if you work outside your home country for a long time, your personal and professional networks there will atrophy. It' is important to keep them up somehow, perhaps by working in your home country every so often.

### *Do you think there are any particularly important trends or growth areas in international development that someone interested in a career in this field should keep in mind?*

A consistent theme from the people we interviewed was that climate and environmental considerations will only get more important. The societal impacts of climate change are going to be massive, and development professionals will need to be prepared to address them. Integrating environmental analysis and climate change mitigation is a growth area in the sector.

Several respondents also mentioned the importance of data and information management. The development sector is getting better at these tasks, but there is considerable room to grow, and people with skills in these areas will be highly sought after.

Relatedly, David suggested that information ecosystems will be an important area for governance work in the coming years. How politicians and publics use and misuse information has already impacted societies around the world, and finding ways to grapple with these challenges deserves more attention. He also sees public health as an area that will receive greater focus.

Robin mentioned that newer donors like China and India are becoming ever more important, as are newer actors such as the big management consultancies like McKinsey and PwC. As these consultancies' involvement in development programming grows, gaining a background with such an organization may be advantageous.

Merit cited a growing understanding of intersectional issues as important, for example integrating disability or LGBTQI elements into programming. Hence people early in their careers would do well to understand these issues better. She also sees early childhood education as a growth area.

Kizzy pointed to locally-grown solutions and adaptive management as growing in importance. She has seen how younger generations in some countries are finding ideas or solutions that are better than what come from outside. Similarly, management and evaluation are changing because programs and events in general are moving faster. Her advice is to learn about adaptive management.

Andrew suggested there will be good career opportunities for people who are "specialized yet holistic." This means having a specific field of expertise, but also being able to integrate across specialties to embrace complexity and pull together a wide variety of insights. One potential example is with the field of human-centered design, which is increasingly being applied in development. Promising solutions are also coming out of social change labs and innovation incubators.

A related trend is insights from behavioral psychology and behavioral economics being built into development programming. These "nudges" may comprise one element of discrete projects, but also governments and other development actors are creating entire teams of people with behavioral expertise. So this is another promising area in which to develop skills.

### Any other advice for people thinking about a career in this field?

David advised that you should have a clear idea of what you are passionate about. Figure out whether it is a part of the world, or an issue, or something else. Then follow the lead of the people who are doing relevant work, and figure out how you can be a part of it. Remember to be led by your passions, not by your desire for success. As Andrew put it, you need to have an appetite to make a difference, but not just from your desk. You need to get out there in the world.

Jessica agreed that you should work on issues that you are interested in and that you care about. Having a strong motivation is important because sometimes the work itself can be very difficult, even depressing. Therefore, you should also keep a realistic perspective on what you can achieve. You might not make a big impact – and you should not expect that you will. Setting realistic expectations helps you avoid burn out. Jessica's recommendation was that "making an impact" should not be your motivation; instead, you should do something that accords with your values.

A realistic perspective implies recognizing that impact is often incremental. You might work months or years and see only minor changes. In fact, much development work is the day-to-day details of project management. Those details may not be very inspiring in themselves, but such small steps are how much positive social change moves forward. The upshot is again that you should work on things that speak to your values and passions, rather than have starry-eyed dreams about how you are going to transform the world.

Kizzy echoed this idea by commenting that the field is full of many brilliant people who work really hard. Therefore, you should not expect that you will be able to effect big changes. Probably, many people have already been working on the same problems you are interested in for years. A lot of the solutions may already be known, but getting through the politics, the implementation, is where the real work has to be done.

Ciaran similarly cautioned that you will burn out if you cannot manage your own empathy. Do not barge into situations with your own goodness, which can be offensive to locals, but is also often counter-productive, since if you cannot find the right professional balance vis-à-vis your own empathy, you will not last long in the profession. He also mentioned that you should beware of your own naivete in the sense that sometimes wanting to help people can actually do harm.

This admonition relates to Merit's warning to beware of the traps of the white savior and white privilege. You should think very carefully about your own motivations and expectations before you start work in some society where you are an outsider. Why are you going there? Who else is in the room when decisions are made? Are there any locals participating? Even if you are not white, if you are from a high-income society, you may be bringing in all kinds of inappropriate cultural assumptions. Your position as an international employed by a development organization can also create problems with privilege. Sometimes, the locals have to teach the internationals their jobs, because the internationals come for a set period of time, without deeply understanding the context, yet the internationals and not the locals are making the decisions.

Finally, Arturo said that you should not be scared of numbers, statistics, or data. You will need them! You will need them when planning strategies as well as when trying to evaluate whatever impact your projects might be having.

### How important is prior field experience for getting a job in international development?

On the whole, our respondents agreed that field experience is extremely important. It gives you contextual knowledge and credibility, and it is harder to get a job if you do not have at least some field experience. There are some nuances, however. If you have strong, specialized technical skills, then field experience may not be as critical. Also, your field experience should be relevant to the location and issues you want to work in. Extensive experience with gender programming in Chile will not help you much if you are applying for governance work in Cambodia.

How can you get valuable field experience before starting your career? Studying abroad during your education is one way. Volunteering or doing an internship for an extended period of time (at least three months) is another. Some entry-level development jobs can also provide opportunities for occasional work in the field.

### How important is fluency in a second language?

According to our respondents, the simple answer to this question is "it depends," namely on where you want to work. In Latin America, being fluent in Spanish or Portuguese is essential. Likewise, in most of the Middle East and North Africa, you need proficiency in Arabic. Beyond that, the picture becomes more complicated. Russian can be helpful but not essential in parts of the former Soviet Union, likewise with French in Francophone Africa. In much of Asia and the Pacific, if you are working with elites (whether in government or NGOs), English is enough in most cases. If you are working more in the community, then you will likely need the local language.

There are two additional points to keep in mind. The first is that even if you do not end up using a language besides English professionally, attaining fluency in a second or third language has enormous benefits both cognitively and in terms of your outlook on the world. It should broaden your horizons and your cultural competencies. Second, Jessica notes that what may be most helpful for native English speakers is to have an excellent command of their own language. For example, being a good writer has proven a valuable skillset for many organizations she has worked with.

### Any advice on mentors and internships?

With mentors, you should not be afraid to ask someone to help you. While not everyone will respond positively, many people will enjoy sharing what they know, and it becomes an opportunity for more senior people to "give back." The best idea is to seek out mentors with experience in the specialty you want to get into. Besides whatever specifics you learn from them, they can also help you build your professional network. Remember, too, that you can learn from people at all levels of an organization: they do not have to be senior, and you should definitely look beyond your own direct boss. Some organizations have formal mentorship programs.

With internships, they can be very useful as a foot in the door. It is an increasingly common way to gain valuable experience, so if you can do an internship, it will probably be worthwhile. However, internships can be controversial because if they are unpaid or underpaid not everyone can afford to work for free. Some organizations have "fairer" internships that offer a decent stipend and/or limit the work hours so that the intern can also hold a better paying job on the side. Ultimately, some under-resourced, struggling NGOs may not be able to afford to pay interns, but these organizations are still doing good work and could provide good experience. So, it comes down to your own situation as to whether you can afford to do an internship. In any case, David cautions that you should beware a sense of entitlement. Be prepared to do rote work at an entry level. That is how you learn and get ahead.

## Biographies

**Arturo Aguilar** is a lifelong human rights defender whose work to end corruption and impunity spans government, philanthropy, civil society, and international NGOs. Currently the Central America Program Director with the Rockefeller Brothers Fund, he previously served as executive director of the Seattle International Foundation. In his home country of Guatemala, he was a member of teams that documented war crimes, and served as a political officer with the International Commission Against Impunity in Guatemala (CICIG), conducting investigations to investigate criminal networks.

**Jennifer Anderson** is a South Asia democracy expert. She has nearly 20 years of international development experience working for USAID, the Carter Center, and the National Endowment for Democracy in countries including Nepal, Bangladesh, Afghanistan, India, and Sri Lanka. Most recently she has provided strategic guidance, technical assistance, and trainings for the Center for International Private Enterprise. Much of her work has focused on strengthening governance and the rule of law. Her educational background is in cultural geography.

**Robin Bush** worked for more than a decade with the Asia Foundation in Indonesia, then became Director of the Asia Regional Office for RTI International, a major research organization that implements development projects. In this position, she led the Knowledge Sector Initiative Program funded by the Australian government. She has also held a research fellowship at the University of Singapore, and completed her PhD in Political Science from the University of Washington.

**Kizzy Gandy** wrote her PhD on the drivers of public opinion about foreign aid, then worked in strategic evaluation for AusAid (the Australian Government's development agency) as well as DFAT (Australia's Department of Foreign Affairs and Trade). During her years at the Behavioural Insights Team in London, she led a variety of international work, such as overseeing a large program to build behavioral insights capability in three developing countries. Her experience includes projects on poverty, anti-corruption, tax compliance, and financial inclusion.

**Merit Hietanen** did her BA at Essex University in Politics and Human Rights, then a Master's in Refugee Studies at Oxford University, and subsequently worked in Gaza and Jordan with UNRWA (the United Nations Relief and Works Agency for Palestine Refugees in the Near East). She also worked for the cross-border operation to Syria for Relief International and the International Rescue Committee, and in Myanmar for UN Women. She has specialized in protection and women's rights issues, with an emphasis on gender-based violence, and most recently has focused on gender aspects of humanitarian response.

**David Holiday** is a Regional Manager of the Central and Latin America Program with the Open Society Foundations. Previously, he worked on USAID-funded democracy and civil society projects in Afghanistan, Uzbekistan, El Salvador, and Guatemala. He has also conducted research and civil society mapping in Central America while with organizations such as Americas Watch and the Washington Office on Latin America.

**Jessica Olney** specializes in community engagement in fragile contexts, particularly in Myanmar and around its borders. As a practitioner, researcher, and facilitator with 15 years of field experience in South and Southeast Asia, she has led studies and written analyses on the Rohingya crisis for DFAT, United Nations Development Program (UNDP), the Asia Foundation, and Peace Research Institute Oslo. She currently serves as Visiting Researcher at the Centre for Peace and Justice, Brac University, in Bangladesh.

**Ciaran O'Toole** is the Southeast Asia and Pacific Program Director at Conciliation Resources, an international organization committed to stopping violent conflict and creating more peaceful societies. He oversees a team of 18 staff members working in the Philippines, Australia, and across locations in the Pacific. He has worked in peace processes at local and national levels in a range of countries including Fiji, Papua New Guinea, and the Philippines. Originally from Ireland, he started his career in the private sector with robotics.

**Andrew Russell** worked for the United Nations Development Program for 29 years. He held posts at UN headquarters in New York City, and in El Salvador, Guatemala, Cyprus, and Kosovo. His primary expertise is with post-conflict and frozen conflict situations, helping to create institutions for sustainable peacebuilding. He also has extensive experience in managing organizational change. As Head of UNDP in Kosovo, he oversaw projects related to employment, environment, and poverty reduction.

# Index